A Century
of Musicals in
Black and White

A Century
of Musicals in
Black and White

An Encyclopedia of
Musical Stage Works
By, About, or Involving
African Americans

BERNARD L. PETERSON, JR.

GREENWOOD PRESS
WESTPORT, CONNECTICUT
LONDON

Library of Congress Cataloging-in-Publication Data

Peterson, Bernard L., Jr.
    A century of musicals in black and white : an encyclopedia of
musical stage works by, about, or involving African Americans /
Bernard L. Peterson, Jr.
        p.   cm.
    Includes indexes.
    ISBN 0–313–26657–3
    1. Musical theater—United States—Dictionaries.   2. Afro-
Americans—Music—Dictionaries.   3. Afro-Americans in the
performing arts—Dictionaries.
ML102.M88P37   1993
782.1'4'08996073—dc20   92–41976

British Library Cataloguing in Publication Data is available.

Copyright © 1993 by Bernard L. Peterson, Jr. and Lena Y. McPhatter

Library of Congress Catalog Card Number: 92–41976
ISBN: 0–313–26657–3

First published in 1993

Greenwood Press, 88 Post Road West, Westport, CT 06881
An imprint of Greenwood Publishing Group, Inc.

Printed in the United States of America

∞™

The paper used in this book complies with the
Permanent Paper Standard issued by the National
Information Standards Organization (Z39.48–1984).

10 9 8 7 6 5 4 3 2 1

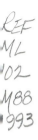

To the memory of my dear departed sister

LORRAINE PETERSON COCKRELL
(1928–1992)

I have chosen this page to pay special tribute to the three chief administrators—past and present—of Elizabeth City State University, Elizabeth City, NC, and their respective first ladies, under whose administrations I served during my twenty-six-year tenure at the university—for the many kindnesses that they have shown me, the honors that they have bestowed upon me, and for their encouragement and support of my endeavors in the theatre, including the research and writing of this book:

CHANCELLOR JIMMY R. JENKINS AND DR. FALEESE MOORE JENKINS

THE LATE CHANCELLOR MARION DENNIS THORPE AND MRS. LULA THORPE

PRESIDENT EMERITUS WALTER N. RIDLEY AND MRS. HENRIETTA RIDLEY

CONTENTS

PREFACE

A Century of Musicals in Black and White is a comprehensive encyclopedia that provides information, as available, on more than twelve hundred musical stage works by, about, or involving black Americans. Included are shows with contributions by black librettists, lyricists, composers, musicians, producers, performers, and other theatre artists, and/or that contain materials of a thematic nature relevant to the black experience either in America or in other nations. Actually the time span exceeds a century as the coverage extends from 1873 to 1992.

This encyclopedia is the third volume of an ongoing series of books that the writer hopes someday to complete on black contributions to the American stage, films, and television. The first two volumes, already published by Greenwood Press, are *Contemporary Black American Playwrights and Their Plays: A Biographical Directory and Dramatic Index* (1988) and *Early Black American Playwrights and Dramatic Writers: A Biographical Directory and Catalog of Plays, Films, and Broadcasting Scripts* (1990).

Because of the numerous problems which cross-references from volume to volume would entail, the writer has decided to devote this and all future volumes to a single aspect of black participation in the theatre and entertainment media. Just as this volume is devoted exclusively to musical stage works, other discrete volumes will be devoted to such subjects as plays, films, television shows, performers and show people, organizations and performing groups, and other separate aspects of blacks in show business.

A Century of Musicals in Black and White has been so named because of the numerous stage works included which represent a collaboration of white and black artists, including composers, librettists, lyricists, musicians, producers, and performers. To cite only a few examples: Black songwriters contributed music and lyrics to dozens of early white-oriented musical shows, such as *The Belle of Bridgeport* (1900), *Casino Girl* (1900–1901), *The Little Duchess* (1901–

2), *Sleeping Beauty and the Beast* (1901–2), *Sally in Our Alley* (1902), *Nancy Brown* (1903), *An English Daisy* (1904), and ten editions of the *Ziegfeld Follies* (1910–22). White librettists, composers, and lyricists created such memorable shows for black performers as the famous *Blackbirds* revues (1926, 1928, 1930, 1933, and 1939), *Four Saints in Three Acts* (1934), *Porgy and Bess* (1935–36), *Cabin in the Sky* (1940–41), *Carmen Jones* (1943–46), *Lost in the Stars* (1949– 50), *House of Flowers* (1954–55), *Mr. Wonderful* (1956), and *Jamaica* (1957– 58). Blacks and whites collaborated in the creation of such Broadway shows as *Early to Bed* (1943–44), *St. Louis Woman* (1933, 1935, 1946), *Beggar's Holiday* (1946–47), *Street Scene* (1947), *Purlie* (1970–74), *Raisin* (1973–81), and *The Wiz* (1975–76). Black stars have shone brightly in such otherwise predominantly-white shows as *The Gold Bug* (1896), *As Thousands Cheer* (1933), *At Home Abroad* (1935), *Golden Boy* (1964–65), *Jesus Christ Superstar* (1971–73), *Two Gentlemen of Verona* (1973), and *Big River* (1985–89). And, finally, blacks have independently created, produced, and performed in such successful all-black shows as *Clorindy, The Origin of the Cakewalk* (1898), *Silas Green from New Orleans* (c. 1903–c. 1953), *Abyssinia* (1906–7), *The Darktown Follies* (1910–16), *Shuffle Along* (1921–23), *Liza* (1922–24), *Runnin' Wild* (1923–25), *The Chocolate Dandies* (1924–25), *Africana* (1927), *Run, Little Chillun!* (1933, 1938–39), *Hot Chocolates* (1929), *Simply Heavenly* (1957–59), *Ballad for Bimshire* (1963), *Don't Bother Me, I Can't Cope* (1970–73), *Ain't Supposed to Die a Natural Death* (1971–72), *Bubbling Brown Sugar* (1975–78), *Mama, I Want to Sing* (1980–91), and *Jelly's Last Jam* (1992).

The aim of the writer in compiling this encyclopedia has been toward inclusiveness, and unlike many other reference books of a similar nature, wide latitude has been used in choosing shows for inclusion. With the single exception of minstrel shows, all other types of musical shows produced since the 1870s are fully represented: tent and outdoor shows, vaudeville (or variety) shows, operettas, operas, musical comedies and farces, musical plays, musical spectacles, revues, cabaret and nightclub shows, children's musicals, musical skits and one-act musicals, retrospectives of early black music and musicians, one-man and one-woman shows, dance revues, and even a musical without songs!

Aiming at inclusiveness, the author has adopted three entry styles: Long entries of several paragraphs mark the most important and noteworthy shows, especially those significant in the history of the black American musical stage. Entries for the majority of shows consist of one full paragraph, providing, wherever possible, succinct but relatively complete information. Shows for which only scant information has been located are identified in short entries of one or two sentences.

Depending upon information available, the following format is loosely followed for each type of musical stage work included in this encyclopedia:

1. Present title of musical. If the title is in a foreign language, or in dialect, the standard English equivalent is given in quotation marks, within parentheses.

2. Other titles by which the musical has been known, such as original title, revised title, or alternate title.

3. Inclusive dates of the musical's production history, with dates of important revivals.

4. Genre or classification of the musical. This is given in quotation marks (with source) if taken from the author's subtitle, the producer's publicity, or from reviews of the production.

5. Length of musical, in acts, scenes, or the equivalent, if known. If not given, the show is presumed to be full length.

6. Author(s) or coauthors of book and lyrics, composer(s) of music, and other collaborators, if known. If authorship is not known, the name of the producer(s) or the leading performer is given as the originator of the show.

7. Title and author of original work on which the musical was based, if adapted or dramatized (including date, if known).

8. Circumstances that led to the writing of the work, if commissioned or written under the aegis or tutelage of some individual or group.

9. Description of musical or synopsis of plot, and/or themes and subjects, including leading performers, if pertinent.

10. Significance of the musical, if applicable, and/or awards received by the musical itself, the collaborators, the production artists, and/or the performers.

11. Production history, including identification of black producers, all directors, selected theatre artists, and best-known actors featured in the cast (including their roles). In long entries, all important cast members are usually listed.

12. Songs, musical numbers, and specialty numbers, if known. These are often followed by names of performers (in parentheses) or by names of composers and lyricists, where given in sources consulted.

13. Location of published or unpublished librettos, scores, songs, recordings, etc., if available from publishers, or deposited in established collections or archives.

14. Sources of important commentary or criticism (including reviews) for further reference, if these may lead to more detailed information on the musical than is included in the entry; and other library sources not previously cited.

This preface is followed by a list of abbreviations and symbols used in this volume. Several additional features supplement the encyclopedia entries. The appendix comprises a chronology, subdivided by decade, of all musical shows included in the main body of the encyclopedia, with the most significant shows highlighted. An extensive bibliography of information sources follows this appendix. The encyclopedia concludes with three indexes: an index of names, primarily of individuals and small performing groups (including prominent duos or two-person teams); an index of songs and musical numbers; and a general index of subjects, themes, genres, and other pertinent categories which may be of interest to users of this encyclopedia.

ACKNOWLEDGMENTS

Appreciation is hereby expressed to the following individuals who assisted me in various capacities in the completion of this encyclopedia.

To my longtime editor and mentor at Greenwood Press, Marilyn Brownstein, for her grand conception of this project which greatly exceeded my ability to achieve. But, as Robert Browning so aptly put it, " . . . a man's reach should exceed his grasp,/or what's a heaven for?'' (*Andrea Del Sarto*).

To James V. Hatch, playwright, drama historian, bibliographer, professor at New York University, and curator of the Hatch-Billops Collection, for his many pioneer writings on black theatre, for the loan of artifacts from his vast collection of taped interviews and transcripts, and especially for his personal assistance in the solution of numerous practical problems that arose in connection with the writing of this book.

To Errol Hill, author, playwright, and Willard Professor of Drama Emeritus of Dartmouth College, for his efforts to secure foundation support for the completion of this encyclopedia, for his loan of artifacts from his Caribbean collection, for his many writings on the theatre which have been of inestimable value in the development of this project, and for his helpful suggestions for locating pertinent materials on the black musical stage.

To Hobson Thompson, Jr., Head Librarian of the Legler Branch of the Chicago Public Library, for furnishing information on theatrical activity in and around the Chicago area, and for making available to me all the research facilities of his library. As my longtime friend, he is also credited with assisting me over a period of twenty years in the research for this and all of my previous writings.

To Attorney William D. Butts of Newport News, VA, and Professor of Criminal Justice at Elizabeth City State University, for helping me keep abreast of numerous musical productions that came to his attention, as well as articles and reviews on black theatre, culled from his daily reading of national newspapers and magazines; and for availing me of his vast knowledge of black music and its impact on the musical stage.

To my sister, Lena McPhatter of New York City, for her generous support of this project in every way, for keeping me informed of all dramatic events in the New York City area that came to her attention through the media and the mails, and for the many boxes of magazines and newspaper clippings mailed to me during the period that I have been working on this book.

To Claude Green, Administrative Librarian of the G. R. Little Library, Elizabeth City State University, and to the following members of his excellent library staff: Patricia Hines, Jutta Chaudhury, Odessa Williams, Kathy Turner, Berthel Penrose, Rebecca Ware, Burnella Griffin, Brenda Sawyer, David Bibb, Cornelius Goodwin, Michael Williams, James Blount, Reginald Riddick, Jackie King, and Frieda Burke—for loan of books, periodicals, and research materials from that library and from other libraries in the University of North Carolina Library System through interlibrary loan; and for making available to me their personal assistance in the location of information needed for this book.

To my colleagues (past and present) in the Department of Language, Literature and Communication at Elizabeth City State University, for their encouragement, support, and assistance in all phases of this research; and for the use of photocopying, typing, and other facilities within the Department: Anne M. Henderson, Chairperson; her secretary Robin Beamon Joyner; and the following faculty members: Robert E. Thorne, Hazel G. Spellman, Venus E. and Carlton Deonanan, Glenda Davis, Samuel C. Moore, Shawn Smith, and Stephen S. Marsh.

To my good friend and colleague, Carol C. Jones, Director of the University Honors Program of Elizabeth City State University, and to her secretary Edna Bonds, for many services, including the use of photocopying facilities.

To Gladys Banks for photocopying services; to James B. and Anne M. Law for research and typing, respectively; to Augustus Sutton and Russell A. Gray, for research assistance; to Casper McDaniel, my principal researcher during the past eight years—especially for his donation of black magazines and clippings of daily newspapers on the black musical stage; and to Larnell Sutton and Jessie Wrighten for clerical assistance.

To the following patrons and benefactors whose financial assistance and other support made it possible for me to get through the rough times: William T. and Dorothy Skinner, William Hartsfield, Herman H. Barrow, Jr., Robert D. Williams, my sister Lena McPhatter and her mate Roger Gore, Russell Gray, and my beloved brother-in-law Dr. Kermit O. Cockrell.

And, finally, I wish to extend a special thanks to my excellent production editor, Margaret Hogan, and to my extremely careful and precise copy editor, Juanita Lewis, for their meticulous care in reviewing and editing my manuscript. By pointing out numerous inconsistencies and inaccuracies in titles of shows, production dates, theatrical names, and use of abbreviations, which they insisted that I correct, I believe that they (along with Marilyn Brownstein) deserve credit as true collaborators in the creation and refinement of this encyclopedia. I, nevertheless, take full responsibility for all errors that remain.

ABBREVIATIONS

Two types of abbreviations are used with regularity throughout this encyclopedia: (1) Bibliographical Abbreviations and (2) General Abbreviations.

BIBLIOGRAPHICAL ABBREVIATIONS

Most Frequently Cited References and Sources

The following abbreviations are used for the most frequently cited books, periodicals, and library collections. These abbreviations may or may not be followed by the author's last name and the date of publication in parentheses. Full publication information is included in the information sources at the back of the encyclopedia.

AmMusTh	*American Musical Theatre: A Chronicle*, by Gerald Bordman. New York, 1986.
BesPls	*The Best Plays of 1894–99/1990–91* (The Burns Mantle Theatre Yearbooks). New York, years as indicated.
BioDAfMus	*Biographical Dictionary of Afro-American and African Musicians*, by Eileen Southern. Westport, CT, 1982.
BlkDr	*Black Drama: The Story of the American Negro in the Theatre*, by Loften Mitchell. New York, 1967.
BlkMagic	*Black Magic: A Pictorial History of the Negro in American Entertainment*, ed. by Langston Hughes and Milton Meltzer. Englewood Cliffs, NJ, 1967.
BlkManh	*Black Manhattan*, by James Weldon Johnson. New York, 1930.
BlkMusTh	*Black Musical Theatre: From "Coontown" to "Dreamgirls,"* by Allen Woll. Baton Rouge, 1989.

BlksBf	*Blacks in Blackface: A Source Book on Early Black Musical Shows*, by Henry T. Sampson. Metuchen, NJ, 1980.
BlkThUSA	*Black Theatre, U.S.A.*, ed. by James V. Hatch and Ted Shine, consultant. New York, 1974.
CLAJ	*College Language Association Journal*
DANB	*Dictionary of American Negro Biography*, ed. by Rayford W. Logan and Michael R. Winston. New York, 1982.
DBlkTh	*Dictionary of the Black Theatre: Broadway, Off-Broadway, and Selected Harlem Theatres*, by Allen Woll. Westport, CT, 1983.
FTP/GMU	Federal Theatre Project Collection, Research for the Federal Theatre Project, George Mason University, Fairfax, VA
Ghost	*The Ghost Walks: A Chronological History of Blacks in Show Business, 1865–1910*, by Henry T. Sampson. Metuchen, NJ, 1988.
HarlRenD	*The Harlem Renaissance: A Historical Dictionary for the Era*, by Bruce Kellner. Westport, CT, 1984.
Hatch-Billops	Hatch-Billops Collection, New York
JWJ/YUL	James Weldon Johnson Memorial Collection, Yale University Library, New Haven, CT
LC	Library of Congress, Washington, DC
Moorland-Spingarn	The Moorland-Spingarn Collection, Howard University, Washington, DC
MusBlkAms	*The Music of Black Americans*, by Eileen Southern. New York, 1971; rev. 1983.
NegAmTh	*The Negro in the American Theatre*, by Edith J. R. Isaacs. New York, 1947.
Neg&Dr	*The Negro and the Drama*, by Frederick W. Bond. Washington, DC, 1940.
NegMus&M	*Negro Musicians and Their Music*, by Maud Cuney-Hare. Washington, DC, 1936.
NegPlaywrs	*Negro Playwrights in the American Theatre, 1925–1959*, by Doris Abramson. New York, 1969.
NewRepub	*New Republic*
Newswk	*Newsweek*
NYorker	*New Yorker*
100 Yrs	*The Tom Fletcher Story: 100 Years of the Negro in Show Business*, by Tom Fletcher. New York, 1954.
Schomburg	The Schomburg Collection, Schomburg Center for Research in Black Culture, New York Public Library
TC/NYPL	Theatre Collection (also Billy Rose Theatre Collection), Performing Arts Research Center, New York Public Library

| *ThArts* | *Theatre Arts* (Monthly) |
| *ThMag* | *Theatre Magazine* |

Other Bibliographical Abbreviations

The following abbreviations are also used for citing many references and sources not listed above.

Am(s).	America, American(s)
&	and
Anth.	Anthology
ASCAP	American Society of Composers, Authors and Publishers
AUDELCO	Audience Development Committee
Bk.	Book
Blk(s).	Black(s)
Bull.	Bulletin
Cath.	Catholic
diss.	dissertation
Dr.	Drama
ed.	editor, edited, edition
Eve.	Evening
FTP	Federal Theatre Project
Harl.	Harlem
Illus.	Illustrated
J.	Journal
Mag.	Magazine
Mass.	Massachusetts
MC	Music Collection
Morn.	Morning
Mus.	Music, Musical
N.	News
Neg.	Negro
NY or N.Y.	New York
NYPL	New York Public Library
Pitts.	Pittsburgh
Pl(s).	Play(s)
Playwr(s).	Playwright(s)
Pop.	Popular
Q.	Quarterly

qtr.	quarter
Ren.	Renaissance
Rev.	Review
Sat.	Saturday
SF	San Francisco
St.	Street
TC	Theatre Collection
Th.	Theatre
Trib.	Tribune
Yr(s).	Year(s)
Yrbk., YrBk	Yearbook, Year Book

GENERAL ABBREVIATIONS

No attempt is made to list all the general abbreviations used in this encyclopedia. Most can be found in a standard American collegiate or unabridged dictionary. Only the most frequently used abbreviations are listed below.

A. & I.	Agricultural and Industrial
A. & M.	Agricultural and Mechanical
A. & T.	Agricultural and Technical
adapt., adaptn.	adapted, adaptation
AEA	Actors Equity Association
ANT	American Negro Theatre
ANTA	American National Theatre and Academy
Bway	Broadway
c.	circa
Coll.	College
dir.	directed, director
ICCC	Inner City Cultural Center
Lib.	Library
NAACP	National Association for the Advancement of Colored People
NYU	New York University
orig.	original
PASLA	Performing Arts Society of Los Angeles
perf(s).	performance(s)
perfd.	performed
prod.	produced
prodn(s).	production(s)

pseud.	pseudonym
pub., pubs.	published, publishers
sched.	scheduled
TOBA	Theatre Owners [and] Booking Association
UCLA	University of California at Los Angeles
Univ.	University
unperfd.	unperformed
unprod.	unproduced
unpub.	unpublished
USO	United Service Organization
WPA	Works Projects/Progress Administration
YMCA	Young Men's Christian Association
YMHA	Young Men's Hebrew Association
YUL	Yale University Library
YWCA	Young Women's Christian Association

SYMBOLS

1. Type and symbols used with titles:
    a. ***BOLDFACE ITALICIZED CAPITALS*** are used as entry headings in the main body of the encyclopedia.
    b. ***Boldface italic type*** is used in entry headings to indicate other titles by which the work has been known, such as alternate titles, original titles, and revised titles.
    c. Double virgules (//) are used to separate entry headings from other titles by which the work has been known.
    d. Asterisks (*) before titles indicate that the title is the subject of a main entry in the encyclopedia, which can be consulted separately for more information or for comparison.
    e. ''Double quotation marks'' are used for song titles within a musical work. They are also used for translations of foreign titles or titles in dialect. These are usually given within parentheses.
    f. 'Single quotation marks' are used for titles of sketches, scenes, and specialty numbers within a musical work.
2. Symbols used with names:
    a. A degree sign (°) before a person's name indicates that the person is known or believed to be white or nonblack. (This symbol is omitted from the names of such world-famous writers as Shakespeare or Aristophanes, whose racial identities are well known.)
    b. A person or collaborator may be assumed to be black if no symbol is used with his or her name. However, in a few instances, this omission may also indicate that the racial identity of that person is not known. (In a work of this type, where racial identity is desirable, no practical method has been found to assure correct identification of all persons associated with each musical, and the writer regrets any misidentifications that may result from the use or omission of a symbol.)

ENCYCLOPEDIA OF MUSICAL STAGE WORKS

A

ABRAHAM FROM ALABAM' (1929). Touring vaudeville comedy. Prod. by W. Henri Bowman, who costarred as singer and straight man with comedian Leroy White. Also in the cast were "Dinah" Scott and Mae Williams.

ABRAHAM THE BARBER (1922). Vaudeville comedy. Prod. and perfd. by Eddie Hunter in Harlem and on tour. With members of the Eddie Hunter Co., featuring singer/dancer Evon Robinson, singer/actress Madeline Belt, Eddie's wife Nina Hunter, veteran actors Alec Lovejoy and William "Babe" Townsend, and female impersonator Andrew Tribble.

ABYSSINIA / / Alternate title: *In Abyssinia* (1906–7). African-inspired musical comedy. 2 acts [14 scenes]. Book and lyrics by Jesse A. Shipp and Alex C. Rogers. Music by Will Marion Cook and Bert Williams. Additional lyrics by Earl C. Jones. Based on prodn. ideas by Bert Williams and George Walker.
    Successful Williams & Walker musical, modeled on their earlier success, **In Dahomey* (1902–5), which was their first show to introduce native African elements. In *Abyssinia*, African culture is presented in a more dignified way than it had been in the earlier show.
    The plot revolved around the journey of a group of black American tourists from Kansas, led by Rastus Johnson (Walker), who has recently won $15,000 in a lottery, and spends it by taking his friends on a European tour. After the group is driven out of Paris because of some violation of French law, they decide instead to visit ancient Abyssinia (Ethiopia), the land of their ancestors. Abyssinia is depicted as an exotic and majestic nation, then ruled by the powerful King Menelik II, whose methods of punishment for breaking his laws are somewhat stern and barbaric. The party first arrives at Borema Springs, a camping place outside the capital, Addis Ababa. In the prodn., the opening scene was a spectacular mountain pass, with a "real waterfall," requiring that Williams & Walk-

er's entrance be delayed until the middle of the scene in order to let the audience admire the scenery. In the second scene—a colorful Abyssinian bazaar—a camel and a lion were used as "props," and "real asses" were used by the party for transportation. Scene 3 moves to King Menelik's audience chamber, where at 5 A.M. each morning he conducts all affairs of state. Scene 4 takes place in the King's throne room, on the occasion of the Queen's birthday, which is a festive one, leading to a happy ending. During the course of the play, the Americans are portrayed as objects of ridicule, running into a number of hilarious and terrifying complications arising from the contrasts between the Abyssinian and American cultures, especially with regard to their differing systems of justice. The plot makes extensive use of mistaken identities and comic misunderstandings, and trouble always seems to follow Williams wherever he goes. In the end, all misunderstandings are cleared up, and the Americans leave their new-found friends with a rousing finale.

Prod. by °Melville B. Raymond at the Majestic Theatre, New York, opening Feb. 21, 1906, for 31 perfs.; dir. by Shipp. Then went on tour for one year, using as many as four different companies carrying abbreviated versions of the show, playing in such theatres as the Great Northern in Chicago (six weeks, June 16–Aug. 4, 1906), the Park Theatre in Indianapolis (opening Oct. 27, 1906), the Grand Theatre in St. Louis (two weeks, opening Nov. 26, 1906), prior to closing early in 1907. The orig. cast included: Bert Williams (Jas, or Jasmine, Jenkins), George Walker (Ras, or Rastus, Johnson), Charles H. Moore (Elder Fowler, a Baptist pastor), Lottie Williams (Miss Primly), Hattie McIntosh (Callie Parker, Ras' aunt), George Catlin (Wong Foo, a Chinese cook), Maggie Davis (Serena, Miss Primly's niece), W. Henri Strange (Menelik II, King of Abyssinia), Jesse A. Shipp (Tegulet, Menelik's chief justice), Alex C. Rogers (Bollaso, Tegulet's nephew, a captain in Menelik's army), J. E. Lightfoot (Zamish, Tegulet's trusted servant), Annie Ross (Tai Tu, Queen of Abyssinia), Aida Overton Walker (Miriam & Market Girl), Lavinia Rogers, Ada Guigesse, Aline Cassel, Craig Williams, Charles Young, Charles L. Moore, William Foster, William C. Elkins, Hattie Hopkins, Katie Jones, and Charles Gilpin (who later became a noted actor) in the Male Chorus.

Principal songs and musical numbers: "Nobody" (the showstopper: B. Williams), "The Island of By and By" (a sentimental ballad: A. O. Walker & Abyssinian Maids), "Here It Comes Again" (the "It" meaning "trouble": B. Williams), and "Let It Alone" ("if it don't concern you": B. Williams), "Overture to Abyssinia" (a medley of African and native melodies), "Song of Reverence to the Rising Sun" (a Rimski-Korsakov-type melody: Chorus), "Jolly Jungle Boys" (to introduce the servants of Menelik: C. Young & Male Chorus), "The Lion and the Monk (Die Trying)" (A. O. Walker & Abyssinian Maids), "The Tale of the Monkey Maid," "Where My Forefathers Died" (H. McIntosh & Chorus), "Holiday in the Market" (Chorus), "Answers You Don't Expect to Get" (L. Williams, with A. Rogers & B. Williams), "I'll Keep a Warm Spot in My Heart for You" (A. O. Walker), "It's Hard to Find a King Like Me"

(G. Walker), "Ode to Menelik," "The Capture of Yaraboo" (about Menelik's slaying of a rival chieftain: Williams & Walker & Chorus), and "Goodbye, Ethiopia" (finale).

Dance and specialty numbers: Menelik's birthday tribute to Queen Tai Tu: 'Dance of the Falasha Maids' and 'Dance of the Amhara Maids' (arranged and led by A. O. Walker, assisted by the Dixie Ballet and the Drum Majors).

Unpub. libretto in Music Collection/LC. No complete score. Some individual vocal-piano scores pub. by Gotham-Attucks Music Co., New York, 1905–8; copies of "Nobody" and "The Island of By and By" in Moorland-Spingarn. **FURTHER REFERENCE:** *AmMusTh* (Bordman). *Blk. Art* Fall 1977. *BlkDr* (Mitchell). *BlksBf* (Sampson). *Boston Transcript* 4–3–1906. *Freeman* (Indianapolis) 10–27–1906. *Ghost* (Sampson). *Just Before Jazz* (Riis). *Nobody* (Charters). Riis diss. *ThMag* 4–1909. Playbill in TC, Philadelphia Free Lib. *Abyssinia* folder in Harvard Theatre Collection.

ABYSSINIA (1987). Gospel musical. Book by °Ted Kociolek and °James Rascheff. Music by Kociolek. Lyrics by Rascheff. Based on a novel by Joyce Carol Thomas. About a young, black rural Oklahoman singer who loses her voice and struggles successfully to regain it. Prod. on Eastern tour, Aug.–Sept. 1987, with perfs. at the Arena Stage, Washington, DC, and the Norma Terris Theatre, Chester, CT; dir. by Tazewell Thompson.

ACE HIGH REVUE (1927). Touring revue. Prod. by Mae Wilson. Cast included comedian Joe Byrd and veteran performer Ernest Whitman. **FURTHER REFERENCE:** *BlksBf* (Sampson).

ACE OF CLUBS (1928). Touring vaudeville show. Prod. by Harry Thomas and William Parvus. Cast included comedian "Dollar Bill" Jones, Patterson & Patterson, Daisy Brown, Violet Field, Charlotte Goodman, Lillian Jackson, Ike Perkins, Mary and Edella Johnson, and Harry Smith.

ACES AND QUEENS (1924–25) / / Revised as *Lucky Sambo* (1925–26). Musical farce, comedy. Book, lyrics, and music by Porter Grainger and Freddie Johnson.

A touring show, which was later retitled, revised, and prod. on Bway as *Lucky Sambo*. Both versions tell the story of an oil swindle, combined with a love story. The oil is discovered in the backyard of some country homes. The swindlers are eventually jailed, the lovers united, and the town celebrates at a midnight cabaret.

Prod. by Foster & Marino, *Aces and Queens* toured the TOBA circuit, 1924–25; dir. by Freddie Johnson. Fred Tunstall was musical dir.; Harold Douglass was stage manager, assisted by Billy Andrews. Cast: Rudolph Gray (John Whitby, Owner of Whitby's Hotel), Grace Smith (June Whitby, his Daughter, in love with Jack Stafford), Henrietta Lovelass (Mrs. Whitby), E. E. Pugh (Turkey Bosom, a Porter at Whitby's Hotel), Joe Byrd (Rufus Perkins, another Porter), Billy Andrews (Sam Houston, a Big Town Slicker), James Fuller

(George Brown, a Detective), Thaddeus Drayton (Jack Stafford, June's Sweetheart), Lelia Wilson (Jacqueline Thompson, the Town Vamp), Rufus Greenlee (Cafe Proprietor), Grace Smith (doubling as Dancing Nan), and others: Dancing Daisies and Dancing Waiters.

Songs and musical numbers: "Happy" (opening ensemble: Chorus), "Stop" (Smith & Chorus), "Dandy Dan" (Greenlee), "Anybody's Men [sic] Has Been My Man" (Wilson), "June" (Smith & Drayton), Dance Specialty (Clifton [sic]), "Will You Love Me While You're Gone" (Andrews & Mildred Brown), "Aunt Jemima (I'm Going Home)" (Wilson & Plantation Folk), "Black Bottom" (dance: Greenlee), "Coal Oil" (Andrews & Town People), "Not So Long Ago" (Brown), "Strolling" (Greenlee & Girls), "Dreary, Dreary, Rainy Days" (Lovelass & Chorus), "Midnight Cabaret" (Dancing Waiters), "Don't Forget Bandanna Days" (Smith & Chorus), "Havin' a Wonderful Time" (Wilson & Chorus), Specialty (Greenlee & Drayton), "Take Me Back to Dixie Blues" (trio: Wilson, Lovelass & Brown), "Runnin' " (Pugh & Byrd), "Dancing" (Smith & Chorus), and "Keep a Diggin' " (Chorus).
FURTHER REFERENCE: *BlksBf* (Sampson).

ADAM (1983). Musical biography. Subtitled "A . . . Musical Drama about Adam Clayton Powell, Jr." Book by °June Tansey (Mrs. Richard Ahlert). Music and lyrics by °Richard Ahlert.

Focuses on the forces which contributed to the fall from power of the flamboyant Harlem congressman and its devastating effect upon the Harlem community. Lionel Mitchell, critic of the *NY Amsterdam N.* (1–29–1983), criticized the book as "not political enough," stating that it "downplays the atmosphere in which [Powell] was unseated in Congress," and "avoids the real issues that caused the House club to destroy [his] power."

Prod. Off-Bway by Woodie King, Jr., and the New Federal Theatre, at the Henry Street Playhouse, New York, Jan. 20–Feb. 6, 1983; dir. by Don Evans. Choreography and musical staging by Dianne McIntyre; choral and dance arrangements by Annie Joe Edward; and orchestra and solo arrangements by Neal Tate. Cast included Reuben Green (Powell); S. Epatha Merkerson (Addie Carmichael); Jackée Harry (now known as Jackée, as Powell's fictitious wife, Rachel); °Frederick Beals, °Jim Keels, and °Bill Rose (white congressmen); °Raymond Stough (Mr. Sam [House Speaker Sam Rayburn]); Keven Ramsey, Robin Wilson, Jeff Bates, Randy Flood, and Hugh Harrell II (all as Adam Clayton Powell, Sr.); Rosetta Jefferson (Serena Crawford & Dancer), and Kevin Anthony Wynn (dancer).

ADAM AND EVA, INC. (early 1930s). A musical satire on the creation. By Ralph Matthews. Music by Rivers D. Chambers. Prod. in Baltimore by Sheldon D. Hoskins and the Adam and Eve Prodn. Co., prior to 1934. Other musicals by Matthews, also prod. in Baltimore by Hoskins, with music by Chambers, include *Shadows on the Moon* and *Looking at the Stars* (a satire on Hollywood).

ADAM AND EVE AND THE APPLE (pre-1950). Opera. 1 act. Libretto by Langston Hughes. Apparently unperfd. Libretto in JWJ/YUL.

ADAM AND EVE IN HARLEM (1929). Vaudeville revue. Prod. by Leonard Harper at the Apollo Theatre in Harlem, Nov. 1929.

ADJOAH AMISSAH (1957). African-inspired musical drama. 2 acts. By Maya Angelou. Set in Ashanti, Ghana, in 1958, it apparently concerned the freedom movement in that country. Unprod.

AFRICA (1944). Tribal operetta. By Asadata Dafora Horton. Perfd. at the YMHA, New York, 1944. Choreographed and danced by Horton.

AFRICANA (1922). Musical comedy. 2 acts [12 scenes]. Written, prod. by, and starring George Taylor, as principal comedian. The plot turns on a fraudulent scheme by two crooks to gain a thousand dollar reward which has been offered by an Ethiopian princess to whoever finds her missing brother. Toured with the following cast: Coley Grant, Billy English, Chick McIntosh, Charles and Lillian Barry, Sadie Long, and Lizzie Maylor.

AFRICANA (1927). Musical revue. 2 parts [12 scenes]. Conceived and prod. by Earl Dancer, who also contributed comedy sketches. Lyrics by Dancer and Donald Heywood. Music by Heywood. A reworking of Heywood and Dancer's earlier touring show, *Miss Calico* (1926), starring Ethel Waters, with a new title, a larger cast, a few changes in format, and additional music and lyrics.

This show boosted Waters to stardom, by permitting white Bway theatregoers to witness for the first time the singing, dancing, and comedy routines which she had perfected after many years of playing only vaudeville and nightclub circuits. Among the highlights of her performance were the "shimmy and shake," a dance in which she specialized, and her singing of the hits of the show, "Shake That Thing," "Dinah," "Take Your Black Bottom Outside," and "I'm Coming Virginia."

First prod. on Bway at Daly's 63rd St. Theatre, opening July 11, 1927, for 77 perfs. Dances and ensembles staged by Louis Douglas; orchestra direction by Allie Ross. Orig. cast featured Waters, Billy Mills, Henry Winifred, Margaret Beckett, Bobby and Baby Goins (athletic and esthetic dancers), Mike Riely [*sic*], Paul Bass, Al Winkins, Ed Pugh, Louis Douglas, Edna Barr, Taskiana Four, and Eddie & Sonny.

Apparently moved to New York's National Theatre for a very short run; then on tour, reportedly closing after a few weeks. Other cast members who appeared during the course of the musical's run include [James] Mordecai & Burnham, Taylor & Johnson (blackface comedy team known as the Two Black Dots), Pickaninny Hill and Snow Fisher (cakewalking champions), Glenn & Jenkins (dancers), the African Jazzers (musicians, dir. by Allie Ross), Paul Meers (character actor), James Bass, Theresa Mason, Columbus Jackson, Paul Floyd, Robichaux, the Southland Syncopators (orchestra), the Africana Eight [or Octette, or Girls], and the Ten Little Bananas.

Program of one of the later perfs., after some of the principals had left the cast: Orchestral Overture—'African Medley' (Southland Syncopators). Part I, Scene 1—Entree, 'African Cargo' (Taskiana Four & Africana Girls); 'Son of Aunt Hagar' (Mordecai & Burnham), Dance, 'Bugle Blues' (Pugh); 'Weary Feet,' introducing song "I'm Coming Virginia" (Waters); 'Tap Drill by Aunt Hagar's Children' (Waters & Johnson). Scene 2—Dance Specialty, 'A Step a Second' (Taylor & Johnson). Scene 3—Dance, 'At the Railroad Station' (Glenn & Jenkins, as porters). Scene 4—'The Original Black Bottom Dance' (Waters & Girls); Black Bottom Tap Dance (Taylor & Johnson). Scene 5—Sketch, 'Judgement Day' [Scene: The Courtroom in Catch Air, Miss. Time: Any Monday Morning. Cast: Defense Attorney (Mordecai), Prosecutor (Bass), Officer Allblack (Pugh), His Honor the Judge (Jackson), One Lung (Floyd), Sadie Go About (Beckett), and A Suspicious Character (Meers)]. Scene 6—Song, "[Here Comes My] Show Boat" (Waters), 'Dance of the Tambourines' (Africana Girls); 'A Little Minstrel and Spiritual Harmony' (Africana Eight); Finale, 'The Cake Walk Strut' (Fisher). Part II, Scene 7 ('The Mississippi')—Song, "Time Ain't Long" (Africana Octette), Song, "Smile" (Waters). Scene 8—'Shine 'Em Up!' (Fisher, Robichaux, Taylor & Johnson). Scene 9—'Porter and Ex-Porter' (Glenn & Jenkins). Scene 10 ('A Romantic Interlude')—Song, "Clorinda" (Bass & Barr) [Performers: The Boy (Beckett), The Girl (Mason), Clorinda Girls and Boys (Taskiana Four)]. Scene 11—'Some Songs You Have [at] Home on Your Records' (Waters). Scene 12 ('Harlem Transported to Paris')—[Scene: Chez Florence, a colored Parisian Cafe. Master of Ceremonies (Bass); Specialty (African Jazzers), 'Banana Maidens à la Josephine Baker' (Beckett & the Little Bananas); 'The Broom Dance' (Glenn & Jenkins); 'The Count and Countess' (Waters & Heywood); Song, "Africana Stomp" (Waters, Heywood & Girls); Grand Finale (Company)].

Ethel Waters' hit song, "I'm Coming Virginia," is recorded by Columbia (14170), with Will Marion Cook's orchestra. Vocal-piano score for "Clorinda" pub. by Robbins Music Corp., New York; copy in Moorland-Spingarn.
FURTHER REFERENCE: *His Eye Is on the Sparrow* (Waters). *NYT* 7–12–1927. *Variety* 7–13–1927. *Africana* file in Philadelphia Free Lib.

AFRICANA (1934). African-inspired musical. Billed as a "Congo Operetta." 2 acts [25 scenes]. Book, music, and lyrics by Donald Heywood, who appropriated the title from his successful 1927 show cited above.

The plot revolves around the cultural conflict and enmity that develops between the Oxford-educated son of a Belgian Congo king and his people when the son returns home after graduating from the university with plans to reform and modernize his country. Although the prince is warmly welcomed and feasted by his father, who goes along with his plans, he is opposed by the woman witchdoctor when he tries to persuade his countrymen to discard their belief in witch-craft and to adopt Christianity. When the prince falls in love with the half-white daughter of a missionary, the witchdoctor succeeds in turning the people against him. The king finally sides with the people and threatens to disinherit his son if he does not give up both the girl and his plans for reform.

Prod. by °Perry-Wood at the Venice Theatre, New York, opening Nov. 26, 1934, for only 3 perfs.; dir. by °Peter Morrell, with music conducted by Hey-wood. Cast included Walter Richardson (Prince Soyonga), Jack Carr (King Yafouba), Heshla Jamanya (Princess), Gertrude [or Gretchen] Branch (Mission-ary's Daughter), Abram Coss (African Dancer), Howard Gould, Joseph ("Joe") Byrd, Earl Carter, Olivette Miller, Nita Gale, Dan C. Michaels, Barrington Guy, and the Four Virginians. The opening night was disrupted by an incident which proved to be a disaster for the show. While conducting the opening number, Heywood was attacked with an iron pipe by Almany Dauoda Camaro, a man in a full dress suit, who claimed that he had cowritten the show, but had received no credit. The incident interrupted the show for more than an hour. Although the court later ruled in favor of Heywood, the annoyed critics all reported the attack, considering it a better show than the musical itself, thus causing it to fold after only three perfs.

Songs and musical numbers included "Clorinda," "Stop Beating Those Drums," "No Peace in My Soul," and "Just a Promise." Music for "Clorinda" pub. by Robbins, New York, 1927; copy in Moorland-Spingarn.
FURTHER REFERENCE: *BlksBf* (Sampson). *NYT* 11–28–1934.

THE AFRICAN AMERICAN (1990). Musical drama. Prod. by Jane Kennedy-Overton and her husband Bill Overton on national tour in the fall of 1990. Cast included the Overtons and their daughter Savannah Re.

THE AFRICAN CHIEF (1949). Cantata. By J. Harold Brown. Based on °Wil-liam Cullen Bryant's poem. Prod. by the Karamu Theatre, Cleveland, Dec. 4, 1949; conducted by Brown.

AN AFRICAN KRAAL (1903). Opera. 1 act. Composed by H. Lawrence Free-man. Apparently unperfd. His best-known operas include *The Martyr* (1893), *Valdo* (1905–6), *Vendetta* (1911–23), and *Voodoo* (1912–28).

AN AFRICAN PRINCE (1920). Tabloid musical comedy. Prod. by the Quality Amusement Co., New York.

A wealthy hog farmer moves his family from Kansas to Harlem, where his daughters long to get into high society, and where he hopes to purchase a high government position in a newly formed African nation. His shiftless playboy son dupes him by pretending to introduce him to an African prince (actually one of the son's Harlem buddies) who has supposedly come to America to select some important members of his country's new government. The resulting experience, which motivates much of the comedy, causes the father to abandon his dream and return to life as a Kansas hog farmer.

Presented at the Lafayette Theatre in Harlem, and on the touring circuit of the Quality Amusement Co., 1920. Cast included Charles Olden (Augustus Keene Shaver), J. Frances Mores (Erastus Underholt), Edward Thompson, Lionel Monagas, Will A. Cook, A. B. DeComathiere, Alice Gorgas, Susie Sutton, Edna Scott, and Ethel Pope.

Of the 20 songs from the show, only two are known: "Lonesome at the Cabin" (Mores) and "Any Time, Any Day, Anywhere" (Scott).

AFRICAN PRINCES (1901). Ragtime musical play. By J. Ed. Green. Prod. by the Rag Time Opera Co., at Traction Park, Birmingham, AL, opening July 20, 1901, on double bill with the author's *Medicine Man*.

AIN'T DOIN' NOTHIN' BUT SINGIN' MY SONG (1979). Musical entertainment. Lyrics and music by Johnny Brandon. Orchestrations by Neal Tate. Prod. at Theatre Off Park, New York, Oct. 11–28, 1978, for 12 perfs.; dir. by Lucia Victor. The integrated cast included black actor Pi Douglass.

AIN'T MISBEHAVIN' (1978–82; revived 1988). Retrospective revue. Based on the music of Thomas "Fats" Waller. 2 parts. Conceived and dir. by °Richard Maltby, Jr. Based on an idea by °Murray Horowitz and Maltby. Music researched, supervised, and originally perfd. by Luther Henderson.

Included some thirty of jazz pianist "Fats" Waller's most memorable songs, borrowing its title from one which was first introduced in *Hot Chocolates* in 1929. The show, which originated as a small cabaret revue at the Manhattan Theatre Club, became so popular that it moved to Bway. Two songs, "I Can't Give You Anything But Love" and "Sunny Side of the Street," which were usually credited to °Jimmy McHugh, were identified as written by Waller and sold to McHugh.

Waller, whose best-known onstage image was that of a fat man wearing a jauntily angled derby hat, was portrayed by Ken Page. The other members of the Bway cast were Nell Carter, who was boosted to stardom and her own television sitcom "Gimme a Break," Andre De Shields, Armelia McQueen, and Charlaine Woodard. The *NYorker* described the show as "a rip-roaring musical tribute by a superb small company whose energy would suffice to light Manhattan." Winner of 1978 Tony Awards for best musical, outstanding actress (Carter), and best director of a musical. Voted best musical by the NY Drama Critics, Drama Desk, and Outer Critics Circle.

First prod. at the Manhattan Theatre Club, New York, Feb. 8–March 5, 1978; Irene Cara, Carter, De Shields, McQueen, and Page. Opened on Bway, May 9, 1978; with Carter, De Shields, McQueen, Page, and Woodard. Moved to the Plymouth Theatre on Bway, May 8, 1978, with the same cast, for a total Bway run of 1,604 perfs. Was also taken on transcontinental tour with both the orig.

and a new cast that included Teresa Bowers, Yvette Freeman, Ben Harney, Adrian Lenox, and Ken Prymus. Other performers who moved in and out of the show during its long orig. run include Avery Sommers, Alan Weeks, Deborah (Debbie) Allen, Frank Owens, Hank Jones, Zoe Walker, Roz Rayan, Jason Booker, and Lonnie McNeil. Prod. as an NBC Special, June 21, 1982; with the orig. cast. Prod. at the Downtown Cabaret Theatre of Bridgeport, CT, Nov. 2–24, 1984; with Ramona Jackson, Ursula Wallace, and Karnell Oliphant; dir. by Debra Bier. Revived at the Ambassador Theatre, New York, 1988; with the orig. Bway cast.

Songs and musical numbers: "Ain't Misbehavin'," "Lookin' Good but Feelin' Bad," "Tain't Nobody's Bizness If I Do," "Honeysuckle Rose," "Squeeze Me," "Handful of Keys," "I've Got a Feelin' I'm Fallin'," "How Ya Baby," "The Jitterbug Waltz," "The Ladies Who Sing with the Band," "Yacht Club Swing," "When the Nylons Bloom Again," "Cash for Your Trash," "Off-Time," "The Joint Is Jumpin'," "Spreadin' Rhythm Around," "Lounging at the Waldorf," "The Viper's Drag," "Mean to Me," "Your Feet's Too Big," "Ain't That Right," "Keepin' Out of Mischief Now," "Find Out What They Look Like," "Fat and Greasy," "Black and Blue," and Finale.

Orig. cast recording, RCA Victor (CBL–2–2966).

FURTHER REFERENCE: *Blk. Pop. Mus. in Am.* (Shaw). *NY* 8–29–1988. *NY Sunday N.* 4–23–1978. *NYT* 5–7–1978; 5–10–1978; 5–21–1978. *Time* 6–5–1978; 5–7–1978; 5–10–1978; 5–21–1978.

AIN'T SUPPOSED TO DIE A NATURAL DEATH (1971–72). Musical of black ghetto life. Also classified as a rock musical. Subtitled "Scenes from Blackness." 2 acts. Book, music, and lyrics by Melvin Van Peebles.

An urban black version of *The Threepenny Opera*, peopled with well-known ghetto types, including prostitutes, pimps, panhandlers, drunks, cops, and racial militants, to show what happens when the American dream is unachievable in a world of injustice, violence, and poverty. The author paints a dynamic portrait of impoverished black street life, using the rhythms of jazz, rock, soul, and the precursors of rap. Selected by Burns Mantle as a "Best Play" of 1971–72. Earned for Van Peebles a Drama Desk Award, 1971–72, as most promising book writer of a musical. Recipient of two Tony nominations, for best book and best score for a musical. Recipient of a Grammy Award for best score from the original cast show album (see below). Beatrice Winde won a *Theatre World* Award; Minnie Gentry won a Tony Award.

First prod. by Paul Carter Harrison at Sacramento State Coll., 1971. Prod. on Bway by Charles Blackwell and others at the Ethel Barrymore Theatre, New York, Oct. 21, 1971–July 30, 1972, for 325 perfs.; dir. by Gilbert Moses, who received a Drama Desk Award and a Tony nomination. Cast: Gloria Edwards, Dick Williams, Ralph Wilcox, Barbara Alston, Joe Fields, Marilyn B. Coleman, Arthur French, Carl Gordon, Madge Wells, Lauren Jones, Clebert Ford, Sati

Jamal, Jimmy Hayeson, Toney Brealond, Beatrice Winde, Albert Hall, Garrett Morris, Bill Duke, and Minnie Gentry.

Prod. by the Theatre of Universal Images in Newark, NJ, May 1983; dir. by Chuck Patterson. With Antonio Fargas.

Songs and musical numbers: "Just Don't Make No Sense," "Coolest Place in Town," "You Can Get Up Before Noon Without Being a Square," "Mirror Mirror on the Wall," "Come Raising Your Leg on Me," "You Gotta Be Holdin' Out Five Dollars on Me," "Sera Sera Jim," "Catch That on the Corner," "The Dozens," "Funky Girl on Motherless Bway," "Tenth and Greenwich," "Hey Hey (Chuckle) Good Mornin' Sunshine," "You Ain't No Astronaut," "Three Boxes of Longs Please," "Lily Done the Zampoughi Every Time I Pulled Her Coattail," "I Got the Blood," "Salamaggis Birthday," "Come on Feet Do Your Thing," and "Put a Curse on You."

Excerpts from the lyrics of 9 of the show's 19 numbers pub. in *BesPls 1971–72*. Book, words, and music pub. by Samuel French, New York, 1971. Pub. as a novel with lyrics by Bantam Books, New York, 1973. Cast recording by A & M Records (SP–3510).

FURTHER REFERENCE: *Blk. World* 4–1972. *Cue* 11–27–1971. *DBlkTh* (Woll) 4–1972. *Dissent* Winter 1973. *Mass. Rev.* Winter 1973. *Newsday* 10–21–1971. *Newswk* 11–1–1971. *NYorker* 10–30–1971. *NYT* 10–21–1971; 11–7–1971; 7–29–1972. *Playboy* 8–1972. *Sat. Rev.* 11–13–1971.

AKOKAWE ("Initiation") (1970). African-inspired theatrical collage. 2 acts. Presentation of traditional African writings through drama, poetry, dance, and song. Selected and dir. by Afolabi Ajayi (Nigerian actor, producer, and playwright). A series of vignettes which focused on the conflicts between African and European culture and the dissatisfactions of African expatriates in Europe. Prod. Off-Bway jointly by the Mbari-Mbayo Players (an African group) and the Negro Ensemble Co., at St. Marks Playhouse, New York, May 19–June 1970, for 44 perfs. With Frances Foster, Esther Rolle, Clarice Taylor, and Amandina Lihamba, a Tanzanian actress. Presented at the Drama Workshop of the Harlem School of the Arts, at St. James Presbyterian Church, also 1970. A special feature of the Mbari-Mbayo Players was the playing of traditional African music on traditional instruments, with lyrics in Yoruba, Swahili, and English.

ALABAMA BLOSSOM (1904). White-oriented musical show. Main authorship unknown. Prod. New York, 1904, with an all-white cast. Featured one song, "Gimme de Leavin's," with lyrics by James Weldon Johnson and music by Bob Cole; pub. by Joseph W. Stern, New York; copy in Moorland-Spingarn.

ALABAMA BOUND (1920–21). Vaudeville revue. Book by Irvin C. Miller, who also prod. and costarred in the show.

An outstanding edition of Miller's *Broadway Rastus* revues (1915–28), involving a black character named Broadway who is constantly scheming of ways to make money. In this edition, Broadway (played in blackface by Miller) and

Gang (Emmett Anthony) travel from New York to Alabama, using their wits to secure food and shelter along the way. Among the more hilarious and memorable scenes are their spending a terrifying night in a graveyard, a visit to a bakeshop when both are penniless and starving, and at a carnival where, without musical training, they obtain employment in the band. The show featured a chorus of beautiful girls with whom the two men also become intermittently involved.

Prod. on tour, 1920–21, opening at the Lafayette Theatre in Harlem in early 1921. Cast included William E. Fountain, Ida Brown, Anita Wilkins, Mildred Smallwood, Ernest Whitman, Ferdo Robinson, and Lena Leggett.

Songs and musical numbers: "The Dog" and "Musical Rass" (Anthony); "Alabama Bound Blues" (Anthony & Robinson); "Come Back to Me Daddy," "Baby Blues," and "Gingham Girl" (Brown); "Dreamy Eyed Girl" (Fountain); "Good Night My Dear" (Fountain & Brown); "When Honey Sings an Old Time Song" (Wilkins); "Day by Day" (Brown & Chorus); "Answer" (Miller, Smallwood & Chorus); "Sundown" (Churchill & Girls); "Love Is a Fable" (Wilkins & Fountain); "McGory Girl" (Whitman); and "Home Again" (Company).

FURTHER REFERENCE: *J. & Guide* (Norfolk) 3–12–1921.

ALABAMA FANTASIES (1925). Musical show. Prod. in Harlem by bandleader Sam Wooding, March 1925; with music by his band, Wooding's Chocolate Kiddies.

A LA CARTE (1927). White-oriented musical revue. Sketches mainly by Pulitzer Prize–winning playwright °Paul Kelly. Music and lyrics mainly by °Herman Hupfield. With additional music and lyrics by Henry S. Creamer and James P. Johnson. According to *AmMusTh* (Bordman), Kelly's sketches concerned theatrical gossip, women golfers, and vacationing in Atlantic City. Prod. by °Rosalie Stewart at the Tremont Theatre, New York(?), opening July 25, 1927; and at the Martin Beck Theatre, New York, opening Aug. 17, 1927, each for a short run. Dances and ensembles staged by °Sam Rose; orchestra dir. by °Carl C. Gray. Musical numbers by Creamer & Johnson were "Kangaroo," "Stepping Out with Lulu," and "Whiskers."

FURTHER REFERENCE: *James P. Johnson* (Brown). *NY Herald Trib.* 8–18–1927.

A LA CARTE (1928). Touring revue. Prod. by Walter Douglass. Cast included actor/dancers Ralph Cooper and Eddie Rector, composer-comedian Billy Higgins (who may have written the music for the show), actor Alec Lovejoy, Roscoe "Red" Simmons, Margaret Beckett, and Theresa Brown.

ALICE (1978). Black-oriented musical adaptation. Concept, book, and direction by Vinnette Carroll. Music and lyrics by Micki Grant and others. Based on °Lewis Carroll's *Alice in Wonderland* and *Through the Looking Glass*. Presented in a pre-Bway tryout at the Forrest Theatre, Philadelphia, May 31–June 11, 1978. Cast included Deborah (Debbie) Allen (Alice), Cleavant Derricks, Clinton

Derricks-Carroll, °Alice Ghostley, and Paula Kelly. Closed prior to reaching Bway. (See also *But Never Jam Today*.)

ALL ABOARD (1922). Musical show. Prod. Oct. 1922, and cited in *Billboard* (J. A. Jackson's Page) 10–17–1922.

ALLAH (1932–47). Opera. 1 act. By H. Lawrence Freeman. Part of his tetralogy entitled *Zululand*. Unperfd. His best-known operas include *The Martyr* (1893), *Valdo* (1905–6), *Vendetta* (1911–23), and *Voodoo* (1912–28).

ALL GIRL REVUE (c. 1928). Musical revue. Prod. in Harlem by Irvin C. Miller; with an all-female cast.

ALL NATION'S REVUE (1927). Touring revue on an international theme. Prod. by Irvin C. Miller, who costarred with Margaret Simms.

THE ALL NIGHT STRUT! (1979). Retrospective musical entertainment. 2 acts. Conceived, dir., and choreographed by °Fran Charnas. Music by various black and white songwriters. Musical direction and orchestrations by °Michael Dansicker. Prod. by Ashton Springer and others at Theatre Four, New York City, Oct. 4–7, 1979, for 13 perfs., including 7 previews. The integrated cast of four consisted of Andrea Danford, Tony Rich, °Jess Richards, and °Jana Robbins. Songs and musical numbers include "Chattanooga Choo Choo," "Minnie the Moocher," "Brother Can You Spare a Dime?," "In the Mood," "Gimme a Pigfoot and a Bottle of Beer," "Fascinating Rhythm," "Ain't Misbehavin'," "Tuxedo Junction," "Juke Box Saturday Night," "Hit That Jive Jack," "It Don't Mean a Thing," and "Lullaby of Broadway."

ALL THE KING'S MEN (1974). Black-oriented musical adaptation. By Vinnette Carroll. Music and lyrics by Malcolm Dodds. Based on the play of the same title by °Robert Penn Warren. About the rise and fall of a Southern demagogue, reminiscent of °Huey Long. Prod. by the Urban Arts Corps, New York, opening May 14, 1974; dir. by Carroll.

ALMANAC (1953). Musical revue. Bway show prod. by °John Murray Anderson. With an integrated cast that featured Harry Belafonte in his stage debut.

ALMOS' A MAN (1985). Musical adaptation. By Parris Barclay. Based on a short story by Richard Wright. Set in South Arkansas during the depression era, this musical depicts how a young black field hand's dream of becoming a man turns to tragedy. Prod. by the Soho Repertory Theatre, New York, April 12–May 5, 1985; dir. by Tazewell Thompson. The integrated cast featured Rodd A. Rolle; with J. Jefferson, Tamari Tumi, David Toney, and Kobi Powell (racial identities not known).

AMEN CORNER (1983). Musical adaptation. Book by °Philip Rose and °Peter Udell, who also wrote the lyrics and prod. the orig. show. Music by Garry Sherman. Based on James Baldwin's play *The Amen Corner* (1954).

About the loss of power of a woman pastor of a Harlem storefront church when her members begin to question her spiritual leadership, especially after the return of her long-absent jazz musician husband.

First prod. on Bway at the Nederlander Theatre, Nov. 10–Dec. 4, 1983, for 29 perfs.; dir. by Rose. Choreography by Al Perryman; musical direction by Margaret Harris. Cast included Rhetta Hughes (Margaret Alexander), Jean Cheek (Sister Moore), Ruth Brown (Odessa), Keith Lorenzo Amos (David), Helena-Joyce Wright (Sister Boxer), Chuck Cooker (Brother Boxer), and Roger Robinson (Luke).

Again prod. by the Philadelphia Drama Guild, at the Annenberg Theatre, Nov. 28–Dec. 21, 1986; dir. by Ed Cambridge. Richardo Martin, musical dir. Featured Cynthia Belgrave (Margaret Alexander) and Antonio Fargas (Luke).

According to Gerald Bordman (*AmMusTh*, p. 708), the orig. show was "filled with rousing gospel music. Unfortunately, the uplifting songs underscored how flaccid the rest of the play was."

Songs and musical numbers included "Amen Corner" (Margaret), "That Woman Can't Play No Piano" (David & friends), "In the Real World" (Brother Boxer, later by Sister Boxer), "We Got a Good Thing Goin' " (Luke & David), "In His Own Time" (Sister Boxer, Brother Boxer, Sister Moore, Odessa & Congregation), "Heat Sensation" (Luke), "Everytime We Call It Quits" (Luke, later Luke & Margaret), "Somewhere Close By" (Odessa), "Leaning on the Lord" (Sister Moore, Brother Boxer, Sister Boxer, Odessa & Congregation), "I've Already Gone" (Davis), "Love Dies Hard" (Margaret), and "Rise Up and Stand Again" (Margaret).
FURTHER REFERENCE: *NY Amsterdam N.* 11–5–1983.

AMERICA MORE OR LESS (1976). Bicentennial musical. By Amiri Baraka, °Frank Chin, and °Leslie Siko. Conception, lyrics, and continuity by °Arnold Weinstein. Music by °Tony Greco. Prod. by the American Conservatory Theatre, at the Marine's Memorial Theatre, San Francisco, opening April 21, 1976, for 20 perfs.

AN AMERICAN ROMANCE (1927). Opera. Written and composed by H. Lawrence Freeman. Unperfd. His best-known operas include *The Martyr* (1893), *Valdo* (1905–6), *Vendetta* (1911–23), and *Voodoo* (1912–28).

A . . . MY NAME IS ALICE (1984). Musical entertainment. 2 acts. Conceived and dir. by °Joan Micklin Silver and °Julianne Boyd. Musical direction by °Michael Skloff. Prod. by the Women's Project, New York (theatre unknown), Feb. 24–March 11, 1984, for 12 perfs.; moved to the Village Gate, New York, March 30, 1984, for a long run. The integrated cast of five women included two blacks: Charlaine Woodard and Alaina Reed. White cast members were °Mary Gordon Murray, °Roo Brown, and °Randy Graff. Scenes and musical numbers dealt mainly with women's interests, such as 'For Women Only Poems,' 'Good Thing I Learned to Dance,' 'Welcome to Kindergarten Mrs. Johnson,' 'Ms. Mae,' 'Harbour Lady,' 'Pretty Young Men,' 'I Sure Like the Boys,' 'I Am Woman,' 'Sisters,' and 'Friends.'

ANCHORMAN (1988). Musical drama. Subtitled "A Blues Operetta." Written and dir. by Paul Carter Harrison. Music by Julius Hemphill. About the coming-of-age of a black teenage track star, whose personal sacrifice leads to victory. Prod. by the American Folk Theatre, at Theatre Four, New York, opening Feb. 6, 1988. Cast included Peter DeMaio, Giancarlo Esposito, Al Freeman, Jr., Micki Grant, Michael Shelle, and Craig Thompson.

AND PEOPLE ALL AROUND (1967). Musical drama. Book by °George Sklar. Music and lyrics by Booker T. Bradshaw, Jr. Based on the murder of the three civil rights workers in Mississippi during the early 1960s. First prod. by the Bristol Old Vic Theatre, England, 1957. Again prod. by the John Fernald Co., at the Meadow Brook Theatre, Rochester, MI, a suburb of Detroit, in 1968. Although the play was not well received in Rochester, Bradshaw's music and lyrics received great praise.

ANDRÉ CHARLOT'S REVUE OF 1924 (1924). White-oriented musical revue. Music and lyrics by °Noel Coward and others. Sketches by various non-black writers. Introduced an additional song by Noble Sissle and Eubie Blake. London revue transferred to Bway Jan. 8, 1924, for 173 perfs. The all-white cast included °Beatrice Lillie, °Gertrude Lawrence, and °Jack Buchanan. Sissle & Blake's song, "You Were Meant for Me (I Was Meant for You)," sung by Lawrence and Buchanan, was a popular romantic ballad that Lawrence and Coward had previously introduced to London audiences in a revue called *London Calling* (1923). In that show, the couple perfd. a dance to the Sissle & Blake music, which had been choreographed by °Fred Astaire. Musical score pub. by Harms, New York; copy in Moorland-Spingarn.
FURTHER REFERENCE: *BesPls 1923–24. NewRepub* 3–12–1924. *NYT* 1–10–1924. *ThMag* 3–1924.

ANITA BUSH COMPANY (1922). Musical show and troupe. Managed, prod. by, and costarring veteran actress Anita Bush, possibly at the Lafayette Theatre in Harlem. Company and cast included Billy Mitchell, the Wallace Family (Doris, Raymond, and Baby Hazel), Seba Banks, Corrine Sneed, Kitty Stevens, and Marie Harris.

ANKLES AWAY (1953). Musical comedy. Bway show with a predominantly white cast, in which Thelma Carpenter appeared briefly as a "bordello madam," and sang one song.

ANNIE GET YOUR GUN (1946). Musical comedy. Bway show, with a predominantly white cast, in which three blacks had minor parts: John Garth, Leon Bibb, and Clyde Turner.

ANNIE OAKLEY (1924). Tabloid musical comedy. Prod. and possibly written by Quintard Miller and Marcus Slayter. Title is taken from the theatrical slang use of Oakley's name to mean a free or complimentary ticket of admission. About two naive brothers whose fun-loving wives are determined to see the world and enjoy life to the fullest. They take their husbands on a wild pursuit of pleasure and dissipation which nearly leads to disaster and ruin. Prod. in Harlem and on tour, 1924. Cast included Miller and Slayter, Eddie Lemons and Amon Davis (as the two brothers), Carrie Yates and Rosa Henderson (as their wives), and Bill Causby.

ANONYMOUS (1984). Musical drama. By °Vincenzo Stornaiuolo. Set in the year 2000, the story centers around the choosing of a black American Pope, after the Cardinals of Vatican City have exhausted all other efforts to select a suitable pontiff. Prod. by the AMAS Repertory Theatre, New York, Oct. 25–Nov. 18, 1984; dir. by the author. Featured Maura Miller, Dirk Lumbard, Steven Cates, Janice Lorraine, and Louise Edeiken (racial identities unknown).

THE ARKANSAS SWIFT FOOT (1930). Touring show which featured blues singer Ma Rainey.

ARMS AND THE GIRL (1950). Musical comedy. Book and lyrics by °Herbert and °Dorothy Fields. Music by °Morton Gould. Bway show with a predominantly white cast, in which Pearl Bailey had a supporting role as a runaway slave. *ThArts* (undated clipping) reported that with her songs she "ran away with the show three times."

ARRIVAL OF THE NEGRO (1920). Operetta. By J. Berni Barbour. Prod. at the Lutheran Abyssinia Church in New York, 1926.

ASK YOUR MAMA (1969). Billed as a "Jazz-Mood Piece." Adapt. posthumously from the works of Langston Hughes. Prod. at the Greenwich Mews Theatre, New York, Oct. 18, 1969.

AS THOUSANDS CHEER (1933). Satirical revue. Sketches by °Moss Hart. Music and lyrics by °Irving Berlin.

The most successful Bway revue of the 1930s, which featured Ethel Waters among the stellar cast of otherwise white performers. Presented in the form of a daily newspaper, the various sections being presented through headlines, songs, and sketches. The performers all played well-known personalities in the news. Waters' salary was reportedly the highest ever paid a woman of any color on Bway.

Prod. on Bway by Sam H. Harris, at the Music Box Theatre, opening Sept. 30, 1933, for 400 perfs.; dir. by °Hassard Short. Choreography by °Charles Weidman. Waters and Hamtree Harrington were the only blacks in the cast, which also included °Marilyn Miller (as Barbara Hutton and Joan Crawford), °Helen Broderick (as Queen Mary, Mrs. Herbert Hoover, Aimee Semple MacPherson, and the Statue of Liberty), and °Clifton Webb (as Douglas Fairbanks, Jr., John D. Rockefeller, Mahatma Gandhi, and Prince Mdivani).

Songs sung by Waters included "Harlem on My Mind," in which she portrayed Josephine Baker in Paris expressing her longing to return home; "Heat Wave," a torrid song in which she gave a musical weather report; "To Be or Not to Be," a more traditional song; and "Supper Time," which she described in *His Eye Is on the Sparrow* as the first "dirge" sung on Bway—the lament of a black woman whose husband has been lynched, sung while she is preparing supper.

FURTHER REFERENCE: *AmMusTh* (Bordman). *BlkMusTh* (Woll). *EncycMusTh* (Green). *HarlRenD* (Kellner). *His Eye Is on the Sparrow* (Waters).

ATHALIA (1915–16). Opera. Prologue, 3 acts. Written and composed by H. Lawrence Freeman. Set in America. Unperfd. His best-known operas include *The Martyr* (1893), *Valdo* (1905–6), *Vendetta* (1911–23), and *Voodoo* (1912–28).

AT HOME ABROAD (1935). Musical revue. Lyrics by °Howard Dietz. Sketches by Dietz, °Dion Titheridge, °Raymond Knight, and °Marc Connelly. Music by °Arthur Schwartz.

This integrated musical, starring Ethel Waters, used a world cruise as the basis of tying together the various songs and sketches; most of the performers played the natives of various countries visited by the travelers.

Prod. at the Winter Garden Theatre, New York City, opening Sept. 19, 1935, for 198 perfs. Other cast members (all white) included °Beatrice Lillie, °Eleanor Powell, °Reginald Gardiner, and °Eddie Foy, Jr.

Waters sang a song entitled "Thief in the Night," which Gerald Bordman (*AmMusTh*, p. 494) described as "a torchy lament, subtly leavened with humor," and perfd. in a musical sketch called "The Hottentot Potentate," in which she described how a Harlem woman became empress of an African nation, through a bit of "trickeration."

FURTHER REFERENCE: Alkire diss. *AmMusTh* (Bordman). *His Eye Is on the Sparrow* (Waters).

AT HOME WITH ETHEL WATERS (1953). Celebrity one-person show. Starring Ethel Waters, accompanied by her pianist, Reginald Beane. A spartan prodn. in which Waters sang songs that she had introduced in her past shows—*ˊPlantation Revue*, *ˊRhapsody in Black*, *ˊAs Thousands Cheer*, and *ˊCabin in the Sky*— and a selection of other standards from her repertoire. Prod. at the 48th St. Theatre, New York, opening Sept. 22, 1953, for only 23 perfs.; dir. by Richard Barr. Cast recording by Monmouth-Evergreen (MES–6812).

AT JOLLY COON-EY ISLAND (1896–97). Subtitled "A Merry Musical Farce." 1 act [40 min.]. Book, music, and lyrics by Bob Cole and William "Billy" Johnson.

The opening skit of the orig. *ˊBlack Patti Troubadours* show; significant as the first musical comedy of record by Cole, and the show in which he introduced his famous tramp character, Willie Wayside, who was to reappear in Cole's more successful *ˊA Trip to Coontown* (1897–1901). This script and the music were withdrawn from the Black Patti show after one year, because of a dispute between Cole and the management. (See also next entry.)

The show was set on the boardwalk of the well-known Coney Island resort. The scenery by Harley Merry & Sons, as indicated on the program, was a faithful reproduction of the scene on canvas. The audience was then introduced to various character types that customarily frequented the seaside resort. According to the Indianapolis *Freeman* (12–12–1896), some of these included the " 'bathing girl,' 'the coon singer' and 'buck dancer,' the 'Bunco [sic] Man' . . . , the 'Couchee Couchee' girls from the midway, and many other peculiar characters." According to the reviewer, "song, story and dance reign[ed] supreme for forty minutes."

Prod. on transcontinental tour by the Black Patti Troubadours, 1896–97, under the management of °Voelckel & Nolan. Charles Hoffman was musical dir.; Bob Cole was stage manager. Cast: Henry Wise (Rube Green, an Alabama Sport), Bob Cole (Willie Wayside, a tramp), Billy Johnson (Jim Flimflammer, "looking for the best of it," & Silas Kalssimine, "the red hot man"), Charles L. Moore (Rev. Sly, a reformer), Jennie Reed (Widow Dean, another reformer), David Rastus (Michael McSweeney, "the pride of the police force"), C. J. Mahoney (Teddy, the handsome waiter), Coley Grant (Cheeky, a news boy), Anthony D. Byrd (Prof. Knowitall, a museum barker), Ben Underwood (William Jackson, a photographer), James Jones (Sam Thomas, a cabman), Sadie De Wolf (Liz Leary, the belle of Avenue A), and a chorus of 40 trained singers.

Songs and musical specialties: Opening Chorus, "At Jolly Cooney Isle" (Company), "Belle of Avenue A" (Stella Wiley), "The Three Little Kinkies" (Davis & Overton), Comic Song (Cole), "Black Four Hundred's Ball" (Johnson), "Black Gal Mine" (Henry Wise), Quintette: "4–11–44" (Johnson, Cole,

Wise, Misses De Wolf & Overton), "Honey Does You Love Your Little Man" (Grant, Byrd, & Oriole Septette), "Red Hots" (Johnson), and "Down to Coney Isle" (Finale: Company).

AT JOLLY COON-EY ISLAND (NEW EDITION) / / Also called *At Gay Coon-ey Island* (1898). Musical skit. 1 act. By Ernest Hogan. Music arranged by J. A. Raynes.

A new version of Bob Cole and William "Billy" Johnson's original opening skit of the *Black Patti Troubadours* show which had been withdrawn from the show by Cole after a dispute with the management (°Voelckel & Nolan). Cole was sued for ownership rights to his musical and won the case. (See preceding entry.)

The plot of Hogan's new ed. apparently differed little from that of Cole's. It, too, was set on the boardwalk of the famous Coney Island resort and featured character types that usually frequented such vacation spots—bathers, hustlers, mashers, flirts, policemen, vendors, etc.— interspersed with comedy acts, songs, and dances.

Prod. on transcontinental tour as part of the Troubadours show, under the management of Voelckel & Nolan, apparently opening in March 1898, where it played at the Los Angeles Theatre in California, through Dec. 1898; later it played at the Park Theatre in Indianapolis. Hogan was stage dir.; Raynes was musical dir. Cast: Ernest Hogan (Jim Jollies, "the real thing"), Will Frazier (Mayor Fullweather, "a man with political aspirations"), Will H. Pierce (Mark U. Hanna, a political promoter), Anthony D. Byrd (Andy Fake, a con man), Charles L. Moore (Parson Parker, a reformer), James (Jim) Burris (Percy Nobrains, a masher), E. G. Belle (Hard Tocatch), H. S. Wooten (Waite Forme), Jessie Williams (Officer Ketchum, "one of the finest"), Walter Richardson (Stanley Sausage, a waiter), Gus Hall (Openair Spieler), Carrie Meredith (Jennie January), Eugenia Wadsworth (Miss Aflat Badnote), Helen King (Miss Highnote), Mattie Phillips (Miss Eyewrite Coonsong), Alice Mackey (Malinda Interview, a reporter), Laura Meredith (Miss Fullweather, Mayor's Wife), Pearl Meredith (Cleo De Mudd), Carrie Carter (Miss Wondore Dressingroom), Soune Suretobite, a bull terrier (Himself), Fakirs, Three Card and Thimble Riggers, and Members of the Coney Island Museums.

Songs and musical numbers: "Hot Time in the Old Town Tonight" (Company), "My Coal Black Lady" (Gus Hall), "Three Little Pumpkin Colored Coons" (Laura, Carrie, and Pearl Meredith; King & Carter), "Enjoy Yourselves" (Hogan), "Roxey Ann Dooley" (Jessie Mitchell), "Before She Fell" (Mackey), Buck Dancing (Company), "Coney Island" (Company), and "The Mayor's Haps and Mishaps" (Finale: Company).

ATLANTIC CITY FOLLIES (1926). Touring revue. Prod. by and costarring Billy Mitchell. Cast also included blackface comedians Johnson & Taylor (the Two Black Dots), comedian Reed C. Moore, singer Luther Toy, Delois Mitchell (Mrs. Billy Mitchell: soubrette), and 6 chorus girls.

ATLANTIC CITY FOLLIES OF 1946 (1946). Presumably a touring show. Prod. by Joe "Ziggie" Johnson; choreographed by Hortense Allen. Cast included dancer "Peg Leg" Bates, Marva Louis (wife of heavyweight boxing champion Joe Louis), and Coleridge Davis and his orchestra.

AT THE BEACH (1918). Tabloid musical comedy. Prod. by Billy King at the Grand Theatre, Chicago, 1918; then on tour. Cast included King, Howard Kelly, Bessie Brown, Gertrude Saunders, and Ernest Whitman.

AUNT JEMIMA'S REVUE (1927). Touring blackface revue. Starring Ella Ringgold as Aunt Jemima, and "Dollar Bill" Jones as Old Black Joe. Cast also included comedian Johnny Williams, Baby Lewis (soubrette), and 6 chorus girls. **FURTHER REFERENCE:** *BlksBf* (Sampson).

B

BABY BLUES (1919–20). Musical comedy. 2 acts [17 scenes]. Book and lyrics by Alex C. Rogers. Music by C. Luckeyth Roberts.

About the exploits of a gold-digging woman named Lulu Darrling—called "Baby Blues" by her friends—who marries a homely, rough, uneducated, wild, and good-for-nothing man because he has received $11,000 from the sale of some land he inherited from his father.

Prod. by the Quality Amusement Co., New York, and presented in the East and Midwest in theatres owned or controlled by that corporation. Cast: Ida Brown (Lulu Darrling/"Baby Blues"), "Dink" Stewart (Wash Wadson, the man she marries), Alex Rogers (Granny Wadson, Wash's grandmother), Lavinia Rogers (Mrs. Darrling, "Baby's" mother), James "Jim" Burris (Sid Green), Estelle Cash (Dilsey Dorsey), Al F. Watts, Perry Solston, Lottie Harris, Elida Welsh, Theresa West, and Jesse Paschall.

The show's 18 songs and musical numbers included "Baby Blues," "Rock-a-By-Baby Blues," "The Rain Song," "The Wedding," "Jewel of the Nile" (Stanford), and "Daddy Moon" (Woody).

BACKBITERS (1924–25). Tabloid musical. Prod. in Harlem by Flournoy E. Miller and Aubrey Lyles (Miller & Lyles), who costarred as the principal comedians. Cast also included Mildred Smallwood, Henrietta Lovelass, Percy Verwayen, and Oswell Lyles (son of Aubrey).

BACK IN THE BIG TIME (1986). Dance musical. By Johnny Brandon and °Abe Kroll. About the "comeback" of a former black vaudeville dancing star. Prod. at the South Street Theatre, New York, Oct. 1986; dir. by Bernard Johnson. Choreography by Henry LeTang. Featured dancer Harold Nicholas of the Nicholas Brothers dancing team.

BALLAD FOR BIMSHIRE (1963). Caribbean-inspired musical. 2 acts [prologue & 11 scenes]. Revised and retitled *Calalou* (1978). Book by Irving Burgie (also known as "Lord Burgess") and Loften Mitchell. Music and lyrics by Burgie.

An island love story, set in Barbados (nicknamed Bimshire), which tells of the romantic involvement of a seventeen-year-old native girl with an American playboy. Focuses on the young girl's dreams and aspirations, and especially on her love for her native country. Scenes of island life and customs are presented, including bars and night life; and important questions of colonialism, racism, and nationalism are also raised.

Prod. Off-Bway, with backing mainly by black investors, at the Mayfair Theatre, located in the basement of the Paramount Hotel, Oct. 15–Dec. 15, 1963, for 74 perfs; dir. by Ed Cambridge. Choreography by Talley Beatty; Carl Byrd was stage manager; and Dick Campbell, company manager. Later prod. in Cleveland, OH. Revised and prod. under the title *Calalou*, 1978. Orig. cast: Frederick O'Neal (Neddie Boyce), Ossie Davis (Sir Radio), Robert Hooks (Dennis Thornton), Christine Spencer (Daphne Byfield, the young girl), Miriam Burton (Iris Boyce), Alyce Webb (Vendor), Ural Wildon (Grafton), Jim Trotman (Spence), Clebert Ford (Howie), Sylvia Moon (Millie), Jimmy Randolph (Johnny Williams), Fran Bennett (Matron), °Joe A. Calloway (Arthur Roundville), Lauren Jones (Maude), Hilda Harris (Hilda), Charles Moore (Watchman), and Eugene Edwards (Lead Man).

Songs and musical numbers: "Ballad for Bimshire," "Street Cries," " 'Fore Day Soon in the Mornin'," "Lately I've Been Feeling So Strange," "Deep in My Heart," "Have You Got Charm?," "Hail Britannica," "Welcome Song," "Belle Plain," "I'm a Dandy," "Silver Earring," "My Love Will Come By," "Chicken's a Popular Bird," "Pardon Me, Sir," "Yesterday Was Such a Lovely Day," "The Master Plan," "Chant," "Vendor's Song," and "We Gon' Jump Up."

Orig. cast recording (selections) issued by London in both monaural (48002) and stereo (78002).

FURTHER REFERENCE: Alkire dis. *BlkDr* (Mitchell). *NY Herald Trib.* 9–10–1963.

BALLAD OF A BLACKBIRD (1968). Musical biography. Book by Loften Mitchell. Lyrics by W. F. Lucas. Based on the life and career of the late Florence Mills, who appeared in the first edition of °Lew Leslie's *Blackbirds* (1926), but died before the show reached Bway. In an earlier musical, *Dixie to Broadway*, she sang the song that was to become her trademark, "I'm a Little Blackbird Looking for a Bluebird," for which she received a nightly standing ovation. Projected for Bway showing in 1967, but apparently is still unprod.

BALLAD OF THE BROWN KING (1960). Black-oriented Christmas cantata. By Langston Hughes. Music by Margaret Bonds. The story of the dark king among the three wise men of the Bible. Dedicated to Martin Luther King, Jr. Much of this material was reworked into Hughes' more successful song play, *Black Nativity* (1961–64). Prod. at the Clark Auditorium of the New York City YMCA, Dec. 11, 1960.

BAL NÈGRE (1946). Dance revue. Assembled and choreographed by Katherine Dunham. Caribbean-inspired, all-black dance show, with Katherine Dunham and her dance troupe. Opened at the Belasco Theatre, Nov. 7, 1946.

BAMBOOLA (1929). Musical revue. Billed as ''A Unique Afro-American Musical Comedy.'' 2 acts. Book and staging by °D. Frank Marcus. Music and lyrics by Marcus and °Bernard Martin. Also called *Bombolla* by some sources. Not to be confused, however, with *Bamboula* (1921).

Song-and-dance revue, named after a popular dance of African origin, with many comedy skits and specialty numbers. One of the numbers was a tribute to Bill Robinson, which presented an imitation of Robinson's famous dance routines by the show's top dancers—including his tapping all the way up and down a staircase. Another of the sketches portrayed a Harlem rent party. The plot revolved around a girl from Savannah, GA, who goes to New York where she makes it big in show business, stars in a show entitled *Bamboola*, and marries the show's composer in a jazz-wedding finale.

Synopsis of scenes: Act I, Scene 1—Front yard of the Frost home on the outskirts of Savannah; Scene 2—Stage entrance of the Jackson Theatre, New York; Scene 3—Stage of the Jackson Theatre on the opening night of *Bamboola*. Act II, Scene 1—Anna's dressing room; Scene 2—Stage of the Jackson Theatre, immediately following.

Prod. without success by °Irving Cooper at the Royale Theatre on Bway opening June 26, 1929, for 34 perfs.; with choreography by °Sam Rose and Tim Brymn. Cast included Isabell Washington (Anna Frost), Mercedes Gilbert (Rhodendra Frost), Monte Hawley ('Lije Frost), Percy Winters (Sampson Frost), Hilda Perleno (Sheila Nesbit), George Randol (Ludlow Blossom), Ray Giles (Deputy Sheriff), John Mason (Sambo), ''Dusty'' Fletcher (Dusty), Ray Giles (Stage Doorman & Preacher), Cora Mereno (First Pedestrian & Anna's Maid), Ruth Krygar (Second Pedestrian), Billy Andrews (J. Quentin Creech, ''the Star''), Billie Cortez (Myrtle Wyms, ''the Soubrette''), Brevard Burnett (Tom Gin, ''the Chief Comedian''), Revella Hughes (''the Song Bird''), the Harmonizers, Cecil Mack's Southland Singers, the Swanee Four, Bamboola Dusky Damsels, and the Bamboola Steppers.

Songs and musical numbers: ''Evenin' '' (Mack's Singers), ''Ace of Spades'' (Perleno, Winters & Ensemble), ''Dixie Vagabond'' (Randol & Ensemble), ''Rub-a-Dub Your Rabbit's Foot'' (Washington), Dance (Bragg & Ensemble), ''Somebody Like Me'' (Washington & Randol), ''Tailor Made Babies'' (Cortez, Bragg & Ensemble), ''Tampico Tune'' (Perleno, Hughes, Andrews, ''Derby'' [a dancer] & Girls), ''Song of Harlem'' (Washington & Swanee Four), ''Shoutin' Sinners'' (Cortez, Perleno, Burnett, Fletcher, Southland Singers & Swanee Four), ''Anna'' (Washington, Andrews & Ensemble), and ''Hot Patootie Wedding Night'' (Washington & Company).

Other specialty numbers: 'One Man Crap Game' (Burnett); 'Mason & Fletcher's *Strange Inter-Feud* (With Due Apologies to the Theatre Guild)' (a parody of Eugene O'Neill's *Strange Interlude*, with Mason, Fletcher, Krygar, Cortez

& Lawrence); 'Two in One' (two skits: 'Clothes Make the Man,' with Perleno, Georgina Spelvina, & Hawley, and 'The Suicide,' with Fletcher & Cortez); 'The Wall Between' (skit, with Fletcher, Perleno, Burnett, Mason, Giles & Lawrence); 'Wedding Procession' (Ensemble); and additional specialties by Mack's Singers, Swanee Four, ''Derby,'' Winters & Mereno, Johnny Bragg, Timoney Gladstone, and the Steppers.
FURTHER REFERENCE: *BlksBf* (Sampson) [under title *Bombolla*]. *NY Post* 6–27–1929. *Variety* 7–3–1929; 7–17–1929.

BAMBOULA (1921). African-inspired tabloid musical comedy. 2 hours. Book by Salem Tutt Whitney and J. Homer Tutt (Whitney & Tutt). Music and lyrics by James Vaughan and Edgar Powell. Not to be confused with *Bamboola* (1929). On hearing a few bars of a strain of music (''Bamboula''), a fanatical music professor (probably from Howard University, as in several other Whitney & Tutt musicals), decides that the melody is of ancient African origin, and sets out on an expedition to the African continent to prove his theory. Accompanying him are Jasper Jazz and Raspberry Razz (Whitney & Tutt in blackface), and an assortment of other characters. In Africa, the travelers have a number of hilarious and frightening experiences before the professor proves his theory.

Prod. by Whitney & Tutt in Harlem and on tour, 1921; with the *Smart Set Co.* Principal cast: Alonzo Fenderson (Professor Loveling), Salem Tutt Whitney (Jasper Jazz), J. Homer Tutt (Raspberry Razz), Alexander White (A Henpecked Husband), and Emma Jackson (Sally Swift, a flirt).

Principal song: ''Bamboula.''
FURTHER REFERENCE: *Competitor* 8/9–1920.

BAMVILLE DANDIES (1926). Tabloid musical. Prod. by and starring S. H. Dudley. Presented at a Harlem Theatre on the same bill with Dudley's film, *Easy Money.*

BANDANA BABIES (1930). Touring revue. Prod. by Boise de Legge, with an all-black cast, headed by Bessie Smith and Ma Rainey.

BANDANA LAND / / Also *Bandanna Land* (1907–9). Musical comedy. 3 acts. Book and lyrics by Jesse A. Shipp and Alex C. Rogers. Music by Will Marion Cook. With additional songs by Bert Williams, J. Leubrie Hill, Mord Allen, Tom Lemonier, Joe Jordan, Cecil Mack, Alex Rogers, and Chris Smith.

Successful Williams & Walker musical, starring Bert Williams and George Walker, about a ''black scare'' real estate, get-rich-quick scam which backfires on the perpetrators. Mose Blackstone (Alex Rogers), the main perpetrator of the scam, organizes a black syndicate (the T.S.C.R.O. Company) for the purpose of real estate investment. The idea is to buy some farmland and sell it to the white townspeople for a street railway at a considerable profit. But he can only raise half the cash; the other half is obtained from Skunkton Bowser (Williams), a simple-minded minstrel performer who has just inherited a small fortune. Blackstone decides to trick both the townspeople and Bowser out of their money by selling only half the land to the railway company, and advising the company of his plan to turn the other half into a riotous amusement park for blacks— unless the company buys the rest of the land for twice the original amount. In the end, however, Skunkton, on the advice of his "guardian" (Walker), backs out of the original deal, and they (Williams & Walker) "turn the tables" on both Blackstone and the townspeople by completing the sale with the railway company themselves and pocketing the profits.

Significant as the last musical in which Williams & Walker appeared as a team; Walker became ill in 1909 and died in 1911. The show was almost universally praised for its good, clean humor and its songs. Included a cakewalk finale at the end of Act II.

Prod. by °F. Ray Comstock at the Majestic Theatre, New York, opening Feb. 3, 1908, for 89 perfs.; dir. by Shipp and Rogers. Musical numbers were staged by Ada Overton Walker (Mrs. George Walker). The principal cast included Bert Williams (Skunkton Bowser), George Walker (Bud Jankins), Alex Rogers (Amos Simmons—owner of some farmland), Ada Banks (Mandy Lou), Hattie McIntosh (Sophie Simmons), Charles H. Moore (Pete Simmons), Ada Walker (Susie Simmons), Muriel Ringgold (Cynthia), Maggie Davis (Julia Smothers), Bessie Vaughan (Sue Higgins), Ida Day (Babe Brown), Katie Jones (Becky White), Minnie Brown (Angelina Diggs), James E. Lightfoot (Mr. Wilson), Sterling Rex (Mr. Jones), J. Leubrie Hill (Sandy Turner), Lloyd G. Gibbs (Deacon Sparks), Lavinia Rogers (Sadie Tompkins), and Henry Troy (Fred Collins, Jr.).

Went on tour, beginning July 1908, first playing the Savoy Theatre in Atlantic City, then the Belasco Theatre in Washington, DC. In March 1909, opened in Philadelphia; in April 1909, played the Yorksville Theatre in Brooklyn.

Songs and musical numbers: [+]"In Bandana Land," " 'Taint Gwine to Be No Rain" (Rogers), "Late Hours" (Williams), [+]"I'd Rather Have Nothin' All of the Time Than Something for a Little While" (Williams), "You Is You Is You" (Williams), [+]"Bon Bon Buddy (The Chocolate Drop)" (made famous by G. Walker), "It's Hard to Love Somebody When Somebody Don't Love You" (A. O. Walker), [+]"Red Red Rose" (Abbie Mitchell Cook), "Just the Same" (Henry Troy), [+]"Dinah," "Corn Song," "Kinky," [+]"Any Old Place in Yankee Land Is Good Enough for Me," "The Sheath Gown in Darktown," "At Peace with the World," "Salome Dance," [+]"Fas', Fas' World," and "The Right Church But the Wrong Pew." Songs marked with a plus sign ([+]) in *Selections from Williams & Walker's Musical Comedy Success, "Bandana Land,"* pub. by Gotham-Attucks, New York, 1907–9; copy in Moorland-Spingarn.

FURTHER REFERENCE: *AmMusTh* (Bordman). *BlkDr* (Mitchell). *BlkMagic* (Hughes & Meltzer). *BlkManh* (Johnson). *BlkMusTh* (Woll). *DBlkTh* (Woll). *Just Before Jazz* (Riis). *Nobody* (Charters). *NY Dramatic Mirror* 2–3–1908. *NYT* 2–4–1908. Riis diss. *Bandana Land* folder in Harvard Theatre Collection.

BANDANNA DAYS (1928). Touring revue. A stereotypical black revue prod. by °Jack Goldberg on the Majestic Theatrical Circuit, 1928. Cast included Hooten & Hooten, Julia Moody, Ralph DeMont, Billy McLaurin, Bee Middleton, Larry Seymour, Ruth Trent, and Willie Williams.

BARCA! MEN OF LIGHTNING (1982). African-inspired musical. Book and lyrics by Ken Grimes. Music by Carlton Bacon. Based on the story of Hannibal, his son Hamilcar, and their father-son relationship, written after two years of research by Grimes. Hannibal was the black Carthaginian general (247–183 B.C.) who led the elephants over the Alps in an attempt to conquer Rome. The elephants were portrayed by dancers. Prod. by the Black Arts Co., Denver, CO, at the Community House Theatre, July 28–Aug. 7, 1972; dir. by John McCallum, under a grant from the Colorado Council of Arts and Humanities and the Eastside Action Movement Summer Youth Employment Program.

BARE FACTS (1927). Musical revue. Presumably a "girlie" show, prod. in Harlem by Quintard Miller, who also costarred. Cast included Margaret Simms, Joe Russell, Troy "Bear" Brown, Edgar "Sambo" Conners, and Gladys Ferguson.

THE BARRIER (1950). Opera. Also called a musical drama. Libretto and lyrics by Langston Hughes. Musical score by °Jan Meyerowitz. Based on Hughes' play *Mulatto* (1930) and his earlier short story "Father and Son," both concerning the tragic conflict between a white plantation owner and his mulatto son in the Deep South.

Cora Lewis, the black housekeeper of Col. Thomas Norwood, a southern plantation owner, has borne three children by him, all of whom have been sent to the North for the betterment of their lives, and to avoid the embarrassment that their presence would cause the colonel. The eldest son Bert, however, refuses to remain in the North, and comes home defiantly to establish his rightful heritage as the colonel's son. His return precipitates an angry confrontation between father and son, in which Bert kills the colonel, and is in turn meted out southern justice by an angry mob of townspeople in the presence of his mother.

First perfd. by the Columbia Univ. Opera Workshop, at Brander Mathews Theatre, New York, Jan. 18, 1950. With Muriel Rahn (Cora Lewis), °Paul Ross (Col. Thomas Norwood), and Robert Goss Lewis (Bert Lewis, Cora's mulatto son).

After a prodn. at the Univ. of Michigan, and an out-of-town tryout in Baltimore, the opera opened on Bway at the Broadhurst Theatre, Nov. 2–4, 1950, for 4 perfs. Cast (some racial identities uncertain): °Lawrence Tibbett (Col. Thomas Norwood), Muriel Rahn (Cora Lewis), Wilston Clary (Bert Lewis), Lorenzo Herrera (William), Charlotte Hollman (Sally Lewis, Cora's daughter), Dolores Bowman (Livonia Lewis, Cora's daughter), Reri Grist (Maid), John Diggs (House Servant), Laurence Watson (Sam), °Victor Thorney (Talbot, Plantation Overseer), Richard Dennis (Fred Higgins), °Robert Tankersley (Plantation Storekeeper), Jesse Jacobs (Undertaker), Stuart Hodes (Assistant to the Undertaker).

Libretto possibly in JWJ/YUL.

FURTHER REFERENCE: *BesPls 1949–50; 1950–51; 1952–53. Christian Science Monitor Mag.* 11–11–1950. *Commonweal* 11–24–1950. *Mus. Am.* 2–1950. *Newswk* 1–30–1950. *NYorker* 1–28–1950; 11–11–1950; *Phylon* 2nd qtr. 1950; 2nd qtr. 1951. *School & Society* 2–25–1950. *ThArts* 1–1951. *Time* 1–30–1950.

A BAYOU LEGEND (1941). Opera. Composed by William Grant Still. Libretto by Verna Arvey, the composer's wife. Based on a Mississippi legend concerning a man who falls in love with a spirit. First perfd. by Opera South in Jackson, MS, 1974. A film version was telecast on PBS in 1981.

BAYOU LEGEND (1975). Musical adaptation. 2 acts [18 scenes]. By Owen Dodson. Music and lyrics by °Jack Landron. Based on Dodson's play by the same title (1948), which was in turn based on °Henrik Ibsen's *Peer Gynt*.

A fantasy set in a Louisiana bayou in the 1800s, which draws upon folklore and legend to make the Peer Gynt story relevant to African Americans.

First prod. in the musical version by the AMAS Repertory Theatre at the Church of St. Paul & St. Andrew, New York, Jan. 10–26, 1975, for a limited engagement of 12 perfs.; dir. by Shauneille Perry, who had previously directed the orig. play at Howard Univ., Washington, DC, in 1975. Musical dir., Neal Tate; choreographer, Deborah (Debbie) Allen; asst. choreographer, Clinton Turner Davis. Cast: Carolyn Byrd (Naomi, Bijou's mother), Zaida Coles (Maud), Lori Chinn (Teaka, Bettesue & Tulip), Billy Davis (Willie Silver & Second Councellor), Clinton T. Davis (Yancey & Third Councellor), Ernie Adano (Bijou's Father, Ballon & Molder), Ted Goodridge (Grave & Zempoaltepec), Karen Grannum (Sophie-Louise), Yvette Johnson (Bijou & Orleander), °Jack Landron (Reve), Edward Love (Troy & First Councellor), Emett [also Emmett] "Babe" Wallace (Apocalypse & Old Priest), Tom White (King Loup & Man), Dorian Williams (Charlotte & Clove), Sundra Williams (Mrs. Candymayme), and Binky Wood (Hethabella & Woman).

Songs and musical numbers: "Alligator Dance," "Rice Hulling Song," "I Wasn't Born to Die No Common Way," "You Only Fool Me Cause I Want You To," "Le Carabine," "Sophie-Louise," "I'm Bad," "King of the Rock," "I Belong Right Here," "My Only Son," "I Cut Their Throats," "Teaka's Dance," "Hello Out There," "Reason Died Last Night," "Something in the Wind," "Graveyard Chant," and "Another Way."

BEALE STREET TO BROADWAY (1920). Touring revue. Prod. by Aaron Gates. Cast included Gertrude Saunders, dancer Ida Forsyne, blackface comedienne India Allen, and comedians Gulfport & Brown (Billy Gulfport and Will Brown).

BEGGAR'S HOLIDAY (1946–47). Musical adaptn. Book and lyrics by °John Latouche. Music by Duke Ellington.

A completely integrated, nonracial adaptn. of °John Gay's eighteenth-century musical play, *The Beggar's Opera*, in contemporary setting and modern dress. It was the product of black-white cooperation and collaboration on every level—in the writing, production, and performance. In the underworld setting, where thieves, prostitutes, pimps, and other motley characters live side by side, the mixture of races was perfectly natural and unself-conscious. In addition, black actress Mildred Smith was cast as the love interest of white leading performer °Alfred Drake, which was a Bway "first." Avon Long was the featured dancer, and according to *AnthANT* (Patterson, p. 222), among "a mixed cast of dancers," he "almost danced away the show."

Co-prod. by Perry Watkins and °John R. Sheppard, Jr. (the black-white producing combination), opening at the Broadway Theatre, New York, Dec. 26, 1946, for 108 perfs.; staged by °Nicholas Ray. The integrated cast featured Alfred Drake (Macheath), Mildred Smith (Lucy Lockit), °Zero Mostel (Peachum), °Jet MacDonald (Polly), °Bernice Parks (Jenny), and Avon Long. Other blacks in the cast were Archie Savage, Albert Popwell, Marie Bryant, Tommie Moore, Royce Wallace, Claire Hald, Enid Williams, Bill Dillard, Lewis Charles, and Rollin Smith.

Ellington's music was reviewed with only faint praise, and his songs (which included "Tomorrow Mountain") apparently were not memorable.

FURTHER REFERENCE: *AmMusTh* (Bordman). *Cath. World* 2–1947. *Commonweal* 1–17–1947. *Newswk* 1–6–1947. *NYorker* 1–4–1947. *NYT* 12–22–1946; 12–27–1946; 1–26–1947; 2–2–1947. *Phylon* 2nd qtr. 1947. *ThArts* 3–1947. *Th. Bk. of the Yr. 1946–47* (Nathan). *Time* 1–6–1947.

THE BELIEVERS (1968). Subtitled "The Black Experience in Song." 2 acts. Written by Josephine Jackson and Joseph A. Walker. Music and lyrics by Dorothy Dinroe, Jackson, Anje Ray, Walker, and Ron Stewart.

A chronicle of the black struggle in America from "The Gone Years" to "The Then and Now," using music as a means of telling the story. According to *DBlkTh* (Woll, p. 15), "The libretto . . . examined black history from its roots in Africa, to the era of American slavery, and to the northward and urban migration in the twentieth century."

Presented by Jesse DeVore and Harold L. Oram, in association with °Gustav Henninburg, at the Garrick Theatre in New York City, opening May 9, 1968, for 310 perfs.; dir. by Barbara Ann Teer. Perfd. by The Voices, Inc., whose cast included Jackson, Walker (Narrator), Dinroe, Ray, Stewart, DeVore, Benjamin Carter, Barry Hemphill, Sylvia Jackson, Shirley McKie, Don Oliver, Veronica Redd, and James Wright.

Songs and musical numbers included tribal chants, slave songs, revival music, jazz blues, and street cries. Among the specific song titles were "This Old Ship," "What Shall I Believe in Now?," "City Blues," "Early One Morning

Blues,'' "Children's Games,'' "School Don't Mean a Damn Thing,'' "Burn This Town,'' and "Learn to Love.''

Cast recording by RCA Victor (LSO–1151).

FURTHER REFERENCE: *NYT* 6–10–1968.

LA BELLE HELENE (1986). Musical adaptation. By John Fearnley. Based on the Offenbach operetta about Helen of Troy. Prod. by the AMAS Repertory Theatre, New York, Feb. 1986; dir. by Fearnley.

THE BELLE OF BRIDGEPORT (1900). White-oriented musical farce. 3 acts. Book mainly by °Glen MacDonough. Music and lyrics mainly by Bob Cole, James Weldon Johnson, and J. Rosamond Johnson. Additional songs by Will Accooe.

About a woman's efforts to save her lover, who, as her father's secretary, has been falsely accused of theft.

Prod. on Bway at the Bijou Theatre, opening Oct. 29, 1900, for 45 perfs.; starring °May Irwin, who commissioned the featured songs, and °Raymond Hitchcock.

The Cole & Johnson Brothers' contributions included "Louisiana Lize,'' apparently their first pub. score; "Ma Mississippi Belle'' (musical score pub. by Joseph W. Stern; copy in Moorland-Spingarn); "Why Don't the Band Play?,'' "Magdaline, My Southern Queen,'' "I Ain't Gwinter Work No More,'' and "I Must-a Been a-Dreamin'.'' Accooe's songs included "My Dandy Soldier Boy'' and "Mabel Moore.''

FURTHER REFERENCE: *AmMusTh* (Bordman).

THE BELLE OF CORNVILLE (1896). Romantic opera. The premiere prodn. of the Afro-American Opera Co., a musical organization established in 1986. It made its debut at Friedberg's Opera House in Chicago. Edna Alexander was a member of the company, which included 12 soloists, a chorus of 75 voices, and a full orchestra.

BENBOW'S NEW YORK COLORED FOLLIES (1928). Vaudeville revue. Prod. by William M. Benbow on tour of the U.S. and Trinidad in 1928. The cast of 32 featured members of the Benbow Family (including F. W. Benbow and Master Richard Benbow, Jr.), Leon Diggs, Henrietta Leggett, and Don Dawleigh's Nine Jazz Kings.

BESSIE (1975). Musical retrospective of blues singer Bessie Smith, her lifestyle, and her music. Prod. in New York and on tour, starring singer Linda Hopkins.

BESSIE, BILLIE & BO (1975). Musical retrospective of Bessie Smith, Billie Holiday, and Bill "Bojangles" Robinson. Prod. by an independent theatre group in Chicago, featuring singers Jeanne Carroll and Inez Davis, and veteran dance instructor Jimmy Payne.

BESSIE SMITH REVUE (1926). Touring show. Prod. by and starring blues singer Bessie Smith. Cast also included blackface comedians Mason & Henderson and their wives; character actor George Wiltshire; the Taskiana Quartet, also called the Taskiana Four; actor Lloyd Hollis; and 5 chorus girls.

BETWIXT AND BETWEEN (1920s). Tabloid musical. By Salem Tutt Whitney and J. Homer Tutt, who were the principal comedians. Prod. on tour of black movie houses in the South, between feature motion pictures.

BEULAH BENBOW'S DANCING FOOLS (1922). Touring dance revue. Prod. by dancer Beulah Benbow, who costarred with Floyd Young.

BIG DEAL (1986). Musical adaptation. Written, dir., and choreographed by °Bob Fosse. Based on an Italian film, *Big Deal on Madonna Street*. Set in the 1930s, it concerned a bumbling Chicago gang of crooks as they make preparations for their big heist. Prod. at the Broadway Theatre, New York, May–June 1986. The all-black cast included Cleavant Derricks, Loretta Devine, Alan Weeks, and Desiree Coleman.

BIG MAN (1974). Folk musical, subtitled "The Legend of John Henry." Cowritten by jazz-musician brothers Julian "Cannonball" Adderley and Nat Adderley. About the mythical black railroad worker who could beat all others in the laying of railroad tracks, with the help of his legendary hammer, until his skill was challenged in a contest with a steel drill. World premiere in a concert version at Carnegie Hall, New York City, July 1976. With Joe Williams in the title role, Robert Guillaume, and Randy Crawford. Cast recording by Fantasy (F–79006) issued in 1975.

BIG RIVER (1985–87). Musical adaptation. 2 acts. Book by °William Haupman. Music and lyrics by °Roger Miller. From the novel *The Adventures of Huckleberry Finn*, by °Mark Twain. A retelling of Twain's famous story, which also features Huckleberry's friend Tom Sawyer and his slave companion, Jim. The action takes place in the Mississippi River Valley some time in the 1840s. Recipient of Tony Awards for best musical, book, score, director, scenic design, lighting design, and for featured black actor Ron Richardson, who played the role of Jim. Richardson also received a Drama Desk Award. Prod. at the Eugene O'Neill Theatre, New York, opening April 25, 1985, for a long run, ending in 1987; dir. by °Des McAnuff. Other blacks in the cast included Carol Dennis (Alice, a slave) and Jennifer Leigh Warren (Alice's daughter). The predominantly white cast was headed by °Gordon Connell (Mark Twain), °Daniel H. Jenkins (Huckleberry Finn), and °John Short (Tom Sawyer). Among the show's 17 musical numbers was the well-known civil rights anthem, "Free at Last."

BILLY NONAME (1970). Musical drama. 2 acts [15 scenes]. Book by William Wellington Mackey. Music and lyrics by Johnny Brandon.

Semiautobiographical musical about a young black writer named Billy (the author's name is William) whose life parallels black history from the 1930s through the civil rights movement of the 1960s. The play concerns his search for identity, as he moves from Billy Noname in Act I to Billy Somebody in Act II. Donny Burks perfd. the title role, for which he won a *Theatre World* Award.

Prod. Off-Bway at the Truck & Warehouse Theatre, March 2–April 12, 1970, for 48 perfs.; dir. by Lucia Victor; choreography by Talley Beatty. Cast included Donny Burks (Billy), Hattie Winston (Dolores), Andrea Saunders (Louisa), Andy Torres (Li'l Nick), Charles Moore (Big Nick), Roger Lawson (Young Billy), Thommie Bush (Young Tiny), Eugene Edwards (Rev. Fisher & Mr. Milton), Alan Weeks (Tiny Shannon), Glory Van Scott (Barbara), and Urylee Leonardos (Harriet).

Songs and musical numbers: "King Joe," "Seduction," "Billy Noname," "Boychild," "A Different Drummer," "Look Through the Window," "It's Our Time Now," "Hello World," "At the End of the Day," "I Want to Live," "Manchild," "Color Me White," "We're Gonna Turn on Freedom," "Mother Earth," "Sit In—Wade In," "Movin'," "The Dream," "Black Boy," "Burn, Baby, Burn," "We Make a Promise," and "Get Your Slice of Cake."

Orig. cast recording by Roulette (SROC–11).

FURTHER REFERENCE: *NYorker* 3–14–1970. *NYT* 3–4–1970. *Playboy* 3–4–1970.

BILLY STARS & KID JUPITER (1980). Billed as "A Sci-Fi Jazzical" (science fiction jazz musical). Written and dir. by William Electric Black (Ian Ellis James). Music by °Paul Shapiro. Prod. at the Theatre for the New City, New York, June 26–July 13, 1980.

BINGO (1985). Musical adaptation. Book by Ossie Davis and Hy Gilbert. Music by °George Fischoff. Lyrics by Gilbert. Based on William Brashler's book, *Bingo Long's Traveling All Stars and Motor Kings* (which was also made into a film in 1976). About the black baseball team of the 1930s. Prod. by the AMAS Repertory Theatre, New York, Oct. 24–Nov. 17, 1985; dir. by Davis. Choreography by Henry LeTang; musical director, Neal Tate. Featuring Norman Matlock. Also presented at the AUDELCO Black Theatre Festival, New York, Oct. 16–19, 1986.

BIRTH OF THE BLUES (1929). Blues musical. Touring show. Prod. by and costarring Ringgold & Watts. Cast also included Felton & Felton, Hodge & Hodge, Babe Manley, Anita Watkins, and Dan Dawley's Tornado Band.

BLACK AMERICA (1895). Outdoor plantation extravaganza. Conceived, prod., and staged by Billy McClain, under the management of °Nate Salisbury, best known previously as the producer of the Buffalo Bill Cody Wild West Show.

The largest aggregation of black talent in a single show during the nineteenth century. The first all-black summer show. In an authentic plantation setting, *Black America* sought to present an arcadian picture of southern black life during the days before the Civil War, in a manner which had never been observed by northern whites. According to Thomas Lawrence Riis (Ph.D. diss., 1981, p. 45), "The plantation atmosphere was executed in impressive detail, with log cabins built in the park, poultry and livestock present, and even genuine cotton plants to add a finishing touch."

Among the featured entertainments were several jubilee choirs, 63 vocal quartets from all over the country, numerous individual soloists and instrumental performers, dancers (jig, buck and wing, cakewalk, etc.), solo acts, boxing exhibitions, foot racing, cotton picking, voodoo rituals, and a marching band from the U.S. Ninth Cavalry.

Prod. outdoors in Ambrose Park in South Brooklyn, NY, during the summer of 1895, with two shows daily—an afternoon and an evening perf.; with a company of over 365 blacks. Among the leading performers were the star, Billy McClain; his wife, singer Cordelia McClain; comedian Billy Farrell; dancer Charles Walker, partner of Dora Dean; and Victor Herbert and band.

A modified and abbreviated version of this show was taken on the road, beginning in 1896, retitled *Darkest America*, starring McClain, and prod. by °Al G. Fields.

FURTHER REFERENCE: *Just Before Jazz* (Riis). *MusBlkAms* (Southern). *NYT* 5–26–1985. *100 Yrs* (Fletcher). Riis diss.

BLACK AND BLUE (1989–90). Retrospective musical of the jazz age. 2 acts. Conceived and dir. by °Claudie Segovia and °Hector Grezzoli. Music and lyrics by various black and white composer-lyricists, including black songwriters Creamer & Layton, Andy Razaf, J. Leubrie Hill, Louis Armstrong, Duke Ellington, Porter Grainger, Shelton Brooks, Thomas "Fats" Waller, Eubie Blake, W. C. Handy, and others.

An opulent revue of the golden age of jazz music, which was described by *Ebony* (9–1989, p. 128) as "an exciting, energetic all Black ensemble of talent. It features stylish music, breathtaking dance routines, elegant costumes and memorable singing, complete with bits of bawdy humor. In short, *Black and Blue* celebrates the rich Black culture of dance and music in Paris between World War I and World War II when Black American artists—notably Josephine Baker—received much acclaim." Recipient of 10 Tony nominations, including best leading actress in a musical for both leading singers, Ruth Brown and Linda Hopkins. Brown actually won the award, as did Cholly Atkins, Henry LeTang, Frankie Manning, and Fayard Nicholas—the latter four for best choreography.

Originally created in France, where it opened at the Theatre Musical de Paris,

c. 1986, and became a smash hit, running for eight months. Prod. on Bway at the Minskoff Theatre, Jan. 26, 1989, for a long run that had not concluded in June 1990. The cast of over 40 singers, dancers and musicians costarred singers Ruth Brown, Linda Hopkins, and Carrie Smith; legendary tap dancers Bunny Briggs, Ralph Brown, Lon Chaney, and Jimmy Slyde; and an array of talented young dancers, including Savion Glover and Kyme (one name only).

Songs and musical numbers: Act I—Blues: "I'm a Woman" (Hopkins, Brown & Smith), 'Hoofers A Capella' (dance number), "Royal Garden Blues" (musicians), "St. Louis Blues" (Brown), "Everybody Loves My Baby" (dancers), "After You've Gone" (Hopkins & dancers), "If I Can't Sell It, I'll Keep Sittin' on It" (Brown), "I Want a Big Butter and Egg Man" (Smith & dancers), "Rhythm Is Our Business" (dancers), "Mystery Song" (dancers), "Stompin' at the Savoy" (dancers), "Black and Tan Fantasy" (dancers), "Come Sunday" (Hopkins), "Daybreak Express" (musicians), " 'Tain't Nobody's Business If I Do" (Brown & Hopkins), "That Rhythm Man" (dancers). Act II—'Swingin' to "Wednesday Night Hop" ' (dancers), "I'm Getting 'Long Alright" (Hopkins), "Memories of You" (dancers), "Body and Soul" (Brown), "I'm Confessing" (dancers), "Am I Blue" (Smith), "I Can't Give You Anything But Love" (dancers), "East St. Louis Toodle-oo" (dancers), "In a Sentimental Mood" (dancers), "Black and Blue" (Brown, Hopkins, Smith & dancers), "Finale" (Company).

FURTHER REFERENCE: *Ebony* 9–1989. *NY Post* 1–25–1989; 1–27–1989. *Time* 2–6–1989.

BLACK AND WHITE REVUES (1924–26). Series of integrated touring revues. Prod. by °Jimmy Cooper on the Columbia Burlesque Circuit, mid-1920s. As described by Henry T. Sampson, these revues consisted of two parts, one black and one white, with about 20 performers in each part. Butterbeans & Susie (Jodie and Susie Edwards) were the stars of the black segment, and Sidney Bechet was instrumentalist and comedian. According to Sampson, "These shows were very popular in the South and Midwest and in many cities were performed before segregated audiences with the Blacks occupying balcony seats in white theatres" (*BlksBf*, p. 352).

BLACKBERRIES OF 1932 (1932). Musical revue. 2 acts. Book by Eddie Green and Lee Posner. Music and lyrics by Donald Heywood and °Tom Peluso.

Song-and-dance revue, imitative of °Lew Leslie's successful *Blackbirds* revues. Billed as "a dancical [*sic*] revue presented to you as you expected to see it" (Program). Included a stereotypical opening number on lazy riverbank, a minstrel finale, and a sketch about a Harlem rent party. Critics were in agreement that the show lacked both originality and vitality.

Prod. by °Max Rudnick at the Liberty Theatre, New York, opening April 4, 1932, for 24 perfs.; dir. by Ben Bernard; choreography by Sidney Sprague and Lew Crawford. Music by Sam Wooding's Chocolate Kiddies. Cast: Green, Tim

Moore, Mantan Moreland, Dewey "Pigmeat" Markham, Gertrude Saunders, Jackie (later "Moms") Mabley, Monte Hawley, Alice Harris, Dusayne Brown, Sam Paige, Johnny Lee Long, John Dickens, Thelma Meers, Harold Norton, Gertrude Harvey's Bon Bons, the Midnight Steppers, the Three Yorkers, and the Three Bubbles.

Songs and musical numbers included "Brown Sugar," "Harlem Mama," "The Answer Is No," "Blackberries," "First Thing in the Morning," and "Love Me More—Love Me Less." Vocal-piano score for "Brown Sugar" by Heywood & Peluso, pub. by Remick, New York; copy in Moorland-Spingarn. **FURTHER REFERENCE:** *NY Sun* 4–5–1932. *NYT* 4–5–1932.

BLACKBIRDS OF 1926 / / Also known as *Lew Leslie's Blackbirds of 1926* (1926–27). Musical revue. Presumably 2 acts. Words and music by °George W. Meyer.

The orig. ed. of the famous *Blackbirds* revues, prod. by °Lew Leslie, and developed from floorshows at the Plantation Club, a Harlem cabaret attended exclusively by whites. Although little is known of this ed., it has become celebrated because it starred Florence Mills, and was her last show before her untimely death from appendicitis in 1927. It was in this show that she sang "I'm a Little Blackbird Looking for a Bluebird," which became known as her theme song.

Prod. for six weeks, with great success, at the Alhambra Theatre in Harlem. It was then taken to Europe, where it played for five months in Paris and six months in London, making Mills an international star. It was reportedly seen several times by England's Prince of Wales. The cast included Mills (who was replaced by Mabel Mercer when she left the show), Aida Ward, Edith Wilson, Johnny Nit, Winfred & Mills, Joyner & Foster, Leonard Harper, and the Three Eddies.
FURTHER REFERENCE: *BlkMusTh* (Woll).

BLACKBIRDS OF 1928 / / Also known as *Lew Leslie's Blackbirds of 1928* (1928–29). Musical revue. Prologue & 2 parts. Lyrics by °Dorothy Fields. Music by °Jimmy McHugh. A second company, organized in 1929, used the title *Blackbirds of 1929*.

The second of a series of all-black song-and-dance shows, interspersed with blackface comedy skits, prod. by °Lew Leslie under the title of *Blackbirds*. This ed. was the first to reach Bway. The orig. ed., *Blackbirds of 1926*, had been presented in Harlem, London, and Paris, starring Florence Mills; Leslie had planned to star her in this ed., but she died in 1927. Adelaide Hall was chosen as her replacement, and a tribute to Mills was included among the featured numbers. Bill Robinson also starred in this ed. He was hired at the last minute, however, and was able to appear in only one number; nevertheless, his dancing was one of the highlights of the show. Tim Moore was the principal comedian.

Although this was an all-white creation for all-white consumption, it was the most successful edition of *Blackbirds*, and is significant as the longest-running all-black revue in Bway history up to its time.

Among the featured scenes and prodn. numbers were 'Scene in Jungleland' (in which Hall introduced the hit song "Diga Diga Do," later used with great success by Lena Horne in the film version of *Stormy Weather*); 'Playing According to Hoyle' (the show's famous blackface poker skit); 'Porgy' (a musical travesty of the Heyward play, which years later was made into *Porgy and Bess*); 'We Must Have "It" ' (a "parody in black" of °Elinor Glyn's novel, *It*—written and staged by Salem Tutt Whitney), 'Magnolia's Wedding Day' (a mock wedding, with a male bride); 'Earl Tucker, Giving His Conception of the Low Down Dance' (a "snake hip" dance specialty); 'Picking a Plot' (a stereotypical graveyard sketch); 'Getting Married in Harlem' (another wedding sketch); 'Wilton Crawley Accompanied by His Low Down Clarinet' (an acrobatic dance with a clarinet solo); and 'A Memory of 1927' (the tribute to Florence Mills).

After a lengthy tryout in several large cities, it opened on Bway at the Liberty Theatre, May 9, 1928, for 518 perfs.; prod. and dir. by Lew Leslie; orchestral arrangements by Will Vodery and others. Cast of the orig. prod.: Adelaide Hall, Bill Robinson, Aida Ward, Tim Moore, Mantan Moreland, Eloise Uggams, Chester Jones, Earl Tucker, Ruth Johnson, Crawford Jackson, Elisabeth Welsh (or Elizabeth Welch), Marjorie Hubbard, Blue McAllister, Lloyd Mitchell, Wilton Crawley, Billie Cortez, George W. Cooper, Mamie Savoy, Harry "Shorty" Lucas, Willard McLean, Baby Banks, Philip Patterson, Joseph Attles, the Blackbird Chorus, the Cecil Mack Choir, and the Plantation Orchestra.

A second company was organized as *Blackbirds of 1929*, with Harriet Calloway in the role created by Adelaide Hall, and John Worthy and Ed Thompson performing the dance steps which Bill Robinson perfd. on Bway. The rest of the cast included Sandy Burns, Beebee Joyner, Clarence Foster, Hilda Perleno, Rollin Smith, Henry "Gang" Jines, Derby Wilson, Maggie Jones, and Myrtle Watkins.

A prodn. opened in London in 1928, with Eddie Hunter, Eva Sherman, Anita Ward, Anita Edwards, Norman Astwood, and Johnny Nit. Another played successfully in Paris in 1929.

Songs and musical numbers: "The Call of the South" (Mack's Choir), "Shuffle Your Feet" (Johnson & Hubbard), "Dixie" (Ward & Company), "Diga Diga Do" (Hall's hit song), "I Can't Give You Anything But Love" (the best-known song from the show—which was written by "Fats" Waller and sung by Ward & Jones), "Doing the New Low Down" (Robinson's big tap-dancing number), "I Must Have That Man" (another song hit, sung by Hall), and "Here Comes My Blackbird" (in tribute to Mills, sung by Hall, McAllister, Jackson & Chorus).

Cast recording by Columbia (OL–6770), with Robinson and Hall of the orig. cast, Duke Ellington and his Orchestra, Cab Calloway, the Mill Brothers, the

Cecil Mack Choir, Don Redman and his Orchestra, and Ethel Waters in songs from the prodn. recorded during the period. Also featured explanatory notes by Miles Kreuger.

FURTHER REFERENCE: Alkire diss. *BlkMusTh* (Woll). *BlksBf* (Sampson). *Life* 7–12–1928. *NY Mirror* 5–19–1928. *NYT* 5–10–1928; 10–26–1928; 3–1–1929. *ThMag* 7–1928. *Variety* 5–16–1928. *Vogue* 7–1–1928.

BLACKBIRDS OF 1930 / / Also known as *Lew Leslie's Blackbirds of 1930* (1930). Musical revue. Presumably 2 acts. Book by Flournoy E. Miller and °Al Richards. Music by Eubie Blake. Lyrics by Andy Razaf. With additional music and lyrics by Spencer Williams, Clarence Williams, °Will Morrissey, and °Clarence Todd.

The third ed. of °Lew Leslie's famous *Blackbirds*, a series of all-black revues featuring songs, dances, and blackface comedy skits. This ed., "Glorifying the Negro," is especially significant because of its mainly black authorship, and because it featured Ethel Waters as the female star. The show was typical of Leslie's revues, which were aimed primarily at white audiences and exploited many of the stereotypes which were then prevalent in white-sponsored black revues. Among these were the traditional life of the Mississippi opening number; the usual plantation scene; the African primitive number; the customary trip to Harlem night spots; the blackface comedy skits; the parody of a well-known black show (in this instance *The Green Pastures*); and an all-black version of a white literary work (*All Quiet on the Western Front*, turned into a skit called 'All's Quiet on the Darkest Front'). Although the show was highly praised for its songs, the comedy scenes, which were mainly of the minstrel type, were reviewed unfavorably. The show, consequently, failed at the box office.

Opened on Bway at the Royale Theatre, Oct. 22, 1930, for 57 perfs. Blake conducted the Blackbird Orchestra; Cecil Mack conducted the Blackbird Choir. The cast featured Ethel Waters, Flournoy Miller, Mantan Moreland, Minto Cato, Tim Moore, Jimmy Baskette, Henry "Broadway" Jones, the Berry Brothers, Buck & Bubbles, Eloise Uggams, Neeka Shaw, Mercia Marquiz, Crawford Jackson, Blue McAllister, Marion Harrison, Estelle Bernier, and Mametta Newton.

Following its unsuccessful Bway run, it was presented in Philadelphia and Newark, before closing "in the red."

Principal songs, mainly by Razaf & Blake (most pub. by Shapiro, Bernstein & Co., New York), include the two showstoppers: "Memories of You" (Cato) and "You're Lucky to Me" (Waters); "My Handyman Ain't Handy No More" (Waters), "Roll, Jordan" (Mack's Choir), "Cabin Door," "Mozambique," "Take a Trip to Harlem," "We're the Berries," "That Lindy Hop," "Dianna Lee," "Green Pastures" (the latter by Morrissey & Razaf), and "Papa-De-Da-Da" (a New Orleans stomp by Todd, Williams & Williams, pub. by Clarence Williams Music Pub. Co.). Music for several songs is located in Moorland-

Spingarn. Miss Waters' two songs are recorded on Columbia Records (CL–2792).
FURTHER REFERENCE: *BlkMusTh* (Woll). *Bookman* 12–1930. *Life* 11–14–1930. *NY Herald Trib.* 10–23–1930. *NYorker* 11–1–1930. *NY Sun* 10–23–1930. *NYT* 11–23–1930. *Variety* 10–29–1930.

BLACKBIRDS OF 1933 / / Also known as ***Lew Leslie's Blackbirds of 1933*** (1933–34). Musical revue. Prologue & 2 acts. Sketches by °Nat N. Dorfman, °Mann Holiner, and °Lew Leslie. Music and lyrics by °Alberta Nichols, °Joseph Young, °Ned Washington, and °Victor Young. Revised as ***Blackbirds of 1934***.

Fourth ed. of the famous Lew Leslie's *Blackbirds*, a series of all-black shows, featuring songs, dances, and comedy skits designed for all-white audiences. This ed. boasted Bill Robinson as guest star. The plot was built around the producing of a *Blackbirds* revue. The Prologue shows the prospective performers rushing from their homes, parties, and various locations on the street to audition for parts in the latest *Blackbirds* show. Act I depicts the assembling of the cast, and their rehearsal by the stage director (played by Lionel Monagas). Act II is the show itself. Among the sketches were parodies of several Bway shows and films, including *Design for Living, Dinner at Eight* (called 'No Dinner at Eight'), the °Gilbert & °Sullivan *Mikado*, and °Eugene O'Neill's *Emperor Jones*. The critics were not impressed by either the skits or the songs. Only Bill Robinson's tap dancing was universally praised by reviewers.

Prod. by the Sepia Guild Players at the Apollo Theatre on Bway, opening Dec. 2, 1933, for 25 perfs.; staged by Leslie. Other cast members included Edith Wilson, Eddie Hunter, John Mason, Speedy Smith, Katherine Perry, Toni Ellis, Musa Williams, Mary Mathews, Phil M. Scott, Martha Jones, Eloise Uggams, the Cecil Mack Choir, and the Blackbirds Chorus.

A revised version billed as *Blackbirds of 1934* added Tim Moore to the cast. It apparently went on tour.

Songs and musical numbers: "A Hundred Years from Today," "I Just Couldn't Take It, Baby," "Your Mother's Son-in-Law," "I'm Walkin' the Chalk Line," "Doin' the Shim Sham," "Tappin' the Barrel," "Victim of the Voodoo Drums," "Let Me Be Born Again," and "What—No Dixie?" Three additional songs were added to the revised edition: "Rhapsody in Blue," "Great Gettin' Up Morning," and "Christmas Night in Harlem."
FURTHER REFERENCE: *BlksBf* (Sampson). *NY Sun* 12–3–1933. *NYT* 12–3–1933; 12–4–1933; 8–26–1934. *Time* 12–11–1933.

BLACKBIRDS OF 1939 / / Also known as ***Lew Leslie's Blackbirds of 1939*** (1939). Musical revue. 2 acts. Dialogue by °Nat N. Dorfman and °Fred F. Finklehofte. Conceived, prod., and staged by °Lew Leslie. Lyrics by °Dorothy Sachs, °Johnny Mercer & others. Music by °Rube Bloom & others. Orchestrations by °Ferde Grofé. Vocal arrangements by J. Rosamond Johnson.

The fifth and final ed. of Lew Leslie's famous *Blackbirds* revues, begun in

1926, and issued in 1928, 1930, 1933, and 1939, respectively. Although this ed. featured the singing and dancing of Lena Horne (then a promising newcomer), it was the least successful version, lasting for only one week on Bway. Calling itself "A Harlem Rhapsody," this show followed the unvarying formula that Leslie had used with varying success in previous eds. There were the comic antics of Hamtree Harrington, Dewey "Pigmeat" Markham, Tim Moore, and Joe Byrd (one of their sketches was a Harlem bridge game); the lively dancing numbers of Ralph Brown (in a jungle holiday), Whitey's Lindy Hoppers, Van Grana's Swing Ballet, and Taps Miller; the songs of the vivacious Horne (whose best number was "You're So Different"); and the renditions of Rosamond Johnson's Choir (which included °George Gershwin's "Rhapsody in Blue").

Prod. on Bway at the Hudson Theatre, opening Feb. 11, 1939, for 9 perfs. In addition to the principals named above, the cast included Laurene Hines, Kate Hall, Norman & Blake, and Rosetta Crawford.

Other songs included "Thursday" (Horne), "Name It and It's Yours," "I Did It for the Red, White, and Blue," and "Dixie Isn't Dixie Anymore."
FURTHER REFERENCE: *NY Daily Mirror* 2–13–1939. *NYT* 11–13–1938; 2–13–1939.

BLACK BOTTOM (1920). Musical revue. Presumably written or coauthored by Perry Bradford. The title suggests that the show featured the popular dance called the "Black Bottom." No record of prodn. Among the musical numbers was "We'll Meet Again," a waltz ballad, pub. by Bradford, New York; copy in Moorland-Spingarn.

BLACK BOTTOM REVUE (1927). Vaudeville revue. Prod. by °Jack Goldberg at the Lincoln Theatre in Harlem, 1927; featuring singer Clara Smith. Cast also included Green & Green, Happy Holmes, "Nuggie" Johnson, "Washboard" Johnson, Clarence Paison, Quinton Redd, Ruth Trent, Ana White, and Williams & Ferguson.

BLACK BROADWAY (1980). Retrospective musical revue. 2 parts. Prod. by °George Wein, Honi Coles, Robert Kimball, and Bobby Short. Songs by various composers and lyricists, black and white. Orchestrations and musical arrangements by Dick Hyman.

The re-creation of an old-time black revue, featuring musical numbers introduced by black composers and performers from 1899 to 1946, some of them sung by the original stars. As described by Arnold Shaw (*Blk. Pop. Mus. in Am.*, p. 299):

Black Broadway was a vaudeville-style song-and-dance salute not only to the old music but to some of the artists who had performed it. Onstage was John Bubbles, of Buck & Bubbles, and the original Sportin' Life in [*]*Porgy and Bess*, who appeared despite being partially paralyzed but sat in a chair as he reprised "It Ain't Necessarily So." Adelaide Hall, who starred in [*]*Blackbirds of 1928*; Elisabeth Welch, celebrated as the popularizer of Cole Porter's "controversial" ballad, "Love for Sale"; and Edith Wilson who starred in [*]*Hot Chocolates* in 1938 with Fats Waller and Louis Armstrong, also appeared.

Presented by the Newport Jazz Festival at Town Hall in New York City, May 4–20, 1980, for 25 perfs. Musical direction by Frank Owens, who conducted a 19-piece band. Cast: John Bubbles, Nell Carter, Honi Coles, Adelaide Hall, Gregory Hines, Bobby Short, Elisabeth Welch, Edith Wilson, Charles "Cookie" Cook, Leslie "Bubba" Gaines, Mercedes Ellington, Carla Earle, Terri Griffin, Wyette Turner, and a chorus of 4 beautiful ladies.

Songs and musical numbers: "Runnin' Wild," "Under the Bamboo Tree," "Oh Say Wouldn't It Be a Dream," "Broadway in Dahomey," "The Unbeliever," "Doin' the Low-Down," "When the Lights Are Low," "Solomon," "Love for Sale," "Creole Love Song," "I Must Have That Man," "Digga Digga Do," "I Can't Give You Anything But Love," "Ill Wind," "Between the Devil and the Deep Blue Sea," "As Long As I Love," "Brownskin Gal in the Calico Gown," "Jump for Joy," "Cotton Club Stomp," "There's a Boat That's Leavin' Soon for New York," "It Ain't Necessarily So," "Black and Blue," "He May Be Your Man," "Tan Manhattan," "Charleston Rag," "Silver Rose," "I'm a Little Blackbird," "Charleston," "I've Got a Feeling I'm Falling," "Legalize My Name," "Taking a Chance on Love," "Heat Wave," "You're Lucky to Me," "Suppertime," "Honey in the Honeycomb," "Dinah," "Stormy Weather," "Sweet Georgia Brown," and "Memories of You."
FURTHER REFERENCE: *AmMusTh* (Bordman). *Blk. Pop. Mus. in Am.* (Shaw). *Newswk* 5–26–1980. *NYT* 5–2–1980. Playbill in TC/NYPL.

BLACK CIRCLES 'ROUND ANGELA / / Also prod. as ***Black Circles***, and as ***Black Circles, Black Spirits*** (1970–74). Topical musical. 1 act. By Hazel Bryant.

A frequently prod. and frequently revised musical which remained in the repertory of Bryant's Afro-American Total Theatre for several years. It concerned a confrontation, in the setting of a beauty parlor, between four women—Safronia, Sweetthing, Peaches, and Aunt Sarah—representative of four vastly different black female lifestyles, as depicted in the recording of "Four Women," made by Nina Simone several years ago. As described by *NY Amsterdam N.* (3–9–1974, p. D-14), "Vignettes and speeches of Angela Davis serve as the catalyst, while the women engage in a verbal brawl occasionally, defending their roles. Angela's role, however, is that of a spiritual entity interspersed throughout the performance, causing each woman to reflect as her words are spoken." Apparently the musical was revised with other "spiritual entities" in the background, during the course of its long run.

First prod. as *Black Circles 'Round Angela* at the International House, New York, Feb. 19 and 22, 1970. Again perfd. under this title at the Afro-American Studio Theatre in Harlem, Feb. 1973. Perfd. as *Black Circles* at the Halsey St. Block Assn., Brooklyn, Aug. 26, 1971. Perfd. as *Black Circles, Black Spirits* at the Martinique Theatre, New York, March 1974. Unpub. script of *Black Circles 'Round Angela* in Schomburg.

(THE) BLACK COWBOYS (1969). "A horse opera in jazz form" (*Blk. World* 4–1976). Music by Sam Rivers. Libretto by Emory Taylor. Part of a longer work called *The Black West* (1969). First prod. by the Afro-American Singing Theatre, New York, Aug. 17–22, 1970; with appearances at a location on 109th Street, Sarah D. Roosevelt Park, Tompkins Square, Mt. Morris Park, and Demroach Bank Shell at Lincoln Center, New York City. Again prod. by the Harlem Jazz Opera (now known as the Harlem Opera Society), New York, 1975. Presented Nov. 18–19, 1971, at the Harlem YWCA, New York City. Presented as a part of *The Black West*, at the Billie Holiday Theatre, Brooklyn, NY, Nov. 8, 1972.

BLACK DIAMOND EXPRESS (1928). Musical revue. Prod. by and starring singer Mamie Smith at the Lafayette Theatre in Harlem, 1928. Cast also included Joe Russell, Amon Davis, and Lorenzo and Rae Tucker.

BLACK EXPO (1969). Billed as "the first comprehensive entertainment series of Black performing artists and companies." A demonstration of black American experience in dance, vocal interpretation, instrumental jazz, the drama, pantomime, soul, and gospel music. Opened April 22, 1969, at New York City Center, presented by the City Center of Music and Drama, and Summer on Wheels.

BLACK LOVE (1975). Topical musical. By Clarence Young III. Described by *Blk. World* (4–1976) as "a musical with some social commentary." Its theme was love, which the show suggests can be achieved "once the barriers to it are removed" (Ibid.). Prod. by Theatre West (of Dayton, OH) in Washington, DC, 1973.

BLACK MAGIC ANYONE? (1971). Musical play. Approximating 3 acts. By Beatrice W. Emeruwa (Leatrice El). Utilized poetry, chants, ritual, and music to explore the conflict between the old-time religious beliefs of Sister Williams and the mysticism of Madame Zenobia—as contrasted with Sister's son, who is inclined toward radicalism and Islam. Presented as a work-in-progress by the Negro Ensemble Co. at St. Marks Playhouse, New York, for 2 perfs., opening Jan. 19, 1971; dir. by Buddy Butler. Also presented in Cleveland, OH, at the First One World Theatre Project, 1971, also dir. by Butler; and at the Second One World Theatre Project, 1973, dir. by the author and her sister, Anna Boles-El.

BLACK NATIVITY / / Orig. title: ***Wasn't It a Mighty Day?*** (1961–64). Subtitled "A Christmas Song Play." 2 acts. By Langston Hughes.
    The birth of Christ and the spread of the gospel celebrated in the black idiom with gospel music, spirituals, pantomime, dance, drama, and narration. (Included some material from Hughes' Christmas cantata, *Ballad of the Brown King* [1960].) Act I ('The Child Is Born') is a pageant of the nativity. Act II ('The

Word Is Spread') takes the form of a revival meeting with praises and songs to the glory of the infant Jesus. Winner of the Catholic Dove Award at Cannes, France.

The change of title caused a mild controversy among the cast, resulting in the resignation of Carmen de Lavallade and Alvin Ailey from the show, on the grounds that the new title (prior to the wide acceptance of the term *black*) might be viewed as sacrilegious and racist.

First prod. Off-Bway at the 41st St. Theatre, opening Dec. 11, 1961; moved to the New York Theatre, Jan. 9–28, 1962, for a total of 57 perfs.; dir. by Vinnette Carroll. Featuring Alex Bradford (as Balthazar & preacher) and Marion Williams & the Stars of Faith. Other cast members included Howard Sanders (Narrator), Cleve Thompson (Joseph), Cleo Quitman (Mary), Henrietta Waddy (Woman), Carl Ford (Shepherd), Princess Stewart (Angel), Calvin White (Melchior), and Kenneth Washington (Caspar).

After closing Off-Bway, went on European tour. Presented at the Festival of Two Worlds in Spoleto, Italy, July 1962. Opened in London at the Criterion Theatre, Aug. 14, 1962. Toured elsewhere in England, Oslo, Copenhagen, Hamburg, and Brussels. Returned to New York for 7 perfs., during the Christmas season at Philharmonic Hall, Lincoln Center, Dec. 23–30, 1962. Resumed European tour, opening in Paris at the Theatre Elysees, Jan. 3, 1963, followed by a six-month tour through Italy, Germany, the Netherlands, Belgium, Switzerland, and Sweden. Returned to the U.S., opening in Boston, Oct. 14, 1963, and closing in Chicago, Jan. 12, 1964.

Prod. Off-Off-Bway by the Afro-American Studio, in repertory, during the 1968–89 season; dir. by Ernie McClintock. This prodn. was considered an "Off-Off-Bway Best" by *BesPls 1968–69*.

Telecast by WABC-TV, New York, Dec. 23, 1973, with members of various New York theatre groups associated with the Black Theatre Alliance. Choreography by Milo Timmons; Andy Cooper, musical dir. Featuring Earlise Vails (Mary), Suave Mitchell (Joseph), and Lee Cooper (lead singer).

Prod. by the Richard Allen Center for Culture and Art of New York City at the Vatican in Rome, in a special perf. for Pope John Paul II, on Dec. 23, 1982; dir. by Hazel Bryant.

Other productions were by the Theatre of Universal Images, Newark, NJ, 1984, dir. by Mike Malone; the Alliance Theatre, at the Marquand Chapel, Yale Divinity School, New Haven, CT, 1986, dir. by Vincent J. O'Brien; the Crossroads Theatre, New Brunswick, NJ, 1986, dir. and choreographed by Mike Malone; and the Paul Robeson Theatre, North Carolina A & T State Univ., Greensboro, NC, 1986 (where it is now an annual event).

Songs and musical numbers: "Joy to the World," "My Way Is Cloudy," "No Room at the Inn," "Most Done Travelling," "Oh, Jerusalem, in the Morning," "Poor Little Jesus," "What You Gonna Name Your Baby?," "Wasn't That a Mighty Day," "Christ Was Born," "Go Tell It on the Mountain," "Rise Up, Shepherd, and Follow," "What Month Was Jesus

Borned In?,'' "Sweet Little Jesus Boy,'' "Oh Come All Ye Faithful,'' "If Anybody Asked You Who I Am,'' "Children, Go Where I Send Thee,'' "Meetin' Here Tonight,'' "Holy Ghost, Don't Leave Me,'' "We Shall Be Changed,'' "The Blood Saved Me,'' "Leak in the Building,'' "Nobody Like the Lord,'' "His Will Be Done,'' "Said I Wan't Gonna Tell Nobody,'' "Get Away Jordan,'' "Packing Up,'' and "God Be With You.''

Cast recording by Vee Jay (VJS–8503). Unpub. script in Schomburg.

FURTHER REFERENCE: *BlkMagic* (Hughes & Meltzer). *Blk. Th.* #3, 1970. *Ebony* 4–1982. Hicklin diss. *Milwaukee J.* 11–3–1963. *Nation* 1–5–1963. *Newswk* 9–3–1962; 1–5–1963. *NY Herald Trib. Mag.* 10–27–1963. *NY Post* 12–12–1961. *NYT* 12–12–1961; 8–15–1962; 1–24–1964. *Sepia* 6–1965.

BLACKOUTS OF 1929 / / Also known as *Ken Murray's Blackouts of 1929* (1929). Harlem revue. Featured actor-composers Shelton Brooks and Billy Higgins, who apparently wrote music for and perfd. in this show.

(THE) BLACK PATTI TROUBADOURS / / Also known as *Black Patti's Troubadours* and the *Black Patti Musical Comedy Co.* (c. 1896–1915). Touring musical comedy company, which toured for about 20 years under the management of °Voelckel & Nolan, with a series of seasonal shows built around and featuring the popular concert singer, Sissieretta Jones, known as the Black Patti (after the white opera star, °Adelina Patti).

The shows combined elements of the minstrel stage, the musical comedy, and the serious musical concert. Part I consisted of an hour-long farce (which was changed from season to season and frequently revived). Part II consisted of two parts, a "Vaudeville Olio" which presented a miscellaneous collection of comedy, songs, and specialty acts, followed by an "Operatic Kaleidoscope," featuring Black Patti, other soloists, and a chorus in operatic and choral selections. In the beginning, Jones did not appear in the farces or sketches; but in later years, some of these were built into three-act musical comedies in which she was the principal star, and the operatic elements were fully integrated into the show.

Among the skits, sketches, and full-length musical comedies prod. by the Troubadours (and included as separate entries in this encyclopedia) are the following: *At Jolly Coon-ey Island (1896–97), with book, music, and lyrics by Bob Cole and William "Billy" Johnson; *At Jolly Coon-ey Island (New Edition) (1898), by Ernest Hogan, with music arranged by J. A. Raynes; *A Spanish Review (1898), conceived and arranged by Bob Cole and William "Billy" Johnson; *A Ragtime Frolic at Ras-bury Park (1899), written by the Troubadours; *A Darktown Frolic at the Rialto (1900), written by the Troubadours; *A Filipino Misfit (1902), written by the Troubadours; *Darktown's Circus Day (1903), book originally by Bob Cole, later revised by others; *Cooney Dreamland (1904), by Bob Cole; *The Prince of Bungaboo (1907–8), written by Salem Tutt Whitney: *Captain Jasper (1907–13), written by Will A. Cook, with music by various composers; *Blackville Strollers* (1908–9), with book, music, and lyrics by Salem Tutt Whitney & J. Homer Tutt; *A Trip to Africa* (1908, 1910–11), written by John Larkins; *In the Jungles* (1911), book by Will A. Cook and Al F. Watts, music by Will Marion Cook and Alex C. Rogers; and *Lucky Sam from Alabam* (1914), book and music mainly by Harrison Stewart.

The Black Patti Troubadours show was first presented at a theatre in New York, presumably Proctor's 58th Street Theatre, Sept. 26, 1896, followed by annual tours throughout the U.S., including the South, where it was one of the few shows to play successfully. Principals in the first season's cast included Madame Sissieretta Jones, Bob Cole and his wife Stella Wiley, and members of Cole's All Star Stock Co., which included the following vaudevillians: Billy and Willie Farrell (cakewalk dancers), Tom Brown, Fred Pifer, Mamie Flowers (operatic soprano), William "Billy" Johnson, Mattie Wilkes, Gussie L. Davis, Will Proctor, Ada Overton Walker (wife of George Walker), and Ernest Hogan. Cole and his troupe left the show after the first year because of a dispute with the management. Hogan left the cast to star in *Clorindy*, then later rejoined Black Patti for a long run.

Other stars who appeared with the show during its 20-year run include Henry Wise, Charles L. Moore, Alice Mackey, Charles Bougia, Ida Forsyne, J. Ed Green, John Rucker, Anthony Byrd, Slim Henderson, Muriel Ringgold, Jeannette Murphy, and Ethel Williams.

For more information, consult separate show titles.

FURTHER REFERENCE: *BlksBf* (Sampson). *Ghost* (Sampson). *Just Before Jazz* (Riis). *Nobody* (Charters). Riis diss.

BLACK PICTURE SHOW (1975). Musical play. Book by Bill Gunn, who also dir. Music and lyrics by Sam Waymon—also musical dir. and vocalist.

The tragedy of a promising black poet-playwright, who compromises his intellectual integrity for the financial rewards and glamour of making Hollywood films. In the setting of a psychiatric unit of a Bronx hospital, it reviews the playwright's life to discover what caused his intellectual decay. Earned for Dick Anthony a Tony nomination.

Prod. by the New York Shakespeare Festival and °Joseph Papp, at the Vivian Beaumont Theatre, Lincoln Center, New York, Jan. 6–Feb. 9, 1975, for 41 perfs. Cast: Albert Hall (J.B.), Dick Anthony (Alexander), Graham Brown (Norman), Carol Cole (Rita), Paul-David Richards (Philippe), Linda Miller (Jane), and Sam Waymon (Vocalist).

Songs and musical numbers: "I'm So Glad," "Mose Art," "Bird of Paradise," "Variation on 'Chopin in E Minor'," "Memory," "Bitch in Heat," "Digits," "Science Fiction," "Vintage '51," "Afghanistan," "Terminate," "Black Picture Show," and "I Feel So Good."

FURTHER REFERENCE: *DBlkTh* (Woll).

THE BLACK POLITICIAN (1904–8). Musical comedy. Book by S. H. Dudley and °S. B. Cassion. Music and lyrics by James Reese Europe and Cecil Mack.

The plot revolves around a contest between two candidates for mayor of Marco, GA—Remus Boreland and Ephraim Grindle. Grindle, the worthier of the two candidates, hires Hezekiah Doo, also known as the Black Politician (played by Dudley) to manage his campaign and entrusts him with his campaign funds, which are stolen, however, by two con artists from a stranded burlesque troupe. The Black Politician makes good the funds by winning in a horse race, and Grindle is elected mayor; while Hezekiah wins the love of the rival candidate's daughter. This was the prodn. in which Dudley first led a mule onstage as part of his act.

Prod. as a touring show by °Gus Hill's *Smart Set Co.*, 1904–8. Tom Logan was stage manager; and Jim Reese Europe, musical dir. Cast: James (Jim) Burris (Walter Tiese, manager of the Overland Burlesquers, a stranded troupe), Tom Logan (Remus Boreland, a candidate for mayor), Irvin Allen (Ephraim Grindle, another candidate), John Smith (Silas Jackson, a one-legged Civil War veteran), Will Carrington (Cephas Knott, a sheriff), Will Ramsey (Ephraim's son), Jennie Pearl (Palora Boreland, Remus' daughter), Rosa Lee Tyler (Flossie Conn, leading lady of the Burlesquers), and Alberta Ormes (Samantha Grindle, Ephraim's wife). Other characters include Jimmy Blackburn (a race horse), Peanuts (a mule), Jockeys, Society Ladies, Spanish Maids, Politicians, and Race Track Officials.

Songs and musical numbers: Medley of Vocal Gems (Company), "When I Rule the Town" (Allen), "Spooney Sam" (Burris), "The Darktown Band" (Matt Johnson, as a Politician), "Help Yourself" (Jennie Pearl), "Don't Take Him Away" (Ensemble), "Races, Races" (Company), "Liking Ain't Like Living" (Rosa Lee Tyler & Chorus), "Down Manilla Bay" (Ella Jones, Florence Greene [as Spanish maids] & Chorus), "Hezekiah Doo" (Jennie Pearl & Dudley), "The Smart Set Carbineers" (Robert Williams [as a Track Official] & Chorus), "Society" (Company), "Lolita" (Tyler), "I Don't Like School" (Female Chorus), "Crow" (Dudley & Scholars), and Grand Medley Finale (Company).

FURTHER REFERENCE: *BlksBf* (Sampson).

BLACK PROPAGANDA (1920s). Military revue. By J. Berni Barbour. One of several of his musical stage works which toured the western part of the United States during the 1920s.

BLACK RHYTHM (1936). Billed as "a Negro Musical Comedy." 2 acts. By Donald Heywood.

The thin plot revolves around an amateur night in Harlem in which a number of specialty acts are presented. Jeni LeGon and dancer Avon Long were among the principal stars.

Prod. on Bway by Earl Dancer and °J. H. Levey at the Comedy Theatre, New

York, opening Dec. 19, 1936, for 6 perfs.; staged by Dancer & Heywood. Cast: Jeni LeGon (Jenny), Maude Russell (Laura), William Walker (Mr. Heydon), Alec Lovejoy (Cornbread), Babe Matthews (Babe), Walter Richardson (David Songbird), Avon Long (Rhythm), Franklin Klien (Mr. Feinstein), Speedy Wilson (Bodidly), Joe Byrd (Dusty), Geneva Washington (Eva), Eddie Baer (Slim), John Foss (Eugene), Sammy Gardner (Toby), Sinclair Brooks (Swing), Walder Davis (Ghichi), Clarence Albright (Money), Eddie Matthews (Joe Michaels), Ina Duncan (Wardrobe Sal), Woodrow Wilson (Van Bugg), and Barrington Guy (Sonny).

Only one song from the show is known: "Back in Circulation," pub. by Mills, New York, 1938; copy in Moorland-Spingarn.
FURTHER REFERENCE: *NYT* 12–21–1936. *Time* 12–28–1936.

BLACK RITUAL (1940). Dance drama. Subtitled "Obeah." By choreographer °Agnes de Mille. Inspired by witchcraft or voodoo practices of West African or Caribbean origin. Prod. by the New York City Ballet Theatre, in its first season, at the City Center, New York, and perfd. by 16 black girls to the music of Darius Milhaud's "Creation of the World."

BLACK SCANDALS (1928). Musical revue. By George Smithfield. Song-and-dance show which, in spite of some "good hoofing," the *NYT* (10–27–1928) considered to be "amateurish," "pretentious," and "mirthless." The music consisted of popular songs of the period. Prod. with an all-black cast at the Totten Theatre, New York, opening Oct. 26, 1928, for a very short run.

A BLACKVILLE CORPORATION (1910, revived 1915). Musical comedy. 2 acts. Adapt. by J. Leubrie Hill from *Bandana Land* (1907–9) by Alex C. Rogers, Jesse A. Shipp, and Will Marion Cook; costarring Williams & Walker.

An updated version of the earlier show, in which Hill had been a cast member, along with Alex C. Rogers, one of the orig. authors who was also in this show. Like its predecessor, *A Blackville Corporation* concerned a get-rich-quick real estate scheme perpetrated by a bogus corporation headed by Bankus Blackville, through which its members buy up some property in a peaceful residential neighborhood, then create such a disturbance by their social activities that the neighbors hopefully will buy it back at double the original investment. In *Bandana Land*, the neighborhood was white. Here the neighbors are apparently black, and the property is located near a church. The scam is eventually foiled by another schemer, and the tables turned on the original perpetrators.

First prod. by Hill in Harlem and on the road in 1910. Only 5 members of that cast are known: Leubrie Hill (in his orig. role as Sandy Turner), Louis Mitchell, Leona Mitchell, and the comedy team of Brown & Shelton.

Revived in 1915, prod. and staged by Hill, presumably as a touring show, with the following cast: Hill (Sandy Turner), Alex C. Rogers (Jasper Jenkins, a landowner), Mme. Fairfax (Matilda Jenkins, Jasper's wife), Anthony Byrd

(Rube Jenkins, his son), Evon Robinson (Mandy Jenkins, his daughter), Sarah Byrd Green (Diana Jenkins, a second daughter), Mattie Harris (Sue Jenkins, a third daughter), Dink Stewart (Bankus Blackville, corporation head); Members of the Church: Emmett Anthony (Elder Sparks), Toots Davis (Brother Jackson), Will Madeleff (Brother Morgan), Joe Hatch (Brother Wilson), Willie Gross (Brother Black), Eddie Rector (Brother Brown), Harry Stafford (Brother Green), Hamilton White (Brother Watson); Others: Charles Olden (Country Green), Fred Cox (Mose Lewis), and Al Steward (Lawyer Tom Collins).

The orig. songs from *Bandana Land* may have been used. Only one additional song from this show is known: "The Harlem Prince," sung by Robinson & Company.

BLACKVILLE STROLLERS (1908–9). Musical comedy. 1 act. Book, music, and lyrics by Salem Tutt Whitney and J. Homer Tutt (Whitney & Tutt).

One of the opening skits of the *Black Patti Troubadours* show. About a stranded troupe of touring players traveling by foot, called the Blackville Strollers, under the management of Miss Sureta Walkback, played by Tutt. The setting is a railroad station, where the players interact with other travelers and station personnel, and possibly put on a show to raise money for their train fares.

Prod. on transcontinental tour by the Troubadours, as part of their show, 1908–9. Opened at Boonton, NJ, in early Sept. 1908 with the following cast: J. Homer Tutt (Sureta Walkback, manager of the Blackville Strollers), William A. Cook (Count-de-Ties, a "dusty Knight of the Road"), Charles Bougia (Percy Harold, who "just can't see it"), Gus Hall (Allah Board, conductor), Sarah Green (Mandy Martina, leading lady of the Strollers), Marie Bell (Sara Heartburn, understudy), Jeanette Murphy (Sal Salome, "looking for a position"), Anthony Byrd (Aunt Jemima, "going to town"), Beatrice Hodge (Flossie), Ruby Taylor (Glossie), Ada Alexander (Cynthe), Daisy Brown (Pliney), Vera Davenport (Margie), Theresa Burroughs [Brooks] (Pansy), Loretta Wooden (Blossom), Irene Gaines (Crissy), Slim Henderson (Head Porter), Henry Wooden (Head Waiter), James Goodman (Station Agent), and Salem Tutt Whitney (Silas Green).

Although the *Blackville Strollers* remained in the repertoire of the Troubadours through 1909, Whitney & Tutt left the show in Dec. 1908 to form their own company, the *Smart Set Co.*, at the New Lincoln Theatre in Knoxville, TN, where Whitney was hired as manager, producer, and stage director. There they presented a new version of their show, with an abbreviated title (*The Strollers*), starring Whitney & Tutt in their customary roles as Silas Green and Sureta Walkback.

The Troubadours continued to present the show under its original title, and in March 1909 it was presented in Los Angeles, CA, and in April in San Francisco; it received good reviews in both cities. The *Los Angeles Daily Times* (2–27–1909) praised the comedy of Tim Owsley as Silas Green and Billy Young as Ned Walkback, the latter character apparently changed to a man after Tutt left the show. The *San Francisco Call* (4–17–1909) praised Owsley's comedy and songs, and stated that "in his burlesque scene with Charles Bougia he was a great jet joke." The *Call* also praised the singing of Sarah Green, in her role as the leading lady of the Strollers.

BLACKVILLE TWINS (1889–91). Minstrel farce. Authorship unknown. First prod. by Richards & Pringle's Georgia Minstrels, 1889, with the following cast: William Ganze (Elmia, one twin), Fred J. Piper (Jemina, the other twin), W. G. Huff (Parson Black, the father), J. A. Watts (Mama Black, the mother), Frank Mallory (Juke, one accepted suitor), William Eldridge (Bud, the other accepted suitor), Billy Kersands (Dr. Cutum, the family physician), Billy Farrell (Zuke Sheppard, rival suitor), J. S. Johnson (Tony Darce, another rival suitor). Again perfd. by the Hyers Sisters' Musical Company in the East, 1891; with the twins played by the Sisters.

BLAZMATAZZ (1987). Retrospective musical entertainment. Conceived, choreographed, and dir. by Osayande Baruti. Billed as "a sparkling blend of the best black music gems from the American stage and screen." Among the black artists whose musical contributions were saluted were Billie Holiday, Lena Horne, Cab Calloway, and Diana Ross, as well as the stars of such shows as *Carmen Jones*, *Lady Sings the Blues*, *Cabin in the Sky*, and *Stormy Weather*. Harold Nicholas, of the famed Nicholas Brothers, was the featured dancer. Prod. by the Theatre of Universal Images, Newark, NJ, April–May 1987. Asst. choreographer, Lilitte Bennett. Cast included Roger Lawson, Frederick Owens, Reena Phillips, Ronnell Bay, Gail Lou, Valencia, Emanuel Bennett, Cheryl Hayes, Miles Watson-Leverett, and Doug Frazier. Also presented at other locations in New Jersey, including the NJ Theatre Jubilee at Liberty State Park, Jersey City, Aug. 19–23.

BLESS YOU ALL (1950). White-oriented musical revue. Bway show in which Pearl Bailey appeared in Dec. 1950, in a supporting comedy/singing role. Brooks Atkinson of the *NYT* (12–15–1950) called her style of humor "only tepidly funny," but wrote that she could make a song "take on a piquant personality."

BLOOMER GIRL (1944–46). Musical of pre-Civil War Americana. Book by °Sig Herzig and °Fred Saidy. Lyrics by °E. Y. Harburg. Music by °Harold Arlen. The story of °Dolly Bloomer, mid-nineteenth century suffragette and inventor of the woman's undergarment named for her. The musical also dealt with her supposed interest in the rights of Negroes, particularly escaped slaves, expressed in at least one of the songs, "Man for Sale." Prod. at the Shubert Theatre, New York, Oct. 5, 1944, for 654 perfs; starring °Celeste Holm. The integrated cast included three blacks in the roles of runaway slaves: Dooley Wilson, Richard Huey, and Hubert Dilworth.

BLUE BABY (1927–28). Touring revue in at least two eds. Prod. by Irvin C. Miller. Toured the South with the following cast, which appeared in both eds.: Edgar Martin, Elizabeth Smith, Billy Young, Teddy[e] Frazier, Albert Jackson, and Louise Williams. The *1927 ed.* also included Lovie Austin, Alfred "Slick" Chester, and the Blue Baby Dancing Girls. The *1928 ed.* also included Billie & Mona.

BLUE HOLIDAY (1945). Variety show. Also called a musical pageant. Prod. by °Alvin Shapiro and °Doris Cole.

This show, which presented excerpts from former black plays and musicals, featured Ethel Waters and Josh White. Waters, whose performance was not well-received by the critics, sang a medley of her best-known songs and performed a scene from *Mamba's Daughters*, in which she had starred in 1939. White received high praise for his renditions of "The House I Live In," "Evil-Hearted Man," "Free and Equal Blues," and "Hard Time Blues."

Opened on Bway at the Belasco Theatre, May 21, 1945, for 8 perfs.; dir. by °Joe Hack. Other members of the all-black cast included Bill "Bojangles" Robinson, Mary Lou Williams, Timmy Rogers, Josephine Premice, Willie Bryant, Muriel Gaines, Lillian Fitzgerald, Lavinia Williams, Talley Beatty, Mildred Smith, Evelyn Ellis, the Three Poms, the Chocolateers, the Hall Johnson Choir, and the Katherine Dunham Dancers.

Songs and musical numbers (not listed above) include "I Want to Give It All to the Stage," "Blue Holiday," "That's Where My Heart Will Be," "Sleep Time Lullaby" (by Al Moritz), "Yours Is My Heart Alone" (by Franz Lehart), and a Duke Ellington medley which included "Mood Indigo," "Sophisticated Lady," and "Solitude." The Katherine Dunham Dancers appeared in two numbers: 'Voodoo in Haiti' and 'Fiji Islands.'
FURTHER REFERENCE: *NYT* 5–23–1945.

BLUE MONDAY BLUES (1922) / / Revised as *135th Street* (1925). Blues opera of black life, perfd. by whites in blackface. Music by °George Gershwin. Lyrics by °B. C. DeSylva. Orchestrations by black arranger Will Vodery; new orchestrations later by °Ferde Grofé.

A tragedy of jealous love à la "Frankie and Johnny," set in a Harlem bar, in which Vi, her lover Joe (a gambler), and Tom (a jealous rival) are the chief characters. When Joe learns that his mother is ill down South, he sends her a telegram and awaits a reply. When the reply arrives, Vi, having been told by Tom that the message is from another woman, shoots and kills Joe, only to discover afterwards that the telegram is from Joe's family informing him that his mother is dead.

First prod. as *Blue Monday Blues*, as part of *°George White's Scandals* of 1922, but was dropped after the opening perf. because of its length and the mixed reviews that it drew from critics. This one perf. was presented at the

Globe Theatre in New York, Aug. 29, 1922; with an all-white cast in blackface that included °Jack McGowan, °Coletta Ryan, and °Richard Bold.

The music was arranged by Vodery, whose orchestrations, once believed lost, are located in the George Gershwin Collection housed in the Music Collection/ LC. Revived in a concert perf. as *135th Street*, presented by °Paul Whiteman, with new orchestrations by Ferde Grofé, at Carnegie Hall in 1925. The all-white cast of singers included McGowan from the orig. prodn., °Blossom Seeley, °Charles Hart, and °Benny Fields.

FURTHER REFERENCE: *NY Eve. J.* 8–29–1922. *NY Eve. World* 8–29–1922. *NY Mail* 8–29–1922. *NY Sun* 8–29–1922. *NY Telegraph* 8–29–1922.

BLUE MOON (1926). Musical comedy. 1 act. Book and lyrics by Irvin C. Miller and Donald Heywood. Music by Heywood. Touring show prod. by Miller. The cast of 20 included Princess Mysteria and her partner Rinal, William ''Babe'' Townsend, Henrietta Lovelass, and Edna Barr.

BLUES FOR A GOSPEL QUEEN (1986). Book and lyrics by Don Evans. Gospel-oriented musical. Music by John Lewis. Possibly based on the life of Mahalia Jackson, and may be an earlier version of the same author and composer's *Mahalia (1978). Prod. by Marjorie Moon at the Billie Holiday Theatre, Brooklyn, NY, Nov. 1986.

BLUES IN THE NIGHT (1980). Blues musical. 2 acts. Conceived and dir. by Shelton Epps. Vocal and musical arrangements mainly by Chapman Roberts.

The story of three women and a saloon singer, set in a cheap hotel in Chicago in 1938.

First prod. by the Production Company at Playhouse 46 in New York, March 26–May 11, 1980, for 51 perfs. Choreography by Gregory Hines; vocal and musical arrangements with the assistance of Sy Johnson. Cast: Rise Collins, Gwen Shepherd, °Suzanne M. Henry, and °Davis Brunetti (Saloon Singer).

Prod. by Broadway Productions at the Rialto Theatre, New York, June 2– July 18, 1982, for 53 perfs. plus 13 previews. Cast: Leslie Uggams, Ruth Brown (replaced by Jean Dushon), °Ruth Shapiro, and °Charles Coleman (Saloon Singer).

Prod. on national tour by Blye Tours, Inc., and Bill Fegan Attractions, apparently during the 1983–84 season. Choreography by Mercedes Ellington. Cast: Cinthia White (Woman of the World), Della Reese (Lady from the Road), °Neva Small (Girl with a Date), and °Clem Moorman (Saloon Singer).

Prod. on national tour by M2 Entertainment, opening March 4, 1985, in Blacksburg, VA, and closing March 24, 1985, in Woodlands, TX. Choreography also by Mercedes Ellington. Cast: Eartha Kitt (Woman of the World), Carrie Smith (Lady from the Road), °Liz Larson (Girl with a Date), and °Clem Moorman (Saloon Singer).

Revised and prod. at the Minetta Lane Theatre, New York, for an open run beginning Sept. 14, 1988. Cast included Carol Woods, Brenda Pressley, Kathleen Rowe McAllen, and Lawrence Hamilton.

Songs and musical numbers: "Blue Blues," "Four Walls Blues," "I've Got a Date with a Dream," "New Orleans Hop Scop Blues," "Stompin' at the Savoy," "Taking a Chance on Love," "It Makes My Love Come Down," "Lush Life," "Take Me for a Buggy Ride," "Wild Women Don't Have the Blues," "Lover Man," "Willow Weep for Me," "Kitchen Man," "Low," "Take It Right Back," "Jam Session," "Blues in the Night," "Dirty No-Gooder's Blues," "Baby Doll," "Nobody Knows You When You're Down and Out," and "I Gotta Right to Sing the Blues."

BLUES LIFE OF BILLIE HOLIDAY (1970s). Musical biography. By Paul R. Allen. About the troubled life of the famed blues singer. Prod. by the Black American Theatre, Washington, DC, later known as the American Theatre, during the 1970s.

BLUE STEEL (1935). Opera. Written and composed by William Grant Still. His first opera, which utilized Negro spirituals, folk music, and jazz. No record of performance.

BOARD OF EDUCATION (1918). Tabloid musical. Written by Billy King, in collaboration with J. Berni Barbour.

Two con artists travel from town to town, receiving free accommodations by pretending that they are members of the Board of Education. Their fraudulent schemes are eventually impeded by a detective who has been on their trail for some time. After an action-filled climax, the crooks are finally arrested.

Prod. by Billy King at the Grand Theatre Chicago, with members of the Billy King Stock Co., which included King and Howard Kelly as the two hustlers, Gertrude Saunders, and the Girl Quartet.

Songs include "Working for the Very Last Time" (King), "Wait Till the Cows Come Home" (Saunders), "Sleep, Kentucky Home" (Quartet), and "Land of Cotton" (finale).

THE BODY BEAUTIFUL (1958). Musical. Book by °Josephine Stein and °Will Glickman. Music by °Jerry Bock. Lyrics by °Sheldon Harnick. Bway show with a predominantly white cast, in which Lonnie Satin and Barbara McNair had nonracial roles as a boxer and his wife.

A BOGUS PRINCE (1903). Musical farce. Written by Sidney Perrin. The plot apparently revolved around the arrival of a bogus prince in a small town, where he is presumably in search of an heiress for a bride. He is eventually exposed as a fraud by a young man whose sweetheart (the daughter of a wealthy farmer) has been chosen by the prince as his prospective wife. Presumably an earlier version of *The Emperor of Dixie*. Prod. by the Jolly Set Co. at Proctor's 23rd

St. Theatre, New York. Cast included Bob Slater, Sidney Perrin, Black Carl Dante, Bobby Kemp, Walter Crumbly, May Lange, Midget Price, Cecil Reese, Marie Willis, James Slater, Emma Chacon, and Eugene Butler.

BOMBAY GIRLS (1915–23). Touring revue in at least five eds.: 1915, 1917, 1921, 1922, and 1923. Prod. by and costarring Drake & Walker (Henry Drake and Ethel Walker). With members of the Great Eastern Stock Co. *1917 ed.* Also featured Russell Lee and Willie Hampton. *1923 ed.* Included James Rutherford, Helen Battle, and Edwards & Edwards.
FURTHER REFERENCE: *Billboard* (J. A. Jackson's Page), 8–16–1921; 7–22–1922.

BON BON BUDDY, JR. (early 1922) / / Later revised as **Liza* (1922–24). Musical comedy. 2 acts [12 scenes]. Book by Irvin C. Miller. Music by Maceo Pinkard.

An earlier, tryout version of *Liza*, the title borrowed from the theme song of George Walker ("Bon Bon Buddy" introduced in **Bandana Land*) as a tribute to the Williams & Walker musicals of the turn of the century. The scenes move from the stage of the Lafayette Theatre in Harlem to various locations in Bowling Green, KY—the home of a young dandy named Bon Bon Buddy, Jr. (played by George Wright). Irvin C. Miller and Emmett "Gang" Anthony performed in blackface as Rastus and Rasmus.

Prod. at the Lafayette Theatre in Harlem, for a long run in early 1922; dir. by Miller and Eugene Field. Other cast members include Gertrude Saunders (Liza Norris), William DuMont (Sheriff), Lydia Brown (Alice Dole), William Simms (Jim Norris), Adrian Joyce (Jason Davis), Parker Ramsey (Uncle Pete), Quintard Miller (Uncle Plummer), Theopolis Miller (Uncle Epheas), Alice Brown (Agneria), Elizabeth Terrell (Aunti Jemima), Doe Doe Green (Sam Johnson), Eugene Field (Bad Man), Fred Falls (Oscar Wilber), and Mary Baines (Soubrette). Chorus: 8 Show Girls, including Bee Freeman; 5 Dandies, including Lloyd Mitchell; and 12 Dancing Girls (also called Struttin' Girls).

Songs and musical numbers: Opening Number (onstage of the Lafayette Theatre): "Struttin' Town," "Creole Girls from the Follies," "Bandana Girls," and "Dixie Girls" (Chorus); "Give Me Plenty" (Saunders), "I'm the Sheriff" (DuMont & Chorus), "Bound Me in My Mammy's Arms" (Brown & Chorus), "The Dog" (Anthony), "Forget All Your Troubles (and Smile)" (Simms & Chorus), "Liza" (Wright, Saunders & Chorus), "The Day Bert Williams Said Goodby" (Wright, Saunders & Chorus), "Just Another Barber Shop Choral" (Anthony), "My Old Man" (Anthony), "Who's Tendin' to the Fireman's Fire" (I. C. Miller), "Raggedy Blues" (Brown & Chorus), "For a Girl Like You" (Brown & Girls), "Bon Bon Buddy, Jr." (Wright & Dandies), "Love Me (While Loving Is Good)" (Saunders), "Ticklin' Time" (Brown & Chorus), "Dance" (Barnes), and "Walk You Baby Doll" (Company).
FURTHER REFERENCE: *BlksBf* (Sampson).

THE BON TON MINSTRELS (1917). Vaudeville show. Prod. by Frank Montgomery and sponsored by the Quality Amusement Co. Presented at the Lafayette Theatre, New York, then on tour. Cast included Montgomery, Fanny Wise, George Stamper, Florence McClain, and Dewey Weinglass.

BON TON REVUE (1926). Touring revue. Prod. by and starring Susie Sutton. Cast included dancers/impersonators Coleman Titus and Richard Huff, Billy Gunn, Harold Brown, Eunice Washington, and the Novelty Quartet.

BORN HAPPY (1943). Musical revue. 2 acts. Special songs by °Lew Pollock and °Charles Newman. Orchestrations by °Lew Katzman and °Charles Koff.

The musical biography of a mythical dancer, starring Bill Robinson. Scenes 1 and 2 of Act I take place in a maternity hospital where the dancer was born. The action moves slowly to 'Harlem After Dark,' where Robinson and the Born Happy Chorus perf. a musical number entitled "I Can't Do Without Love," written by °Deke Moffett. This is followed by a rendition of several songs by Velma Middleton (a song stylist), the Delta Rhythm Boys (Decca recording artists), dances by Whitey's Jitterbugs, and the first act finale by the Born Happy Chorus. Act II begins with a scene outside a church in the Deep South, followed by several secular songs and dances, and then the big dance number by Robinson (billed as 'Mr. Born Happy Himself') just before the finale.

No prodn. information on this obscure Robinson revue has been located. It was probably prod. on the road in an unsuccessful attempt to reach Bway. Other cast members included Emmett [or Emett] "Babe" Wallace (the dancer's father); Johnny Virgel (Dr. Flash); John Mason (Rev. "Spiker" Bruce); the Three Peppers; Pot, Pan and Skillet (eccentric dancers); and singers Thelma Oliver, Rose Murphy, Mabel Scott, Judy Carol, Jimmy Anderson, and Holmes & Jean.

Other songs and musical numbers: "Smoke Gets in Your Eyes" (Holmes & Jean), "The Chee Chee Girl" (Murphy), "You Can Hear a Pin Drop" (Carol & Anderson), "Delightful, Delicious, Delovely" (Three Peppers), and "Is There a Latin in the House" (Carol, Oliver & Chorus).

BOTTOMLAND (1927). Musical revue. Called by the author "a musical comedy in three acts with special music" (*NY Post* 4–28–1927). Book, lyrics, and music by Clarence Williams.

Conceived as a starring vehicle for the Clarence Williams Trio, consisting of Williams, Eva Taylor, and Sara Martin, who were recording artists for Okey Records as well as radio performers, and according to Williams, it was written in compliance with "the thousands of requests from radio friends" (*NY Post*).

The threadbare plot concerned a talented southern woman, May Mandy Lee, who yearns to be a professional singer. After receiving glowing letters from one of her hometown friends, Sally, who claims to be a successful singer in New York, Mandy leaves her happy home and family in Bottomland and travels to New York's Harlem, where she discovers that Sally is actually a down-and-out alcoholic, barely eking out a living singing in a third-class cabaret. The nightclub setting provided an opportunity for staging several of the songs and specialty numbers. Other music was liberally sprinkled throughout the show, which caused the *NYT* (6–28–1927) to quip: "About every tenth line in the book is a song cue."

Prod. by Williams at the Princess Theatre in New York City, opening June 27, 1927, for 21 perfs. Cast: Eva Taylor (May Mandy Lee), Sara Martin (Mammy Lee), James A. Lilliard (Pappy Lee), Louis Cole (Jimmy), Katherine Henderson (Tough Lilly), Slim Henderson (Joshua), John Mason (The Dumb Waiter), Charles Doyle (Henry Henpeck), "Nuggie" Johnson (Shiftless Sam), Raymond Campbell (Skinny), Edward Farrow (Rastus), Olive Ortiz (Sally), Willie Porter (Mammy Chloe), Emanuel Weston (Kid Slick), Edwin Tandel (Policeman Doolittle), Craddock & Shadney (Specialty Act), and a "Pickaninny" Chorus.

Songs included "Steamboat Days," "Shootin' the Pistol," "Bottomland," "You're the Only One," "Come on Home," "Dancing Girl," "Any Time," and "When I March with April in May." "Bottomland" and "Shootin' the Pistol," which received high praise from the critics, were both recorded by Williams on Paramount label (12517), with trumpeter Ed Allen and trombonist Charlie Irvis.

FURTHER REFERENCE: *Billboard* 7–9–1927. *NY Herald Trib.* 6–28–1927. *NY Post* 6–28–1927. *NYT* 6–28–1927.

BOWMAN'S COTTON BLOSSOMS (1919). Touring vaudeville show. Prod. on tour by W. Henri Bowman. S. H. Dudley was the agent; W. Henri Bowman, straight man; Leroy White, comedian; Bonnie Bell Drew, leading lady; Johnny Sawyer, leading man; Sam P. Gardner, character actor; and James Phoenix, dancer. Comedienne Jackie (later "Moms") Mabley was one of the 5 chorus girls, which also included Sweetie Mae.

THE BOYS AND BETTY (1908). White-oriented musical play. 3 acts. Book and lyrics by °George V. Hobart. Music by °Silvio Stein. With an additional song by Will Marion Cook. About a woman who runs away to Paris to escape from a loveless marriage, sets up a shop, becomes rich, and is able to divorce her husband and find true love. Prod. by °Daniel V. Arthur at Wallack's Theatre, New York, Nov. 2, 1908, for 17 weeks; with an all-white cast headed by °Marie Cahill. Then went on tour. Cook's song, presumably sung by Cahill, was "Whoop 'er Up with a Whoop La La."

BREEZY TIMES (1922). Touring vaudeville revue. Book, lyrics, and orchestra direction by Herbert Byron. Prod. by Clarence Muse, who also directed and costarred. Cast included his wife Ophelia Muse, comedian Billy Walker, Leon Diggs, and Susie Sutton.

BRER RABBIT WHOLE (1984). Musical. Book and lyrics by George Houston Bass. Music by Robert L. Holmes, Jr. A research-based revue centered around the Uncle Remus stories. Showcase prodn. at Fisk Univ., Nashville, TN, Oct. 11–13, 1984. Premiered by Rites & Reason at Brown Univ., Providence, RI, March 8–24, 1985; dir. by Bass.

BRINGING UP HUSBAND (1920). Touring vaudeville revue. Prod. and perfd. by comedian Hambone Jones. Cast also included Virginia Liston and Sam H. Gray.

BROADWAY BREVITIES (1926). Touring revue. Not to be confused with the more famous *Broadway Brevities [of] 1920*, starring Bert Williams. This show was prod. by and costarred comedians Quintard Miller and Marcus Slayter.

BROADWAY BREVITIES [OF] 1920 (1920). Musical revue. Written and prod. by °George LeMaire. Additional music by Chris Smith. Financed by Bert Williams.

Starring vehicle for Williams, written by a white actor who had appeared with him in the *Ziegfeld Follies*, and who perfd. as his straight man in this prodn. According to Ann Charters (*Nobody*, p. 144), this show gave Williams "an opportunity to perform in longer skits, and these comedy routines were interspersed between acts by 'specialty people.' " In his funniest sketch, Williams purchased a pair of "yella" shoes, throwing away his old pair before leaving the store, only to return later, limping in pain, to retrieve the discarded shoes and throw away the new pair. °Eddie Cantor, who had also perfd. in the *Ziegfeld Follies*, appeared in a popular sketch entitled 'The Osteopath's Office,' which he had used in the *Follies*, but °Ziegfeld sued and the sketch was dropped from *Brevities*. This was the last show in which Williams appeared before his death in 1922.

Prod. on Bway at Shubert's Winter Garden Theatre, opening Sept. 29, 1920, for a run of 13 weeks.

Only three of Williams' songs are known: "The Moon Shines on the Moonshine" by Frances De Witt and Robert Hood Bowers, "I Want to Know Where Tosti Went (When He Said Goodbye)" by Chris Smith, and "You'll Never Need a Doctor No More" also by Smith—the latter pub. by Skidmore Mus. Co., 1921; copy in Moorland-Spingarn.

BROADWAY FLAPPERS (1927). Touring revue. Prod. by and starring Rosa Johnson. Cast also included blackface comedians "Slick" Porter and "Kid Country," Willie Townsend (possibly William "Babe" Townsend), Marie Hampton, James Miller, Bennie Robinson, and May Smith.

BROADWAY GOSSIPS (1920). Vaudeville revue. 10 scenes. Prod. in Harlem by comedian/showman Quintard Miller, who also starred in the prodn. Cast included B. B. (or Beebee) Joyner, comedian Doe Doe Green, Cleo Mitchell, Aaron Gates, Joe Carmouche, Lulu Whidby, and Theresa Burroughs Brooks.

A BROADWAY MUSICAL (1978). Musical "spoof." 2 acts [9 scenes]. Book by °William F. Brown. Music by °Charles Strouse. Lyrics by Lee Adams. A satire of the making of white-authored black musicals. Prod. unsuccessfully at the Lunt-Fontanne Theatre, New York, opening Dec. 21, 1978, for only 1 perf. and 14 previews; prodn. supervised by °Gower Champion. Blacks in the integrated cast included Lee Riley, Irving Allen Lee, Jackée Harry, Tiger Haynes, and Larry Marshall. Among the 13 musical numbers was one called "The 1934 Hot Chocolate Jazz Babies Revue."

BROADWAY RASTUS (1915–28). Touring revue in at least eight eds.: 1915, 1919, 1920, 1921, 1923, 1924, 1925, and 1928. Books mainly by Irvin C. Miller. Songs by various composers and lyrics (some named below).

The series of shows on which Miller's more successful *Put and Take* and *Alabama Bound* (both 1921) were based—built around the exploits of a character named Rastus King (also called "Broadway"), played by Miller in blackface, who is constantly scheming of ways to make some easy money.

Toured the black theatrical circuits, with seasonal revisions, from 1915 to 1928. Among the performers who appeared in one or more eds. were Emmett "Gang" Anthony, Esther Bigeou, May Boyd, Flo Brown, Frank Brown, James Calloway, Gallie DeGaston, S. H. Dudley, Jr., Billy Ewing, William E. Fountain, Charles Gibbs, Aurora Greeley, James Hicks, Juanita Hicks, Westley Hill, Henry "Gang" Jines, Eloise Johnson, Russell Lee, the Leggett Sisters (Lena, Josephine & Henrietta), Leon the Magician, Cecil Rivers, Trixie Smith, Blanche Thompson (Mrs. Irvin C. Miller), Lulu Whidby, Leigh Whipper, Ernest Whitman, and Lilly "Pontop" Yuen.

1915 ed. Lyrics by Whipper; music by Homer C. Brown, assisted by Rob Ricketts and W. C. Handy. Synopsis of scenes: Scene 1—Interior of the Elite Cafe; Scene 2—At the corner of 31st and State Streets; Scene 3—Interior of the Blue Ribbon Hotel. Cast: James Hicks (John Miller, a baker), Juanita Hicks (Sadie Williams, a student), I. C. Miller (Rastus King), Jines (Mose Smith, his pal), Carrie Purnell (Mabel Durant, a somnambulist), Boyd (Madame Durant, her mother), Westley Hill (Keen Johnson, a detective), Gibbs (Happy Ben, a town character), Bigeou (Ethel Morris, a popular girl), Johnson (Mae West, her friend), Ewing (Archive Love, a popular young man), Calloway (Dandy Man, a sport), Frank Brown (Wallace Page, a promoter of fairs), Lee (Dave Wallace, a booster), Whipper (Bill Mays, manager of the Birth of an Onion), and Billy Young (La Esmarelda, a fortune teller). Songs include "Bye-and-Bye" and "Whip-o-will" (Ewing), "Every Woman's Got a Man But Me" (Young), "Some Day" and "You Go Your Way and I'll Go Mine" (Bigeou), "Every

Goodye Ain't Gone,'' "Every Shut Eye Ain't Sleep," "I Was Mad [or Made] for You," "Can't Stop Lovin' You Now," "Chinese Blues," "Clutching Hand," "Dandy Man," "Texas Tommy," and "Just to Be Near Salvation Nell."

1919 ed. Cast included Flo Brown, I. C. Miller, Rivers, Thompson, and Yuen.

1920 ed. Cast included I. C. Miller, Thompson, the Leggett Sisters, Fountain, Anthony, Q. Miller, Leon the Magician, Whitman, and the Charlie Williams Jazz Band.

1921 ed. See *Put and Take* (1921) and *Alabama Bound* (1921).

1923 ed. Lyrics by Pousseau Simmons; music by W. Alston Morgan. Dir. by Q. Miller. Cast included I. C. Miller, Q. Miller, and Smith.

1924 ed. Cast included Anthony, Rivers, Greeley, Thompson, I. Brown, Lloyd Mitchell, and John Henderson.

1925 ed. 2 acts [3 scenes]. Music by Maceo Pinkard. Music dir. by Clarence Marks. Cast included I. C. Miller, Thompson, Flo Brown, Rivers, Greeley, DeGaston, Yuen, and Chorus. Songs and musical numbers: "Levee Nights" (Ensemble), "Going South" (Flo Brown, Rivers & Chorus), "Black Bottom Dance" (Yuen & Chorus), "Orange Grove" (Rivers & Chorus), "Savannah" (Greeley, Brown & Chorus), "Runnin' Wild Blues" (Ensemble), "Hello" (Liza Girls), "Planning" (John Henderson), "Too Tired" and "Daddy" (Greeley & Chorus). Other specialty numbers: Comedy act (DeGaston & Yuen), Specialty act (Rivers & Flo Brown), Eccentric dance (Lloyd Mitchell).

1928 ed. Cast included Anthony, I. Brown, Dudley, and chorus.

BROADWAY RASTUS (1937). Touring revue starring blues singer Bessie Smith. The show in which she was appearing at the time of her tragic death. It was touring the South, and was scheduled to open in Darling, MS, on Sept. 26, 1937, when Smith was killed as a result of an automobile accident.

BROADWAY REVUE (1930). Musical revue. Starring blues singer Bessie Smith. Toured the TOBA circuit through the South in 1930, closing in the spring of 1931.

THE BROADWAY ROUNDERS (1921). Vaudeville revue. 2 acts [16 scenes]. One of the hit shows of the 1920s, prod. by Frank Montgomery in Harlem and on tour, starring Montgomery and his wife Florence McClain. Cast also included Leon Diggs, Margaret Scott, and acrobats Wells & Wells (Al Wells and his wife Laura). Songs included "All by Myself" (McClain), "Feeling Mighty Gay," "Jack Johnson Blues," "Sadie from Hackensack," and "Mabel." (See also *Harlem Rounders.*)

FURTHER REFERENCE: *Billboard* (J. A. Jackson's Page) 10–8–1921.

BROADWAY RUNS THROUGH HARLEM—II (1986). Musical revue. Written and dir. by Jerry Love. Apparently the second ed. of a musical retrospective of Harlem shows and performers. Prod. by the HADLEY Players, New York, July 18–Aug. 10, 1986. (HADLEY is an acronym for Harlem Artistic Development League Especially for You, a Harlem group founded and dir. by Gertrude Jeannette.)

BROADWAY STRUTTERS (1922). Musical revue. Prod. Jan. 1922, and cited in *Billboard* (J. A. Jackson's Page) 1–28–1922.

THE BROADWAY VAMPS (1924). Touring revue. Prod. by Thomas Mason. Starring members of the Townsend family: William "Babe" Townsend, Kid Townsend, and Flossie Townsend.

BRONZE MANIKINS (1941). Touring revue. Prod. by Don Kay. Cast included Vivian Henderson, Ernest "Baby" Seals, "Flip" Murdoci, and the Royal Bermudian Orchestra.

BROWN BABIES (1925). Touring show. One of the lesser known shows of veteran producer Irvin C. Miller.

BROWN BEAUTIES (1924–26). Touring revue in at least two eds. Prod. mainly by Mae [or Mary] Wilson. *1924 ed.*: Cast included Wilson and Charlie "Fat" Hayden. *1926 ed.*: Co-prod. with Jessie Cobb. Cast included Wilson, Joe LaRose (straight man), "Sleepy" Harris (comedian), R. E. Foster (vocalist), Clentonia Babb (soubrette), William Benton Overstreet (piano act), Eva Overstreet, and Antonio Grant (chorus boy).

BROWN BUDDIES (1930). Musical comedy. 2 acts. Book and lyrics by °Carl Rickman. Music mainly by Joe Jordan and Millard Thomas. With additional songs by Porter Grainger, J. C. Johnson, J. Rosamond Johnson, and Shelton Brooks.

Starring vehicle for the great Bill "Bojangles" Robinson. About the adventures of a company of black soldiers during World War I, taking them from the mud flats of East St. Louis to the trenches of France, and back home again. They are followed by a group of black YMCA entertainers from their hometown, including Adelaide Hall as the leading lady who becomes romantically involved with Robinson. A USO camp show perfd. during the second act permitted Robinson to show off his talents in an extended tap-dancing routine, along with other specialty acts.

Prod. at the Liberty Theatre, New York, opening Oct. 7, 1930 for 111 perfs.; staged by Ralph Rose. Charles L. Cook, musical conductor. Cast: Bill Robinson (Sam Wilson), Adelaide Hall (Betty Lou Johnson), Shelton Brooks (Deacon Siccamore), John Mason (Spider Bruce), Thomas Mosely (Matthews), "Little

Ferdie'' Lewis (Hamfat), Ada Brown (Mammy Johnson), Alma Smith (Jessie Watkins), Andrew Tribble (George Brown), Putney Dandridge (Ukelele Kid), Walter Braggsdale (Bill Jones), Maurice Ellis (Pete Johnson), Ethel Jackson (Mabel), Nancy Sharpe (Woman), Sam Jones (Policeman), Hank Smith (Trumpeteer), William E. Fountain (Lt. Pugh), Joseph Willis (Houstin Charlie), James A. Lilliard (Capt. Andrews), Carroll Tate (Medical Officer), Pete Thompson (Orderly), Edgar Brown (Guard), Red & Struggy (Pvts. Red & Struggy), Thomas Wye (YMCA Man), and Archie Toms (Corporal). The cast also included Soldiers, Sailors, Dixie Dancing Girls, and a male chorus.

Songs and specialty numbers: Act I overture, ''Brown Buddies'' (Company), ''Gettin' Off'' (Ukelele Kid & Jessie), ''Happy'' (Sam & Betty Lou), ''Brown Buddies'' (Sam & Boys), ''When a Black Man's Blue'' (Mammy & Boys), Tap-dancing specialty (Sam), ''Sugar Cane'' (Ukelele Kid & Jessie), ''My Blue Melody'' (Betty Lou), ''Carry On'' (Capt. Andrews & Company); Act II opening chorus (Company), ''Dance Away Your Sins'' (Mammy & Ensemble), ''I Lost Everything Losing You'' (Lt. Pugh), ''Sweetie Mine'' (Dixie Dancing Girls), Comedy specialty (Red & Struggy), ''Give Me a Man Like That'' (Betty Lou), ''In Missouria'' (Ukelele Kid & Boys), ''Taps'' (Sam & Girls), and Finale (Company).

FURTHER REFERENCE: *NY Daily N.* 10–8–1930. *NY Eve. World* 10–8–1930. *NY Herald Trib.* 10–8–1930. *NY Post* 10–8–1930. *NYT* 10–8–1930. *Variety* 10–15–1930. *Brown Buddies* file in Theatre Collection, Philadelphia Free Lib.

BROWN GAL (1929). Touring revue. Prod. by John Henderson, who costarred with dancer Queenie Price (she played the title role). Cast also included the Hokum Kids on banjoes and saxophone, singer Inez Drew, and celebrity impersonator George ''Hoss'' Crawford. Musical numbers included ''Diga Diga Do'' and ''Shy Violets,'' both danced by Price.

BROWNSKIN MODELS (1925–c. 1954). Annual touring revue. Prod. by Irvin C. Miller, who costarred in several early eds.

Popular show in frank imitation of such successful white revues as *Artists and Models* and the *Ziegfeld Follies*—to glorify the brownskin girl. Featured gorgeously gowned dancing girls and posing models, funny comedy routines, lively songs, and other specialty acts.

Originated from the stage of the Lafayette Theatre in Harlem in 1925. The cast of that show included Miller, Lilly Yuen, Margaret Bolden, H. L. Pryor, Eva Metcalf, Edna Barr, Bee Freeman, Hazel McPherson, George ''Hoss'' Crawford, and Cecil Rivers. Songs included ''Painting a Picture of You'' (Rivers), ''Argentine'' (Chorus), and ''Mary Ann'' (Metcalf). Comedy routines included a monologue by Miller, a skit entitled 'Relief Bureau' with Crawford and the girls, and a bedroom comedy skit with the entire company.

Toured the country annually, with seasonal revisions, until the onset of World War II, playing the large black and white theatre chains. During the war, it toured the USO circuit of army camps. After the war, it continued to tour in an abbreviated version until Miller's retirement in 1954.

Among other performers who appeared in one or more eds. were Shelton Brooks, Troy "Bear" Brown, Jesse James, "Lollipop" Jones, Pearl Mc-Cormack, George Randol, Joe Russell, Ernest "Baby" Seals, Margaret Simms, Mildred Smallwood, Blanche Thompson, Wells & Wells (Al and Laura Wells), and George Williams.

BROWN SKIN QUINAN REVUE (1925). Musical revue. Prod. by °Lew Leslie. A forerunner of the famous *Blackbirds* revues, prod. at the Plantation Club, New York. Cast included Florence Mills, Johnny Nit, U. S. Thompson, Will Vodery's Orchestra, Edith Wilson, Leonard Harper, Archie Cross, Henry Winfred, and Billy Mills.

BROWN SKIN VAMPS (1924). Touring revue. Prod. by Billy McLaurin. Viola Williams was leading lady; and Boy Lee was soubrette. Cast also included Joe Clark, "Little Bits" Hall, Catherine Jackson, Guy Jackson, Buster Lee, and Margaret Warren.

BROWNSKIN VAMPS (1926). Touring revue. Prod. by Lew Payton. Josephine Oliver was soubrette; Paul C. Floyd, straight man; and Freda Griffin, muscle dancer. Cast also included Artis McGinty, Grace Conoway, Myrtle Dillard, Dick Webb, and 7 chorus girls.

BROWN SUGAR (1927). Musical comedy. Book by Marcus Garvey and Sam Manning. About a beautiful brownskin girl who is courted by two suitors—a rich prince from India and an ordinary mechanic. The scenes shift from America to India, and much of the comedy and drama arises from the contrasts between the two suitors and their vastly different cultural backgrounds. Prod. by Amy Ashwood Garvey (Mrs. Marcus Garvey) as a touring show. With Manning and Mercay Marques as the mechanic and the prince respectively.

BUBBLE ALONG (1930). Musical comedy. One of many imitators of the famous *Shuffle Along* revue of 1921. Prod. at the Garrick Theatre, New York, in June 1930, for a very short run.
FURTHER REFERENCE: *NYT* 6–3–1930.

BUBBLING BROWN SUGAR (1975–78). Retrospective musical revue. Subtitled "A Musical Journey Through Harlem." 2 acts. Based on a concept by Rosetta LeNoire. Book by Loften Mitchell. Featuring the best-known songs of several composers, lyricists, and singers, including Eubie Blake, Duke Ellington, Billie Holiday, Bert Williams, Andy Razaf, Cab Calloway, "Fats" Waller, Earl "Fatha" Hines, Shelton Brooks, and J. C. Johnson. New songs by Danny Holgate, Emma Kemp, and Lillian Lopez (racial identities not known).

One of the earliest Bway musicals to explore the history of black entertainment, focusing on the all-black musical revues that flourished in Harlem from 1910 to the beginning of World War II. The thin plot, as described by Alex Bontemps (*Ebony* 2–1976, p. 129), concerns "a young man who has just graduated from college and is eager to leave Harlem, [which] he believes has no history and no future." To change his mind, "a trio of veteran entertainers [take] him on an imaginary tour of Harlem in its hey-day," where they visit such famous nightspots as the Cotton Club, the Savoy Ballroom, and Small's Paradise, as well as a house rent party and other places of entertainment.

First prod. by the AMAS Repertory Theatre, playing Off-Bway and on tour for a year, 1975–76. Featuring Joseph Attles, Ethel Beatty, Avon Long, and Vivian Reed. Prod. on Bway by Ashton Springer and others at the ANTA Theatre, March 2, 1976–Dec. 31, 1977, for 766 perfs.; dir. by Robert M. Cooper. Choreography by Billy Wilson, who was nominated for a Tony Award as best choreographer. Cast: Avon Long (John Sage & Rusty); Josephine Premice (Irene Paige); Vivian Reed, who won a *Theatre World* Award, a Drama Desk Award, and a nomination for a Tony Award as best actress in a musical (Marsha & Young Irene); Joseph Attles (Checkers & Dusty); Ethel Beatty (Ella); Barry Preston, who won a Clarence Derwent Award (Charlie & Count); Lonnie McNeil (Skip & Young Checkers); Vernon Washington (Bill, Time Man, Bumpy & Emcee); Newton Winters (Ray & Young Sage); Carolyn Bird (Carolyn, Gospel Lady & Female Nightclub Singer); Alton Lathrop (Gene & Gospel Lady's Son); Dyann Robinson (Helen); Charlise Harris (Laura); Anthony Whitehouse (Tony, Walter & Dutch); Chip Garnett, who also won a *Theatre World* Award (Jim & Male Nightclub Singer); and Barbara Rubenstein (Judy & Dutch's Girl).

Its first touring company opened June 22, 1976, at the Shubert Theatre in Chicago and closed at the National Theatre in Washington, DC, Oct. 9, 1977. A second touring company opened Aug. 23, 1977, at Uihlein Hall, Milwaukee, WI, and closed April 22, 1978, at the National Arts Center, Ottawa, Canada. Prod. by the Papermill Playhouse, Milburn, NJ, during the 1977 season. Prod. in London, Paris, Central Europe, the Netherlands, Germany, on other extensive U.S. tours, and by numerous independent groups throughout the United States.

Songs and musical numbers: "Harlem '70," "Bubbling Brown Sugar," "That's What Harlem Is to Me," "Harlem Sweet Harlem," "Nobody," "Goin' Back in Time," "Some of These Days," "Moving Uptown," "I'm Gonna Tell God All My Troubles," "His Eye Is on the Sparrow," "Swing Low, Sweet Chariot," "Sweet Georgia Brown," "Honeysuckle Rose," "Stormy Monday Blues," "Rosetta," "Sophisticated Lady," "In Honeysuckle Time," "Solitude," "C'mon Up to Jive Time," "Stompin' at the Savoy," "Take the 'A' Train," "Harlem Time," "Love Will Find a Way," "Dutch's Song," "Brown Gal," "Pray for the Lights to Go Out," "I Got It Bad and That Ain't Good," "Harlem Makes Me Feel," "Jim, Jam, Jumpin' Jive," "There'll Be Some Changes Made," "God Bless the Child," and "It Don't Mean a Thing."

Libretto and score pub. by Broadway Play Pub. Co., 1984. Cast recording released by H & L Records (HL–69011). (Winner of a 1977 Grammy Award.) **FURTHER REFERENCE:** *BlkMusTh* (Woll). *DBlkTh* (Woll). *Ebony* 2–1976. *NY Amsterdam N.* 3–6–1976. *NYT* 3–25–1977.

BUBBLING OVER REVUE (1928). Touring revue. Prod. by and costarring Mitchell & Rector (Leila Mitchell and Julia Rector). Cast also included Dewey Weinglass, Lawrence Lomax, Bertha Roe, and Tommy Woods.

BUBBLIN' OVER (1928). Touring revue. Featuring blackface comedians "Boll Weevil" and Willie Richardson. Johnny Williams was straight man; Ola Mae Waters, soubrette; and Tillie Johnson, character woman. Chorus of 4 included Mary Bell, Vernon Hogan, Valetta Ridgel, and Jessie Tanner.

BUCK WHITE (1969–70). Comedy with music. Book and musical score by Oscar Brown, Jr. Based on the play *Big Time Buck White* (1969), by °Joseph Dolan Tuotti.

Musical play of the "black power" movement, dealing with the confusion and conflict which develop within a black social organization called B.A.D. (for Beautiful Allelujah Days), when a so-called militant black leader addresses its membership. In the Bway version, the title role was played by heavyweight boxing champion Muhammad Ali, who received mixed revues for his performance—although the audience apparently loved the show. Black critic Kushauri Kupa (*Blk. Th.* #4, 4–1970, p. 43) felt that Ali had demeaned himself as a genuine black hero by accepting a part that presented a militant leader as a buffoon.

First prod. at the Committee Theatre, San Francisco, opening Feb. 12, 1969, for a successful run; dir. by and starring Oscar Brown, Jr., as Buck White.

Prod. on Bway by °Zev Bufman and High John Productions, at the George Abbott Theatre, opening Dec. 2, 1969, for 7 perfs.; dir. by Brown and Jean Pace. With Ali as Buck White. Other cast members included Herschell Burton (Hunter), Davis Moody (Honey Man), Ted Ross (Weasel), Charles Weldon (Rubber Band), Don Rich (Jive), Eugene Smith (Whitey), and Don Sutherland (Black Man). Act I of this prodn. was also presented Off-Bway, at the Village Gate Theatre, Jan. 8–18, 1970, for 18 perfs.

Songs and musical numbers: "Honey Man Song," "Money, Money, Money," "Nobody Does My Thing," "Step Across That Line," "H.N.I.C." [for Head Nigger in Charge], "Beautiful Allelujah Days," "Tap the Plate," "Big Time Buck White Chant," "Better Far," "We Came in Chains," "Black Balloons," "Look at Them," "Mighty Whitey," and "Get Down."

Cast album of the San Francisco prodn. was released by Buddah Records. **FURTHER REFERENCE:** *BesPls 1969–70. Blk. Th.* #4 4–1970. *NYT* 11–23–1969; 12–3–1969; 12–4–1969; 12–7–1969.

BURGLETON GREEN VS. SPARK PLUG (1923). Tabloid musical. Written and prod. by Billy King. Presented with members of the Billy King Stock Co. at the Grand Theatre, Chicago, 1923. Cast included King, Esther Bigeou, Clarence Muse, Chick Beamon, Frank Kirk, Alice Ramsey, and the Beauty Chorus.

BUSINESS BEFORE PLEASURE (1922). Musical show. Prod. during the summer of 1922, and cited in *Billboard* (J. A. Jackson's Page) 6–24–1922.

BUT NEVER JAM TODAY (1969–70, 1979). Musical adaptation. 2 acts [16 scenes]. Conceived and dir. by Vinnette Carroll.

An African-American version of °Lewis Carroll's *Alice in Wonderland* and *Through the Looking Glass*.

First prod. by the Urban Arts Corps, New York, opening April 24, 1969, as part of New York's Black Expo. This prodn. was also presented at the City Center, New York City, "for the Summer 1970 tour of . . . parks and streets" (Program notes). Music by Gershon Kingsley; lyrics by Robert Larimer; choreography by Talley Beatty; associate choreographer, Herman Howell. The integrated cast included Marie Thomas (Alice), °Tommy Pinnock (White Rabbit), °Marvin Camillo (Caterpillar & Humpty Dumpty), Joseph Perry (Black Queen), Lola Holman (Cheshire Cat, Two of Spades & Gryphon), Verna Gillis (First Cook), Winston Savage (Second Cook), °Cynthia Towns (Duchess & White Queen), Sherman Hemsley (Mad Hatter & Seven of Spades), Thelma Drayton (March Hare), °Wai Ching Ho (Dormouse), Alex Alexander (Five of Spades, Queen of Hearts & Mock Turtle), Sterling Roberts (King of Hearts), °Burt Rodriguez (Knave of Hearts), °Danny Barrajanos (Herald, Citizen & Drummer), Dance Corps (Members of Jury); 12 dancers, including Hope Clarke; and other Citizens.

Prod. in a pre-Bway tryout, entitled *Alice, May 1–June 1, 1978.

Prod. on Bway—with book by Vinnette Carroll and Bob Larimer; lyrics by Larimer; and music by Bert Keyes and Larimer—at the Longacre Theatre, July 31–Aug. 5, 1979, 16 perfs., including 9 previews. Choreography by Beatty; choral arrangements by Cleavant Derricks. Cast: Marilyn Winbush (Alice), Cleavant Derricks (Caterpillar, Cook, Tweedledee & Seven of Spades), Lynne Thigpen (Persona Non Grata), Lynne Clifton-Allen (Black Queen), Jeffrey Anderson-Gunter (White Rabbit, Cheshire Cat & Mock Turtle), Reginald Vel Johnson (Duchess, Humpty Dumpty & King of Hearts), Jai Oscar St. John (Mad Hatter, Tweedledum, and Two of Spades), Sheila Ellis (March Hare, Cook & Five of Spades), Celestine DeSaussure (Dormouse & Cook), Charlene Harris (White Queen & Queen of Hearts), Clayton Strange and Garry Q. Lewis (Guards), and Brenda Braxton and Clayton Strange (Mushrooms).

Musical numbers (Bway prodn.): "Curiouser and Curiouser," "Twinkle Twinkle Little Star," "Long Live the Queen," "A Real Life Lullaby," "The More I See People," "My Little Room," "But Never Jam Today," "Riding for a Fall," "All the Same to Me," "I've Got My Orders," "God Could Give

Me Anything," "I Like to Win," "And They All Call the Hatter Mad," and "Jumping from Rock to Rock."

BUTTERBEANS AND SUSIE REVUE (1928). Vaudeville revue. Prod. by and costarring Butterbeans & Susie (Jodie and Susie Edwards), and toured major cities of the Midwest for the Consolidated Booking Office. Also in the cast were Gertrude "Baby" Cox, Billy Mitchell, Russell Lee, Daisy Wright; the Johnson, Wells & Blue Chorus; and a chorus of 7.

BY THE BEAUTIFUL SEA (1954). White-oriented musical romance. Book by °Betty Smith and °George Abbott. Music by °Dorothy Fields and °Arthur Schwartz. About an old vaudeville star who now runs a boardinghouse for theatre people on Coney Island. She falls in love with one of the boarders whose wife and daughter are also living in the home. Prod. at the Majestic Theatre in New York, opening April 4, 1954, for 270 perfs.; starring °Shirley Booth as Lottie Gibson, the vaudevillian, and °Dennis Evans as her boarder. May Barnes, a black actress, appeared as housekeeper of the boardinghouse. According to Miles Jefferson (*Phylon*, 3rd qtr. 1954, p. 257), "Miss Barnes . . . does not have anything very exciting to do . . . except to belt two songs over the footlights in a way to bring down the house."

BY THE SAD SEA WAVES (1899). White-oriented musical comedy. Dialogue mainly by °Harry Bulger and °J. Sherri Matthews. Included an additional song by Ernest Hogan. Concerned two unemployed teachers, desperate for work, who accept positions as music instructor and athletic director, respectively, in an insane asylum which they believe to be a regular school. Prod. on Bway at the Herald Square Theatre, opening Feb. 28, 1899, costarring the authors (as Boston Budge and Palmer Coin). Included a popular dance song, "La Pas Ma La," by Hogan, sung by °May Irwin, who was also featured in this prodn.

C

THE CABARET (1913). Tabloid musical comedy. Prod. by Flournoy E. Miller and Aubrey Lyles at the Pekin Theatre, Chicago, 1913. Cast included Miller & Lyles, Lizzie Wallace, Lottie Grady, Jerry Mills, Kid Brown, the Pekin Trio, Cook & Bernard, Davis & Walker, Clarence M. Jones, Jordan & Jones, and Johnny Woods.

CABARET FOR FREEDOM (1960). Nightclub revue. Written and prod. by Maya Angelou and Godfrey Cambridge, who also costarred in the show. Topical revue in support of the civil rights movement and as a fund-raiser for the Southern Christian Leadership Congress (SCLC). Prod. Off-Bway at the Village Gate, during the summer of 1960, sponsored by the Emergency Committee for the Southern Freedom Struggle; dir. by Hugh Herd. The integrated cast included unemployed actors, singers, dancers, and musicians.

CABARET PRINCE (1930). Musical comedy. 4 scenes. Written and prod. by Quintard Miller and Marcus Slayter.
   Subtitled "A Spectacular Musical Comedy Drama of Life in New York City." Scene 1—A private party room of the Blue Bird Night Club; Scene 2—In front of a fashionable restaurant; Scene 3—The Blue Bird Night Club; Scene 4—A street in New York; Scene 5—A gambling room at the Blue Bird.
   Toured the South, 1930. Cast: Lloyd Curtis (Manager of the Blue Bird Night Club), Edith Spencer (Cora Blake), Lottie Gee (Mary Doyle), Marcus Slayter (Billy Dexter), Aurora Greeley (Sally, an entertainer), Amos Davis (Steve Randolph), Gallie DeGaston (Boddidly), Leroy Broomfield (Larry), Irene Poindexter (Daisy), Quintard Miller (Rastus Jones).
   Songs and musical numbers: Opening—"Cabaret Nights" (Miller & Slayter Girls), "Get Out and Get Under" (Spencer & Girls), "To Be with You" (Broomfield, Greeley & Chorus), "Anytime" (Hawkins & Chorus), "Deep Henderson"

(Miller & Slayter Girls), and Finale (Company). Other specialty numbers were perfd. by Slayter, Gee, Greeley & Broomfield.

CABIN IN THE SKY (1940–41). Musical fantasy. 2 acts. Book by °Lynn Root. Lyrics by °John Latouche. Music by °Vernon Duke.

Another white-conceived, pseudo-folk parable of black life in the South, presumably inspired by *The Green Pastures*, and based on the age-old battle between good and evil for the soul of the main character, Little Joe Jackson (Dooley Wilson). In response to the prayers of his faithful wife, Petunia Jackson (Ethel Waters), De Lawd grants Joe a six-month reprieve from death, during which he must redeem himself from his past sins or suffer eternal damnation. Petunia does everything in her power to keep her no-good husband from falling into the traps that Lucifer, Jr. (Rex Ingram) has set for him, the most irresistible of which is the seductive dancing vamp, Georgia Brown (Katherine Dunham). Petunia is assisted by De Lawd's General (Todd Duncan). Joe is almost successful, until he gets into an argument with Petunia and accidentally shoots her. In the end, Joe finally makes it through the Pearly Gates to "The Cabin in the Sky" through the powerful entreaties of the forgiving soul of Petunia, who precedes him.

Prod. at the Martin Beck Theatre, New York, opening Oct. 25, 1940, for 155 perfs.; dir. by George Ballanchine and Albert Lewis. In addition to Waters, Wilson, Duncan, Ingram, and Dunham, the cast also featured the Katherine Dunham Dancers, with Talley Beatty dancing opposite Dunham; J. Rosamond Johnson, who trained the singing chorus and had a small role as Brother Green; Georgia Burke (Lily), Milton Williams (Fleetfoot), J. Louis Johnson (John Henry), Al Moore (Dude), Al Stokes (Devil's Messenger), Wilson Bradley (Messenger Boy), Dick Campbell (Domino Johnson); and Earl Sydnor, Earl Edwards, and Maurice Ellis (as 3 Henchmen).

Prod. in an unsuccessful Off-Bway revival in 1963, featuring Rosetta LeNoire as Petunia and Ketty Lester as Little Joe.

Prod. in a film version by MGM, 1944; dir. by Vincente Minnelli. Cast featured Eddie Anderson (Little Joe Jackson), Ethel Waters (Petunia Jackson), Lena Horne (Georgia Brown), Rex Ingram (Lucifer, Jr.), Louis Armstrong, Ruby Dandridge, Willie Best, Butterfly McQueen, Mantan Moreland, Oscar Polk, Kenneth Spencer, Ernest Whitman, and the Hall Johnson Choir.

Songs and musical numbers: Act I—"The General's Song" (Lawd's General & Saints), "Pay Heed" (Lawd's General), "Taking a Chance on Love" (Petunia), "Cabin in the Sky" (Petunia & Little Joe), "Holy Unto the Lord" (Petunia, Little Joe, Parson Green and Church members), "Dem Bones" (Petunia, Helen & Church members), "Do What You Wanna Do" (Lucifer, Jr., and Imps), Reprise: "Taking a Chance on Love" (Petunia & Saints). Act II— "Fugue" (Lawd's General & Saints), "My Old Virginia Home on the Nile" (Petunia & Little Joe), (Vision) Egyptian Ballet (Dunham Troupe), "It's Not So Good to Be Bad" (Lawd's General), "Love Me Tomorrow" (Georgia Brown

& Little Joe), "Love Turned the Light Out" (Petunia), Lazy Steps (Dunham Troupe), Boogy Woogy (Dunham Troupe), "Honey in the Honeycomb" (Georgia Brown & Boys), and "Savannah" (Petunia: dance with Archie Savage).

Libretto and musical score commercially unavailable. Cast recordings by Capitol (SW–2073) and Columbia (CSP–CCL–2792).

FURTHER REFERENCE: Alkire diss. *BlkMusTh* (Woll). *BlksBf* (Sampson). *EncycMusTh* (Green). *DBlkTh* (Woll). *His Eye Is on the Sparrow* (Waters). *NYT* 11–3–1940.

THE CABLE (1975). Musical comedy. 5 acts. By Townsend Brewster. Musical adaptn. of the *Rudens* of Plautus, his only comedy which takes place in Africa. Concerns a long-lost daughter who has fallen into the clutches of a panderer, telling how she escapes, finds her parents, and becomes reunited with her true love. Pub. by Continental Play Service, New York, 1975.

CALL ME MISTER (1946). Musical revue. By °Harold Rome. About returning GIs after World War II. Included three black actors who dramatized the problems of black veterans in postwar society: Lawrence Winters, Bruce Howard, and James Young. Prod. at the National Theatre, opening April 18, 1946, for a long run; with a predominantly white cast.

CANARY COTTAGE (1920). Vaudeville farce. Music by Shelton Brooks and °Earl Carroll. Lyrics by °Oliver Morosco.

About the romantic affairs of a fickle blackface lover (played by Brooks), first with a wealthy matron, then with a rich widow's beautiful daughter, and finally with the housekeeper of Canary Cottage.

Prod. by the Panama Amusement Co., Chicago, 1920, as a touring show. Cast included Brooks (Jerry Summerfield), Billy Moss ("Jag"), Ollie Powers (Sam Asbestos, in blackface), Evelyn Preer (Pauline Hugg), Alberta Hunter (Betty Fay), Margaret Lee (Widow), Birleanna Blanks (Mrs. Hugg), and Charles Shelton (Mile [*sic*] Flanagan, a boy).

Songs included "Wake Up with the Blues" (Hunter) and "It Ruined Marc Anthony" (Hunter, Preer & Lee).

THE CANNIBAL KING / / A reworking of some of the materials from *Jes Lak White Fo'ks* (1901). Comic opera. 2 acts. Concept and music by Will Marion Cook. Additional contributions, including music and lyrics by a number of collaborators, including James Weldon Johnson, J. Rosamond Johnson, Paul Laurence Dunbar, Bob Cole, and Willis Accooe. After a number of disputes between Cook and some of his collaborators, the work was eventually completed.

The plot turns upon the farcical efforts of a former black headwaiter at an elite white southern hotel, who suddenly becomes rich and now tries to school his people in the social graces to make them more acceptable in high society.

Apparently it had a short run at a theatre in New York in Aug. 1901, then went on tour. Opened in Hartford and in Indianapolis, both in Nov. 1901. Cast included Cole, J. R. Johnson, William "Billy" Johnson, Henry Wise, Coley Grant, Ernest Hogan (presumably in the title role), Theo Pankey, Lewis Salisbury, Reginald Burleigh, "Kid" Frazier, Abbie Mitchell [Cook], Aida Overton [Walker], Kati Milton, Mamie Grant, Muriel Ringgold, Cecil Watts, Anna Cook, Mollie Dill, Odessa Warren, Willie Dancy, Midget Price, Gertie Peterson, George Archer, John Boyer, the Alabama Comedy Four, and a chorus of 40 singers.

See Cook's *Jes Lak White Fo'ks* for songs which may have also been included in this work.

FURTHER REFERENCE: *Freeman* (Indianapolis) 11–9–1901.

CAN'T HELP SINGING (1982). Musical retrospective. Billed as "A Salute to Jerome Kern." Presented at the St. Regis–Sheraton/King Cole Room, New York, April 5–June 26, 1982; dir. and staged by °Michael Lichtefeld. Musical dir., °Keith Herrmann. The predominantly white cast, headed by °Judy Kaye, included two black singers—Armelia McQueen and Ken Page.

CAN'T TAKE HER NOWHERE (1991). Gospel musical. 2 hrs. By Ron Harris.

The sixth musical by the Virginia Beach composer. About a much-married woman named Louisa who is at the altar again with her new husband, Lenny, determined to make a go of it this time. Described by the *Virginian-Pilot* (Norfolk, VA, 12–12–1991) as "a Christian comedy full of infectious, emotion-packed tunes that push along the plot. True to Harris' inspirational style, there's a happy ending."

Premiered at the Center Theatre, Norfolk, VA, Dec. 13–15, 1991; dir. by DeShera Rainey, who portrayed Louisa. The 15-member cast also included Vincent Epps (Lenny & choreographer) and Jill Holly Jenkins (Louisa's mother).

Music was provided by a 6-piece band, which included the composer's 14-year-old son AaRonn Harris, a saxophonist. The 10 songs included "Pay It No 'Tension," described by the composer as the mother's attempt "to pick up Louisa's spirits, since people are talking about her," and "Tonight's the Night," the groom's "honeymoon fantasy," sung by Lenny to a calypso beat.

CAPTAIN BOGUS OF THE JIM CROW REGIMENT (1913). Tabloid musical comedy. Military comedy about the misadventures of a phony army captain, a popular theme of the period. Prod. by the Star Stock Co., at the Star Theatre, Savannah, GA. Cast included Bradford & Bradford, Mabel Johnson, Papa String Beans, William & Rajou, and the Williams Sisters.

CAPTAIN JASPER (1907–13). Billed as "A Rapturous, Melodious Musical Comedy." 2 1/2 hrs. Written by Will A. Cook. Music by various composers.

One of the favorite full-length musical shows of the *Black Patti Troubadours*, about the heroic deeds of a brave army captain in the Philippines. The complicated plot revolves around the theft of some secret documents by a Major Drummond, which are eventually recovered by Captain Jasper. The characters move from the U.S., where the theft is discovered, to the Philippines, where the thief has absconded with the papers, and back to the U.S., where the documents are recovered and returned to their rightful owners, thus averting sabotage of a U.S. military fortress in the Philippines and restoring a valuable deed of land to a young woman as her rightful inheritance.

First prod. by the Troubadours, opening in 1907, and apparently remained in the company's repertory until around 1913. The orig. cast featured Sissieretta Jones (Black Patti), Julius "Happy" Glenn, Sarah (Byrd) Green, Will A. Cook, Al F. Watts, Charles C. Bougia, and Jeannette Murphy.

Songs and musical numbers, which ranged from sentimental to ragtime, included "Sun-Blest Are You," "The Nightingale," "Sugar Babe," "The Belle of New York," "Goodbye, Rose," "O Golden Land," "Shakey Rag," "I Am By Myself," "When Old Glory Waves," and "Lady Angeline."
FURTHER REFERENCE: *Freeman* (Indianapolis) 5–17–1913.

CAPTAIN RUFUS (1907, revived 1914). Musical comedy. Book by J. Ed. Green and Alfred Anderson. Music originally by H. Lawrence Freeman.

Military comedy set in the Philippines, about the misadventures of a phony army captain—a popular theme of musicals of the pre–World War I period.

First presented by the Pekin Stock Co., at the Pekin Theatre, Chicago, opening July 20, 1907; prod. and staged by Green. With choreography by William "Billy" Johnson. Also presented at the °Hurtig & Seamon Musical Hall Theatre in New York City opening Aug. 12, 1907, for a two-week engagement. Orig. cast: Harrison Stewart (Capt. Rufus), J. Ed. Green (Colonel), Dan Wromley (Sergeant), Jerry Mills (Maj. Drummond), Charles H. Gilpin (Lt. Stokes), Jennie Ringgold (Colonel's Daughter), Lottie Grady (Filipino Girl), Lawrence Chenault (West Point Cadet), Russell White (Russell Wallace, war correspondent), and Matt Marshall (billed as Rufus' Manager?). Musical numbers included "The Tale of the Monkey and the Snake," "The Voodoo King," "Morning Is Dawning," "Girls of the U.S.A.," "I've Got Good Common Sense," "Chief of the Aggregation," "Song of the Witches," "You Ain't Said Nothin' Yet," and "The Lily."

Revised and revived in 1914 by the Pekin Stock Co.; prod. by Jerry Mills (who played Maj. Drummond in the orig. prodn. and presumably repeated his role). Toured the U.S. and Europe with the Dark Town Entertainers, a troupe managed by Laura Bowman, wife of Sidney Kirkpatrick, who played the role of Capt. Rufus. Other cast members included Charles Liverpool (Leon Carlos, a Filipino man), Lizzie Wallace (Cheteka Castro, a Filipino girl), Bessie Tribble (Lucy, Colonel's daughter), Mayme Carter (war correspondent), Charles Moore (Col. Warsaw), Leon Crosby (Lt. Stokes); others: Andrew Tribble, Jack Smith, George Hall, Lem Crosby, Sergeant W. Jones, D. Acklen, and the Pekin Orchestra under the direction of Beecher Todd. Musical numbers included "Amazon Land" (Wallace), "My Mandiline [*sic*]" (Crosby), "You Ain't Said

Nothin' Yet'' (A. Tribble), "Tale of the Monkey and the Snake" (Carter), "Chief of the Aggregation" (Smith), "The Sword and the Flag" (Kirkpatrick), "Just for a Night" (B. Tribble & Company), and "Back to the U.S.A." (Company).

CARIBBEAN CARNIVAL (1947). Billed as "The First Calypso Musical Ever Presented." Music and lyrics by Samuel L. Manning and °Adolph Thenstead. An all-black revue featuring the music and dances of the West Indies, choreographed by Pearl Primus. Prod. at the International Theatre, New York, opening Dec. 5, 1947, for 11 perfs. Perfd. by Pearl Primus, Josephine Premice, Claude Merchant, Sam Manning, Pamela Ward, Billie Allen, Alex Young, Eloise Hill, the Smith Kids, the Trio Cubana, Peggy Watson, the Duke of Iron, Curtis James, Fred Thomas, Padjet Fredericks, and Dorothy Graham.

CARIB SONG (1945). Musical of West Indian life. Book and lyrics by °William Archibald. Music by °Baldwin Bergersen.

An interpretation of Caribbean dances by Katherine Dunham and her dance troupe. Built around "the old hackneyed story of the youthful, spirited erring wife, her jealous, unromantic husband and her glamorous passionate lover . . . , weighed down with an overload of pseudo-exotic and interminable dances, trite dialogue and music of little if any originality" (Miles Jefferson, *Phylon* 2nd qtr. 1946, pp. 187–88).

Prod. at the Adelphi Theatre, New York, opening Sept. 27, 1945, for 36 perfs. Featured cast: Dunham (Wife), Avon Long (Fisherman), Harriet Jackson (Singer), Mabel Sanford Lewis (Fat Woman), Mercedes Gilbert (Tall Woman), William Franklin (Husband), Elsie Benjamin (Fish Woman), La Rosa Entrada (Shango Priest), Vanoye Aikens (Leader of Shango Dancers), Tommy Gomez (Boy Possessed by a Snake), and Katherine Dunham Dancers.

Songs and musical numbers: "Go Sit by the Body," "This Woman," "A Girl She Can't Remain," "Market Song," "Water Movin' Slow," "Basket, Make a Basket," "Today I Is So Happy," "Can't Stop the Sea," "You Know, Oh Lord," "Go Down to the River," and "Oh, Lonely One."

Cast recording by Inspirational Records (B-401-6).

FURTHER REFERENCE: *Carib Song* file in Theatre Collection, Philadelphia Free Lib.

CARMEN (1950). Translation of the Bizet opera. By Townsend Brewster. Broadcast by the NBC Television Opera, 1950. Repeated as the first opera telecast in compatible color, 1953, and as part of the Highlights of Opera Historical Educational Television Series, 1957.

CARMEN JONES (1943–46). Adapted musical play. Based on Georges Bizet's opera *Carmen*. Libretto and lyrics by °Oscar Hammerstein II. Music by Bizet.

The most successful and longest-running all-black musical of the 1940s, which utilized a World War II setting for the jazzed-up version of Bizet's immortal classic. As in the orig. opera, the plot turns on the triangular love affair between the heartless and passionate Carmen and the two men who love her. Seville is turned into the American South; Carmen's cigarette factory becomes a defense plant for the making of parachutes; Don Jose, a soldier-guard, becomes Joe, a corporal in the army; and Escamillo, the bullfighter, becomes Husky Miller, the prizefighter. Although the recitatives were turned into dialogue, a few cuts were made, and new words were put to the arias, the play remained quite faithful to the original, and the result was highly praised by most (white) critics.

Several black writers, artists, and critics, however, found fault with the Hammerstein adaptn. The late actress Diana Sands (*Look* 1–9–1968) was disturbed by the treatment of black women, and considered that the musical employed "one of the oldest racist clichés: the Negro whore." James Baldwin found that black male-female relationships were misrepresented, and that the love affair between Carmen and Joe was "a sterile and distressing eroticism . . . because it is occurring in a vacuum between two mannequins" (*Notes of a Native Son*). In this regard, it might be noted that the bestial and violent Husky Miller is portrayed as sexually potent; while the decent and gentle Joe is portrayed as lacking in passion and aggressiveness. Loften Mitchell was disturbed by the deliberate insertion of stereotypes into the Hammerstein libretto that were not in the orig. opera (*BlkDr*, p. 120). Two stereotypes that can be pointed out (other than those already noted) include the use of minstrel elements in the minor characters (such as Rum and Dink, Husky Miller's fight manager and sidekick) and the use of black dialect throughout (as evidenced by the titles of musical numbers below).

Prod. by °Billy Rose at the Broadway Theatre, New York, opening Dec. 2, 1943, for a long run of 502 perfs.; dir. by °Hassard Short and °Charles Friedman. Choreography by °Eugene Loring. Orig. cast: Muriel Rahn and Muriel Smith (alternating as Carmen; later replaced by Inez Matthews and Urylee Leonardos), Luther Saxon (Joe), Carlotta Franzell (Cindy Lou [Michaela in the Bizet score]), Napoleon Reed (Cpl. Morrell), Robert Clarke (Foreman), Jack Carr (Sgt. Brown), Sibol Cain (Sally), Edward Roche (T-Bone), William Jones (Tough Kid), Cozy Cole (Drummer), Melvin Howard (Bartender), Edward Christopher (Waiter), June Hawkins (Frankie), Jessica Russell (Myrt), Edward Lee Tyler (Rum), Dick Montgomery (Dink), Glenn Bryant (Husky Miller), P. Jay Sidney (Mr. Higgins), Freddye Marshall White (Miss Higgins), Alford Pierre (Photographer), Urylee Leonardos and Ethel White (Card Players), Ruth Crumpton (Dancing Girl), William Dillard (Poncho), Sheldon D. Hoskins and Randolph Sawyer (Dancing Boxers), Melvin Howard (Bullet Head), and Tony Fleming (Referee).

After a brief tour, the show was revived on Bway, May 2, 1945; on April 7, 1946; and on May 31, 1956, for limited engagements.

Prod. as a film, dir. by °Otto Preminger, 1954; with Dorothy Dandridge (Carmen), Harry Belafonte (Joe), Pearl Bailey, Roy Glenn, Diahann Carroll, and Brock Peters.

Songs and musical numbers: "Lif' 'Em Up and Put 'Em Down," "Honey Gal o' Mine," "Good Luck," "Dat's Love," "You Talk Just Like My Maw," "Carmen Jones Is Goin' to Jail," "Dere's a Cafe on de Corner," "Beat Out Dat Rhythm on a Drum," "Stan' Up and Fight," "Whizzin' Away Along de Track," "Dis Flower," "If You Would Only Come Away," "De Cards Don't Lie," "Dat Ol' Boy," "Poncho de Panther from Brazil," "My Joe," "Get Yer Program for de Big Fight," and "Dat's Our Man."

Libretto pub. by Alfred A. Knopf, 1943. Cast recording issued by Decca (DL–8014/MCA 2054).

FURTHER REFERENCE: Alkire diss. *DBlkTh* (Woll). *Life* 5–18–1944. *NY Herald Trib.* 12–3–1943. *NY Morn. Telegraph* 12–4–1943. *NYT* 8–23–1942; 11–14–1943. *Phylon* 1st qtr. 1945. *ThArts* 2–1944; 3–1944. *Women's Wear Daily* 12–3–1943. *Carmen Jones* file in Theatre Collection, Philadelphia Free Lib.

CARNATION (1914). Tabloid musical. Written and prod. by Billy King. Perfd. by the Billy King Stock Co., at the Star Theatre, Savannah, GA, 1914, where it played for one week.

CAROLINA NIGHTS (1928). Vaudeville revue. Book by comedian Doe Doe Green, who also costarred. Touring show which also featured Evelyn Preer, Arthur D. Porter, Paul C. Floyd, Edward Thompson, Gladys Thompson, Arlyne Brooks, Alonzo McLane, Frankie Watts, and 8 chorus girls.

CARTOONS FOR A LUNCH HOUR (1978). Musical. Book and lyrics by Loften Mitchell. Music and additional lyrics by Rudy Stevenson. Prod. at the Perry St. Theatre, New York, 1978; dir. by Akin Batunde. Choreography and musical staging by Frank Hatchett. With an integrated cast that included Arlena Rolant, Clinton Derricks-Carroll, and °Anthony Whitehouse. Among the 20 musical numbers were "This Angel's Arrivin'," "Wanna Go to Heaven," "Hail to Peter," "Heaven in Your Eyes," and "A Party at Peter's Place."

THE CASINO GIRL (1900–1901). White-oriented musical comedy. Book by °Harry B. Smith. Music mainly by °Ludwig Englander. With additional songs by Will Marion Cook and Will Accooe, among other composers.

Commissioned especially for the Casino Theatre on Bway, to glorify one of its famous chorus girls. About a former Casino chorine who is pursued by an amorous English earl to Cairo, Egypt, where she has a number of adventures before the earl is made to realize that she does not love him.

Prod. by °George Lederer at the Casino Theatre, New York, opening March

19, 1900, for 51 perfs., with an all-white cast. Revived Aug. 6, 1900, for 40 perfs.; then toured the U.S. before traveling to London's West End, where it apparently had a short run before closing.

Cook's songs included "Whatever the Hue of Your Eyes," "Down de Lover's Lane," and "Bygone Days Are Best." Accooe contributed only one known song, "Love Has Claimed Its Own."

CATCHING THE BURGLAR (1918). Tabloid musical. Written and prod. by Billy King.

After the home of a wealthy family has been robbed several times, a bungling detective is hired to apprehend the criminal. He finally arrests the man being robbed, allowing the burglar to escape.

Presented by the Billy King Stock Co., at the Grand Theatre, Chicago, 1918. Cast included King (as the detective), Howard Kelly, Bessie Brown, Leon Brooks, Blaine Brown, and James Thomas.

Musical numbers include "My Place of Business" (King), "I Wish You Good Luck" (Miss Brown), "Before the World Began" (Brooks), "I Miss the Mississippi Miss" (Thomas), and "Our Own Broadway" (Mr. Brown & Company).

CAVALCADE OF THE NEGRO THEATRE / / Adapt. for radio as **Jubilee: A Cavalcade of the Negro Theatre** (1940–41). A celebration of black music. Theatre and radio scripts by Langston Hughes and Arna Bontemps. Described by the *Dictionary Catalog of the Schomburg Collection* (New York Public Lib.) as "utilizing Creole melodies, spirituals, folk songs, blues and especially written numbers by [°]Thomas A. Dorsey and Duke Ellington." Prod. at the Negro Exposition, Chicago, IL, July 4–Sept. 4, 1940; copy in Moorland-Spingarn. Adapted as a radio script, entitled *Jubilee: A Cavalcade of the Negro Theatre*, and prod. as a CBS Showcase Program in 1941; typescript without music in Schomburg.

(A) CELEBRATION (1985–86, revived 1988). Musical retrospective. Subtitled "The African American Tradition Through Words and Songs." Conceived and dir. by Shauneille Perry. A musical journey from the beginnings of the tradition to the 1980s. Prod. by Roger Furman's New Heritage Repertory Theatre, New York, in association with Danva Prodns., Feb. 18–24, 1985. Featuring guitarist Clebert Ford, Carolyn Byrd, Andre Robinson, Jr., and Fran Salisbury. Prod. at the American Place Theatre (APT), New York, as part of *Jubilee! A Black Theatre Festival*, for 91 perfs., May 14–June 24, 1985; dir. by Perry. With Byrd, Salisbury, Robinson, and Ford of the orig. cast, plus pianist Thomas Riggsbee. Twice revived at APT, Jan. 28–Feb. 23, 1986, and Feb. 9–28, 1988; with essentially the same cast and credits. Presented on a secondary school tour of Bermuda, sponsored by the Ministry of Education and Community Cultural Affairs, Feb. 1–6, 1988; with Salisbury, Byrd, and Andre Robinson of the orig. cast plus Ronnie "Pepsi" Robinson and Loni Berry, pianist. Prod. by the National Black Touring Circuit, at various locations in New York State, Spring 1988. Cast included Nora Cole, Robin Sutton, Kim Sullivan, and Lee Coward, pianist.

THE CENSUS TAKER (1910). Musical comedy. Written by Jerry Mills. Music by Sam Stewart.

The contrived plot tells the story of a young woman of 16 who has been left a large fortune on the death of her father, which she is to receive only after she marries or comes of age. Both she and her inheritance are placed in the charge of her uncle, who is determined to carry out her father's wishes. The lady conceives of a scheme to get her money by persuading a handsome young census taker to pretend to marry her, for which he will receive a considerable sum. She pays him a hundred dollars as a down payment. The uncle uncovers the plot and is about to have the young man arrested, but by this time the couple have really fallen in love and the uncle finally consents to the marriage.

Prod. at the Pekin Theatre, Chicago, opening Oct. 22, 1910. Cast included Mills, Fanny Wise, Sidney Perrin, Goldie Crosby, Tom Brown, and Marguerite Ward.

CHAMPAGNE CHARLIE (1901). White-oriented musical play. Written by °Augustus Thomas. Included several songs by Bob Cole, J. Rosamond Johnson, and James Weldon Johnson. Prod. apparently on the road, 1901, starring °Peter Dailey and an all-white cast. Cole & Johnson's songs—all pub. in their album, "Song Successes Introduced by Peter F. Dailey in the New Successful Comedy 'Champagne Charlie' by Augustus Thomas," by Cole & Johnson (Joseph W. Stern & Co., New York, 1901)—include "I Don't Want to Be No Actor Man" (music by Cole), "Gin" (music by J. R. Johnson), "My Castle on the Nile" (music by J. R. Johnson), "Nobody's Looking But de Owl an' de Moon" (music by J. R. Johnson); copy in Moorland-Spingarn. "Gin," a minstrel song, was also pub. separately by Howley, Haviland & Dresser; copy also in Moorland-Spingarn.

CHANGES (1973). Topical musical. Book by Vantile Whitfield (Motojicho). Music and lyrics by Valerian Smith.

Musical of black life which, according to Jeanne-Marie A. Miller (*Blk. World* 4–1974, pp. 59–60), "makes use of language styles familiar to Blacks—the 'dozens,' tall tales, street rhymes." She compares it ("in some places faintly") to Melvin Van Peebles' *Ain't Supposed to Die a Natural Death.* Among the problems and themes dealt with are the generation gap that exists between young blacks and their middle-class parents with regard to racial assimilation, the slaying of black youths by white policemen, and the necessity for black self-esteem and self-discovery.

Prod. by the DC Black Repertory Co., Washington, DC, opening Dec. 6, 1973, for 47 perfs.; dir. by Motojicho.

According to Miller (ibid.), "The music ran the gamut of Black music, the dancers were at their energetic best." Two memorable songs were "God Help My Child," sung by a distressed mother, and "Mississippi Mud," a plaintive folk song, sung at the grave of a murdered black youth.

CHANGES (1980). Musical. No intermission. Conceived, dir., and co-prod. by °Dorothy Love. Lyrics by °Danny Apolinar. Music by °Addy Fieger. About the changes that occur in the lives of two couples (one black, one white) in a large city from one New Year's Eve to the next. Prod. at Theatre DeLys, New York, Feb. 19–24, 1980, for 7 perfs. The integrated cast included °Kelly Bishop, °Larry Kert, Irving Allen, and Trina Parks. The 22 songs and musical numbers included "Have I Got a Girl for You," "Have I Got a Guy for You," "Happy New Year," "Keep Love Away," "All of a Sudden It's Spring," "Love Ain't So Hot," "Love Is a Whole Other Scene," and "Merry Christmas to Me."

CHANGE YOUR LUCK (1930) / / Orig. title: *Darktown Affairs* (1929). Musical comedy. 2 acts. Book by Garland Howard. Music and lyrics by J. C. Johnson. Additional music by Maceo Pinkard.

A satire on Prohibition in which a number of specialty acts are assembled around a thin plot about an undertaker/bootlegger (Evergreen Peppers), who hides his liquor in empty formaldehyde cans in his funeral parlor and also has financial involvement in prostitution in the community. He justifies his iniquities on the grounds that the good he does for the town and the church more than compensates for his illegal activities during the week. The plot is complicated by a love triangle in which Peppers' partner, an underworld character (Diamond Joe), and a corrupt revenue agent (Hot Stuff Jackson) both compete for the hand of Josephine (Evergreen Peppers' daughter).

Toured as *Darktown Affairs* (1929) before being revised under its present title and prod. by °Cleon Throckmorton at the George M. Cohan Theatre, New York, opening June 6, 1930, for 17 perfs.; dir. by Stanley Bennett. With choreography by Lawrence Deas and Speedy Smith. Both prodns. featured Leigh Whipper as Evergreen Peppers (the undertaker), Garland Howard as Hot Stuff Jackson, and Speedy Smith as Skybo Snowball, proprietor of the Sundown Hotel. In this prodn. Hamtree Harrington was the principal comedian (Ebenezer Smart), and Alberta Hunter (who later rose to stardom) was a singer (Mary Jane). Other characters: Alec Lovejoy (Big Bill), Jimmy Thomas (Cateye), Alberta Perkins (Malindy), Sam Cross (Profit [*sic*] Jones), Cora La Redd (Bandana Babe Peppers), Sterling Grant (Romeo Green), Neeka Shaw (Josephine Peppers), Mabel Grant (Mathilda), Millie Holmes (Passionate Sadie), Emma Maitland (Rat Row Sadie), Aurelia Wheeldin (Tack Annie); Dorothy Embry, Mary Mason, and Lillian Cowan (Sisters of Mercy: Dottie, Mary & Lil); Henry Davis, James Davis, and Van Jackson (Hot Poppers Henry, Jimmy & Van); Bertha Row (Ansy), Gertie Chambers (Percolatin' Gertie), Yank Bronson (Short Dog, the Hoofer), Sammy Van (Charleston Sam, the Hoofer); Louis Simms and Buster

Bowie (Bellboys: Shake a Hip & Shake a Leg); J. Louis Johnson (Capt. Jones); S. W. Warren, Charles Gill, Billy Cole, and C. P. Wade (The Four Flash Devils); Stanley Bennett and His Syncopators, Dancing Girls, Levee Maids, Rat Row Rowdies, Roustabouts, Stevedores, High Yellows and Seal Skin Browns, Church Folks and Citizens of Sundown; and Members of the Uplift Club.

Songs and musical numbers: Act I—Opening Chorus (Ensemble), "Sweet Little Baby o' Mine" (Josephine, Hot Stuff, Simms & Bowie, & Ensemble), "Can't Be Bothered Now" (Bandana Babe, Four Hot Peppers & Sisters of Mercy), "Ain't Puttin' Out Nothin' " (Bill & Malindy), "Religion in My Feet" (Sundown Trio, Four Flash Devils, Sammy Van & Ensemble), "You Should Know" (Josephine, Romeo & Ensemble), "Waisting Away" (Mary Jane & Diamond Joe), "Walk Together, Children" (Profit Jones & Uplift League), "Honesty" (Romeo, Josephine, Sundown Trio & Dance Sextet), "Mr. Mammy Man" (Josephine, Hot Stuff & Girls), Dance Specialty (Louise Simms & Buster Bowie), "My Regular Man" (Bandana Babe, Sammy Van & Ensemble), "I'm Honest" (Romeo & Sundown Trio), Act I Finale (Company). Act II—"We're Here" (Malindy & Ensemble), Low Down Dance (Diamond Joe, Sammy Van & Girls), "Open That Door" (Snowball & Passionate Sadie), "Change Your Luck" (Smart & Mary Jane), "Percolatin' " (Bandana Babe & Girls), Dance Specialty (Gertie), "Travelin' " (Profit Jones, Mary Jane & Ensemble), "St. Louis Blues" (Four Hot Peppers), "What Have I Done?" (Josephine & Romeo), Dance (Romeo, Hot Stuff & Josephine), "Rhythm Feet" (Louis Simms & Buster Bowie), Finale (Company).

Unpub. prompt book in TC/NYPL.

FURTHER REFERENCE: *BlkMusTh* (Woll). *BlksBf* (Sampson). *NewRepub* 6–25–1930. *NY Eve. World* 6–7–1930. *NYT* 6–7–1930. *Philadelphia Record* 1–15–1930.

CHAPPELLE AND STINNETTE REVUE (1922). Touring vaudeville revue. Prod. by and costarring the dancing team of Chappelle & Stinnette (Thomas Chappelle and Juanita Stinnette). Music was provided by the Jazz Hounds, which included Bobby Lee (piano), Percy Glasco (clarinet), Seymour Errick (cornet), and Fleming & Faulkner (trombone and banjo, respectively).

CHARLESTON DANDIES (1926–27). Musical revue in at least two eds. Prod. by Clarence Muse, who also costarred. Apparently originated in Chicago. Toured the country on the TOBA Circuit, 1926–27. Presumed to be an earlier version of Muse's *Chicago Plantation Revue* (1927). *First ed. (1926).* Cast included Norman Astwood, Andrew Tribble, Hardtack Jackson (blackface comedian), Crawford Jackson, and chorus of 3 women and 2 men. *Second ed. (1926–27).* Advertised as "an elaborate, scenic and costumed production," with "two carloads of equipment," "35 people," "funny comedians," "Peppy dance numbers," "original tunes," and "a sizzling hot beauty chorus—12 real steppers" (Advt., 8–23–1926, reprinted in *BlksBf*, p. 410). Cast included comedians Roscoe Montella and "Skeeter" Winston; dancers Roscoe "Red" Simmons, Frisco

& Al, and "Static" & Harry Hamilton; "real stars," including Pauline Montella, Dolly Allen, Marie Gonzales, Chicago [Harmony] Four, Charleston King, and "Kid Lips." Chorus included Lillian Stokes of the 1926 ed. Music was played by the Maryland Ramblers, an 11-piece jazz band "direct from [the] Green Cat Club" in New York City.

CHARLESTON FRICASEE (1926). Musical revue. Harlem show prod. by and costarring Quintard Miller and blackface comedian Marcus Slayter. Cast also included Amon Davis, Montrose Brooks, George Wiltshire, Enez Davis, Emma Hawkins, Robert Rice, Tendelayo, and Bessie Wright.

THE CHARLESTON STEPPERS (1922). Touring dance revue. Featuring Vivian Brown, Helen Dolly, Mose Williams, Floyd Young, and Rose Young.

CHARLESTON SYNCOPATORS (1926). Touring revue. Prod. by and costarring Bruce & Skinner (Madame Bruce and Herbert Skinner). Cast also included Troy "Bear" Brown, Odel Irvin, and Josie Austin.

CHARLOT'S REVUE OF 1924. See *ANDRÉ CHARLOT'S REVUE OF 1924*.

THE CHARMING WIDOW (1918). Tabloid musical comedy. Prod. by Bob Russell. An early show in which Florence Mills appeared. Toured throughout the South with members of the Bob Russell Stock Co., originally based at the Pekin Theatre in Savannah, GA. Cast included Blanche Thompson, Cora Green, Carolyn Williams, and Mills.

CHICAGO FOLLIES / / Also known as *Tim Moore's Chicago Follies* (c. 1916– c. 1928). Musical revue in several eds. Prod. by Tim Moore, who also starred as principal comedian. Toured the U.S. for many years, with members of the Tim Moore Co. Information on only three eds. has been located: *1916 ed*. Cast also included Moore's wife Gertrude (Gertie) Moore (leading lady), Kid Brown (straight man), Campbell Brownie (boy), Ethel Watts (soubrette), and Eddie Stafford (character actor). Chorus included Eva Smith, Jessie Cowan, and Florence Seals. *1921 ed*. Mentioned in *Billboard* 7–2–1921 (J. A. Jackson's Page). *1928 ed*. Cast also included Jackson & Rector, Julia Davis, and Raymond Shackelford.

CHICAGO LOOP (1926). Musical comedy. 2 acts. Music by James P. Johnson. Lyrics by Henry Creamer and Ted Wing. Apparently unprod. Copyright by Henry Creamer, 1926; copy in LC.

CHICAGO PACEMAKERS (1926). Touring vaudeville revue. Featured "Ragtime" David Wiles and the Humming Bird Beauty Chorus.

CHICAGO PLANTATION REVUE (1927). Musical revue. Prod. by Clarence Muse in Chicago and on tour. Apparently a metamorphosis of Muse's *Charleston Dandies*, which toured the TOBA Circuit 1926–27. Cast of this show included Roscoe "Red" Simmons, Roscoe Montella, Pauline Montella, Marie Gonzales, "Skeeter" Winston, and the Chicago [Harmony] Four, all of whom had perfd. with the *Charleston Dandies*. Also in the cast were Johnny Jones and the Valley Inn Orchestra.

CHIEF OUTLANCHETTE (1918). Tabloid musical melodrama. Book by Billy King. Involved a half-caste Indian who is in love with a beautiful heroine. She is, of course, abducted by the villain, saved by the hero; the lovers are united, and the story ends happily. Perfd. by the Billy King Stock Co., at the Grand Theatre, Chicago. Cast: Leon Brooks (Hero), Bessie Brown (Heroine), Jerry Mills (Villain), James P. Reed (Indian Chief), Howard Kelly (Wild Bill), and Billy King (Handy Man & Comedian).

(THE) CHILDREN OF THE SUN (1919–20). African-inspired musical comedy. 2 acts [10 scenes]. Book by Salem Tutt Whitney and J. Homer Tutt, assisted by George Wells Parker, a black Omaha, NE, archaeologist, historian, and author. Music by James Vaughan.

While on an archaeological research tour, the dean of Howard University discovers a document which claims that the black race originated from a lost people called the Children of the Sun, and that when the site of these ancestors is found, a mountain of gold will also be discovered. Believing that the Children of the Sun will be found in the Far East, an expedition immediately travels through Japan, Persia, India, and Egypt, but fails to find the lost site. A second expedition headed by Whitney & Tutt, playing the roles of Abe and Gabe Washington, travels to Ethiopia, where they discover the true site of the ancestors of the black race, and also learn of the fabulous wealth still undiscovered in King Solomon's mines.

Prod. on tour by Whitney & Tutt's *Smart Set Co.* under °Klaw & Erlanger bookings, 1919–20; starring Whitney & Tutt. Other members of the cast included Edward Tolliver, Carrie King, Virginia Wheeler, May Olden, Julia Moody, Alice Smith, Bertha Roe, and Grace Howell.

Songs and musical numbers included "Woman All Go for Mine" (Tutt & Ladies), "We're Travelin'," "Dear Old Dixie Home," "Come and Dance with Me," and "Something About You I Like."

CHINA TOWN (1920). Musical comedy. 2 acts. Written and prod. by Billy King and the Darktown Follies Co. Presented at the Grand Theatre, Chicago. Orchestra dir. by Marie Lucas. Cast included King, George Catlin (Chinese impersonator), Lottie Gee, Will A. Cook, Leon Diggs, Dink Stewart, Jesse Paschall, Evon Robinson, Percy Colston, Helen Baxter, A. Thiggs, Lillian Gardner, Lottie Harris, and May Crowder. Musical numbers included "After You're

Gone" and "Ruling Power" (Stewart), "Some Day" and "China Town" (Crowder), "Japanese Sandman" and "Gay White Way" (Stewart), "Old Home Jim" (Paschall), "Sweet Sixteen" and "My Dream of the U.S.A." (Diggs), "Kentucky Home" (Cook), "Acalon" (Thiggs), "High Jinks" (Gardner & Chorus), "Don't Take My Blues Away" (Baxter), "Margie" (Harris), and "Rose" (Colston).

CHOCOLATE BLONDES (1929). Harlem revue. Presumably featuring fair-skinned chorines with blonde hair. Prod. either at the Lafayette or Lincoln Theatre. The cast was headed by "blues shouter" Mattie Hite and dancer Eddie Rector.

CHOCOLATE BOX REVUE (1925–26). Musical revue in at least 2 eds. Prod. by John Gibson at his Standard or Dunbar Theatres in Philadelphia, then on tour. *1925 ed.* Cast included Berthel Gibson, the Gibson Trio, Roy B. Arthur (called "That Grasshopper Comedian"), Johnny Stevens, Gladys Kirkland, Rastus Brown, Marie Kitchen, Happy Bolden, Fats Johnson, and Will Silbey. *1926 ed.* Cast included Baby Corrine and Little Albert.

CHOCOLATE BROWN (1921). Topical musical revue. Prod. by Irvin C. Miller, in Harlem and on tour. Special music and lyrics by Spencer Williams. About the problems of southern blacks who migrate to the North—particularly crime and unemployment; with a message to northern blacks to help their southern brothers adjust to their new environment. Cast included William E. Fountain, Andrew Tribble, Mildred Smallwood, Mary Bradford, Percy Colston, Archie Bross, and the Broadway Four.
FURTHER REFERENCE: *Billboard* 7–30–1921. *Chicago Whip* 5–28–1921.

THE CHOCOLATE DANDIES (1924–25) / / Orig. title: *In Bamville* (1923–24). Musical comedy. 2 acts [12 scenes]. Book by Noble Sissle and Lew Payton. Music and lyrics by Sissle and Eubie Blake (Sissle & Blake).
    A reworking of their earlier show, *In Bamville*, for Bway prodn., written mainly by Sissle & Blake, the lyricist and composer of the more successful *Shuffle Along* (1921). This was a lavish prodn., with tuneful lyrics, lively music, beautiful chorus girls, and funny comedy routines. Josephine Baker was a comedy chorus girl, and Lena Horne was in the chorus line. The plot was built around horse racing, and is described by Gerald Bordman (*AmMusTh*, p. 391) as follows:

Mose Washington (Lew Payton), who owns a race horse named Dumb Luck, falls asleep before the race and dreams his horse has won him a small fortune. He becomes president of Bamville's bank, only to have a run on the bank start. He wakes up to discover Dumb Luck has not won. The big money has gone to Dan Jackson's Rarin'-to-Go, and with his winnings Dan (Ivan H. Browning) has also won the hand of Angeline Brown (Lottie Gee). The race was shown onstage, using three horses on a treadmill.

Toured for about six months as *In Bamville* before opening on Bway at the Colonial Theatre, Sept. 1, 1924, for 96 perfs., which was not enough time to recoup its losses. Julian Mitchell was stage dir., and Eubie Blake perfd. at the piano. Cast: Amanda Randolph (Mandy Green, the Deacon's Wife), Pauline Godfrey (Sammy, Mandy's Baby), Addison Carey (Black Joe, Jr.), Josephine Baker (That Comely Chorus Girl), J. Mardo Brown (Struttin' Drum Major and His Bamville Band), W. H. Hann (Bill Splivins, Plantation Owner), William Grundy (Mr. Hez Brown, President of Bamville Fair), Inez Clough (Mrs. Hez Brown, the Wife), Lottie Gee (Angeline Brown, the Daughter), Elizabeth Welsh (or Elisabeth Welch: Jessie Johnson), Valaida Snow (Manda, Bill Splivins' Niece), Fred Jennings (Uncle Eph), Noble Sissle (Doddy Hicks), Ivan H. Browning (Dan Jackson), Ferdie Robinson (Shorty), Russell Smith (Johnny Wise), Lew Payton (Mose Washington), Johnny Hudgins (Joe Dolks), Lee J. Randall (Silas Green, the Deacon), George Jones, Jr. (Bookmaker), Charlie Davis (Snappy), Curtis Carpenter (Sandy, Scarecrow's Jockey), and John Alexander & Chick Fisher (Jump Steady [a horse]). Other Characters: In the Bank—Robinson (Bank Policeman), Jennings (Porter), Snow (Secretary), Richard Cooper (Cashier), Percy Colston (Bookkeeper), Carey (Auditor); At the Wedding— Mildred Smallwood (Mischief), Baker (A Deserted Female), and Lloyd Keyes (Her Bunco Attorney).

Songs and musical numbers: "Mammy's Little Chocolate Cullud Chile," "Have a Good Time Everybody," "That Charleston Dance," "The Slave of Love," "I'll Find My Love in D-I-X-I-E," "There's No Place as Grand as Bandana Land," "The Sons of Old Black Joe," "Jassamine Lane," "Dumb Luck," "Breakin' 'Em Down," "Dancing Pickaninnies," "Thinking of Me," "All the Wrongs You've Done to Me," "Manda," "Run on the Bank," "You Ought to Know," "Jazztime Baby," and "There's a Million Little Cupids in the Sky."

Piano scores for Sissle & Blake's songs are pub. by Harms, Inc., New York, 1924. "All the Wrongs You've Done to Me," by Lew Payton, Chris Smith, and Edgar Dowell, pub. by Clarence Williams Music Co., New York, 1924. Copies of several songs from this show are in Moorland-Spingarn.

FURTHER REFERENCE: *AmMusTh* (Bordman). *BlkMusTh* (Woll). *Messenger* 11– 1924. *NY Herald* 1–20–1924. *NYT* 9–2–1924. *Opportunity* 11–19–1924. *ThMag* 11– 1924. *Variety* 4–2–1924; 9–24–1924.

CHOCOLATE KIDDIES (1925). Musical revue. Music and lyrics by Duke Ellington and Joe Trent. Prod. on European tour, 1925; music perfd. by Ben Bernie and his orchestra. With an all-black cast headed by Adelaide Hall. The hit song from this show was "Jig Walk," a popular song written for the Charleston, the dance craze of the 1920s; lyrics by Trent, melody by Ellington; pub. by Robbins-Engle, New York; copy in Moorland-Spingarn.

THE CHOCOLATE SCANDALS (1923, 1927). Touring revue in at least two eds. Both featured Sam Russell, Sarah Martin, and Doc Straine. *1923 ed.* Cast also included Halen [*sic*] Stokes and Gill & Warner (billed as the Two Ebony Nights). *1927 ed.* Cast also included the Ali Brothers & Jackson, and Curtis Mosby's Dixieland Blue Blowers.

CHOCOLATE SCANDALS (1931). Touring vaudeville revue. Prod. by Al Davis. Cast included Mantan Moreland, Shelton Brooks, Percy Verwayen, Kitty Aublanche, Lottie Brown, the Smart Brothers, and Hanna Sylvester.

CHOCOLATE TOWN (1923). Touring revue. Prod. by Raymond Day; dir. by Coy Herndon. Cast included Herndon, Leon Diggs, Billy Arnette, Jazz Warren, Bessie Brown, Frank "Pork Chops" Gibson, Cecilia Coleman, Louise Washington, "Rastus" Brown, the Charles Trice Trio, and the Flapper Chorus. Music was provided by W. Kelly's orchestra and Ernest Montagua's 18-piece band. Songs included "Hot Lips" (Coleman), "Bell in the Light House" (Gibson), "Jennie's Jubilee" (Brown), "Old [*sic*] Lang Syne" (Trio), "Tomorrow Moonshine" (Warren), and "Long Gone" (Arnette). A comedy sketch, 'The Oklahoma Wild Cat Oil Co.,' was perfd. by the company.

THE CHOICE (pre-1968). Musical. Book by John Ashby. Music and lyrics by Dorothy Ashby. Based on a story of black ghetto life. Presented by the Ashby Players at the Dexter Theatre, Detroit, MI; dir. by John Ashby.

THE CHOREOGRAPHY OF LOVE (1946). Comic opera. 1 act. Libretto by Townsend Brewster. Musical score by °Mitzi Goldreyer. About two shy young people in New York's Central Park, who fall in love but are unable to communicate their feelings. They finally do so through dance. Prod. at Queens Coll., New York, 1945. Broadcast over WNYC Radio, New York, Feb. 16, 1946.

A CHRISTMAS MIRACLE / / Orig. title: ***A Southern Star*** (1958). Opera. 1 act. Libretto by Owen Dodson. Musical score by Mark Fax. Begun in 1950; completed in 1958. Twice perfd. at Howard Univ., Washington, DC, by Phi Kappa Lambda National Music Fraternity, March 1958. Libretto of *A Southern Star* in JWJ/YUL.

CHRISTMAS REVELS (1933). Musical revue. Starring blues singer Bessie Smith. Presented as the Lafayette Theatre's holiday prodn., at the Harlem Opera House, New York, during the 1933 Christmas season.

CHUCKLES (1922). Touring vaudeville revue. Book by comedian William (Bill) "Bodidley" Pierson, who also perfd. Music by Johnny Anderson and his Orchestra. Cast included Clittle Adams, Lottie Bolds, Helen Boyd, Lena Boyd, George Bronson, Fern Calswell, Janet Cooper, Richard Count, Edna Douglass, Milton Douglass, Herman Higgs, Lelia Johnson, Epsie Lee, James Moore, Joy

Morris, T. A. Perkins, Victoria Powell, Mae Provost, Catherine Reese, Bessie Ricketts, Charlotte Strange, and Alice Walker.

CIRCUS DAY REVUE (1928). Touring revue. Built around a circus plot, and featuring Slim Thompson, Hilda Rogers, King Knapple, and Dewey Miles.

THE CIRCUS SHOWMAN (1929). Vaudeville revue. Prod. in Harlem by veteran showman Irvin C. Miller, April 1929.

CLARA SMITH REVUE (1928). Musical revue. Prod. at the Lincoln Theatre, New York; starring singer Clara Smith.

CLASS STRUGGLE IN SWING (1939). Topical cabaret musical. Sketches and songs by James P. Johnson, Aarons & Stratton, and Lewis Allen. Lyrics attributed to Langston Hughes. Apparently prod. at the Theatre Arts Committee (TAC) Cabaret, Nov. 7, 1939.
FURTHER REFERENCE: *NY Herald Trib.* 10–6–1939.

CLORIFENA'S WEDDING DAY (1922). Vaudeville entertainment. Prod. by and costarring comedians Joe Simms and Robert Warfield. Cast also included Edna Hicks, James Edwards, Eloise Johnson, and Lovie Taylor.

CLORINDY, THE ORIGIN OF THE CAKEWALK / / Alternate title: *Clorindy, or, The Origin of the Cakewalk* (1898). Musical comedy sketch, called by the composer a Negro Operetta. Conceived by Will Marion Cook, who also wrote the orig. sketch, composed the music, wrote some of the lyrics, and conducted the orchestra. Most lyrics and a libretto (not used) by Paul Laurence Dunbar. Written as a starring vehicle for Williams & Walker, who were unable to appear in the Bway prodn., but who did take it on the road after the show closed in New York.
   A love story set on a Southern plantation, described by the composer as "a story of how the cakewalk came about in Louisiana in the Eighteen Forties" (*ThArts* 9–1947). A landmark show that attempted to depart from the minstrel tradition by demonstrating the true artistry of the Negro as creator and performer. Although more of a vaudeville revue with minstrel elements than a true operetta, it did help to pave the way for white acceptance of later black musicals. It was probably the first to fully exploit the possibilities of syncopated ragtime music in the theatre; the first to introduce the cakewalk (a staple of the minstrel stage) to sophisticated New York audiences; the first all-black show to play at a major Bway theatre; and the first to have a white theatre orchestra led by a black conductor.
   First prod. on Bway by °George W. Lederer at the Casino Roof Garden (an open-air theatre patronized exclusively by whites, on the roof of the renowned Casino Theatre). Opened on July 5, 1898 (one week after its scheduled premiere

on June 28, which was postponed because of heavy rain). It was presented as an afterpiece to an entertainment called *Rice's Summer Nights*. Because of the circumstances of its prodn., the entire libretto by Dunbar had to be virtually eliminated, and only the songs and dances were retained. It was an instant "hit," which the *New York Times* called "sensational" (*AmMusTh* [Bordman], p. 158), and continued to run for most of the summer. The cast of 26 orig. participants, later increased to 40, was headed by Ernest Hogan, the veteran minstrel comedian, and the beautiful Belle Davis. Also in the show was Abbie Mitchell (then age 14), who took over the lead at some point, and later became Mrs. Will Marion Cook.

Songs and musical numbers included an Overture (title unknown), "The Hottes' Coon in Dixie" (a swaggering "coon" song: Hogan), "Who Dat Say Chicken in Dis Crowd?" (which received 10 encores on opening night: Hogan), "Jump Back, Honey, Jump Back!" (a love song also receiving several encores: Davis), "On Emancipation Day," "That's How the Cake-Walk's Done," "Love in a Cottage Is Best," "Dance Creole," and the rousing 20-minute choral and cakewalking finale, "Darktown Is Out Tonight," after which, according to the composer, "the audience stood up and cheered for at least ten minutes" (*ThArts* 9–1947). It was the song hit of the show, which "was being whistled and sung all over town" (*Paul Laurence Dunbar and His Song* [Cunningham], pp. 177-78).

After its successful Bway run, Hogan left the show, and *Clorindy* was incorporated as an afterpiece into Williams & Walker's new show, *Senegambian Carnival*, with Williams & Walker as Hogan's replacement. The combined show toured some of the major cities in the East, including Boston, Philadelphia, Cincinnati, and Washington, DC, without much success, before finally closing.

The libretto of *Clorindy* is in the MC/LC. Music and lyrics pub. by M. Witmark & Sons, New York; copies in Moorland-Spingarn. Excerpts, including overture and medley selections, arranged for piano by F. W. Meacham, also pub. by Witmark, 1899; copy in Schomburg.
FURTHER REFERENCE: *Just Before Jazz* (Riis). *Nobody* (Charters). *NYT* 10–6–1898. Riis diss. *ThArts* 9–1947 ("Clorindy, the Origin of the Cakewalk," by Will Marion Cook, pp. 61–65; reprinted in *AnthANT* [Patterson] and *Readings Blk. Am. Mus.* [Southern]).

CLUB ALABAM REVUE (1926). Cabaret revue, which originated at Club Alabam, a Harlem nightspot. Prod. by and costarring "Doc" Straine and Bessie Brown. Musical dir., Aaron Thompson. Also in the cast were Helen Stokes, Clifton & Batis, Henry Myres, Robert Wade, C. J. Davis, and 7 chorus girls.

CLUB FIFTY (1986). Cabaret revue. Written and dir. by Adam Wade and Jeree Palmer. A celebration of life after 50. Prod. at the Kopia Dinner Theatre, Philadelphia, PA, March 6–April 27, 1986. Musical dir., Donna Brown; choreographer, Ty Stephens. Featuring Gail Gaddie, John Hines, George Lowe, Brenda Smith, Hazel Stith, and the Dancing Dictators.

CLUB HOLLYWOOD REVUE (1931). Cabaret revue. Touring show, prod. by Irvin C. Miller. Cast included Evon Robinson and Gertrude Saunders.

CLUB KENTUCKY REVUE (1927). Cabaret revue. Touring show, prod. by and starring dancer/choreographer Leonard Harper. Cast also included Blanche Thompson, Radcliffe & Radcliffe, Hunter & Ledman, and "Jazz Lips," Jr.

THE COAL HEAVERS (1922). Touring show. Prod. by the James Crescent Players. Cast included Freddie James (age 13), Tillie James, Crawford Jackson, Willie Glover, and Frank Delyon.

COCK O' DE WORLD (1931). Musical comedy. 3 acts. Adapt. by Langston Hughes from a play by Kaj Gynt. Music by Duke Ellington. Concerns the travels of a black seaman from New Orleans through the West Indies to France, where he has a number of bizarre experiences and encounters with racism that make him happy to return to the United States. Incomplete copy of script in JWJ/YUL.

THE COCKTAIL SIP (1973). Comic opera. 1 act. Libretto by Townsend Brewster. Musical score by Noel Da Costa. Musical parody of *The Cocktail Party* by °T. S. Eliot, with the setting changed to Newark, NJ, and the guests to pseudosophisticated blacks. Unprod.

COCKTAILS OF 1932 (1932). Vaudeville revue. Prod. in Harlem and on tour; starring comedian Dewey "Pigmeat" Markham.

COLORED ARISTOCRACY (1891). Musical show. Prod. by the Hyers Sisters' Musical Comedy Co. on tour of the East., Oct. 1891; starring Anna Madah Hyers and Emma Louise Hyers.

THE COLORED ARISTOCRATS (1908). Musical comedy. Book by Flournoy E. Miller and Aubrey Lyles (Miller & Lyles). Music by Sidney Perrin.
    The plot revolves around the social snobbery and rivalry within an all-black community. This was the show in which Miller & Lyles first introduced the blackface characters Steve Jankins and Sam Peck, which they were to use and portray in many of their future shows, including *Shuffle Along.
    Prod. by Irvin C. Miller and Miller & Lyles as a touring show, 1909. Cast: Flournoy Miller (Steve Jenkins), Aubrey Lyles (Sam Peck), Irvin C. Miller (Harry Fast), Cliff Green (Dodson Moseby), Cassie Burch (Matilda Moseby), Arthur Malone (Frank Cole), Carmen Lawson (Rose Littlejohn), Vivian Forrest (Laberta Birdsong), Alice Christy (Mrs. Bootnose), Eva Simpson (Mrs. Fainty), Georgia Hutchinson (Mrs. Hatchethead), Edith Gordon (Mrs. Solate), Julia Turner (Mrs. Meddlesome), Sourthey DeJole (Mrs. Nuffsed), Clyde Brooks

(Policeman 13-13-13), Alfonso Walker (Jim, the Lime Man), and Thomas Pierson (Happy Harry).

Songs and musical numbers: "Why Moses Never Saw the Promised Land," "Caroline," "Fare Thee Well," "Dreamy Day," "Chocolate Mandy," "Meet Me by the Candy Pole," "For the Last Time, Call Me Sweetheart," and "Pleading Eyes."

THE COLORED MUSEUM (1986). Musical satire. Described by *NYT* (11–3–1986) as a "near-musical revue." 11 sketches. By George C. Wolfe.

In the context of a museum of black culture, a series of 12 exhibits come alive, satirizing the stereotypes and myths of black life. Among those skits that are relevant to the musical stage are one of Josephine Baker and a parody of black song-and-dance musicals. Winner of the Dramatists Guild Award, 1986.

World premiere at the Crossroads Theatre, New Brunswick, NJ, opening March 26, 1986; dir. by Lee Richardson. Again prod. by the New York Shakespeare Festival/Public Theatre, at the Susan Stein Shiva Theatre, opening Oct. 7, 1986; also dir. by Richardson. Featured cast included Loretta Devine, Tommy Hollis, Reggie Montgomery, Vicilyn Reynolds, and Danitra Vance.

A televised version was aired in 1991.

Pub. by Broadway Play Publishing, New York, 1987.

FURTHER REFERENCE: *Newswk* 11–17–1986. *NY* 11–17–1986. *NYT* 11–3–1986. *Variety* 11–12–1986.

COME ALONG MANDY (1923–24). Musical farce. Book and lyrics by Salem Tutt Whitney and J. Homer Tutt (Whitney & Tutt). Music by Donald Heywood.

Concerned a dispute over boundary lines between two pieces of property in Hopeville, GA, owned by Zack and Sudds, played by Whitney & Tutt. The situation becomes more complicated when the deeds to both parcels of land are stolen by a thief posing as a lawyer. Much of the action concerns the chase of the thief, and Mandy (one of the characters) is invited to "come along" on the trip which finally ends in the capture at a social affair in Harlem.

Prod. at the Lafayette Theatre in Harlem, Dec. 1923, apparently continuing until 1924; starring Whitney & Tutt. Other characters include Al LaBabor, the thief; Lovey Joe, a peacemaker; and Lucinda and Krispy, who pose as detectives.

FURTHER REFERENCE: *Messenger* 2–1924.

COMIN' UPTOWN (1979). Musical adaptation. 2 acts [13 scenes]. Book by °Philip Rose and °Peter Udell. Lyrics by Udell. Music by °Garry Sherman.

A black American adaptn. of °Charles Dickens' *A Christmas Carol*, with the action transferred to Harlem, 1979. In this version, dancer Gregory Hines plays the part of Scrooge, a heartless slumlord.

Prod. at the Winter Garden Theatre, New York, Dec. 20, 1979–Jan. 27, 1980, for 45 perfs. plus 19 previews; dir. by Rose. Choreography by Michael Peters. Cast: Hines (Scrooge), John Russell (Bob Cratchit & Deacon), Larry

Marshall (Tenant's Representative), Saundra McClain (Mary, Recreation Center Director & Christmas Present), Robert Jackson (Minister), Tiger Haynes (Marley), Larry Marshall (Christmas Past), Frances Lee Morgan (Time), Loretta Devine (Young Mary), Duane Davis (Young Scrooge), Vernal Polson (His Assistant), Ned Wright (Reverend Byrd), Esther Marrow (Gospel Singer), Virginia McKinzie (Mrs. Cratchit & Deacon's Wife), Shirley Black-Brown and Allison R. Manson (Cratchit Daughters), Kevin Babb (Tiny Tim), Robert Jackson (Christmas Future), and Salvation Army Trio: Deborah Lynn Bridges, Deborah Burrell, and Jenifer Lewis.

Songs and musical numbers: "Christmas Is Comin' Uptown," "Now I Lay Me Down to Sleep," "Get Your Act Together," "Lifeline," "What Better Time for Love," "It Won't Be Long," "Get Down Brother Get Down," "Sing a Christmas Song," "Have I Finally Found My Heart?," "Nobody Really Do," "Goin' Gone," "One Way Ticket to Hell," and "Born Again."

THE CONFESSION STONE (1968). Subtitled "A Song Cycle." By Owen Dodson. Music by Noel Da Costa. Musical portrayal of several biblical characters, including Mary, the mother of Jesus. First prod. at Carnegie Hall, New York, Feb. 3, 1968; then at the Canadian Expo, and other places in the United States; sung by Canadian contralto Maureen Forrester. Prod. by Theatre Off Park, New York, opening Feb. 14, 1979, for 8 perfs.; dir. by Dodson. Featuring Ruth Attaway.

THE CON MAN (1918). Tabloid musical. Written and prod. by Billy King.

About a rich widow who wishes to buy a pet on which to lavish her affections and her money. A con man tries to swindle her by disguising his accomplice as a dog. Much of the comedy comes through attempts to prove that the dog is well trained by putting it/him through a number of tricks.

First presented by the Billy King Stock Co., at the Grand Theatre, Chicago, 1918; then on tour. Cast included King (accomplice), Howard Kelly (con man), Bessie Whitman (widow), James P. Reed, and Ernest Whitman.

Musical numbers included "You're Just Like a Mother to Me" (E. Whitman), "Rolling Stones" (Reed), "Real King Mama" (B. Whitman), and "Cotton Bales" (King).

CONNIE'S INN FROLICS (1926–27). Cabaret show in two eds. Prod. by Connie's Inn, New York. Featured in both eds. were Emmett "Gang" Anthony, Sam Cross, Alta Oates, John Dancy, and Jennie Dancy. *1926 ed*. Other cast members included George Taylor, Archie Crow, Billy Young, "Baby" Johnson, and Octovia Sumpter. This ed. featured a comic sketch, 'Twenty Minutes to Hell,' with Anthony & Cross. *1927 ed*. Prod. by °George Immerman (°Connie Immerman's husband). Cast also included Mantan Moreland, Johnny Lee, Baby Lee, and Ruth Payne.

CONRACK (1987). Musical adaptation. Book by Granville Burgess, with Anne Croswell and Lee Pockriss. Based on *The Water Is Wide* by Pat Conroy. About the experiences of a young, idealistic white man, who is engaged to teach seven black children on Yamacraw Island off the coast of South Carolina. Prod. by the AMAS Repertory Theatre, New York, Oct. 15–Nov. 8, 1987.

COONEY DREAMLAND (1904). Musical comedy skit. 1 act. By Bob Cole.

One of the opening skits of the *Black Patti Troubadours* show. A sequel to Cole's earlier one-act musical skit, *At Jolly Coon-ey Island* (1896–97). According to a review in the Indianapolis *Freeman* (8–16–1903), *Cooney Dreamland*

served to introduce the strongest set of colored comedians ever brought together in one performance. Bob Cole . . . has excelled his former efforts in giving a higher grade of comedy than has heretofore [been] accorded to life at Coney Island. "Dreamland" is a dream, and a highly legitimate one, if we must not consider it second cousin to a circus. Expressing the farcical side of Negro life . . . , [Cole] can be credited with having presented a musical Negro comedy quite as genuine as white comedies of the same class.

Prod. on tour as part of the Troubadours' show, 1904. In Aug., it played in Indianapolis, IN, where it was reviewed above. Cast included comedian John Rucker (billed as the Alabama Blossom), Anthony Byrd (Dinah Jones, Rucker's wife), James Crosby (an overgrown boy; also a Shanghai rooster with wings and feathers), Charles Bougia (an Italian organ grinder), Mattie Phillips (singer/dancer), Ida Forsyne (A Kaffir queen), James Worles (singer), Bobby Kemp (singer), W. H. Steward (a monkey), Will A. Cook (a tramp), Harry Reed (a policeman), and the chorus.

Songs and musical numbers: "All Aboard for Dreamland" (Company), "When the Coons Have a Dreamland of Their Own" (Crosby), "Big Indian Chief" (Chorus), "Maiden of Timbuctoo" (Forsyne), "Dollie" (a love song: Worles), and "Lazy Moon" (a serenade: Kemp & Chorus).

COONTOWN CARNIVAL (1900). Musical farce. By Bob Cole. Cited by Fannin Belcher (Ph.D. diss., 1945, p. 116). No record of prodn.

THE COTTON BROKERS (1920). Touring vaudeville show. Prod. by the Hambone Jones Co. Cast included comedian Hambone Jones, Virginia Liston, and Sam H. Gray.

COTTON CLUB PARADE (1935). Musical revue. Book, lyrics, and prodn. by °Ted Koehler. Music by °Rube Bloome. Dances by Leonard Harper and Elida Webb. Orchestrations by Will Vodery, Claude Hopkins, and Alex Hill. Prod. at the Cotton Club, New York, with the following stellar cast: Nina Mae McKinney, Flournoy E. Miller, Mantan Moreland, Butterbeans & Susie, Juano Hernandez, Lena Horne, Emmett "Babe" Wallace, the Three Rhythm Queens, the Rhythm Rascals, and Claude Hopkins' Orchestra.

COTTON CLUB PARADE OF 1933 (1933). Night club revue. One of the Cotton Club's most famous shows, starring Ethel Waters. It was in this show that Waters first sang °Harold Arlen and °Ted Koehler's "Stormy Weather," a black woman's lament about her unfaithful man. Prod. at the Cotton Club, New York, 1933.

COTTON LAND (1924). Touring show. Music by James P. Johnson. Cast included Johnson, Billy Higgins, Gertrude Saunders, Dick ("Dickie") Wells, Billy Mitchell, Jimmy Mordecai, the Three Browns, and the Cotton Land Chorus.

COTTON TOPS (1921). Vaudeville show. Cited in *Billboard* (7–2–1921) when it was then being produced.

A COUNTRY COON (c. 1900). Vaudeville farce, which the authors originally called "A Pastoral Comedy." 4 acts. By Ernest Hogan and Allan Dunn. Later copyrighted as a musical farce comedy, 3 acts. Cited by Fannin Belcher (Ph.D. diss., 1945, p. 116). No record of prodn.

COUNT YOUR BLESSINGS (1989, revised 1990). Gospel musical. Book and lyrics by James M. Brown. Music by William "Butch" Oatman, Bryant Pugh, and Scott Parker. Originally described by *Blk. Masks* (Sept./Oct. 1989) as "about a young woman's struggles to pick a mate of her choosing versus God's choice of a mate for her." Prod. at the West Side Complex, Dr. Martin Luther King, Jr. Blvd. and Marmora Ave., Atlantic City, NY, Oct. 1989; dir. by Al (Suavae) Mitchell. Rev. Charles Lyles, vocal and musical director. Featuring Rev. Richard Brown, Jennifer Trott, Gwen Fleming, and Bill Greene. Revised as "a love story about a young African American woman who has just finished law school and falls in love with her first client, a street-wise rap artist" (*Blk. Masks*). Musical direction by William "Butch" Oatman. Arrangements and orchestration by Bryant Pugh and Rev. Charles R. Lyles. Prod. at the Aronow Theatre, City College (CCNY), New York, Jan. 27, 1990, for a lengthy run. Featuring the orig. cast plus Kay Wright and Levi Peterson.

COURTED INTO COURT (1896–97). White-oriented musical farce-comedy. By °John McNally. With interpolated, so-called coon songs by Ernest Hogan and Ben Harney.

Centered around the divorce proceedings of an actress whose case is brought before a judge who hopes to marry her himself; in addition, her husband's father is involved in the plot as a rival suitor.

Prod. at the Bijou Theatre, New York, opening Dec. 29, 1896, continuing its run into 1897. The all-white cast included °May Irwin (the actress), °John C. Rise (her husband), °Joseph Sparks (the judge), and °Raymond Hitchcock (the father-in-law).

The two black-authored songs sung by Irwin were "All Coons Look Alike to

Me'' (the grandfather of the coon song genre), written and composed by Hogan, and ''Mr. Johnson, Turn Me Loose'' (a ragtime classic), written and composed by Harney.

CRAZY QUILT REVUE (1929). Touring vaudeville revue. Prod. Oct. 1929, starring heavyweight champion Jack Johnson. This was the same year that he won the championship.

CREOLE BELLES (1921–26). Touring vaudeville revue in at least three eds. The first two eds. were owned and managed by Ed(ward) Lee. The third was prod. by Jimmy Cooper. *1922 ed.* (opened in 1921). Cast included Albert Allen, Edward Bonner and his band, Jessie Brooks, Landow Crosby, Lavinia Moore, Pace & Pace, Bessie Stones, and Josephine Thomas. *1924 ed.* Joe Brown as stage manager; A. C. Davis, musical dir. Cast included [Joe] Stevens & Lockhard (comedians), William Pace (straight man/singer), Prince and Princess Alimonia (magicians), and chorus. *1926 ed.* Cast included ''Doc'' Straine, Billy Cumby, Bessie Brown, Grace Smith, Barrington Carter, C. Westley Hill, the Dancing Browns, and the Famous Runnin' Wild Quartet.

CREOLE FOLLIES [REVUE] (1922–23). Vaudeville revue. Prod. by the Coleman Brothers Creole Follies Co., at the Lafayette Theatre in Harlem; then on tour. Cast included Billy Higgins, Emmett (or Emett) ''Gang'' Anthony, Blanche Thompson, Johnny Hudgins, Lulu Whidby, Lucille Hegamin (as the ''Cameo Girl''), Freeman & McGinty, Mildred Martine, and W. C. Richardson.

CREOLE JAZZ BABIES (1922). Touring revue. Prod. by and starring comedian Slim Henderson. Also in the cast were comedian Royal Sutton, straight man Frank King, singer Rosa Henderson, singer/dancer Isabel Dabner, dancer Marietta Foster, and 4 chorus girls.

CREOLE REVUE (1922–24). Touring revue in at least two eds. The *1922 ed.* was cited in *Billboard* 6–24–1922. The *1924 ed.* was prod. by and costarred James Berry (who also was orchestra dir.) and Earl Hailstock (also straight man); stage manager was Roger Bell (also comedian). Cast included Marie Bell (Mrs. Roger Bell: leading lady), Catherine Ross (soubrette/blues singer), Charles Duffis (straight man/member of chorus). Chorus also included Eleanor Hamilton and Louie Kepplinger.

THE CREOLE SHOW / / *Sam T. Jack's Creole [Burlesque] Company* (1890–97). Transitional musical show—between minstrelsy and the vaudeville revue. Also called the first black burlesque show (although not a true ''girlie'' show). Conceived and developed by Sam Lucas. Prod. by °Sam T. Jack. With orig. sketches, songs, and specialty numbers by various participating black songwriters, sketch artists, comedians, and musicians.

A forerunner of the later all-black musical comedies and revues that were to rule the stage for the next few decades, this was the first show utilizing a minstrel format to feature black women in the traditionally all-male semicircle. There were three women conversationalists (or interlocutors), who sat in the center, flanked on each side by 8 chorus girls, with males on each end and in the orchestra.

The innovative influence of *The Creole Show* cannot be underestimated, although this innovation is sometimes overstated. This was not the first show to feature black women on the stage. The Hyers Sisters had appeared in several shows prior to 1890. But, because of the first-class booking and promotion of *The Creole Show* by a white theatrical manager, it had a great influence on all black shows to follow. As stated by Henry T. Sampson (*BlksBf*, pp. 70–71):

It was the first large black company to present burlesque entertainment and the first to feature beautiful, lavishly costumed black women in the leading roles, supported by a talented male and female cast. The show significantly increased the status of black women performers and opened up more opportunities for them. Following Jack's lead, minstrel company managers began to use more women. . . . The success of *The Creole Show* also inspired other black and white managers to put their own "Creole" shows on the road. Thus Blacks quickly expanded into another department of American show business.

The Creole Show followed the customary minstrel pattern of three parts. Part I consisted of the banter between the interlocutors (conversationalists) and the comedians, and individual and group songs and dances by the chorus. Part II consisted of the Olio, or variety show, including a number of sketches and specialty acts. Part III was an afterpiece, or burlesque.

The 1890 show opened with a First Part entitled "Tropical Reveries," with the chorus dressed as natives, and apparently included jokes, songs, and dances on a tropical theme. The three Conversationalists, dressed in male attire, were Florence Brisco, Florence Hines, and Mrs. Sam Lucas. The ladies in the chorus were Annie Pearl, Lizzie Scott, Laura Hinton, May Vorshall, Mattie Wilkes, Nina St. John, Eloise Pousett, Mamie Laning, Sara LaRue, Sadie D. Watts, Sadie Terry, Belle Davis, Mazie Brooks, Sadie Jones (Mrs. Irving Jones), Susie Grundy (Mrs. James Grundy), and a Miss Vaija (or Vija). The Olio (or Second Part) included sketches, songs and specialty acts, which the Indianapolis *Freeman* reported as "very fine and called for numerous encores." Little is known of these specialties except that Sam Lucas was the leading comedian, and he and his wife perfd. in a musical sketch; Irving Jones is credited with writing and singing "Home Ain't Nothing Like This"; Black Carl Dante (or Danti) performed magical tricks; James Grundy danced with his wife Susie; and the Mallory Brothers (Frank and Edward) were featured musical instrumentalists. The Third Part consisted of a burlesque entitled "The Beauty of the Nile, or Doomed by Fire," written by William R. Watts, and perfd. mainly by the "Creoles." The cast included Watts (Nafara), Hines (Cheop), Burnell Hawkins (Grip), I. Jones (Zeno), LaRue (Isis, the Queen), Brisco (Amasis, King of Thebes), Laning

(Kermach), Pousett (Dinon), St. John (Amon), Vorshall (Zoilous), and Viaja [or Vija] (Yeason).

The show was organized in New York in 1899. It opened at a theatre in Haverhill, MA, Aug. 4, 1890, also playing at the Howard Theatre in Boston, before opening in Brooklyn, NY, at Proctor's Novelty Theatre, Aug. 25, 1890. In 1890 it also played in New York City at the Old Standard Theatre in Greeley Square, which was on the edge of the Bway zone. In 1891 it opened in Chicago, at Sam T. Jack's (the producer's) Opera House. From there it toured the major vaudeville houses on Jack's burlesque circuit. During the 1892 season, Lucas and his wife left the show, which continued to tour the country. The 1893 season was an important one, during which a number of new cast members joined the show, including Charles E. Johnson and Dora Dean, the famous dancing team whose specialty was the cakewalk, which they perfd. with great style and grace; the multitalented Bob Cole, who became the youngest stage manager of the show at age 21, and Stella Wiley, a young dancer who later became Mrs. Cole; Tom and Hattie McIntosh, and a number of other talented performers. The show continued for four more seasons, closing in 1897. Among others who were with the show for one or more seasons were Billy and Cordelia McClain (sketch artists), Fred Piper, Billy Jackson, George Wilson (blackface comedian), the Golden Gate Quartette, Charles Hunn and his future wife Mary Bohee, Sherman Coats, Billy Johnson, and the team of Smart & Williams (George Smart and George Williams).

FURTHER REFERENCE: Belcher diss. *BlksBf* (Sampson). *Freeman* (Indianapolis) 9–20–1890; 1–1–1897. *Ghost* (Sampson). *Haverhill* (MA) *Eve. Gazette* 8–4–1890. *Just Before Jazz* (Riis). *Nobody* (Charters). *NY Dramatic Mirror* 9–6–1890; and various other dates, from 1891 to 1896. Riis diss.

CRISPUS (1986). Musical biography. Subtitled "A Musical Based on the Life of Black Revolutionary War Hero, Crispus Attucks." Book and music by Chuck Patterson and °Gerard La Torraca. Musical arrangements by Robert L. Arrington. Prod. by the Theatre of Universal Images, at the Van Houton Theatre, New Jersey Institute of Technology, Newark, NJ, May 1986; dir. by Chuck Patterson. With Frederick B. Owens (Crispus) and Gwendolyn Fleming.

CROESUS AND THE WITCH (1971). Musical adaptn. of a fable. 1 act. Book by Vinnette Carroll. Music and lyrics by Micki Grant. A West Indian version of the Croesus legend, teaching children how Croesus saved himself from destruction by the cruel witch Hecuba by using his mind power. Prod. by the Urban Arts Corps (UAC) of New York, opening Aug. 10, 1971, at Ft. Green Park; remained in UAC's repertory through 1975; dir. by Carroll. Libretto and musical score pub. by Broadway Music Publishing, New York, 1984.

FURTHER REFERENCE: *NYorker* 9–4–1971. *NYT* 4–27–1971.

THE CRYSTAL TREE (1980–81). Musical drama. Book and lyrics by Doris Julian. Music by Luther Henderson. Prod. by the AMAS Repertory Theatre, New York, 1980–81, dir. by Billie Allen. Choreographer, Walter Raines. Cast: Albert S. Bennett, T. Renee Crutcher, Jean DuShon, Val Eley, Leon Summers, Jr., Grenoldo Frazier, Dolores Garcia, Ira Hawkins, Norman Matlock, Andre Morgan, Christine Spencer, Vanessa Thornton, and Marta Vidal.

CURLEY McDIMPLE (1967). Musical comedy. 2 acts. Book by °Mary Boylan and °Robert Dahdah. Music and lyrics by Dahdah. A parody of Shirley Temple's optimistic film character, set in Sarah's boardinghouse in New York City during the 1930s. Prod. at the Bert Wheeler Theatre, New York, opening Nov. 22, 1967, for 991 perfs.; dir. by Dahdah. Starring °Bayne Johnson in the title role. The cast included two blacks in servant roles: Don Emmons as Jimmy, and Butterfly McQueen as Hattie. McQueen's role was especially written for her and eliminated when she left the cast.
FURTHER REFERENCE: *NYT* 11–23–1967; 1–14–1968; 5–9–1968; 11–25–1969.

CUTE ROOT (1980s). Comic opera. 1 act. By Townsend Brewster. About a young man who wins the woman he loves in spite of her preference for a visiting African. Commissioned by the Harlem Opera Society, but apparently unprod.

THE CZAR OF DIXIE (1908). Minstrel farce. Prod. by the Lincoln Stock Co., Knoxville, TN.

A series of songs and specialty numbers assembled around a thin plot about a con man posing as the Czar of Dixie. He is eventually exposed by the arrival of the real Czar. A popular plot of the period. (See *The Emperor of Dixie* [1908].)

Presented at the Lincoln Theatre in Knoxville, TN, April 1908. Cast: George Center (Pusesedo, Czar of Dixie), Sank Simms (The Real Czar), Sam P. Gardner (Czar's Valet), Mabel Brown (Juliette, the Czar's Niece), Annie Grinder (Soubrette), Miss Center, Miss Love, Kid Love, Miss Dean, and George Lewis.

Songs and musical numbers: "When the Band Was Playing Dixie" (Simms), "Dinah Green" (Gardner), "Slumberland" (Miss Center), "Warm Spot" (Miss Love), "School Days" (Miss Brown), and "Build a Nest for Birdie" (Kid Love). The program also included Kid Love as "Conversationalist" (i.e., interlocutor), assisted by Miss Center, Miss Dean, and George Lewis; a sketch entitled 'The Show Is on the Road' performed by the Centers; a monologue by Lewis; and a song and dance by Grinder.

D

DADDY! DADDY! (1980). Subtitled "A Blues Drama with Music." 2 acts. Written and dir. by Tad Truesdale. Music co-composed with and arranged by Gerald Cook. In the setting of a rural community in the South during the 1920s, the story concerns the efforts of a black father to hold together both his family and his farm during the Depression. Nominated for an AUDELCO Award in 1981 for choreography by Danna Manno. Prod. by La Mama E.T.C. (Experimental Theatre Club), New York, 1981. Featured members of the cast included Ronald Ballard, Charles Evans Berry, Henry E. Bradley, Mary Louise, Mackie Lowe, Sarallen, and Gwen Sumpter.

DADDY GOODNESS (1979). Musical adaptation. 2 acts [14 scenes]. Book by Ron Milner and Shauneille Perry. Lyrics by Milner. Music by Ken Hirsch. Based on the play of the same title by Richard Wright and °Louis Sapin.

In a small Louisiana town during the heat of the summer, a drunken man, thought to be dead, is proclaimed to be the Messiah, after he seems miraculously to come back to life. A church of New Faith is established to spread the joy and good news of his resurrection.

Prod. by Ashton Springer and Motown, in association with others, opening in an out-of-town tryout, at the Forest Theatre in Philadelphia, Aug. 16, 1979, and closing at the National Theatre in Washington, DC, Oct. 7, 1979, before reaching Bway. Dir. by Israel Hicks; choreography and musical staging by Louis Johnson. Cast: Clifton Davis (Thomas), Freda Payne (Lottie), Ted Ross (Daddy Goodness), Rod Perry (Sam), Carol-Jean Lewis (Ethel), Arthur French (Jeremiah), Dan Strayhorn (Luke), Sandra Reaves-Phillips (Annie & Mary), Ann Duquesnay (Night Club Singer), Clebert Ford (Pastor Weeks), Stefanie Showell (Daughter), Clyde Williams (Willis), Roslyn Burroughs (Mrs. Perkins), Brenda J. Davis (Mother), and the following Dancer/Singers: Vikki Baltimore, Dwight

Baxter, Gary Easterling, Brenda Garrett, Charles "C.B." Murray, Nancy-Suzanne, Mabel Robinson, Wynonna Smith, and Ned Wright.

Songs and musical numbers: "Goodness Don't Come Easy When You're Bad," "I Got Religion," "Hungry," "Spread Joy," "Lottie's Purification," "We'll Let the People Decide," "One More Step," "People Make Me Cry," "I Don't Wanna Do It Alone No More," "Daddy's Decision," "Don't Touch That Dial," and "You're Home."

DAFFY GIRLS (1921–22). Vaudeville revue. Touring show prod. by and co-starring Mills & [Maude] Frisby. Cast also included blues singer Zarelda Larue and her husband, straight man John Larue; blackface comedians Rastus Brown and Doris Hudson; and singers Terri Williams and Green & Jene Fradley. Songs included "Chick" (the Fradleys), "High Yellow and Seal-Brown" (Mills, Frisby, Hudson, Brown & Z. Larue), and "Tuck Me to Sleep" (Williams).
FURTHER REFERENCE: *Billboard* (J. A. Jackson's Page) 3–26–1921.

DANCIN' (1978–81). Musical entertainment. 3 acts [13 scenes]. Conceived, choreographed, and dir. by °Bob Fosse. Dance musical which featured two black dancers, Wendy Edmead and Bruce Anthony Davis, in an otherwise predominantly white cast. Prod. at the Broadhurst Theatre, New York, opening March 27, 1978; then moved to the Ambassador Theatre, where it continued its long run through May 1981. One of the pertinent dance numbers was "Mr. Bojangles."

DANCING DAYS (1928). Touring dance revue. Prod. by and costarring co-median Joe Simms. Music by the Clarence Jones Orchestra. Cast also included blackface comedienne Catherine Brown, Laura Bailey, Reginald York, and William Simpson.

DARKEST AMERICA (1896–89). Musical extravaganza. 2 acts. First prod. and managed by °Al G. Fields and °Oliver Scott; then by °John Vogel, who leased the rights in 1897 and purchased the show in 1898. Believed to be a modified and abbreviated version of *Black America*, an outdoor plantation ex-travaganza prod. in 1895.

A touring musical show, described by the *St. Louis Post Dispatch* (5–1897) as "partly vaudeville and partly spectacular," which "began with scenes in slavery and conclude[d] with a swell function in Washington." *The Colored American* (Washington, DC, 11–4–1896) called it a "delineation of Negro life, carrying the race through all their historical phases from the plantation . . . into reconstruction days and finally painting our people as they are today, cultured and accomplished in social graces." (To illustrate the latter observation, the finale included selections from grand opera.)

Rehearsals began in Aug. 1896, under the direction of Frank Dumont. Toured the West during the fall of 1896. Played the Bijou Theatre in Washington, DC, in Nov. 1896. Then apparently toured the theatrical circuits for the rest of the first season. The orig. cast of 50 performers included the costars Sam Lucas (principal comedian) and his wife, Marie Lucas (violinist/cornetist), who left the show after only a few months; John Rucker and Billy Miller (comedians and monologists); Clifford Brooks (comedian); Florence Hines (male impersonator); Laurence E. Chenault (featured tenor); James Crosby (singer/dancer); the Charleston Shouter; the Magnolia Quartet; Professor Henderson Smith and his military band; and Frank M. Hailstock, orchestra leader.

Under Vogel's proprietorship, the show continued to tour successfully for 3 more years. Toward the end of its run, in April 1899, it was combined with Vogel's Mastadon Minstrels, and an olio was added to the orig. 2 acts, in which the minstrels perfd. their specialties. Other performers during the 4-year run included George Titchner, the McCarver Bros., Cicero Reed, Black Carl (Carl Dante, magician), Herbert LaShe (slack wire artist), and Billy McClain (comedian).

Featured acts cited in some reviews included Rucker's portrayal of an aged character named Uncle Amos Jackson, and Chenault's impersonation of ''Golden Hair Nell,'' as well as his renditions of selections from grand opera.
FURTHER REFERENCE: *BlksBf* (Sampson). *Ghost* (Sampson).

DARKEST AMERICANS (1918–19). Musical comedy. 2 acts. Book and lyrics by Salem Tutt Whitney and J. Homer Tutt (Whitney & Tutt). Music by C. Luckeyth Roberts.

The dean of Howard University, Kelly Miller, has been lost on an archaeological expedition, and two students, Abe and Gabe (played by Whitney & Tutt), who have been enrolled at the university under false pretenses, are commissioned to search for the lost dean. Their search takes them to many parts of the world, where they have a number of hilarious and terrifying adventures before the dean is found.

Prod. by Whitney & Tutt's *Smart Set Co.* in Harlem and on tour, 1918–19. Featured cast included Whitney (Abraham DuBois Washington), Tutt (Gabriel Douglass), Alonzo Fenderson (Professor, Howard U.), Alfred F. Watts (Dean Kelly Miller), Wilbur White (R. Verson, journalist), Ed Tolliver (President of the U.S.A.), Sammy Lewin (Red Cap), Emma Jackson, Virginia Wheeler, William E. Fountain, Lee ''Boots'' Marshall, Carrie King, Estelle Cash, Edna Gibbs, Helen Jackson, and Ora Dunlop.

Songs and musical numbers included ''Jolly Jazz Joy Ride,'' ''Blue Fever,'' ''That Creole Flower Garden of Mine,'' and ''The Sambos Will Get You If You Don't Watch Out.''

DARKEYDOM. See *DARKYDOM.*

DARKTOWN AFFAIRS (1929) / / Later revised as *Change Your Luck* (1930). Musical farce-comedy. 2 acts. Book, lyrics, and music by Garland Howard, Mae Brown, Speedy Smith, and Jesse A. Shipp. Musical director, Stanley Bennett.

A number of specialty acts are assembled around a thin plot about an undertaker/bootlegger (Evergreen Peppers) who hides his liquor in empty cans of formaldehyde in his funeral parlor. The plot is complicated by the rivalry of a probation officer (Hot Stuff Jackson) and a gigolo (Diamond Joe) for the hand of the undertaker's daughter (Sally Ann Peppers).

Synopsis of scenes: Act I, Scene 1—Interior of Evergreen Peppers' funeral parlor and living room, Sundown, LA; Scene 2—Low Down Street; Scene 3—Sundown Hotel. Act II, Scene 1—Rat Row, across the river; Scene 2—The Stroll; Scene 3—Interior of Evergreen Peppers' funeral parlor: The Social Function Jamboree.

Toured as a road show in 1929. Cast: Leigh Whipper (Evergreen Peppers), Garland Howard (Hot Stuff Jackson, the Dixie Dude probation officer), Mae Brown (Sally Ann Peppers, Evergreen Peppers' angel child), Speedy Smith (Jack Snowball, proprietor of Sundown Hotel), Hattie Noles (Milindy, cook at Sundown Hotel and owner of a Hoggery across the river in Rat Row), Robert Davis (Diamond Joe, the gigolo), Kitty Brown (Liza, "just a gal"), Ada Banks (Pinky, a tot), Joe Loomis (Sweet Singing Eddie), Andrew Copeland (Officer Green), Zudora DeGaston (Sarah Go About), Leo Broadner (Detective Smart), Andrew Fairchild (Prophet Jones), Angie Mitchell (Pansy Sunshine), Moxie & Al (Just Two Hot Papas), Teddy & Eddie (Bellboys), Coley Grant (Black Bill, bad man), Frank Carter (Duksy Chinberry); Sam Lee, Aril Doe, and Jim Glover (Members of the Literary Club: Miscellaneous Frank, Keystone Atterbury, and Juniper Wheatley); Showgirls, Maids, Dancers, Expressmen, Toughs, Rustabouts, Village Choir, Rat Row Rowdies, etc.

Songs and specialty numbers: Act I—Overture, Opening Chorus (Company), "Home Brew" (Ensemble), "How About Me?" (Hot Stuff, Sally Ann, Pansy, Dock & Chorus), "Your Sins Will Find You Out" (Liza and Diamond Joe), "Loving Friends" (Hot Stuff & Ensemble), "Page Mr. Jackson" (Sally Ann & Teddy), Hot Foot Dance (Teddy), Social Function Stomp (Milindy), 'Chicken Bone' (comedy act: Snowball), "Liza" (Eddie & Literary Club), "Sally Ann" (Sally Ann, Hot Stuff & Ensemble). Act II—"Milindy" (Company), "Kicking the Mule" (Sarah, Gals & Red Lincoln[?]), "Foolishness" (Smart & Pinky), "Walk Together" (Ensemble), "Function Bound" (Al & Moxie), "Going to Miss Me" (Snowball and Sarah), "Under the Moon" (Eddie), Dance Porto Rico (Hot Stuff & Sally), "Milindy Blues" (Milindy), "Wedding Day" (Liza), Sally Ann Revival (Company), Finale.

DARKTOWN AFTER DARK (1919). Touring revue. Prod. by and starring musician Perry Bradford.

THE DARKTOWN BAZAAR (1924). Touring vaudeville revue. Prod. by and costarring Allen & Stokes (Arthur Allen and Helen Stokes). Al Wells, stage manager. Cast also included comedian Harry Brooks (who perfd. with Allen as Brooks & Allen), straight man Raymond Jefferson, Tylas Bailey, Anna Brock, Jennie Finch, Amelia Smith, and Luella Wells.

THE DARKTOWN FOLLIES (best known for the 1913–14 ed.) / / Also known as *The Darktown Follies in "My Friend from Kentucky"* and *The Darktown Follies in "My Friend from Dixie" and "Here and There"* (1910–16). Frequently revised musical revue. 3 acts. Book mainly by J. Leubrie Hill and Alex C. Rogers. Music and lyrics mainly by Hill and Will Vodery.

The Darktown Follies, especially the 1913–14 ed., which evolved from several separate musical comedies, was considered one of the best shows of its time, and, according to James Weldon Johnson (*BlkManh*, p. 173), "drew space, headlines, and cartoons in New York papers; and consequently it became the vogue to go to Harlem to see it. This was the beginning of the nightly migration to Harlem [by whites] in search of entertainment." Florenz Ziegfeld was one of the visitors to *The Darktown Follies*, and he purchased the rights to produce the grand finale at the end of the show and several song numbers in his own *Ziegfeld Follies.

The final plot of the metamorphosed show (often called *The Darktown Follies of 1914*) revolved around Jim Jackson Lee, son-in-law of a rich black plantation owner (Jasper Green) in Leesburg, VA, who is persuaded by a smooth-talking young businessman (Bill Simmons) from Kentucky to desert his shrewish, domineering wife (Mandy Lee), mortgage their home (owned by her father), and flee to Washington, DC, where he has been assured, for a healthy fee, that he will be introduced into high society as a single man and elected to the presidency of the Washington Colored Men's Business League (an office which he already holds in Leesburg). Unknown to Jim, his father-in-law Jasper and a host of his friends and neighbors have come to Washington on vacation, followed by Mandy Lee (with her children) in search of her errant husband. Their presence in Washington serves to complicate and eventually foil Jim's plans for finding a new life and marrying into Washington society, and he is forced to return with his family to Leesburg.

Much of the production history of this show is sketchy and unreliable. It apparently developed from Hill's 2-act musical *My Friend from Dixie* (which was originally titled *Our Friend from Dixie*). This was prod. under its orig. title in 1910, and under its new title in 1911, where it ran for a few weeks in Brooklyn, NY, and Newark, NJ, before premiering at the Howard Theatre in Washington, DC, where it remained for a year before going on the road in 1912. As *My Friend from Dixie*, the show gained immediate recognition because of the stereotypical portrayal of Mandy Lee, the six-foot-tall wife of Jim Jackson, by the author J. Leubrie Hill, who also prod. and dir. the show. Other members of the orig. cast were Evon Robinson (Hill's wife), C. Luckeyth Roberts (then a teenager), Tiny Ray, Will Brown, Quetta Watts, Virgie Richards, Dick Shelton, Pop Riley, Henry Hutchison, Ida Jones, Charles Odum, Mayme Butler, Walker Thompson, Jockey Murray, Frances Johnson Pendleton, Lena Stanford (the future Mrs. C. Luckeyth Roberts), and William Kelly.

After playing on the road for a year, *My Friend from Dixie* was revised and expanded, with the assistance of Alex C. Rogers, to a 3-act musical, and retitled

My Friend from Kentucky. It opened in Harlem at the Lafayette Theatre in Oct. 1913 as *The Darktown Follies in "My Friend from Kentucky,"* but was widely known simply as *The Darktown Follies*. It remained at the Lafayette until Feb. 1914, attracting the attention of white theatregoers from downtown New York, the New York press, and Florenz Ziegfeld, as previously noted. Principal cast and characters: Sam Gaines (Jasper Green, rich colored plantation owner of Leesburg, VA), Edna Morton (Juliette Lee), Adel Johnson (Susie Lee), Daisy Brown (Emmaline), Anna Pankey (Clemantine), Tiny Ray (Jimmy Moon, a very shy country lad), Julius Glenn (Jim Jackson Lee, Jasper Green's son-in-law), J. Leubrie Hill (Mandy Lee, Jasper's eldest daughter and Jim's wife), Will Brown (Bill Simmons, the friend from Kentucky, a representative of the Colored Men's Business League), Jennie Schepar (Madame Langtree, a society matron of Washington, DC), Evon Robinson (Miss Lucinda Langtree, Madame's younger daughter), Alice Ramsey (Miss Lillian Langtree, Madame's older daughter [and the show's featured singer]), Effie Hollman (Katie Krew, a society reporter for the Washington *Busy Bee*), Ethel Williams (Carrie Nation Brown, president and treasurer of the Colored Women's Suffragettes, a friend of the Langtrees [and a featured dancer]), Katie Wayne (Hannah Belmont Johnson, vice-president and secretary of the Colored Women's Suffragettes, also a friend of the Langtrees), Johnny Peters (chauffeur), Eugene L. Perkins (Mose Lewis, a prominent lawyer of Leesburg), Theodore Pankey (Dr. Moore, a physician), Billy Moore (Officer Jones), Grace Johnson (Spikie, a newsboy), Ray Webster (Shine, a bootblack), Will Thomas (cab driver), Eddie Stafford (Red Cap Sam), Pauline Parker (Lady Ensom), Arthur V. Carr (Head Waiter Thompson), and Eddie Rector (as a specialty dancer and member of the chorus, who later replaced Eddie Stafford as Red Cap Sam).

After its Harlem run, the show was cut to a 40-minute sketch and combined with another one-act musical sketch, *Here and There*, with book and lyrics by Alex C. Rogers, and music by J. Leubrie Hill. Under the blanket title *The Darktown Follies in "My Friend from Dixie" and "Here and There,"* the show moved downtown, where it played to white audiences, first opening at the Grand Opera House on 23rd St. and Eighth Ave. During the week of June 1, 1914, it opened at Hammerstein's Victoria Theatre, where it was expected to remain for a long run; however, the show suffered much from the cutting, and remained at Hammerstein's for only one week. It then went on to the Bijou Theatre on Bway, where the 3-act version was apparently restored. It was still playing in 1915 as *The Darktown Follies of 1915*.

During the season of 1919–20, the Quality Amusement Co. presented a revival of *My Friend from Kentucky* at the Lafayette Theatre in New York, with Andrew Tribble in the role of Mandy Lee, the part originally played by Hill. The show was prod. by Evon Robinson (Mrs. J. Leubrie Hill), with Dink Stewart also in the cast. It was revived again by Evon Robinson. Principal members of the cast were Dink Stewart, Jim Towel, LeRoy Morton, Rudolph Fraction, Billie Henderson, Margaret Anderson, Isador Kenney, James Smith, Fred Gordon, India

Allen, Blondie LaMarr, Coleen Morton, Viola (last name not given), Constance Anderson, Evon Robinson, and Frank DeCarlos.

Songs and specialty numbers: The main feature of the show was its dancing. According to *Jazz Dance* (Stearns & Stearns, p. 127), "*Darktown Follies* exploded with a variety of dancing, some of it topical and much of it new to the New York stage." Among the songs and dance numbers purchased by Ziegfeld for inclusion in his *Follies* were "Night Time Is the Right Time," [+]"Dear Old Dixie" (sung by Sam Gaines in Act I), [+]"Rock Me in the Cradle of Love" (sung by Alice Ramsey in Act II), and "At the Ball, That's All," the grand finale of the show, during which "the whole company formed an endless chain that passed before the footlights and behind the scenes, round and round, singing and executing a movement from a dance called 'ballin' the jack' " (*BlkManh* [Johnson], p. 174).

Songs marked with a plus sign ([+]) above were written by J. Leubrie Hill, with piano scores pub. by Jerome H. Remick, New York, 1913–14; copies in Moorland-Spingarn.

FURTHER REFERENCE: *BlkManh* (Johnson). *BlksBf* (Sampson). *Born with the Blues* (Bradford). *Chicago Defender* 11–30–1914. *Jazz Dance* (Stearns & Stearns). *Just Before Jazz* (Riis). Riis diss.

A DARKTOWN FROLIC AT THE RIALTO (1900). Billed as a "Farcical Absurdity." 1 act. One of the opening skits of the *Black Patti Troubadours* show which was prod. on tour of the U.S. and Canada, opening at the Theatre Royal in Montreal in Sept. 1900. Cast included Irvin Jones, James White, Cecil and Al F. Watts, and Black Patti (Sissieretta Jones) herself.

DARKTOWN FROLICS (1921). Touring revue. Featured Madame Branin, Carrie Hall, Beatrice Howe, Tucker & Gresham, and "Rare Back" (billed as S. H. Dudley's Mule).

DARKTOWN JUBILEE (1922). Vaudeville farce. Written and prod. by Billy King. Courtroom comedy in which the defendant is accused of kidnapping the plaintiff. Presented by the Billy King Stock Co., at the Grand Theatre, Chicago. Cast included King (Judge), Ida Cox (Defendant), Anna Belle (Plaintiff), Susie Brown (Attorney), Rebecca "Dink" Thomas (Dope Fiend), and "Doc" Straine (Officer of the Court).

THE DARKTOWN POLITICIAN (1915). Musical comedy. Touring show written and prod. by Salem Tutt Whitney, who starred in the title role. Music by T. L. Corwell, S. T. Whitney, and J. Homer Tutt. Cast also featured Tutt and Blanche Thompson in supporting roles. Included 5 songs and musical numbers.

DARKTOWN PUZZLES (1925). Touring vaudeville revue. Prod. by and co-starring "Strawberry" Russell. Cast also included Billy Maxey, Margaret Scott, "Ragtime" Billy Tucker, Gold & Goldie, and DeLoach & Corbin.

DARKTOWN SCANDALS (1927). Musical revue. Prod. in Harlem and on tour by Eddie Hunter. Under the guise of organizing a steamship company in a small southern town, Rastus Lime (played by Hunter) is actually operating a gin mill. He is eventually arrested and imprisoned, but successfully escapes in the end. Cast also included Sidney Easton, Billy Mitchell, Martha Copeland (singer/dancer), Julia Moody, Raymond Campbell, Edward Farrow, and Maggie Johnson.

DARKTOWN SCANDALS (1936). Touring vaudeville revue. Featured Ida Cox, Bell & Bell, "Peg Leg" Jefferson, and the Cotton Pickers Swing Band.

DARKTOWN SCANDALS OF 1921 (1921–22). Vaudeville revue. Touring show prod. by Quintard Miller. Cast included B. B. Joyner, Lulu Whidby, Clarence Foster, Margaret Lee, Theresa Burroughs Brooks, Billy Higgins, Tom Cross, Earl Evans, James Howell, Clarence Jackson, Margaret Jackson, Grace Johnson, and George Lynch.
FURTHER REFERENCE: *Billboard* (J. A. Jackson's Page) 4–9–1921.

DARKTOWN'S CIRCUS DAY (1903). Musical comedy skit. 3 scenes. Book originally by Bob Cole; later revised by others.
   One of the opening skits of the *Black Patti Troubadours* show, consisting of a number of specialty acts around a thin circus plot. The atmosphere of the circus is established by candy merchants, circus spielers, peanut vendors, animal attendants, policemen, actors, actresses, freaks, monkeys, bears, elephants, and others. The Poo-Bah of Darktown takes his wife and children to see the circus, which is also attended by the other citizens of Darktown. Troubles abound at the circus which complicate the plot. The specialty acts are presented, which include M'mselle Hoplightly, "the queen of the arena"; Henri Tenori, "from the opera"; Percy Hamfat, an actor; a slack wire performer; and other acts.
   Prod. on tour as part of the Troubadours show, under the management of °Voelckel & Nolan, presumably opening in March 1903 and continuing throughout the year. °Anton Gloeckner, musical dir. Cast: John Green (Josiah Johnson, the Poo-Bah), Anthony D. Byrd (Marish Johnson, his wife), Will A. Cook and Charles Bougia (Primus and Reuben Johnson, their sons), James Crosby (Little Willie Johnson, their youngest), Ida Forsyne (M'mselle Hoplightly), J. Ed Green (Prof. Blackenback, the circus owner), Bobby Kemp (Handy Andy, circus handyman), Leslie Triplett (policeman 7–11), Mack Allen (Bill Barber, circus spieler and slack wire equilibrist), James Worles (Henri Tenori, opera singer), J. P. Reed (Percy Hamfat, actor), Belles of Darktown, and other personnel and animals associated with a circus as indicated in description above.
   Songs and musical numbers: "When the Circus Comes to Town" (Chorus), "Strolling Around the Circus Tent" (Company), "Castle on the Nile" (Crosby & Company), "What Became of the Monk" (Kemp, Byrd, Crosby & Triplett),

"Mandy" (Forsyne & Chorus), "Ain't Going to Stay Here Any Longer" (Green & Chorus), "Under the Bamboo Tree" (Lewis & Kemp), Finale, Buck Dancing Contest.

DARKYDOM / / Also known as *Darkeydom* (1914–15). Musical revue. Book by Henry Troy. Lyrics by Henry Creamer and Lester Walton. Music co-composed and co-conducted by Will Marion Cook and James Reese Europe. Prod. by Walton.

A series of sketches and specialty acts, featuring Flournoy E. Miller and Aubrey Lyles (the comedy team of Miller & Lyles), re-creating their popular roles as Steve Jenkins and Sam Peck. One of the sketches apparently involved their adventures as hoboes on a train on which the president of the railroad line is also riding. In order to evict the hoboes, the engineer pulls the train onto a side track which luckily prevents a train wreck; and the grateful president attempts to reward the hoboes, instead of punishing them.

Apparently toured the theatres of the Quality Amusement chain, including the Howard Theatre in Washington, DC, 1914–15, prior to its premiere at the Lafayette Theatre in Harlem, beginning Oct. 23, 1915, where it had a successful run. Loften Mitchell (*BlkDr*, p. 68) reported that "the premiere was attended by many whites in coaches," and "it looked like a Broadway opening." According to Mitchell, some of the sketches were sold to Bway producers. Other featured players were Abbie Mitchell (Mrs. Will Marion Cook, who played Mrs. Top Note, a teacher of music), Cliff Green (Mose Montgomery, a barber), Fannie Wise (Mrs. Ethel Green, a manicurist), Hilda Offley (Mrs. Hazel Black, an air insurance agent), Henry Shaw (a valet), Frank Walker (Ah Sing, a "Chinaman"), Allie Gilliam, Will A. Cook, dancer Ida Forsyne, and singers Opal Cooper, Nettie Anderson, Lillian Grade, and Helen Baxter.

Songs and musical number included "Cairo" (Wise), "My Lady's Lips" (Mitchell), "Mammy" (Cooper), "The Ghost Ship" (Thompson), 'Scaddle de Hootch' (dance: Ida Forsyne), "Magnolia Time" (Anderson), "Dreamy Town" (Grade), "Rat-a-Tat" (Baxter), "All Kinds of People Make a Town," "Arcadia," "Bamboula," "Chop Suey Sue," "Drive the Blues Away," "Keep Off the Grass," "Life," "Live and Die in Dixieland," "My Gal from the South," and "Naughty Moon."
FURTHER REFERENCE: *Freeman* (Indianapolis) 10–23–1915; 10–30–1915. *Just Before Jazz* (Riis). *NY Age* 10–28–1915; 10–21–1915. Riis diss. *Variety* 11–5–1915.

DASHING DINAH (1927). Touring revue. Prod. by and costarring Eddie Lemons. Cast also included male impersonator Jack "Ginger" Wiggins, J. Homer Hubbard, Charles Barry, Christina Gray, Leroy Phillips, Isadore Price, Rogers & Rogers, and Willie Taylor.

A DAY IN THE LIFE OF JUST ABOUT EVERYONE (1971). Musical entertainment. 26 scenes. Music and lyrics by °Earl Wilson, Jr. Additional dialogue by °Michael Sawyer. Prod. at the Bijou Theatre, New York, March 9–14, 1971, for 7 perfs. With an integrated cast that featured °Earl Wilson, Jr. (Smitty) and °June Grable (Penny), and their four friends and acquaintances: Dickie Evans, DeMarest Grey, °Daniel Fortus, and °Bennett Kinsey.

DEAR OLD SOUTHLAND (1932). Musical show. Prod. at the Lafayette Theatre in Harlem; with blues singer Mary Stafford.

DE BOARD MEETIN' (1925). Musical comedy. 1 act. Book and music by Porter Grainger and Leigh Whipper. A church pastor is brought before the board for misappropriation of church money, selling liquor, and making passes at the women. Prod. in Harlem and toured the TOBA circuit briefly. Script without music in Schomburg.

DE CIDER MAN (1909). Touring vaudeville show. Prod. by Edward Denton.

DEEP CENTRAL (1932). Book by John Larkins and Alec Lovejoy, who also costarred in the prodn. Cast included Mae Johnson.

DEEP HARLEM (1928–29). Musical revue. 1 act. Conceived by Earl Dancer. Book by Salem Tutt Whitney and J. Homer Tutt. Lyrics by Tutt and Henry Creamer. Music by Joe Jordan.

A musical history in song and dance of blacks in America from their noble origins in the kingdoms of Africa, through the various trials and tribulations of slavery and plantation life, to the chorus lines and cabarets of Harlem during the 1920s. In spite of this valiant effort to present black history and culture through the medium of a popular revue, the critics were not impressed.

First opened at a theatre on 57th Street in New York City in 1928. Prod. by Samuel Grisman at the Biltmore Theatre on Bway, Jan. 7, 1929, for 8 perfs.; dir. by Creamer. Cast included Andrew Bishop, Chappie Chappelle, Whitney & Tutt, Columbus Jackson, Sterling Grant, John Mason, William Edmondson, Billy Andrews, Howard Elmore, Cutout & Leonard, Ivy Black, Virginia Branum, Rosa White, Juanita Stinnette, Mabel Ridley, Neeka Shaw, Marietta Warren, Mary Welch, Louise Williams, Mary King, Alice Gorgas, Carrie Huff, Inez Glover, Gertrude Gardeen, and Lena Wilson. Also in the first prodn. were Pearl McCormack and Doe Doe Green.

FURTHER REFERENCE: *Inter-State Tattler* 1–7–1929. *NY Herald Trib.* 1–13–1929. *NY Post* 1–8–1929. *NY Sun* 1–8–1929. *NYT* 1–8–1929. *NY Telegram* 1–9–1929.

DEEP RIVER (1926). Subtitled "A Native Opera." Book and lyrics by °Laurence Stallings. Music by °Frank Harling.

Dealt primarily with Creole life in New Orleans in the mid-1830s, a few days before the annual Quadroon Ball, where traditionally the socially elite Creole men come to select the most beautiful ladies as their mistresses. The story focuses on one of the quadroon ladies, the beautiful Mugette, who is certain to have a number of interested suitors. She is desired by three men—Brusard, a cruel and treacherous Creole; Colonel Streatfeld; and his brother Hazard—the latter of whom she secretly desires as her lover. The rivalry between Brusard and the two brothers leads to a duel in which the colonel is killed by Brusard, and Hazard avenges his brother's death by fatally wounding Brusard. To escape prosecution, Hazard flees from New Orleans, leaving Mugette with no prospective suitor at the ball.

Opened on Bway at the Imperial Theatre, Oct. 10, 1926, for 32 perfs.; prod. and dir. by °Arthur Hopkins. All of the major characters were played by whites, except the role of Octavie, an elderly quadroon who serves as a chaperone to the younger ladies, played by veteran black actress Rose McClendon. Two other blacks had minor, atmospheric roles. Jules Bledsoe had a singing role as Tirzan, for which he received good notices, but was not directly involved in the plot. Charlotte Murray played a bit part as a voodoo queen.

Songs and musical numbers: "Ashes and Fire," "Cherokee Rose," "De Old Clay Road," "Dis Is de Day," "Love Lasts a Day," "Po' Lil' Black Chile," "Serenade Creole," "Soft in de Moonlight," and "Two Little Stars."

DE GOSPEL TRAIN (1940). Musical comedy. By J. Homer Tutt. With musical settings by Donald Heywood. Lyrics by J. Homer Tutt and Henry Creamer. Music by Joe Jordan. Rewritten from *Jim Crow*, an unprod., unpub. musical (c. 1934) by Salem Tutt Whitney, J. Homer Tutt, and Heywood. Concerns the fate of the passengers on a Jim Crow railroad car headed from the South to Washington, DC. Unprod., unpub. script (without music) in Schomburg.

DE OBEAH MAN ("The Witch Doctor") (1986). Billed as "A new magical tropical musical, loosely based on Molière's *The Doctor in Spite of Himself*." By Charles Douglass. Prod. by the Actors Studio, New York, 1986. Cast featured Delores Hall, Ann Duquesnay, Jimmy Justice, and Gilbert Price.

DE ORGANIZER (1938). Blues opera. 1 act. Libretto by Langston Hughes. Music by James P. Johnson. Propaganda, written to support efforts to organize a labor union of sharecroppers in the South. Prod. by the Harlem Suitcase Theatre, New York, 1939. Unpub. librettos JWJ/YUL and Schomburg. For more information, see also *The Organizer*.

DERBY DAY IN DIXIE. See *THEY'RE OFF*.

DESIRES OF 1927 (1926). Musical revue. Lyrics and music by Andy Razaf and J. C. Johnson. Book and staging by Irvin C. Miller. Prod. by Miller in Harlem, 1926, and may have toured until 1927. Cast included Adelaide Hall, J. Homer Tutt, Henry "Gang" Jines, Arthur Porter, Bee Freeman, Mabel Ridley, Arlyne Brooks, Stewart Hampton, William McKelvey, Clarence Nance, Frankie Watts, and Jacqueline White.

THE DEVIL (1922). Musical morality. Prod. by and starring Quintard Miller. The Devil leads a young man on a downward path of sin and debauchery, until he reaches bottom in a Chinese pleasure den. He is rescued by a faithful young friend (whom the Devil is unable to seduce) who shoots their way out of the den. Prod. in Harlem and on tour. Cast included Miller (Young Man), Purcell Cuff (Devil), Henrietta Lovelass (Poverty), "Monkey" Jim Johnson (Friend), Marion [*sic*] Ablaunche (Soubrette), Helen Chapelle (Purity), and Eugene Shields (One Lung, a "Chinaman").

DEVIL'S FROLICS (1929). Vaudeville revue. Music by Addison Carey's Band. Harlem show, which opened in Nov. 1929. Cast included John "Rareback" Mason, Gallie DeGaston, Jackie (later "Moms") Mabley, Putney Dandridge, Doris Rheubottom, and "Jelly Beans" Smith.

THE DEVINE [*sic*] (1924). Touring show. Cast included Sarah Martin, Julian Costello, White & Moore, and the Davenport Trio.

DIARY OF LIGHTS (1987). Subtitled "A Musical Without Songs." By Adrienne Kennedy. Music by °Gib Veconi. According to producer's publicity, it concerns "the youthful idealism of a young black couple on the inter-racial Upper West Side." This prodn. coincided with the Alfred Knopf publication of Kennedy's book, *People Who Led to My Plays*. New York premiere held at Aaron Davis Hall, City College of New York, June 5–14, 1987, for 8 perfs.; dir. by David Willinger. Choreography by Tracy Hendryx. Cast included Maria Bethea, Lori Ann Brown, Gabrielle Danchick, David Fritsch, Allen Griggsby, Traci Kindell, Janine Lucas, Ivan Moore, and Kenny Moore.

DINAH (1923–24). Musical comedy. 2 acts [10 scenes]. Book by Irvin C. Miller, who also prod. the show. Music and lyrics by Tim Brymn and Sidney Bechet.

Song-and-dance show, significant for introducing the black bottom, a dance which originated in Nashville and achieved a popularity in New York second only to the Charleston.

The incredible plot revolves around a young woman named Dinah Lee, whose inheritance, which was to be invested in some dance hall stock, is apparently stolen by her uncle. However, the money turns out not to have been stolen, but lost in a haunted house on its way to being delivered by the uncle to the bank. The recovered money is invested in the dance hall, and its opening is a gala occasion which gives an opportunity to display the latest dances, including the black bottom.

Opened at the Lafayette Theatre in New York in late 1923, starring Gertrude Saunders (as Dinah), Irvin C. Miller (as Sambo Smith, the leading comedian), and Ethel Ridley (as Corine, the dancer who introduced the black bottom). Other cast members included Lemuel Jackson (Policeman), Will A. Cook (Uncle Joe Davis), Florence Brown (Lucinda), May Barnes (Mandy), Uncle Simms (Diral Davis), Cecil Rivers (Walter Davis), Sterling Grant (Sambo Johnson), Archie Cross (Uncle Amos), Doe Doe Green (Sam Sykes), Billy Mills (Slow Kid), Harry Smith (Just Different), and Alonzo Fenderson (Harry Jenkins). The Chorus consisted of 8 Dinah Girls, 8 Honey Girls, and 6 Dandy Sambos.

Of the 18 songs and musical numbers reportedly in this show, only one is known: "Ghost of the Blues," by Brymn & Bechet; vocal-piano score pub. by Clarence Williams, New York, 1924; copy in Moorland-Spingarn.
FURTHER REFERENCE: *Messenger* 1–1924.

DIXIANA (1926). Touring revue. Prod. by Johnny Lee Long, who costarred with Catherine Patterson.

DIXIE BREVITIES (1926–28). Musical revue in at least three eds.: 1926, 1927, and 1928. Written by Quintard Miller and Marcus Slayter. Prod. in Harlem and on tour. *1926 ed.* Book by Miller. Music by Slayter and Inez Dennis. Cast included Dennis, Covan & Florence (Willie and Florence Covan), George Wiltshire, Montrose Brooks, and Andrew Fairchild(s). *1927 ed.* Cast included Dennis, Covan & Florence, and Fairchild(s). *1928 ed.* Cast included Dennis, Brooks, Wiltshire, Lottie Gee, Edith Spencer, Robert "Snow" Rice (blackface dancer), and Willie DeGaston. Only one song from the 1928 ed. is known: "No Foolin' " (Wiltshire).

DIXIE FLYER GIRLS (1922). Touring revue. Prod. by and costarring Jimmy Cox. Cast also included Buster Lee, Baby Ernestine Jones, Anna Mae Cox, Louise Howard, Pearl Jones, Roy Lee, Margaret Lyon, and Gladys Williams.

DIXIE FOLLIES (1934). Touring revue. Featuring Wilton Crawley, William Brown, the Three Brown Buddies, Joyner & Foster, and the Two Tan Tippers.

DIXIE GIRLS (1921). Touring revue. Prod. by Pal Williams. Cast included Billy Mack, his wife Mary Mack, the producer's wife Madame Williams, Floyd Young, and Olivia Zalette.

DIXIE GOES HIGH HAT (1938). Musical comedy. Written and prod. by Flournoy E. Miller. Miller (Steve Jenkins) and Mantan Moreland (Ceason Jones) starred in this musical, which took them in an airplane from an all-black village named Jim Town to the jungles of Africa, where they had a number of terrifying and hilarious experiences. This show also featured Dorothy Dandridge, who later became an important film star. Prod. on tour with the following additional cast: Mae Turner (Ma Jenkins), Margaret Robinson (Georgia), Dorothy Dandridge (Sally Jenkins), Otis Rene (Harry Hopkins), Rudolph Toombs (Marmadulie Sylvane), Spencer Williams (Elder Moore), Leonard Christmas (Half Dollar Bill), Juneda Carter (Cindy), Marcus Slayter (Jackson), Quintard Miller (Mose), Jessie Cryner (Socrates), Leonard Dixon (Solomon), and George Cooper (Owl).

DIXIE ON PARADE (1930). Touring revue. Prod. and possibly written by Noble Sissle. Music was perfd. by Sissle's Paris Ambassadeurs. Cast included George "Hoss" Crawford, Marshall Rogers, Dewey Weinglass, Wilton Crawley, the Lucky Seven Trio, and the Chocolate Steppers.

DIXIE STRUTTERS (1926). Touring revue. Featuring "String Beans" Price, Inez Saunders, Joe Slater, and Johnson & Rector.

DIXIE TO BROADWAY / / Orig. title: *From Dover to Dixie* (1923–25). Musical revue. 2 acts. Book by °Walter DeLeon, °Tom Howard, °Lew Leslie, and °Sidney Lazarus. Music by °George W. Meyer and °Arthur Johnstone. Lyrics by °Grant Clarke and °Roy Turke. Additional music by Will Vodery.

First developed by Lew Leslie at the Plantation Club in New York, as the *Plantation Revue*; which combined with a white revue for a successful tour of England. The combination of two revues was called *From Dover to Dixie*. The first half was white (Dover); the other half was black (Dixie). The Bway version was expanded from the second half of the original show.

This show was significant as the first black revue built around a female star (Florence Mills), rather than around two male blackface comedians, as was the usual custom. It was also the last major New York appearance of Florence Mills before her untimely death. It consisted mainly of skits, songs, and specialty dancing by individual performers and the black chorus of eight males and eight females.

First prod. in London under its orig. title, 1923. Prod. on Bway, under its present title, at the Broadhurst Theatre, opening Oct. 29, 1924, for 77 perfs., closing in early 1925. Featured members of the cast were Mills, Shelton Brooks, Hamtree Harrington, Vodery, Cora Green, Johnny Nit, Willie Covan, U. S. Thompson, the Chocolate Drops (chorus girls), the Plantation Steppers (chorus boys), and the Plantation Orchestra. Other performers were Danny Small, Maude Russell, William DeMott, Byron Jones, Lew Keane, Walter Crumbly, Alma Smith, Billy Cain, Juan Harrison, Charlie Walker, Ethel Moses, Gwendolyn Graham, Anita Rivera, Ralph Love, Marion Tyler, Jerry Clarke, Aida Ward,

Eva Metcalf, Natalie Caldwell, Snow Fisher, Dick Whalen, Sam Vanderhurst, Charles Foster, and Winfred & Brown.

Synopsis of scenes and musical numbers: Act I, Scene 1—Prologue, 'Evolution of the Colored Race'; Scene 2—'Put Your Old Bandanna On' (dance specialty: Small, Russell, Chocolate Drops & Steppers); Scene 3—"Dixie Dreams" (Mills & Company); Scene 4—'A Few Minutes in Front of the Curtain' (dance: Steppers); Scene 5—'Treasure Castle,' a skit by Tom Howard (Cast: Sam [Harrington], Slim [Brooks], Carlie [Small], Svengali [DeMott]); Scene 6—"He Only Comes to See Me Once in a While" (song: Green); Scene 7—'Jungle Nights in Dixieland' (in which Mills stopped the show with her singing, dancing, and what an unidentified reviewer called "her native grotesqueries"); Scene 8—'Prisoners Up-to-Date' (skit in which Jones, Keane & Nit in chains and convict suits executed a clever tap dance); Scene 9—'The Right of Way,' a traffic skit by DeLeon and Leslie in which a real Oldsmobile was used onstage (Cast: The Cop [Crumbly], The Victim [Harrington], Mr. and Mrs. [Brooks & Russell], Miss High Hat [Green]); Scene 10—"Mandy, Make Up Your Mind," one of the important songs, involving a wedding scene (Cast: The Groom [Mills], The Bride [Smith], Others: Bridesmaids, Maids of Honor, and Best Men); Scene 11—'Hanging Around' (comedy skit: Harrington & Green); Scene 12—"Jazz Time Came from the South" (Mills, Smith & Cain); Scene 13—Finale, Act I (reprise): "Jazz Came from the South" (Company). Act II, Scene 14—"If My Dream Came True" (song: Harrison); Scene 15 (continuation)—"If My Dream Came True" (Series of six episodes in which performers imitate famous stage personalities: George M. Cohan [Covan], Eva Tanquay [Smith], Gallagher & Shean [Thompson], George Walker [Fisher], and Bert Williams [Brooks]; Scene 16—Specialty (Brooks); Scene 17—'Darkest Russia' (satirizing the Chauve Souris, a Russian dance group, to the jazzed-up tune of "The Parade of the Wooden Soldiers": Mills, Small, Chocolate Drops & Steppers); Scene 18—'The Sailor and the Chink' (skit: Winfred & Brown); Scene 19—'Dixie Wildflowers' (Green & Chocolate Drops); Scene 20—"I'm a Little Blackbird Looking for a Blue Bird" (the showstopper, sung by Mills, which became her theme song); Scene 21—'A Nice Husband,' skit by Sidney F. Lazarus (Cast: Maid [Russell], Georgette [Green], Freddie [Harrington], Jimmy [Brooks]); Scene 22—Dance Specialty, Thompson & Covan; Scene 23—'Trottin' to the Land of Cotton Melodies' (dance specialty: Green, Small & Company); Scene 24—Finale (Company).

Sheet music of many songs in MC/NYPL.

FURTHER REFERENCE: *BlkDr* (Mitchell). *BlkMusTh* (Woll). *DBlkTh* (Woll). *HarlRenD* (Kellner). *Jazz Dance* (Stearns & Stearns). *NYT* 10–30–1924. Theatre program and other primary materials in TC/NYPL.

THE DIXIE VAGABOND (1928). Touring vaudeville entertainment. Featured Roscoe Montella, Pauline Montella, Lillian Westmoreland, Ernest Whitman, Lilly Yuen, Hazel Lee, Marion Moore, and 6 chorus girls.

DR. BEANS FROM BOSTON (1912). Musical farce. Book by S. H. Dudley and Henry Troy. Music by Will H. Vodery. Lyrics by Henry Creamer.

The setting is Bay Shore in Buckroe Beach, VA, a famed summer resort for blacks at the turn of the century, where Gym(nasium) Butts, an ex-minstrel comedian, has come into possession of a drugstore which he has purchased by selling his famous "show-business" mule. Although Gym has no knowledge of drugs, he passes himself off as a druggist from Boston named Dr. Beans. Gym falls in love with the beautiful Susie Lee, and gains access to a love potion which he dispenses in copious amounts to Susie, hoping to win her love. Everything goes fine, until the real Dr. Beans comes to the resort town on the night of a big dance, and complicates the plot. Although Gym loses the drugstore in a crap game, he wins the love of Susie, regains his mule, and the story ends happily.

Prod. by Dudley and his *Smart Set Co.*, apparently opening at °Hurtig & Seamon's Music Hall in New York early in 1912, for a brief engagement. Then went on tour of the black theatre circuit, with engagements in Pittsburgh, Cincinnati, Atlantic City, NJ (at the Apollo Theatre in March), and Washington, DC (for two weeks at the Howard Theatre, beginning April 8). Cast: S. H. Dudley (Gymnasium Butts, ex-minstrel), Dudley's Mule (Patrick, Butt's friend), Arthur Talbot (Mr. Waterbury Lee, proprietor of Bay Shores Hotel), Daisy Martin (Susie Lee, his Daughter), Jim Burris (Bill Simmons, a Hustler), Henry Troy (Larry Smith, a Druggist), Roley Gibson (Jimmy Quickstep, a Messenger), William Ramsey (Alex, a Waiter), Frank DeLyons (Dr. Beans from Boston), Ella Revans (Madam Sahara Heartburn, Primadonna), Robert Williams (Queen Sophenia, a Fortune Teller & Jessie Jenkins, a Telephone Agent), Hattie Burris (A Cash Girl), and Jessie Harris (A Drug Clerk). Other characters include Bathing Girls, Babies, Auto Girls, Matrons, and Boys.

Songs and musical numbers: Act I—Opening Chorus (Ensemble), "Sunshine" (Martin & Chorus), "Messenger Boy" (Gibson & Male Quartette), "Virginia" (Burris & Chorus), "Bathing" (Revans & Girls), "Rain" (Finale: Company). Act II—"Idle Dream" (Opening: Chorus), "Dearest Memories" (Troy & Chorus), "Let's Make Love" (Martin & Chorus), "Dr. Beans from Boston" (Dudley & Chorus), 'Old Virginia Dance' (dance: Dudley, Martin & Chorus). Act III— "Drinking" (opening: Chorus), "Eternity" (Troy), "What Did I Say That For?" (Dudley), Grand Finale (Chorus).

DR. HERB'S PRESCRIPTION, OR IT HAPPENED IN A DREAM (1911). Musical farce. Written and prod. by Jesse A. Shipp. Presented at the Pekin Theatre, Chicago. Cast included Shipp, Allie Gilliam, Shelton Brooks, Hattie McIntosh, Fannie Wise, Ada Banks, Lottie Grady, William "Billy" Johnson, Charles Gilpin, Will[iam] C. Elkins, Jerry Mills, Daisy Brown, Gertie Brown, W. D. Coleman, Katie Jones, Ethel Marlowe, and Clarence Tisdale.

DOCTOR JAZZ (1975). Jazz-inspired musical. 2 acts [20 scenes]. Book, music, and lyrics mostly by Buster Davis. Prod. at the Winter Garden Theatre, New York, opening March 19, 1975, for 5 perfs.; direction and choreography by Donald McKayle. With an integrated cast that included Lillian Hayman (as Georgia Sheridan) and Lola Falana (as Edna Mae Sheridan).

DR. KNIGHT (1908). Musical comedy. 3 acts. Written by and costarring Flournoy E. Miller and Aubrey Lyles (Miller & Lyles). Music arranged by James T. Brymn. Prod. at the Pekin Theatre, Chicago, 1908; staged by J. Ed. Green. With Harrison Stewart in the title role.

DON'T BOTHER ME, I CAN'T COPE (1970–73). Musical entertainment. Described by Arnold Shaw (*Blk. Pop. Mus. in Am.*, p. 30) as ''a Spiritual/Blues/Gospel–oriented show.'' 2 acts. Conceived and dir. by Vinnette Carroll. Book, music, and lyrics by Micki Grant.

Award-winning musical which deals with the black and universal problem of coping with life. Utilizes songs and dances based on jazz, blues, gospel, rock, calypso, and traditional ballad rhythms. Winner of an Outer Circle Award, two Obie Awards, two Drama Desk Awards, and an NAACP Image Award, 1972. Nominated for a Tony Award.

First presented by the Urban Arts Corps in small theatres around New York City and elsewhere during the 1970–71 season, prior to its world premiere at Ford's Theatre in Washington, DC, where it opened Sept. 15, 1971, for 32 perfs. Original cast: Alex Bradford (gospel singer), Micki Grant, Bobby Hill, Arnold Wilkerson, Charles E. Campbell, Marie Thomas, Carl Bean, and Willie James McPhatter.

Opened on Bway in a slightly revised version of the orig. prodn., at the Playhouse Theatre, April 19, 1972, transferring to the Edison Theatre, June 13, 1972, where it continued its run, closing Oct. 23, 1973, after 1,065 perfs. Bway cast: Alex Bradford, Hope Clarke, Micki Grant, Bobby Hill, and Arnold Wilkerson. Singers: Alberta Bradford, Charles Campbell, Marie Thomas, Pat Lundy, and D. Morris Brown. Dancers: Thommi Bush, Gerald G. Francis, Ben Harney, and Leona Johnson.

Prod. by the Center Theatre Group at the Mark Taper Forum, Los Angeles, opening Aug. 10, 1972, for 54 perfs. Transferred to the Huntington Hartford Theatre, Los Angeles, for a long run; featuring Paula Kelly. Also prod. at the Happy Medium Theatre, Chicago, 1972; with a different cast, featuring Loleatta, a singer formerly with Albertine Walker's Caravans. Prod. as a guest prodn. at the American Conservatory Theatre, San Francisco, opening July 21, 1973, for 56 perfs. Again prod. at Ford's Theatre, Washington, DC, opening April 23, 1973, for more than 44 perfs.

Cast recording by Polydor (PD–6013), with liner notes by Ed Padula. Libretto and score pub. by Samuel French, New York, 1972.

Songs and musical numbers: "I Gotta Keep Movin'," "Harlem Streets," "Lookin' Over from Your Side," "Don't Bother Me, I Can't Cope," "When I Feel Like Movin'," "Help," "Fighting for Pharoah," "Good Vibrations," "Love Power," "You Think I Got Rhythm?," "They Keep Coming," "My Name Is Man," "Questions," "It Takes a Whole Lot of Human Feeling," "Time Brings About a Change," "So Little Time," "Thank Heaven for You," "Show Me That Special Gene," "So Long Sammy," and "All I Need."
FURTHER REFERENCE: *America* 5–13–1972. *Ebony* 2–1973. *Nation* 5–8–1972. *NYorker* 4–29–1972. *NYT* 10–8–1970; 4–20–1972; 5–7–1972; 12–3–1972. *Time* 5–8–1972.

DON'T GET GOD STARTED (1987–88). Subtitled "A Gospel Revival." By Ron Milner. Prod. at the Longacre Theatre, New York, Dec. 1987–Jan. 1988.

DON'T PLAY US CHEAP! (1970–72). Musical of Harlem life. Book, music, and lyrics by Melvin Van Peebles. Based on his novel *La Fête à Harlem* ("The Party in Harlem," 1967).

The setting is a Harlem apartment. The plot revolves around two inept demons, Trinity (Joe Keyes) and David (Avon Long), who are unsuccessful in their attempts to break up Miss Mabell's (Esther Rolle) wild Saturday night party. Recipient of a Tony nomination for best book for a musical.

Premiered at San Francisco State Coll., Nov. 1970. Presented on Bway at the Ethel Barrymore Theatre, May 16–Oct. 1, 1972, for 164 perfs.; prod. and dir. by Van Peebles. Other cast members of the Bway prodn. (not named above)— all guests at the party: Thomas Anderson, Joshie Jo Armstead, Nate Barnett, Frank Carey, Frank Dunn, Mabel King, George "Oopee" Cooper, Rhetta Hughes, and Jay Vanleer.

Made into a film in New Mexico; also prod. by the author, and premiered in Atlanta, GA.

Songs and musical numbers: "Some Days It Seems That It Just Don't Even Pay to Get Out of Bed," "Break That Party," "8 Day Week," "Saturday Night," "I'm a Bad Character," "You Cut Up the Clothes in the Closet of My Dreams," "It Makes No Difference," "Quittin' Time," "Ain't Love Grand," "The Book of Life," "Know Your Business," "Big Future," "Feast on Me," "The Phoney Game," and "Smash Him."

First pub. in French as a novel, *La Fête à Harlem*, by Jerome Martineau, Paris, 1967. Pub. in English as a novel with lyrics, under the title *Don't Play Us Cheap: A Harlem Party*, by Bantam Books, New York, 1973.

Cast recording by Stax (STS 2–3006).
FURTHER REFERENCE: *Cue* 5–27–72. *Mass. Rev.* Winter 1973. *NY Daily News* 9–24–1971; 1–8–1972. *NY Mag.* 6–5–1972. *NYorker* 5–27–1972. *NY Post* 2–5–1972. *NYT* 5–17–1972; 5–18–1972. *Variety* 5–24–1972.

DON'T YOU WANT TO BE FREE? (1937; revised 1963). Musical pageant. First called "A Poetry Play"; revised as "A Negro History Play." 1 long act. By Langston Hughes.

"Agit-prop" musical history of blacks in America, utilizing poetry, dramatic sketches, spirituals, blues, work songs, and jazz or swing rhythms of the piano to support the theme that the oppression of blacks continues even in modern times. According to Fannie Ella Frazier Hicklin (Ph.D. diss., 1965, p. 256), "A white man, who first appears as an Overseer during the era of slavery, reappears in succeeding episodes as tenant farmer, the 'boss' of a hotel, a landlord, a butcher, an editor, insurance man, a factory foreman, and a sergeant in the army." The lyrics draw heavily upon two of Hughes' books of poetry, *The Weary Blues* (1926) and *The Dream Keeper* (1932). Significant as one of the longest-running plays in the Harlem community.

First prod. by the author's Harlem Suitcase Theatre, opening in May 1938, at the IWO (International Workers Order) Center, 317 W. 125th St., where it established a record run of 135 perfs., playing mainly on weekends; dir. by Hughes. Cast featured Robert Earl Jones, father of James Earl Jones (Young Man); Amos Lange, alternating with Jay Loftin (Boy); Grace Johnson (Girl); Ernest Goldstein, alternating with Clarence Nathan (Man); Tony Harper (Woman); Mary Savage (Mulatto Girl); Edith Jones (Wife); and Clifford Brown (Husband).

The Harlem Suitcase Theatre prodn. was presented for one perf. Off-Bway by the New Theatre League, at the Nora Bayes Theatre on June 10, 1938.

Prod. by the New Negro Theatre, a group founded by the author in Los Angeles, 1939, for 15 perfs. Also presented by several college and univ. theatre groups, including Wilberforce, Howard, and Talladega, and by little theatre groups in New Orleans, Pittsburgh, and Chicago.

Instrumental music included piano, drums, and cymbals—the latter two used mainly in the African sequences. Spirituals and traditional music, sung by the Chorus and some of the characters, included "Go Down Moses," "Nobody Knows the Trouble I've Seen," "In That Great Gettin' Up Morning," "John Brown's Body," and "Sometimes I Feel Like a Motherless Child." During one section of the play, which the author called "the blues sequence," several of his poems on the blues were recited. Hughes indicated that these should be "accompanied by an expert, old-time, stompdown blues-piano player who should continue the same rhythm throughout the entire sequence, played softly but shrewdly and steadily through the spoken portions" ("Production Notes" reprinted in Edwin Leon Coleman, Jr., Ph.D. diss., 1971, p. 211). The final song of the play, sung by the entire company, was "Who Wants to Come Join Hands with Me?," and the stage directions indicate that "as they sing the audience joins with them, and various members of the audience . . . , white and black, come forward to link hands with the characters . . . until the players and the audience are one" (Pub. script).

Script pub. in *One-Act Play Mag.* 10–1938, and in *BlkThUSA* (Hatch & Shine,

1974). Typescript of the revised 1963 Centennial (of the Emancipation Proclamation) Version, with music by Sammy Heyward, is located in Schomburg. Other scripts in JWJ/YUL and in the Archives and Manuscript Div., State Historical Soc. of Wisc. at Madison.
FURTHER REFERENCE: *AnthANT* (Patterson). *BesPls 1937–38*. *BlkDr* (Mitchell). *BlkMagic* (Hughes & Meltzer). Coleman diss. *Crisis* 11–1938. Hicklin diss. *NegPlaywrs* (Abramson). *ThArts* 8–1942.

DOROTHY FIELDS (1986). Retrospective revue of the career, songs, and shows of white lyricist °Dorothy Fields, who, with composer °Jimmie McHugh, wrote songs for several black revues, including the Cotton Club revues, *Blackbirds of 1928*, and *Singin' the Blues* (1931). Prod. at the Minskoff Theatre, New York, Winter 1986; dir. and choreographed by °Bob Fosse. Featuring dancer/choreographer Debbie Allen.

DOTS AND DASHES (1926). Touring revue. Prod. by Ocey Wilson. Cast included Arty Bell, Edward DeGaston, Irene & May, Scott & Evans, Gladys Smith, and Williams & Williams.

DOVER TO DIXIE. See *DIXIE TO BROADWAY*.

DOWN IN THE VALLEY (1969). Musical. By °Kurt Weill. Prod. by the Afro-American Singing Theatre, at the Brooklyn Academy of Music, Brooklyn, NY, Feb. 1, 1969.

DOWN ON BEALE ST. (1973). Musical. By Levi Frazier, Jr. In two versions, one full-length, the other, shorter. The short version deals only with the legendary Beale Street of Memphis, TN. The longer version combines the life of W. C. Handy, Father of the Blues, with the story of Beale Street. Prod. in Memphis at LeMoyne-Owens Coll., 1973; Memphis State Univ. Lab Theatre, 1974; WKNO-TV, 1974; Mid-America Mall, at May Festival, 1978; Memphis State Univ., Main Stage, 1979; Martin Luther King Performing Arts Center, 1982; and WLOK Radio, 1979. Prod. in New York at the Richard Allen Center for Culture and Art, 1980.

DO YOUR STUFF (1932). Touring revue. Prod. by Ralph Thomas. Dances choreographed by Sammy Dyer, who also costarred. Cast included singer Ruby Mason, the Three Rhythm Ramblers and the Three Brown Brothers (dancers), banjoist Patti Patterson, Eva Waters, Wiona [*sic*] Short, the Four Cotton Pickers Quartet, the Blanche Walton Choir, and "Tiny" Parham and his Grandles Life Orchestra.

DREAMGIRLS (1981–89). Musical retrospective. 2 acts [8 scenes]. Book and lyrics by °Tom Ewen. Music by °Henry Krieger.

Tony Award–winning musical inspired by the black musical history of the Motown era of the 1950s, 1960s, and 1970s, and particularly by the triumphs and tribulations of the famed Supremes, who rose from the ghetto to achieve national fame. Although the names of the characters and some of the incidents have been changed for obvious legal reasons, the real-life story of the Supremes is clearly recognizable in the plot and in the relationships of the characters. For example, the character of Effie, who is dropped from the group because she does not have sufficient "crossover" appeal, is reminiscent of Florence Ballard, who was dropped from the Supremes for unexplained reasons. In the case of the fictional Effie, the reasons given are that she is (1) too fat, (2) too black, and (3) not glamorous enough to appeal to white audiences. This role, played by Jennifer Holliday, earned for her a 1982 Tony Award as best actress. Other Tonys were won for best book, lighting, choreography, actor (Ben Harney), and supporting actor (Cleavant Derricks).

Prod. on Bway at the Imperial Theatre, opening Dec. 20, 1981, for nearly four years, closing Aug. 4, 1985, after 1,522 perfs.; dir. and choreographed by °Michael Bennett; Michael Peters, co-choreographer. Toured extensively during and after its Bway run. Had a long run at the Shubert Theatre in Los Angeles, CA, 1983–84. Revived at the Ambassador Theatre, New York, 1987; and continued to tour through 1989. Bway cast: Deborah Burrell, Vanessa Bell, Tenita Jordan, and Brenda Pressley (The Stepp Sisters), Cheryl Alexander (Charlene), Linda Lloyd (Joanne), Vondie Curtis-Hall (Marty), Ben Harney (Curtis Taylor, Jr.), Sheryl Lee Ralph (Deena Jones), Larry Stewart (The M.C.), Joe Lynn (Tiny Joe Dixon), Loretta Devine (Lorrell Robinson), Obba Babatunde (C. C. White), Jennifer Holliday (Effie Melody White), Cleavant Derricks (James Thunder Early), Sheila Ellis (Edna Burke), Tony Franklin (Wayne), David Thomé (Frank, press agent), Deborah Burrell (Michelle Morris), Joe Lynn (Jerry, nightclub owner), Larry Stewart (Mr. Morgan); and the following groups of characters: Little Albert and the Tru-Tones, Dave and the Sweethearts, the Five Tuxedos, Les Style, Film Executives, Fans, Reporters, Stagehands, Guests, and Photographers.

Songs and musical numbers: "I'm Looking for Something," "Goin' Downtown," "Takin' the Long Way Home," "Move," "Fake Your Way to the Top," "Cadillac Car," "Steppin' to the Bad Side," "Party Party," "I Want You Baby," "Family," "Dreamgirls," "Press Conference," "Only the Beginning," "Heavy," "It's All Over," "And I Am Telling You I'm Not Going," "Love Love You Baby," "Dreams Medley," "I Am Changing," "One More Picture Please," "When I First Saw You," "Got to Be Good Times," "Ain't No Party," "I Meant You No Harm," "Quintette," "The Rap," "I Miss You Old Friend," "One Night Only," "I'm Somebody," "Faith in Myself," and "Hard to Say Goodbye My Love."

Orig. Bway cast recording by Geffen Records, a division of Warner Bros. Records, Inc., 1982.
FURTHER REFERENCE: *Ebony* 5–1982.

DREAM GIRLS AND CANDIED SWEETS (1929). Musical revue. Prod. at the Alhambra Theatre in Harlem, Sept. 1929; starring blues singer Clara Smith.

DREAM LOVERS (1899). Operatic romance. 1 act. Libretto by Paul Laurence Dunbar. Music by Samuel Coleridge Taylor. Serving as a background for 6 musical numbers, the loosely constructed plot, according to Thomas Pawley (*Blk. World* 4–1975, p. 79), revolves around the love of "Torado, a mulatto prince from Madagascar, baritone" for "Catherine, a quadroon lady, soprano." No record of prodn. Pub. by Boosey & Co., London, 1898.

A DREAM OF ENCHANTMENT (1926). Musical play. 3 acts. By Estelle Ancrum Foster. Pub. by Presser, Boston, 1926.

THE DREAM TEAM (1985). Musical. Book by Richard Wesley. Music by Tom Tierney. Lyrics by John Foster. About the rivalry between two brothers who play basketball, when only one is picked for the newly integrated major leagues. Premiered at the Norma Terris Theatre, Goodspeed-at-Chester, CT, April 23–May 19, 1985; dir. and choreographed by Dan Sieretta. Featuring Gilbert Price and James McDaniel.

THE DUFFERS (pre-1986). Musical. Book by John Ashby. Music and lyrics by Dorothy Ashby. The story was drawn mainly from ghetto life. Prod. by the Ashby Players at the Dexter Theatre, Detroit; dir. by John Ashby.

DUMB LUCK (1922). Musical revue. 2 acts [12 scenes]. Prod. by the Louis Rosen Producing Co., under the proprietorship of °Louis Rosen (a theatrical costumer) and the management of Arthur G. Moss (of the team of Moss & Frye).

An elaborately staged musical, costarring Moss & Frye (Edward Frye) as two traveling salesmen who flee from their hometown in Honeysuckle, SC, to escape prosecution for some infraction of the law. They travel to a number of exotic places, including New Orleans and Argentina, where they sell their products and enjoy the festivities and adventures which each place has to offer. They finally return to Honeysuckle, where, instead of being arrested, they are treated as heroes and their return is celebrated by the whole town.

Toured the New England states in 1922, opening in Stamford, CT, on Sept. 11, and folding in Worcester, MA, on Sept. 23, stranding the large company of 100, including a 10-piece orchestra (dir. by Robert W. Ricketts). The troupe was finally rescued by the producers of *Shuffle Along*, through the efforts of Noble Sissle and his wife, who raised $700 to enable the cast to return to New York. The cast included Ethel Waters, Revella Hughes, Justa (toe dancer), India

Allen (in blackface), Joe Bright (County Sheriff), Cleo Desmond (Mother), Alberta Hunter, Boots Marshall, Inez Clough, Ethel Williams, Lottie Taylor (Bert Williams' niece), A. B. Comathiere, J. Lawrence Criner, Jesse A. Shipp, Dick Wells, Ruby Mason, Will Elkins, and a Male Glee Club.

Also prod. as a film short.

Songs and musical numbers included "My Old Kentucky Home," "Little Red Shawl," "Melody of Love," and "Argentina Says Farewell."

FURTHER REFERENCE: *Billboard* 10–14–1922 (J. A. Jackson's Page). *BlksBf* (Sampson).

DUSKY FOLLIES (1928). Vaudeville revue. Stereotypical black show prod. by °Jack Goldberg. Toured the Majestic Circuit, 1928. Cast included Skeeter Winston, Lovie Austin, Lena Cury, and Jan Jeanet.

DUSTY MILLER REVUE (1925). Touring revue. Prod. by and starring comedian Dusty Miller. Cast also included James Phoenix (straight man), Henry Mitchell, Belle Johnson Murray, Tillie Marshall, Henry Mitchell, Daisy Randolph, and 5 chorus girls.

E

EARL CARROLL'S VANITIES (1926, 1930). White-oriented musical revue. 5th and 8th eds. of the famous Bway revue series prod. by impresario Earl Carroll at his Earl Carroll Theatre in New York. Both eds. featured musical numbers by James P. Johnson. The 1926 ed. included "Alabama Stomp," and the 1930 ed. included "Rhumba Rhythm."

FURTHER REFERENCE: *AmMusTh* (Bordman). *BesPls of 1926–27; 1930–31.*

EARLY TO BED (1943–44). Musical comedy. Book and lyrics by °George Marion, Jr. Music by Thomas "Fats" Waller.

Racy, burlesque entertainment set in and around a West Indian brothel in Martinique, called The Angry Pigeon, run by an ex-schoolteacher. When the place is visited by a famous bullfighter and his son, and a track team for its training quarters, Madame Rowena (°Muriel Angelus) pretends that her house of ill repute is a finishing school for young ladies, a deception that provides a number of plot complications. There were only four blacks in this otherwise white-oriented show: Jeni LeGon, a dancer, who played one of the prostitutes; Bob Howard, a comedian, who played a handyman; and two other dancers, David Bethea and Harold Cromers, who appeared as a gardener and caddy respectively. As reviewed by black critic Miles Jefferson (*Phylon* 1st qtr. 1945, p. 44),

In this pictorially gorgeous but essentially dull and tasteless show Jeni LeGon and Bob Howard managed to be amusing in parts which retraced old stencils. Miss LeGon was a kind of undefined lady in waiting, to honor her position with a hyperbole, and Mr. Howard was a corpulently jolly species of Redcap transplanted in Martinique.

This was "Fats" Waller's last big show on Bway, and probably his last score.

Tried out in Boston in May 1943. Opened on Bway, June 17, 1943, for 382 perfs. With a predominantly white cast that included °Muriel Angelus, °Mary Small, °Richard Kollman, °George Zoritch, °John Lind, and °Jeanne Kean.

Both Waller's music and Marion's lyrics were described by Gerald Bordman (*AmMusTh*, p. 537) as "flaccid" and "lackluster." However, there were several song hits: "The Ladies Who Sing with the Band" (a showstopper, sung by Angelus & others), "There's a Man in My Life" (a love paean also sung by Angelus), "When the Nylons Bloom Again" (sung by Howard), "High-De-Ho-High" (sung by LeGon & Howard), and three other songs of record: "Early to Bed," "Slightly Less Than Wonderful," and "My Old World Charm."
FURTHER REFERENCE: *Ain't Misbehavin'* (Kirkeby). *Cath. World* 8–1943. *Newswk* 6–28–1943. *NYorker* 6–26–1943. *NYT* 6–18–1943. *ThArts* 10–1943. *Time* 6–28–1943.

EBONY FOLLIES (1928). Touring revue. Prod. by and starring S. H. Dudley. Dir. by his son, S. H. Dudley, Jr., who also perfd. in the show. Cast also included Madame Tolliver, Lonnie Fisher, Ozie McPherson, Cash & Smith, the Georgia Brownskin Peaches Chorus, and the Cyclonic Jazz Band.

EBONY SCANDALS (1932). Musical revue. Prod. in New York City, then went on tour of the Keith Circuit. Cast included May [or Mae] Barnes, Julia Noisette, Cecil Rivers, Flo Brown, Bowie & Simms, Leviana Mack, Freddie Seymour, and Sarah Smith.

EBONY VAMPIRES (1925–26). Touring vaudeville revue in at least two eds. Prod. mainly by Billy Watts. Cast of both eds. featured Watts & Wills (Mme. Patti Wills, contralto, formerly Pattie Williams) and Alonzo Johnson. *1925 ed.* Cast also included Bertha Hill, Mary Hicks, and Bennie Johnson. *1926 ed.* Co-prod. by Wills. Cast also included Charles Shaw, Rosetta Branum, Mildred Crimes, and Rosa Tucker.

ECHOES OF A PLANTATION (1931). Musical show. Prod. by Earl Dancer. Plantation musical, staged by the Fred Whittaker American Legion Post No. 372, Los Angeles, as a benefit for the Black Boy Scouts of that city. Cast included Eddie "Rochester" Anderson, Clarence Muse, Hattie McDaniels, Stepin Fetchit, and Butler's Old Time Southern Singers.

ECSTATIC EBONY (1939). Touring revue. Prod. by and costarring actor Ralph Cooper. Cast also included Dewey "Pigmeat" Markham, Edith Wilson, Reginald Fenderson, Shirley Howard, Myrtle Quinland, Williams & Grant, Ernestine & Pal, and Leroy White's Band.

ELIZABETH WELCH: TIME TO START LIVING (1986). Billed as "An Evening of Music and Song." Starring the veteran black singer/actress Elizabeth Welch. Presented at the Lucille Lorten Theatre, New York, April 1986, for a limited engagement. Welch sang songs of °Cole Porter, °Hoagy Carmichael, °Jerome Kern, and others.

ELSIE (1923). White-oriented musical comedy. Book by °Charles W. Bell. Music and lyrics by Noble Sissle, Eubie Blake, and others. Prod. on Bway, April 2, 1923, for 40 perfs.; staged by °Edgar McGregor. With an all-white cast, including °Margaret Zender, °Stanley Ridges, and °Vinton Freedley. Songs by Sissle & Blake included "Baby Bunting," "Everybody's Strutting Now," "I Would Like to Walk with a Pal Like You," "Jingle Step," "My Crinoline Girl," "A Regular Guy," "Sand Flowers," "Two Hearts in Tune," and "Wish You"; musical scores pub. by M. Witmark, New York; copies in Moorland-Spingarn.
FURTHER REFERENCE: *AmMusTh* (Bordman). *BesPls* 1922–23. *NY Clipper* 4–11–1923. *NYT* 4-3-1923.

E-MAN (1987). Musical adaptation. Billed as a musical comedy-drama. By Michael Dagley. With additional material, special effects, and music by Lenga Tooks (joint pseudonym for *Lawrence Edward aNd George Arnold Tooks*). Free adaptn. of the anonymous medieval morality play *Everyman*. Prod. by Theatre-in-Progress and the Lenga Tooks Musical Workshop, New York, opening April 30, 1987, at the ACAR Theatre in Harlem; staged and dir. by Randy Frazier. Featuring James Foster, Betty Vaughan, Cyrus Simmons, and Patricia A. Clement.

THE EMPEROR OF DIXIE (1908). Musical farce. 2 acts. Authorship not known. Probably written by Sidney Perrin, in collaboration with Walter Crumbly, since Perrin had written an earlier musical play with a similar plot entitled *A Bogus Prince* (1903), and Crumbly had also been in the cast of that play.
The plot is conjectured to turn on the arrival in a small village of Prince Black, who is "in search of an heiress." "A wealthy old farmer," Amos Johnson, and his wife Betty, "who craves notoriety," are presumably in hopes that the Prince will choose their daughter Lina as his bride; but Lina is in love with Bill Skeemar. In order to keep his sweetheart from marrying the prince, Bill disguises himself as the Emperor of Dixie and exposes the prince as a fraud. Jack Johnson, the heavyweight champion, who had a stint in vaudeville, was in the cast.
Apparently prod. at the Pekin Theatre in Chicago, 1908. Cast: An unknown actress (Lina Johnson), Walter Crumbly (Bill Skeemar, Lina's sweetheart), E. L. Henderson (Plain Sam), S. H. Lane (Amos Johnson), Odessa Crosby (Betty Johnson), Carlene Jefferson (Mandy, Betty's cousin, the village flirt), Corrine Brown (Sally Thompson, Betty's sister), Sidney Perrin (Eph Thompson, Sally's mischievous son), Arthur Rhoads (Professor Quickstep, a poet, vocalist, and dancing master), Jack Johnson (Captain Hardy, on furlough), Mena Caldwell (Phoebie, the Captain's sweetheart), T. White (Vardefoots, a village character), F. L. Mitchell (Prince Black), Bill Bradley (Skagga, a village laborer), Ada Fisher (Areta), Leona Miller (Tulip), Daisy Miller (Lucy), and Myrtle Freeman (Mme. Belle).
Songs and musical numbers: Act I—Opening Chorus (Company), "When De

Dinner Horn Blows'' (Perrin, Rhoads, White & Crumbly), ''I've a Never Dying Love All for You'' (Crumbly), ''The Emperor of Dixie'' (Crumbly), ''When the Trees Shed Their Leaves in the Fall'' (Johnson & Caldwell), ''Give Me My Three Nickels'' (Henderson), ''When the Band Played Old Yankee Doodle Dandy'' (Crumbly & Chorus). Act II—Opening Chorus, ''Drink and Be Merry'' (Company), ''The Tallaho Song'' (Company), ''Salam'' (Mitchell & Chorus), ''All Hail the Prince'' (Company), ''Much Obliged to You'' (Henderson), and ''Emperor of Dixie'' (Finale: Company).

AN ENGLISH DAISY (1904). White-oriented musical comedy. 2 acts. By °Seymour Hicks and °Walter Slaughter. Rearranged for American prodn. by °Edgar Smith. Added score by °A. M. Norton. With additional songs by Bob Cole and the Johnson Brothers (James Weldon Johnson and J. Rosamond Johnson). About two unemployed boardinghouse lodgers who are about to be evicted unless one of them consents to marry the landlord's niece. Prod. on Bway at the Victoria Theatre, opening Jan. 18, 1904, for a run of approximately one week; with an all-white cast. The Cole & Johnson Bros. songs included ''Big Indian Chief'' and ''Prepossessing Maid.''

EPHRAHAM JOHNSON FROM NORFOLK (1908). Musical comedy. 3 acts. Book by Flournoy E. Miller and Marion Brooks, who also costarred in this prodn.

The familiar plot centers around an attempt by a group of con artists to bilk an unsuspecting widow out of her money, by pretending to be prospective suitors.

Prod. by the Bijou Stock Co., at the Bijou Theatre in Montgomery, AL, in April 1908. Cast: James Moore (Ephraham L. Johnson, the man from Norfolk), Flournoy E. Miller (Bill Smart, who is ''looking for money''), Marion A. Brooks (Harry Blue, Eph's friend, also from Norfolk), Master Dazzel (Johnny Fast, a young man who has ''strayed from home''), Henderson Bowen (Harry Wilkes, a social leader), Irvin Jones (Dick Stopen, a bungling detective), Ivy Hubbard (Mrs. Flanders, the widow), Carmen Lawson (Fanny Lenox, a news reporter), and Blanch Arlington (Barth Lewis, who is ''very stylish'').

Songs and musical numbers: Act I—''Society'' (opening chorus: Company), ''Hard to Love Somebody When Somebody Don't Love You'' (Arlington), ''Here Today but When Tomorrow Comes, I'll Be Gone'' (Miller & Chorus), ''On One Summer Night'' (Dixie Mattison & Boys). Act II—''Since You Called Me Dear'' (C. W. Atkins), ''I'd Like to Know Your Address'' (Miller & Lawson), ''Darktown Grenadiers'' (Bowen & Chorus). Act III—''What Will Your Answer Be'' (opening chorus: Bowen & Chorus), ''I Want You'' (Hubbard & Moore), and ''Nuf Sed'' (Moore & Hubbard).

ESPRIT DE CORPS II (1980s). Subtitled ''A Musical Variety Show.'' Written by various authors. Dir. by Jeffrey W. Nickelson, assisted by Donnie L. Betts. Included the following skits and specialty numbers: 'Morning,' by Richard Koonce; 'Three Plus Three Equals Five Daddy,' by Leslie A. Nickelson; 'Car 99,' by Jeffrey W. Nickelson and Donnie L. Betts; 'On the Wings of Love,' by

Jeffrey W. Nickelson; 'The Interrogation of Mr. Nicks (A Headache),' written by Richard Lauchman; 'The Telethon,' by Timothy Betts and Jeffrey D. Nickelson; 'Dance,' by Hugo & Janice Sayles; and 'Silky Smooth,' by Richard Koonce, Lynette Nickelson, Crystel Niedel, and Jeffrey W. Nickelson. Prod. by DC West, Inc., at the Bonfils Theatre in Bobans Cabaret, Denver, CO, in July, during the early or mid-1980s.

ESTHER (1957–58). Biblical opera. 3 acts. Libretto by Langston Hughes. Musical score by °Jan Meyerowitz.

Based on the Book of Esther and other sources, telling the story of Queen Esther and her defense of her exiled Jewish people. Commissioned by the Fromm Music Foundation.

First prod. by the Univ. of Illinois at the Urbana Music Festival, March 17, 1957. Prod. by the New England Conservatory of Music, Boston, 1958.

Libretto, both in English and a separate German translation by Jean Geiringer, and a full musical score, pub. by Associated Music Pubs., Inc., New York (date unknown).

FURTHER REFERENCE: *Mus. Am.* 3–1958.

ETHIOPIA (1920s). Opera. By J. Berni Barbour. Toured the western part of the U.S. during the 1920s.

ETHIOPIA SHALL WIN (1924). Touring revue. Prod. by comedian Joe Bright. Cast included Theresa Burroughs Brooks and ''Bobbie'' Toliver Bright.

EUBIE! (1978–80). Musical retrospective. Based on the music of Eubie Blake. With lyrics primarily by Noble Sissle. Conceived and dir. by Julianne Boyd.

A vaudeville salute to the songs of the then 95-year-old black composer, who, in the words of Gerald Bordman (*AmMusTh*, p. 690), ''had re-emerged from obscurity to become a beguiling raconteur on television.'' As Bordman continued:

Most of his music remained steadfastly forgotten, with only ''I'm Just Wild About Harry'' and ''Memories of You'' retaining their precarious hold on popularity. If most of his songs were, as *Variety* noted, ''basically routine,'' they were brought to life with all the colorful razzmatazz that an economically pinched Broadway would allow, although some tastelessly contemporary orchestrations and that ubiquitous modern outrage, amplification, often hampered an appreciation of their delicacy. Still, there was enough to appreciate and enjoy.

Presented on Bway by Ashton Springer, in association with others, at the Ambassador Theatre, Sept. 20, 1978–Oct. 7, 1979, for 437 perfs. Choreographer and musical staging, Billy Wilson; choreographer and tap choreographer, Henry LeTang; orchestrations, Neal Tate. Cast: Ethel Beatty, Deborah Burrell, Leslie Dockery, Lynnie Godfrey, Gregory Hines, Maurice Hines, Mel Johnson, Jr.,

Lonnie McNeil, Janet Powell, Marion Ramsey, Alaina Reed, and Jeffery V. Thompson.

Went on national tour, simultaneously with the Bway prodn., playing major U.S. cities, including Los Angeles, Baltimore, Wilmington, Cincinnati, St. Louis, and Denver, from Jan. through Apr. 1979, resuming its run in Los Angeles in the fall of 1979. Cast: Robert Anderson, Danny Miller Beard, Cab Calloway (who joined the company for performances in St. Louis), Pi Douglass, Millie Foster, Winston DeWitt Hemsley, Donna Ingram, Jennifer Lewis, Bernard Manners, Gail Nelson, Kaaren Ragland, and Roderick Spencer Siberg.

Presented in a second touring prodn. by Tom Mallow in association with James Janek, opening during Aug. 1979 in Huntsville, AL, and closing in March 1980 in Providence, RI. Cast: Susan Beaubian, Chris Calloway, Keith Alan Davis, Tony Franklin, Jackée Harry, Marva Hicks, Donna Patrice Ingram, Bernard Manners, Robert Melvin, Francine Claudia Moore, Keith Rozie, Deborah Lynn Sharpe, Roderick Spencer Silbert, and Vernon Spencer.

Songs and musical numbers: "Goodnight Angeline," "Charleston Rag," "Shuffle Along," "In Honeysuckle Time," "I'm Just Wild About Harry," "Baltimore Buzz," "Daddy," "There's a Million Little Cupids in the Sky," "I'm a Great Big Daddy," "My Handyman Ain't Handy No More," "Low Down Blues," "Gee, I Wish I Had Someone to Rock Me in the Cradle of Love," "I'm Just Simply Full of Jazz," "High Steppin' Days," "Dixie Moon," "Weary," "Roll Jordan," "Memories of You," "If You've Never Been Vamped by a Brownskin, You've Never Been Vamped at All," "You Got to Git the Gittin While the Gittin's Good," "Oriental Blues," "I'm Craving for That Kind of Love," "Hot Feet," Finale.

Orig. cast album by Warner Bros. Records (HS–3267).

FURTHER REFERENCE: *Newswk* 10–28–1978. *Reminiscing with Sissle and Blake* (Kimball & Bolcom).

AN EVENING WITH JOSEPHINE BAKER (1974). Celebrity one-person show. Josephine Baker in a program of songs. Presented at the Palace Theatre, New York, opening on New Year's Eve, 1974, for a one-week stay. According to Gerald Bordman (*AmMusTh*, p. 676), "Although she was surrounded by an array of competent musical-hall talent, Miss Baker was indeed the whole evening even if to some her glamor and material (much of which she had offered in her 1964 appearance [*Josephine Baker*]) were more than a bit frayed."

EVERYBODY'S TALKING (1926). Touring revue. Prod. by Salem Tutt Whitney. Cast included Mabel Ridley, Mae Austin, Arlyne Brooks, Marion Davis, Ida Foster, Charlie Hawkins, Rosa Knight, Emma Marshall, Clarence Nance, Selma Sayles, Julia Thomas, and Frankie Watts.

EXPERIMENT IN BLACK (1955). Musical and dramatic revue. By William B. Branch. Prod. at a Harlem cabaret (presumably Club Baton), starring Isabel Sanford, Elwood Smith, Johnny Barracuda, and Irene Senior.

EXPLOITS IN AFRICA (1919). African-inspired tabloid musical. Written and prod. by Billy King. Music composed and dir. by J. Berni Barbour. Originally presented at the Grand Theatre, Chicago, with members of the Billy King Stock Co.; then apparently taken on tour, including the Lafayette Theatre in Harlem. Cast included King, Billy Higgins, Margaret Scott, Ernest Whitman, Theresa Burroughs Brooks, and Gertrude Saunders. Musical numbers included "Bleeding Moon" (Scott & Whitman), "You Can't Get Lovin' When There Ain't No Lovin' " (Brooks), and "Itsy Bitsy Doll" (Saunders). Birleanna Blanks appeared in the New Lafayette Theatre prodn.

THE EX-PRESIDENT OF LIBERIA (1901–9). Musical comedy. 2 acts. Written, prod., and staged by Salem Tutt Whitney, who also starred in the title role.
   Whitney's first touring musical show, which apparently had a flexible plot, with seasonal revisions, built around the fraudulent schemes of a man pretending to be the Liberian ex-president.
   First prod. in 1901, under the management of °Ed Dale, owner of the Dale Hotel, Cape May, NJ. Whitney was understudied by his brother, J. Homer Tutt.
   In the 1902 prodn., which was prod. by the Oriental Troubadours Musical Comedy Co., Dale continued as general manager. In that year, William A. Baynard became musical dir., and his wife Emma A. Baynard became the prima donna and soubrette. Other cast members included Walter Jones (dancer/acrobat), Charles Puggesley (billed as "The Colored Aristocrat," and assistant to Whitney), Nettie Taylor ("Queen of Instrumentalists"), Montrose Douglass (bicycle & unicycle stunt artist), and Ben Toledo (juggler).
   In the 1904 prodn., also prod. by the Oriental Troubadours Co., Whitney, William and Emma Baynard, and Nettie Taylor remained with the cast. Alice Cassell was prima donna. This ed. also included a chorus of ten.
   In the 1909 ed., prod. by Salem Tutt Whitney's Lincoln Stock Co., at Lincoln Theatre, Knoxville, TN, the cast was listed as follows: Whitney (Ex-President), J. Homer Tutt (Money King), Mabel Brown (Lady Winterbottom), W. A. Baynard (Senator Mock Anna), Sam Gardner (Runneminn), Sank Simms (Spot Cash), and Nettie Taylor (Widow Burymore).

F

THE FACE AT THE WINDOW (1917). Tabloid musical. Written and prod. by Billy King. Perfd. at the Grand Theatre, Chicago, with members of the Billy King Stock Co., including King, Gertrude Saunders, Howard Kelly, Weber & Wilson, and the Blackstone Quartet.

FADE OUT—FADE IN (1964). Musical comedy. Book and lyrics by °Betty Comden and °Adolph Green. Music by °Jules Styne. A starring vehicle for °Carol Burnett, in which she plays an awkward, plain, but stagestruck girl trying to break into Hollywood films during the 1930s, with the help of a second-rate black singer/dancer. They develop a hilarious routine in which Burnett impersonates Shirley Temple, with Tiger Haynes as Bill "Bojangles" Robinson, in a song and dance entitled "You Mustn't Be Discouraged." Prod. on Bway, opening around June 8, 1964, for 271 perfs.

FANCY TRIMMINGS (1928). Touring revue. Prod. by Addison Carey. Cast included Billy Higgins, Ernest Whitman, Johnny Lee Long and his wife, Putney Dandridge, and George Green.

FAN FAN FOLLIES (1925). Touring revue. Prod. by Earl B. Westfield (a musician and recording artist with Black Swan Records). Starring Lean [sic] Kinbrough.

FANTICIES OF 1927 [sic] (1927). Touring revue. Featuring Earl Howard, "Baby" Juanita Johnson, Margaret Johnson, and the Strand Serenaders.

FAN WAVES (1934). Musical extravaganza. Starring blues singer Bessie Smith. Opened at the Apollo Theatre in Harlem, Feb. 3, 1934, with the proceeds going to the Harlem Children's Fresh Air Fund. In addition to Miss Smith, the cast featured comedians Dusty Fletcher and Gallie DeGaston, Meers & Meers (dancing team), "Norma" (fan dancer), and Ida Cox (blues singer, billed as "The Sepia Mae West") who appeared in a special prodn. with 16 chorus girls.

FAST AND FURIOUS (1931). Musical revue. 2 acts [27 scenes]. Assembled, prod., and dir. by °Forbes Randolph. Sketches by Randolph, °John Wells, Zora Neale Hurston, Tim Moore, Clinton "Dusty" Fletcher, and Jackie (later "Moms") Mabley. Music and lyrics by Joe Jordan, who also dir. the orchestra, J. Rosamond Johnson, Porter Grainger, °Mack Gordon, °Harry Revel, °John Dellavo, °Leighton Brill, and °Sigmund Herzig.

According to the producer's program notes, on entering the theatre, spectators were able to "witness the inhabitants of Waycross [GA] engaged [in] 'woofing,' " which he explained as "a term employed by the Negroes of the South to describe their animated, self-laudatory conversation." While waiting for the performance to begin, they were able to listen to "songs never heard in the North," including "John Henry" and "East Coast Blues," which, according to the producer, "originated in the colored work camps of the South."

Although this revue included some elements of sociological significance among its numerous sketches and dance routines, it failed to appeal to white New York audiences and critics, as being either too white or too black. The critic for the *Outlook & Independent* (9–30–1931) complained that "the darkies... most of the time are forced to sing second-rate Broadway-Hebraic songs with dismal consequences," and were allowed only "about twenty minutes... to be themselves." The reviewer for the *NY American* (9–16–1931) admitted that "the so-called colored show is going definitely out of fashion" and that he not only "failed to appreciate the geniality and animal humor and vital athletics of their jumbles," but added: "I can't forgive some of them for being so successful in the past."

According to the producer's program notes, on entering the theatre, spectators were able to "witness the inhabitants of Waycross [GA] engaged [in] 'woofing,' " which he explained as "a term employed by the Negroes of the South to describe their animated, self-laudatory conversation." While waiting for the performance to begin, they were able to listen to "songs never heard in the North," including "John Henry" and "East Coast Blues," which, according to the producer, "originated in the colored work camps of the South."

Prod. on Bway at the New Yorker Theatre, New York, Sept. 15, 1931, for only 7 perfs. Featured cast included Melva Boden, Louis Deppe, Clinton "Dusty" Fletcher, Forbes Randolph Choir, Baby Goins, Edna Guy, Juano Hernandez, Midgie Lane, Tim Moore, Jackie Mabley, Emma Maitland, Etta Moten, Al Richards, Grace Smith, Helmsley Winfield, and Aurelia Wheeldin. Other performers: Jean Donnell, Senorita Ofelia Diaz, Maurice Ellis, Ruby Elzie, Fast and Furious Quartet, Marion Hairston, Gilbert Holland, Edward Jones, Russell Lee, Larri Loerear, Penwood Lovingood, Gracie Smith, Chickieta Martin, Lee "Boots" Marshall, Lloyd Mitchell, Alexander Moody, Orlando Roberson, Earl Shanks, Thomas Smith, Clarence Todd, Carl H. Taylor, Joe Willis, Wilhelmina Wade, Joe Willis, Billy Wallace, Frank Walker, Frederick A. Wheeldin, Lilly "Ponton" Yuen, and Maurice Young.

Synopsis of sketches: 'The Last Word' by Tim Moore (The Husband [Moore],

The Wife [Goins]). 'In the Cigar Store' by Clinton Fletcher (Proprietor [Fletcher], 1st Customer [Smith], 2nd Customer [Hernandez], 3rd Customer [Lee]). 'Theatre Pantomime,' with apologies to Mazie Gay, "Cochran's Revue," London, 1929. 'The Court Room' by Zora Neale Hurston (Judge [Moore], Clerk of Court [Ellis], Prosecuting Attorney [Todd], Lawyer [Mitchell], Officer Simpson [Boden], John Barnes [Hernandez], Cliff Mullins [Lee], Mrs. Mullins [Mabley], Jessie Smith [Maitland], Eva [Moten]). 'The Silent Bootlegger' by Clinton Fletcher (The Bootlegger [Fletcher], 1st Customer [Smith], 2nd Customer [Goins], Detective [Todd]). 'Raid on Jake's' by Tim Moore (Jake [Moore], Dizzy [Boden], 1st Guest [Moten], 2nd Guest [Shanks], Two Detectives [Hernandez & Willis], Other Guests [Ellis, Wallace, Mitchell & A. Wheeldin]). 'Scene on 135th Street' by Jackie Mabley (Mrs. Smith [Mabley], Mr. Smith [Boden], Detective [Ellis], Policeman [Willis]). 'Jacob's Ladder,' conceived and written by Rosamond Johnson and Allie Wrubel (Elder Simmons [Deppe], Cigarette Girl [Shaw], Rhythm Girl [Hairston], Cabaret Dancer [Lane], Singing Waiters [Todd, Willis, Mitchell & Shanks], Number King [Holland], Danny [Winfield], Sisters and Brothers of the Church [Forbes Randolph Choir], Guests at the Cabaret). 'Football Game' by Zora Neale Hurston (Capt. of Howard's Team [Moore], Capt. of Lincoln's Team [Fletcher], Referee [Deppe], Cheerleaders [Mabley & Hurston], Lincoln's Wrestler [Holland], Howard's Wrestler [Hernandez], Teams, Bands, Chorus & Choir). 'Pansies' by Lottie Meaney (Young Man [Winfield], Business Man [Lee], Garner [Marshall], Flowers: Orchid [Boden], Violet [Donnell], Forget-me-not [Moody], Lily [Loerear], Daffydill [sic] [Lovingood], Dancing Pansies [Smith, Jones, Walker & Young]). 'Poker Game' by Zora Neale Hurston (Nunky [Fletcher], Tush Hog [Moore], Too Sweet [Todd], Sack Daddy [Lee], Black Baby [Ellis], Peckerwood [Hernandez], Mrs. Dilson [Mabley]; Hell: 1st Asst. to the Devil [F. Wheeldin], 2nd Asst. to the Devil [Taylor], The Devil [Smith], Imps, Angels, and Sojourners in Hell; Heaven: The Lord [Deppe], Angel Gabriel [Ellis], Angel Michael [Lee], Singing by Messrs. Shanks, Willis, Todd & Mitchell). 'Macbeth' by John Wells and Wm. Shakespeare (The Doctor [Boden], Gentlewoman [Moten], Lady Macbeth [Mabley], Servant [Shanks], Seyton [Hernandez], Macbeth [Moore], Messenger [Willis], Young Siward [Ellis], King of Scotland [Fletcher], Prompter [Todd]).

Songs and musical numbers: Overture (sung by Fast and Furious Quartet and Rosamond Johnson Quartet). "Fast and Furious" (sung by Smith, danced by 4 dancing boys & Chorus, music and lyrics by Gordon & Revel). "Walking on Air" (sung by Roberson, danced by Martin, Wade & Chorus, music and lyrics by Gordon & Revel). "Frowns" (sung by Deppe, music and lyrics by Gordon & Revel). "The Three Dames Ziegfeld Failed to Glorify" (sung by Marshall, Boden & Donnell, music and lyrics by Grainger). "Rhumbatism" (sung by Yuen & Mabley, danced by Yuen & Chorus, music and lyrics by Gordon & Revel). "So Lonesome" (sung by Roberson, music and lyrics by Jordan & Johnson). "Gymnasium" (sung by Shaw, danced by Shaw, Mabley & Chorus, boxing by A. Wheeldin & Maitland, music and lyrics by Gordon & Revel).

"Madrassi Nautch" (East Indian street dance, through the courtesy of Miss Ruth St. Denis; danced by Guy). "Shadows on the Wall" (sung by Moten; Shadows: Todd, Willis, Shanks, Mitchell & Hairston). "Happy Ending" (sung by Elzy, music and lyrics by Gordon & Revel). "Hot Feet" (sung by Shaw, danced by Richard, Lane & Chorus, music by Gordon & Revel). "Asaka-Saba" (Dance of the Moods: danced by Winfield, music by Grainger). "Snowball Blues" (Forbes Randolph's Choir and Dancing Girls). Others: "Where's My Happy Ending?," "Boomerang" (Jordan & Johnson), "Hot Hot Mama," "Pansies on Parade," "Let's Raise Hell" (Grainger), "Modernistic" (Grainger & Dallavo), and "Ham What Am" (Brill & Herzig).
FURTHER REFERENCE: *BlkMusTh* (Woll). *DBlkTh* (Woll). *NY Herald Trib.* 9–16–1931. *NYT* 9–16–1931. *Variety* 9–22–1931.

FAT TUESDAY (1975). Musical comedy. By Roger Furman. Based on a nonmusical comedy entitled "Drawers Down, Bottoms Up," by Dee Robinson, who wrote the music and lyrics. The title is taken from the English rendition of *Mardi Gras*. Centers on the activities in a New Orleans brothel during the 1930s. Prod. by the New Heritage Players, New York, in repertory, opening Oct. 1975, dir. by Furman. Won AUDELCO Awards in 1976 for Louis Meyers (performer) and Joseph Gandy (scenic designer).

FIESTA (1969). Children's musical. 1 act. By Kelsie E. Collie. To find truth and happiness, a young man goes on an odyssey to a South American village where he prevents a fiesta from becoming a disaster when it is discovered that someone has stolen the ceremonial donkey. Written as part of the author's MFA thesis at George Washington Univ., Washington, DC, where it was presumably prod. in 1969.

THE 5TH DIMENSION, WITH JO JO'S DANCE FACTORY (1974). Musical show. Prod. at the Uris Theatre, New York, Nov. 27–Dec. 8, 1974, for 15 perfs. Featuring the Fifth Dimension (a black vocal group) and Jo Jo's Dance Factory.

A FILIPINO MISFIT (1902). Subtitled "A Farcical Skit in One Act."
    One of the opening skits of the *Black Patti Troubadours* show, set on a jungle island in the Philippines.
    Prod. as part of the Troubadours show, opening Jan. 1, 1902, at the Los Angeles Theatre, Los Angeles, CA, as one stop on a transcontinental tour. Cast: John Rucker (Bo-Ho, a Filipino Misfit), Leslie Triplet (Ho-Ho, another Filipino Misfit), Anthony D. Byrd (Zambolo, Ambassador to the Azore Islands), Al F. Watts (Brother Jungle, a Missionary), J. P. Reed (Sa-Bo, Governor of the Azores), Will A. Cook (Officer Monk, on the Governor's staff), Laura Bailey (Priscilla, Governor Sa-Bo's daughter, looking for a husband), James Crosby (Capt. Rufus), Charles C. Bougia (Bill O'Fare), Gustav Hall (Faro Bill, Secretary

to the Ambassador), Cecil Watts (Mrs. Jungle, the missionary's wife), Ida Larkins (Miss O So Ot, "a warm member"), Ida Forsyne (Miss Tom Arlie, from Texas), Henrietta Hicks (Miss Co-Co), Sarah Green (Miss Lo Lo), Jeannette Murphy (Miss Do Do), Ida Butler (Miss Po Po), Eva Moore (Miss Lo Do), Barney, the terrier mascot (as himself), Soldiers, Pleasure Seekers, etc.

Songs and musical numbers: "The Honolulu Dance" (Company), "Meeting at the Old Town Hall" (Bailey, C. Watts, A. Watts, Reed & Chorus, assisted by the Coonville Band), "We Need the Money" (Triplet & Rucker), "My Alabama Lady Love" (Triplet, Rucker, Butler & Larkins), "My Drowsy Babe" (Green, Forsyne & Chorus), "As the Boys Go Marching By" (Chorus), "Kiss-kiss-kiss" (Dougle Quartet), Finale—Buck Dance.

THE FINAL REHEARSAL (1917–18). Tabloid musical. Written and prod. by Billy King. Perfd. at the Grand Theatre, Chicago, and on tour. With members of the Billy King Stock Co., including Howard Kelly, Gertrude Saunders, Blaine & Brown, and Genevieve Stearn.

FINIAN'S RAINBOW (1947). Musical comedy. Book by °E. Y. Harburg & °Fred Saidy. Lyrics by Harburg. A satire on race relations and bigotry in the Deep South, in which blacks were cast in minor roles, as a gesture of racial goodwill. Prod. on Bway at the 46th St. Theatre, opening Jan. 10, 1947, for 725 perfs. The integrated cast included Maude Simmons, William Greaves, and a group of black singers and dancers.

FIORETTA (1929). White-oriented musical. Book by °Earl Carroll and °Charlton Andrews. Lyrics and music by °G. Romilli. Included a popular song, "Dreamboat," by Jo Trent. Prod. on Bway, Feb. 5, 1929, for 111 perfs. With an all-white cast that included °Leon Errol, °Fanny Brice, °Dorothy Knapp, °Jan Brennan, and °Lionel Atwell.

FIREWORKS OF 1930 (1930). Musical revue. Music by "Fats" Waller and James P. Johnson (as Jimmie Johnson). Prod. and staged by Emory Hutchins at the Lafayette Theatre in Harlem, opening June 28, 1930, playing through the July 4 holiday. Cast included George Dewey Washington, Mamie Smith, and about 40 other performers. Music perfd. by "Fats" Waller and Jimmy Johnson's Syncopators.

THE FIRST (1981). Musical biography. 2 acts. Book by °Joel Siegel and °Martin Charnin. Music by °Bob Brush. Lyrics by Charnin. About the events in the life of baseball player Jackie Robinson that led to his entry into the major leagues. The action occurs between 1945 and 1947. Prod. on Bway at the Martin Beck Theatre, Nov. 17–Dec. 12, 1981, for 37 perfs. plus 33 previews; staged and

dir. by Charnin. Choreography by Alan Johnson. With David Alan Grier as Robinson and Lonnette McKee as his wife, Rachel.
FURTHER REFERENCE: *DBlkTh* (Woll).

THE FIRST LADY (1992). Gospel musical. Written and dir. by Chip Fields. From a story by Barry Henderson. About the wife of a church pastor who takes over her husband's ministry after he dies of a heart attack, thus dividing the church because of the opposition of several key members. The situation is complicated when a young, handsome ne'er-do-well, who strongly resembles her late husband, joins the church, after being released from prison for drug trafficking, and makes romantic overtures toward the lady minister. Prod. by Dimensions Unlimited, Inc., in association with the New Regal Theatre Foundation, at Constitution Hall in Washington, DC, March 10–15, 1992; costarring Vickie Winans and Louis Price, a Motown recording artist.

FIVE FOOLISH VIRGINS (pre-1950). Opera. 2 acts. Libretto by Langston Hughes. Musical score by °Jan Meyerowitz. Copy in JWJ/YUL.

5-6-7-8. . . . DANCE! (1983). Dance musical. Written by °Bruce Vilanch. Orig. songs by David Zippel & Wally Harper. Prod. at Radio City Music Hall, New York City, June 15–Sept. 5, 1983, for 149 perfs. With an integrated cast featuring Armelia McQueen.

FLAT STREET SA'DAY NIGHT (1985). Musical drama. 2 acts. Book by Frank Solomon. Music and lyrics by Lenga Tooks (joint pseudonym for *Lawrence Edward aNd George Arnold Tooks*). Based on Solomon's novel, *A Hell of a Life,* set in Allendale, SC, in the 1940s and 1950s, and concerned with events that occurred in jukebox joints on Flat Street, a real street, where blacks socialized and vented their frustrations after working all week in the fields. Prod. by Theatre-in-Progress, New York, and presented Off-Bway at the Arts for Living Center, Henry St. Settlement, in the facilities of the New Federal Theatre, May 16–June 30, 1985, and July 11–Aug. 4, 1985. Also presented in Allendale, SC, at the Allendale Primary School, July 5 and 6, 1985, at the invitation of the mayor. Winner of five AUDELCO Awards for choreography (Sheryle R. Jones), outstanding perf. in a musical by a female (Patricia A. Clement), outstanding perf. in a musical by a male (Steve Beckman), outstanding musical creator (Lenga Tooks), and musical prodn. of the year (Frank Solomon and Lenga Tooks).
FURTHER REFERENCE: *The State* (Columbia, SC) 8–26–1985.

FLOWER DRUM SONG (1958). Musical. Book by °Oscar Hammerstein II and °Joseph Fields. Lyrics by Hammerstein. Music by °Richard Rodgers. Based on a novel by Chin Y. Lee. Explores the conflict between the traditions of the older Chinese-Americans in San Francisco and the younger generation. Prod. on Bway at the St. James Theatre, opening Dec. 1, 1958, for 600 perfs. The integrated cast included black actress Juanita Hall as Madam Liang.

FLY BLACKBIRD (1960–62). Musical of the civil rights movement. 2 acts. Book by C. Bernard Jackson. Music by Jackson and °James V. Hatch.

An outgrowth of the sit-in movement of 1960, this musical is a satire of the conflicts within the ranks of a group of blacks in the Deep South as to the most effective methods of securing civil rights. The issues are those with which the students were wrestling at the time, which, according to James V. Hatch, one of the coauthors, were violence vs. nonviolence; now or wait; confront or conform; new vs. old; and integration vs. separation (*BlkThUSA* [Hatch & Shine], p. 671).

According to C. Bernard Jackson, the librettist, the play advocates a mature, wise, and reasonable course of action, and voices the need for "caution, patience, restraint, and due process" (*BlkThUSA* [Hatch & Shine], p. 671).

Developed from a one-act play presented in the Shoebox Theatre in Los Angeles in the autumn of 1960, which found an audience among the young and politically active. First prod. as a two-act musical at the Metro Theatre, Los Angeles, Feb. 10, 1961; with a cast of student performers, many of whom went on to professional stage and film careers, including Micki Grant, Thelma Oliver, Jack Crowder, and Camille Billops.

Prod. Off-Bway in a revised and expanded version, with additional material by the director, Jerome Eskow, at the Mayfair Theatre, for 127 perfs., opening Feb. 6, 1962; with Avon Long in the leading role. Winner of an Obie Award, 1961–62.

Cast: Avon Long (William Piper), Elwood Smith (Police Officer Jonsen), Robert Guillaume (Carl), Mary Louise (Josie), Thelma Oliver (Susie), Chele Abel (Gladys), Micki Grant (Camille), William Sugihara (George), Paul Reid Roman (Paul), Jim Bailey (Lou), Gail Ziferstein (Gail), Jack Crowder (Palmer), Gilbert Price (Roger), Glory Van Scott (Big Betty), Michael Kermoyan (Mr. Crocker), and Helen Blount (Police Matron Jonsen); Others: Lodge Members, Students, Crocker Boys and Crocker Girls.

Prod. at the Inst. in Black Repertory Theatre, Univ. of Calif.–Santa Barbara, Summer 1968.

Songs and musical numbers: Overture and Opening Scene, "All in Good Time," "Now," "I'm Sick of the Whole Damn Problem," "Who's the Fool?," "The Right Way," "Couldn't We?," "The Housing Cha-Cha," "Natchitoches, Louisiana," "Fly Blackbird," "The Gong," "Rivers to the South," Entr'acte—"The Lilac Song," "The Twilight Zone," "The Crocker Boy's Song," "Mister Boy," "Old White Tom," Burial Sequence, Reprise—"Natchitoches, Louisiana," "Who's the Fool?," and "Wake Up."

Book and lyrics of the revised Bway script pub. in *Blk. Teacher and the Dramatic Arts* (Reardon & Pawley). Book and lyrics of the orig. script pub. in *BlkThUSA* (Hatch & Shine). Orig. cast album released by Mercury (OCM-2206; OCS-6206).

[For other musicals by C. Bernard Jackson, consult *Contemporary Blk. Am. Playwrs. and Their Pls.* (Peterson).]

FURTHER REFERENCE: Alkire diss. *America* 3–10–1962. *Nation* 3–3–1962. *NYorker* 2–17–1962. *NYT* 2–6–1962. *ThArts* 5–1962.

FLYING DOWN TO HARLEM (1934). Touring revue. Coproduced by and costarring "Rubber Leg" Williams, the Three Cyclones, and "Uke" Bob.

FLY ROUND, YOUNG LADIES (c. 1920s). White-oriented musical. Main authorship unknown. Included two songs by Cecil Mack: "You for Me, Me for You," and "The Camel Walk." Prod. New York, during the 1920s.

FOLIES BERGERE REVUE / / Also called *Will Morrissey's Folies Bergere Revue* (1930). Musical revue. Music by Eubie Blake and °Will Morrissey. Prod. at the Gansevoort Theatre, New York City, opening April 15, 1930, for a brief run. The integrated cast included dancers from the *Folies Bergères*, Paris.
FURTHER REFERENCE: *NYT* 4–16–1930.

FOLLIES AND FANCIES OF 1920 (1920). Touring revue. Prod. by and featuring dancer Frank Montgomery and his wife/partner, Florence McClain. Laura Brown was also in the cast.

FOLLIES OF THE STROLL (1920s). Musical revue. Book and lyrics by Alex C. Rogers. Music by C. Luckeyth Roberts. Prod. New York during the 1920s.

FOLLOW ME (1923–24). Musical revue. Prod. by °I. M. Weingarden, at the Lafayette Theatre, New York, Dec. 1923, then on tour. Cast included Valaida Snow (mistress of ceremonies), Billy Higgins, Ernest Whitman, Clifford Ross, Alice Gorgas, Julia Moody, Susie Sutton, Mamie Smith, Ollie Burgoyne, Edna Hicks, the Follow Me Four, the Pony Ballet, and the Regular Chorus.
FURTHER REFERENCE: *Billboard* (J. A. Jackson's Page) 7–14–1922. *BlksBf* (Sampson).

FOLLY TOWN (1920). Musical revue. Prod. in New York, by °William K. Wells and °Jesse Greer, opening May 17, 1920; starring comedian °Bert Lahr. According to *HarlRenD* (Kellner, p. 126) and *NYT* 5–18–1920, this ambitious show featured an integrated cast which included ten black performers ("in a riot of jazz") among an assortment of comedians, vaudevillians, singers, dancers, and showgirls. No information concerning the names of individual black performers or their contributions.

45 MINUTES TO BROADWAY (1916). Musical show. Prod. by the Lafayette Players at the Lafayette Theatre in Harlem, 1916. Cast included Abbie Mitchell, William "Babe" Townsend, Susie Sutton, Laura Bowman, Walker Thompson, Tom Brown, Alice Gorgas, and Susie Smith.

4–11–44 (1926) / / Title later changed to ***Struttin' Hannah from Savannah*** (1927–28). Musical comedy. Book by Eddie Hunter, who was also the principal comedian.

After stealing some money from his wife, which he uses to bet on the number 4–11–44, a henpecked husband (Hunter) hides behind a well and falls asleep. He dreams that he is in Harlem enjoying the good life, living off his wife's money. During his dream, a number of the specialty acts are perfd. The climax comes when his wife has him arrested for theft, and just as he is being taken off to jail, he wakes up, realizing that it has all been a dream.

First prod. as *4–11–44*, and apparently taken on tour with the following cast: Andrew Tribble, Nina Hunter, Grayce Rector, Alberta Perkins, Norman Astwood, Aurora Greeley, Emma Jackson, George Cooper, Billy Mitchell, and Claude Lawson.

Prod. in Harlem and on tour, under its changed title, by Will Mastin (Sammy Davis, Jr.'s uncle) and "Virgie" Richards. Cast included Hunter (husband), Richards (Creola), Chick MacIntosh (Mandy), Charlie Smith (Sam Green), Mastin (Bill Simmons), Daisy Randolph (Child), Rastus Airship (Rastus), C. C. Parker (Mandy's father), Mae Larkin (contortionist), Cecil Smith (banjoist), and a chorus of 8 ladies.

FOUR SAINTS IN THREE ACTS (1934, revived 1952). Redundantly described by the librettist as "An opera to be sung." But according to black drama historian °Edith J. R. Isaacs (*NegAmTh*, p. 92), it was "actually . . . a sung-dance, striking and original in both form and content." 4 acts (in spite of the title). Libretto by °Gertrude Stein. Music and lyrics by °Virgil Thomson.

Perhaps the most controversial musical of the 1934 season, possibly because its libretto was totally incomprehensible to most critics and members of the audience, and possibly because of the novelty of an all-black cast. According to the opera's director °John Houseman (in his autobiography, *Run-Through*, p. 105), Thomson felt that blacks alone "possess the dignity and poise, the lack of self-consciousness that proper interpretation of opera demands. And they are not ashamed of words."

The opera was apparently typical of Stein's enigmatic style in using words for their sounds and suggestions rather than for their conventional meanings. This did not endear her to Broadway critics, however, who universally discredited the libretto, while praising the music and the singing.

The story focused on two Spanish saints—in four acts, rather than three—a characteristic Steinian touch. One of the saints, St. Theresa of Avila, was represented by two performers, one portraying herself and the other her male alter ego. Act I focused on the incidents in her life. The second featured saint was St. Ignatius Loyola, whose vision of the Holy Ghost is presented in Act II. Act III dealt with the landscape of Barcelona; and Act IV was a summary by the chorus of the preceding themes and motifs of the opera, which apparently concerned the saintly qualities of the saints. Black choir director Eva Jessye was the choral director.

In addition to the music, the critics also praised the lavish costumes of lace and gold, and the settings of oil cloth, cellophane, and gauze by set designer °Florine Stettheimer, as well as the stylized choreography of °Frederick Ashton.

First prod. on Bway at the Forty-Fourth Street Theatre, opening Feb. 20, 1934, for 48 perfs.; dir. by John Houseman. Cast: Beatrice Robinson-Wayne (St. Theresa I), Bruce Howard (St. Theresa II), Edward Matthews (St. Ignatius), John Diggs (St. Chavez). Others: Altonell Hines, Abner Dorsey, Bertha Fitzhugh Baker, Leonard Franklin, Randolph Robinson, David Bethe, Kitty Mason, Thomas Anderson, Charles Spinnard, Margaret Perry, Flossie Roberts, Edward Batten, Florence Hester, and George Timber. This prodn. also played briefly in Chicago with the orig. cast.

Revived in 1952, under the auspices of the ANTA (American National Theatre and Academy), with the following cast: singers Rawn Spearman, Martha Flowers, Leontyne Price, and Betty Allen; and dancers Arthur Mitchell and Louis Johnson.

According to black reviewer George W. Streator (*Crisis* 4–1934, p. 103), the music was "a strange mixture of sacred and vulgar sequences. At times one feels 'churchy,' and at times one wants to guffaw. But at no time is one quite certain what it is all about." Gerald Bordman (*AmMusTh*, p. 487) described the music as having "a simple folk-like quality [which] drew its inspiration strongly from the church hymns of Thomson's southern background."

Libretto pub. 1934. Cast recording by RCA-Victor (LM 2756).

FOXY GRANDPA (1902). White-oriented musical comedy. Book by °R. Melville Baker. Music and lyrics by °Joseph Hart. With an interpolated song by Tom Lemonier and Richard H. Gerard. Prod. at the 14th St. Theatre, New York, opening Feb. 17, 1902, for 1,920 perfs. With an all-white cast that included Joseph Hart and Carrie DeMar. They introduced "with great success" "I'll Be Your Dewdrop Rosey," a popular song with music by Lemonier and words by Gerard; musical score pub. by M. Witmark, New York; copy in Moorland-Spingarn.

FRANKENSTEIN: NEW WAVE (1985). Rock musical. Book, music, and direction by William Electric Black (Ian Ellis James). Based on °Mary Shelley's *Frankenstein*. Described by the *NY Native* (11–4/10–1985) as "a kind of big fun blend of *Cats* and *Rocky Horror* with tremendous reverence for its source [Shelley's novel]." According to the reviewer, the monster reminded him of "Truman Capote on acid," and there were "gay overtones" in Dr. Frankenstein's relationship with Henry Clervel. Prod. at the Kraine Gallery Theatre, New York, Sept.–Nov. 1985.

FRED DOUGLASS' RECEPTION (1896). Musical prodn. Written and staged by J. Ed. Green. Perfd. by the Black American Troubadours at Havelin's Theatre, Chicago, in the summer of 1896.

FREE AND EASY (1873). Variety show. One of the earliest black musical shows of record. Featured Lyles & Lyles, a musical comedy team. Apparently prod. on tour. Cited in *NegMus&M* (Cuney-Hare).

FREE AND EASY (1959–60). Blues opera. Adapt. by °Harold Arlen from *St. Louis Woman*, a musical by Arna Bontemps and Countee Cullen, with music by Arlen and lyrics by Johnny Mercer (prod. on Bway, 1946). According to *Compl. Bk. of the Am. Mus. Th.*, rev. ed. (Ewen, p. 51), "The entire structure [of *St. Louis Woman*] was extended to make the work more of an opera than a popular musical production." Arlen added several songs which he had previously written for other prodns., such as "That Old Black Magic" and "Blues in the Night," and made extensive revisions of the orig. play, hoping to make it more successful. Opened in Amsterdam, Dec. 1959, with presentations in Brussels and Paris, with the intention of being brought to Bway, but closed early in 1960, after only a brief run.
FURTHER REFERENCE: *NYT* 12–15–1959. *World of Mus. Comedy*, rev. ed. (Green).

THE FROG FOLLIES (1913). Musical revue. Prod. by Will Marion Cook, J. Rosamond Johnson, and James Reese Europe. Prod. New York, 1913, with members of the famous black club, The Frogs (a theatrical association). Cast included Bert Williams, Julius Glenn, Henry Troy, James Reese Europe's Band, Harper & Gilliam, Alex Rogers, Sam Lucas, Lloyd Gibbs, Jesse A. Shipp, Charles Gilpin, Barber & William [*sic*], S. H. Dudley, and Kelly & Catlin.

THE FROLICS (1923). Musical revue. Prod. by Leonard Harper. Musical dir., Allie Ross. Presented in Harlem, presumably at the Lafayette Theatre. Cast included Harper & Blanks (Osceola Blanks, Leonard Harper's wife), Mason & Henderson, Eva Metcalf, Ada Bricktop Smith, [Billy] Mitchell & Moore, Johnny Virgel, Aida Ward, the Byron Brothers, Fred Davis, the Three Eddies, Rosa Henderson, and Roy White. The show included 20 songs, 12 dancing numbers, and 4 specialty numbers.

FROM BALTIMORE TO TURKEY (1924). Musical revue. Prod. by Joe Bright in Harlem and on tour. Cast included Bright, Dink Stewart, Andrew Tribble, and Theresa Burroughs Brooks.

FROM DOVER TO DIXIE. See *PLANTATION REVUE* and *DIXIE TO BROADWAY*.

FROM SPEEDVILLE TO BROADWAY (1916). Musical revue. Prod. by Frank Montgomery, under the sponsorship of the Quality Amusement Co. Presented at the Lafayette Theatre in Harlem and on tour of the Quality Amusement Co. circuit. Cast included Montgomery, Franny Wise, George Stamper, Florence McClain, Dewey Weinglass, Mae Brown, Blanche Harris, Howard & Mason, Hattie James, Josephine Lazzo, Dave and Gertrude Stuffin, Earl West, Lillian Williams, and Clarice Wright.

FUN AT THE PICNIC GROUNDS (1921). Touring show. Prod. by blackface comedian Hardtack Johnson.

FUN FESTIVAL (1926). Touring musical show. Prod. and perfd. by Lonnie Fisher. Cast included Fisher's wife, "Stompy" Watson, and "Lollipop."

THE FUNHOUSE (1968). Theatrework with music. By George Houston Bass. Prod. by the Long Wharf Summer Theatre, New Haven, Sept. 1968, with incidental music, including soloists, chorus, and instrumental ensemble, by Noel Da Costa.

FUN IN A MUSIC SHOP (1920). Touring vaudeville entertainment. Prod. and perfd. by the Gains Brothers Variety Players Company.

FUNNYHOUSE OF A NEGRO (1984). Musical version of the author's play by the same title (1963). By Adrienne Kennedy. Music by Carmen Moore. Musical arrangements by Luther Henderson.

The title of the play provides an insight into the basic problems of the 1960s with which it dealt—the black rejection of the various labels by which the race had been identified in the past, especially Negro and colored; and the search for one's racial heritage or identity. The plot concerns the unsuccessful attempt by a mulatto girl (Sarah) to resolve the psychological conflicts of her biracial (Negro/white) identity, and of bringing together the many facets of her divided self—which are symbolically represented by the various historical figures who visit her in the surrealistic rooming house (i.e., "funnyhouse") where she resides. Among these figures are Queen Victoria, Jesus Christ, Patrice Lumumba, and the Duchess of Hapsburg—who apparently symbolize Victorian morality, Christianity, African ancestry, and, possibly, the longing to be descended from a great and noble family.

The orig. play without music won for Kennedy a Stanley Award in 1963 from Wagner Coll. in Staten Island, NY, and an Obie Award in 1964, when it was prod. Off-Bway at the East End Theatre, Jan. 14–Feb. 9, 1964, for 64 perfs.; dir. by Michael Kahn, and featuring Billie Allen as Sarah.

Billie Allen dir. the musical version of the play, which was prod. by the Undergraduate Dept. of Drama at New York University, Nov. 28– Dec. 2, 1984. (Luther Henderson, the arranger, is Allen's husband.)

The music by Carmen Moore was inspired by the play's stream-of-consciousness technique, according to the composer, who was interviewed by Mel Tapley of the *NY Amsterdam N.* (12–1–1984): "It's an exciting project," said Moore. "I heard the music immediately. The logic of how it's written—its kind of stream of consciousness is the way I write." He further stated in the Tapley interview that he "used a quartet with keyboards and synthesizer," and that a "lot of the music is related to the 19th Century—Queen Victoria," which was author Kennedy's favorite period of literature. Moore stated that in the music for *Funnyhouse* he also used "ragtime, jazz, salon, 20th Century with the synthesizer," and, "finally, African drums."

FUNNY MONEY (1930). Musical show. 2 acts [7 scenes]. Prod. by Tim Owsley, who also wrote lyrics. Special music by F. B. Woods and George Gillins.

At the time of writing this show, Owsley was producer of *Silas Green from New Orleans*, the longest-running black show in the history of the American musical theatre. This show included Silas Green as one of the characters, and possibly incorporated other characters and situations from the orig. show.

Synopsis of scenes: Act I, Scene 1—The front yard of the Green home; Scene 2—A nearby street; Scene 3—A public graveyard; Scene 4—A nearby street; Scene 5—The city park; Scene 6—Another street. Act II, Scene 7—The living room of the Green home.

Prod. on tour, 1930. Cast: Leroy "Kike" Gresham (Mr. Meddla), Manzie Campbell (Lila Bean), Fred Wiggins (Silas Green), Princess White Durrah (A Street Angel), Frank Keith (Hubbard), Mildred Scott (Wife), Mose Penny (Man), Evelyn White (Woman), Sean Johnson (Lawyer), Freddie Durrah (Officer), Frank Smedelay (Uncle Ruco), Katie Bryant (Miss Watsey), Bertle Davis (Miss Ritsen), Other Townspeople, and Special Added Attractions: Allie Johnson (wire artist), Tim Green & Roberta (comedian/singers), Bobby Gillins and Katie Bryant (special dancing chorus).

Songs and musical numbers: "The Same Old Silas," "All the Time in Dixie," "A Little Kiss," "Whoopee," "In Love with You," "Absence," "Dance of the Ghost," "Steppin'," "For Sale," "It's All Over Now," "Blue," and "Can't Help It."

G

GAY HARLEM (1927). Musical revue. Prod. by Irvin C. Miller at the Lafayette Theatre in Harlem prior to June 1927. The *NY Amsterdam N.* (as quoted in *HarlRenD* [Kellner], p. 134) criticized the show for its "wanton display of human flesh," and stated that it was a blend of "loose morals and lasciviousness"; but the *Messenger* (6–1927, p. 193) defended it against these charges, calling it a "highly entertaining lampoon of the more picturesque phases of [Harlem] life." The cast included Louise Williams, Ruby Mason, Bill Cumby, Elizabeth Smith, Ethel Dudley, Charles Alexander, Ike Paul, and Claude Winifrey.

GEECHIE (1922). Subtitled "A Dusky Romance in Three Acts." Book and lyrics by Henry Creamer. Music by Jimmy Johnson [James P. Johnson]. Copyright by Creamer, 1926; copy in LC.

GEE WHIZ (1929). Touring revue. Featuring blues singer Alice Ramsey, singer/dancer Evon Robinson, dancer "Cut Out" Ellis, and George Green (juvenile).

GENTLEMEN, BE SEATED! (1963). Contemporary minstrel show. Book by °Jerome Moross and °Edward Eager. Music by Moross. Lyrics by Eager. The events leading from slavery to the Civil War are retold in the format of a minstrel show. Avon Long was the only black with a leading role (Mr. Tambo). Other blacks were cast mainly in the roles of slaves and minstrels. Prod. by the New York City Center of Music and Drama at the New York City Center, opening Oct. 10, 1963, for 3 perfs.; dir. by °Robert Turoff. Other leading performers (all white) included °Dick Shawn (Mister Interlocutor), °Charles Atkins (Mr. Bones), and °Alice Ghostley (The Comedienne).

GEORGE STAMPER'S REVUE (1929). Touring revue. Prod. by and starring dancer/choreographer George Stamper. Cast also included PeeWee & Eddie, Mabel Richards, Audrey Thomas, and the Wilber DeParis Orchestra.

GEORGE WASHINGTON BULLION (1910). Musical comedy. Presumably 3 acts. Written and prod. by Salem Tutt Whitney. The adventures of George Washington Bullion, owner of a tobacco plantation in Bowling Green, KY. Prod. on tour by Whitney & Tutt's *Smart Set Co.*, 1910. (See also *George Washington Bullion Abroad* [1915].)

GEORGE WASHINGTON BULLION ABROAD (1915). Musical comedy. 3 acts. Book, lyrics, and prodn. by J. Homer Tutt. Music by Salem Tutt Whitney, Tutt, and James Vaughan.

A new adventure for the title character of *George Washington Bullion* (first prod. in 1910), which takes him (with an entourage of his family and friends) from his tobacco plantation in Bowling Green, KY, by ship and by raft to "The Rajah's Garden" in the Orient and back home again.

Prod. on tour by Whitney & Tutt's *Smart Set Co.*, 1915. Also presented at the Lexington Theatre in New York, c. 1915. Cast: Salem Tutt Whitney (George Washington Bullion), J. Homer Tutt (Sam Cain, Bullion's Friend), Luke A. Scott (Chameleon Norman, Detective—who creates five different characters), Ethel Scott (singer), Will Dixon (Grafton Smooth, a Slick Article), Frank Jackson (Captain Raymond, Captain of the Vessel), Sam Gardner (Jack Snow), George McClain (Jed Simpkins), Sam Grey (Willie Little), George Boutte (Ephram Howe & asst. stage manager), O. D. Carter (Poor Little Henpecko), Will Brown (First Mate), Edward Marshall (Second Mate), Julian Costello (Amanda Henpecko), Blanche Thompson (Geraldine Shantz, the New Schoolteacher), Ethel Marshall (Mrs. Dewar), Hattie Ackers (Moana Sweet, Bullion's Ward), Ethelyn Proctor (Louis Dillingham, Smooth's Confederate), Irene Tasker (Martha Bullion, George's Sister), Emma Jackson (Clover Leaf, Schoolgirl), Josie Graham (Susie Young), Mattie Lewis (Emany Poorly), Mamie Palmer (Militant Parkfurst), Tom Hall (Zabastic), Will Norwood (Happy Sam), Theodore Peyton (Peter Joy), and Other Characters: 8 Oriental Dancing Girls, Plantation Hands, Deck Hands and Sailors, Guards, School Girls, Waiting Maids, and Society Belles.

Songs and musical numbers: Act I—Opening Chorus, "Dinner Bells" (Company), "Golden Days" (song and dance: Carter, Boutte, Ackers, Palmer & Chorus), "Love Me Anywhere" (Proctor, Dixon & others), "Shine on Southern Moon" (Thompson & School Girls), "Don't Do That to Me, Dear" (Whitney & Ackers), "Dog Gon I'm Young Again" (Old Folks), "Italy and My Rose" (Scott), "Levee Pastimes" (Boutte, Carter, Palmer & Graham), "Goodbye My Old Kentucky Home" (Ensemble & soloists: Thompson & King). Act II—Opening Chorus, "We're Sailing Along" (Ensemble), "Moonlight Pace" (modern dance: Tutt, Thompson & Chorus), "The Deep Blue Sea" (F. Jackson), "Help Cometh from Above" (Octette: Principals), "Allah Oh! Allah!" (Company), "Body Guards of the Prince" (song and drill: 8 Guards), "Dance of Death" (E. Scott & L. Scott), "Manyana" (Thompson & Chorus), "No Matter How Good You Treat the World You Never Get Out Alive" (Whitney), "Going Back to Dixieland" (Company & Soloists: Dunlap, E. Jackson, H. Jackson, & Wheeler). Act III—"Strutting Sam" (Tutt & Chorus), "Gin, Gin, Gin" (toast: Whitney), and "When You Hear the Old Kentucky Blues" (Finale: Company). "Manyana" pub. by Joseph W. Stern, New York, 1915; copy in Moorland-Spingarn.

GEORGE WHITE'S SCANDALS (1921, 1922, 1926, and 1931 eds.). Series of white-oriented annual revues presented, dir. and choreographed by °George White. Music by various composers. These four eds. are significant because of their black content.

1921 ed. Included a popular sketch and songs about black life on the old plantation, with Theresa Gardella as Aunt Jemima and comedian °Lou Holtz in blackface. Prod. at the Liberty Theatre, New York, 1921.

1922 ed. For one perf., this ed. included a blackface jazz opera, composed by °George Gershwin, entitled *Blue Monday Blues* (see separate entry), about black life during the 1920s, with music arranged by black musician Will Vodery. It was presented as the opening number of Act II. The opera was dropped from the show after opening night, ostensibly because of its length, and later presented at Carnegie Hall in 1925, under a new title and with different orchestrations. Vodery's orchestrations are located in the George Gershwin Collection, Music Collection/LC. Prod. on Bway at the Globe Theatre, 1922.

1926 ed. A lavish prodn., built around the theme "Birth of the Blues," which included W. C. Handy's "The Memphis Blues" and "St. Louis Blues," as well as George Gershwin's *Rhapsody in Blue.*

1931 ed. Included a song, with music by °Ray Henderson and lyrics by °Lew Brown, entitled "That's Why Darkies Were Born," sung by °Everett Marshall in blackface. The song was a philosophical justification of black subservience, assuming that blacks were born to perform cheerfully the menial labor that whites did not wish to do. °Ethel Merman was also in this show, which was prod. on Bway at the Apollo Theatre, 1931.

FURTHER REFERENCE: *AmMusTh* (Bordman). *BesPls 1921–22; 1931–32. BlkMusTh* (Woll).

GEORGIA PEACHES (1929). Touring revue. Prod. by Jenkins & Idaho (Hezekiah Jenkins and [Bertha] Idaho Jordan), who also costarred. Cast also included Willie Holmes, Herman Higgs, Willie Mitchell, and Jessie Wilson.

GEORGIA RED HOTS (1924–26). Touring revue in at least two eds. Prod. by Jimmy Cox (principal comedian). *1924 ed.* Cast also included Anna Mae Cox (leading lady), Parlee Cox, Baby Ernestine Jones (singer), Leroy Johnson (comedian), Master Henry Thomas (dancer), Billy Wright (straight man), Mabel Granger, and Madam Pearl Jones (pianist). *1926 ed.* Cast also included Gertrude "Baby" Cox, Betty Snow, Clarkston (strong man), and Lee & Eckart.

GET HAPPY (1925–27). Touring revue in at least three eds.: 1925, 1926, and 1927. Prod. by William Benbow. *1925 ed.* Cast included Benbow, Shorty Edwards, Deatta [*sic*] Robinson, Margie Cohen, Odell Irvins, "Rastus" Winfield, and Elnora Mantley. *1926 ed.* Cast included Benbow, Edwards, Mabel Jones, Henrietta Leggett, Ozie Stennis, and Zue [*sic*] Robinson and his Jazz Band. *1927 ed.* Toured Cuba, presumably with the same cast as the 1926 ed.

GET-IT-FIXED (1925). Touring revue. Prod. by and costarring comedian Joe Bright. Cast also included Dink Stewart, Andrew Tribble, Eddie Lemons, Maybella Brown, and Millie Holmes.

GET LUCKY (1934–35). Musical revue in at least two eds. Prod. in Harlem and on tour mainly by Quintard Miller. *1934 ed.* Book by Quintard Miller and Flournoy E. Miller. Cast included Q. Miller, Billy Mitchell, Sammy Ayer, Oliver Childs, Cook & Brown, Margaret Cosby, Hattie Knowles, Joseph Stubbs, and Margaret Watkins. *1935 ed.* Co-prod. by Marcus Slayter, who also costarred with Q. Miller. Also in the cast were Butterbeans & Susie, Billie Hunter, Joe Paige, the Three Red Hots, and the Hot Dixie Club Orchestra.

GET SET (1923; revived 1926). Musical revue. 2 acts. Book by Joe Bright. Music and lyrics by Donald Heywood and Porter Grainger. Additional music by Rob Ricketts and William Benton Overstreet. Dances by Lee "Boots" Marshall and John Dancy.

Ethel Waters appeared in this revue, which revolved around the efforts of the wife of a Kentucky soldier of fortune to get into society. Synopsis of scenes: Act I—Lawn and garden of Mr. Douglass, Louisville, KY. Act II, Scene 1—Lobby, Dunbar Hotel; Scene 2—State Street, Chicago; Scene 3—Ball Room, Star Casino, Chicago.

Prod. in Harlem and on tour, 1923, by the Harlem Producing Co. (consisting of Joe Bright in partnership with °Mann & Luigi). Revived in 1926. Most of the following cast members appeared in both prodns.: Lawrence Chenault (Fred Douglass, Soldier of Fortune), Henry Rector (Officer L. C. All), Walter Richardson (Grafton Smooth, a Schemer), Bennie Clark (Bud Feret, a Secret Service Man), Hilda Thompson (Mrs. Douglass, "Trying to Get into Society"), Jennie Plate (Clementina, a Flapper), Ruby [or Rubie] Mason (Dolly Jess, Town's Fashionplate), Mabel Johnson (Mandy Snow, a Lady of Color), Rose Brown (Dot, "the Pride of the Town"), Ida Anderson (Madam LaRue, a Society Leader), Tootsie Delks (Dolly Springtime, a Village Belle), Ella Deas (Senorita Lopez, "a Butterfly" from Old Madrid), Louise Dunbar (Pansy Blossom, from Boston), Mattie Harris (Madam Jack, of the Opera), Edna Scotron (Marie Antoinette, from Paris), Lloyd G. Gibbs (Messenger Boy, "all His Life"), Joe Bright and Joe Russell (Isthmus and Peninsula, "Two Unbleached Americans"),

Ethel Williams (singer), Jessie Lawson (singer), Ethel Waters ("the Famous Black Swan Recording Star"), and Donald Heywood (accompanist).

Songs and musical numbers: Act I—Opening (Company), "Tee-dle-oo" (Brown & Dancing Girls), "Two Eyes in Dixie" (Clark & Chorus), Dancing Specialty (Richardson & Chorus), "They Won't" (Bright & Ponies), "Hoo Che Ans" (Deas & Senoritas), "Jigi Hoo" (Bright & Brown), "Melody of Love" (Richardson & Mason), "Old Kentucky Blues" (Russell & Dancing Girls), Finale, Act I (Mason & Company). Act II—"Pay Day" (Ensemble), "Strolling" (Company), "Get Set" (Williams), "Shake It" (Delks & Dancing Girls), "Linda Lee" (Lawson & Dandies), "Georgia" (Russell), "Jimmie and Charlie" (Mason, Boys & Girls), 'The Treat of the Evening' (Ethel Waters), 'A Few Moments With . . . ' (Heywood & Richardson), Grand Finale, "Let's Forget Bandana Days" (Company).

GETTIN' HOT (1928). Touring revue. Prod. by and costarring dancer/choreographer Speedy Smith. Cast also included Sadie Crawford, Zudora DeGaston, Jessie Love, George Lynch, Pete Peterson, and Billy Wilson.

GINGERSNAPS (1929–30). Musical revue. Equivalent of 2 acts. Book and lyrics by J. Homer Tutt, Donald Heywood, and George Morris. Music arranged by Heywood and perfd. by his Band. Dances arranged by George Stamper.

Using the metaphor of gingersnaps in a carton, the show consisted of two "Cartons" of "Snaps." The first carton (or act) consisted of 7 snaps; the second of 11 snaps. The snaps were a series of comedy skits, dance numbers, and songs. Dances were perfd. mainly by the Five Hot Shots, the Snapperettes, Bobby DeLeon, and Frank "Pimples" Davis. Songs were rendered mainly by Barrington Guy, Roscoe "Red" Simmons, and the Southland Choir. Among the skits were 'A Foul Deed' (about the purloining of a chicken), 'In and Out Again' (a prison skit), 'Sambo's in the Movies' (a parody of stereotypes in Hollywood films), a 'Travesty on [the film] "Hallelujah",' 'My Jungle Home' (a spoof of Tarzan), 'Change My Luck' (a scene between a janitor and a scrubwoman), and 'He Always Gets His Man' (a skit on the Canadian mounted police). Critics found the show amateurish, glum, and inept. The *NYT* (1–1–1930) considered the sketches humorless and pointless, and only the dancing was praised.

The show may have toured prior to opening at the Belmont Theatre in New York on Dec. 31, 1929, for 7 perfs. Cast included J. Homer Tutt, Vivian Baber, Barrington Guy, Roscoe Simmons, Donald Heywood, George Stamper, Selma Smith, Bobby DeLeon, John Lee, James Monday, Bertha Wright, Walter Meadows, Boots Swan, Frank Davis, and the Southland Choir.

Songs and musical numbers: "Let's Make Hey, Hey (While the Sun Is Shinin')," "Big Boy, I Gotta Belong to You," "I'll Do Anything for Love," and the finale, "You're Something to Write Home About."

THE GIRL FROM DIXIE (1902). White-oriented musical comedy. 2 acts. Book by °Harry B. Smith. Written as a starring vehicle for his wife, °Irene Bentley. Music and lyrics by several writers, headed by Bob Cole, J. Rosamond Johnson, and James Weldon Johnson. °A. E. Aarons, the orig. composer, resigned from the show when he learned that he would be working with a team of black songwriters.

About a well-born but impoverished southern belle who is courted by a titled Englishman whose love she spurns. She, in turn, is attracted by a young man who believes that she is an heiress, and who spurns her when he finds out that she is not.

Prod. at the Madison Square Theatre, New York, opening Dec. 14, 1903, for 26 perfs.; costarring Bentley in the title role and °Frederick Gottschalk as the spurned Englishman who apparently finally wins the girl.

Cole and the Johnson Brothers contributed 6 songs, including "When the Moon Comes Peeping O'er the Hill," sung by Bentley, and pub. by Joseph W. Stern, New York; copy in Moorland-Spingarn.
FURTHER REFERENCE: *AmMusTh* (Bordman). *BesPls 1899–1909*.

THE GIRL FROM PHILLY (1924). Touring revue. Prod. by and costarring Drake & Walker (Henry Drake and Ethel Walker [Mrs. Drake]). Cast also included Alta Oats, Willie Drake (straight man), George Crawford, and "Sambo" Reid.

THE GIRL FROM UTAH (1914). Musical play. Book by °James T. Tanner. Lyrics by °Adrian Ross and °Percy Greenback. Music by °Paul Rubens and °Sidney Jones. With several additional musical numbers by °Jerome Kern, and one song by Chris Smith and James Reese Europe. About a woman who runs from Utah to London to escape an objectionable marriage to a Mormon. There she meets an actor, a butcher, and (to be expected) the Mormon who has followed her. The story ends happily when the Mormon agrees that the actor would make her the best husband, and returns to Utah. Prod. by °Charles Frohman on tour, prior to opening at the Knickerbocker Theatre, New York, Aug. 24, 1914, for 120 perfs. Returned for a second engagement in the summer of 1915. During its tour, the Chris Smith/James Reese Europe song was added—"Balling the Jack," which was first introduced in *The Darktown Follies*.

THE GIRL WITH THE BEAUTY SPOT (1923). Touring revue. Featuring India Edwards, Will Jeedman, Josephine Leggett, Sylvia Mitchell, Medell Thomas, and Edward Williams.

THE GIRL WITH THE GREEN EYES (c. 1903). White-oriented musical revue. Authorship unknown. Included a song by Sidney L. Perrin. Prod. by Charles Frohman in New York City, with an all-white cast that included °Clara Bloodgood, who sang "I Wants to Be Some Kind of a Show Girl Too," by Perrin; pub. by M. Witmark, New York; copy in Moorland-Spingarn.
FURTHER REFERENCE: *BesPls 1899–1909*.

GOD IS A (GUESS WHAT?) (1968–69). Subtitled "A Morality Play with Music." Presented without intermission. By Ray McIver. Music by Coleridge-Taylor Perkinson.

Employs elements of the minstrel show and vaudeville routines to satirize race relations in the Deep South. The lynching of a black man is averted in the nick of time by the personal intervention of God, who turns out to be (guess what?) . . . neither black nor white.

Prod. by the Negro Ensemble Co., at St. Marks Playhouse, New York, Dec. 17, 1968–Jan. 12, 1969, for 32 perfs.; dir. by Michael A. Schultz. Choreography by Louis Johnson. Cast included Arthur French (1st End Man), David Downing (2nd End Man), Julius W. Harris (Jim), Theodore Wilson (Officer), Clarice Taylor (Reba), William Jay (Boy), Frances Foster (Lady), Graham Brown (Voice), Allie Woods (Man), Judyann Jonsson (1st Extraordinary Spook), Hattie Winston (2nd Extraordinary Spook), Rosalind Cash (3rd Extraordinary Spook), Esther Rolle (Cannibal), Norman Bush (Priest), Mari Toussaint (Acolyte), and Graham Brown (Bla-Bla [God]).

Songs and musical numbers include "A Mighty Fortress," "The Lynch-Him Song," "The Sonny-Boy Slave Song," "The Black-Black Song," "The Golden Rule Song," "God Will Take Care," "The Darkies' Song," "The Sit Down Song," and "The Lynchers' Prayer."
FURTHER REFERENCE: *NYT* 12–18–1968; 12–19–1968; 12–29–1968.

GOD'S CREATION (1989). Subtitled "A Gospel Musical." By William Hardy, Jr. Described by *Blk. Masks* (Summer 1989) as "A foot-stomping, hand-clapping celebration depicting Biblical events." Prod. at Symphony Space, New York, July 8–Aug. 26, 1989.

THE GODSONG (1976). Subtitled "A Gospel-Rock Revival of James Weldon Johnson's *God's Trombones*." Also called a new American opera. Adapt. by Tad Truesdale, who also composed the music.

One of many musical adaptns. of Johnson's volume of 6 sermons retelling some of the major stories of the Bible, from the creation to the crucifixion. According to the *Soho Weekly News* (New York, 1–13–1977), "There's little that's original but quite a bit that's good," and goes on to praise the choral singing, conducted by J. Hamilton Grandison, the choreography of John Parks, and the performances of Loretta Devine, Rudy Lowe, Marcia McBroom (as Eve), Gaetan Young (as Satan), and Barbara Montgomery.

Prod. by AMAS Repertory Theatre, March 4, 1976; dir. by the author. Prod. by La Mama E.T.C. (Experimental Theatre Club), Dec. 30, 1976, with the principals named above. Prod. by the Macedonia AME Church at Queens Coll., New York, 1978. Prod. by the Hospital Workers Union, Local 1199, at Hunter Coll., New York, 1979. Listed as a new American opera in the *Metropolitan Opera's Central Opera Service Bulletin* (vol. 22, no. 2). Excerpts of the score were presented in a Composers' Workshop sponsored by the Metropolitan in

Lake George, NY, on Aug. 17, 1983. A prodn. was being planned by Woodie King, Jr., at the New Federal Theatre, Fall 1984, to be dir. by Tom O'Horgan, with the author playing the leading role of Narrator/Minister, and to tour nationally beginning in the spring of 1984; no record of the actual prodn.

GOD'S TROMBONES (1988–89). Gospel musical adaptn. of James Weldon Johnson's *God's Trombones* (1927). By Vinnette Carroll. Presumably based on Carroll's previous adaptns. of the same work, including *Trumpets of the Lord* (1963) and *The Great Gettin' Up Morning* (1963). First prod. at the Shubert Theatre, Philadelphia, Sept. 20–25, 1988; dir. by Carroll. With Ossie Davis, Al Freeman, Jr., Germaine Hawkins, and Theresa Merritt. Prod. and dir. by Woodie King, Jr., in association with the New Federal Theatre, at the Theatre of Riverside Church, New York, Oct. 4–Nov. 26, 1989. Featuring Theresa Merritt and Trazana Beverly; Dianne McIntyre, movement consultant.

GO GET IT (1922). Touring show. Prod. by and starring comedian S. H. Dudley. Cast featured Slim Henderson, John "Rareback" Mason, Sam H. Gray, Aaron Gates, Virginia Liston, Eva Metcalf, Grace Smith, the Wizard Quartet, and Oliver Blackwell's Jazz Orchestra.

GO BETTER REVUE (1925). Touring revue. Prod. by and starring blackface comedian John "Rareback" Mason. Cast also featured Eva Metcalf, female vocalist "Bobby" Covington, actress Blanch McLancom, Willie DeLoach, Mary Wood Mason, and Perry & Perry.

GO-GO (1923). White-oriented musical comedy. 2 acts. Book by °Harry L. Cort and °George E. Stoddard. Music by C. Luckeyth Roberts. Lyrics by Alex C. Rogers.
　　The plot turns on the confusion caused by two sisters—one living in France, the other in the U.S.A.—whose mutual boyfriend does not realize that they are twins until late in the show. Described by *Crisis* (6–1942, p. 194) as "the fastest white show on record," because of the energy of its syncopated jazz numbers.
　　Prod. successfully on Bway by °John Cort at Daly's Theatre, opening March 12, 1923, for 140 perfs., before being taken on the road. The all-white cast included °Josephine Stevens (as both twins) and °Bernard Granville (as the boyfriend).
　　Songs, which were considered competent but not outstanding, except for one number, "Rosebuds and You," included "Doggon[e] Whippoorwill," "Go-Go Bug," "Mo'lasses," "Struttin' the Blues Away," "Uno," and "When You Dance"; music and lyrics pub. by Shapiro, Bernstein & Co., New York; copies in Moorland-Spingarn.

GOIN' DOWNTOWN TO SEE JESUS (1978). "Disco-Gospel Musical" (Author). By Sylvia Woingust Branchcomb. According to Branchcomb, it was "written for the goddess of song, world renowned 'Queen Yahna,' and contains the message that "Jesus is within 'Love.' " First prod. in Yonkers, NY, Dec. 1978; then was taken on an extended tour of Africa, Egypt, Greece, and Germany, where it was twice presented at the Berlin Philharmonic to standing-room-only audiences. Also presented in Italy, France, Austria, Switzerland, Jamaica, and the Philippines.

GOIN' TO TOWN (1934). Musical revue. Prod. in Harlem, with a cast that included eccentric and acrobatic dancer Jazzlips Richardson, blues singer Ada Brown, singer Jimmie Baskette, Bill Bailey, Harry Swangegen, the Brown Buddies Chorus, and Russell Wooding's Choir.

THE GOLD BUG (1896). Subtitled "A Musical Farce." Book and lyrics by °Glen MacDonough. Music by °Victor Herbert, who later became a well-known composer of operettas. With interpolated comedy materials and songs by Williams & Walker (Bert Williams and George Walker).

Predominantly white, thinly disguised vaudeville show, combining elements of comic opera, burlesque, and farce. The plot was built around the appointment of a former government agent for Indian affairs—a man with a few skeletons in his closet and no knowledge of naval affairs—as Secretary of the Navy, in reward for his generous campaign contributions. The complications spring from the diastrous naval reforms which he institutes, as well as certain aspects of his past (including embezzlement of funds and desertion of his Indian wife by whom he has fathered a child) which come to light after his appointment. Most of the show takes place aboard a naval cruiser called *The Gold Bug*, where the incidental variety acts are also conveniently staged. (There is no relationship between this musical—as is often stated in print—and Edgar Allan Poe's short story of the same title.)

Significant as the first musical show in which Williams & Walker appeared. Prior to this, while performing their vaudeville act in the Midwest, they had received a telegram from the producers promising them an engagement in this show if they could get to New York by September 14, 1896. However, after their arrival, when they performed their act before a group of the producers' friends, they were told that their material was mediocre and that they would not be used. After an unsuccessful first-night opening, however, the couple were engaged on the second night, in a last-minute effort to save the show. Although they were a big hit, this did not prevent the show from folding after only one week.

Prod. on Bway by °Canary & Lederer (Thomas Canary and George W. Lederer) at the Casino Theatre, Sept. 21–26, 1896, for approx. 6 perfs.; dir. by °Max Freeman. The otherwise all-white cast included °Max Figman (Willet Float, Secy. of the Navy), °Molly Fuller (Wawayanda, his half-blood daughter), °Marie

Cahill (Lady Patty Larceny, a divorcée in search of a sixteenth husband), °Henry Norman (Doolittle Work), and °Robert Fisher (Constant Steel, a corrupt politician).

Principal songs and musical numbers by MacDonough & Herbert included "One for Another," "The Owl and the Thrush," "The Gold Bug March," and "When I First Began to Marry, Years Ago" (successfully sung by Cahill, who also stopped the show with two dance numbers perfd. with her ex-husbands).

No information is available concerning the musical interpolations of Williams & Walker, who were not an integral part of the show, and were not even listed by name on the program. According to °Allen Woll (*BlkMusTh*, pp. 34–35), "Their ragtime melodies offered a sharp contrast to Herbert's operetta-style score. In fact, many members of the orchestra claimed that they were unable to play the newfangled music."

FURTHER REFERENCE: *BesPls 1894–99. BlksBf* (Sampson). *Nobody* (Charters). *NY Dramatic Mirror* 9-25-1896; 10-3-1896.

GOLDEN BOY (1964–65). Dramatic musical adaptation. 2 acts [18 scenes]. Conceived and prod. by °Hilliard Elkins. Book by °Clifford Odets and °William Gibson. Based on Odets' play by the same title (1937). Music by °Charles Strouse. Lyrics by °Lee Adams.

A starring vehicle for Sammy Davis, Jr., begun by Odets, and completed by Gibson after Odets' death. The new musical updated the orig. script to the 1960s, and changed the story from that of a struggling young Italian violist who becomes a prizefighter to that of a black boxer struggling to overcome racial prejudice and to succeed and be accepted in the white world. On his way up, he has a romance with his manager's beautiful blonde mistress, played by Paula Wayne.

After a lengthy tryout tour, during which the show was completely revised, it opened on Bway at the Majestic Theatre, Oct. 20, 1964, for 569 perfs. Cast: Sammy Davis, Jr. (Joe Wellington), Billy Daniels (Eddie Satin), Louis Gossett (Frank), Johnny Brown (Ronny), Lola Falana (Lola), °Paula Wayne (Lorna Moon), °Kenneth Tobey (Tom Moody), °Ted Beniades (Roxy Gottlieb), °Charles Welch (Tokio), Roy Glenn (Mr. Wellington), Jeannette DuBois (Anna), Terrin Miles (Terry), Buck Heller (Hoodlum), Benny Payne (Benny), Albert Popwell (Al), Jaime Rogers (Lopez), Mabel Robinson (Mabel), Lester Wilson (Les), Don Crabtree (Drake), Maxwell Glanville (Fight Announcer), °Bob Daley (Reporter), °Ralph Vucci (Driscoll).

Prod. at the Auditorium Theatre in Chicago, April 23–May 25, 1968. Opened in London after closing in Chicago. Cast featured Davis in his orig. role, with the following changes in some of the roles: °Gloria DeHaven (Lorna Moon), Hilda Haynes (Ma Wellington [not listed in above cast]), Altovise Gore (Anna), and Ben Vereen (Fight Announcer).

Songs and musical numbers: "Workout," "Night Song," "Everything's Great," "Lorna's Here," "Here's a Party Going On," "Don't Forget 127th Street," "Tour," "This Is the Life," "Yes, I Can!," "Trio," "I Want to Be with You," "No More," "You're No Brother of Mine," "The Fight," and "What Became of Me?"

Libretto pub. by Atheneum; available from Samuel French. Cast recording issued by Capitol (SVAS 2124).

FURTHER REFERENCE: Alkire diss. *NYT* 11–8–1964.

GOLDEN BROWN REASONS OF 1926 (1926). Touring revue. Featuring Sarah Martin, Alvin Beman, Josephine Byrd, Happy Cole, John Henderson, Herby Leonard, Pete Nugent, Willie Rogers, Rogers & Rogers, Annie White, and 10 men and women in the chorus.

GOODBYE EVERYBODY (1918). Tabloid musical. Written and prod. by Billy King. Presented at the Grand Theatre, Chicago, then on tour; with members of the Billy King Stock Co., including Ernest Whitman, Bessie Brown, Howard Kelly, Blanche Thompson, Leon Brooks, and James Thomas.

THE GOOD MR. BEST (1897). White-oriented musical comedy. Authorship unknown. Included a song by Sidney L. Perrin and Charles Hillman. Prod. New York, 1897, with an all-white cast. The Perrin and Hillman song was "Mammy's Little Pumpkin Colored Coon[s]," a plantation slumber song; musical score by M. Witmark, New York; copy in Moorland-Spingarn.

FURTHER REFERENCE: *BesPls 1894–99.*

GOOD TIMES TONIGHT (1916). Touring revue. Prod. by and costarring Drake & Walker (Henry Drake and Ethel Walker [Mrs. Drake]). Cast also included male impersonator Jack "Ginger" Wiggins, Madeline Cooper, and William Bally.

GOREE (1989). Musical show. By Matselmela Manaka. A proud and joyful presentation of the African experience through song and dance. Joint production of the New Federal Theatre and the Theatre of Universal Images, presented at the Theatre of the Riverside Church, New York, Sept. 13–24, 1989; dir. by John Kani. Featuring Sibangile Khumalo and Nomsa Manaka.

THE GOSPEL AT COLONUS (1983). Musical adaptation of Sophocles' *Oedipus at Colonus*. 2 parts. Based on the version by °Robert Fitzgerald, also incorporating passages from *Oedipus Rex* and *Antigone*. Adapt. and dir. by °Lee Breuer. Music composed and arranged by °Bob Telson. First prod. by the Brooklyn Academy of Music at the Carey Playhouse, Brooklyn, Nov. 8–20, 1983, for 14 perfs. Returned for two additional weeks, Dec. 15–31, 1983, for 16 perfs. Reopened at Houston, TX, Grand Opera. Cast: Morgan Freeman (Messenger), Clarence Fountain (Oedipus), Isabell Monk (Antigone), Carl Lumbly (Theseus), Jevetta Steele (Ismene), Robert Earl Jones (Creon), Kevin Davis (Polynices); Chorus: Clarence Fountain and the Five Blind Boys of Alabama, J. J. Farley and the Original Soul Stirrers, J. D. Steele Singers, and Institutional Radio Choir. Opened on Bway at the Lunt-Fontanne Theatre, March 24, 1988. The 60-member cast featured many of the orig. cast members, including Morgan Freeman, Robert Earl Jones, Isabell Monk, Javetta Steele, and the Five Blind Boys, plus some of the country's greatest gospel singers.

THE GOSPEL GLORY. See *GOSPEL GLOW.*

GOSPEL GLOW / / Orig. title: *The Gospel Glory* (1962). Orig. subtitle: "A Passion Play." 1 long act, revised from its former 2-act version. By Langston Hughes.

Title revised to distinguish it from *Tambourines to Glory*, one of Hughes' more important plays. Described by the author (program notes), as "the first Negro passion play, depicting the life of Christ from the cradle to the cross." Utilized spirituals, gospel hymns, and pantomime for the purpose of telling the story.

First prod. under its orig. title at Washington Temple, Church of God in Christ, Brooklyn, NY, opening Oct. 26, 1962, for 2 perfs.; and in Westport, CT, 1962, for 1 perf. Prod. by the Wheatley Players at the dedication of the Don Valles Theatre, Cleveland, 1973.

Unpub. scripts of *The Gospel Glory* in Schomburg, JWJ/YUL, and in the Archives and Manuscripts Div., State Historical Soc. of Wisc., at Madison; earlier drafts also in JWJ/YUL.

THE GOSPEL OF THE HARLEM RENAISSANCE (1989). Musical retrospective. Written, dir., and prod. by Titus Walker. Based on the historical events of the Harlem Renaissance. Presented by the Ujamaa Black Theatre, at the Lincoln Square Theatre, New York, Aug. 2–6, 1989.

GOSSIPING LIZA (1931). Musical show. Featuring blues singer Bessie Smith. Prod. at the Standard Theatre in Philadelphia, opening July 6, 1931, for a two-week engagement; with a cast of 40.

THE GRAFTERS (1907). Musical comedy. Staged and possibly written by J. Ed. Green. Music by Joe Jordan and James T. Brymn.

About the difficulties encountered by a prosperous Washington, DC, businessman who wishes to use his money to improve his position in society. He falls victim to a number of schemers, including two con men who persuade him to invest his wealth in a stranded opera company.

Prod. by the Pekin Theatre, Chicago, March 1907. Cast included Harrison Stewart (Dusty Graball, a schemer), J. Ed. Green (Grafton Meatball, another schemer), J. Francis Mores (Terrible Turk), Lou Pennington (The Ambassador), Don Wormley (The Man with the Money), Lottie Grady (The Belle of San

Domingo), Aubrey Lyles (The Song Book Seller), and Nettie Lewis (The Soubrette).

Musical numbers included "Graft," "You Ain't Gotta Chance in the Dark," "Acting Ain't What It's Cracked Up to Be," "The Belle of San Domingo," "Every Day'll Be Sunday Bye and Bye," and "The Candle and the Star."

GREAT DAY (1929). Musical play. 3 acts. Book by °John Wells and °W. Carey Duncan. Lyrics by °William Rose and °Edward Ellison. Music by °Vincent Youmans, who also prod. the show.

White-oriented musical set on and around a plantation in New Orleans, which utilized a number of blacks in comedy, singing, and atmospheric roles as plantation hands, pickaninnies, etc., including baritone Louis Deppe (as Elijah), the comedy team of Miller & Lyles performing some of their blackface routines, and an energetic chorus called the Jubilee Ensemble, under the direction of Will Marion Cook and Russell Wooding.

Prod. on Bway at the Cosmopolitan Theatre, opening Oct. 17, 1929, for 36 perfs.

Songs included "Without a Song" and "Great Day," sung by Deppe and the plantation hands (chorus).
FURTHER REFERENCE: *AmMusTh* (Bordman). *BlksBf* (Sampson). *NYT* 8–9–1929; 10–18–1929; 11–3–1929.

A GREAT DAY IN N'ORLEANS / / *A Great Day in New Orleans* (1929–30). Conceived and staged by Flournoy E. Miller. Music by Jimmie Johnson (James P. Johnson). Opened in Philadelphia at the Pearl Theatre, Dec. 30, 1929, with a view to Bway prodn., "but never made it to New York" (*Chicago Defender* 1–4–1930). Included a company of 50 singers and dancers, and one known musical number: "Modernistic."

THE GREAT MacDADDY (1972–74). Dramatic musical odyssey. Also called "A Ritualized African/American event" (Prog. notes). By Paul Carter Harrison. 2 acts. Based on the novel *Palm-Wine Drinkard* by Amos Tutuola.

After the death of his father, a wealthy bootlegger, MacDaddy goes on a journey in search of the secret formula of a palm wine that was the basis of his father's successful business, which he hopes to learn from the Spirit of Wine. His odyssey takes him to a number of different places in the U.S. Midwest, West, and South, where he becomes involved with a number of different characters, including an unfriendly character called Scag (which is another name for heroin), who reappears throughout his journey in various disguises. Recipient of an Obie Award, 1973–74, as a distinguished play.

Prod. by the State Univ. of California/Sacramento, May 1972. Prod. by Black Arts/West, Seattle, WA, 1973. Prod. Off-Bway by the Negro Ensemble Co., at St. Marks Playhouse, New York, Feb. 12–April 14, 1974, for 72 perfs.; dir. by Douglas Turner Ward. With David Downing in the title role, later replaced by Robert Hooks and Cleavon Little, and Al Freeman, Jr., in the part of Scag. Revived by NEC, April 5–May 22, 1977, for 56 perfs.; again dir. by Ward. This revival had previously been presented in St. Croix and St. Thomas, Virgin Islands.

Pub. in the author's *Kuntu Drama* (Grove Press, New York, 1974).

GREAT TEMPTATIONS (1927). Touring revue. Prod. by Donald Heywood and Jimmy Marshall. Cast included "Dink" Stewart, Villa Colston, Percy Verwayen, Lottie Brown, the Four Melody Maids, Monroe & Daley, Edna Barr, Geraldine Gooding, Adell Hargrave, and Mildred Mitchell.

THE GREEN PASTURES (1930–35). Musical fantasy. 2 acts [18 scenes]. By °Marc Connelly. Based on °Roark Bradford's *Ol' Man Adam an' His Chillun.* Music by the Hall Johnson Choir.

A pseudo-folk fable and religious pageant which offered to white theatregoers what Sterling Brown (*Neg. Poetry and Dr.*, p. 119) has described as "Marc Connelly's version of what Roark Bradford said was a Negro preacher's version of God," in stories of the Old Testament as they might be interpreted to uneducated, Southern rural Negro churchgoers. Although it is comfortable today to point out the numerous stereotypes which this play perpetuated from the minstrel stage, as well as its distortion of the religious beliefs of the folk-Negro, the importance of *The Green Pastures* in the history of the American theatre cannot be overestimated. It was the most newsworthy play of its time, considered a masterpiece of American drama which won for the author a Pulitzer Prize in 1930. It had a record run on Bway and toured the country for a combined period of nearly five years altogether. It made a star of black actor Richard B. Harrison as "de Lawd" and, according to Edith J. R. Isaacs (writing in both *ThArts* and *NegAmTh*), made his name the "most famous of all Negro theatre names." Most of all, it provided jobs for dozens of black actors, actresses, singers, and other theatre artists during the depression era, which was also the theatre's most difficult decade.

The play, of course, was criticized by many blacks, who, according to Leonard C. Archer (*Blk. Images in the Am. Th.*, pp. 63–64), "did not like the basis for generalizing that all Negroes believed in a Black heaven, a Black God, and celestial fish fries." Oddly enough, one of the criticisms voiced against the play by the NAACP, through Dr. W.E.B. Du Bois, editor of *Crisis* (5–1930, pp. 162–63), was that although "in *Green Pastures*, Marc Connelly has made an extraordinarily appealing [and] beautiful play based on folk religion of Negroes," "some whites will not like it because it is too human and tragic with all its humor. But more Negroes will view it aghast because it will seem sacrilegious." Black playwright, critic, and educator Randolph Edmonds also supported this view in *Opportunity* (10–1930, p. 303):

[Negroes] cannot see how a fish-fry could represent [their] idea of heaven when they have been told all their lives about the golden stairs and pearly gates. God being Black is something they have never heard except as a humorous part of the Garvey [Back-to-Africa] Movement. They conclude that *Green Pastures* is just another play making fun of the Negro.

All in all, however, the prevailing view of black critics was similar to that of Sterling Brown (*Neg. Poetry and Dr.*, p. 119), who felt that the play was universal in its religious appeal:

Discerning critics have seen in *The Green Pastures* a statement in simple terms of the relationship of *anyone* and his God. . . . If the play is not accurate truth about the religion of the folk-Negro, it is movingly true to folk life. Reverend Mr. Deshee's Sunday school; the fishfry (which, though placed in heaven, is delightfully true to the delta country); Noah's wish for the second "kag"; young gamblers starting with "frozen" dice; honkey-tonk cabarets, magicians, country folk, city scoffers, the pure in heart, and the sinful; all of these make *The Green Pastures* a vivid resumé of folk types and folk experience. Most majestic of the folk scenes is the exodus: here in these marching people with their faces turned toward hope is a spectacle symbolic and moving. *The Green Pastures* is fantasy, but it is likewise simple profound reality. [emphasis added]

Synopsis of scenes: Act I—Scene 1, The Sunday School; Scene 2, A Fish Fry; Scene 3, A Garden; Scene 4, Outside the Garden; Scene 5, A Roadside; Scene 6, A Private Office; Scene 7, Another Roadside; Scene 8, A House; Scene 9, A Hillside; Scene 10, A Mountain Top. Act II—Scene 1, The Private Office; Scene 2, The Mouth of a Cave; Scene 3, The Throne Room; Scene 4, The Foot of a Mountain; Scene 5, A Cabaret; Scene 6, The Private Office; Scene 7, Outside a Temple; Scene 8, Another Fish Fry.

Prod. on Bway at the Mansfield Theatre, Feb. 26, 1930–Aug. 29, 1931, for 557 perfs.; then went on U.S. tour until 1935. Cast: Charles H. Moore (Mr. Deshee); Alicia Escamilla (Myrtle); Jazzlips Richardson, Jr., Howard Washington, and Reginald Blythwood (First, Second & Third Boys); Frances Smith (Cook); J. Homer Tutt (Custard Maker, Ham & High Priest); Anna Mae Fritz (Mammy Angel & Second Woman); Josephine Byrd (Stout Angel, Voice in Shanty & First Cleaner); Edna Thrower (Slender Angel); Jesse A. Shipp (Archangel & Abraham); Westley Hill (Gabriel); Richard B. Harrison (De Lawd); McKinley Reeves (Choir Leader); Daniel L. Haynes (Adam); Inez Richardson Wilson (Eve); Lou Vernon (Cain); Dorothy Randolph (Cain's Girl); Edna M. Harris (Zeba); James Fuller (Cain the Sixth); Louis Kelsey (Boy Gambler); Collington Hayes (First Gambler); Ivan Sharp (Second Gambler & First Scout); Susie Sutton (Noah's Wife); Milton J. Williams (Shem); Dink Thomas, Anna Mae Fritz, Geneva Blythwood & Benveneta Washington (Women); Freddie Archibald (Flatfoot); Stanleigh Morrell (Japeth & Joshua); Florence Fields (Second Cleaner); Edgar Burks (Jacob); Alonzo Fenderson (Moses); Mercedes Gilbert (Zipporah); Reginald Fenderson (Magician); George Randol (Pharaoh); Walt McClane (General); Emory Richardson (First Magician); Arthur Porter (Head

Magician); Ivan Sharp (First Scout); Billy Cumby (Master of Ceremonies); Jay Mondaaye (King of Babylon); Ivan Sharp (Prophet); Leona Winkler, Florence Lee, Constance Van Dyke, Mary Ella Hart, and Inez Persand (King's Favorites).

Prod. in a film version by Warner Brothers, 1936; with Rex Ingram as De Lawd.

Songs and musical numbers: (A background of spirituals sung by the Hall Johnson Choir.) Act I—"Oh, Rise and Shine," "When the Saints Come Marchin' In," "Cert'n'y Lord," "My God Is So High," "Hallelujah!," "In Bright Mansions Above," "Don't You Let Nobody Turn You Roun'," "Run, Sinner, Run," "You Better Min'," "Dere's No Hidin-Place Down Dere," "Some o' Dese Days," "I Want to Be Ready," "De Old Ark's a-Moverin," "My Soul Is a Witness," and Entr-Acte—"City Called Heaven." Act II—"My Lord's a-Writin' All de Time," "Go Down, Moses" (Bass solo by Cecil T. McNair), "Oh, Mary, Don't You Weep," "Lord, I Don't Feel Noways Tired," "Joshua Fit de Battle of Jericho," "I Can't Stay Away," "Hail de King of Babylon!," and "Death's Gointer Lay His Cold Icy Hands on Me."

FURTHER REFERENCE: Alkire diss. Archer diss. *BesPls 1929–30; 1934–35; 1950– 51. Blk. Images in the Am. Th.* (Archer). *BlkManh* (Johnson). *BlkMusTh* (Woll). *BlksBf* (Sampson). *Catholic World* 5–1930. *Crisis* 5–1933. *Dramatics* 3–1971. *Golden Bk. Mag.* 5–1930. *Literary Dig.* 3–22–1930. *Nation* 3–26–1930; 4–9–1930. *NegAmTh* (Isaacs). *NewRepub* 3–19–1930; 6–18–1930. *New Th.* 7–1935. *NY Eve. Post* 3–21–1930. *NY Herald Trib.* 3–5–1930. *NYT* 2–27–1930; 3–9–1930. *NY Telegraph* 2–28–1930. *Opportunity* 5–1930; 10–1930; 9–1931. *Outlook* 3–12–1930. *Phylon* 1st qtr. 1959; 2nd qtr. 1959. *Wall St. J.* 3–31–1930. Woods diss.

A GUEST OF HONOR (1903). Ragtime opera. Written and composed by Scott Joplin. The first opera, now lost, by Joplin, who also wrote and composed **Treemonisha* in 1907. Advertised as "the most complete and unique collection of words and music produced by any Negro writer" (*Freeman* [Indianapolis] 9– 1903). According to *BioDAfMus* (Southern, p. 221), two of "its big numbers were 'The Dude's Parade' and 'Patriotic Parade.'" According to *DANB* (p. 370), it

was performed in 1903 in St. Louis by a group billed as Scott Joplin's Ragtime Opera Company, and presumably it was the chief attraction of their projected tour of towns in Missouri, Nebraska, Iowa, Illinois, and Kentucky, as announced in the *New York Dramatic Mirror*. At some undisclosed time, all traces of the score . . . unaccountably vanished. This unsolved mystery has tantalized successive generations of Joplin's admirers, who persist in believing that it will someday be found. On the basis of Joplin's known perfectionist standards, it is not entirely unlikely that he might have had second thoughts about his unpublished score and destroyed it himself.

GULLAH (1984). Musical. By Alice Childress. Music composed by her husband Nathan Woodard. Based on her drama *Sea Island Song* (1977), originally commissioned by the South Carolina Arts Commission. About the Gullah-speaking people of the Georgia Sea Islands off the coast of South Carolina. Prod. at the Univ. of Massachusetts, Amherst, Spring 1984.

GUYS AND DOLLS (all-black version, 1976). Musical revival with an all-black cast. Book by °Jo Swerling and °Abe Burroughs. Music and lyrics by °Frank Loesser.

One of several black versions of musicals originally prod. with a white cast. According to *BlkMusTh* (Woll), among the new features of this revival were "new orchestrations, more reminiscent of the 1970s, . . . and new choreography by Willy Wilson."

Prod. at the Broadway Theatre, July 21, 1976, for 239 perfs.; dir. by Wilson. Cast: Robert Guillaume (Nathan Detroit), Norma Donaldson (Miss Adelaide), Ken Paige (Nicely-Nicely Johnson), Ernestine Jackson (Sister Sarah Brown), James Randolph (Sky Masterson), Christophe Pierre (Benny Southstreet), Sterling McQueen (Rusty Charlie), John Russell (Harry the Horse), Clark Morgan (Lt. Brannigan), Jymie Charles (Augie the Ox), Emett Wallace [also Emmett "Babe" Wallace] (Arvide Abernathy), Irene Dutcher (Agatha), Alvin Davis (Calvin), Marion Moore (Matha), Derrick Bell (Joe Biltmore & Waiter), Andy Torres (M.C. & Drunk), Prudence Darby (Mimi), Edye Byrdie (Gen. Cartwright), and Walter White (Big Jule).

H

HAARLEM NOCTURNE (1983). Musical retrospective. 2 acts. Conceived by Andre De Shields. Cowritten and dir. by DeShields and °Murray Horowitz. Vocal arrangements by °Marc Shaiman. A celebration of New York City's history through songs, dances, and production numbers. Prod. by LaMama E.T.C. (Experimental Theatre Club), New York, 1983, where it had a long and successful run. Expanded for Bway, opening at the Latin Quarter, Oct. 30–Dec. 30, 1984, for 64 perfs., where, according to Arnold Shaw (*Blk. Pop. Mus. in Am.*, p. 299), it "brought the famous and capacious Latin Quarter back into operation." Starring De Shields, and featuring Debra Byrd, Ellia English, Marc Shaiman, and Freida Williams. Music included jazz, blues, gospel, pop, R&B, and rock. Among the sketches and production numbers were 'New York Is a Party,' which is a description of the musical itself; 'The Sermon,' about racism in America; and 'Jungle Hiphop,' which makes the same point with music and humor.

HALLELUJAH, BABY! (1967–68). Musical history. 2 acts. Book by °Arthur Laurents. Music by °Jule Styne. Lyrics by °Betty Comden and °Adolph Green.

A musical pageant of racial problems in the United States, both in and out of the theatre, which apparently promised more than it delivered, as "the majority of [daily newspaper] reviews," according to Stephen Robert Alkire (Ph.D. diss., p. 498n), "faulted the book's simplistic and superficial treatment of black-white relations," and "reviews in weekly periodicals were even more harshly critical."

As the four main black characters move agelessly through the five historical decades, they shift their various roles in accordance with the prevailing race relationships of that decade. As Alkire further points out, "The intended effect is somewhat akin to that of time-lapse photography, for it enables the audience to perceive quickly and with clarity the authors' vision of the American Negro's long march toward equality."

Leading roles were played by Leslie Uggams (Georgina), Robert Hooks (Clem), Allen Case (Harvey), and Lillian Hayman (Momma). During the course of moving through the ages, Georgina plays a maid in a Civil War drama, a chorus girl in a Harlem nightspot, a servant during the depression, a performer in a voodoo version of *Macbeth* prod. by the Federal Theatre Project during the 1930s, an entertainer with a USO troupe during World War II, a stage star during the 1950s, and the first tenant in a newly integrated apartment building in the 1960s. Other characters move similarly in their relationships to each other and to the historical decade in which they appear. The production permitted a variety of musical, dancing, and singing styles, and many changes of costume. Winner of a Tony Award as best musical.

Prod. on Bway at the Martin Beck Theatre, opening April 26, 1967, for 283 perfs.; dir. by °Burt Shevelove. The rest of the cast (some racial identities uncertain) included °Justin McDonough (Captain Yankee), Lou Angel (Calhoun), Barbara Sharma (Mary), °Frank Hamilton (Mister Charles), °Marilyn Cooper (Mrs. Charles), Winston DeWitt Hemsley and Alan Weeks (Tip and Tap, dancers), Bud Vest (Prince), Carol Flemming (Princess), Darrell Notara (Sugar Daddy), °Chad Block (Official), °Alan Peterson (Director), Ann Rachel (Brenda), Hope Clarke (Maid), Clifford Allen, Garrett Morris, and Kenneth Scott.

Songs and musical numbers: "Back in the Kitchen," "My Own Morning," "The Slice," "Farewell, Farewell," "Feet Do Yo' Stuff," "Watch My Dust," "Smile, Smile," "Witches Brew," "Another Day," "I Wanted to Change Him," "Being Good Isn't Good Enough," "Talking to Yourself," "Hallelujah Baby!," "Not Mine," "I Don't Know Where She Got It," and "Now's the Time."

No pub. libretto. Cast recording by Columbia (KOS–3090).
FURTHER REFERENCE: Alkire diss. *BlkMusTh* (Woll). *NYT* 4–20–1967; 5–14–1967; 4–14–1968.

THE HALL OF FAME (1902). White-oriented musical comedy. 3 acts. By °Sidney Rosenfield. Music by °A. Baldwin Sloane and °Mae A. Sloane. Included a song by J. Rosamond Johnson and James Weldon Johnson. Prod. by the °Sire Brothers at the New York Theatre, New York, Jan. 30, 1902, for 152 perfs. With an all-white cast that included °Marie Dressler. The Johnson Brothers song was "Angemina Green."

HAM'S DAUGHTER (1932). Musical drama. Written and prod. by Dennis Donoghue. A reworking of his earlier musical *Malinda* (1929), with a view to Bway prodn. (Music may have been by Reginald Loving and Earl Westfield, as in the orig. prodn.)

The thin plot, similar to that of *Malinda*, concerns a naive young woman who is lured from her strongly religious home in the South, where she also has a devoted fiancé, to New York's Harlem, by a swindler who promises to help her realize her lifelong dream of becoming a professional singer. There he deserts her, and she has a number of devastating and disillusioning experiences before being rescued by a clever detective who takes her back to her family and her lover.

Presented at the Lafayette Theatre, New York, 1932, for a short run, but was unsuccessful in its effort to reach Bway. The cast was headed by Mary Jane Watkins (Eliza Jones, the singer), Alvin Childress (Slick Harris, the Swindler), and Lorenzo Tucker (Ned Daniels, the faithful lover). Other cast members: Thurston Lewis (Dad Jones), Trixie Smith (Mother Jones), Robert Johnson (Rastus), Marty Crossman (Detective Jim Bronson), Speedy Smith (Smitty), Millie Holmes (Emma), Ponchita Aublaunche (Kitty), Gwendolyn Clarke (Lola), Thomas Lee (Sam Wheeler & Prison Keeper), Allen Cohen (Police Officer), Victor Archer (Rev. Washington), Lawrence Lomax (Brother Amos), M. Holmes (Sister Freeman), Queenie Estwick (Margaret), and Dorothy Harris (Sister Mary).

THE HAM TREE (1911). Musical farce. 3 acts. Prod. by William M. Benbow and the Alabama Chocolate Drop Co. Cast included William and Edna Benbow, Mose Graham, and Rebecca Kinzy.

A HAND IS ON THE GATE / / Orig. title: *An Evening of Negro Poetry and Folk Music* (1966, revised 1976). Theatrical collage. 2 parts. Conceived, arranged, and dir. by Roscoe Lee Browne. Readings from the works of black authors and renditions of folk songs, to tell the story of the black man from his roots in Africa through slavery to his present status in America. First prod. Off-Bway, under its orig. title, by the New York Shakespeare Festival, at the Delacorte Theatre in Central Park, Aug. 15, 1966, for 1 perf. Opened on Bway, under its present title (taken from a poem by Arna Bontemps), at the Longacre Theatre, Sept. 21, 1966, for 21 perfs. Cast: Leon Bibb, Roscoe Lee Browne, Gloria Foster, Moses Gunn, Ellen Holly, James Earl Jones, Josephine Premice, and Cicely Tyson. Prod. as an all-black showcase by the Ohio Univ. School of Theatre, Athens, OH, during the 1968–69 season. Prod. Off-Bway by the Afro-American Studio, opening Nov. 1974, continuing through 1975; dir. by Ernie McClintock. Revived, under the title *A Hand Is on the Gate—'76*, March 5, 1976; also dir. by McClintock. Cast recording of the Bway prodn released by Verve/Folkways (FVS 9040–2).

HANG TOUGH (c. 1989). Musical drama. By Useni Eugene Perkins. Music by Ernest McCarty. Deals with the struggle of a young man who must choose between a lucrative basketball career and preparing himself for other important options in life. Prod. by the ETA Creative Arts Foundation, Chicago, c. 1989; dir. by Songodina Ifatunji.

HANSEL AND GRETEL (1950). Translation of the Humperdinck opera. By Townsend Brewster. Broadcast by the NBC Television Opera, 1950.

HAPPY DAYS (1924). Touring vaudeville revue. Featuring the Dancing Demons, Bill H. Ward, and Frank R. Murphy.

HAPPY DAYS IN DIXIE (1925). Touring vaudeville revue. Prod. by and costarring comedian Joe Carmouche and his partner Cleo Mitchell. Cast also included comedian S. H. Dudley, "Buckwheat" Stringer, "Sugarfoot" Mitchell, Zachariah White, George Green, Nathaniel Lane, and James Cash.

HAPPY GIRLS (1912–13). White-oriented musical revue. With music by Will Vodery. Prod. New York, with an all-white cast.

HAPPY GO LUCKY (1924). Touring vaudeville revue. With Madeline Ashton, Thomas A. Brooks, the Kelso Brothers, Juggling Delisle, Arlove Johnson, and Chester Nelson.

HAPPY GO LUCKY (1928). Touring vaudeville revue. Featuring Johnson & Lee, George Williams, Henry Williams, and William & Brown.

HAPPY SAM FROM BAM (1912). Musical comedy. Book and lyrics by Irvin C. Miller. Music by Henry Paschal, who also dir. the chorus. Prod. by black vaudevillian John Rucker's company in New Orleans, at the Temple Theatre, Dec. 1912. Company included Miller, Wallace and Nina Stovall, the Valeria Sisters (Lillian and Maye), J. C. Boone, J. Francis Mores, La Belle Glean, Esther Bigeou, Tillie Johnson, Beatrice F. Moore, Israel James, and George Allen. Songs and musical numbers, staged by Miller and J. Francis Mores, included "Goodbye Rose," "Dearest Memories," "You're My Baby," "The Undertaker Man," "Gee Whiz," "It's Tough to Be Poor," "Last Man," and "Molasses and Candy."

HAPPY TIMES (1930). Musical revue. Featuring blues singer Bessie Smith. This was the last big show that she starred in. Prod. at the Standard Theatre in Philadelphia, opening Aug. 11, 1930, for a run of 6 weeks.

HARDTACK JACKSON'S COMPANY (1922). Touring vaudeville revue. Prod. by and costarring blackface comedian Hardtack Jackson. Cast also included Joseph Jones, Baby Benbow, Eugene Jones, Peggy Richards, Jack Richards, Ida Wilson, Marie Biddings, and the Little Alton Choristers.

HARLEM BROADCAST (1936). Touring vaudeville revue. Prod. by veteran showman Irvin C. Miller. Cast included Marcus Slayter, comedian S. H. Dudley, Margaret Simms, Estelle Blackman, and Delores Smith.

HARLEM BUTTERFLIES (1926). Touring revue. Prod. by and costarring Quintard Miller and Marcus Slayter. Cast also included Inez Dennis, Amon Davis, Helen Dolly, and Emma Hawkins.

HARLEM CALVACADE (1942). Retrospective vaudeville revue. Assembled and prod. by °Ed Sullivan. With sketches, music, and lyrics by various black contributors named below. A nostalgic (but unsuccessful) attempt to re-create the atmosphere of a typical Harlem revue of the 1920s, with its lively dance routines, low blackface comedy, and past song hits, but the audience no longer found these palatable. Opened on Bway at the Ritz Theatre, New York, May 1, 1942, for 49 perfs.; staged by Sullivan and Noble Sissle. Music dir. by Will Vodery. Cast included Sissle, Flournoy Miller, Amanda Randolph, Tom Fletcher, and a host of other black stars.

HARLEM DARLINGS (1929). Touring vaudeville revue. Prod. by Charlie Davis. Cast also included Eva Metcalf, comedian Joe Byrd, Emmett Anthony, Cooper & Hunter, Sammy Payne, and Roscoe "Red" Simmons.

HARLEM EXPRESS (1945). Touring vaudeville revue. Prod. by veteran showman Irvin C. Miller. Cast included musician Shelton Brooks, the Three Hot Flashes, Billie Young, Margaret Simms, Irvin's brother Quintard Miller, Marion Davis, Boots Bryant, and Madeline Carter.

THE HARLEM FOLLIES (1927). Touring vaudeville revue. Prod. by Jack Gee. Bessie Smith starred in this show, and film star Lorenzo Tucker was in the chorus. Cast also included Clarence Smith, Dina Scott, "Long" Johnnie Madlock, James Collins, Tucker & Tucker, Louise Alexander, the Red Hot Chorus, and dancers Gert Darlin and Phillips.

HARLEM FROLICS (1925–27). Musical road show. Organized by and starring blues singer Bessie Smith. Toured for three years throughout the South, with annual revisions.

HARLEM GIRL (1930). Touring revue. Prod. by veteran showman Irvin C. Miller. Cast included musician Shelton Brooks and comedian Hamtree Harrington.

HARLEM HEYDAY (1973). Musical retrospective. A re-creation of the Harlem of the twenties and thirties, in songs, dances, and humor, for the 1970s generation. Prod. Off-Bway and on tour of colleges and universities by Voices, Inc., 1973, dir. by Roger Furman. Songs, all written by blacks, included "Honeysuckle Rose," "In My Solitude," "Love Will Find a Way," "I'm Just Wild about Harry," "Do Nothing 'Til You Hear from Me," "Darktown Strutter's

Ball,'' "Sweet Georgia Brown," "Nobody," "There'll Be Some Changes Made,'' and "Please Don't Talk about Me When I'm Gone.''

HARLEM HOTCHA (1932–33). Cabaret revue. Conceived and prod. by °Connie Immerman. Music by James P. Johnson. Lyrics by Andy Razaf. Presented in 1932 as a featured floorshow at Connie's Inn, one of the most popular Harlem nightclubs, frequented by white clientele. Connie's Inn Orchestra dir. by Don Redman. Also played for four weeks at the Lafayette Theatre in Harlem in March 1933; special orchestral arrangements by Sam Wooding. Cast of the Lafayette prodn. included Earl "Snakehips" Tucker, Bessie Dudley, "Jazzlips" Richardson, Paul and Barbara Meeres, the Lucky Seven Trio, Lillian Cowan and the Dixie Nightingales, Roscoe Simmons, and the Eight Dancing Fools. Musical numbers by Razaf & Johnson, all pub. by Handy Bros. Music, 1932, include "Aintcha Got Music" (a rhythmic spiritual), "Get Off," "Harlem Hotcha," +"I Was So Weak, Love Was So Strong," "Madame T.N.T.," "My Headache," +"Stop That Dog," "Summer Was Made for Lovers," and +"Yours, All Yours." Songs marked with a plus sign (+) are located in Moorland-Spingarn. **FURTHER REFERENCE:** *NY Amsterdam N*. 3–8–1933; 3–10–1933. *NY Sun* 11–12–1932.

HARLEM IS HEAVEN (1937). Touring show which featured Christola Williams.

HARLEM ON PARADE (early 1940s). Musical revue. By Noble Sissle and Eubie Blake (Sissle & Blake). Toured USO circuits during the early years of World War II.

HARLEM ROUNDERS (1925). Vaudeville revue. 2 acts. Prod. by Frank Montgomery. Musical dir., J. Rosamond Johnson.
   Popular revue of the mid-1920s, described by the *Inter-State Tattler* (3–6–1925) as "the cleverest combination put together [at the Lafayette Theatre] since the days of Leubrie Hill,'' producer of *Darktown Follies*.
   Prod. at the Lafayette Theatre in Harlem, Feb.–March 1925, for several weeks. Cast included Billy Higgins, Florence McClain (Mrs. Frank Montgomery), Billy Gulfport, Abbie Mitchell, Kitty Brown, Ed Peat, Will Brown, Eloise Bennett, Eddie & George, William Thrill, Dewey Weinglass, Jessie Crawford, George Phillips, J. Rosamond Johnson and his Troubadour Band, the Southern Four, the Bunch of Beauties and the Dancing Boys (chorus).
   Synopsis of scenes and musical numbers: Act I, Scene in Dixie—"Trucking Cotton" (Higgins, Gulfport, Peat & Men); "Honey Bunch" (K. Brown & W. Brown); "Alabam' " (McClain & Chorus); Comedy Scene (Higgins, McClain & Peat); "Too Tired" (K. Brown & Girls). Olio—Specialty (Peat), "Effervescing Lady" and "The Mysterious Bowl" (Bennett & Girls). Olio—Specialty,

"Follow the Swallow" (Eddie & George). Scene in Italy—Italian Number, "Rose of Montmartre" (Mitchell); "Does My Sweetie Do What I Want To?" (McClain); Hotel Chateau, Comedy Safe Robbery Scene (Higgins, Gulfport, and Lion[?]). Olio—Selections (Southern Four). Scene in Mexico—Indian Jazz (McClain & Indian Squaw); Specialty (K. Brown); "Phoebe Brown" (Bennett & Mexican Girls); Specialty (Gulfport); "Step on It, Johnny" (Brown & Company). Act II, Apache Scene—Apache Dance (Bennett & Thrill); Specialty (Higgins). Charleston Scene—"Charleston Town" (McClain & Charleston Rose Buds); 'Bomb Hit' (skit: Higgins, Brown, Gulfport, Peat, Eddie & George). Old Broadway Scene—Specialty (Weinglass, Crowford & Phillips; 'Holdup Scene' (Higgins, McClain, Gulfport, B. Brown, Eddie & George, K. Brown, & Peat). Monte Carlo Scene—J. Rosamond Johnson & his Troubadours. Russian Scene—Specialty (Gulfport & Brown), "Song of Songs" (Mitchell & Chorus), Russian Dancers (Weinglass, Dancing Demons & Chorus), Burlesque (Higgins, Gulfport & Brown, Peat). Finale (Company).
FURTHER REFERENCE: *Billboard* (J. A. Jackson's Page) 3–7–1925. *Inter-State Tattler* 6–3–1925. *"Keep A-Inchin' Along"* (Van Vechten).

THE HARLEM SCANDALS (1926). Touring revue. Prod. by and costarring Billy Cumby. Cast also included Bee Freeman, Jimmy Marshall, Edith Young, May Dewit, Eleanor Wilson, Jerry Wiley, Irene Louder, and Cooper & Thomas.

HARLEM SCANDALS (1934). Touring revue. Prod. by veteran showman Irvin C. Miller. Cast included Alta Oates, Edgar Martin, Ernest "Baby" Seals, one-legged crutch dancer Jesse James, Fred Jennings, and Teddy & Estelle.

HARLEM STRUTTERS (1925). Dance revue. Prod. in Harlem by classic dancer Ollie Burgoyne, who also perfd. in the show. Ida Forsyne was one of the featured dancers; Katherine Jacks was soubrette; Harrison Blackburn perfd. as a one-man circus; and the Harmony Four Quartet was the featured vocal group.

THE HARLEM STRUTTERS (1927). Touring revue. Prod. by and costarring comedian Clinton "Dusty" Fletcher. Cast also included ukelele king "Hard Back," Willie Mae, Marie Miller, comedian "Dollar Bill" Jones, Billy McKensey, and the "Won't Don't" Orchestra.

AN HAWAIIAN IDYLL (1916). Operetta. 3 acts. By Alice Moore Dunbar-Nelson. Music arranged by Etta A. Reach. Prod. as a Christmas entertainment at Howard High School, Wilmington, DE, Dec. 1916.

THE HEART BREAKERS (1917–18). Tabloid musical. Written and prod. by Billy King. King (as a detective) has been hired by a young woman's parents to spy on their daughter to prevent her from courting the man she loves. First presented at the Grand Theatre, Chicago, 1917, perfd. by the Billy King Stock Co. Again presented by the same group in 1918, with the following cast: King,

Howard Kelly, Georgia Kelly, Bessie Brown, Gertrude Saunders, James Thomas, and a group called the Beaus and Belles. Musical numbers include "Hid Away" (King), "Cotton Picking Time" (Brown), "Little Lump of Sugar" (Saunders), "Flirtation" (Beaus & Belles), and "Going Carolina" (Company).

HEARTS OF MEN (1922). Touring show. Prod. by Quintard Miller.

HEEBEE JEEBIES (1927). Touring vaudeville revue. Prod. by Jimmy Cooper; starring Butterbeans & Susie (Jodie and Susie Edwards). Featured in the show were the Five Crackerjacks, Gulfport & Brown, Brown & Marguerite, Octavia Sumler, Florence Parham, and Eddie Heywood and his orchestra.

HELLO DIXIE (1925). Touring vaudeville revue. Prod. by Andrew Downey. The show featured Gus Smith (J. Augustus Smith) and his wife Genee Jones, comic dancer George Williams, Broadway Eddie, Buck Price, Carrie Crutchfield, and Cecilia Coleman.

HELLO DIXIELAND (1920). Musical revue. Written and staged by Billy King. Prod. at the Grand Theatre, Chicago. Cast included King, Arthur Bruce, Lelia Mitchell, Birleanna Blanks, Clarence Beasley, and Charles Williams. Songs and musical numbers included "Mandy" (Bruce), "Yama" (Mitchell), "Don't Take My Blues Away" (Blanks), "Rose" (Hickman), "Come Back, Mandy" (Beasley), and the song whose title was to become one of the popular phrases of the Black Renaissance, "Hey, Hey" (Williams & Company).

HELLO, DOLLY! (all-black version, 1967–71). Musical comedy. 2 acts [15 scenes]. Book by °Michael Stewart. Based on *The Matchmaker* by °Thornton Wilder. Music and lyrics by °Jerry Herman.

Starring vehicle for Pearl Bailey as Dolly Levi, and Cab Calloway as Horace Vandergelder, in the well-known Thornton Wilder classic which tells the story of a middle-aged marriage broker who successfully makes a match for herself, while pretending to find a suitable mate for a wealthy Yonkers, NY, widower— who believes that he is going to get a young, beautiful milliner for his bride. Dolly removes her competition by matching her up with one of Vandergelder's employees, and the milliner's helper with another young man in Vandergelder's employ. She also arranges a match for Vandergelder's niece and the young man that she has been forbidden to marry. The big scene occurs in the Harmonia Gardens Restaurant in New York City, where the three other couples are assembled—all hiding from Vandergelder, who comes to meet his bride-to-be. After a series of comic disasters, matters are straightened out for a happy romantic conclusion. The show's big number, "Hello, Dolly!," is sung as she makes her entrance into the restaurant down a flight of stairs, while being greeted by the management and the dancing waiters as their favorite customer.

The show became a symbol of improved race relations in the theatre in the

1960s, and demonstrated that blacks could play roles originally written for white actors, and that these roles could be redefined by the black experience in such a way as to bring new dimensions and charm to many shows. As a result of the new vitality brought to *Hello, Dolly!* by Pearl Bailey, President Lyndon Johnson (who had used the title song as his campaign theme song, changing the words to "Hello, Lyndon") was on hand, along with Lady Bird, to greet Bailey when the show was brought to Washington, and they joined her on the stage for a rousing finale, which included a march around the orchestra seats.

In spite of the show's success, there were many critics who thought that an all-black cast was out of date during a period when integration was being sought by blacks in all areas of the theatre. But none could deny that the all-black *Hello, Dolly!* was a rousing success and a positive step toward opening up better employment opportunities for blacks on the Bway stage.

Opened on Bway at the St. James Theatre in Nov. 1967 for a long run, sharing the stage with the orig. version starring °Carol Channing, which began its long run in 1964. The Bway run was followed by a U.S. tour that lasted until 1971. Dir. by °Gower Champion. Cast: Pearl Bailey (Mrs. Dolly Gallagher Levi), Mabel King (Ernestina), Roger Lawson (Ambrose Kemper), Dianne Conway and Barbara Harper (Horse), Cab Calloway (Horace Vandergelder), Sherri "Peaches" Brewer (Ermengarde), Jack Crowder (Cornelius Hackl), Winston DeWitt Hemsley (Barnaby Tucker), Emily Yancy (Irene Molloy), Chris Calloway (Minnie Fay), Marie Bryant (Mrs. Rose), Morgan Freeman (Rudolph), Walter P. Brown (Judge), James Kennon-Wilson (Court Clerk), and Others: Townspeople, Waiters, etc.

Songs and musical numbers: "I Put My Hand In," "It Takes a Woman," "Put On Your Sunday Clothes," "Ribbons Down My Back," "Motherhood," "Dancing," "Before the Parade Passes Me By," "Elegance," "Waiters' Gallop," "Polka Contest," "It Only Takes a Moment," "So Long, Dearie," and "Hello, Dolly!"

Orig. cast album of the black version issued by RCA (ANL1–2849).
FURTHER REFERENCE: *NYT* 7–29–1967; 11–5–1967; 4–25–1968.

HELLO EVERYBODY (1930). Touring revue. Prod. by and costarring Henry Drake and Ethel Walker (Drake & Walker [Mrs. Drake]). Cast also included Sam "Bilo" Russell, Baby & Billy English, and the Harmony Four.

HELLO 19– [followed by specific year] (1919–22). Series of musical revues in at least four eds. Touring show prod. by Frank Montgomery, the star comedian.

Hello 1919 (1919–20). 2 acts [11 scenes]. Co-prod. by Florence McClain (Mrs. Frank Montgomery), who also costarred. As described by the *Chicago Whip* (7–4–1920), this edition began with

a minstrel scene [onstage] with Mr. Butler [endman] and Mr. Thomas [endman] sitting on miniature boxes on each side of a semicircle. At the center of the semicircle a gentleman [the interlocutor] was being interrupted by someone sitting in the audience with whom he took issue. After much nonsense, the gentleman in the audience was invited on the stage to do what he could and it proved to be none other than Frank Montgomery (the star comedian), who makes a nice prologue speech, accompanied by a sweet musical strain, and then the show began. The second act takes place in the Capitol, Palm Beach, the Boardwalk and a hotel lobby in the Island of Yap (last scene).

Cast included Early West, Tiny Ray, Clarence Robinson, Raymond Miller, Ardelle Townsend, Dink Thomas, Alice Ramsey, Willie Ingram, Millie Holmes, Marie Rich, May Bird, Willie Bird, and Nona Burke. Songs and musical numbers included "Hello Everybody" (West, Ray, Robinson & Miller), "Impossible" (Thomas), "Ballyhoo Baby" (Townsend), "Distinguished Ball" (Broadway Octet: Ray, West, W. Bird, Ingram, Holmes, Rich, M. Bird & Burke), "Yo Son" (M. Bird & Chinese Girls), "Sand Dunes," and "Great Big Baby Boy." Apparently toured under the same title, with a different cast, into 1920. Co-prod. by Florence McClain. Cast included Montgomery, McClain, Gus Butler, Dink Thomas, and Daisy Martin.

Hello 1921 (1921). Lyrics and music by Montgomery and Marie Lucas. Additional lyrics and music by McClain and Jim Vaughan. Musical arrangements by Lucas. Dance arrangements by Montgomery. Cast included Montgomery, McClain, Blondie Robinson, Chinese Walker, Toots Hoy, Pat Ford, Wells & Wells, Royal Sutton, James Jasper, Josie Graham Austin, Johnny Virgel, Alexander Peel, Eleanor Wilson, and the Montgomery Beauty Chorus.

Hello 1922. No information. Cited in *Billboard* (J. A. Jackson's Page) 7–2–1921.

HELLO, PARIS (revised ed. 1911). White-oriented "musical revuette." (Not to be confused with the orig. ed., which opened during the summer of the same year.) Dialogue (book) by °William LeBaron. Music by J. Rosamond Johnson. Lyrics by J. Leubrie Hill. Prod. at the Folies Bergere Theatre, New York, opening Sept. 22, 1911, for 8 perfs. With an all-white cast that included °Harry Pilcer, °James J. Morton, °Nita Allen, °Minerva Coversale, and °Zeke Colvan. Featured songs by Johnson & Hill included "You're the Nicest Little Girl I Ever Knew" (conversational song/dance), "Look Me Over" (syncopated rhythm), "Loving Moon" (romantic ballad), "The Siberian Dip" (dance number), "That Aeroplane Rag," and the title song, "Hello, Paris."

HELLO RUFUS (1922). Musical show. Cited in *Billboard* (J. A. Jackson's Page) 7–15–1922.

HELLO SAMBO (1926). Touring vaudeville show. Prod. by comedian Jules McGarr, who also costarred. Cast included "Kid Lips," Dorothy Scott, Jimmy Howell, Ethel Ogburn, Mabel Dilworth, "Buckwheat" Stringer, Melvin Hunter, and Beulah Benson.

HELLO SUE (1921). Touring vaudeville revue. Prod. by comedian Sandy Burns. Featuring members of the Sandy Burns Co.

HELLO SUE (1922). Tabloid musical. Book by Billy King. Music by William Overstreet. Prod. at the Grand Theatre, Chicago, with members of the Billy King Stock Co., including King, George "Hoss" Crawford, Marshall Rogers, Margaret Scott, and Rebecca "Dink" Thomas.

HENRI BOWMAN'S COTTON BLOSSOMS (1922). Touring vaudeville revue. Prod. by W. Henri Bowman, who also costarred with his partner, comedian Leroy White. Cast also included Bonnie Bell Drew as leading lady, James Phoenix, and Jessie Wilson.

HERE AND THERE. See *THE DARKTOWN FOLLIES.*

HERE 'TIS (1941). Touring revue. Book by Jesse James. Music and lyrics by Eddie Hunter and J. C. Johnson, who also perfd. Cast included "Peg Leg" Bates, Crip Heard, Joe Jordan and his Orchestra, Charlie Davis, Marion Worthy, and Deanie Larey.

HERE WE ARE (1928). Touring vaudeville revue. Prod. by Ed. E. Daley. Cast included Brown & Jones, Buster Newman, Grace Rector, Kitty Aublanche, and Spencer Barnes.

HER FIRST ROMAN (1968). Musical adaptation. 2 acts [prologue & 13 scenes]. Book, music, and lyrics by Ervin Drake. Based on °George Bernard Shaw's *Caesar and Cleopatra*. Starring vehicle for Leslie Uggams, who played Cleopatra. Prod. at the Lunt-Fontanne Theatre, New York, Oct. 20–Nov. 2, 1968, for 17 perfs. plus 21 previews; dances and musical scenes staged by °Daina Krupska. Cast also included Claudia McNeil as Ftatateeta and °Richard Kiley as Caesar. The 15 musical numbers included "What Are We Doing in Egypt?," "Hail to the Sphinx," "Her First Roman," "I Cannot Make Him Jealous," and "Caesar Is Wrong."

HEY, HEY! (1926–27). Musical comedy. Written and prod. by Amy Ashwood Garvey (Mrs. Marcus Garvey). Title based on a catch-phrase of the Harlem Renaissance. Described by cultural historian Harold Cruse as "composed of African, West Indian and American Negro folk elements, blended together (the author believed) in aesthetic, as well as historical unity" (*The Crisis of the Neg. Intellectual* [Cruse], p. 821). Two American black men, played by Sam Manning and George McClendon, having been evicted from their homes by their wives, travel to Africa (which they believe to be the original Garden of Eden) to try to locate their true soulmates, or the women who were originally made from their ribs. They find that the lovemates they are searching for are their own wives. Prod. at the Lafayette Theatre, New York, Nov. 1, 1926, for a limited engagement. Cast also included Alberta Bryne and Evelyn Ray as the wives. Apparently toured in 1927 with Sam Manning, Sam Davis (father of Sammy Davis, Jr.),

Charlotte Ringgold, Dorothy McClemont, Catherine Beas, and the Cottonbelt Four.
FURTHER REFERENCE: *Messenger* 12–1926.

HIDE AND SEEK (1924). Touring musical comedy. Prod. by Salem Tutt Whitney and J. Homer Tutt (Whitney & Tutt). Perfd. by the *Smart Set Co.

HIGH FLYERS (1921). Touring vaudeville revue. Written and prod. by song-writer Sidney Perrin. Cast included George Wiltshire, Iris Hall, Brooks & Jackson, "One String" Willie, Allen & Stokes, Margreto Rice, and Ike Thompson's 10-piece orchestra.

HIGH JOHN DE CONQUER (1969). Folk musical. Script by Marc Primus, who also dir. Music written and conducted by Bobby Banks. Based on the folk legend of High John the Conqueror. Prod. by the Afro-American Folkloric Troupe, at City Center, New York, opening April 23, 1969.

HIGH LIFE SCANDALS (1922). Touring vaudeville revue. Prod. by Benbow & Cohen (Beulah? Benbow and Margie Cohen). Featured Cohen, Harry Brown, George Green, Henrietta Lovelass, John Dunsey, May Smith, Mattie Miles, Bell and Dorothy Waters, and Macklin White.

HIGHLIGHTS OF HARLEM (1928). Vaudeville revue. Prod. at the Lincoln Theatre, New York, featuring Trixie Smith.

A HIP RUMPLESTILTSKIN (1969). Juvenile rock/soul musical. By Clay Goss. Hip, black version of the well-known fairy tale. Prod. by the Dept. of Recreation, Washington, DC, 1969; by Ebony Impromptu, Washington, DC, 1971; by Theatre Black, at the Third Annual Black Theatre Alliance Festival, held at Brooklyn Academy of Music, 1973; and by Summer in the Parks of New York City, 1974.

HIS EXCELLENCY, THE PRESIDENT (1914–15) / / A revised version of *The Wrong Mr. President* (1913–14). Musical comedy. 2 hrs. Book, lyrics, and music by Salem Tutt Whitney.
   The plot is presumably similar to that of *The Wrong Mr. President*, which turned on a story of two down-and-out "gentlemen of leisure" (Whitney & Tutt), who pose as the president and secretary of the Republic of Haiti at a swank reception, where they get into all kinds of difficulty, until the real president and secretary arrive, and the bogus Haitian officials are exposed. Tutt is not listed among the cast members of this revised version, which suggests that only Whitney was involved in the fraudulent scheme.
   Prod. by the *Smart Set Co.* in New York and on tour, 1914–15. Blanche Thompson was in the 1914 ed. Cast of the 1915 ed. included William "Babe" Townsend (His Excellency, O. Saymore), Salem Tutt Whitney (Dud White),

Greenberg Holmes (Monsieur LaFritz), Helen Harper (Mandy Simpkins), Frank Jackson (Senator Comeback), Pauline Parker (Lady Winterbottom), and Emma Jackson and Babe Brown (who performed a Letter Dance).

Songs included "All I Ask Is to Forget You," "Come Out, Sue," "For Honor," "Good Advice," "Have Patience, Don't Worry," "I'm Just a Pickaninny All Dressed Up," "The Intruder," "The Love You Can't Forget," "Romance Espanola," "The Smart Set Tango," "We Welcome Thee," "What You Need is Ginger Springs," and "When Your Country Calls to Arms."

HIS HONERY, THE JUDGE (1927). Vaudeville entertainment. Touring show that featured the Our Gang Revue Co.

HIS HONOR, THE BARBER (1909–11). Musical comedy. 3 acts [17 scenes]. Book by °Edwin Hanford. Music and lyrics by James T. Brymn, Chris Smith, and James Burrus (who was also a member of the cast).

Loosely modeled on the Williams & Walker and Cole & Johnson musicals, this show featured a series of vaudeville acts and comedy sketches built around the thin plot of Raspberry Snow (played by Dudley), who wishes to become barber to the President of the United States and to marry the beautiful Lady (or Lily) White. He goes to the White House, and is tranquilized by a navy doctor and forcibly evicted. He then falls asleep on the White House steps and dreams that he has bet on a racehorse, won a large sum of money, and that the president has invited him to the White House to be his barber. Just as he is about to realize his ambition, he awakens to find himself still on the White House steps. According to Gerald Bordman (*AmMusTh*, p. 266), the show was praised for its ragtime music.

One of the few black shows to reach Bway between 1910 and 1920. Organized in New York in 1909, it toured theatres in the South successfully, prod. by Barton & Wiswell. Orig. cast: S. H. Dudley (Raspberry Snow), Andrew Tribble (Babe Johnson), James Burrus (Mose Lewis), Lawrence Chenault (Capt. Percival Dandelion), Aline Cassals (Caroline Brown), Jennie Pearl (Lady White), Alberta Ormes [Mrs. S. H. Dudley] (Ella Wheeler Wilson), and Dudley's famous mule "Patrick."

Prod. by S. H. Dudley's *Smart Set Co.* on Bway at the Majestic Theatre, opening May 9, 1911, for 15 perfs.; dir. by and starring Dudley (Raspberry Snow). Cast: James Burrus (Mose Lewis), Will Grundy (Capt. Percival Dandelion), James Lightfoot (Wellington White), Elizabeth Hart (Lily White), Ella Anderson (Carolyn [Caroline] Brown), Alberta Ormes (Ella Wheeler Wilson), Andrew Tribble (Babe Johnson), Will Everly (a lion), George McClain (a bear), John Warren (a monkey), Aida Overton Walker (principal comedienne & specialty performer).

Songs and musical numbers: "Come After Breakfast [, Bring Your Lunch, and Leave 'Fore Supper Time]" (Dudley's famous song hit, which he included in most of his shows), "Merry Widow Brown" (sung by the character Carolyn

Brown, first portrayed by Aline Cassals), "The Isle of Love" (sung by Lady [or Lily] White, first portrayed by Jennie Pearl), "Rainbow Sue," "Consolation Lane," "Crybaby Moon," "Caroline Brown," "Corn Shucking Time," "Golly, Ain't I Wicked," "His Dream Is Over," "I Like That," "Let Him Dream," "Pickaninny Days," "Puerto Rico," "That's Why They Call Me Shine," and "Watermelon Time."

FURTHER REFERENCE: *AmMusTh* (Bordman). *Freeman* (Indianapolis) 1–8–1910. *Just Before Jazz* (Riis). *NY Age* 9–28–1911. *NY Dramatic Mirror* 5–10–1911. *NYT* 5–9–1911. Riis diss.

HIS HONOR, THE MAYOR (1918). Musical show. Prod. by the Lafayette Players, at the Lafayette Theatre, New York, 1918. Cast included Laura Bowman, Walker Thompson, and Sidney Kirkpatrick.

HIT AND RUN (1924). Touring vaudeville revue. 2 acts [18 scenes]. Prod. by and costarring dancer/choreographer Speedy Smith and actor Barrington Carter (Smith & Carter). Cast also included Andrew Tribble, Al Young, Sam Cook, Marion Davis, Estelle Floyd, Sterling Grant, Johnny Nit, Charles Prime, Garland Howard, George Myric, Charles Young, Mamie Lewis, and Howard Cook. Featured 24 songs and 4 specialty numbers.

HITS AND BITS (1922–24). Tabloid musical in at least two eds.: 1922 and 1924. Written and prod. by Billy King. The *1922 ed.* was presented at the Grand Theatre, Chicago, with members of the Billy King Stock Co., including Marshall Rogers, Margaret Scott, and Sarah Martin. Cast of the *1924 ed.* included "Buzzin' Sparrow" Harris and his wife, Alberta Harris.

HOLIDAY IN DIXIE (1916–22). Vaudeville revue in at least 2 eds.: 1916 and 1922. Touring show prod. by Will Mastin (Sammy Davis, Jr.'s uncle). *1916 ed.* Cast included Mastin, Vergie Richards, C. Owen, Cora Hunter, Alice Owen, Essie Wallace, Burt Smith, Sam Bailey, Arthur Malone, and Miles Williams. *1922 ed.* Cast included Ida Forsyne.

FURTHER REFERENCE: *Billboard* (J. A. Jackson's Page) 2–11–1922.

HOLLYWOOD REVUE (1930). Touring revue. Prod. by and starring film star Stepin Fetchit (Lincoln Perry) as principal comedian.

HOLLYWOOD REVUE (1939). Touring revue. Prod. by and costarring Flournoy E. Miller, surviving partner of the Miller & Lyles comedy team. In this show Miller was now teamed with film star and comedian Mantan Moreland. Edith Wilson was also in the cast.

HONEY (1924). Tabloid musical comedy. 2 acts [7 scenes]. Book by Flournoy E. Miller and Aubrey Lyles (Miller & Lyles). Music and lyrics by Porter Grainger, Rob Ricketts, and Joe Trent. Orchestra dir., J. Rosamond Johnson. Choral dir., Ricketts. Unsuccessful Miller & Lyles show, which toured in 1924. Cast featured Miller & Lyles, Doe Doe Green, Eddie and Julia Rector, Elizabeth Williams, Alma Daniels, Edgar Conners, Alonzo Fenderson, May Dent, George Stamper, Dorothy Rhodes, Juanita Boyd, and Zenaide Anderson.

HONEYMOON CRUISE (1935). Touring revue. Prod. by Earl Partello. Cast included Bea Moore, Ernestine McLain, Marie Wade, and Monzella Lewis.

HOOLA-BOOLA (1922). Vaudeville revue. Prod. in Chicago and on tour by Clarence Muse. Cast included "Babe" Townsend, Gladys Jordan, Evelyn Riley, E. C. Caldwell, Lena Wilson, Elsie Fisher, Dorothy Sweetny, Etta Thomas, and Carrie Hutt.

HOT CHOCOLATES / / Also known as *Connie's Hot Chocolates* (1929, revived 1935). Billed as "A New Tanskin Revue." 2 acts [20 scenes]. Book and lyrics by Andy Razaf. Sketches by Eddie Green. Music by Thomas "Fats" Waller and Harry Brooks.

This was a fast, funny revue, featuring comedians Eddie Green and "Jazzlips" Richardson, dancer Baby Cox, singer Margaret Simms, and jazz musician/trumpeter Louis Armstrong as a member of the orchestra. This show introduced "Ain't Misbehavin'," which later had a Bway revue named after it. It was one of the few shows of the late 1920s to create a sensation on Bway. Originating as a Harlem cabaret revue, it consisted of a series of sketches and musical numbers, which included lively singing, memorable solos, and choral singing.

First prod. by °Connie and George Immerman at their Harlem nightclub, Connie's Inn, before being brought to Bway where it opened at the Hudson Theatre, June 20, 1929, for 219 perfs.; staged by Leonard Harper and the Immermans. Revived 1935 (location unknown). The orig. cast (in addition to the above) included Edith Wilson, Jimmie Baskette, Billy Higgins, Cab Calloway, the Six Crackerjacks, Sam Wooding's Jubilee Singers, LeRoy Smith and His Orchestra, the 16 Hot Chocolate Drops (chorus girls), and the 8 Bon Bon Buddies (chorus boys).

Synopsis of scenes and musical numbers: Prologue (at Connie's Inn) (Porter [Richardson], Head Waiter [J. E. Lightfoot], Doorman [Clarence Todd], First Waiter [Jesse Wilson], Second Waiter [J. W. Loguen], Attendant [Thomas R. Hall], Master of Ceremonies [Baskette], Guests, Orchestra, Entertainers, 'Waltz Divine' [Paul and Thelma Meeres], The Club Revue: 'Pickaninny Land' [Parham, Crackerjacks, Hot Chocolate Drops & Bon Bon Buddies]). Act I, Scene 1—"Song of the Cotton Fields" (Wooding's Jubilee Singers), "Sweet Savannah Sue" (Simms, Paul Bass, Hot Chocolate Drops, Bon Bon Buddies & Jubilee Singers); Scene 2—'The Unloaded Gun' (sketch: Green, Bill Maxey & Baskette);

Scene 3—'Say It with Your Feet' (dance: Cox, Hot Chocolate Drops & Bon Bon Buddies); Scene 4—"'Ain't Misbehavin' '" (Simms, Calloway & Singers); Scene 5—Specialty (Rowland Holder); Scene 6—'Big Business' (boxing sketch: Kid Licorice [Richardson], Manager [Green], Promoter [Higgins], Reporter [Billy Maxey], Gamblers [Jesse Wilson, Dick Campbell & J. E. Lightfoot], Referee [Thomas R. Hall], Moving Picture Magnate [A. A. Haston]); Scene 7—"Goddess of Rain" (sung by Jimmie Baskette, danced by Louise Cook & Ensemble); Scene 8—"Dixie Cinderella" (Cox & Maxey); Scene 9—Negro Spiritual (Singers); Scene 10—Harlem Street Scene (Maxey, Calloway, Bernice Aiken, LaRoma Bradley & Frances Hubbard); Scene 11—"Black and Blue" (Wilson & Calloway); Scene 12—"That Rhythm Man" (Paul Meeres & Company), Finale Specialty (Louise Cook, Paul & Thelma Meeres). Entre'Acte—Trumpet Solo by Louis Armstrong. Act II, Scene 1—'The Wedding of the Rabbit and the Bear' (skit: Hostess [Wilson], Bunnies [the Meeres], Bear [Cox], Rabbit [Florence Parham], Fox [Calloway], Monkeys [Mary Prevall, Louise Williams & Natalie Long], Pussy-Cat [Simms], Frogs [Midnight Steppers], Sister Twister [Louise Cook], Jackass [Maxey], Zebras [Bon Bon Buddies], and Birds [Singers]); Scene 2—'Somewhere in Harlem' (sketch: Wilson, Green, Higgins, Baskette & Louise Williams); Scene 3—"Can't We Get It Together?" (Cox & Parham); Scene 4—"Redskinland" (sung by Baskette, specialty dance by the Meeres); Scene 5—(specialty: "Jazzlips" Richardson; Scene 6—'Traffic in Harlem' (sketch: Chaufferettes [Hot Chocolate Drops], Motorcycle Cops [Bon Bon Buddies], Sergeant [Maxey], Lieutenant [Richardson], Captain [Higgins], Specialty [Crackerjacks], Entertainer [Simms], Cabaret Girls [Hot Chocolate Drops], "Snake Hips' Dance" [Simms & Girls]); Scene 7—'In a Telegraph Office' (sketch: Clerk [Baskette], Hallow [Green]); Scene 8—"Off Time" (Simms, Bon Bon Buddies & Company).

Featured songs from this show, pub. by Mills, New York, included "Ain't Misbehavin'," which became a hit, and "That Rhythm Parade"; piano-vocal score of the latter is located in Moorland-Spingarn. Other songs were "Black and Blue," "Song of the Cotton Fields," and "Sweet Savannah Sue." Cast recording by Smithsonian (P–14589).

FURTHER REFERENCE: *Ain't Misbehavin'* (Kirkeby). *BlkMagic* (Hughes & Meltzer). *NYT* 6–21–1929. *Outlook* 7–31–1929. *ThMag* 8–1929.

HOT CHOPS (1923). Touring vaudeville revue. Book and music by Joe Trent. Prod. by °Nat Nazarro; dir. by Frank Montgomery. Cast included Buck & Bubbles (Ford Washington Lee and John William Sublett), George McGlennon, Sam Russell, Tony Green, Willie Spencer, B. Wiggins, Jean Starr, Gene Kane, and E. McKinney. Songs included "Hot Chops" (Buck & Bubbles) and "Moanin' and Groanin' '" (McGlennon on clarinet).

HOT DOGS (1922). Touring revue. 2 acts [12 scenes]. Prod. by and starring Irvin C. Miller. Cast also included Evon Robinson, Wilbur Blanks, Madeline Belt, Joe Peterson, Troy Brown, Doe Doe Green, May Barnes, B. B. Joyner, Clarence Foster, and Jimmy Ewell.

HOT ELLA (1929). Touring vaudeville revue. Prod. by and starring Ella B. Moore. Cast also included Brown & Brown, Jones & Johnson, Boyd & Boyd, Martin & Martin, and Lorine Winn.

HOTEL NOBODY (1917). Tabloid musical. Written and prod. by Billy King. Presented at the Grand Theatre, Chicago, with members of the Billy King Stock Co., including Howard and Georgia Kelly.

HOT FEET (1924). Vaudeville dance revue. Prod. by Jimmy Cooper in Harlem, at either the Lincoln or the Lafayette Theatre. Cast included Emmett Anthony, Bessie DeSota, Reuben Brown, Octavia Slayter, Joe Peterson, Gertie Miller, Sam Cross, Ida Roley, Bob Thompson, Hilaria Friend, and the Four Dancing Fools.

HOT FROM HARLEM (1931). Touring vaudeville revue. Starring Bill "Bojangles" Robinson. Cast also included Neeka Shaw, Jelli Smith, Putney Dandridge, Mary Prevall, and John Mason.

HOT HEELS (1930). Touring vaudeville revue. Prod. by °Louis Azorsky. Cast included Snake Hips, Jr., Buster Lee, George Cooper, Jr., Buddy Green, Billy Griffin, Marie Moore, and the Two Dancing Demons.

THE HOT MIKADO (1939). A swing version of °Gilbert and °Sullivan's classic operetta. Conceived and prod. by °Michael Todd. Book by °Hassard Short. Lyrics by °Dave Greggory and °William Tracy. Modern orchestral arrangements by °Charles L. Cook. Dances by °Truly McGee.

The second of the two most important black versions of *The Mikado*, both prod. on Bway in 1939. The first was *The Swing Mikado*, prod. by the WPA Federal Theatre Project in Chicago in 1938, which was so popular in that city that it was brought to New York the following year. When producer Mike Todd was turned down on his bid to purchase the rights to that show, he decided to bring out his own version, and was able to better his competition by casting the then 61-year-old Bill Robinson in the title role, decking him and the show with such expensive and gaudy trappings that they literally outshone the WPA version. As reported in Art Cohn's biography of Todd (*The Nine Lives of Michael Todd*, New York: Pocket Books, 1958, p. 72), Todd dressed Robinson from head to foot in solid gold (derby, suit, cane, and shoes), built a special floor of Bakelite for him to dance on, and provided onstage a volcano that really erupted and a waterfall of soap bubbles 40 feet tall—thus giving *The Hot Mikado* what Allen Woll (*BlkMusTh*, p. 182) has described as "a Broadway sheen that the FTP show could not hope to duplicate."

Prod. at the Broadhurst Theatre, opening March 23, 1939, for 85 perfs. That same year it played to capacity audiences at the New York World's Fair, then toured the country. Cast: Bill Robinson (The Mikado), Bob Parrish (Nanki-Poo, his son, in love with Yum-Yum), James A. Lilliard (Pish-Tush, a Noble Lord), Eddie Green (Ko-Ko, the Lord High Executioner), Maurice Ellis (Pooh-Bah, The Lord High Everything Else); Three Sisters, Wards of Ko-Ko: Gwendolyn Reyde (Yum-Yum), Frances Brock (Pitti-Sing), and Rosetta LeNoire (Peep-Bo); Rose Brown (Katisha, Prospective Bride-to-Be of Nanki-Poo), Freddie Robinson (Messenger Boy), and Vincent Shields (Red Cap); Others: Singing Girls, Singing Boys, Dancing Girls, Jitterbug Girls, Jitterbug Boys, "Tap-a-Teers," Guards, and Quartet.

Songs and musical numbers (Sullivan's music set to modern tempos): Act I— "If You Want to Know Who We Are" (Ensemble), "A Wandering Minstrel" (Nanki-Poo, Male Chorus, & Tap-a-Teers), "Our Great Mikado" (Pish-Tush, Male Chorus, & Tap-a-Teers), "Young Man Despair" (Pooh-Bah, Pish-Tush, & Nanki-Poo), "Behold the Lord High Executioner" (Ko-Ko & Male Chorus), "I've Got a Little List" (Ko-Ko & Male Chorus), "Comes a Train of Little Ladies" (Girls' Chorus), "Three Little Maids" (Yum-Yum, Pitti-Sing, Peep-Bo, Tap-a-Teers, Dancing Girls, & Jitterbugs), "So Pardon Us" (Yum-Yum, Pitti-Sing, Peep-Bo, Pooh-Bah, Pish-Tush, & Girls' Chorus), "Were You Not to Ko-Ko Plighted" (duet: Yum-Yum & Nanki-Poo), Finale of Act I (Nanki-Poo, Ko-Ko, Pish-Tush, Pooh-Bah, Yum-Yum, Pitti-Sing, Peep-Bo, Katisha, & Ensemble). Act II—"Braid the Raven Hair" (Ensemble), "The Moon and I" (Yum-Yum & the Harmoneers), "Here's a How-de-do" (Yum-Yum, Nanki-Poo, & Ko-Ko), "I'm the Emperor of Japan" (Mikado & Katisha), "My Object All Sublime" (Mikado), "Flowers That Bloom in the Spring" (Pitti-Sing, Yum-Yum, Nanki-Poo, Pooh-Bah, & Ko-Ko), Dance (Tap-a-Teers, Dancing Girls, & Jitterbugs), Dance (Mikado and Dancers), "I, Living I" (Katisha), "Titwillow" (Ko-Ko), and Finale of Act II (Company).
FURTHER REFERENCE: *BlkMusTh* (Woll). *NYT* 3–24–1939. *Variety* 4–12–1939.

HOT RAGS (1985). Ragtime musical retrospective. With Scott Joplin ragtimes. Co-prod. by °Rinaldo Tazzini and the Brooklyn Opera Society, and presented for four perfs., opening May 18, and continuing through May 26, 1985, at Prospect Hall in Brooklyn, NY. The premiere perf. was a Ragtime Gala Evening headed by singer/actress Pearl Bailey, which included dinner and dancing, to raise funds for the Brooklyn Opera Society and its Scott Joplin Memorial Scholarship. Choreography was by Henry LeTang. Costarring in *Hot Rags* were Ed Pierson, of the New York City Opera Co., and Ernestine Jackson, a Bway singer/actress.

HOT RHYTHM (1930). Musical revue. Subtitled "A Sepia-Tinted Little Show." 2 acts [25 scenes]. Sketches by Dewey "Pigmeat" Markham, °Will Morrissey, Johnny Lee Long, and others. Lyrics by Donald Heywood. Music by Porter Grainger. An additional song by Eubie Blake.

A Harlem song-and-dance show starring Mae [or May] Barnes, Johnny Hudgins, Eddie Rector, Edith Wilson, and Pigmeat Markham, which attempted unsuccessfully to imitate the type of smart, intimate all-white revue typified by *The Little Show* (1929) starring °Fred Allen, °Libby Holman, and °Clifton Webb, and the °André Charlot London revues starring °Noel Coward and °Gertrude Lawrence. The *NYT* critic (8–22–1930) praised the singing of Wilson, but considered the show "tasteless, pointless and a soggy rehash of preceding white and negro entertainments."

Prod. at the Times Square Theatre, New York, opening Aug. 21, 1930, for 73 perfs. Musical dir., Maurice Coffin; master of ceremonies, Eddie Rector. In addition to the above, the cast included Johnny Hudgins, Arthur Bryson, Johnny Lee Long, George Wiltshire, Amon Davis, Jarahal, Doris Rheubottom, Laura Duncan, Revella Hughes, Ina Duncan, Inez Seeley, Hazel Van Vlerah, Sam Paige, Slaps Wallace, Lois Simms, Buster Bowie, Al Vigal, Hilda Perleno, Willie Taylor, Billy Sheppard, Hendricks Mattingly, King Washington, Joseph Brown, St. Clair Dodson, Natalie Long, Mel Dumas, Freddie Waithe, Llewelyn Ransom, Larri N. Lorear, Madeline Belt, Tousaint Duers, Roland Smith, Ladies of the Ensemble, and Singers.

Synopsis of scenes and musical numbers: Act I, Scene 1—'Tree of Hope' (actors' wishing tree: Songs by Vigal & Dumas). Scene 2—Specialty (Nora Green, Seeley, Simms, Bowie, Dodson, & Taylor). Scene 3—'A Harlem Rent Party' (Long, Markham, Wiltshire, Wilson, Van Vlerah & Rheubottom; "Mama's Gotta Get Her Rent," sung by Wilson). Scene 4—"Say the Word That Will Make You Mine" (sung by Barnes). Scene 5—'A Harlem Spelling Bee' (Rheubottom, Wiltshire, & "a no-good brat"). Scene 6—"Loving You the Way I Do" (sung by Hughes, Vigal, Barnes, Bryson & Ensemble). Scene 7—'Rector Rhythm. 100° Fahrenheit' (Rector, Belt & Ensemble). Scene 8—"The Penalty of Love" (Seeley, Davis, Taylor, Wiltshire, Dumas, Sheppard, Long, & Markham; sung by Duers & Ensemble; Condemned man, Sheppard; Broadcaster, Hudgins). Scene 9—"Since You Went Away" (sung by Perleno & Vigal; danced by Simms & Bowie). Scene 10—'A Certain Lady on Trial' (Barnes, Long, Markham, Davis, Wiltshire, Dodson & Rector). Scene 11—Revella Hughes Trio, with Ina and Laura Duncan ('in sepia melodies' arranged by Hughes). Scene 12—'Floradora Sextette (A la Harlem)' (Ensemble: Post-Graduates & Hudgins). Scene 13—'Jarahal' (a gangster incident). Scene 14—The Cave, a hot spot in Harlem ([a]—Rector Girls; [b]—"Albany," sung by Belt; [c]—'A Harlem Skate,' J. McGarver; [d]—'Tumbling Around,' Baby Goins; [e]—'The Tornado,' Mr. Bryson; [f]—Finale, Sepia Vanities: 'Beautifying Harlem'). Act II, Scene 1—(a) "Up in the Sky" (sung by Seeley & Vigal); (b) 'Afro Fresh Air, Inc' (skit: Long & Markham). Scene 2—'In the Air' (?). Scene 3—'Anywhere in Africa' ("Tropical Moon," sung by Hughes & Ensemble; Dramatic Interlude, Sheppard). Scene 4—Sam Paige and Slaps (presumably a comedy skit). Scene 5—"Hungry for Love" (sung by Perleno; Cupid's Hospital: Nurses—Hughes with Laura & Ina Duncan; Dr. Smith, Wiltshire). Scene 6—Episodes of a Broadway Producer (Wilson, Vlerah, Wiltshire, Vigal, Markham & Rector). Scene 7—"Hot Rhythm" (sung by Barnes & Girls). Scene 8—'Miss

Wilson Struts Her Stuff' (Rector & Belt). Scene 9—'Othello—Put on the Spot' (Barnes, Long, Markham & Davis); 'Another Strange Interlude' (musical); 'Mr. Hudgins on the Old Sole Hour' (Hudgins). Scene 10—'Steppin' on It' (Rector & Belt); 'Arthur Bryson Shakes a Foot' (Bryson). Scene 11—Finale (Company).

"Loving You the Way I Do," with music by Eubie Blake, lyrics by Jack Scholl and Will Morrissey, pub. by Shapiro, Bernstein & Co., New York, 1930; copy in Moorland-Spingarn.
FURTHER REFERENCE: *Life* (New York) 9–12–1930. *NYT* 8–22–1930. *Variety* 8–27–1930.

HOT RHYTHM (1932). Touring vaudeville revue. Prod. by and starring Russian-style dancer Dewey Weinglass. Cast also included Sandy Burns, Billy Higgins, and George Wiltshire.

HOT STUFF OF 1933 (1933). Vaudeville revue. Starring Butterbeans & Susie (Jodie and Susie Edwards). Prod. at the Lincoln Theatre in Philadelphia. Bessie Smith, the blues singer, also shared top billing in this prodn.

A HOT SUMMER NIGHT (1984). Musical drama. Written and dir. by Grenoldo [Frazier]. In the glamorous setting of New Orleans, during the period from 1917 to the present, it explores the reasons that a romantic relationship went wrong. Prod. by LaMama Experimental Theatre Club (E.T.C.), Dec. 28, 1983–Jan. 12, 1984.

HOTTENTOT REVUE (1925). Touring vaudeville revue. Prod. by and co-starring Petway & Rector (Eddie Rector and Ed. Peat, comedian/singer/dancer). Cast also included "Onions" Jeffrey, Aaron Thompson, Aconia Turner, Shirley Abby, and the Ten Dixie Dandies Band.

HOTTENTOTS OF 1930 (1929–30). Touring vaudeville revue. Featured dancer Beulah Benbow, Lilly Yuen, Marion Moore, Midget George Brown, and Rastus Airship.

HOTTEST COON IN DIXIE (1906). Vaudeville show. 2 parts. Book and lyrics by °Ferdos & °Carter. Music by °George Bryant.

Touring show, organized along minstrel lines, featuring comedian Andrew A. Copeland in the title role. The first part apparently involved a horse racing plot. Cast: Copeland (Jeff Jackson, Hottest Coon in Dixie), H. M. Prince (Lilly Snow White, "Jeff's means of support"), Josephine Lazzo (Mamie Brown, "just back from college"), Thomas Deaker (Parson Brown, "typically Southern"), L. E. Gideon (Nancy Brown, Parson's wife), Emma Prince (Sue Simpkins, "very kittish"), Sidney H. Carter (Will Daily, club man), J. A. English (Jube Jones, "race horse tout"), Clarence Dotson (Rastus Brown, "just for fun"), Amos Scruggs (Miss Eater), Earl Burton (Mose Jenkins, "the law"), and Will Burton

(Isaac Murphy, jockey). The second part, the Olio, included the following specialties: Queen Dora (Manipulation in flames), Clarence Dotson (Song and dance), Marvelous Petitts (Magic), Dixie Comedy Four (Musical selections), and the Great English (Hoop manipulator).

Songs and musical numbers: "My Old Kentucky Home" (Edyth Drake and Chorus), "Allus de Same in Dixie" (Josephine Lazzo and Chorus), "All Wise Chickens Follow Me" (Copeland), "Love Me and the World Is Mine" (Irving Richardson), "I Like Your Way" (Sidney Carter & Chorus), "I Don't Know Where I'm Going, But I'm on My Way" (Prince), and "Sweet Mamie" (Copeland & Chorus).

THE HOTTEST COON IN DIXIE (1911–12). Vaudeville revue. May have been a revival of the 1906 show cited above, or a different show using the same title. Toured for two seasons with the following cast: Harry Morgan, Bud Halliday, Alan Richardson, Viola Harris, Otis Benson, and Alex Wheeler's Rag Time Band.

HOUND DOG PARTY (1974). Variety show created and perfd. by workshop members of the AMAS Repertory Theatre, New York. Prod. New York, June 9, 1971, under the direction of Rosetta LeNoire.

HOUSE OF FLOWERS (1954–55, revived 1968). Caribbean-inspired musical. 2 acts. Book by °Truman Capote. Lyrics by Capote and °Harold Arlen. Music by Arlen. Based on Capote's short story of the same title.

A lavishly staged starring vehicle for Pearl Bailey, who played the part of a bordello madam (Mme. Fleur), whose house of prostitution, located in the West Indies, is undergoing hard times. The title is based on the name of the madam and the fact that each of the prostitutes is named after a flower. Mme. Fleur's house not only faces competition from another bordello run by Mme. Tango (Juanita Hall), but is eventually forced to close when an epidemic of mumps breaks out on the island, brought on by visiting sailors during Mardi Gras week.

Mme. Fleur tries to recoup her investment by "selling off" one of her most beautiful and innocent girls, Violet (played by Diahann Carroll), to a rich white shipping merchant as his mistress. To do this, she gets rid of Violet's young island lover, the handsome Royal (played by Rawn Spearman), by having him abducted aboard a ship, and reports that he has drowned at sea. Royal escapes, however, and returns just in time to prevent his sweetheart from going away with the shipping merchant. All ends happily for the lovers and Mme. Fleur. Her establishment is returned to its former glory when Mme. Tango's girls all sail away on a lengthy world cruise.

First prod. on Bway, at the Alvin Theatre, Dec. 30, 1954–May 22, 1955, for 165 perfs.; dir. by °Peter Brook. Cast: Pearl Bailey (Mme. Fleur), Diahann Carroll (Violet, whose real name is Ottilie), Juanita Hall (Mme. Tango), Geoffrey Holder (The Champion), Frederick O'Neal (The Houngan), Alvin Ailey (Alvin),

Dolores Harper (Tulip), Ada Moore (Gladiola), Enid Mosier (Pansy), Winston George Henriques (Do), Solomon Earl Green (Don't), Miriam Burton (Mother), Ray Walston (Captain Jonas), Leu Comacho & Margot Small (The Sisters Merinque), Mary Mon Toy (Mamselle Honolulu), Glory Van Scott (Mamselle Cigarette), Rawn Spearman (Royal), Don Redman (Chief of Police), Carmen deLavallade (Carmen), and Dino DiLuca (Monsieur Jameson).

Revived Off-Bway, with a revised script and 5 new songs, at the Theatre De Lys, opening Jan. 28, 1968, for a short run.

Songs and musical numbers (Bway prodn.): "Waitin'," "One Man Ain't Quite Enough" (Bailey), "Madame Tango's Tango," "A Sleepin' Bee" (Carroll), "Bamboo Cage," "House of Flowers," "Two Ladies in de Shade of de Banana Tree," "What Is a Friend For?" (Bailey), "Mardi Gras," "I Never Has Seen Snow," "Husband Cage," "Has I Let You Down?" (Bailey), "Voudou," "Slide, Boy, Slide," "Don't Like Goodbyes," "Turtle Song," and "Bamboo Cage" Finale.

Cast recording of the orig. Bway version issued by Columbia (CSP–COS–2320), 1954; 1968 revival by United Artists (VAS–5180). The Off-Bway version was recorded by Columbia Artists (5180), 1968. A much revised libretto was pub. by Random House, New York, 1968.

FURTHER REFERENCE: Alkire diss. *NY Herald Trib.* 12–31–1954. *NY J. American* 12–31–1954. *NY Post* 12–31–1954. *NYT* 12–31–1954.

HOUSE PARTY (1973). Subtitled "A Musical Memory." Conceived by Rosetta LeNoire. Music by °Manny Cavaco, Jr., and °John Lenahan. Prod. by the AMAS Repertory Theatre, New York, April 15–May 13, 1973, for 15 perfs.; with an integrated cast.

HOW COME? (1923, revived 1925). Musical revue. Billed as "A Girly Musical Darkcomedy." Book by Eddie Hunter. Music and lyrics by Hunter, Will Vodery, Henry Creamer, and Ben Harris.

Song-and-dance revue, in imitation of *Shuffle Along* (1921), with sketches built around a thin plot of embezzlement of funds from the Mobile Trust Chicken Corporation, by Hunter (in blackface as Rastus Skunkton Lime), who is the secretary. For this he is eventually jailed. One of the outstanding comic scenes was his attempted jailbreak, a noisy affair, during which he is not aware that the jailer is both deaf and nearly blind. Another of the sketches deals with a shoeshine parlor fronting for a bootlegging establishment. Although the show was not a success, it is significant because of its Bway opening at the downtown Apollo Theatre, where black patrons were permitted to sit in a special reserved section on the first floor.

First prod. at the Attucks Theatre in Norfolk, VA, Jan. 15, 1923, touring from there to Washington, DC, and then to Philadelphia, where it was presented at the Dunbar Theatre on Jan. 29. Blues singer Bessie Smith joined the show for a week during its Dunbar appearance, performing as herself, singing between the acts. She was fired after a run-in with Hunter, and was replaced by Alberta Hunter for the Bway run. Opened on Bway at the Apollo Theatre, April 16, 1923, for 32 perfs. Cast also included Sidney Bechet, the jazz musician, featured in the role of the chief of police; Andrew Tribble, as Deacon Long Track; Chappelle & Stinnette, the song and dance team; and the noted dancer Johnny Nit. Other performers were Alice Brown, Amon Davis, Rastus Wilson, Leroy Broomfield, Nat Cash, and Alfred "Slick" Chester.

Revived 1925 with the following cast: Eddie Hunter, Barrington Carter, Caroline Williams, Nina Hunter, Madlyn Odlum, Leroy Broomfield, Billy Higgins, Doe Doe Green, Nona Marshall, George Lynch, George W. Cooper, Emma Jackson, Norman Astwood, Alberta Perkins, Amy Spencer, Jessica Zack, Mabel Gant, Adrian Joyce, and Dutch Victor.

Included 23 songs, 5 of which were blues.

FURTHER REFERENCE: *NY Commercial* 4–17–1923. *NY News* 4–18–1923. *NYT* 4–17–1923. *NY Telegram* 4–17–1923. *NY World* 4–18–1923.

HOW NEWTOWN PREPARED / / Spelled also as *Newton* (1916). Musical comedy. 2 acts. Book and lyrics by Salem Tutt Whitney and J. Homer Tutt (Whitney & Tutt). Music by Whitney & Tutt, Taylor L. Corwell, and Clarence G. Wilson.

A military comedy about a voluntary army of old black Civil War veterans of Newtown, headed by Colonel George Washington Bullion (a character who appears in a number of Whitney & Tutt musicals). The veterans (a standby army only) are tricked into fighting in the Spanish-American War, and find themselves on the wrong side, fighting against the Allies. They experience many tribulations before they are finally rescued and returned to the U.S.A.

Prod. on tour by Whitney & Tutt's *Smart Set Co.*, 1916. Cast: Salem Tutt Whitney (George Washington Bullion), J. Homer Tutt (Sam Cain, Bullion's Friend), Al Watts (Pedro Gomez, a Mexican Spy), Dave Liston (Eagle Eye, Indian Chief), Julian Costello (Said Pasha, Turkish Prince), Sam Gardner (Major Bragg, Civil War Relic), Tommy Hall (Elder Toots, Newtown Pastor), Alonzo Fenderson (Captain Marmon), Sam Gray (Eph Snow, New Oracle); Veterans: Lee Marshall (Pvt. Arsenal), Nathan Cash (Cpl. Remington), Charles Hicks (Sgt. Duposal), O. D. Carter (Lt. Krupp), Charles M. Lawrence (Maj. Bragg), Albert Crane (Col. Hullabaloo); Others: Helen Clinton (Martha Bullion), Mattie Lewis (Moana Sweet, Bullion's Ward), Carrie King (Louise Dillingham, Society Lady), Julian Costello (Samantha Haskfort, Suffragette), Emma Jackson (Peggie Flipp, News Dispenser), Helen Jackson (Margaret Simpson), Estelle Cash (Mandy Lee), Sweetie May (Lucinda Thompson), Blanche Thompson (Senora Flores, Secret Service Agent); Soldiers, Farmhands, Turks, Sailors, Citizens, etc.: Edna Gibbs, Juanita Hicks, Josie Graham, Ora Dunlop, and Virginia Wheeler.

Songs and musical numbers: Act I—Opening chorus (Company), 'Grand Old Veterans in the U.S.A.' (Gardner & Veterans), 'Study in Black and White' (Tutt

& King), Girls Quartette (King, E. Jackson, H. Jackson & Lewis), 'Old Veterans Jubilee' (Carter, Gray, Marshall & Gardner), "The Wedding of the Flower and the Bee" (Tutt & Cash), "All I Want Is Plenty of Loving" (Young & Chorus), "My Sweet Hawaiian Home" (Thompson & Male Quartette), "Sweet Melody Blues" (Sweetie May & Chorus), Buck Dancing (Carter & Marshall), "Little Boy, Little Girl" (Dunlop, Wheeler, Hicks, H. Jackson, Gray, Fenderson, Hicks & Cash), and Finale Farewell (Thompson, Whitney, Tutt & Ensemble). Act II—"The Tar's [sic] Farewell" (Soldiers & Nurses), "The Zoo" (Thompson, Tutt & Chorus), "Help Cometh from Above" (Thompson, Whitney, Tutt, Lewis, Gardner & Liston), "Ode to Allah" (Chorus), "Turkish Drill" (Turkish Soldiers), "Turkey" (Tutt, Thompson & Company), "The Pasha's Dream" (Costello), "If I Could Make the Sun Stand Still" (Whitney), and "Dixie Land Is Calling Me" (Company).
FURTHER REFERENCE: *BlksBf* (Sampson).

HOW'S YOUR SEX LIFE (1977). Musical satire. By Alice Browning. Prod. at the International Black Writers Conference, Chicago, June 1977; dir. by Jimmidee Smith.

HOW TO BE A JEWISH MOTHER (1967–68). Musical revue. 2 acts. Conceived by °Seymour Vall. Based on a book by °Dan Greenburg. Music by °Michael Leonard. Lyrics by °Herbert Martin. Two-character show, starring °Molly Picon and Godfrey Cambridge. (Tiger Haynes was Cambridge's standby.) Prod. at the Hudson Theatre, New York, Dec. 28, 1967–Jan. 13, 1968, for 21 perfs. Songs and musical numbers: "Once the Man You Laughed At," "Laugh a Little," "Since the Time We Met," "The Wedding Song," and "Child You Are."

HOW TO BE HAPPY THOUGH MARRIED (1977). Musical satire. By Alice Browning. Prod. by the International Black Writers Conference, Chicago, 1977.

HOW TO STEAL AN ELECTION (1968). Subtitled "A Dirty Politics Musical." 2 acts. Book by °William F. Brown. Music and lyrics by °Oscar Brand. Prod. at the Pocket Theatre, New York, Oct. 13–Dec. 22, 1968, for 89 perfs. The integrated cast of 8 performers included Clifton Davis. 19 songs and musical numbers.

HOW'VE YOU BEEN (1925). Touring revue. Music by Donald Heywood. Dances by George Stamper. Prod. by Pollock Productions. Cast featured Sidney Easton ("The Happy Bootblack") and Lottie Brown.

HUCKLEBERRY FINN (1902). White-oriented musical adaptn. of °Mark Twain's novel. Included two black-authored songs, one by Cecil Mack (R. C. McPherson) and Tim Brymn (James T. Brymn), and the other by Bob Cole and J. Rosamond Johnson. Prod. by °Klaw & Erlanger in New York, 1902; with an all-white cast. Mack & Brymn's song was "Good Night Lucinda," introduced by °John C. Slavin in this prodn.; pub. by Shapiro, Bernstein & Co., New York; copy in Moorland-Spingarn. The Cole & Johnson song was "The Animals' Convention."

HUMMIN' SAM (1933). Vaudeville revue. Written by °Ellen Nutter. Music and lyrics by °Alexander Hill.
    Unsuccessful musical about horse racing, starring Gertrude "Baby" Cox and Edith Wilson, supported by Lionel Monagas and Lorenzo Tucker. Unfavorably reviewed by *NYT* [date unknown], which considered it amateurish.
    Prod. at the New Yorker Theatre, opening April 8, 1933, for only one perf.; dir. by Carey & Davis. Cast: Cox (Hummin' Sam), Speedy Smith (Uncle Ned), Alonza Bozen (Totem), Bunny Allen (Hot Cakes), the Two Chesterfields (First Jockey, Second Jockey), Lionel Monagas (Yellow George), Lorenzo Tucker (Edward Holton), John Lee (Mr. Conners), Sandy [*sic*] (Mike), Jones & Allen (Caesar and Cicero), Al Wells (Mr. Carter), Flo Brown (Mae Carter), Cecil Rivers (Freddie Marlowe), Edith Wilson (Nina May), Hannah Sylvester (Clara), J. Mardo Brown (Drum Major), and Louise Cook (Miss Jitters).
    Songs and musical numbers: "Steppin' Along," "Harlem Dan," "How the First Song Was Born," "They're Off," "Pinching Yourself," "Change Your Mind About Me," "If I Didn't Have You," "In the Stretch," "Jubilee," "A Little Bit of Quicksilver," "Answer My Heart," "Stompin' 'Em Down," "I'll Be True, But I'll Be Blue," "Jitters," "Fifteen Minutes a Day," "Ain'tcha Glad You Got Music?," "Dancing, and I Mean Dancing."

HUMPTY DUMPTY (1904–8). White-oriented musical spectacle. By °J. Hickory Wood and °Arthur Collins. Adapt. to the American stage by °John McNally. Music and lyrics mainly by Bob Cole, J. Rosamond Johnson, and James Weldon Johnson.
    An Americanized version of one of the most popular Drury Lane pantomimes imported from London, which were extravagant in their marvelous effects and lavish scenery. The central action involved the search for a lost ring, which brought the characters into numerous adventures involving kingdoms in the sea, magic forests, and castles inhabited by monsters, giants, fairies, and animals.
    Prod. by °Klaw & Erlanger at the New Amsterdam Theatre, New York, for 132 perfs., opening Nov. 14, 1904, and closing in March 1905. With an all-white cast, including °Frank Moulan, °Maude Lillian Berry, °Nellie Daly, and °John McVeigh.
    Cole & the Johnson Brothers' songs, all pub. by Joseph W. Stern, New York, in *Selections from Humpty Dumpty* (1905), arranged for piano by Andor Pinter,

include "Peter Piper," "Any Old Tree," +"Mexico," "When the Harvest Moon Is Shining on the River," +"Sambo and Dinah" (a black love song— the most popular number in the show), "The Banana Man," "In Sweet Loveland," and "On Lalawana's Shore." One additional song by Johnson & Johnson alone is +"The Pussy and the Bow-Wow," also pub. by Stern. The pub. collection and those individual songs marked with a plus sign (+) are located in Moorland-Spingarn.

FURTHER REFERENCE: *AmMusTh* (Bordman). *BesPls 1899–1909. Just Before Jazz* (Riis). Riis diss. Program and reviews in the Archives of the Museum of the City of New York.

THE HUNTER HORSE (1919). Touring vaudeville revue. Prod. by comedian Sandy Burns. Featuring members of the Sandy Burns Stock Co.

THE HUSBAND (1907–9). Musical comedy. Book and lyrics by Flournoy E. Miller and Aubrey Lyles (Miller & Lyles). Music by Joe Jordan. Additional music and lyrics by Tim Brymn, Bob Cole, and J. Rosamond Johnson.

About the domestic problems of a married couple and the concern of their friends.

Originated at the Pekin Stock Co. in Chicago, where Miller & Lyles were the resident writers. Opened at the Pekin Theatre, Chicago, on April 22, 1908. Cast included Harrison Stewart (The Husband), Lottie Grady (The Wife), Jennie Ringgold (Friend of the Wife), Nettie Lewis (The Maid), Jerry Mills (Mr. Durant), Charles Gilpin (Dishrag), Matt Marshall (Friend of the Family), and Elvira Johnson (Hannah). Other members of orig. cast were May White, Pearl Brown, George White, J. F. Mores (singer), Beulah White, Adolph Henderson, George Day, Madeline Cooper, Oma Crosby, Pauline Freeman, and John Turner. After its run in Chicago, it was sent to New York with J. Ed. Green as producer, and with Miller & Lyles in the cast. Opened at °Hurtig & Seamon's Music Hall Theatre, New York, Aug. 12, 1907, for a run of 2 weeks.

Revived by the Pekin Stock Co., Chicago, 1909, with Stewart, Grady, Ring-gold, Lewis, Mills, Gilpin, Marshall, Mores, and Johnson in their orig. roles. Cast also included Ada Smith (Cook) and C. B. Winfrey (Butler).

Songs and musical numbers (of the 1909 prodn.) included "Lulu" and "Oh, You Kid" (Lewis); "Good Evening, Caroline" (Johnson); "You Dear" (Mores); "Dissipation," "Take Your Time," and "I've Got Good Common Sense" (Stewart); "Friend of the Family" (Marshall); "Mine, All Mine" (Ringgold); and the two interpolated songs: "Susanna" by Cole & Johnson (Lewis) and "Running Wild" by Brymn (Johnson).

THE HYMIE FINKLESTEIN USED LUMBER COMPANY (1973). Musical comedy. By Margaret Ford Taylor Snipes (Mrs. Kenneth E. Snipes) and Ernie Fann. First prod. by the Karamu Theatre, in the Arena Theatre, Summer 1973. Revised and restaged by Karamu Theatre for a run of 4 weeks, opening Sept. 28, 1983.

I

I AM (1973). Blues musical. Written by Ann Early, partly with inmates of C-76, Riker's Island, NY, where it was prod. in 1973.

I HAVE A DREAM (1989). Musical biography. Based on the life of Dr. Martin Luther King, Jr. By °John Greenfield. Prod. by the National Black Touring Circuit, at the African Peoples Theatre Festival, Birmingham, England, Aug. 30–Sept. 2, 1989. Also perfd. at the National Black Theatre Festival in Winston-Salem, NC, Aug. 17, 1989. Cast featured Lee Coward, Chequita Jackson, Herman LeVerne Jones, Nick Sercy, Bruce Strickland, Diane Weaver, and Dwight Witherspoon.

I'M LAUGHIN' BUT I AIN'T TICKLED (1976). Musical. Conceived and dir. by Vinnette Carroll. Music by Micki Grant. Based on poetry anthologized in *A Rock Against the Wind* (ed. Lindsay Patterson, 1973). Prod. by the Urban Arts Corps, New York, May and Dec. 1976.

IN ABYSSINIA. See *ABYSSINIA* (1906–7).

IN BAMVILLE (1923–24) / / Later revised as *The Chocolate Dandies* (1924–25). Musical comedy. 2 acts. Book by Noble Sissle and Lew Payton. Music and lyrics by Sissle and Eubie Blake (Sissle & Blake). Music perfd. at the piano by Blake.

An earlier tryout version of *The Chocolate Dandies*, which toured for several months before being revised. The story line was built around horse racing, and the race was effectively staged with real horses moving on treadmills. The plot revolved around a race horse owner who dreams that one of his thoroughbreds has won a fortune, which enables him to become president of the Bamville Bank and marry the girl that he loves. When he wakes up, he discovers that his horse has lost the race, and he has lost the girl. Act I occurred on the last day of the Bamville, Mississippi, fair, with the action moving from the street to the stables at the fairgrounds, to the betting ring, to the paddock where the horses are assembled, and finally to the Bamville Race Track, where the race takes place. Act II occurred on the evening of the same day, and moves from a lawn party at Bill Spliven's plantation home, to the street, to the Bamville County Bank, to an interlude at Sissle & Blake's studio, to the wedding of Dan and Angeline on the stage of the Bamville Opera House. Josephine Baker appeared in the cast of this show, which featured the authors and Valaida Snow.

Toured for approximately six months, with performances in Chicago, 1923, and at the Lyceum Theatre in Rochester, NY, March 10, 1924. Cast: Amanda Randolph (Mandy Green, the Deacon's Wife), Gwendolyn Fenster (Sammy, Mandy's Baby), Addison Carey (Black Joe, Jr.), Josephine Baker (That Comedy Chorus Girl), J. Mardo Brown (Struttin' Drum Major and His Bamville Band), W. A. Hann (Bill Splivens, Plantation Owner), William Grundy (Mr. Hez Brown, President of Bamville Fair), Inez Clough (Mrs. Hez Brown, the Wife), Lottie Gee (Angeline Brown, the Daughter), Elizabeth Welsh (or Elisabeth Welch: Jessie Johnson), Valaida Snow (Manda, Bill Spliven's Niece), Fred Jennings (Uncle Eph, Trainer of Rarin' to-Go), Noble Sissle (Dobby Hicks, Race Horse Tout), Ivan H. Browning (Dan Jackson, Owner of Rarin' to-Go), Ferd[ie] Robinson (Shorty, Dumb Luck's Jockey), Russell Smith (Johnny Wise, Village Rube), Lew Payton (Mose Washington, Owner of Dumb Luck), Johnny Hudgins (Joe Dolks, Owner of Jump Steady), Lee J. Randall (Silas Green, the Deacon), George Jones (Bookmaker), Charlie Davis (Snappy, Rarin' to-Go's Jockey), and Curtis Carpenter (Sandy, Scarecrow's Jockey). Other characters: In the Bank—Robinson (Bank Policeman), Jennings (Porter), Snow (Secretary), Richard Cooper (Cashier), Percy Colston (Bookkeeper), Claude Lawson (Draft Clerk), Carey [sic] (Auditor); At the Wedding—Mildred Smallwood (Mischief), Baker (A Deserted Female), Lloyd Keyes (Her Bunco Attorney), Town Flappers, Bank Clerks, Citizens, Clerks, Four Harmony Kings (Quartette), Bamville Opera House Band, Jazzy Jassmines, Bandanaland Girls, Bamville Vamps, and Syncopated Sunflowers.

Songs and musical numbers: Act I—"Have a Good Time, Everybody" (Opening Chorus), "That Charleston Dance" (Welsh), "Fate Is the Slave of Love" (Gee & Browning), "I'll Find My Love in D-I-X-I-E" (Sissle & His Dixie Darlings), "Bandanaland" (Randall, Smith & Bandanaland Girls), "The Sons of Old Black Joe" (Syncopated Sunflowers), "Breakin' 'Em Down" (Joe Smith [jazz cornetist], Valaida Snow & Girls) "Jockey's Life of Mine" (Davis & Jockeys). Act II—"Dixie Moon" (Jones & Chorus), "Manda" (Snow & Syncopated Sunflowers), "Thinking of Me" (Gee & Browning), "Land of Dancing Pickaninnies" (Davis & Bamville Picks), Selections (Four Harmony Kings), "Take Down Dis Letter" (Payton), 'In Their Studio—A Few Minutes with Chocolate Dandies' (Sissle & Blake and Their Struttin' Co.).

FURTHER REFERENCE: *BesPls 1923–24. BlksBf* (Sampson). *NYT* 3–16–1924.

IN DAHOMEY (1902–5). Musical farce. 3 acts [later reduced to a prologue and 2 acts]. Book by Jesse A. Shipp. Lyrics by Paul Laurence Dunbar and others. Based on production ideas by Bert Williams and George Walker (Williams & Walker). Music by Will Marion Cook. Additional songs by James Weldon Johnson, Paul Laurence Dunbar, J. Leubrie Hill, Al. Johns, Alex C. Rogers, James Vaughan, °Henry von Tilzer, and Bert Williams.

The most famous, most successful, and longest-running Williams & Walker show, which ran almost continuously for four years. The first black show to play in Bway's Times Square [cf. *Clorindy, the Origin of the Cakewalk*]; the first major show to introduce native African elements; and the first to give a command perf. at Windsor Castle and Buckingham Palace in London.

The plot, which underwent several changes during its long run, thus preventing a definitive description, originally turned on a fraudulent scheme by a black syndicate to colonize some land in Dahomey (a former republic of West Africa, now known as Benin) as a haven for dissatisfied American blacks. Williams & Walker somehow become involved in the scheme, and the events move through three successive acts from Boston (where the syndicate was organized) to Florida (where the funds are obtained and the emigrants recruited) and thence to Dahomey (where their contact with the natives makes them abandon plans for colonization and return home).

For its European and American tour, the show was shortened to a prologue and two acts, in order to accommodate a "Grand Cakewalk Finale." The Prologue took place in Dahomey, Act I in Boston, and Act II in Florida, where the colonization plans are finally abandoned.

Previewed Sept. 8, 1902 in Stamford, CT, prior to its premiere at the Globe Theatre in Boston, Sept. 12, 1902; then played for several months on the road. Made theatrical history when it opened on Bway at the New York Theatre in Times Square, Feb. 18, 1903, for 53 perfs. Played in Philadelphia for 2 weeks. Then it was taken to London in April 1903, where it ran for 9 months (the number usually given is 7) at the Shaftsbury Theatre from May 16, 1903, to Feb. 13, 1904, for about 200 perfs.; a celebration having been given after its 150th perf. on Sept. 29, 1903. Although the show was well received by London theatregoers, it did not become a hit until after two command performances before King Edward—the first at Windsor Castle in early or mid-June 1903, which "so pleased the King that he commanded [the company] to give a special matinee at Buckingham Palace on June 23rd, the occasion being the ninth birthday of Prince Eddy, the King's grandson" (*BlksBf* [Sampson], p. 297). Following its London triumph, it toured the English provinces for about 5 months before returning to the U.S., opening at the Grand Opera House, New York, Aug. 27, 1904. Toured the U.S. for 40 weeks, traveling to many western, southern, and eastern cities, including Portland, San Francisco, St. Louis, and Boston, closing in June 1905. A second company, featuring Dan Avery and Charles Hart, again took the abandoned Williams & Walker show to Europe in Aug. 1904, returning in 1905.

Cast of the 1903 London production, including character descriptions from the program: Prologue (In Dahomey)—Charles Moore (Je-Je, a caboceer), William Elkins (Menuki, Messenger of the King), William Barker (Mose Lightfoot, Agent of Dahomey Colonization Society), Soldiers, Natives, etc. Acts I and II—Bert A. Williams (Shylock Homestead, called "Shy" by his friends), George Walker (Rareback Pinkerton, "Shy's" personal friend and advisor), Pete Hampton (Hamilton Lightfoot, president of a colonization society), Fred Douglas (Dr. Straight [in name only], street fakir), William Barker (Mose Lightfoot, brother of Hamilton, thinks Dahomey a land of great promise), Alex Rogers (George Reeder, proprietor of an intelligence office), Walter Richardson (Henry Stampfield, letter carrier, with an argument against immigration), George Catlin (Me Sing, a Chinese cook), J. A. Shipp (Hustling Charley, promoter of Get-the-Coin Syndicate), Richard Conners (Leather, a bootblack), J. Leubrie Hill (Officer Still), Green Tapley (White Wash Man), Theodore Pankey (Messenger Rush, but not often), Abbie Mitchell (Pansy, Daughter of Cecilia Lightfoot, in love with Leather), Mrs. Hattie McIntosh (Cecilia Lightfoot, Hamilton's wife), Mrs. Lottie Williams (Mrs. Stringer, dealer in forsaken patterns and editor of fashion notes in "Beanville Agitator"), Aida Overton Walker (Rosetta Lightfoot, a troublesome young thing), Colonists, Natives, etc.

Songs and musical numbers: Musical score pub. by Keith, Prowse & Co., Ltd., London, 1902, which contains the following songs [NOTE: The composer's name is marked with a plus sign ($^+$).]: Prologue—"My Dahomian Queen" (F. B. Williams & $^+$J. L. Hill), "Caboceers Entrance" ($^+$W. M. Cook). Act I—"Swing Along" (opening chorus) ($^+$Cook), "Molly Green" (C. Mack & $^+$W. M. Cook), "On Broadway in Dahomey Bye and Bye" (A. Rogers & $^+$Al. Johns). Act II—"I Wants to Be a Actor Lady" (V. Bryan & $^+$H. von Tilzer), "Brownskin Baby Mine" (C. Mack & $^+$W. M. Cook), "Leader of the Colored Aristocracy" (J. W. Johnson & $^+$W. M. Cook), "Society" ($^+$W. M. Cook), "I'm a Jonah Man" ($^+$A. Rogers), "The Czar" (W. M. Cook), "On Emancipation Day" (P. L. Dunbar & $^+$W. M. Cook), "Chocolate Drops" ($^+$W. M. Cook), "Happy Jim" (Cakewalk) ($^+$J. Vaughan).

Other songs used during the course of the musical's long run include "Captain Kidd," "Dat Girl of Mine," "Dear Luzon," "For Florida," "Good Evenin'," "I Want to Be a Real Lady," "I May Be Crazy But I Ain't No Fool," "[In] My Castle on the River Nile," "My Lady Frog," "Me and De Minstrel Ban'," "A Rich Coon's Babe," "Returned," "She's Dancing Sue," "That's How the Cakewalk's Done," "Vassar Girl," "When Sousa Comes to Town," "Who Dat Say Chicken in Dis Crowd," and "Why Adam Sinned."

Libretto in Music Collection/LC.

FURTHER REFERENCE: *AmMusTh* (Bordman). *Blk. Art* Fall 1977. *Blk. Perspectives in Mus.* Spring 1983. *Harl. Ren.* (Huggins). *Life* 3–12–1903. *Nobody* (Charters). *NYT* 2–19–1903. *Phylon* 2nd qtr. 1950. Riis diss. *ThMag* 4–1906. *In Dahomey* folder in Harvard Theatre Collection.

IN DE BEGINNING (1977). Biblical-inspired musical. The Genesis story in music and verse. By Oscar Brown, Jr. Prod. at the Body Politic Theatre, Chicago, Aug. 3, 1977.

IN ETHIOPIAVILLE (1911–13). Musical farce. Book, lyrics, and music by Frank Montgomery.

This show, starring Montgomery as the leading comedian, was built around the theft of a jewel case from Old Man Joseph Green, which occurred after Green had decided to move with his family from the South (Ethiopiaville) to Boston. Detectives are called in to find the stolen case; but before they can arrive, two former minstrel men, now down on their luck, decide to impersonate the detectives, locate the case, and claim the reward. In spite of their ineptness, they accidentally find the missing case, and avoid being arrested for impersonating the detectives.

This was apparently Montgomery's first important show, prod. by the Dixie Flyers Company, which he organized in 1911, and apparently toured until 1913. Cast of the 1911 ed. included Montgomery, Russell Smith, Eddie Stafford, James Brown, Elwood Wooding, Sallie Jones, Maude Hudson, Bessie Stafford, Mayme Brown, Bonnie Clark, Florence McClain (later Mrs. Montgomery), and Senora McClain (presumably her mother).

Cast of the 1913 ed.: Montgomery (Shylock Holmestead), Ed Lea Coleman (Dandy Jones Pinkerton), Charlie Ross (Joseph Green), Florence McClain (Georgiana Green), Emma Morton (Semantha Green), Charles Nickerson (George Augusta Stokes, a Policeman), Lila Moore (Eliza Jones, a Nurse), Belle Smedley (Lucinder Jones, the Lady from Boston), Sollie [*sic*] Jones (Little Willie Jones, the Village Pest), Edna Coleman (Sadie Green, His Little Sweetheart), Harry MacDonald ("Nick Carter," King of Detectives); Village Boys and Girls: Sadie Thompson, Blanche Thompson, Mary Thompson, Will Duncan, Elwood Wooding, Mamie Garrett, George Smith, Bessie Bullard, and Beah Moore; Billy Ewing and Chorus.

Songs and musical numbers: "Bless Your Everloving Little Heart" (Ewing), "Peace Wid the World" (Montgomery), "Musical Moon" (Ewing & Chorus), "On the Mississippi," "Dixie," "Syncopated Boogie Boo," "Oh, Ho, in the Morning," "Old Boston Town," "Crazy About Some Boy," "Out Old Man," "I Wonder Why They Call Me Snowball," and "When Will I Plant the Tree."

IN HONOLULU (1922). Touring vaudeville revue. Prod. by Mae Kemp and her Ragtime Steppers Co. Cast included Kemp, "Skunk" Tom Bower, Zachariah White, Lyons Daniels, Elmer Lloyd (straight man), Billy Nichols, Hector Patterson, Louise Patterson, Viola Dorsey, Eloise Howard, Hazel Wallace, and Estelle Carroll.

IN MEXICO (1921). Touring vaudeville revue. Prod. by and starring comedian Doe Doe Green. Musical dir., Lovey ''Percey'' Saunders. Also in the cast were Arthur Williams, Kid Bruce, Rosa Lee Saunders, Helen Butler, Mary Jackson, Ed Pickett, Bobby Wilson, Louise Wilson, and Coleman Titus.

INNER CITY (1971–72). Billed as ''A Street Cantata.'' 2 acts [10 scenes]. Music by °Helen Miller. Lyrics by °Eve Merriam. Based on Merriam's book, *The Inner City Mother Goose*. Conceived and dir. by °Tom O'Horgan. Musical of urban underclass life, set in New York City during the 1970s; and featuring Linda Hopkins, who won a Tony Award as best supporting actress. Included 46 songs and musical numbers, mainly nursery rhymes revised to fit events of the 1970s. According to the publisher of the libretto and score, ''these modern tales catalog urban ills using a fascinating parade of characters: a local congressman, a prostitute, a cop, a drug pusher, and many others'' (Samuel French, *Basic Catalog of Plays*). Prod. on Bway at the Ethel Barrymore Theatre, Dec. 19, 1971–March 11, 1972, for 97 perfs. and 24 previews. The integrated cast of 10 included 5 blacks: Hopkins, Carl Hall, Delores Hall, Paulette Ellen Jones, and Larry Marshall.

Libretto and score pub. by Samuel French, New York, c. 1972.

IN NEWPORT (1904–5). White-oriented musical comedy. 2 acts. Book by °John J. McNally. Music and lyrics by Bob Cole, James Weldon Johnson, and J. Rosamond Johnson.

The plot revolves around the efforts of a private detective to thwart a blackmail scheme against an errant husband who has written a love letter to a French girl.

Prod. on Bway at the Liberty Theatre, New York, opening Dec. 26, 1904, for 24 perfs., closing after a three-week run, in Jan. 1905. The all-white cast included °Fay Templeton (as the girl), °Peter F. Dailey (as the detective), °Lee Harrison (as the husband), and °Joseph Coyne (as a stereotypical English stage simpleton).

Songs by Cole & the Johnson Brothers included ''How a Monocle Helps the Mind,'' ''Lindy,'' ''Mary Was a Manicure,'' ''Nobody But You,'' ''Peggy Is a New Yorker Now,'' ''Scandal,'' ''Spirit of the Banjo,'' ''When I Am Chief of Police,'' and ''Women.''

FURTHER REFERENCE: *AmMusTh* (Bordman). *BesPls 1899–1909*. *Just Before Jazz* (Riis). Riis diss.

IN OLD KENTUCKY (c. 1900–c. 1915). Predominantly white touring show, which used black musicians and dancers. Organized and prod. by °Charles L. Dazy. According to Eileen Southern (*MusBlkAms*, 1st ed., p. 274), this was a ''long-lived show,'' ''based on a plot about thoroughbred horses and plantation life in Kentucky and which used black singers and dancers in the stable scene. An added feature in the scene was a so-called 'pickaninny band' composed of small boys playing brass instruments.'' Opened each season at the old Academy of Music in New York City, then went on U.S. tour, playing mainly in small cities, towns, and villages. John Brister organized the first Negro boys' brass band in Cincinnati. In 1910 the Original Pickaninny Band was under the direction of John Powell.

IN OLD VIRGINIA (1922). Musical show cited by *Billboard* (J. A. Jackson's Page) 9–9–1922.

THE INSANE ASYLUM (1921). Vaudeville revue. Touring show prod. by Eddie Hunter and the Standard Stock Co., at the Standard Theatre in Philadelphia, and on tour of the vaudeville circuit. Cast included Jim Burris, Evon Robinson, Lottie Harris, Theodore Robinson, Marcus Slayter, Madeline Belt, Elizabeth Moulton, Fred Hollins, Charles Lawrence, Alfred Curtis, Maggie Crosh, Bee Palmer, Marie Warren, and Mae Lambert.

IN SLAM (1922). Touring vaudeville revue. Starring Byrd & Byrd.

IN THE DRAFT (1918). Tabloid musical. Written and prod. by Billy King. Presumably on a World War I theme. First prod. at the Grand Theatre, Chicago, with members of the Billy King Stock Co., including Howard Kelly, James P. Reed, and Gertrude Saunders.

IN THE HOUSE OF THE BLUES (1986). Billed as "A Black Women's Blues Musical." By David Charles. Deals with the 1920s and 1930s. Prod. by the New Federal Theatre, New York, Dec. 1986; dir. by Buddy Butler. Musical dir., John McCallum. Featuring Debra Byrd, David Cannell, Crystal Lilly, and Larry Marshall.

IN THE JUNGLES (1911). Musical comedy. Presumably 3 acts. Book by Will A. Cook and Al F. Watts. Music by Will Marion Cook and Alex C. Rogers.

A Baptist missionary society hires a detective to rescue one of its missionaries (Sissieretta Jones) who has been lost in the jungles. A con man is also involved in the plot, apparently intending to gain a reward by locating the lost woman first. The rescue takes several characters to the jungles, where, after a number of trials and vicissitudes, the woman is discovered safe, having been made a queen by the Gumbula tribe. Through the efforts of a detective, she is returned to the U.S.

Written for and prod. by the *Black Patti Troubadours*, on U.S. tour, 1911; staged by Jerry Mills. Cast included Sissieretta Jones [Black Patti] (Missionary/ Queen Le-Ku-Li), Will A. Cook, Al F. Watts, Julius Glenn, Charles Bougia, Jeannette Murphy, and William and Marie Greer.

Songs and musical numbers: "My Jewel of the River Nile" and "Home, Sweet Home" (Black Patti), "Never Let the Same Bee Sting You Twice" (Glenn), "Plant a Watermelon by My Grave" (Glenn), "Roll a Little Pill for

Me'' (Cook), ''Baby Rose'' (Black Patti), ''Love Is King'' (Black Patti & Bougia), ''Ragtime Love'' (M. Greer), ''Let the Juice Ooze Through'' (Glenn), ''Oh, Say Wouldn't That Be a Dream'' (Glenn), and ''My Dreamland'' (Glenn). **FURTHER REFERENCE:** *Freeman* (Indianapolis) 9–30–1911. *NY Age* 5–14–1911.

INTO THE WOODS (1988). Billed as ''A Fairy-Tale Musical.'' Written and dir. by °James Lapine. Music and lyrics by °Stephen Sondheim. Based on stories from the Grimm Brothers and other classic frightening fairy tales. Prod. at the Martin Beck Theatre, New York, Spring and Summer 1988. With an integrated cast that featured Phylicia Rashad as the Witch.

IN ZULULAND (1907). African-inspired musical show. Written, prod., and staged by J. Ed. Green. Music by Joe Jordan, Will Marion Cook, and James T. Brymn. Musical numbers staged by William ''Billy'' Johnson. Presented at the Pekin Theatre, Chicago, opening June 29, 1907; featuring Harrison Stewart in the leading role.

ISABEL RISING / / Orig. title: *Evita Del Barrio* (1979). Fantasy-laden musical melodrama. By Houston Brummit. About life in the theatre and the power of the imagination. The four principal roles weave in and out of the legends of Isabel and Eva Peron, Catherine of Russia, and Tito Luciardo. Songs include both orig. Latin-like popular songs and Bway operating scores. Showcased under its orig. title as a musical play, with only 5 songs, at El Porton Theatre, New York, July 1979. Revised under its present title as a full-length musical, which is still apparently unprod.

IT'S ABOUT TIME (1989). Billed as ''A Father and Son Musical.'' Written by and costarring Oscar Brown, Jr., and Oscar Brown III. On the theme of growing up and growing old. Prod. at the Ebony Showcase Theatre, Los Angeles, Spring 1989, for an indefinite run.

IT'S A PLENTY (1929). Touring vaudeville revue. Featured Roscoe ''Red'' Simmons, Al Watts, Eva Metcalf, Mary Clemons, Amanda Randolph, S. H. Dudley, Jr., Swan & Lee, and the Alhambra Girls.

IT'S FUN TO BE BLACK (1973). Children's musical. By Alice Browning. Prod. by the Actors of America, at Malcolm X Coll., Chicago, during the 1973–74 season.

IT'S SO NICE TO BE CIVILIZED (1978–80). Musical entertainment. 2 acts. Book, music, and lyrics by Micki Grant.

Deals with the lives and romantic involvements of people on Sweetbriar Street—in the black section of an inner city. Sharky, a streetwise character, introduces himself and his neighbors: a young couple expecting their first child, a bag lady, a street gang, and a grandma who wonders who's going to teach the children and who lets the world know that "I've Still Got My Bite," referring to her own sexual desires. The love story involves Sharky and a nightclub owner named Mollie, who are lonely and disillusioned, and need each other. A white social worker comes into the street, trying to interest the youth gang in painting a mural on a tenement wall. Though he is at first met with hostility, he finally succeeds in winning over the gang.

First prod. by the AMAS Repertory Theatre, New York, 1978; dir. by Jeffrey Dunn. Choreography by Fred Benjamin; musical supervision and arrangements by Danny Holgate; choral arrangements and direction by Chapman Roberts. The integrated cast (racial identities not known) included Charles Berry, Karen G. Burke, David Cahn, Claudine Cassan, Jean Cheek, Kevin DeVoe, Eugene Edwards, Joey Ginza, Dwayne Grayman, Paul Harman, Sundy Leake, Carol Lynn Maillard, Brenda Mitchell, Ennis Smith, Cassie Stein, and Diane Wilson.

Prod. on Bway at the Martin Beck Theatre, June 3–8, 1980, for 7 perfs. and 23 previews; dir. by Frank Coraso. Choreography by Mabel Robinson; musical dir., Coleridge-Taylor Perkinson. Cast: Obba Babatunde (Sharky), Vivian Reed (Mollie), Larry Steward (Larry), Vickie D. Campbell (Sissy), Carol Lynn Maillard (LuAnne), Mabel King (Grandma), Stephen Pender (Mr. Anderson), Dan Strayhorn (Blade), Eugene Edwards (Rev. Williams), Deborah Burrell (Mother), Juanita Grace Taylor (Dancing Bag Lady); and the Ensemble of 11 men and women.

Songs and musical numbers: "Step into My World," "Keep Your Eye on the Red," "Wake-Up Sun," "Subway Rider," "God Help Us," "Who's Going to Teach the Children?" (King), "Out in the Street," "Welcome Mr. Anderson," "Why Can't Me and You?," "When I Rise," "World Keeps Going Round," "Antiquity," "I've Still Got My Bite" (King), "Look at Us," "The American Dream," "Bright Lights," "It's So Nice to Be Civilized," "Like a Lady," and "Pass a Little Love Around."

Libretto and music pub. by Samuel French, New York.
FURTHER REFERENCE: *AmMusTh* (Bordman).

J

JACK (1985). Subtitled ''A Musical Fantasy.'' Book and lyrics by °Chris Ann Melli and °Jill Wess. Music by Wess. A young man's search for manhood takes him and the audience on a magical and surrealistic odyssey through the city. Prod. by the Theatre of Universal Images, Newark, NJ, June 5–23, 1985; and at the Harry deJur Henry Street Settlement Playhouse, in association with the New Federal Theatre, July 5–Aug. 4, 1985; dir. by William Ebron.

JACQUES BREL IS ALIVE AND WELL AND LIVING IN PARIS (1968–71). Musical entertainment. 2 acts. Production concept, English lyrics, and additional material by °Eric Blau and °Mort Shuman. Adapted from works of Jacques Brel, and based on his lyrics and commentary. Prod. at the Village Gate Theatre, opening Jan. 22, 1968, and continued through 1971. The orig. cast (all-white) included °Eli Stone, Mort Shuman, °Shawn Eliot, and °Alice Whitfield. Robert Guillaume (of TV's ''Benson'' fame) succeeded Shuman during the course of the play's run. 25 songs and musical numbers.

THE JAIL BIRDS (1929–30). Vaudeville revue. Prod. by and costarring Drake & Walker (Henry Drake and Ethel Walker). Toured for two seasons. Cast of the *1929 ed.* also included George Williams, Flora Wilson, ''String Beans'' Price (comedian), Coristine Daniels (soubrette), Elenor Wilson (female lead), Jay Goines (character impersonator), 10 Female Dancers, and 4 Male Dancers. Cast of the *1930 ed.* included Sam ''Bilo'' Russell, Helen Stokes, Billie and Baby English, Lucy Strayhorne, the Kennetts, and the Harmony Four. This ed. opened in Harlem at the Apollo Theatre during the Fourth of July weekend, with a cast of 60. Also on the program was blues singer Bessie Smith.

JAMAICA (1957–58). Caribbean-inspired musical. Book by °E. Y. Harburg and °Fred Saidy. Lyrics by Harburg. Music by °Harold Arlen.

Starring vehicle for Lena Horne, originally written as a folk play for Harry Belafonte, who withdrew from the prodn. because of illness. Sidney Poitier was also offered the part before it was rewritten to suit the talents of Miss Horne, and °Ricardo Montalban was chosen as the leading man, which changed the play's focus to an interracial romance, although Montalban was considerably suntanned for the role.

A typical island romance, involving the love of Koli, a poor, handsome fisherman, for the beautiful Savannah, whose main desire is to leave the island and go to New York, where life is more modern and full of conveniences that require only a "push of de button." The love story is also complicated by the arrival of a young hustler who plans to capitalize on the pearl-diving industry, and Savannah sees him as an opportunity to fulfill her lifelong dream to leave the island. Although Savannah does visit New York in a dream sequence, she actually remains with her island suitor after he saves her brother's life during a hurricane. Miss Horne's performance and stage presence were universally praised by all New York daily newspapers.

Prod. on Bway by °David Merrick at the Imperial Theatre, opening Oct. 31, 1957, for 558 perfs.; dir. by °Robert Lewis. The interracial cast included Lena Horne (Savannah), Ricardo Montalban (Koli), Ossie Davis (Cicero), Josephine Premice (Ginger), Adelaide Hall (Grandma Obeah), Augustine Rios (Quico), Roy Thompson (Snodgrass), Hugh Dilworth (Hucklebuck), Erik Rhodes (Governor), James E. Wall (Lancaster), Joe Adams (Nashua), and Alvin Ailey and Christyne Lawson (Leading Dancers).

Principal songs and musical numbers: "Savannah," "Pretty to Walk With," "Push de Button," "Cocoanut Sweet," "Pity the Sunset," "Take It Slow, Joe," "Ain't It de Truth?," "Leave the Atom Alone," "Napoleon," "I Don't Think I'll End It All Today," and "Little Biscuit."

Libretto not pub. Orig. cast recordings by RCA Victor (LOC 1036; LSO 1103) and Time-Life (STL–AM11).

FURTHER REFERENCE: Alkire diss. *BlkMusTh* (Woll). *NYT* 10–27–1957. *NY World-Telegraph & Sun* 11–1–1957. *Sat. Rev.* 11–16–1957. *Variety* 11–6–1957.

JANE WHITE, WHO? . . . (1980). Celebrity one-person show. Billed as "An Autobiographical Musical." 2 acts. By veteran actress Jane White and °Joe Masteroff. Musical dir., Roger Leonard. Prod. at One Sheridan Square, New York, Jan. 29–March 28, 1980, for 51 perfs.; starring Jane White.

JAZZBO BROWN (1980). Black-oriented musical adaptation. 2 acts. Book, music, and lyrics by °Stephen H. Lemberg.

A black version of the °Al Jolson film *The Jazz Singer* (1927), *Jazzbo Brown* concerned the dilemma of a young dancer/singer and son of a Harlem minister who wants to go on the stage in spite of his father's opposition. The action moves back and forth between the father's church and a Broadway theatre during a two-day period in 1924.

Prod. by °Barbara Gittler and °Morris Jaffee at the City Lights Theatre, New York, June 24–Aug. 24, 1980, for 44 perfs., apparently expanded from a workshop prodn. at the same theatre. Dir. and choreographed by Louis Johnson. Cast: Andre De Shields (Jazzbo Brown), Chris Calloway (Cab Calloway's daughter: Maxine McCall), Jerry Jarrett (D. D. Daniels), Zulema (Rachel Brown), Ned Wright (Rev. Brown), and Charles Bernard, Deborah Lynn Bridges, Rodney Green, Janice Nicki Harrison, Dennis A. Morgan, Gayle Samuels, Wynonna Smith, and Alicia C. Sneed.

Songs and musical numbers: "Jazzbo Brown," "Broadway," "I'm Bettin' on You," "Million Songs," "Born to Sing," "He Had the Callin'," "Bump Bump Bump, The Same Old Tune," "When You've Loved Your Man," "The Best Man," "Give Me More," "When I Die," "Dancin' Shoes," "Precious Patterns," "Funky Bessie," "Harlem Follies," "First Time I Saw You," "Pride and Freedom," and "Take a Bow."

THE JAZZ EXPRESS (1923). Touring revue. Prod. by and costarring Salem Tutt Whitney and J. Homer Tutt (Whitney & Tutt). Cast also included Julian Costello, Maude DeForest, and Alma Daniels. The song hit from this show was "Betwixt and Between," composed by Donald Heywood.

JAZZ OPERA. See **MONEY**.

JAZZ REGIMENT (1929). Touring revue. Featuring Gertrude Saunders and Sam Gorman.

JAZZ SET (1980). Jazz-inspired musical. By Ron Milner. Musical score by Max Roach. About the members of a jazz sextet. First prod. at the Mark Taper Forum, Los Angeles, 1980. Prod. at the New Federal Theatre, New York, July 1982; dir. by Norman Riley.

JAZZ TOWN CAPERS (1928). Touring vaudeville revue. Prod. by and costarring Marshall Rogers. Cast also included Fess Williams, Margie Lorraine, Joyce Robinson, Rookie Davis (blackface comedian), Walter Richardson, Aggie & White, and Jimmie Bertrand.

JELLY'S LAST JAM (1992). Dramatic and musical retrospective. 2 acts [12 scenes]. Book by George C. Wolfe. Music by Jelly Roll Morton, arranged by Luther Henderson, who also composed additional music. Lyrics by Susan Birkenhead.

Based on the life and music of the late jazz great Jelly Roll Morton, a mixed-blood musician who thought of himself as the inventor of jazz, and was not comfortable in either the black or the white world. Praised by Clive Barnes (*NY*

Post 4–27–1992) as "the most original musical to hit Broadway in years." A review of Jelly's life on the eve of his death, by a sort of voodoo devil called Chimney Man. As Jelly's life is dissected, people from his past move in and out, and his music is celebrated. According to *Connoisseur* magazine (5–1991), Wolfe considered Morton, who "was famous for being insufferable and overbearing," as representing "the asshole in all of us." As the reviewer continues, Wolfe's concept "embraces the exasperating Jelly . . . as well as the gifted one."

Developed at the Crossroads Theatre in New Brunswick, NJ, 1991, and first presented at the Mark Taper Forum in Los Angeles, Winter 1991–92. Opened on Bway at the Virginia Theatre in late April 1992; dir. by Wolfe. Choreography by Hope Clarke; tap choreography by Gregory Hines and Ted L. Levy. Cast: Keith David (Chimney Man); Mamie Duncan-Gibbs, Stephanie Pope, and Allison W. Williams (The Hunnies, Figures of Fate); Gregory Hines (Jelly Roll Morton); Savion Glover (Young Jelly); Victoria Gabrielle Platt and Sherry D. Boone (The Sisters); Adrian Bailey, Mary Bond Davis, Ralph Deaton, Ann Duquesnay, and Melissa Haizlip (The Ancestors); Mary Bond Davis (Miss Mamie, An Old-Time Blues Singer); Reuben Santiago-Hudson (Buddy Bolden, A Musician); Brenda Braxton (Too-Tight Nora); Gil Prichett II (Three Finger Jake); Ann Duquesnay (Gran Mimi); Stanley Wayne Mathis (Kack the Bear, Jelly's Side-Kick); Ken Ard (Foot-in-Yo-Ass Sam); Tonya Pinkins (Anita); Don Johanson and Gordon Joseph Weiss (The Melrose Brothers); Jelly's Red Hot Peppers (Sextet); and Crowd. Tony Awards were won by Gregory Hines, for best leading actor, and Tonya Pinkins, for best featured actress. Tony nominations were also received by George Wolfe, for best book and best director; Luther Henderson, for best original score; Hines, Levy, and Clarke, for best choreography; and Toni-Leslie James, for best costume design.

Scenes and musical numbers: Act I, Scene 1 (The Jam)—"Jelly's Jam" (Hunnies & Crowd), "In My Day" (Jelly & Hunnies); Scene 2 (In the Beginning)—"The Creole Way" (Ancestors & Young Jelly), "The Whole World's Waitin' to Sing Your Song" and "Street Scene" (Jelly, Young Jelly & Crowd); Scene 3 (Goin' Uptown)—"Michigan Water" (Miss Mamie & Buddy Bolden), The Banishment ("Get Away Boy" and "Lonely Boy Blues") (Gran Mimi, Young Jelly & Jelly); Scene 4 (The Journey to Chicago)—"Somethin' More" (Jelly, Jack, Chimney Man, Hunnies & Crowd), "That's How You Jazz" (Jelly, Jack & Crowd); Scene 5 (Chicago!)—"The Chicago Stomp" (Jelly, Peppers, Chimney Man, Hunnies & Crowd); Scene 6 (Jelly 'n' Anita)—"Play the Music for Me" (Anita), "Lovin' Is a Lowdown Blues" (Hunnies); Scene 7 (The Midnite Inn)—"Dr. Jazz" (Jelly & Crowd). Act II, Scene 1 (Chimney Man Takes Charge); Scene 2 (The New York Suite)—"Good Ole New York" (Chimney Man, Hunnies, Jelly & Crowd), "Too Late, Daddy" (Jelly & Crowd), "That's the Way We Do Things in New Yawk" (Jelly & Melrose Bros.), Jelly's Isolation Dance (Jelly & Young Jelly); Scene 3 (The Last Chance)—"The Last Chance Blues" (Jelly & Anita); Scene 4 (Central Avenue); Scene 5 (The Last Rites)—"The Last Rites (Jelly, People of His Past & Chimney Man).

JERICHO (1984). A topical musical. By °Judy Brussel. Music by °Buck Brown. About the assassination of five civil rights leaders and labor organizers. Benefit premiere for the Greensboro (NC) Civil Rights Fund, at Symphony Space, New York, Nov. 9, 1984. Showcase prodn. at the 18th St. Playhouse, New York, Nov. 11–28, 1984; dir. by Jerry Campbell. Featuring Evelyn Blakey, Juanda LaJoyce Holley, and Molly Stark (racial identities not known).

JERICO–JIM CROW (1963–64, revived 1968). Called by the author "A Song Play." Presented without intermission. By Langston Hughes.

The history of segregation (Jim Crow) in America from slavery to the sit-in demonstrations of the 1960s, told through freedom songs, gospel music, spirituals, poetry, and narrative. The character of Jim Crow reappears in various guises throughout the play, as slaveholder, redneck sheriff, fundamentalist preacher, and segregationist.

First prod. Off-Bway by the Greenwich Players, under the auspices of °Stella Holt, in coordination with CORE (Congress of Racial Equality), SNCC (Student Non-Violent Coordinating Committee), and the NAACP, at the Sanctuary of the Village Presbyterian Church–Brotherhood Synagogue, New York City, Dec. 28, 1963, through April 1964, for about 40 perfs.; dir. by William Hairston and Alvin Ailey; music dir. by Hugh Porter. Cast: Gilbert Price (Young Man), Hilda Harris (Young Girl), Joseph Attles (Old Man), Rosalie King (Old Woman), William Cain (Jim Crow), and Dorothy Drake (Woman). The Hugh Porter Gospel Singers provided the choral music. Sam Shepherd was percussionist, and Marion Franklin, organist. Also prod. in other churches and halls.

Revived at the Greenwich Mews Theatre, New York, March 9–May 5, 1968, for 5 perfs. on weekends only; dir. by Alvin Ailey and William Hairston. Hilda Harris, Joseph Attles, Rosalie King, and Dorothy Drake appeared in their orig. roles. New cast members were Dion Watts (Young Man) and Barney Hodges (Jim Crow). Hugh Porter was musical dir. and pianist; Marion Franklin, organist; James W. Major, percussionist.

The music incorporated many classic or traditional songs with new lyrics and slants. Among the numbers were two orig. songs by Hughes—"Such a Little King" (sung by King & Harris) and "Freedom Land" (sung by Price). The traditional songs and musical numbers included "A Meeting Here Tonight," "I'm on My Way," "I Been 'Buked and I Been Scorned," "Is Massa Gwine to Sell Us Tomorrow?," "How Much Do You Want Me to Bear?," "Where Will I Lie Down?," "Follow the Drinking Gourd," "John Brown's Body," "Battle Hymn of the Republic," "Slavery Chain Done Broke at Last," "Oh, Freedom!," "Go Down, Moses," "Ezekiel Saw the Wheel," "Stay in the Field," "God's Gonna Cut You Down," "Don't You View That Ship?," "Better Leave Segregation Alone," "My Mind on Freedom," "We Shall Overcome," "The Battle of Old Jim Crow," and "Come and Go with Me."

Orig. cast recording by Folkways/Scholastic FL9671. Unpub. scripts in TC/NYPL and JWJ/YUL.

FURTHER REFERENCE: *BlkMagic* (Hughes & Meltzer). *NY Herald Trib.* 1–14–1964. *NY Post* 1–13–1964. *NYT* 1–13–1963; 2–23–1968. *Village Voice* 1–23–1964.

JERRY BLAND AND THE BLANDELLES FEATURING MISS MARVA JAMES / / Orig. title: **Charles Fuller Presents the Dynamic Jerry Bland and the Blandelles, with the Fabulous Miss Marva James** (1974). Blues-inspired musical. 3 acts. By Charles Fuller. About an aging blues singer attempting to make a comeback. Prod. Off-Bway by the New Federal Theatre, Spring 1977.

JERRY'S GIRLS (1981). Musical revue. 2 acts. By Jerry Herman and Larry Alford. "Starring the music and lyrics of Jerry Herman." Prod. at the Onstage Theatre, New York, Aug. 17–Nov. 11, 1981; dir. by Alford. The integrated cast of four ladies (and Jerry Herman) included one black: Pauletta Pearson. Other cast members were °Evalyn Baron, °Alexander Korey, and °Leila Martin.

JES LAK WHITE FO'KS / / Also *Jes Lak White Folks* (1900). Musical playlet. Book, music, and most of the lyrics by Will Marion Cook. Additional lyrics by Paul Laurence Dunbar.

Brief musical comedy (about 45 minutes in length), with about 6 songs (of which only 5 have been identified). Concerns a black soldier's dream of his daughter's having all the opportunities and privileges of affluent young white women, including the prospect of marrying a foreign prince or duke—until he discovers in his dream that troubles also go along with such social status. When he awakens, he decides that the simple life of black folks is much better. Written for Ernest Hogan, who was unable to assume the role because of a prior engagement.

Prod. without much success at the New York Winter Garden, June 26, 1900. Cast included Irvin Jones (a comedian) as the father and Abbie Mitchell (later Mrs. Will Marion Cook) as the daughter.

Songs, pub. by Harry von Tilzer, New York, c. 1900, included "Colored Girl from Vassar," "Evah Nigger Is a King," "Love Looks Not at Estate," "Spread de News," and "We's a Comin'." Libretto (8 pp.) located in the Music Div./LC.

Much of the material from this show was worked into Cook's comic opera *The Cannibal King* (1901).

JESUS CHRIST—LAWD TODAY (1971). Biblical-inspired musical. By Glenda Dickerson. Music by Clyde Barrett. The Christ story in a black American urban setting. Prod. by the Black American Theatre, Washington, DC, Summer 1971; dir. by Dickerson; with choreography by Debbie Allen. Also presented at Howard Univ. during the 1970s.

JESUS CHRIST SUPERSTAR (1971–73). Rock opera. Subtitled "The Last Seven Days in the Life of Jesus of Nazareth." Conceived and dir. by °Tom O'Horgan. Lyrics by °Tim Rice. Music by °Andrew Lloyd Webber. Prod. by °Robert Stigwood, in association with MCA, Inc., at the Mark Hellinger Theatre, New York, opening Oct. 12, 1971, for 711 perfs. With a predominantly white cast that featured Ben Vereen as Judas Iscariot. Jesus was played by °Jeff Fenholt, and Mary Magdalene by °Yvonne Elliman. Judas's songs included "Heaven on Their Minds," "Strange Thing Mystifying" (with Jesus, Apostles & Women), "Everything's Alright" (with Mary, Jesus, Apostles & Women), "Damned for All Time" (with Annas, Caiaphas & Priests), "The Last Supper" (with Jesus & Apostles), "Judas's Death" (with Annas & Caiaphas), and "Superstar" (Voice of Judas & Company). Libretto pub. in *Great Rock Musicals* (ed. Stanley Richards; New York: Stein and Day, 1979).

JIGFIELD FOLLIES (1927). Touring vaudeville revue. Featured Billy Mitchell, the Calloway Sisters (Harriet and Jenne), Frank Keith (female impersonator), Tommie Davis (toe dancer), Henry Drew, Billy Hayes, Bootsie Wilson, Betty Lockwood, and Lillian White.

JILL REED, READ!? (1980). Children's musical. Book, music, and lyrics by Michael Dinwiddie. Prod. by the Grand Street Settlement, New York.

JIM CROW (pre-1934). Musical drama. By Donald Heywood, J. Homer Tutt, and Salem Tutt Whitney. Concerns the fate of the passengers on a Jim Crow car headed from the South to Washington, DC. Rewritten as *De Gospel Train* (1940); copy of the latter in Schomburg.

JOHN HENRY (1940). Music drama. 3 acts. By °Roark Bradford. Music by °Jacques Wolf. In this version of the story, John Henry demonstrates that he is the strongest black man in 48 states by toting bales of cotton, laying railroad tracks, and defying the advances of wicked women. The innocent Julie Anne is the only woman he loves, and when he thinks that she has been untrue to him, he takes to drink, and in a boastful state of intoxication tries to match his skill in toting cotton with a steam joist. When he drops dead in the attempt, his sweetheart also dies of grief beside him. Prod. at the 44th St. Theatre, New York, Jan. 10–15, 1940, for 7 perfs.; staged by Anthony Brown and Charles Friedman. Choral direction by Leonard de Paur.

JOLLY COON-EY ISLAND. See *AT JOLLY COON-EY ISLAND* (two entries).

JOLLY TIME FOLLIES (1924). Touring vaudeville revue. Featuring Louis Deppe, Vance Dixon, Bo Diddley, and Earl Hines.

JONAH (1966). Biblical-inspired play with music. 2 acts [9 scenes]. By °Paul Goodman. Prod. by the American Place Theatre, New York, Feb. 15–March 6, 1966, for 24 perfs.; dir. by °Lawrence Kornfeld. The predominantly white cast was headed by °Sorrell Booke (as Jonah). Earle Hyman (as An Angel) was the only black with an important role. There were 21 songs and musical numbers.

JONES SYNCOPATED SYNCOPATORS (1923). Touring vaudeville revue. Prod. by and starring Jewish impersonator Joseph Jones. Cast included dancer and blackface comedian Speedy Smith, George Gould, Minnie Lee, Bobby Vinson, Eva Mason, Lilly Yuen, Raymond Jefferson, and Violette Howell.

JOSEPHINE BAKER (1964). Musical revue. Built around the international celebrity. Consisted of songs by Baker, dance routines by Geoffrey Holder, folk dances by the Aviv Dancers, and primitive and modern dances by the Larl Becham Trio.

Prod. by °Sherman S. Krellberg at the Brooks Atkinson Theatre, New York, Feb. 4–16, 1964, for 15 perfs.; staged by °Felix G. Gerstman. Musical dir., °Gershon Kingsley. Cast included the above-named 4 principal persons and groups. Played a return engagement at Henry Miller's Theatre, New York, opening March 31, 1964, for 24 perfs.: with dancer Carmen deLavallade as Holder's partner.

Songs and musical numbers, mainly from Miss Baker's repertoire, included "Avec," "Quand Tu M'embrasse," "Make Believe," "Quando, Quando," "Don't Touch My Tomatoes," "La Seine," "Hello Young Lovers," "Mon Bateau Blanc," "Felicida," "April in Paris" (sung in English and French), "Adios, Adios," "Bill," "Je Pars," "Melodie Perdue," "Lucky Star," "En Emerada," "J'ai Deux Amours," "Hava Neguila," "Fan, Fan," "Dans Mon Village," and "J'attendrai."

JOY (1966). Musical revue. Written, directed, and starred in by Oscar Brown, Jr. Described by *Jet* (2–12–1970) as "a collection of songs in the Brazilian style." First prod. at the Happy Medium, Chicago, 1966. Prod. Off-Bway at the New Theatre, Jan. 27–July 26, 1970, for 208 perfs.; with the author, Judy Pace, and Sivucca (an albino Brazilian performer) on the accordion.
FURTHER REFERENCE: *NYT* 7–19–1970.

THE JOY BOAT (1930). Touring vaudeville revue. Featured comedians Clinton "Dusty" Fletcher and Jackie (later "Moms") Mabley (in blackface), Izzy Ringgold, Johnny Hudgins, Marion Bradford, the Three Aces, Jimmie Baskette, and George Brown.

JOYLAND GIRLS (1921). Touring vaudeville revue. Prod. by and starring comedian Edgar Martin (in blackface). Cast also included Pearl Ray, Peggy Barnette, Helen Thomas, Bobby Bramlet, and Isabelle Foster.

JUDY FORGOT (1910). White-oriented musical. Book and lyrics by °Avery Hopwood. Music by °Silvio Hein. With additional music and lyrics by Will Marion Cook and °Andrew R. Sterling. Based on *The Winking Princess* (author unknown). Prod. on Bway, opening Oct. 6, 1910, for 44 perfs. The all-white cast included °Marie Cahill, °Truly Sattuch, and °Joseph Stanley. The Cook/ Sterling song was "Whoop 'Er Up!," introduced with great success by Cahill; vocal-piano score pub. by Harry von Tilzer Music Publishing Co., New York, 1910; copy in Moorland-Spingarn.

JUMBLE JAZZBO JAMBOREE (1929). Touring jazz show. Featured Watts & Wills (with Billy Watts), the Maryland Harmony Four, Mary Hicks, and Oliver Price's Jazz Wizards Orchestra.

JUMP FOR JOY (1941). Musical revue. Billed as "A Sun-Tanned Revu-sical." 2 acts [29 scenes]. Music mainly by Duke Ellington, with other songs by °Hal Borne and °Otis Bene. Lyrics by °Sid Kuller, Paul Webster, and Hal °Fimberg. Sketches by Kuller and Fimberg.

A wartime hit show prod. in Hollywood, consisting of a series of sketches and songs built around the theme that Uncle Tom is dead and has been replaced by new images (*Blk Playwrs* [Hatch & Abdullah], p. 83).

Prod. by the American Revue Theatre, at the Mayan Theatre in Los Angeles, during the summer of 1941, for a long run. Featured cast: Ivy Anderson, Marie Bryant, Herb Jeffries, Judy Carol, Artie Brandon, Al Guster, the Hi-Hatters, Lawrence Harris, Suzette Johnson, William Lewis, Pot, Pan & Skillet, Otis Renee, Wonderful Smith, Joe Turner, Paul White, and Duke Ellington's Orchestra. Girls of the Ensemble: Artie Brandon, Lucille Battle, Avanelle Harris, Ethelyn Stevenson, Myrtle Fortune, Alice Key, Doris Ake, Hyacinth Cotten, Millie Munroe, Louise Franklin, and Patsy Hunter. Singers in the Choir: Maudie Bilbrew, Eddievies Flenoury, Evelyn Burrwell, Elizabeth Green, Edward Short, Bene Greene, Lawrence Harris, and Roy Glenn. The Hi-Hatters: Clarence Landry, Vernod Bradley, and Udell Johnson.

Program (including cast, scenes, and musical numbers): Act I—Scene 1, "Sun-Tanned Tenth of the Nation," lyrics by Webster, music by Borne and Bene (Company). Scene 2, Prologue (Ellington). Scene 3, 'It's Only Propaganda' (White & Smith). Scene 4, "The Brown Gal in the Calico Gown," lyrics by Webster, music by Ellington (Jeffries [Boy], Carol [Girl], Girls of the Ensemble [Calico Girls], Hi-Hatters [dance]). Scene 5, "Bli-Blip," lyrics by Kuller, music by Ellington (Bryant [Girl], White [Boy]). Scene 6, 'Resigned to Living,' by Fimberg (Johnson [Gertrude], Guster [Noel], Jeffries [1st Caller], Lewis [2nd Caller], Smith [Man]). Scene 7, "Bugle Break" and "Subtle Slough" (Pot, Pan & Skillet). Scene 8, "Chocolate Shake," lyrics by Webster, music by Ellington (White [Bartender], Guster [Boy], Anderson [Girl], and Bryant [Cigarette Girl]). Scene 9, Monologue (Smith). Scene 10, "I Got It Bad and That Ain't Good," lyrics by Webster, music by Ellington (Anderson [singer]). Scene

11, "Two Left Feet," lyrics by Webster, music by Borne (White [Schoolboy], Bryant [Cindy], Harris [1st Sister], Lucille Battle [2nd Sister], Burrwell [Fairy Godmother], Harris [Prince Charming], Jitterbugs [Hi-Hatters, Brandon, Fortune & Munroe]). Scene 12, Joe Turner. Scene 13, 'The Life of Our Time,' by Fimberg (Smith [Carlyle], Franklin [Ephedrine], Pan [Sharpie], Pot [Kit Carson], and Skillet [Johnny]). Scene 14, "Stomp Caprice," music by Mercer Ellington (Guster [dancer]). Scene 15, "Whether or Not" (Pan & Skillet). Scene 16, "Uncle Tom's Cabin Is a Drive-In Now," lyrics by Webster, music by Borne (Glenn [Uncle Tom], Burrwell [Aunt Jemima], Anderson [Hostess], Bryant [Waitress], Hi-Hatters, Ensemble). Act II—Overture. Scene 1, "Jump for Joy," lyrics by Kuller and Webster, music by Ellington (Choir & Ensemble). Scene 2, "If Life Were All Peaches and Cream," lyrics by Webster, music by Borne (Carol & Jeffries [1st Couple], Bryant & White [2nd Couple]). Scene 3, "Nothin'," lyrics by Kuller & Ray Golden, music by Borne (Ivy Anderson [singer]). Scene 4, 'You're in the Army Now,' by Kuller (Glenn [Doctor], White [1st Draftee], Pan [2nd Draftee], Skillet [3rd Draftee], Pot [4th Draftee]). Scene 5, "Concerto for Klinkers," music by Ellington. Scene 6, "Shh! He's on the Beat," lyrics by Kuller & Fimberg, music by Ellington (Glenn [Proprietor], Bryant [Waitress], Smith [Bartender], Cotten & B. Greene [1st Couple], Key & White [2nd Couple], Landry & Johnson [3rd Couple], Harris & Pot [4th Couple], Pan [Cop], Turner [Police Captain]). Scene 7, 'Vignettes,' by Kuller (Ellington [The Duke], Carol & Jeffries [1st Couple], Bryant & Johnson [2nd Couple]). Scene 8, "The Tune of the Hickory Stick," lyrics by Webster, music by Borne (Carol [singer], Guster [dancer]). Scene 9, Willie Lewis. Scene 10, 'Sidewalk Incident' (Smith [Panhandler], White [Passerby]). Scene 11, 'Made to Order,' by Kuller (Pan [1st Tailor], Skillet [2nd Tailor], Pot [Customer]). Scene 12, "Sharp Easter," lyrics by Kuller, music by Ellington. Scene 13, Finale (Entire Cast).

FURTHER REFERENCE: *Mus. Is My Mistress* (Ellington).

JUMP STEADY (1922). Musical comedy. 2 acts [11 scenes]. Written and prod. by Salem Tutt Whitney and J. Homer Tutt, who costarred as two schemers (Samford and Hamford). The story revolves around their effort to swindle one of the characters (played by Amon Davis) out of a large sum of money. Touring show, which apparently was one of the earliest shows in which the great star Ethel Waters appeared (*BlksBf* [Sampson], p. 446). Cast also included Margaret Lee, Henrietta Lovelass, Nelly Brown, Percy Colston, Margaret Simms, Nat Cash, Helen Fenderson, Bessie Simms, Ethel Pope, Leroy Bloomfield, Joyce Robinson, Julia Moody, Elvita Davis, Elizabeth Campbell, Bernice Winston, Hazel Springer, Viola Mandero, Helen Warren, George Randol, Jennie Dancy, Chester Jones, John Dancy, Henry Thompson, Lottie Harris, and Dick Conway. Songs and musical numbers included a song/dance number entitled "Breaking

a Leg" (Harris, Brown, Moody, & M. Simms); "Ja Da Blues" (Moody); "Dear Old Southland" and "Syncopated Blues" (Lee).
FURTHER REFERENCE: *Billboard* (J. A. Jackson's Page) 6–17–1922; 7–8–1922.

JUNEBUG JACK (1991). Musical play. Created jointly by Junebug Productions of New Orleans, LA (the successor to the Free Southern Theatre), and Roadside Theatre of Whitesburg, KY (a touring group from Central Appalachia). The play celebrates the rich cultural heritage of two southern cultures—rural African American and Appalachian mountain—weaving together Junebug stories and Jack tales, the blues, ballads, mountain fiddle tunes, banjo picking, and gospel singing that are popular in the two companies' homeplaces. Toured the eastern and central states during the summer of 1991. The integrated company included two blacks (John O'Neal and Michael Keck) and two whites (°Tom Bledsoe and °Angelyn DeBord).

JR. BLACKBIRDS (1926). Musical revue. Music by Thomas "Fats" Waller. A show which capitalized on one of the hit musicals of the period, *Blackbirds of 1926*, starring Florence Mills. Produced in New York, presumably at the Lafayette Theatre, for a short run in late 1926, then on tour.

JUST A LITTLE SIMPLE (1950). Musical adaptation. By Alice Childress. Based on Langston Hughes' *Simple Speaks His Mind*, about a Harlem character named Jesse B. Semple. Prod. by the Committee for the Negro in the Arts, at Club Baron in Harlem, opening Sept. 1950, for a run of two months.

JUST AROUND THE CORNER (1951). Musical of the depression era. 2 acts. Book by °Abby Mann and °Bernard Drew. Lyrics by Langston Hughes. Music by °Joe Sherman. About a group of likable bums who arrive by boxcar in New York City in 1933, expecting to find prosperity, on the very day that President Roosevelt closes the nation's banks. Prod. in a tryout prodn. at the Ogunquit Playhouse in Maine, during the summer of 1950, featuring Avon Long, but closed prior to reaching New York. Script of Hughes' lyrics in JWJ/YUL.
FURTHER REFERENCE: *Variety* 8–2–1950.

JUST FOR FUN (1923). Touring vaudeville revue. Prod. by and costarring veteran showman Irvin C. Miller. Cast also included composer Will Marion Cook and Ida Andrews.

JUST SO (1986). Musical based on the Rudyard Kipling stories. Prod. at the Jack Lawrence Theatre, New York, 1986; featuring Andre De Shields.

K

KEEP IT UP (1922). Touring vaudeville revue. 2 acts. Prod. by °I. M. Weingarden. Starring Billy Higgins and Clifford Ross. Higgins perfd. in at least two sketches: 'Circus at the Cut Out Inn,' in which he portrayed a hotel porter; and 'The Greedy Man,' a courtroom scene in which he played a judge. Ross impersonated comedian Bert Williams in a song entitled "At the Poker Club." Other members of the cast were Ernest Whitman, Alice Gorgas, Susie Sutton, Lena Leggett, Henrietta Leggett, Edna Hicks, Ollie Burgoyne, Bob "Monk" Brawlet, Al Curtis, and Iola Young.

KEEP MOVIN' (1927). Touring vaudeville revue. Prod. by Ed. E. Daley. Cast included Pauline and Roscoe Montella, "Skeeter" Winston, Onnie Jones, Williams & Scott, Nona Marshall, Billy Young, Troy Brown, and Edgar Haynes.

KEEP SHUFFLIN' (1928). Musical revue. 2 acts [8 scenes]. Book by Flournoy E. Miller and Aubrey Lyles (Miller & Lyles). Lyrics by Henry Creamer and Andy Razaf. Music by Jimmy [James P.] Johnson, Thomas "Fats" Waller, and °Clarence Todd.

Modeled after Miller & Lyles' eminently successful *Shuffle Along* of 1921, this show was also set in Jimtown, and based on the antics of Steve Jenkins and Sam Peck, and is built around a utopian get-rich-quick scheme which also involves a satire on communism. Jenkins and Peck, as two shiftless dreamers, form a group called the Equal Got League, through which they plan a scheme to provide wealth and plenty for everybody (especially themselves) by blowing up a bank and distributing the cash. For a few days everyone lives in luxury and splendor, but the damage to the economy is so great that their money soon becomes worthless and the futility of the whole scheme becomes apparent. Of course, the whole thing is only a dream.

Prod. on Bway by °Con Conrad at the Daly's 63rd St. Theatre, opening Feb.

27, 1928, for 104 perfs.; dir. by Conrad. Orchestrations by Will Vodery; choreography by Clarence Robinson. Johnson was musical dir.; and he and Waller both perfd. at the piano. Jabbo Smith was "behind the bugle." Cast: Flournoy E. Miller (Steve Jenkins), Aubrey Lyles (Sam Peck), Margaret Lee (Mrs. Jenkins), Paul Floyd (Boss), John Gregg (Brother Jones), John Virgel (Mose), Greta Anderson (Grit), Clarence Robinson (Walter), Byron Jones (Scrappy), Evelyn Keyes (Evelyn), Honey Brown (Honey), Jean Starr (Alice), Maude Russell (Maude), Billie Yarbo (Yarbo), Hazel Sheppard (Hazel), Marie Dove (Marie), Gilbert Holland (Bill), and Herman Listerino (Joseph); Others: Ladies of the Ensemble, Jubilee Singers and Dancers, Paraders, Citizens of Jimtown, etc.

Moved to the Windsor Theatre, New York, Sept. 3, 1928, for a short run. Toured as a USO camp show during the 1940s, with a different cast.

Songs and musical numbers: "Teasing Mama" (Creamer & Johnson), "Choc'late Bar" (Razaf & Waller), "Labor Day Parade" (Razaf & Todd),[+] "Give Me the Sunshine" (Creamer, Johnson, & Conrad), "Leg It" (Creamer, Todd, & Conrad), Exhortation Theme from "Yamekraw Negro Rhapsody" (Creamer & Johnson),[+] " 'Sippi" (Creamer, Johnson, & Conrad), "How Jazz Was Born" (Razaf & Waller), [+] "Willow Tree (A Musical Misery)" (Razaf & Waller), "Keep Shufflin' " (Razaf & Waller), "Everybody's Happy in Jimtown" (Razaf & Waller), "Dusky Love" (Creamer & Vodery), "Charlie, My Back Door Man" (Creamer & Todd), "On the Levee" (Creamer & Johnson), Finale—"Skiddle de Scow" (Johnson & Bradford). Other songs added during the course of the show's run include "Harlem Rose" (Conrad & Gladys Rogers), "Pining" (Creamer & Todd), "Washboard Ballet" (Waller), "Got Myself Another Jockey Now" (Razaf & Waller), and " 'Twas a Kiss in the Moonlight" (Creamer, Conrad & Stephen Jones), "Brothers," "Don't Wake 'Em Up," "Bugle Blues," "Deep Blue Sea," "My Old Banjo," "Let's Go to Town," "Pretty Soft, Pretty Soft," "Whoopem Up," and "You May Be a Whale in Georgia."

Songs marked with a plus sign ([+]) pub. by Harms, Inc., New York, 1928; copies in Moorland-Spingarn.

FURTHER REFERENCE: *Ain't Misbehavin'* (Kirkeby). *Billboard* 3–10–1928. *BlkMusTh* (Woll). *BlksBf* (Sampson). *James P. Johnson* (Brown). *NY American* 3–1–1928. *NY Eve. World* 2–28–1928. *NY Graphic* 2–28–1928. *NY J. of Commerce* 2–29–1928. *NY Post* 2–28–1928. *NY Sun* 2–28–1928. *NYT* 2–28–1928. *NY Telegraph* 2–28–1928. *NY World* 2–28–1928. *Variety* 3–7–1928. *Vogue* 5–1–1928.

KENTUCKY SUE (1926). Touring vaudeville revue. Prod. by and starring the dance team of Chappelle & Stinnette (Thomas Chappelle and Juanita Stinnette). Cast also included comedian Doe Doe Green, dancer Dink Thomas, "Babe" Townsend, Billy Maxey, Loveless & McLane, Larry Seymour, Grace Smith, and 17 chorus girls.

KICKS & COMPANY (1961). Musical. 2 acts. Book, music, and lyrics by Oscar Brown, Jr., in collaboration with °Robert Nemiroff. About a Satan-like figure who is working to sabotage the southern sit-in movement. Financed by °Dave Garroway, Lorraine Hansberry, and her husband Nemiroff. Auditioned on "The Dave Garroway" television show, before being prod. at the Arie Brown Theatre, Chicago, where it ran for only 4 perfs., Oct. 11–14, 1961; staged by Hansberry. Cast included Vi Velasco, Lonnie Sattin, and °Burgess Meredith.
FURTHER REFERENCE: *Jet* 3–16–1961; 10–12–1961; 10–26–1961.

THE KIDNAPPER (1917). Tabloid musical. Written and prod. by Billy King at the Grand Theatre, Chicago. With members of the Billy King Stock Co.

KINGDOM OF GOLD (1991). African-inspired musical. Apparently cowritten by members of the Chocolate Chips Theatre Company of Chicago. About an ancient kingdom of Wagandu which thrived in West Africa hundreds of years ago, through which flowed incredible amounts of gold from the mines of Wangara—the location of which was one of the empire's best kept secrets. The musical centers about attempts to discover the gold mines by those who plan to betray the king, and it blends traditional myth and historical fact, to take the audience back to a time that is a part of the cultural heritage of African Americans. Prod. by the Chocolate Chips Theatre Co., at the Dunham Theatre of Kennedy-King City College in Chicago, Feb. 22, 1991.

THE KING OF SPADES (1900). Musical comedy. 2 acts. By Bob Cole. Copyright 1900. Cited by Fannin Belcher (Ph.D. diss., 1945, p. 116). May be in LC. No record of prodn.

KING RASTUS (1900–1905). Billed as "A Farcical Vaudeville Comedy." Also called an "Operatic Comedy." Prod. by Will Isham, with members of John Isham's *The Octoroons* Company, after John Isham's retirement.
    Touring show which starred Billy Kersands in the title role. Cast also included the Mallory Brothers & Brooks, Grace Halliday Mallory, Smart & Williams, and Hattie McIntosh. The critic of the Indianapolis *Freeman* (3–30–1901), who saw the show at the Memphis (TN) Auditorium on March 19, 1901, lambasted it in the following review:

As a whole the show was one that the citizens of this place care not to see repeated. It is a slander on the Negro of America; for example, here are some of their sayings: "Who raised you, a Colored Woman?"; "If a Negro left those things here, give them back to him"; "Say, gal, give me them White folks money"; "That's the reason White folks don't let niggers hold office, because they want to rule the earth." And worse than all was when they say "Every nation has a flag but a coon." Every flag was displayed with honor, then a rag with a chicken and watermelon was displayed, and on it was this inscription: "Our rag," signifying that the Negro would spill his last drop of blood to get into somebody's chicken coop and watermelon patch. The costumes and dancing were very vulgar. The white people enjoyed this flag business and niggers in the white folks yard, but for me, we say shame, shame!

In spite of this unfavorable review, the show continued to tour for several seasons, playing variety and vaudeville houses in the Northeast, East, and Midwest until mid-1905.

KINGS OF KOON-DOM (1898). Musical show. By Bob Cole and William "Billy" Johnson. Apparently a hodgepodge of everything in the "coon" genre, taken from Cole & Johnson's other shows, including *A Trip to Coontown* (1897–1901) and *At Jolly Coon-ey Island* (1896–97). Prod. at Koster and Bial's Music Hall, New York, Aug. 1898, where it was the main attraction, and according to Gerald Bordman (*AmMusTh*), quoting from a contemporary source, the show featured "over twenty of the Darktown contingent." It included one interpolated song from Will Marion Cook's *Clorindy*, "Darktown Is Out Tonight."

KING SOLOMON / / Orig. title: *Song of Solomon* (1951). Biblical opera. 1 act. Libretto by Elmslie (one name). Musical score by J. Harold Brown. Prod. as *Song of Solomon* at Karamu House, Cleveland, in repertory, Sept. 28–Nov. 24, 1951; conducted by the composer.

KITCHEN MECHANICS REVUE (1930). Cabaret revue on a "black domestics" theme. Music by James P. Johnson (as Jimmie Johnson). Lyrics by Andy Razaf. Prod. at Small's Paradise in Harlem, 1930. Orchestra directed by Elmer Snowden. Musical accompaniment by Snowden's band, which included Elmer Snowden (guitar), Gus Aiken and Red Harlen (trumpets), Herb Gregory (trombone), Otto Hardwick and Wayman Carver (reeds), Don Kirkpatrick (piano), and Sid Catlett (drums). Songs by Razaf & Johnson, copyright by Joe Davis, 1930, included "Bantu Baby," "Elevator Papa—Switchboard Mama," "Go Harlem" (pub. by Mayfair Music), "Good for Nothin'," "Kitchen Mechanics' Parade," "Mammy Land," "On the Level with You," "Porter's Love Song to a Chambermaid," "Sambo's Syncopated Russian Dance," "Shake Your Duster," "Slippery Hips," "Swanee Fashion Plate," and "Ya Gotta Be Versatile."

KITCHEN OPERA (1947). Musical comedy on a "black domestics" theme. Music by James P. Johnson. Lyrics by Flournoy E. Miller. No record of prodn. Musical numbers by Miller & Johnson, all pub. by Mills Music, 1947, included "Accusation," "At Home with My Range," "Butler and the Cook Desire," "Butler and the Handy Man," "Chauffeur," "Finale Love," "Handy Man," "Lindy Lou," "Love," "Mandy's Blessing," "Solution," "Spring Cleaning," and "Where Is the Handy Man."

K OF P (1923). Vaudeville revue. Prod. in Harlem by Collington Hayes, who also costarred with his wife, Helen Hayes. About two husbands who pretend to be attending fraternity lodge meetings as an excuse for getting away from their wives for a night out on the town. Cast also included Shelton Brooks, Bessie White, Olivette West, Malachi Smith, and Newell Morse. Musical numbers included "Ghost of Mr. Jazz," "Tomorrow," "Asleep in the Deep," "Got My Habits On," "Da Da Strain," and "Royal Garden Blues."

KOJO AND THE LEOPARD (1973). African-inspired children's musical. By Grace Cooper [Ihunanya]. Concerns a young African boy who completes his tribal initiation into manhood by conquering a leopard. Prod. at school, college, and community theatres throughout the U.S.

KWAMINA (1961–62). African-inspired musical. Book by °Robert Alan Aurthur. Music and lyrics by °Richard Adler.
    A dramatization of the conflict between the past and present in an African village, focusing mainly on an interracial love story, involving an African physician (Kwamina), returning to his country after being educated abroad, and a visiting British medical doctor (Eve), the daughter of a missionary, who is working in the village clinic. The title and the leading character's name are taken from a West African term meaning "Saturday's Child." The love affair is opposed by Kwamina's father, a village chieftain (Nana Mwalla), the British commissioner (Blair) who is also in love with Eve, and most of the African villagers. Unwilling to conduct a clandestine affair in the face of such opposition, the two lovers agree at the end to terminate the affair.
    In spite of the daring theme—an interracial romance involving a black man and a white woman—most critics agreed that the librettist was so restrained in the treatment of his material that the two lovers might as well have been white. *ThArts* (1–1962, p. 14) stated tersely that "*Kwamina* decided to brave a White-Negro Romance and then got scared." The *Toronto Daily Star* (9–5–1961) concluded that "Mr. Aurthur fears the miscegenation theme," and further speculated: "Whatever the reason he never allows their physical intimacy to extend beyond Eve flinging herself into Kwamina's arms at the Act I curtain and walking hand-in-hand at the final curtain. The dialogue is discretion itself."
    Toured in Boston and Toronto prior to opening in New York at the 54th Street Theatre, Oct. 23, 1961, for 32 perfs.; dir. by Robert Lewis. Choreography by °Agnes de Mille. Cast: Brock Peters (Obitsebi, a Tribal Fetish Man), Robert Guillaume (Ako), °Sally Ann Howes (Eve), Terry Carter (Kwamina), Rex Ingram (Nana Mwalla, Kwamina's father, an ailing tribal chief), °Norman Barrs (Blair, the British commissioner), Ethel Ayler (Naii), Joseph Attles (Akufo), Ainsley Sigmond (Kojo), Rosalie Maxwell (Alla), Lillian Hayman (Mammy Trader), Ronald Platt and Edward Thomas (Policemen).
    Songs and musical numbers: "The Cocoa Bean Song," "Welcome Home," "The Sun Is Beginning to Crow," "Did You Hear That?," "You're As English

As,'' "Seven Sheep, Four Red Shirts, and a Bottle of Gin," "Nothing More to Look Forward To," "What's Wrong with Me?," "Something Big," "Ordinary People," "A Man Can Have No Choice," "What Happened to Me Tonight?," "One Wife," and "Another Time, Another Place."

No published libretto. Cast recording by Capitol (SW–1645).

FURTHER REFERENCE: Alkire diss. *BlkDr* (Mitchell). *BlkMusTh* (Woll). *NY Herald Trib.* 10–24–1961. *NY J. American* 10–24–1961. *NY Mirror* 10–24–1961. *NYT* 10–25–1961. *NY World-Telegraph & Sun* 11–7–1961. *Show* 3–1962. *Show Business Illus.* 10–24–1962. *ThArts* 1–1962. *Toronto Daily Star* 9–5–1961; 9–7–1961.

KYKUNKOR [pronounced Ky-KUN-kor] / / Subtitled *The Witch Woman* (1934). African dance opera. 3 acts. Written and choreographed by Asadata Dafora Horton, a native African choreographer/dancer from Sierra Leone.

Developed as "part of a program of research in African arts which aim[ed] to place a racial foundation under modern American Negro dance and music, and also [stressed] the aesthetic values of native traditions and rituals" (*NegAmTh* [Isaacs], p. 95).

The thin plot, which was used primarily as a basis for presenting the native dances and music, "dealt with a curse placed [by a witch doctor] on a bridegroom [the king] (enacted by Dafora) and the attempt to remove it" (*Blk. Dance* [Emery], pp. 249-50). An extant playbill indicates that the dances include the Agunda, a dance of joy; the Eboe, a jester's dance; the Batoo, a dance of challenge; a war dance; and the Jabawa, or festival dance. This work is of significance as the first successful concert performance by black dancers on the American stage. Because of its success, it also led to the founding of an African unit of the WPA Federal Theatre Project in 1937.

First prod. in a little hall on East 34th St. in New York City in May 1934. Again presented at the Little Theatre, 244 West 44th St., New York City, June 18, 1934. Opened at Carnegie Hall, New York City, Dec. 22, 1934. The mixed cast included both native African and black American dancers.

The music was arranged by black pianist Margaret Kennerly Upshur. The drum orchestra was particularly praised by the critics. Henry Krehbiel (quoted in *NegAmTh* [Isaacs], p. 94) wrote that

Berlioz in his supremest effort with his army of drummers produced nothing to compare in artistic interest with [*Kyunkor*'s] harmonious drumming. . . . The fundamental effect was a combination of double and triple time, the former kept by the singers, the latter by the drummers, but it is impossible to convey the idea of the wealth of detail achieved by the drummers by means of exchange of the rhythms, syncopation of both simultaneously, and dynamic devices [*sic*].

FURTHER REFERENCE: *Blk. Dance* (Emery). *NegAmTh* (Isaacs). *NYT* 12–22–1934. *Opportunity* 8–1934.

L

LADY AFRICA (1901–4). Musical comedy with minstrel elements. Written, assembled, and prod. by Al (Albert) and Mamie Anderson (husband and wife vaudeville team). Toured for three years, starring the Andersons. In 1903, it opened in Providence, RI, with a roster including Fannie Winfred, Helen Beckley, Maggie Davis, and the Golden Gate Quartette. In 1904, it was partially resurrected at a Massachusetts summer resort as a minstrel show called *Lady Africa's Minstrels*, which reportedly had a beautifully staged afterpiece called 'On Broadway in Dahomey,' which capitalized upon the Bway success of the Williams & Walker show *In Dahomey* (1903).

THE LADY BARBER (c. 1913). Musical comedy. 2 acts. By Bob Russell and Billy Owens. Prod. by the Russell & Owens Stock Co., at the Pekin Theatre, Savannah, GA, opening March 17, c. 1913. With Russell & Owens, Lena Wiggins, Margie Crosby, Clifford Ross, and Tom Parker (comedian).

LADY DAY (1971–72). "A Musical Tragedy." 2 acts. Book by Aishah Rahman. Music by Archie Shepp. Additional music by Stanley Cowell and Cal Massey. Based on the life and career of Billie Holiday. First prod. at the Brooklyn Academy of Music, 1971. Prod. at the Chelsea Theatre, Brooklyn, Oct. 17–Nov. 5, 1972, for 24 perfs.; dir. by Paul Carter Harrison. Featuring Cecilia Norfleet as Billie Holiday. Also in the cast were Rosetta LeNoire as Mother Horne, and Maxwell Glanville as Mort Shazer.
FURTHER REFERENCE: *NYT* 10–26–1972.

A LADY FOR A DAY (1917). Tabloid musical. Written and prod. by Billy King. Presented at the Grand Theatre, Chicago, with members of the Billy King Stock Co.

A LADY OF CONSEQUENCE (1961–62). Musical play. Libretto and lyrics by Harold Cruse. Musical score by Frank Fields. Scheduled for prodn. around 1962, with Pearl Bailey in the lead, but the planned prodn. did not materialize.

LADY PLUM BLOSSOM (1972). Children's musical. 2 acts. Book by Madeline Davidson. Lyrics by Townsend Brewster. Musical score by Mark Ollinger. Prod. by Oregon State Univ./Corvallis, April 14, 1972. Pub. by Modern Theatre for Youth, Inc., Manhattan, KS, 1973.

THE LAST MINSTREL SHOW (1978). Musical entertainment. 2 acts [6 scenes]. By Joe Taylor Ford. Re-creation of an old-time minstrel show with significant social commentary for the 1970s. The action occurs backstage at the Variety Theatre in Cincinnati, OH, on the night of March 15, 1926. Prod. on tour of the East, opening at the Wilbur Theatre in Boston, March 20, 1978, and closing at the New Locust Theatre in Philadelphia, April 30, 1978. The integrated cast included Della Reese (Black Sally), Gregory Hines (Mr. Shine & J. J. Jones), and Clebert Ford (Mr. Bones & Bert Pine).

L. A. SUNSET (1981). Billed as a "Rock Jazzical." Written, dir., and choreographed by William Electric Black (Ian Ellis James). Prod. at the Nat Horne Musical Theatre, New York, Oct. 15–Nov. 1, 1981.

LATE HOUR [TAP] DANCERS (1929). Musical extravaganza. Featuring blues singer Bessie Smith. Prod. in Harlem, Sept. 1929, opening first at the Lafayette Theatre, then at the Lincoln Theatre the following week. With a cast of 50. Afterwards, apparently went on tour.

LAZY RHYTHM (1931). Touring show. Prod. by the veteran comedy team Miller & Lyles (Flournoy E. Miller and Aubrey Lyles), who also costarred. Cast included composer Shelton Brooks, Eddie Rector, and Louise Cook.

THE LEAGUE OF RHYTHM (1936). Musical revue. Opened at the Apollo Theatre in Harlem, Dec. 1936, featuring blues singer Bessie Smith.

LEAH KLESCHNA (1931). Opera. Written and composed by H. Lawrence Freeman. His best-known operas are *The Martyr* (1893), *Valdo* (1905–6), *Vendetta* (1911–23), and *Voodoo* (1921–28).

THE LEGACY (1987–90). Gospel musical. By Gordon Nelson. Explores the history of gospel music. Prod. by the National Black Theatre of Harlem, for an open run, Oct. 1987–May 1990; dir. by Elmo Terry. Featuring Cheryl Hilliard-Hewitt, Jolianna Daughtrey, Marsha Z. West, Clarice LaVerne Thompson, Lee Hayes, Robert Rowe, Steve Scott, Pasean Wilson, Laura Bowman, Edine Hart, Esther Pulliam, Billie Scott, James McLeod, Conrad Neblett, and Tunde Samuel.

LEONARD HARPER'S REVUE (1929). Touring revue. Prod. by dancer/choreographer Leonard Harper. Cast included Jazzlips Richardson, Baby Cox, Louise Cook, Madeline Belt, Billy Maxey, Leona Williams, the Two Black Dots, Dudley Dixon, the Midnight Steppers, and Louis Anthony's Orchestra.

LET 'EM HAVE IT (1923). Touring vaudeville revue. Prod. by and costarring Byrd & Ewing (comedian Joe Byrd and straight man Billy Ewing). Also in the cast were blackface comedian Louis Talley, Madam Cherrie Blossom, Elsie Fisher, Libby Robinson, Alma Henderson, Gladys Foster, Gladys Jordan, Beulah Getting, and Beatrice Moody.

LET'S GO (1924). Touring revue. Prod. by Fred Clark. Cast included Mabel Kemp, Manny King, Kitty Madison, Burton Sash, and Sammy Thompson's Colored Jazz Band.

LET THE MUSIC PLAY GOSPEL (1989). Gospel musical. With Vy Higginsen (author of *Mama, I Want to Sing*) as hostess and narrator. Prod. at the Heckscher Theatre, New York, Fall 1989, for an open run.

LEVEE DAYS (1928). Touring vaudeville revue. Prod. by Al Rogers. Clarence Austin, musical dir. Cast included the dance team of Chappelle & Stinnette (Thomas Chappelle and Juanita Stinnette), Ollie Burgoyne, Marion Moore, Frank Badham, Willie Porter, Charlie Doyle, George Morton, and Lillian Westmoreland.

THE LIBERTY BELLES (1901). White-oriented musical comedy. 3 acts. By °Harry B. Smith. Additional song by Will Accooe. Prod. by °Klaw & Erlanger at the Madison Square Theatre, New York, opening Sept. 30, 1901, for 104 perfs. With an all-white cast. Included "I'd Like to Be a Gunner in the Navy," by Will Accooe.
FURTHER REFERENCE: *AmMusTh* (Bordman). *BesPls 1899–1909.*

LILY WHITE (1930). Musical revue. Prod. at the Majestic Theatre in Brooklyn, and then on tour. Featuring Trixie Smith.

LIME KILN CLUB (1920). Musical show. Prod. by Billy King and the Darktown Follies Co., apparently at the Grand Theatre, Chicago. Cast included King, Andrew Tribble, Dink Stewart, Will A. Cook, Mattie Wilkes, and E. R. Fraction.

LINCOLN FOLLIES (1926). Musical revue. Prod. at the Lincoln Theatre in Harlem. Featuring Adelaide Hall and Lucille Hegamin.

A LITTLE BIT OF EVERYTHING (1904). White-oriented "Musical Vaude-ville." Also called "The Offenbach Review." By °John J. McNally. Included a series of 6 songs by Bob Cole, J. Rosamond Johnson, and James Weldon Johnson. Prod. by °Klaw & Erlanger at the Aerial Gardens, on top of the New Amsterdam Theatre, New York, June 6, 1904, for 1,920 perfs. The all-white cast was headed by °Peter F. Dailey and °Fay Templeton. The Cole & Johnson Brothers' interpolation was entitled "The Evolution of Ragtime," a series of 6 songs which traced the development of ragtime from its African beginnings to the present (1904). For individual song titles, see *Mother Goose* (1903).

LITTLE BLACK SAMBO (1937). Children's opera. Adapt. from the °Helen Bannerman story by the same title. Music and direction by Shirley Graham Du Bois. Prod. by the Chicago Unit of the WPA Federal Theatre, 1937.

THE LITTLE DUCHESS (1901–2). White-oriented musical comedy. 3 acts. Adapt. by °Harry B. Smith (book and lyrics) from *Niniche*, a French vaudeville-operetta of the 1870s. Music by °Reginald de Koven. With interpolated songs by J. Rosamond Johnson, Bob Cole, and others.

Very loosely built around the thin story of an actress who foils her creditors and the three detectives they have hired to pursue her by impersonating a duchess.

Commissioned and prod. by °Florenz Ziegfeld as a starring vehicle for his wife, °Anna Held. Opened at the Casino Theatre, New York, Oct. 14, 1901, for 136 perfs. With an all-white cast, including Held, °Charles A. Bigelow, °Joseph Herbert, °George Marion, and °Sidney Barrachlough. Revived at the Grand Opera House, New York, 1902.

One of the songs from this show, "The Maiden with the Dreamy Eyes," sung by Held, became Cole & the Johnson Brothers' biggest hits, earning them substantial royalties. It was pub. by Joseph W. Stern, New York; copies in MC/NYPL and Moorland-Spingarn. Other interpolations by them include "Strollin' along the Beach" and "Sweet Salomaa."
FURTHER REFERENCE: *AmMusTh* (Bordman). *BesPls 1899–1909.*

LITTLE GIRL, BIG TOWN (1953). Musical revue. 2 acts. Book and lyrics by Townsend Brewster. Music by °Jacques Urbent, °Mel Waldren, °Jack Gottlieb, and °Anthony Bruno. Depicts the adventures of a newcomer to New York City, and includes a one-act ballet-opera, *Slappy Hooper* (music by Urbent), which tells how Slappy paints a picture of a stove on a billboard that looks so realistic that the city's poor and homeless come to warm themselves by it. Prod. at Queens Coll., New York, May 1, 1953.

LITTLE MISS FIX-IT (1911). White-oriented musical. 3 acts. Book by °William J. Hurlburt. Lyrics and music mainly by °Nora Bayes, °Jack Norworth, and others. With additional lyrics and music by James Weldon Johnson and J. Rosamond Johnson. Prod. on Bway at the Globe Theatre, New York, opening April 3, 1911, for 56 perfs. With an all-white cast, including Nora Bayes, Jack

Norworth, °Grace Field, °Lionel Walsh, °Eleanor Stewart, and °Alice Lloyd. The Johnson & Johnson songs included "Excuse Me Mister Moon" and "If You'll Be My Eve (I'll Build an Eden for You)," sung by Lloyd; musical scores pub. by Joseph W. Stern, New York; copies in Moorland-Spingarn.

THE LITTLE TOMMY PARKER CELEBRATED COLORED MINSTREL SHOW (1988). By Carlyle Brown. An award-winning musical which depicts how a black minstrel company's arrival affects the small town of Joplin, MO, in the late 1800s. Prod. by the St. Louis Repertory Company, St. Louis, MO, Jan. 12–Feb. 5, 1988.

LIZA (1922–24) / / A completely revised version of *Bon Bon Buddy, Jr.* (1922). Book by Irvin C. Miller. Music and lyrics by Maceo Pinkard. With additional lyrics by °Nat Vincent.

The most successful black musical of 1922, which many critics acclaimed as a worthy successor to *Shuffle Along* (1921). Originally tried out at the Lafayette Theatre in Harlem for a lengthy run, in 1922, as *Bon Bon Buddy, Jr.*, after which it was retitled, the story line completely revised, and new musical numbers added. Using the setting of Jimtown (from *Shuffle Along*), the new version was built around the plans of the politically prominent Squire Norris (father of Liza) to erect a statue in the public square as a tribute to the town's late mayor, for which money is being raised. When the funds for the statue are embezzled, suspicion falls upon the new schoolteacher, whose name happens to be Dandy, with whom Liza has fallen in love, because Dandy is now sporting new clothes and seems to have a "wad" of money. In the end, Dandy is exonerated, and his marriage to Liza is formally announced at the ball which takes place in the last scene, where a number of specialty acts are introduced. *Liza* was the first musical to introduce the Charleston song and dance to Broadway, although *Runnin' Wild* (1923–25) is usually credited with that distinction, because that was the show that popularized the dance.

Prod. on Bway by °Al Davis, opening at Daly's Theatre, Nov. 27, 1922, for 169 perfs.; dir. by °Walter Brooks. It apparently remained until the spring of 1923, then went on tour until 1924. In March of 1923, before it closed on Bway, a midnight benefit was given at the Lafayette Theatre in Harlem, for the Harlem Branch of the NAACP, and over $900 was raised on that occasion. Cast: Alonzo Fenderson (Squire Norris), Margaret Simms (Liza), Gertrude Saunders (Nora), William Simms (Uncle Pete), Packer Ramsey (Parson Jordan), Quintard Miller (Judge Plummer), R. Eddie Greenlee (Ras Johnson), Thaddeus Drayton (Dandy), Will A. Cook (The Sheriff), Irvin C. Miller (Ice Cream Charlie), Emmet Anthony (Bodiddily), Billy Mills (Tom Liggett), Doe Doe Green (Sam Sykes), Elizabeth Terrill (Mammy), Maude Russell (Mandy), Snippy Mason (Harry Davis), Donald Fields (Bill Jones); Others: Brown-Skin Vamps, Jimtown Flappers, Dancing Honey Girls, and Struttin' Dandies.

Songs and specialty numbers: Act I, Scene 1—Opening Chorus—"Tag Day"

(Ensemble), "Pleasure" (song: Saunders & Chorus), "I'm the Sheriff" (song: Cook & Boys), "Liza" (song: Drayton, M. Simms, Saunders & Chorus); Scene 2—'Memories' (specialty: Agnes Anthony, Viola Branch, Gladys Taylor, Ethel Taylor & Angeline Hammond); Scene 3—"Just a Barber Shop Chord" (song: The Gang); Scene 4—"That Brown-Skin Flapper" (song: Saunders & Flappers); Scene 5—"On the Moonlit Swanee" (ensemble: Town Folks), "Essence" (dance: Greenlee, Drayton & Boys), "Forget Your Troubles" (dance: Boys & Girls), "My Old Man" (Elizabeth Welch, Anthony & Quintette), "Runnin' Wild Blues" (Saunders, M. Simms, Greenlee, Drayton & Company). Act II, Scene 1—"The Charleston Dance" (song & dance: Maude Russell & Dancing Honey Girls), "Dandy" (song: Simms & Dandies), "My Creole Girl" (song: Greenlee & Girls); Scene 2—"Planning" (duet: M. Simms & Drayton); Scene 3—'The Ghost Dance' (dance: Dotson & Mitchell); Scene 4—"Love Me" (song: Saunders); Scene 5—Dance (Four Steppers), 'Jimtown Speedster' (dance: Fields), Specialty (Anthony), Specialty (Greenlee & Drayton), "Don't Be Blue" (song: Saunders), and Finale (Company).

Libretto in Music Collection/LC.

FURTHER REFERENCE: *AmMusTh* (Bordman). *BlkMusTh* (Woll). *BlksBf* (Sampson). *HarlRenD* (Kellner).

LIZZIE AND PETE OF THE CABARET SHOW (1916). Touring show. Starring Mabel Decard.

LOAD OF COAL (c. 1929). Cabaret musical. Music and lyrics by Thomas "Fats" Waller and Andy Razaf. Prod. at Connie's Inn, New York, around 1929. Introduced "Honeysuckle Rose," which later became a song hit. Two other songs from this show were "My Fate Is in Your Hands" and "Zonky."
FURTHER REFERENCE: *Ain't Misbehavin'* (Kirkeby).

THE LONELY CROWD (1969). Musical revue. Perfd. by the Performing Arts Society of Los Angeles (PASLA) in 1969, under the direction of Vantile Whitfield. The prodn. involved more than 100 teenagers in the area.

THE LONESOME MILE (1917). Tabloid musical. Written and prod. by Billy King. Presented at the Grand Theatre, Chicago, with members of the Billy King Stock Co.

LOOK WHO'S HERE (1927). Musical revue. New York show which featured Jackie ("Moms") Mabley.

LOOSE FEET (1929). Touring revue. Prod. by comedian Joe Carmouche, who also prod. *Happy Days in Dixie* and *A Night in Turkey* (both 1925).

LOST IN THE STARS (1949–50, 1958, 1968, 1972, 1987). Musical tragedy. 2 acts [18 scenes]. Book and lyrics by °Maxwell Anderson. Based on °Alan Paton's novel *Cry, the Beloved Country*. Music by °Kurt Weill.

An ambitious, sentimental, and sympathetic exploration of racial problems in South Africa, which tells the story of a black Christian minister who desperately seeks to save his son from execution by hanging for the accidental shooting death of the son of a staunch supporter of apartheid. Having traveled from his small village to Johannesburg, the minister pleads for his son's life, but to no avail. The white father of the murdered young man seeks only retribution, and refuses to intercede. Unable to save his son, the minister returns to his small village and resigns his pastorate, believing that he has lost his faith in the justness of God. Before the execution takes place, the white father visits the minister and offers his hand in friendship. The two men forgive each other, and find some comfort in their mutual bereavement for the loss of their sons.

Prod. on Bway by the Playwrights' Company, at the Music Box Theatre, opening Oct. 30, 1949, for 273 perfs.; dir. by °Rouben Mamoulian. The principal cast included Todd Duncan (Rev. Stephen Kumalo), Gertrude Jeannette (Grace Kumalo, his wife), Julian Mayfield (Absalom Kumalo, his son), °Leslie Banks (James Jarvis, father of the murdered man), Inez Matthews (Irina, Absalom's girl), °John Morely (Arthur Jarvis, James' son), °Judson Rees (Edward Jarvis, son of Arthur); Others: Georgette Harvey (Mrs. M'kise), Frank Roane (Leader), Joseph James (Answerer), Elayne Richards (Nita), Mabel (Young Woman), Warren Coleman (John Kumalo), Charles McRae (Paulus), Roy Allen (William), William C. Smith (Jared), Herbert Coleman (Alex), °Jerome Shaw (Foreman), William Marshall (Hlabeni), Charles Grunwell (Eland), Sheila Guyse (Linda), Van Prince (Johannes Pafuri), William Greaves (Matthew Kumalo), Gloria Smith (Rose), °Robert Byrn (Policeman), °Biruta Ramoska (White Woman), °Mark Kramer (White Man), °Jerome Shaw (Guard), John W. Stanley (Burton), °Guy Spaull (The Judge), and Robert McFerrin (Villager).

Revived in 1958, 1968, 1972, and 1987. The 1972 revival was brought to New York from the John F. Kennedy Center for the Performing Arts in Washington, DC, and presented at the Imperial Theatre, opening April 18, 1972, for 39 perfs. Cast featured Brock Peters (Stephen Kumalo), °Jack Gwillim (James Jarvis), Gilbert Price (Absalom), and Margaret Cowie (Irina). A film version, starring Brock Peters and Melba Moore, was presented in 1974, dir. by Daniel Mann. Prod. by Ebony Opera, in conjunction with Universal Symphony, at Aaron Davis Hall, New York, Nov. 12, 14, and 20, 1987.

Songs and musical numbers: "The Hills of Ixopo," "Thousands of Miles," "Train to Johannesburg," "The Search," "Little Grey House," "Stay Well," "Trouble Man," "Murder in Parkwold," "Fear," "Lost in the Stars," "Wild Justice," "O Tixo, Tixo, Help Me," "Cry, the Beloved Country," and "Big Mole."

Pub. in *Famous Plays of the 1940s* (Hewes) and *Great Musicals of the American Theatre*, vol. 2 (Richards). Cast recording by Decca (DL 79120).

220

LOUIS

FURTHER REFERENCE: Alkire diss. *BesPls 1949–50; 1963–64; 1967–68. Commonweal* 11–25–1949. *NewRepub* 11–21–1949. *NY Daily N.* 10–31–1948. *NY Herald Trib.* 10–30–1949. *NY World Telegram* 10–31–1949. *Phylon* 2nd qtr. 1950.

LOUIS / / Orig. title: *Satchmo* (1981). Musical biography. Book and lyrics by Don Evans. Music by °Michael Renzi. About the life of Louis "Satchmo" Armstrong. Prod. at the Henry St. Playhouse, New York, Sept. 18–Oct. 4, 1981, for 12 perfs.; dir. by Gilbert Moses. With Norther J. Calloway as Louis.

LOUISIANA BLACKBIRDS (1927). Touring show. Featuring Ma Rainey.

LOUISIANA MESS-AROUND (1926). Touring show. Cast included Madge Young, Travil Tucker, Odelina Johnson, Agnes Levi, Daybreak Nelson, William McConnicoe, Marie Daniels, Stella Young, Susie Taylor, and Margaret Wilkens.

LOVIN' SAM FROM ALABAM' (1920s). Touring show. Starring Rufus Greenlee and Thaddeus Drayton.

A LUCKY COON (1898–99). Ragtime musical show. A Williams & Walker musical, conceived by Bert Williams and George Walker. Music by Will Marion Cook.

A mediocre show, consisting of a new arrangement of much of the material from the company's less successful *Senegambian Carnival* (prod. fall 1898), now built around a thin gambling plot, involving the playing and winning of a lottery. As described by Ann Charters (*Nobody*, p. 40), it was "a hodge-podge of everything in the 'coon line' from buck-dancing and ragtime melodies to selections from the grand opera." It also included a number of specialty acts and a big cakewalking finale which had been featured in *Clorindy*.

Prod. in the winter of 1898, under the management of °Hurtig & Seamon, with a cast of some 60 singers, dancers, variety performers, and musicians, including Williams & Walker, Hodges & Launchmere (singers), the Mallory Bros. (Ed. and Frank, musicians), Goggins & Davis (acrobats), Lottie Thompson (later Mrs. Bert Williams), Carl Dante (Black Carl, the magician), Ada Overton (later Mrs. George Walker), Ollie Burgoyne (dancer), and William C. Elkins.

Played at the Park Theatre, New York, in Dec. 1898, where it may have opened. It was booked mainly for one-night stands in cheap theatres in the East, Middle Atlantic states, and the Midwest, from Jan. 1899 through the spring of 1899. Although a second-rate show, it played to enthusiastic audiences and apparently made money at the box office.

Some of the ideas from *A Lucky Coon* were incorporated into the next Williams & Walker show, *The Policy Players* (1899–1900), also about a lottery winner.

A Lucky Coon continued to be perfd., under the management of Carl Dante and Charles F. Moore, after being discarded by Williams & Walker. In Aug. 1901, it was playing in Bay Shore, Long Island, NY, with the following cast:

Dante, Moore, Charles L. Hart, Allie Brown, Al and Cecil Watts, Yeager &
Yeager, and James White.
FURTHER REFERENCE: *Ghost* (Sampson). *Nobody* (Charters).

LUCKY SAMBO (1925–26) / / A revised version of *Aces and Queens* (1924–
25). Musical farce-comedy. Book, music, and lyrics by Porter Grainger and
Freddie Johnson.

A stereotypical black musical show that had a lengthy tryout as *Aces and
Queens* (1924–25) before being revised and brought to Bway. Sambo Jenkins
(Tim Moore) and Rufus Johnson (Joe Byrd), two porters at a local hotel, are
tricked into buying some stock in a phony oil-drilling scam by Jim Nightengale
(Clarence Robinson), after oil is discovered in some of the slum dwellings in
the all-black section of the town. The swindle is eventually uncovered with the
help of a detective, and the swindler and his cohorts are jailed. However, the
tables are turned when oil is really discovered on the land. The oil swindle plot
is combined with a love story involving June Whitby (Monette Moore), the
daughter of the hotel proprietors, and Jack Stafford (Freddie Johnson), which
ends happily for the couple. The musical ends with a celebration of the discovery
of oil and the forthcoming marriage, by a floorshow at a midnight cabaret, where
a number of specialty acts are perfd.

Toured the TOBA circuit as *Aces and Queens*, 1924–25. Prod. as *Lucky Sambo*
by Harlem Productions, Inc., at the Colonial Theatre, opening June 6, 1925,
for 9 perfs.; dir. by Leigh Whipper. Jesse A. Shipp was stage manager, and
Leonard Harper was dance dir. Cast: Tim Moore (Sambo Jenkins), Joe Byrd
(Rufus Johnson), Westley Hill (John Whitby, hotel proprietor), Gertie Moore
(Mrs. Whitby), Monette Moore (June Whitby), Arthur Porter ("Doc" August),
Freddie Johnson (Jack Stafford), Lena Wilson (Lena March), "Happy" Williams
(Edith Simpson), Billy Ewing (John Law, a Detective), Clarence Robinson (Jim
Nightengale, the Stock Swindler), Porter Grainger (Hitt Keys, a Pianist), Jean
Starr (Vera Blues, a Torch Singer), Amelia Loomis (Nimble Foote, a dancer),
Mildred Brown (Minnie Tree), Anna White (Twilight Gadson), Johnny Hudgins
(Shoo Nuff, a Red Cap), Ernest Whitman (Oil Promoter), and the Three Dixie
Songbirds: Hilda Perleno (first soprano), Amanda Randolph (second soprano),
and Birleanna Blanks (contralto).

Toured the Columbia Theatrical circuit (white) for one year after closing on
Bway, under the management of °Hurtig & Seamon, 1926.

Songs and musical numbers: "If You Can't Bring It," "Dancing in the
Moonlight," "The Big Parade," "Happy," "Stop," "Don't Forget Bandanna
Days," "Anybody's Man Will Be My Man," "Aunt Jemima," "Coal Oil,"
"Charley from That Charleston Dancin' School," "Strolling," "Dreary,
Dreary, Rainy Days," "Take Him to Jail," "Legomania," "Always on the
Job," "Singing Nurses," "Dandy Dan," "Porterology," "Love Me While
You're Gone," "Keep a-Diggin'," "Runnin'," "Midnight Cabaret," "Havin'

a Wonderful Time,'' ''Not So Long Ago,'' and ''Alexander's Ragtime Wedding Day.''
FURTHER REFERENCE: *AmMusTh* (Bordman). *HarlRenD* (Kellner). *NYT* 6–8–1925; 5–26–1926. *Variety* 6–10–1925.

LUCKY SAM FROM ALABAM' (1914). Vaudeville farce-comedy. 3 acts. Book and music mainly by Harrison Stewart, who also costarred with Sissieretta Jones (Black Patti).

This musical was pieced together from several of Harrison Stewart's vaudeville routines, tied together with a thin plot. The story depicts the rise of Sam Toles, a humble whitewash painter, to the ownership of a successful bootblack parlor, and finally to a public school teaching position in Alabama.

Prod. on tour by the *Black Patti Troubadours* in 1914. Cast: Sissieretta Jones (Miss Inez Jones, Principal of the Colored Schools), Harrison Stewart (Sam Toles [''Lucky Sam'']), Will A. Cook (Ray, a Good-Natured Tramp), Viola Stewart (A Lassie), Tillie Seguin (Pansy Wilson), Jeannette Murphy, George Howard, John Grant, and Ethel Williams.

Among the 22 songs and musical numbers: ''Luckstone's Delight,'' ''Tosti's Goodbye!'' (Jones), ''No One,'' ''Hostess of Social Functions'' (Jones & Ensemble), ''Mournful Rag,'' ''Going No Place in Particular'' (H. Stewart), ''Pleading Eyes'' (Williams & Chorus), and ''Watch Your Step'' (Seguin).
FURTHER REFERENCE: *Just Before Jazz* (Riis). *NY Age* 9–24–1914. Riis diss.

LUCKY TO ME (1931). Touring revue. Featuring Ethel Waters, comedian ''Dusty'' Fletcher, Jimmie Baskette, Blue McAllister, Gallie DeGaston, and the Melody Monarchs.

LULU BELLE (1927). Touring vaudeville revue. Prod. by J. W. Jackson. Cast included Alberta Pope, Lionel Monagas, Ollie Burgoyne, Elvira Johnson, Louis Decall, and Percy Wade.

M

MADGE SMITH, ATTORNEY (1900). White-oriented farce with music. 3 acts. By °Ramsey Morris. Musical numbers by Ernest Hogan, °A. Baldwin Sloane, °James O'Dea, °Theodore H. Northrup, °Dave Reed, and °Frances Bryant. Prod. on Bway at the Bijou Theatre, New York, opening Dec. 10, 1900, for 28 perfs., starring °May Irwin. The titles of Hogan's individual songs, sung by Irwin, have not been located, but it is presumed that they were in the "coon" or ragtime genre.

MAE'S AMEES (fractured French for "Mae's Friends") (1969). Musical. 1 act. By Hazel Bryant, Hope Clarke, and Hank Johnson. Prod. by the Afro-American Total Theatre, at the Riverside Church Theatre, New York, Aug. 9–10, 1969, and apparently remained in repertory until Oct. 1969.

MAHALIA (1978–82). Book and lyrics by Don Evans. Musical biography. Music by John Lewis. Based on the life of Mahalia Jackson. First prod. by the New Federal Theatre, at the Henry St. Playhouse, New York, May 31–June 11, 1978, for 14 perfs.; dir. by Oz Scott. With Esther Marrow as Mahalia. Prod. by the Hartman Theatre, Stamford, CT, during the 1981–82 season; dir. by Gerald Freedman; also with Esther Marrow as Mahalia. May have been revised as *Blues for a Gospel Queen* (1986).

MAID IN HARLEM / / Also called **Maid of Harlem** (1920). Musical revue. Prod. at the Lincoln Theatre in Harlem. Cast included Jeannette Taylor and Mamie Smith. Smith sang "Harlem Blues," the first song written by Perry Bradford. With the title changed to "Crazy Blues," it was recorded by OK Records, and was one of the first solo recordings by a black artist.

MAKE ME KNOW IT (1929). Touring show. Featuring A. B. DeComathiere, Ollie Burgoyne, Barrington Guy, Ethel Moses, Vivian Barber, Frances Carter, Lee Bailey, Enid Raphael, Charles Hawkins, Pearl Ford, Walter Dike, Florence Lee, Brevard Burnett, Edna Ellington, James Dunsmore, Lorenzo Tucker, Allen Gillard, Louis Schooler, Frances Carter, Napoleon Whitney, James McAtec, Marion Fleming, Charles Hawkins, and Elmer Snowden's Band.

MAKIN' IT (1970). Musical. Book by Hazel Bryant, Gertrude Greenidge, and Walter Miles. Music by Jimmy Justice and Holly Hamilton. About the trials and tribulations of a young black man from a small town who is trying to make it in show business. Written in 1970. Prod. by the Afro-American Total Theatre, and perfd. at the following locations in New York: International House, Jan. 14–16, 1972; Riverside Church, March 6–12, 1972; Finch Coll. Museum of Art (excerpts), March 1972; as a street theatre prodn. in the five boroughs of New York City, July 31–Aug. 14, 1972, for 20 perfs.; and Lincoln Center Plaza— Street Theatre Festival, Sept. 9, 1972. Also presented in Boston at the "Summer Thing," sponsored by Mayor Kevin White, during the week of Aug. 14, 1972. Remained in repertory until June 10, 1973.

MAKIN' IT (1981). Musical comedy. By Houston Brummit. About a naive young woman who comes to New York to get into show business, where she falls in love with a smooth-talking song-and-dance man and is almost seduced by an unscrupulous producer. Showcased at the Perry St. Theatre, New York, Dec. 1981.

MALINDA (1929) / / Revised as *Ham's Daughter* (1932). Musical melodrama. Book by Dennis Donoghue. Music and lyrics by Reginald Loving and Earl B. Westfield. Tells the story of a Florida schoolteacher (Malinda) who leaves her job, home, and family to find fame and fortune in New York's Harlem. There she falls into the clutches of a professional swindler and other unsavory characters. She is ultimately rescued by a handsome young detective, who is sent by her family to search for her, and they fall in love and marry in the end. The book was criticized by *NYT* (12–4–1929), although the music received faint praise. Prod. unsuccessfully in New York, Dec. 1929.

MAMA DO BLEW (1975). Musical. By George Houston Bass. Music by Thomas Riggsbee and Kambon Obayani. Prod. by Rites & Reason, Brown Univ. at Brown Univ. in Providence, RI, and at Lincoln Center in New York City, July–Aug. 1975; dir. by Brown.

MAMA ETTA'S CHITLIN CIRCUIT (1973). Subtitled "A Soul Revue." 3 scenes. By George Houston Bass. As portrayed by actors, famous black entertainers of the past perform their own specialty numbers. Prod. at Brown Univ., Providence, RI, April 1973.

MAMA, I WANT TO SING (1980–91). Billed as "A Story in Concert Form." Book by Vy Higginsen. Lyrics and additional story by Higgensen and Ken Wydro. Music composed, arranged, and dir. by Grenoldo [Frazier].

Self-advertised as the longest-running black Off-Bway musical ever. Loosely based on the story of Doris Troy, Higginsen's sister, who left the church choir of Mount Calvary in Harlem, against her mother's wishes, to sing rhythm and blues and popular music at age 17.

As described by the author:

Mama, I Want to Sing is the story of a young girl, born and raised in the church, who finds that her talent leads her out into "the world" to sing for all people. The family unit is the key to the story. The girl, Doris Winter, is portrayed by Desiree Coleman, a young rising star with an exceptional gift and classic looks to match. . . . The original music of the play, composed by Grenoldo Frazier, artistically weaves great sounds of the past with satisfying rhythms of the present. Grenoldo also adds his expertise as musical director and key board player. (Publicity release)

Presented in an early workshop version at the AMAS Repertory Theatre, New York, 1980, for 13 perfs.; dir. by Duane L. Jones, with music by Richard Tee.

Rewritten with Higgensen's husband, Ken Wydro, and composer Grenoldo, and first presented by the Molimo Players of Fordham Univ. as a benefit in Jan. 1983, for 4 perfs.

Independently prod. by the coauthors at the Heckscher Theatre, New York, opening in March 1983, where it ran for 8 years before being closed by the City of New York in March 1992—apparently because it was a profit-making enterprise in a public facility originally intended for nonprofit use. Orig. cast: Desiree Coleman (Doris Winter, the young girl who "wants to sing"), Doris Troy (the subject of the musical who now plays her own mother, Mama Winter), Randy Higginsen (Rev. Winter, pastor of the church and Doris's father), Trina Thomas (Sister Carrie, a member of the church), Vy Higginsen (Narrator), Steve Williams (Choir Director), and Choir Members.

At least one touring company took the play on a transcontinental U.S. tour. A sequel, entitled *Mama, I Want to Sing—Part II*, was being planned when the orig. prodn. ended its lengthy run.

MAMIE SMITH REVUE (1924, 1926). Touring revue in at least two eds. Starring blues singer Mamie Smith. The *1924 ed.*, prod. by Ocey Wilson, had the following cast: Mitchell & Harris, Frederick Johnson, Bobby Shields, Ruby Mason, Dewey Weinglass and his Dancing Demons, Ethel Harris, and Billy Gulfport. The *1926 ed.*, prod. by Mamie Smith, featured Ethel Williams Dotson (as soubrette), Clinton "Dusty" Fletcher and Mose Gaston (as principal comedians), "Ace, King and Jack" (which included Herbert and Eugene Taylor, and Daniel Winstead, dancers), and a chorus of 6 women.

MAN BETTER MAN (1960, 1962, 1969). Subtitled "A Trinidad Folk Musical." 3 acts [17 scenes]. By Errol Hill. Music (for the Negro Ensemble Company production) by Coleridge-Taylor Perkinson.

A lighthearted musical of life in Trinidad in 1900, in which a young suitor resorts to voodoo to try to win a stick-fighting contest, hoping to impress the girl that he loves. The *NYT* (7–12–1969) called it "a refreshing Calypso tale" "that shelves for a moment the brow-furrowing issues of the day," and praised the cast of the NEC prodn., headed by David Downing (as the young suitor) and Hattie Winston (as his sweetheart).

Twice prod. by the Yale School of Drama, first in 1960 and again in 1962. Prod. in Trinidad and in England, 1969. Prod. by the Negro Ensemble Co., at St. Marks Playhouse, New York, July 9–20, 1969, for 23 perfs.; dir. by Douglas Turner Ward. Cast: Rosalind Cash (Inez Briscoe), Esther Rolle (Alice Sugar), David Downing (Tim Briscoe), Graham Brown (Portagee Joe), Allie Woods (Swifty), Tony McKay (Hannibal), Samuel Blue, Jr. (Tiny Satin), Arthur French (Crackerjack), Hattie Winston (Petite Belle Lily), Julius W. Harris (Cutaway Rimbeau), Aston Young (Dagger Da Silva), Norman Bush (Coolie), Afolabi Ajayi (Peeloo), William Jay (Pogo), Damon W. Brazwell (Diable Papa), Mari Toussaint (Minee Woopsa), Frances Foster (1st Village Woman), and Clarice Taylor (2nd Village Woman).

Songs and musical numbers: "Tiny, the Champion," "I Love Petite Belle," "One Day, One Day Congotay," "One, Two, Three," "Man Better Man," "Thousand, Thousand," "Petite Lily Belle," "Me Alone," "Girl in the Coffee," "Coolie Gone," "War and Rebellion," "Beautiful Heaven," and "Brisco, the Hero."

Pub. in *Three Plays from the Yale School of Drama* (ed. John Gassner, New York: Dutton, 1964).

MANDY GREEN FROM NEW ORLEANS (1928). Vaudeville farce. Apparently written by Quintard Miller and Marcus Slayter. Prod. by °Jack Goldberg. This show attempted to capitalize on the popularity of *Silas Green from New Orleans*, the longest-running black tent show in the history of the American theatre. It concerned the marital problems of Sam Green, a henpecked husband (played in blackface), and his wife, Mandy, who spends her time as the town vamp while he does the housework. Toured the Majestic Theatrical Circuit in 1928, with a cast of 20, headed by "Babe" Brown, Johnny Stevens, John LaRue, and Harry "Shrimp" Brock.
FURTHER REFERENCE: *BlksBf* (Sampson).

THE MAN FROM BALTIMORE (1934). Vaudeville farce-comedy. 2 acts. Book by °John Raines. Music by °Wen Talbert. Lyrics by °Alonzo Govern.

A white-authored show which attempted to re-create a successful, earlier black-authored show, *The Oyster Man* (1907–8), written by Miller & Lyles and starring Ernest Hogan, who played the role of Rufus Rastus. In both shows, Rufus, an oyster peddler from Baltimore, somehow becomes transported to a mythical island where he becomes king. In *The Oyster Man*, the island was Blazasus. With only the doubling of the z's and the s's, the island in this show was called Blazzassus.

In the plot of *The Man from Baltimore*, a group of Baltimoreans are duped into buying boat passage to the island of Blazzassus, where the scheme's promoter, Samuel Austin, promises them a utopian life of ease and plenty where no one has to work for a living. En route to the island, the boat is shipwrecked and the passengers and crew land on another island, Bahaha, which is inhabited by natives and ruled by a king. (In *The Oyster Man*, the natives were savages.) The foreigners are subject to stern treatment, until Rufus promises to marry the king's daughter and (somehow—possibly by abdication, assassination, or death), Rufus becomes the new king. In this capacity, he is able to bring about a happy ending for everyone; Samuel Austin, the promoter of the scheme, is exposed as a fraud; the group is rescued by a delegation from the U.S.; and a festive celebration is held at the end.

Prod. on tour of the Columbia Theatrical Circuit by Joe Hurtig (of Hurtig & Seamon, which prod. *The Oyster Man*). Cast: Billy Higgins (Rufus Rastus, Oyster Peddler), Joe Brown (Useless, Rufus' Dog & Dogolo, the King's Sacred Dog), Baby Joyce (Matilda Jensarp, Rufus' Best Girl), Dinah Scott (Sunny Sam, Rufus' Side Pardner [sic]), Alfred "Slick" Chester (Ben Gibbs, a Sailor & King of Bahaha), Lionel Monagas (Samuel Austin, Promoter of Blazzassus Scheme), Percy Verwayen (George Ormas, a Detective), Trixie Smith (Aunt Jemima), Hilda Perleno (Angeline Gaillard, Graduate of Tuskegee), Pearl Gaines (Belk Cowan, Angeline's Chum), Sisters of the Flock (played by Hattie King, Dora Thompson, Mabel Howard, Massie Patterson, Bertha Powell, and Violet Anderson), Fred Brown (King's Courier), Virginia Wright and Hazel Cheek (Palm Girls), Billy Anderson, Jerry Pierce, and Robert Lee (three Native Men), John Lee and Lovel Willis (King's Guards), Mabel Howard (Princess Ito, King's Favorite Daughter), Henry Davis (General Debility), Sylvan Greenridge (General Delivery), Pearl Gaines (Seeress), Archie Cross (Minister Pleni Potentiary [sic], from the USA), Trixie Smith (Royal Cook), Willie Alant (Secretary of the Navy), Wen Talbert's Choir (12 singers), Sixteen Oysterettes, Eight Baltimoreans, White Wing Brigade, and Specialties (including the Three Rhapsodians and the Three Ebony Steppers).
FURTHER REFERENCE: *BlksBf* (Sampson).

THE MAN FROM 'BAM (1906–7, revived 1920, 1923). Book originally by Flournoy E. Miller and Aubrey Lyles. Music originally by Joe Jordan and Will H. Vodery.

After winning a fortune at the race track, Jube Johnson, a former Chicago railway worker originally from Mobile, AL, decides to throw a party for some of his friends in Chicago, but does not share his winnings with his wife, Hester. Hester comes to the party, denounces Jube, and tells him that he will have nothing but bad luck for his mistreatment of her. In the next race, Jube loses his winnings by betting on the wrong horse, while Hester wins a fortune on another horse in the same race. Now reduced to poverty, Jube begs his wife to take him back, promising to do better, and all ends happily when she does.

First prod. by the Pekin Theatre in Chicago, 1906; staged by Charles S. Sager. The orig. cast included Charles Sager (Elder Cashingberry), L. D. Henderson (Jube Johnson, the Man from 'Bam), Andrew Tribble (Hester Johnson, Jube's Wife), Joe Weatherly (Henry Johnson), R. T. Thomas (Capt. D. Young), Henry Reed (Pete Jones); Others: the Cook Sisters, Josephine Smith, Irwin Allen, Dolores Thomas, Ethel Jones, George Henry, Ora Griswald, Nina Smith, and Lizzie Wallace.

Songs and musical numbers: "The Man from 'Bam," "I'd Like to Steal You," "Feather Your Nest," "I'm Just from 'Bam," "The Alabama Cadets," and Strolling."

Revived by Joe Jordan, composer of the orig. music, 1920, as a musical in 3 acts, with a different set of characters and cast, and prod. by the Chicago Producing Co., of which Jordan was vice president and manager; Dave Payton was president and treasurer; and Jerry Mills was stage director. Cast: Jerry Mills (Bob Skinner, the Man from 'Bam), Mabel Gant (Hanna), Birleanna Blanks (Mandy Lee), Medill Thompson (Lazy Dancing specialist), Margaret Lee (Matron-singer), Maud Russell (Young Lady-singer), and Louis Taylor (Jack Fairfax).

Revived 1923, with the following cast: Emmett Anthony, B. B. Joyner, Clarence Foster, Alberta Perkins, and Valaida Snow.

MANNEQUINS OF 1927 (1927). Touring revue. Prod. by Johnny Lee Long. Cast included "Baby Kid," Johnny Bodidly, Teddy Smith, Howard Dorsey, Catherine Patterson, and 6 chorus girls.

MA RAINEY AND HER GEORGIA JAZZ HOUNDS (1926). Touring show. Prod. by and starring Ma Rainey. Cast included John "Jiggs" Briedy, whose specialty was singing, dancing, and whistling; "Jolly" Saunders, a juggler; Queen Dora, a dancer; and 3 members of the chorus: Madeline Carter, Margaret McDonald, and Grace McDaniels.

MARRYING MARY (1906). White-oriented musical play. With additional songs by Chris Smith, Cecil Mack, Bob Cole, and J. Rosamond Johnson. Book by °Edwin Milton Royle. Lyrics by °George V. Hobart. Music by °Silvio Hein. Based on the play *My Wife's Husband*. About a lady who has been married three times, each marriage lasting only a few hours. Just as she is trying to choose between a father and son as her fourth mate, all her former husbands appear and help her to make up her mind. Prod. at Daly's Theatre, New York, opening Aug. 27, 1906, where it played for six weeks before going on the road. The all-white cast included °Marie Cahill in the title role, °Roy Atwell, °William

Courtleigh, °Eugene Cowles, and °Virginia Staunton. The most memorable song from this prodn. was "He's a Cousin of Mine," with lyrics by Mack and music by Smith and Hein, sung by Cahill, musical score pub. by Gotham-Attucks, New York; copy in Moorland-Spingarn. Cole & Johnson contributed the music and lyrics to "Hottentot Love Song," also sung by Cahill.

MARTIN (1988). A musical about Martin Luther King, Jr. Written and dir. by Lamar Alford. Through the life of King, this musical also takes a comprehensive look at the moral consciousness and cultural mores of the civil rights movement. Presented in a choral performance, with a cast of 40, by the King Players of the Martin Luther King, Jr. International Chapel of Morehouse College, at LaMama Experimental Theatre Club Annex, New York, Jan. 27–31, 1988; with students and faculty from Morehouse, Spelman, and Clark Colleges.

THE MARTYR (1893). Dramatic opera. 2 acts. By H. Lawrence Freeman. The first opera by an African-American composer. Tells the story of an Egyptian nobleman who abandons the faith of his people and accepts the religion of Jehovah, for which he is imprisoned and burned to death. First perfd. by the Freeman Grand Opera Co., at the Deutsches Theatre in Denver, CO, Sept. 1893. Presented in a concert version in Carnegie Hall, Sept. 21, 1947.

MASCARA AND CONFETTI (1970s–1987). Revue. 2 acts. Book and lyrics by Townsend Brewster. Music by Genovis Albright. Explores the theme of the modern woman, in a New Orleans setting during Mardi Gras. Prod. by the Broadway Tomorrow Musical Theatre, at Second Presbyterian Church, New York, May 11–16, 1987.

THE MAYOR OF DIXIE (1907). Musical play. By Flournoy E. Miller and Aubrey Lyles (Miller & Lyles). Significant as their first play, which later became the book for the 1921 musical comedy sensation, *Shuffle Along*. Prod. at the Pekin Theatre, Chicago, 1907.

THE MAYOR OF JIMTOWN (1923). Touring vaudeville comedy. Prod. by Quintard Miller and Marcus Slayter (Miller & Slayter). Follows a plot similar to that of *Shuffle Along* (1921), and apparently was one of that show's many imitators. Concerns the rivalry of two grocery store operators who are running against each other for mayor of Jimtown. Cast included Miller & Slayter (as the two rival grocers), Emmett Anthony, and Blanche Thompson.

THE MAYOR OF NEWTOWN / / Also *New Town* or *Newton* (1909, 1914). Book, music, and lyrics by Salem Tutt Whitney and J. Homer Tutt. Music by T. L. Corwell, J. Homer Tutt, and Henry Watterson.
   The mayor (Whitney) wishes to bring a number of modern reforms to his town, as suggested by his chief aide and protégé, Ned Jenkins (Tutt), but his

reforms are violently opposed by many of the older citizens who wish to oust him from his job. When he falls in love with the town's new schoolteacher, this only complicates the situation. But the mayor is determined to keep his job, and as he states in two of his songs, "I'm the Mayor of Newton" and "Here I Is and Here I Stay." And with the schoolteacher, he sings a love duet entitled "You, Babe, Only You." The mayor saves his job by accomplishing a deed of heroism.

First prod. by Whitney & Tutt's *Smart Set Co.* on southern tour during the 1909 season. Cast: Salem Tutt Whitney (Lem Lee, His Excellency the Mayor), J. Homer Tutt (Ned Jenkins, Lem's Protégé, a Man With Modern Ideas), Russell Smith (Pedro Manuel, Mexican Half-Breed), Al[fred] Strauder (Ephraim Snow, Shoemaker and Politician), Will Dixon (Major Jinks, Civil War Veteran), Frank Jackson (Eagle Eye, Indian Chief), George Warden (Jeremiah Blackstone, Shyster Lawyer), Sam Grey (Zook Swift, Town Constable), John C. Wright (Elder Toots, Preacher), Blaine Waters (Loco Pete, Bad Man), Charles Olden (Lieutenant Fear, of Newtown Guards), Blanche Thompson (Marie Bellfonte, Coquette), Lena Roberts (Evelyn Stockholm, Schoolteacher), Ethel Marshall (Pocahontas, Indian Princess), Hattie Ackers (Semantha Mandrake, Suffragette Leader), Babe Brown (Alice Darling, Book Canvasser), Ora Dunlop (Phoebe Brown), Nina Marshall (Dolly Dimple), Grace Kneff (Sally Slymley), Emma Jackson (Helen Summer), Alice Russell (Pattie Broenson), Margaret Langford (Freezie Winters), and Stella Moore (Minnie Thanks).

Revived during the 1914 season, in New York and on tour, with the following cast: Salem Tutt Whitney (Mayor), J. Homer Tutt (Ned Jenkins), Ed. Toliver (Pedro Manuel), Leigh Whipper (Major Jinks), Alfred Strauder (Ephraim Snow), Frank Jackson (Eagle Eye), Ethel Marshall (Village Belle), Maybelle Brown (Pocahontas), Hattie Akers (Semantha Mandrake), Babe Brown (A Suffragette), Nettie Taylor (Schoolteacher), Alice Russell (Pattie Broenson), Nina Marshall (Dolly Dimple), Grace Kneff (Sally Slymley); Others: W. Blaine, Fred Redant, John Wilson, Julia Gideon, Cleo Mitchell, Belle May, and Virginia Wheeler.

Songs and musical numbers (combined from both prodns.): "I'm the Mayor of Newtown" (Mayor), "Here I Is and Here I Stay" (Mayor), "Hot Tamale Moon" (Jenkins), "Good Night, Marie" (Village Belle), "Neat Bed Nuff Sed" (Jenkins), "Tell Me, Rose" (Schoolteacher), "I Could Learn to Love a Boy Like You" (Schoolteacher), "You, Babe, Only You" (Mayor & Schoolteacher), "Mexico," "Keep a Movin' Right Along," "That Was Me," and "Those Songs I Love."

MAYTIME REVUE (1930). Touring revue. Cast included Johnny Lee Long, Fat Head, and Grant & Wilson.

ME AND BESSIE (1974–76). Musical retrospective. Conceived and written by Linda Hopkins and °Will Holt.

Essentially a one-woman show, or, as Gerald Bordman (*AmMusTh*, p. 681) called it, "a two-woman show, and one of those women was dead." A starring vehicle for blues and gospel singer Linda Hopkins, in which she narrates the tragic history of Bessie Smith, known as the Empress of the Blues, relates anecdotes and reminiscences, and sings the songs that Miss Smith made famous during her stormy career. Hopkins admits at the beginning, "I ain't Bessie. But you know there's a lot of Bessie in me."

First prod. at the Mark Taper Forum in Los Angeles, 1974. Prod. by the Ford's Theatre Society at Ford's Theatre in Washington, DC, Sept. 15, 1974–Aug. 31, 1975. Opened Off-Bway at the Ambassador Theatre, Oct. 22, 1975, for a lengthy run, eventually transferring to the Edison Theatre, for a total run of 453 perfs.; dir. by °Robert Greenwald. Starring Linda Hopkins as Bessie Smith; with Lester Wilson and Gerri Dean.

Songs: "I Feel Good," "God Shall Wipe All Tears Away," "Moan You Mourners," "New Orleans Hop Scop Blues," "Romance in the Dark," "Preach Them Blues," "A Good Man Is Hard to Find," " 'Tain't Nobody's Bizness If I Do," "Gimme a Pigfoot," "Put It Right Here," "You've Been a Good Ole Wagon," "Trombone Cholly," "Jazzbo Brown," "After You've Gone," "There'll Be a Hot Time in the Old Town Tonight," "Empty Bed Blues," "Kitchen Man," "Mama Don't 'Low," "Do Your Duty," "Fare Thee Well," "Nobody Knows You When You're Down and Out," "Trouble," and "The Man's All Right."

ME AND YOU (1922). Musical revue. Songs by James P. Johnson. Touring show which featured Andrew Tribble, Alec Lovejoy, Dink Stewart, Parker Anderson, and Eddie Gray.

MEDICINE MAN (1901). Musical play. 1 act. By J. Ed. Green. Prod. by the Rag Time Opera Co., at Traction Park, Birmingham, AL, opening July 20, 1901, on double bill with the author's *African Princes*.

MEET MISS JONES. See *SUGAR HILL*.

MELODY LANE GIRLS (1925). Touring revue. Cast included Ernest "Baby" Seals, James Isom, Emma J. Michaels, and Willie Gunn and his Beauty Chorus.

MEMPHIS BOUND! (1945). A swing version of °Gilbert and °Sullivan's *H.M.S. Pinafore*, presented as a play-within-a-play. Book by °Alberg Barker and °Sally Benson. Music adapt. from the orig. score, with new songs, by °Don Walker. Lyrics adapt. or rewritten by °Clay Warnick.

A stereotypical, brassy, white-authored song-and-dance show, conceived as a starring vehicle for the then 67-year-old Bill Robinson, who had previously starred with great success six years earlier in *The Hot Mikado* (1939), a swing version of another Gilbert and Sullivan operetta. This show presented *Pinafore* as a minstrel travesty perfd. by a stranded black showboat troupe whose boat (*The Calliboga Queen*) has been grounded on a sandbar near Memphis, TN, and they have been jailed for not having a proper license. After a speedy trial and acquittal, the troupers decide to put on a show on another showboat to raise the funds to get their boat afloat. As described by °Louis Kronenberger (*PM* 5–25–1945), "They put it on with so much jive, swing, boogie-woogie, abandon and irreverence that half way through it the horrified lady impresario rings down the curtain." The writers also provide a comic romance between Robinson's character and the owner of the showboat, and there is a romantic triangle between the beautiful Lily Valentine (Sheila Guyse), the happy-go-lucky Winfield Carter (dancer Avon Long), and the sterling Roy Baggott (singer Billy Daniels) who truly loves her.

Prod. on Bway by °John Wildberg at the Broadway Theatre, New York, opening May 24, 1945, for 36 perfs.; dir. by °Vinton Freedly and °Robert Ross, with the assistance of black choir dir. Eva Jessye. Cast: Bill Robinson (Pilot Meriwether), Avon Long (Winfield Carter), Edith Wilson (Melissa Carter), Billy Daniels (Roy Baggott), William C. Smith (Hector), Ann Robinson (Chloe), Ada Brown (Mrs. Paradise), Sheila Guyse (Lily Valentine), Ida James (Penny), Thelma Carpenter (Henny), Frank Wilson (Mr. Finch), Timothy Grace (Timmy), Oscar Plante (Sheriff McDaniels), Joy Merrimore (Eulalia), Harriet Jackson (Sarabelle), Charles Welch (Bill), William Dillard (Gabriel), and the Delta Rhythm Boys.

Songs and musical numbers (in addition to the *H.M.S. Pinafore* score): "Gilbert and Sullivan Blues," "Big Old River," "Stand Around the Band," "Old Love and Brand New Love," and "Growing Pains."
FURTHER REFERENCE: Alkire diss. *Life* 6–20–1945. *NY News* 6–10–1945. *NY World Telegram* 5–25–1945. *Time* 6–4–1945.

MENELEK (1936). Opera. By Penman Lovinggood. About the emperor of Abyssinia (Ethiopia) at the turn of the century. Perfd. by the American Negro Opera Association, 1938.

THE ME NOBODY KNOWS (1970–72). Musical of urban ghetto life. 2 acts. Adapt. by °Robert M. Livingston and °Herb Schapiro. From the book of the same title, ed. by °Stephen M. Joseph: an anthology of his New York public school students' writings about life in the ghetto. Music by °Gary William Friedman. Lyrics by °Will Holt.

A long-running, highly acclaimed show which began Off-Bway and moved to Bway after receiving the Obie Award for best musical in 1970. The *NYT* praised it as a "glorious and triumphant" revelation of "the sheer tenacity of the human spirit against oppression, . . . rats, . . . drugs, . . . [and] poverty."

Opened Off-Bway at the Orpheum Theatre, May 18–Nov. 15, 1970; continued its run on Bway at the Helen Hayes Theatre, Dec. 18, 1970, for a total of 586 perfs. Then went on transcontinental tour, where it played until late 1972, with lengthy runs at the Locust St. Theatre in Philadelphia and the Civic Theatre in Chicago. The Bway cast of 12 performers included 5 blacks: Irene Cara, Douglas Grant, Northern J. Calloway, Carl Thomas, and Hattie Winston.
FURTHER REFERENCE: *BesPls 1969–70; 1970–71. DBlkTh* (Woll).

THE MERRY WIDOWER (1908). Musical comedy. Book and lyrics by Victor H. Smalley. Prod. by Robert Motts and the Pekin Stock Co., at the Pekin Theatre, Chicago, April 1908; dir. by J. Ed. Green. Cast: Jerry Mills (Prince Dan-Low, the Merry Widower), Lottie Grady (Phonia), Charles H. Gilpin (Popoven Chickenian, Ambassador), Mae White (Notty Head, his wife), Harrison Stewart (Dish, Messenger of the Embassy), Walter Crumbly (Tipp-Mah, Head Waiter of Mack's Inn), Josephine DeVance (Maid at Mack's Inn), Willie Ingalls (Co-Co), Ada Fisher (Co-La), Madeline Cooper (O-Mee), and Effie King (O-Mii). Songs and musical numbers included "The Merry Widower" (rag and dance: Mills & Grady) and "As Long as the World Rolls By" (contralto solo: King).

MESSIN' AROUND (1929). Musical revue. Billed as "A Modern Musical Novelty." Prologue, 2 parts [11 scenes]. Conceived and staged by °Louis Isquity. Lyrics by Perry Bradford. Music by Jimmy Johnson (James P. Johnson).

A lively but cliché-ridden song-and-dance revue of the late 1920s, praised for Johnson's music (especially "Your Love Is All I Crave") and Eddie Rector's choreography, but criticized for the lack of a star performer of the caliber of Bill Robinson or Florence Mills. Although it received only fair reviews, not all were as condescending as that of the *NYT* (4–23–1929, p. 26), which considered the show's "outstanding claim to distinction" its display of "more gold teeth than any other group of similar size . . . on the whole Atlantic seaboard." Perhaps the "most unique" feature that surprised and delighted the critics was the staging each night of an actual boxing match between two professional women boxers—Emma Maitland, world female champion in the junior lightweight division, and Aurelia Wheeldin, world female champion bantamweight. The outcome of each match was judged on its own merits. But even this novelty was not enough to save the show from mediocrity and an early closing.

After an initial tryout in Boston, it opened at the Hudson Theatre (on 44th St. east of Bway), New York, April 22, 1929, for a run of only 33 perfs. Cast: Paul Floyd, Freda Jackson, Monetta Moore, Arthur Porter, Cora La Redd, James Dwyer, Audrey Thomas, Billy McLaurin, James "Slim" Thompson, Hilda Perleno, Sterling Grant, Walter Brogsdale, William McKelvey, Olive Ball, Jimmy Johnson, Queenie Price, Lena Shadney, Susie Wrote, Emma Maitland, Aurelia Wheeldin, the "Messin' Around" Choir, the Our Gang Kids (dancing waiters), the Maids, and Chorus.

Synopsis of scenes, songs, sketches, and musical numbers: Prologue—"On to Harlem" (Floyd). Part I, Scene 1—*Harlem Street Scene*; Place: Lenox Avenue and 135th Street, New York City; "Harlem Town" (song: Choir), 'I'm the Law' (Floyd), 'Makin' Time' (Maids), 'Papers' (Our Gang Kids), 'Blues' (Moore), Reprise, "Harlem Town" (Company), 'On Parade' (Floyd, Jackson, Moore, Porter & LaRedd), + "Skiddle-De-Scow" (song: LaRedd, Our Gang Kids, Dwyer & Company), "Get Away from My Window" (song: Thomas, McLaurin & Thompson), "Your Love Is All I Crave" (the song hit: Perleno, Grant & Chorus), 'Predictions' (Brogsdale, Floyd, Jackson, Price, Our Gang Kids &

Company), "Shout On" (song: Brogsdale, Porter, Floyd & Choir). Scene 2—Specialty (McKelvey). Scene 3—Telling Fortunes; Place: A Gypsy Camp Fire; Ball (Fortune Teller), Grant (He), Perleno (She), McLaurin (Fortune Seeker), Thompson (His Friend). Scene 4—+"I Don't Love Nobody But You" (song: Choir). Scene 5—*Dynamite*; Floyd (Crook), Thompson (Guardian), McLaurin (Dummy). Scene 6—*Mississippi*; "Roustabouts" (song: Choir & Chorus), "Mississippi" (song: Brogsdale & Company). Part II, Scene 1—*At the Carnival*; Place: Outside the Entrance of Main Tent; Floyd (Barker), Chorus (song: "Circus Days"); Bamboo McCarver (Tapso, the Dancing Skater), McLaurin (Applicant), Thompson (2nd Applicant), James K. Love (Rolo), James Skank (Jolo). Scene 2—*Battle for World's Female Championship*; Maitland (World's Female Junior Lightweight Champion), Wheeldin (World's Female Bantamweight Champion), McLaurin (Maitland's Second), Thompson (Wheeldin's Second), Fred A. Wheeldin (Referee), Company (Spectators). Scene 3—Paying Off; At the Carnival—Same as Act II, Scene 1; Wroten (Ballerina), Floyd (Carnival Barker), McLaurin (1st Second), Thompson (2nd Second). Scene 4—"Spirituals" (the Three Harmony Sisters: Olive, Pearl & Gladys). Scene 5—*Harlem's Midnight Frolic*; Master of Ceremonies (Grant), 'Tapcopation' (dance: LaRedd & Dancing Waiters), +"Sorry (that I Strayed Away from You)" (song: Perleno & Grant), Russian Specialty (Davis), 'Hopping the Buck' (McKelvey), "Put Your Mind Right on It" (song: Moore, Choir, Waiters, LaRedd, Chorus & Others), "Yamekraw" (piano symphony: Johnson), "Whirlwind" (Ebony Trio), "Messin' Around" (song: Moore), and Finale (Company).

Songs marked with a plus sign (+) pub. by M. Witmark & Sons, New York; copies in Moorland-Spingarn.

FURTHER REFERENCE: *BlksBf* (Sampson). *James P. Johnson* (Brown). *Life* 5–17–1929. *NY Eve. Post* 4–23–1929. *NY Eve. World* 4–23–1929. 5–4–1929. *NYorker* 5–4–1929. *NY Sun* 4–23–1929. *NYT* 4–23–1929. *NY Trib.* 4–23–1929. *ThMag* 6–1929.

MEXICO (1921). Touring vaudeville revue. Prod. by and starring comedian Doe Doe Green. Cast included Henrietta Lovelass, May Crowder, Charles Smith, Lovie Taylor, Georgia White, Geraldine Cardwell, Lena Wiggins, and Gene Collins.

MIDNIGHT FOLLIES (1920s). Touring revue with Bessie Smith.

MIDNIGHT FROLIC (1929). Touring vaudeville revue. Featured Mae Bonds, Mabel Hite, Frisco Bowman, and Virginia Mack.

MIDNIGHT IN CHINATOWN (1921). Touring vaudeville revue. Prod. by Luke Scott, who costarred with his wife, Irene Elmo Scott (as Scott & Scott). Songs included "Rusty" and "Sweet Adeline" [*sic*].

THE MIDNIGHT ROUNDERS (1920). White-oriented musical revue. Featured a popular song by Noble Sissle and Eubie Blake, introduced by Helen Bolton in this prodn. Prod. on Bway in 1920, with an all-white cast, featuring °Eddie Cantor. Included "Vision Girl," described in the *Dictionary Catalog of the Jesse E. Moorland Collection* (Howard Univ. Lib.) as "an oriental fox trot song," with lyrics by Sissle and music by Blake, pub. by M. Witmark, New York, 1920; copy in Moorland-Spingarn.

MIDNIGHT STEPPERS (1927). Touring vaudeville revue. Prod. by dancer/ choreographer Leonard Harper. Cast included Joe Byrd, Billy Higgins, the Three Dixie Song Birds (Birleanna Blanks, Amanda Randolph, and Hilda Perleno), Nina May, Dewey Brown, Paulis and Jimmie Johnson (possibly James P. Johnson), the Midnight Steppers (Edward Chenault, Joe Wilson, and Sam Burnham), the Alabama Four (dance group), George Phillips (acrobatic dancer), and Linda Garnette (contortionist).

MIDNIGHT STEPPERS (1928–29). Vaudeville revue. Toured the South starring Bessie Smith. Also in the cast were blues singer Lonnie Johnson, Hattie Noel, Lorenzo Tucker, and the Black and Tan Trio.

MIDNIGHT STEPPERS (1930). Touring vaudeville revue. Prod. by Gertrude Saunders and John Dancy, and starring Saunders. Cast also included the Three Black Sams (dance group), "Peaches" Wilson (soubrette), "Chick" Smith, Teddy Bunn, the Washboard Serenaders, Melvin Hunter, George Williams, William Charleston, James Allen, Norman Wright, Otis Blake, and 10 chorus girls.

MIKADO AMAS (1975). Operetta. Based on °Gilbert & °Sullivan's classic. Adapt. by Rosetta LeNoire. Presented by the AMAS Repertory Theatre, New York, Oct. 14, 1975; dir. by Irving Vincent.

MILINDA'S WEDDING DAY (1924). Touring vaudeville revue. Prod. by and costarring comedian Joe Bright. Also in the cast were Dink Stewart, Andrew Tribble, Theresa Burroughs Brooks, and "Bobby" Toliver Bright.

MIO (1988). Children's musical. By Shauneille Perry. Music by Julius P. Williams. Only the birds know where Mio goes when he does not attend school. Prod. by the Young People's Theatre at Lehman Coll., New York City, April 1988; dir. by Nancy Donato Tietze.

MISS BANDANNA (1927). Touring vaudeville revue. Prod. by and costarring Clarence Muse. About a stagestruck girl who leaves her Mississippi home and her youthful lover to seek fame and fortune in New York. Starring Jackie (later "Moms") Mabley in the title role. Also in the cast were Mabel Ridley, Salem Tutt Whitney, Alice Gorgas, "Onion" Jeffries, George Booker (juvenile), L.

J. Randall, Walter Crumbly, Ollie Burgoyne, Geraldine Gooding, and the Three Brownies.

MISS BROADWAY (1928). Touring vaudeville revue. Prod. by and costarring "Boots" Hope. Cast also included Pete and Minnie Gentry, John "Rastus" Murray, Kid Hawks, Joe Watts, Ruth Carter, Lorraine Lockhart, Georgia Celletta, Rose Morris, Lillian Hayes, and Helen Bush.

MISS BROADWAY (1930). Touring vaudeville revue. Prod. by and costarring comedian Billy "Bodidley" Pierson. Cast also featured Irene Butler, Simmons & Jenkins, Helen Jackie Morrison, Earl Palmer, Ishmael Watkins, "Soap" & "Towel," the Theophile Sisters, Dot Johnson, and Lenora Jones.

MISS CALICO (1926) / / Revised as *Africana* (1927). Tabloid musical. 2 acts. Lyrics, prodn., and staging by Earl Dancer. Music by Donald Heywood.

The orig. show on which the more successful *Africana* (1927) was based, both of which starred Ethel Waters. This was a lively song-and-dance revue, with comedy routines designed to be a showcase for Waters' talents, which thus far had been seen only by vaudeville and nightclub audiences.

Toured for several months in 1926, with a view to reaching Bway. Principal cast: Waters, Alec Lovejoy, Marshall Rogers, Lionel Monagas, Thornton Brown, George Stanton, the White Brothers (Jimmie and Eddie), Ida Hooten, George Hooten, Lew Keene, Margaret Beckett, the Taskiana Four, the Cocoa-Brown Skinned Maids, the Calico Girls, the Calico Syncopators (dir. by Thornton Brown), Louisa V. Jones, the Bamboo Girls, and chorus.

Program (including sketches, songs, and specialty numbers): Act I—Overture (Brown, cornetist); Opening, 'America's Black Cargo' (Taskiana Four, Cocoa-Brown Skinned Maids, Stanton & Lovejoy); "I'm Coming Virginia" (song: Waters); Specialty (White Bros.); 'I'm Satisfied' (specialty: Lovejoy); "Black Bottom" (song and dance: Waters & Calico Girls), 'A Revival Meeting,' written by G. Hooten, staged by Dancer (Cast: Spiritual Singers [Taskiana Four], Sister Few Clothes [Hooten], Elder Full Bosum [Rogers], Sister Get Happy [Waters], and Presiding Elder Low Down [Hooten]); Specialty (Keene); 'A Few Moments with Ethel Waters' (Waters); "Down Home Stomp" (song: Beckett, White Bros. & Chorus); Finale. Act II—'A Few Moments with the Calico Syncopators and Louisa V. Jones' (Thornton Brown, dir.); 'The Dance of the Old Black Crow' (Keene & Girls); 'Sweet Mama, Lulu Belle,' sketch written by Dancer, 'with apologies to Mr. Belasco' (Waters & Monagas); 'Shadows on the Wall' (Stanton & Cocoa-Brown Skinned Maids); Specialty (Taskiana Four); 'Bamborina' (Beckett & Bamboo Girls); 'A Court Scene—from Catch Air, Mississippi,' skit written by Dancer (Cast: Chink [Keene], Policeman—His name is Allblack [Hooten], Prosecuting Attorney [Monagas], Attorney for Defense [White], Judge—Nothing but Years [Lovejoy], Sophie Go Bout [Beckett], A Darktown Divorce Seeker [Waters], Tack Annie [I. Hooten], and Razor Jim [Rogers]); 'The Drill of Aunt

Hagar's Children' (Calico Girls & White Bros.); Specialty, 'Some Songs That You Have Heard in Your Homes' (Waters, Pearl Wright at Piano); Finale (Company).

MISS CREOLA (1929). Touring vaudeville revue. Prod. by and costarring Will Mastin (uncle of Sammy Davis, Jr.). Also in the cast were Sammy Davis's father, Sam Davis (Sr.), Eddie Williams, Rastus Murray, Jessie Cryor, Al Parker, Nora Collins, Obie Smith, Kathleen Bart, and Chick McIntosh.

MISS DINAH OF 1926 (1926). Touring vaudeville revue. Prod. by and costarring Quintard Miller and Marcus Slayter. Also in the cast were dancer Inez Dennis, blues singer Rosa Henderson, singer Annie White, and character actor George Wiltshire. The show featured 8 chorus girls.

MISS GEORGIA BROWN (1925). Touring vaudeville revue. Prod. by and costarring Irvin C. Miller. Also in the cast were Gallie DeGaston, Lilly Yuen, and Aurora Greeley.

MISS INEZ (1929). Touring vaudeville revue. Featured Beulah Benbow, Charlie Smith, Sol and Myrtle Speights, Gladys Dorsey, Anna Rose Turner, Allen & Allen, Randolph Johnson, and Waneta Gonzales.

MISSISSIPPI DAYS (1928). Billed as a "Musical Comedy Triumph." Organized by blues singer Bessie Smith, who starred in this prodn. Prod. at the Lafayette Theatre in Harlem, with a cast of 45. Then went on tour of the Southern Negro theatre circuit.

MISSISSIPPI STEPPERS (1928). Touring vaudeville revue. Prod. by and costarring Hezekiah Jenkins. Cast also included Bertha Idaho [Jordan?], Billie Dedway, Hattie Snow, Herman Higgs, Walter Smith, and Jessie Winston.

MISS NOBODY FROM STARLAND (1920). Musical comedy. 2 acts. Touring show prod. by and starring actor/singer/composer Shelton Brooks. A musical about how a musical is produced. Built around an elaborate plot involving an actress who stows away on a ship in the disguise of an Egyptian princess. She is saved by a wealthy young man who falls in love with her, and she persuades him to back a show which her brother has written. The rest of the show depicts the producing and staging of this show. Reportedly contained more than 20 musical numbers.
FURTHER REFERENCE: *BlksBf* (Sampson).

MISS NOBODY'S HOTEL (1921). Touring vaudeville revue. Prod. by and starring comedian Hardtack Jackson. Cast also included E. E. Pugh and Louise Jackson.

MISS TRUTH (1971–72, revived 1978). Poetic suite. Originally 1 act, presumably revised to a full-length show. Music and lyrics by Glory Van Scott. About the life of Sojourner Truth. First prod. by the Afro-American Studio for Acting and Speech, New York, 1971, with the author in the leading role. Prod. by the Negro Ensemble Co., New York, Jan. 1972. Prod. at the Nat Horne Theatre, New York, Sept. 15–Nov. 5, 1978, for 32 perfs. Cast: Glory Van Scott, Lochandra Aarons, Loretta Abbott, Jamil Garland, Lloyd McNeil, Al Perryman, Ronell Seay, Tina Harrison, Gene Casey, Keith Loving, and Babafumi Akunyun. An early unpub. script in TC/NYPL and Hatch-Billops.

MISS WATERS, TO YOU (1983). Musical retrospective. Book by Loften Mitchell. Based on a concept by Rosetta LeNoire. Music from Ethel Waters' repertoire. Prod. by the AMAS Repertory Theatre, New York, opening Feb. 24, 1983; dir. by Billie Allen.

MR. BLUEBEARD (1903). White-oriented musical extravaganza. 3 acts. Based on the Drury Lane pantomime of the same title, brought over from London by °J. Hickory Wood and °Arthur Collins. Adapt. for the American stage by °John J. McNally. Lyrics by °J. Cheever Goodwin. Music by °Frederick Solomon and °C. Herbert Kerr. Prod. on Bway at the Knickerbocker Theatre, New York, opening Jan. 21, 1903, for 134 perfs. The all-white cast included °Eddie Foy, °Dan McAvoy, °Flora Parker, °Bonnie Maginn, and °William Danforth. Included one black-authored dialect song, ''W'en de Colo'ed Ban' Comes Ma-chin' Down the Street'' (When the Colored Band Comes Marching Down the Street), words by Dunbar, music by Cole & Johnson, pub. by Howley, Haviland & Dresser, New York; copy in Moorland-Spingarn.
FURTHER REFERENCE: *AmMusTh* (Bordman). *BesPls 1899–1909.*

MR. JAZZ FROM DIXIE (1918). Tabloid musical. Written and dir. by Billy King. Presented by the Grand Theatre, Chicago, by members of the Billy King Stock Co.

MR. LODE OF KOAL (1909–10). Musical fantasy. 3 acts. Book and lyrics by Jesse A. Shipp and Alex C. Rogers. Based on prodn. ideas by Bert Williams. Music by J. Rosamond Johnson. Additional music by Williams.

This was the last show in which Bert Williams starred before being engaged for the *Ziegfeld Follies*, in which he perfd. for the next ten years. It was also his first show without his longtime partner George Walker, with whom he had starred in at least seven Williams & Walker shows.

In Act I, Mr. Lode (Williams), who is employed as a coal worker, has been shipwrecked on a mythical island, where the former king (Big Smoke) has been kidnapped, and where the natives believe that someday a new ruler will come to them from out of the sea. When Mr. Lode is washed ashore, he is proclaimed the new monarch. Unhappy about being king, he tries to escape many times, but is prevented from doing so by his strong-arm bodyguards. To pacify him until the coronation, he is given a sleep-inducing fruit to eat, which causes him to dream a wonderful dream that comprises the whole of Act II. In this dream, there is much feasting and dancing, and some of the show's most important songs are sung. In Act III, Mr. Lode is about to be crowned king when the real monarch arrives on the scene, and Mr. Lode is condemned to work in the coal department of the kingdom. Rather than subject himself to this fate, he escapes down the aisle of the audience and disappears from sight.

Prod. on Bway at the Majestic Theatre, opening Nov. 1, 1909, for 40 perfs. Then toured for six months on the road, closing March 5, 1910, at the Cort Street Theatre in Brooklyn. Cast: Bert Williams (Chester A. Lode), Alex Rogers (Buggsy), Tom Brown (Gimlet), Siren Nevarro (Gluter), J. Leubrie Hill (Buttram), Charles H. Moore (Weedhead), Henry Troy ("Cap"), Charles McKenzie (Singlink), J. E. Lightfoot (Sarg), Matt Housley (Blootch), Lottie Grady (Hysteria), Ada Banks (Saylor), Hattie Hopkins (Hoola), Georgia Gomez (Kinklets), Bessie Brady (What), Anita Bush (Ho), Lavinia Rogers (Rubuena), Maggie Davis (Diano), Jessie Ellis (Osee), Ida Day (Discretia), Katie Jones (Giddina), Sterling Rex (1st Lt.), J. M. Thomas (2nd Lt.), Clarence Redd (3rd Lt.), Hattie McIntosh (Woozy, Commander-in-Chief of the Army); Others: Citizens, Guards, Flower Girls, Dancers, etc.

Songs and musical numbers: "The Start," "The Can Song," "My Old Man," +"The Harbor of Lost Dreams," "Mum's the Word, Mr. Moon," "In Far Off Mandelay," "Hodge Podge," "Bygone Days in Dixie," "Lament," "Chink Chink Chinyman," "The Fete of the Veiled Mugs," "Believe Me," "The Christening," "That's a Plenty," and "Blue Law."

Song marked with a plus sign (+) pub. by Will Rositer, Chicago, 1909; copies in Moorland-Spingarn.

FURTHER REFERENCE: *BlksBf* (Sampson). *Just Before Jazz* (Riis). *Nobody* (Charters). *NY Age* 9–16–1909. *NY Dramatic Mirror* 11–13–1909. Riis diss. *ThMag* 11–1915. *Mr. Lode of Koal* folder in Harvard Theatre Collection.

MR. RAGTIME (1914). Musical revue. Billed as a "Farce-comedy." Book by Irvin C. Miller. Music by Will Vodery.

Miller's first musical show, which apparently concerned a big-time New York show producer who comes to New Orleans to look for new talent for a forthcoming show. He stays at the Dumas Hotel, where he discovers that everybody there has talent, including the hotel proprietor, the staff (waitress, manicurist, maids, etc.), the guests, and especially the porter (Kid Brown). They stage a show in the hotel lobby, which provides the basis for the songs, comedy, and specialty acts. According to *BlksBf* (Sampson, p. 110), "Miller and Brown had the leading straight and comedy roles, respectively." The cast also featured the James Sisters (Ethel and Orena), who both had singing roles.

Prod. by Miller and Kid Brown, with Kid Brown's Company, in Chicago and on tour, 1914, apparently playing for a year before closing. Cast: Irvin C. Miller

(James Wilberforce, from New York), Ethel James (Mme. Winfrey, Proprietor of the Dumas Hotel), Eva Hill (Daisy Lewis, Waitress), Tillie Cross (Dora Jones, Hair Dresser), Carrie Caisons (Louise Day, Manicurist), Kid Brown (Thomas Green, Porter), Eleanor Johnson (Sarah Green, His Wife), Orena James (Mabel Webster, Entertainer), Esther Bigeou (Alleen Dean, a Singer), Maids, Guests, Visitors, etc.

Songs and musical numbers: "Ragtime Chimes" (opening chorus: Company), "All Aboard for Dixie Land" (E. James & Chorus), "Croony Melody" (Bigeou & Miller), "Every Road" (O. James & Chorus), "I'm Going to Exit" (Brown), "Bleeding Heart" (E. James), "Flippity Flop" (Brown & Chorus), "When You Sang the Rosary to Me" (Bigeou), "Carmina" (James Sisters), "Long Lost Blues" (Johnson & Company), "Hello Little Miss U.S.A.," "Hesitation Waltz," and Finale (Company).

MR. SAMBO FROM GASTON, SOUTH CAROLINA (1923). Touring vaudeville show. Prod. by the Delaney & Delaney Stock Revue Co., under the proprietorship of Tom and Pearl Delaney. The cast featured the two Delaneys, Catherine Stanley, and Gladys Dorsey.

MR. WONDERFUL (1956–57). Musical showcase. Book by °Joseph Stein and °Will Glickman. Music and lyrics by °Jerry Bock, °Larry Holofcener, and °George Weiss.

Starring vehicle for Sammy Davis, Jr., tailored to showcase his songs and impersonations, and those of the Will Mastin Trio. About a small-time nightclub entertainer who is persuaded to try to make it to Bway stardom; and in spite of his lack of self-confidence, he eventually succeeds. The settings include Union City, NJ; Miami, FL; and New York City.

Prod. at the Bway Theatre, opening March 22, 1956, for 383 perfs. Cast featured Sammy Davis, Jr. (Charlie Welch), Olga James (Ethel, his fiancée), °Jack Carter (Fred Campbell, his best friend), the Will Mastin Trio (with Sammy, his uncle [Will Mastin], and his father [Sam Davis, Sr.]), Pat Marshall, Chita Rivera, and Karen Shepard.

The song hits from the show were "Mr. Wonderful" (sung by James) and "Too Close for Comfort" (sung by Sammy). Other songs sung by Sammy were "Without You I'm Nothing" and "Ethel Baby."

No pub. libretto. Cast recording by Decca (DL 9032).
FURTHER REFERENCE: Alkire diss. *Yes I Can: The Story of Sammy Davis, Jr.* (Davis, Boyar & Boyar).

MRS. PATTERSON (1954–55, 1957). Fantasy, with music. By Charles Seebree and °Greer Johnson. Music by James Shelton. Adapt. from Seebree's 3-act nonmusical fantasy, *My Mother Came Crying Most Pitifully* (1949).

A starring vehicle for Eartha Kitt, who had made her Bway debut two years earlier in *New Faces of 1952*. Tells the story of a 15-year-old black southern country girl, during the 1920s, who lives in a fantasy world in which she dreams of being a rich, white lady like her mother's employer, Mrs. Patterson. In spite of the rave revues for Kitt, the play was considered "banal" by *Phylon* reviewer Miles Jefferson. However, it was one of the few shows on Bway during the 1950s written by a black playwright.

Prod. on Bway at the National Theatre, Dec. 1, 1954–Feb. 26, 1955, for 101 perfs.; dir. by Guthrie McClintic. Cast: Eartha Kitt (Teddy Hicks), Avon Long (Mr. D[evil]), Helen Dowdy (Bessie Bolt), Ruth Attaway (Anna Hicks), Vinie Burrows (Selma Mae), Terry Carter (Willie B. Brayboy), Estelle Hemsley (Aunt Matt Crossy), Emory Richardson (Sylvanus), Enid Markey (Mrs. Patterson), Mary Ann Hoxworth (June Embree), Mary Harmon (Rose Embree), and Joan Morgan (Fern Embree).

Went on a three-month national tour, after closing on Bway. Prod. by the Gilpin Players, Cleveland, Jan. 15–Feb. 16, 1957.

Songs and musical numbers: "Tea in Chicago," "If I Was a Boy," "My Daddy Is a Dandy," "Be Good, Be Good," and "I Wish I Was a Bumble Bee."

Bway cast recording by RCA Victor (LOC–1017).

FURTHER REFERENCE: *NY Herald Trib.* 12–1–1954. *NYT* 12–3–1954. *ThArts* 2– 1955. *Thursday's Child* (Eartha Kitt; New York: Duell, Sloan and Pearce, 1956).

MODERN COCKTAIL (1927). Touring vaudeville revue. Prod. by Norman Thomas. Musical dir., Grant Williams. Cast featured character actress Susie Sutton, aerialists Wells & Wells, straight actor Lloyd Hollis, character actor Coleman Titus, comedians Robert Perry and Willie Richardson, and 7 chorus girls.

MONEY / / Orig. title and genre *Jazz Opera* (1979). Libretto by Amiri Baraka (LeRoi Jones). Musical score by °George Gruntz. Commissioned by the Paris Opera. Prod. as a workshop prodn. by La Mama Experimental Theatre Club (E.T.C.), New York, Jan. 1982, and presented at the Kool Jazz Festival, New York, July 3–5, 1982.

MOOCHIN' ALONG / / Orig. title presumed to be *Sunshine Sammy* (1925). Musical revue. Book by Jesse A. Shipp. Music by Jimmie Johnson (James P. Johnson). Lyrics by Cecil Mack (James P. McPherson).

The details concerning this show have not been located, but it is believed to be a revision of *Sunshine Sammy* by the same writers, which was to star a performer by that name (Sunshine Sammy), and was scheduled for fall prodn. at the Lafayette Theatre in Harlem, when it was previewed by the *NY Amsterdam N.* (9–9–1925). Since Sunshine Sammy is not listed in the cast of *Moochin' Along*, it is conjectured that he dropped out of the show for some reason, and the show's title and opening date were changed accordingly.

Prod. by Billy Mitchell and the Broadway Revue Company at the Lafayette

Theatre, Dec. 7, 1925, for at least one week; stage managed by Dick Conway. With dances staged by Harwell Cook and Roscoe Simmons, Jr. Cast included Billy Cumby, Inez Dennis, Edgar Conners, Alonzo Fenderson, Ollie Burgoyne, Jimmy Marshall, Mattie Harris, Al Majors, Ada Rex, Richard Gregg, Izzie Ringgold, Slim Henderson, Arthur Ames, Arthur Gaines, Ada Gulgnesse, Madge Hall, and Thelma Henderson.

Principal songs are believed to include "You for Me, Me for You from Now On" (pub. by Pickwick Music, ASCAP, 1926); "Everybody's Doin' the Charleston Now" and "Mistah Jim" (both pub. by Irving Berlin, 1928).
FURTHER REFERENCE: *NY Amsterdam N.* 12–2–1925; 12–9–1925.

MOOD INDIGO (1989). "Nostalgic musical revue." By Julian Swain. A retrospective "highlighting the great African American composers and singers such as Duke Ellington, Fats Waller, Eubie Blake, Bessie Smith, Ma Rainey and Big Maybell" (*Blk. Masks* [11/12–1989]). Prod. by the ETA Creative Arts Foundation, Chicago, Nov. 16–Dec. 23, 1989.

MOONSHINE (1922). Musical comedy. 2 acts [11 scenes]. Written and prod. by Billy King.

Elaborately staged song-and-dance show built around the thin plot of a boozing father being pursued by his bootlegger, who does not want his best customer to give up drinking and the life of pleasure that he leads when drunk.

First prod. at the Grand Theatre, Chicago, perfd. by the Billy King Stock Co. Featured cast: King (Billy Booker, the Father), Margaret Scott (Mrs. Sallie Booker, his Wife), Marshall Rogers (Silas Jenkins, the Bootlegger), and Genevieve Stearn (a Vamp); Dancers: Jack "Ginger" Wiggins, Willie Thrill, "Doc" and Jennie Straine, and the Incomparable Steppers (which included Rebecca "Dink" Thomas and Gertrude "Baby" Cox); Instrumentalists: Jasper Johnson's Syncopated Band, Marie Thomas (trombone soloist), and Gertrude Rustill (violinist); Other singers and performers: Bessie Brown, William Gunn, May Bell Brown, and Ike Young.

Songs and musical numbers: "The Dancing Fool," "The Jazzbo Strutt," "Hello Everybody," "The Old Time Ball," "Moonshine Blues," "Just Vamping That's All," "Jazz Me," "Step on It," and the title song "Moonshine."
FURTHER REFERENCE: *BlksBf* (Sampson).

THE MORNING DUKE ELLINGTON PRAISED THE LORD AND SEVEN LITTLE BLACK DAVIDS TAP-DANCED UNTO (1976). Ceremonial entertainment, with blues, jazz, and dance. By Owen Dodson. Music by Roscoe Gill. Several black entertainers are brought back after death to be judged before Jesus for their deeds on earth. Staged reading by the Frank Silvera Writers Workshop at the Martinique Theatre, New York, Jan. 1976. Unpub. script in Hatch-Billops.

MO' TEA, MISS ANN? (1980–81). Book and lyrics by Bebe Coker. Music by Leander Morris. Apparently concerned the subtle racial nuances of the black-white servant-mistress relationship. Prod. by the AMAS Repertory Theatre, New York. Dir. and choreographed by Denny Shearer. Cast: Jimmy Almistad, Suzanne Buffington, Jay Aubrey Jones, Joy Kelly, Boncellia Lewis, Charles Muckle, Herb Quebeck, Zoe Walker, Juanita Walsh, Carmiletta Wiggins, Alonzo G. Reid, and Sundy Leigh Leake. (Racial identities not known.)

MOTHER GOOSE (1903). White-oriented musical extravaganza. Book by °John J. McNally. Music by °George V. Hobart and others. With additional music and lyrics by James Weldon Johnson, J. Rosamond Johnson, and Bob Cole.

°Klaw & Erlanger's prodn. of the Drury Lane extravaganza brought over from London and adapt. for American audiences.

Prod. on Bway at the New Amsterdam Theatre, opening Dec. 2, 1903, for 105 perfs. The all-white cast included °Joseph Cawthorn, °Clifton Crawford, °Harry Bulger, °Leila McIntyre, and °Pat Rooney.

Black-authored songs included "There's a Very Pretty Moon To-Night" by the Johnson Brothers and "The Evolution of Ragtime" by Cole and the Johnson Brothers; the former song pub. by Joseph W. Stern, New York, copy in Moorland-Spingarn. "The Evolution of Ragtime," which traced and illustrated black music from the African dance to its present form of jazz, consisted of six individual songs: "Voice of the Savage" (a Zulu dance), "Echoes of the Day" (a sentimental plantation song), "Essence of the Jug" (black dance music), "Darkies Delight" (a minstrel song), "The Spirit of the Banjo" (instrumental folk song), and "Sounds of the Times" (ragtime dance music).

See also *A Little Bit of Everything.*

A MOTHER-IN-LAW'S DISPOSITION (1917). Tabloid musical. Written and prod. by Billy King. Perfd. by the Billy King Stock Co. at the Grand Theatre, Chicago.

THE MUSIC MAN (1910). Touring revue. Featured Tom Lockhart, Lena Lockhart, the Mitchell Sisters, and Billy Scott (billed as "The Droll Comedian").

MUTT AND JEFF (1922). Vaudeville comedy. 2 acts [14 scenes]. Book by °"Bud" Fisher and °Richard F. Carroll. Based on Fisher's nationally syndicated comic strip by the same title. Music and lyrics by Frank Montgomery and several white songwriters, including °Paul Worde, °Joseph Conoly, and Richard Carroll.

Although no plot information concerning this show has been located, the main characters were Mutt and Jeff, played by comedians Leroy "Stringbeans" Brown and T. H. Hammond. Mutt was the tall one and Jeff was his short companion; both liked to bet on the horse races.

The setting was the race track at Belmont Park, Long Island, NY, and the show was built around a horse-racing theme. The event may well have been the

Belmont Stakes, one of the three races in the Triple Crown. Among the cast of characters were a track official, a horse owner, a sport, his wife (in disguise), a dude, a drunk, a tipster, a blind man, two ladies straight out of Shakespeare (and possibly the "loony bin"), two political refugees from Mexico, and the captain of the ship that brought them to the U.S.

Apparently toured the white theatrical circuits, under the management of Conoly and °Gus Hill (the show's owners). Frank Hill was the musical dir., and Paul Worde was orchestra dir. Cast: Margaret Lee (Chiquita, Daughter of Mexican Rebel President), Lillian Russell (Carmencita, her Aunt), Henry Sapara (Jack Manley, a Sporty Young Man), Joe Russell (Plungy Wiggles, Horse Owner and Man About Town), Ben Williams (Racetrack Gatekeeper), Leroy "Stringbeans" Brown (Mutt, the Long of It), T. H. Hammond (Jeff, the Short of It), Florence McClain (Jacquille Manley [Jack Manley's wife], Posing as a Widow), E. C. Caldwell (A Blind Man), Bee Freeman (Ophelia), Dempale Braxton (Desdemonia Newmonia), Charles Hawkins (A Dude), Frank Montgomery (Captain Jinks of the Good Ship "Hot Tamale"), and Others (Spectators, Spanish Girls, Mermaids, Jingling Joy Jiggers, & High Steppers.

Songs and musical numbers: Act I—"Hello, Belmont Park" (Montgomery & Chorus), "Wild About Rose" (T. H. Hammond), "No One Like You" (Sapara & Lee), "Pretty Melody" (Quintette: Lee, McClain, L. Russell, Sapara & J. Russell), "Echoes of Jazzland" (Russell & Russell), "Two Handsome Men" (Brown & Hammond), "Chiquita" (Sapara & Spanish Girls), "My Cavalier" (Lee), "The Shimmy Wedding" (Ensemble), "The Jockey Jamboree" (Conoly & Carroll), "Widow Kiddo" (J. Russell & McClain), "The Sport of Kings" (Finale: Company). Act II—"Carolina Sue" (opening ensemble: Company), "The Cabaret Entertainers" (Sapara & Lee), "Poor Little Me" (Hammond), "The Tale of the Mermaid" (Lee & Mermaids), Specialty (Montgomery & McClain), "Jefferson Jazz Band" (J. Russell, L. Russell & Jingling Joy Jiggers), "How Long" (Montgomery, High Steppers & Ensemble), and Good Night Number (Ensemble).

FURTHER REFERENCE: *Billboard* (J. A. Jackson's Page), 2–18–1922.

MY FRIEND FROM DIXIE. See *THE DARKTOWN FOLLIES.*

MY FRIEND FROM KENTUCKY (1909). Vaudeville farce-comedy. Book and lyrics by Salem Tutt Whitney and J. Homer Tutt. Music by Taylor L. Caldwell and Whitney & Tutt. (Not to be confused with the show of the same title and similar plot by J. Leubrie Hill [1913]. See *The Darktown Follies.*)

About a socially ambitious and wealthy farmer (Abraham Lincoln Brown) who is duped into leaving his comfortable home in Bowling Green, KY, and moving to the North where his host resides, and where, for a large fee, he is promised that he will be introduced into society, make new friends, meet beautiful girls, and be given a position of rank.

When the gullible Brown arrives in town, he is transported by wheelbarrow to his host and friends, who greet him as "The Man Who Rules the Town." Brown is then carried through a number of comic situations that fulfill to the letter the promises made. For his introduction into society, he is initiated into a fraternal lodge. He meets several beautiful girls in a saloon, including one who meets his fancy (played by Daisy Martin). He is made an officer in the town's standing army, and when his new girlfriend's reputation is impugned, he challenges the offender to a duel, from which he barely escapes with his life. The events of the plot are presumably unraveled satisfactorily at the end.

   Prod. as a touring show with the following cast: Salem Tutt Whitney (Abraham Lincoln Brown), J. Homer Tutt, Sam Gardner, Frank Jackson, Lindsey Lewis, James Woodson, Daisy Martin, Nettie Taylor, Mabel Dehearbe, Nina Marshall, Mamie Gardner, Georgie Davis, Blanche Simms, H. S. Wooten, James Weaver, James Woodson, and Al Stauder.

   Songs and musical numbers: "Come Out, Dear Louise" (Taylor & Sextette), "The Man That Rules the Town" (Whitney), "Strutting Sam" (Tutt & Chorus), "Hymn by the Royal Roosters" (Company), "Way Back in Dixie Land" (Marshall & Ensemble), "My Spanish Maid" (Babe Brown & Spanish Maids), "Smile On, Sue" (Martin & Tutt), "Pride of Company B" (Whitney & Gardner), "Reminiscing of Dixie" (Jackson & Chorus), "Dat's Sufficiency" (Whitney & Martin), and "For Honor" (Company).

MY FRIEND FROM KENTUCKY (1913–14). See **THE DARKTOWN FOLLIES**.

MY GAL (1929). Touring vaudeville revue. Prod. by and costarring Garland Howard. Cast also included Mae Brown, Nettie Hays, Joe Byrd, Al Young, Maxey & Al, Joe Lumes, Clarence Parson, Bob Davis, and the William Elkins Jubilee Choir.

MY MAGNOLIA (1926). Musical revue. 2 acts. Book by Alex C. Rogers and Eddie Hunter. Lyrics by Alex C. Rogers. Music by C. Luckeyth Roberts.
   An ill-fated revue that was criticized by the *NY Herald Trib.* (7–13–1926) for trying to pattern itself after white Bway revues, comparing the performers to "children acting out a play in a nursery." *Variety* (7–14–1926) deplored "the number of encores, given for any excuse," which lengthened the performance, and attributed these to the frequent applause by "colored people . . . spotted throughout the lower floor," and occupying "several boxes." The *NYT* (7–13–1926) disparagingly praised the dancing, which included "charlestons, taps and other convulsions," and commented that "the chorus of men and women, individually and collectively, seemed to look upon dancing as the breath of life." As Gerald Bordman quipped (*AmMusTh*, p. 414): "For the luckless C. Luckeyth Roberts it was apparently the last straw. The score was his third in three years to be given short shrift. He disappeared from the Broadway scene."
   Prod. at the Mansfield Theatre, "closer to Times Square than many Negro

shows of the era'' (Bordman, p. 414), opening July 8, 1926, for only 4 perfs.; dir. by Rogers & Hunter. Dances choreographed by Charley Davis. Cast: Dink Stewart (Henry Upson, Bellboy), Henry "Gang" Jines (Jasper Downson, another Bellboy), Catherine Parker (Magnolia), Adelaide Hall (Jenny), Hilda Rogers (Peggy Switch), Paul Bass (Harvey, Floor Manager), Percy Colston (Jody), Lionel Monagas (Mr. Workem), Barrington Carter (Constable Sapp), George Randol (Johnny Page, a Detective), Claude Lawson (Chef), Alberta Perkins (Daisy Snow), Eddie Hunter (Sherman), Estelle Floyd (Jerry), Lena Sanford Roberts (Widow Love), Mabel Grant (Geraldine), Charles Davis (Lightfoot & Sherman's Brother), Shippy Mason (Snappy), Alex Rogers (Uncle Fi), and George Nanton and Clarence Peters (Crap Shooters).

Songs and musical numbers: "At Your Service," "Baby Mine," "Shake Your Duster," "Pay Day," "Magnolia," "Hard Times," "Spend It," "Jazz Land Ball," "Laugh Your Blues Away," "Gallopin' Dominoes," "Headin' South," "Merry Christmas," "Struttin' Time," "Our Child," "Gee Chee," "Sundown Serenade," "Parade of the Christmas Dinner," "Baby Wants," "The Oof Dah Man," and "Sweet Popopper."

MY PEOPLE (1917–18). Musical comedy. 2 hours. Written, prod., and co-starring Salem Tutt Whitney and J. Homer Tutt (Whitney & Tutt). Music by C. Luckeyth Roberts. Perfd. by the *Smart Set Co.* at the Lexington Theatre in New York and on tour, 1917–18. Cast: T. L. Corwell, B. Hillman, Luke Scott, Sam Gray, Al Watts, Nat Cash, William Fountain, Julian Costello, Wesley Mitchell, Charles Lawrence, Alex White, Edward Marshall, Buster Williams, Emma Jackson, Lena Roberts, Daisy Martin, Carrie King, Estelle Cash, Ora Dunlop, Virginia Wheeler, Gladys Dennis, Ferrell White, Julia Moody, Marion Artie, Theresa West, Mattie Brooks, Jim Lee, Alonzo Fenderson, and Ethel Pope.

THE MYSTERY OF PHILLIS WHEATLEY (1976). Historical musical for children. By Ed Bullins. Depicts the black and white forces that contend for the soul of African-American poet Phillis Wheatley as she begins to achieve international recognition. Prod. by the New Federal Theatre, New York, Feb. 1976; dir. by Elizabeth Van Dyke. Unpub. script in Hatch-Billops.

MY WIFE (1930). Touring vaudeville revue. Prod. by and costarring Henry Drake and Ethel Walker (Drake & Walker [Mrs. Drake]). Cast also included Sam "Bilo" Russell, Lucy Strayhorne, Billy English, and the Harmony Four Quartet.

MY WIFE'S SWEETHEART (1918). Vaudeville revue. Touring show prod. by the Dunnell Bright Co. Cast featured Irvin C. Miller and Esther Bigeou Miller.

N

NADA (1925–47). Opera. By H. Lawrence Freeman. Unperfd. Part of a tetralogy entitled *Zululand*. The composer's best-known operas include *The Martyr (1893), *Valdo (1905–6), *Vendetta (1911–23), and *Voodoo (1921–28).

NANCY BROWN (1903). White-oriented musical comedy. 2 acts. Book and lyrics by °Frederick Ranken, in collaboration with °George Broadhurst. Music mainly by °Henry Hadley. With numerous interpolated songs by Bob Cole, James Weldon Johnson, and J. Rosamond Johnson.

Conceived as a starring vehicle for °Marie Cahill, the plot concerns a marriage broker who arranges profitable matches for the impoverished men of Ballyhoo.

Prod. at the Bijou Theatre, New York, opening Feb. 16, 1903, for 104 perfs.

Songs by Cole & the Johnson Brothers include +"Under the Bamboo Tree," which Cahill had previously introduced in her permanent repertoire; "Magdaline, My Southern Queen," "My Mississippi Belle," "Save It for Me," "The Soldier Is the Idol of the Nation," +"The Katy-did, the Cricket and the Frog," +"Two Eyes," "Octette to Bacchus," "In Gay Ballyhoo," and "Cupid's Ramble." Songs pub. mainly by Joseph W. Stern; those marked with a plus sign (+) are in Moorland-Spingarn.

NATURAL MAN / / Orig. title: *This Ole Hammer* (1936–37, 1941). First prod. as a "Negro folk opera"; latter prod. as a folk drama with music. 8 episodes. By Theodore Browne. Based on the legend of John Henry.

John Henry was one of the best-known black folk heroes, whose legendary strength as a "steel driving" railroad worker, with his legendary hammer, was tested in a contest with a modern steam drill. In the words of Doris Abramson (*NegPlaywrs*, p. 103), "John Henry has become a symbol of indomitable human pride and an expression of the Negro's will to survive impossible odds." Browne's version focuses on the injustices suffered by blacks, and John Henry is portrayed as a militant black man whose belligerence is matched by physical strength. Although he dies in his battle against the machine, he has proven his manhood, and his death is therefore a glorious one; symbolically, he has taken a stand against the American system of social injustice and oppression, even though he has been defeated in the struggle.

Completed in 1936. First prod. as a full-length Negro opera by the Negro Unit of the WPA Federal Theatre in Seattle, WA, Jan. 28–Feb. 28, 1937. Although the WPA cast is not significant, the music of this prodn. is worthy of comment, and is presented in lieu of the cast of characters. According to Evamarii Alexandria Johnson (Ph.D. diss., 1981, p. 83), much of the music was sung by a chorus of 13 singers from backstage over a public address system:

The play was run without intermission, and part of the function of the chorus and the music was to aid in maintaining the desired pace of the show. Songs used were a combination of popular tunes, such as ''Beale St. Blues,'' which was used as introduction to a honky-tonk episode set in Memphis, and folk or ethnic songs of uncertain origin, such as ''John Henry,'' which opened and closed the show, or ''New River Train,'' which led into a scene between John Henry and a gang of railway hobos.

There were also several songs within the action, sung by actors on stage. John Henry has several, including ''This Old Hammer,'' which opened the action of the play. There is also a flirtatious duet between Polly Ann and John Henry which established the tone of that relationship, and in the ''Beale Street'' episode, . . . a sextette of streetwalkers and pimps performed a hymn to their lifestyle.

Again prod. as a folk drama with music by the American Negro Theatre, at the 135th St. Library Theatre (now known as the Schomburg Center/New York Public Library), May 7, 1941, for a short run; dir. by Benjamin Zemach. Cast: Stanley Greene (John Henry, a steel driving man); Five steel drivers: James Jackson (Charley), Maxwell Glanville (Big'N Me), William Lopez Daniels (Hard Tack), Howard Augusta (Jim), and George Lewis (Britt); Ruby Wallace [Ruby Dee] (Polly Ann, John Henry's woman), Alvin Childress (Capt. Tommy Walters, white railway boss), Kenneth Manigault (The Creeper, a black troubadour), Claude Sloan (The Salesman of Steam Drills), Letitia Toole (The Singer), Clair Leyba (Cleo), Mildred Meekins (Susie), Frederick O'Neal (The Preacher), and Alice Childress (Sistuh Bessie). This won for the author a Rockefeller Playwriting Fellowship, 1941.

Full script pub. in *BlkThUSA* (Hatch & Shine, 1974). Federal Theatre Project script in the National Archives, Washington, DC, and in FTP/GMU.

FURTHER REFERENCE: Johnson diss. *List of Neg. Plays* (WPA/FTP). *NegPlaywrs* (Abramson). *NYT* 5–8–1941. Pitts diss. *PM* 5–8–1941. Ross diss.

'NEATH THE SOUTHERN MOON (1927). Touring vaudeville revue. Prod. by and costarring comedian Bill ''Bodidley'' Pierson. Cast also included Hazel Myers, Lovey Austin, Walter Smith, Dink Stewart, and Mann & Cole.

NEGRO NUANCES (1924). Musical comedy. Book by Abbie Mitchell, Flournoy E. Miller, and Aubrey E. Lyles. Music by James P. Johnson and Will Marion Cook. Lyrics by Cook. Orchestra direction by Johnson. Traces the history of blacks from the beginning in Africa to America aboard the slave ships, through the pre–Civil War days, to the Reconstruction period and the era of black participation in minstrelsy. Prod. in Harlem and apparently on tour, 1924. Cast included Miller & Lyles, Mitchell, Lucille Handy (daughter of composer W. C. Handy), and Louis Douglass.

NEIGHBORS (1917). Tabloid musical. Written and prod. by Billy King. Presented at the Grand Theatre, Chicago, with members of the Billy King Stock Co.

NEW AMERICANS / / Orig. title: *The New American* (1920–21). Musical pageant. Written and dir. by Billy King. Dealt with the status of the Negro as the new American. First presented under its orig. title at the Grand Theatre, Chicago, with members of the Billy King Stock Co. Cast included King, Marshall Rogers, and Julia Rector. Presented under its present title by the same group, 1921, opening again at the Grand Theatre, then going on U.S. tour, including the Lafayette Theatre in New York. Cast included King, Maude Russell, Edna Hicks, Margaret Scott, Birleanna Blanks, and Rebecca "Dinks" Thomas. **FURTHER REFERENCE:** *Chicago Whip* 12–18–1920.

A NEW BREED IS NOW THE SEED. See *PAPER BIRD.*

NEW FACES (1952, 1956). A series of annual revues prod. by °Leonard Sillman in New York. The *1952 ed.* introduced Eartha Kitt in her Bway debut, singing a sultry rendition of "Monotonous," about the boredom of the life of luxury and adventure. The *1956 ed.* featured Tiger Haynes in his Bway debut. Both eds. were recorded by RCA Victor: *New Faces of 1952* (LOC 1008); *New Faces of 1956* (LOC 1025).

NEW ORLEANS VAMPIRES (1924–25). Touring vaudeville revue. Prod. by Jim Green, who also costarred. Cast included Roberta Green, Elenora Moore, Catherine Simmons, Emma Thomas, Lucille Smith, Julius Shedrick, Kid Thomas, Blanche Nelson, and the Spencer Anthony Orchestra: James Sykes, Clarence Simmons, Bob Johnson, Charles Mason, and William Turner.

THE NEW YORKERS (1901). White-oriented musical comedy. Book by °Glen MacDonough. Lyrics by °George V. Hobart. Music by °Ludwig Englander. With additional, so-called coon songs by Will Marion Cook and Sidney L. Perrin.

The adventures of a down-and-out New Yorker in Paris, who hopes to marry well by pretending to be a baron.

Prod. on Bway at the Herald Square Theatre, opening Oct. 7, 1901, for 64

250 NEW YORK REVUE

perfs. With an all-white cast, including °Dan Daley, °William Cameron, °Virginia Earle, °Margaret Clark, and °Anna Laughlin.

Black-authored songs included "Dat's All" by Cook; and "My Dixie Queen (Coontown Loyalty)" by Perrin, sung by Laughlin, the latter pub. by M. Witmark, New York, copy in Moorland-Spingarn.

NEW YORK REVUE (1928). Musical revue. Prod. at the Lincoln Theatre; starring Trixie Smith.

NEXT DOOR NEIGHBORS (1928). Musical revue. Prod. at the Lincoln Theatre in Harlem; starring Trixie Smith.

(THE) NIFTIES OF 1928 (1928). Touring vaudeville revue. Prod. and perfd. by actor/singer/composer Shelton Brooks. Cast also included King Hunter, St. Clair Dotson, Ivette, Anna and Wilbur White, Popo Warfield, and Lena Wilson.

A NIGHT AT THE CABARET (1926). Touring vaudeville revue. Prod. by Joe Clark and perfd. by the Joy Makers Co.

A NIGHT IN NEW YORK'S CHINATOWN (1910). Musical comedy. Book by Jesse A. Shipp.

A comedy of lowly life, in a mysterious Chinese setting in New York. Apparently much of the action took place in a cafe, which permitted the use of show girls and the performance of specialty acts.

Prod. by Sam Corker, Jr., at the Pekin Theatre, Chicago, Dec. 1910, with the following cast: Sidney Perrin (comedian/piano player), Tom Brown [later replaced by Frank Walker] (Ah Sing), Jesse A. Shipp (Ling Lee), Charles Gilpin ("buffet boss"), W. W. Elkins (soldier), Jerry Mills ("sleeper"/comedian), Lloyd Gibbs and Carrol Amos (waiters), Mr. Matthews [first name unknown] ("Mocking Bird Rube"), Hattie McIntosh, Fanny Wise, Goldie Crosby, Ada Banks, Gertie Brown, Ethel Marlow, Anna Wills, and the Broadway Girls (chorus).

A NIGHT IN TURKEY (1925). Touring vaudeville revue. Prod. and perfd. by comedian Joe Carmouche and his partner Cleo Mitchell.

THE NIGHT RAID (1918). Tabloid musical. Written and prod. by Billy King. Presented at the Grand Theatre, Chicago, with members of the Billy King Stock Co.; featuring Bessie Brown and Howard Kelly.

1999: THE BEGINNING OF THE END . . . THE END OF THE BEGIN-NING (1980). Billed as "A Modern Morality Play with Music." 2 acts. Book and lyrics by Cecil Alonzo. Music conceived by Alonzo; composed and dir. by JaSun.

A blending of biblical prophecy with predictions of Nostradamus and science fiction, which tells the story of one family caught between the forces of good and evil during the last seven days of time.

Prod. by the Alonzo Players, Brooklyn, NY, in repertory, opening Feb. 1980; dir. by Alonzo. With Greg-Eugene Sullivan as asst. dir. and choreographer. Cast: Nefrete Rasheed, Cheryl Jackson, L. E. Howell, Nathan Gibson, Clifford Robinson, Lawrence Evans, Trenda Browning, James Durant, Gordon Gatherer, and Leslie Louard. Dancers/Robots: Angela Barber, Vincent Carter, Jason A. Ilori, and Sharon Dancell Jenkins.

Songs: Act I (On the Streets of What's Left)—"Hurry Tomorrow," "Robot Song," "He Lives," "Ticket to Heaven." Act II, Scene 1 (Below the Ground in the Only Safe Place)—"Mother Is Crazed," "There Is a God," "Love Can Heal"; Scene 2 (The Final Day/The Last of Seven)—"Perfect Love," "Caught Up to Meet Him," "The Beginning of the End," "Wash Them," and "Seven Days."

NOBODY'S GIRL (1926). Touring vaudeville revue. Starring comedian Hamtree Harrington and Cora Green.

NO CRYSTAL STAIR (1980). Musical choreopoem. By Kenshaka Ali. A collage of poems, songs, and anecdotes depicting the historical struggle of black youth in America. Prod. by AMAS Repertory Theatre, New York, 1980.

NO NAME IN THE STREET (1985, revived 1987). Biblical adaptation. Book, lyrics, and music by Van Dirk Fisher. Musical version of the Book of Job, set in Africa during the 18th century. A Black Experimental Theatre production. First presented at Prospect Heights High School, Brooklyn, NY, April 26–May 19, 1985. Revived at Lincoln Square Theatre, New York, March 5–29, 1987; dir. by the author. Choreography by Collin Walker; musical arrangements by Diedre Murray. Featuring Marvel Lewis-Allen, Gary Anglin, Madeline Harrison, Rosemarie Lindau, and Torri Truss.

NON-SENSE (1925). Touring tabloid musical. Written, prod. by, and costarring Salem Tutt Whitney and J. Homer Tutt. Cast also included Joseph Purnell, Arlyne Brooks, Charles H. Hawkins, Frances Watts, Mabel Ridley, Baynard Whitney, and a chorus of 7 men and women.

NO PLACE LIKE HOME (1910). Musical comedy. Written and prod. by Jesse A. Shipp. Presented at the Pekin Theatre, Chicago, with members of Jesse A. Shipp's Stock Co. Cast featured Sidney Perrin (Willie Brown), Jesse Shipp (Rod Staff), Goldie Crosby (Lucy White), Fanny Wise (Anna Bell), Hattie McIntosh (Mrs. White), Jerry Mills (Mr. White), and Tom Brown (Italian Man).

NORTH AIN'T SOUTH (1923). Musical farce-comedy. Book by Salem Tutt Whitney, J. Homer Tutt, and Jesse A. Shipp. Music by Donald Heywood.

Whitney & Tutt musical about an ambitious group of singers and dancers in a small southern town who want to go on the stage. When a bigshot New York producer (Jesse A. Shipp) spends a night at the town's hotel, the performers put on a show especially for him. The show included singing and dancing, several comedy skits, including one that took place in a graveyard, and a burlesque version of Shakespeare's *Othello* (with Whitney as Othello and Maude DeForrest as Desdemona). Although impressed by the show, the producer is more impressed by one of the beautiful young singers in the group, and invites her to come back to New York with him, where he promises to help her get into show business. The entire group follows them to New York with the expectation of making it on the stage, but are unable to find work. They go back home, completely disillusioned, thinking that the South is a better place for blacks than the North. George Schuyler, critic for the *Messenger* (11–1923), called the music "tuneless," the singing and dancing "bad," and accused the show of perpetuating black stereotypes in the comedy skits.

Prod. by Whitney & Tutt at the Lafayette Theatre in Harlem, in the fall of 1923; dances dir. by Frank Montgomery. In addition to Whitney, Shipp, and DeForrest named above, the cast included George McClennon, Edna Gibbs, Mae Kemp, Hilda Bendischer, Harold Demond, Joe Purnell, Marion Harrison, Frank Shipp, and Lorraine Sampson.

Song and musical numbers included "What Kind of a Woman Does a Man Expect?," "Po' Little Lamb," "Pickaninny All Dressed Up," "On Parade," "Shake a Leg," and "Keep-A-Stepping Along."

NOW I'M A MASON (1914). Musical show. Prod. by Billy King. Presented at the Grand Theatre, Chicago, with members of the Billy King Stock Co.; featuring Bessie Brown and Howard Kelly.

NOYES AND WATTS MUSICAL COMEDY CO. (1921). Touring musical comedy troupe and show. Company included Hazel Gray, Juanita Jones, Evelin Winfield, Sam Rhodes, William Floyd, and Rastus Winfield.

NUT BROWN LADY (1924). Touring vaudeville revue. Prod. by H. D. Collins. Featured Salem Tutt Whitney, J. Homer Tutt, and members of the *Smart Set Co.

O

THE OCTOROON (1902). Opera. 4 acts. Libretto by M. E. Braddon. Musical score by H. Lawrence Freeman. Based on the 19th century melodrama *The Octoroon*, by °Dion Boucicault, which tells the plight of a "tragic mulatto." Earned for the composer the Harmon Award in 1930. Apparently unperfd.

THE OCTOROONS / / Orig. title: ***Isham's Creole Opera Co.*** / / Other previous titles: ***The Royal Octoroons***; ***Isham's Octoroons*** (1895–1900). Transitional musical show. 3 parts. Conceived and prod. by John W. Isham, proprietor and manager.

The second important show to use beautiful black women as chorus girls, replacing the all-male minstrel chorus. The first was °Sam T. Jack's *Creole Show* (1890–97), for which Isham had been the advance agent. Isham then decided to put out a show of his own, which he first called *Isham's Creole Opera Co.*, later changing the name as indicated above, to avoid threatened legal action by Jack. Although the show made a decided break with the typical minstrel show, it still used the three-part minstrel format. The first part consisted of the opening chorus and songs; the second was a loosely constructed burlesque sketch; and the third was a dance finale which included the celebrated cakewalk, a military drill, and a closing chorus-march. As the show progressed, there were various alterations in this three-part format, similar to those that Isham included in his next show *Oriental America* (1896–99).

Organized in New York City, the show toured such theatres as Waldman's Theatre in Newark, NJ; the Empire Theatre in Philadelphia, PA; Howard's Theatre in Louisville, KY; the Brooklyn Music Hall in Brooklyn, NY; the Corning Opera House in Corning, NY; the Park Theatre in Indianapolis, IN; and the Howard Atheneum in New York City. Ernest Graff was co-proprietor with Isham, and treasurer. Will H. Isham (John's brother) was acting manager, and later took over the position of manager in 1900 after John retired. Harry S.

Stafford was master of transportation and electrician. The orig. company, which included 16 men and 17 women performers, included Mme. Flowers (prima donna, known as the Bronze Melba, and called ''the greatest singer of her race''), Fred Piper (operatic baritone), Belle Davis (a well-known ''coon singer,'' called ''the star of her race''), Tom and Hattie McIntosh (sketch artists), the Mallory Brothers (Frank and Ed; novelty performers), Mattie Wilkes (character actress and wardrobe mistress), George Collins (musical director), Aida Overton (later Mrs. George Walker), Stella Wiley, Jesse A. Shipp, William ''Billy'' Johnson, Tom Brown, Shorty May, George Hammond, Bob Kelly, Mazie Brooks, Mamie Emerson, Ed Furber, Arthur Maxwell, and Ed Barber. (Flowers, Piper, Davis, the McIntoshes, and the Mallory Brothers remained with the show for several seasons.) Other performers who joined the show included Sam Lucas (comedian and monologist), Walter Smart and George Williams (Smart & Williams; specialty artists), the Hyers Sisters (operatic duo), Henry Fiddler (character mimic), Harry Jackson (tenor), Billy Jackson (comedian), Bertha Lee (soprano), Berthel & Jones (character sketch artists; called the ''Twentieth Century Swells''), the Spanish Serenaders, Ada Mickey (comedienne), the Brittons (Sadie and Joe; comedy, singing, and dancing performers), Alvin (comedy equilibrist), Ada Sullivan (soubrette), Stella Reinhart Nasher (dancer), the Reese Brothers (acrobats and jugglers), Williams & Melburn (comedy sketch artists), Frank Cushing (in 'Silence and Fun'), William Mozambique English (billed as a ''senegambian comedian''), and Billy Miller (comedy monologue artist).

Some of the outstanding musical and specialty numbers included in the show during its long run were 'The Carnival of Venice' (a giant operatic extravaganza, featuring Mme. Flowers and Fred Piper, 1985); 'Darkville Derby' (a skit about horse racing, 1986; the title changed to 'The Blackville Derby,' 1897); 'Thirty Minutes Around the Opera' (a ''mélange'' of selections from comic and grand opera, 1897–1900); 'Susanna Sampson's Wedding Day' (a comic skit, 1898); 'A Tenderloin Coon' (a ''laughable absurdity'' in two acts, 1898); 'The Ninth Battalion on dress parade, escorted by the Darktown Bandoleers, in a cake walk and jubilee' (1898); '7–11–77' (a skit showing a policy shop in operation, written by Bob Cole, 1899–1900); 'The Booking Agency' (comic sketch by Smart & Williams, 1900); and *King Rastus (vaudeville farce, 1900–1901).

FURTHER REFERENCE: BlksBf (Sampson). Ghost (Sampson).

ODODO (Yoruba word for ''Truth''—Subtitle) (1968–73). Billed as a ''Musical epic.'' 2 acts [14 scenes]. By Joseph A. Walker. Music by Dorothy A. Dinroe (Walker).

Described by BesPls 1970–71 (pp. 28–29) as ''a musical review of the black man's history in North America viewed as repeated episodes of hate and injustice leading to a present status as an inevitable revolutionary—a kind of release of pent-up fury on the stage.''

Prod. by the Afro-American Studio, New York, Sept. 13, 1968. Prod. by the Negro Ensemble Co., at St. Marks Playhouse, Nov. 17–Dec. 27, 1970, for 48 perfs.; dir. by Walker, and choreographed by Walker and Syvilla Fort. Cast: Ray Aranha, Ethel Ayler, Marilyn B. Coleman, Deloris Gaskins, Tonice Gwathney, Robert Jackson, °Jack Landron, Garrett Morris, Roxie Roker, Garrett Saunders, Charles Weldon, and Anita Wilson. Prod. by LaMont Zeno Community Theatre, Chicago, 1973–74 season. Prod. by the Demi-Gods at Howard Univ., Spring 1973.

Pub. in *Blk. Dr. Anth.* (King & Milner). Libretto also available from Samuel French, New York.

OH HONEY (1924). Touring vaudeville revue. Prod. by and costarring Augustus Smith. Music, band, and orchestra dir. by Genee Jones (Mrs. Augustus Smith). George Bascom, company manager. Cast included Leo Boatner, Marie Williams, Ora Carpenter, Viola Walker, Sherman Dirkson, Herbert Latham, Rosetta Swan, Bertha LaJoie, Anna Whitfield, and A. C. Flower.

OH JOY! (1922). Musical comedy. Book, lyrics, and music by Salem Tutt Whitney and J. Homer Tutt.

The only Whitney & Tutt show that was prod. near the Bway district, although the circumstances were somewhat less than ideal. Ethel Waters was scheduled to appear as the star, and indeed was a part of the cast during the rehearsals and tryout period. But because of her difficulty in securing her salary, which was reportedly $125 per week, and on her discovery that the show would be produced in a tent (because no theatre was available), she withdrew from the cast at the last minute, explaining that her days of working in a tent and sleeping with horses were over forever.

Prod. by °Lewis Rogers in a tryout version in Boston during the summer of 1922, starring Miss Waters. Opened in New York on Aug. 3, 1922, minus the star, in a tent-covered theatre, converted from the Van Kelton tennis stadium at the corner of Fifty-Seventh Street and Eighth Avenue, dubbed by the producer the "Bamboo Isle, where it remained for a short run. The cast featured Whitney & Tutt, Andrew Tribble (in the role of Ophelia Johnson), singer Julian Costello, Amon Davis, comedian Emmett Anthony, Alonzo Fenderson, J. Frances Mores, Margaret Simms, Ethel Williams, Lottie Harris, Ethel Pope, dancer Leroy Broomfield, and Johnny Nit. According to Frederick W. Bond (*Neg&Dr*, pp. 53–54), this prodn. received favorable reviews in 21 leading dailies and publications.

Songs and musical numbers: "Georgia Rose," "Valley of the Nile," "What's the Use?," "Smile on Sue," "Da Da Strain," "My Dog," "At the Stage Door," and "Brown Boys Go Marching By."
FURTHER REFERENCE: *Billboard* (J. A. Jackson's Page) 9–23–1922. *BlkMusTh* (Woll). *His Eye Is on the Sparrow* (Waters). *Variety* 8–11–1922.

OH LORD, THIS WORLD (1969). Gospel musical. Subtitled "Get It Together." Book and lyrics by George Houston Baas. Music by Clinton Utterbach. Prod. by the Queen of Angels Players, Newark, NJ, Nov.–Dec. 1969; dir. by Bass. Perfs. also given by several high school and college groups.

OH, MY PRETTY QUINTROON (1975). Jazz opera. Libretto by Townsend Brewster. Music by Sam Rivers. Prod. by the Harlem Cultural Center, New York, 1975.

OH! OH! OBESITY (1984–87). Musical comedy. 2 acts [13 scenes]. Story, lyrics, and music by Gerald W. Deas. Script collaboration (book) and direction by Bette Howard.

About the perils of being and staying overweight, while giving a few pointers about how to solve the problem, written by a medical doctor from Queens, NY. Told in song and dance by characters who know what it means to be obese.

First prod. by the New Federal Theatre, at the Louis Abrons Arts for Living Center, New York, June 7–24, 1984, for 15 perfs. Prod. by the Paul Robeson Theatre, Brooklyn, NY, Nov. 1986, for an open run. Cast: Pepsi Togar (Big Mama [also called Fat Momma], a riotous woman in search of the quickest way to lose weight), W. Paul Davis (Big Daddy [also called Fat Daddy], a self-professed ladies' man, who thinks his weight makes him sexy), Robert Wright and Paris Clark (Blimpie and Fatsie, respectively, their sons), Francine Palmer Johnson (Mrs. Nosh, Big Mama's friend, who encourages her to eat), and Harold Smith (Dr. DoNothing, a quack doctor).

Musical numbers included "I Can't Eat a Thing," "I'm Fat," and "I Fried All Night Long."

OH, YES (1923). Touring vaudeville revue. Cast included Hezekiah Jenkins, S. H. Gray, Virginia Liston, Brown & Jenkins (Hermon Brown and Dorothy Jenkins), and Houze & Houze (Bert and Carrie Houze).

AN OIL WELL SCANDAL (1924). Touring vaudeville comedy. Written and prod. by Freddie Johnson. On a popular theme about the sale of phony stock in an oil well to the people of a small town by a con man who is aided by two unsuspecting dupes, Turkey Bosom and Mose (played by Bill McLaurin and E. E. Pugh). The dupes are accused of and jailed for the crime, until the real culprit is captured. Cast also included Clarence Robinson, Mattie Harris, Ruth Cherry, Tillie Marshall, Daisy Pizarro, Howard Douglass, James Fulton, and Thomas Morris.

OLD KENTUCKY (1932). Touring vaudeville revue. Featured Clara Smith, Muriel Rahn, Hamtree Harrington, George Dewey Washington, and Marjorie Sterner.

THE OLD MAN'S BOY (1913–14). Musical comedy. Prologue, 3 acts. Book by Alex C. Rogers and Henry S. Creamer. "Musical numbers were said to be by '[Negro] composers,' but neither the newspapers nor a December 2 program identified the names of the songwriters" (Riis diss., pp. 290–91).

Showcase prodn., probably conceived by Lester A. Walton (who was involved as one of the producers), "to demonstrate what Negroes can do along dramatic lines" (*NY Age* 5–15–1913, p. 6). It differed from other musical shows in that the Prologue contained no songs and the last act contained only one, which was added later. The singing, dancing, and specialty numbers were confined to Acts I and II. The plot revolves around the son of an old-time vaudevillian, who is scheduled to appear in a Harlem show, just like his father before him. The Prologue takes place in the Old Man's house on the Mississippi levee. Acts I and II occur three weeks later at the Lafayette Theatre in Harlem, where the Negro Players are rehearsing for the show. Act III occurs after the show, back at the Old Man's house in Mississippi.

Prod. by the Negro Players Stock Co. (also referred to as the Pioneer Negro Amusement Co.), opening first at the Casino Theatre in Philadelphia, in Jan. 1913, then at the Empire Theatre in Brooklyn, and at the Lafayette Theatre in Harlem, prior to being taken on tour of the U.S. South, 1913–14; dir. by Creamer. Cast of Prologue and Act III: Alex Rogers (Hiram Wilson, the Old Man), Andrew Bishop (Hiram Wilson, Jr., the Old Man's Boy), Lavinia Rogers (Martha, Hiram Sr.'s wife), Charles Gilpin (Tom Bolden, Hiram Sr.'s Lifelong Friend), Ruth Cherry (Pearl, Hiram Jr.'s Wife), "Himself" (Hiram Wilson III, the Baby), Alice Gorgas (Grace, a Visiting Friend), Jessie Ellis and Grace LeCook (Mary and Emma, Hiram Jr.'s Sisters). Cast of Acts I and II: Henry Creamer (Stage Manager), Andrew Bishop (Hiram Wilson, Jr., Newest Member of the Company), Ruth Cherry (Hiram Jr.'s Wife, Principal Dancer), Billy Harper (Comedian of the Company), Charles Gilpin (Phrenological Vocal Director), Alice Gorgas (The Prima Donna), Cassie Norwood (Assistant Stage Manager), Grayce LeCook (The New Soubrette), Marie Lucas [wife of Charles Lucas] (The Orchestra Director), Cricket Smith (That Scrapping Drummer), Jessie Ellis (LaBelle, a Dancer), Gwendolyn Walton (Gwen, a Dancer), Billie Harper (King Jung-a-boo), Henry S. Creamer (Prime Minister), and Andrew Bishop (Tuff-Tuff, the Court Jester).

Songs and musical numbers: Act I—"June Time" (opening chorus: Company), "Dixie Land March Song" (Ellis & Chorus), "All Day Long" (Edward Brown, Goldie Cisco & Chorus), "Hello Mr. Moon" (Gorgas & Chorus), "Oh, You Devil Rag" (dance: Cherry, Norwood & Company), "You'll Want My Love" (LeCook & Howard Durry), Trombone Solo (Lucas), "Brazilian Dreams" (Ellis & Company), "I Lost My Way" (Harper), "International Rag" (LeCook & Company). Act II—Swanee River Dance (Cherry & Company), Specialty Song (Gorgas), "You've Got to Rag It" (Ellis, Norwood & Chorus), Panama Dance (Cherry & Durry), "Hanging Around and Gone, Gone, Gone" (LeCook), "Uncle Remus at the Races" (Gilpin), "King Love 'Em All" and "The Castle on the Isle of Koal" (Harper & Company). Act III—"Sweet Thoughts of Home" (Gorgas).

FURTHER REFERENCE: *BlksBf* (Sampson). *Just Before Jazz* (Riis). *NY Age* 5–1–1913; 5–15–1913. Program located among Leigh Whipper's papers in Moorland-Spingarn.

OLLIE BURGOYNE AND HER DARKTOWN STRUTTERS (1925). Touring dance revue. Prod. by and starring classic dancer Ollie Burgoyne. Cast included Russian dancer Ida Forsyne, one-man circus performer Harrison Blackburn, the Harmony Four Quartet, and Katherine Jacks (soubrette).

OL' MAN SATAN (1932). Folk allegory with music. 3 acts [37 scenes]. By Donald Heywood.

A crudely constructed drama which sought to capitalize on the success of *"The Green Pastures*. It tried to present the black concept of Satan and the afterlife through the telling of biblical and allegorical stories by a black mother (Ma Jackson) to her small son. The stories are dramatized through a series of scenes, involving the defeat of many well-known biblical characters by various tempters and temptresses, with Satan always behind the action. The show apparently failed in spite of "good dancing, singing and clever antics," as well as "fine acting [by] the cream of colored entertainment" (*Neg&Dr* [Bond], p. 181).

Prod. at the Forrest Theatre, New York, opening Oct. 3, 1932, for 24 perfs.; staged by William A. Shilling. The cast included 125 people, featuring the following: A. B. Comathiere (Satan), Dan Michaels (Saul), Lionel Monagas (Peter), Georgette Harvey (Ma Jackson), Phyllis Hunt (Josh), Edna Thomas (Maggie), Mike Jackson (Gabriel), Laurence Chenault (Moses), Hayes L. Pryor (Noah), Walter Richardson (Davis), Alice Ramsey (Sister Bright), Tressie Legge (Sister Crabtree), Lorenzo Tucker (Teacher), Freeman Fairley (Number Three Imp), Mary Jane Watkins (Becky), Kolly Mitchell (Soldier), Hilda Offley (First David Temptress), Bee Freeman (Second David Temptress), Herbert Ellis (Keeper of Souls), Fred Miller (Farmer), Walter Robinson (Paul), DeKoven Thompson (James), James McPheeters (John); Taylor Gordon, Luther Henderson, and David Bethe (Disciples); Clyde Faison (Noah's Temptress), Florence Lee (Jezebel), Arthur McLean (Maggie's Protector), Ismay Andrews (Sister Johnson), James Cook (Hunchback), Ralph Ramson (Blind Man), Helen Nelson (Mother), Alice Ramsey (Procuress), Wandolf Saunders (Racketeer), Lionel Monagas (Murderer), Ellen Baylor (Primrose), and Cleo Harris (Merrie).

Among the "score of musical numbers" were the following spirituals and songs: "Watermelon Time," "Trouble Don't Last Always," "Time Ain't Long," "I Know the Lord," "Hol' On," "Go Down, Moses," "Ain't It a Shame," "Home Beyond the River," "Blind Man," and "Angel Song."
FURTHER REFERENCE: *NYT* 10–4–1932.

ONCE ON THIS ISLAND (1990). Caribbean-inspired musical. Book and lyrics by Lynn Ahrens. Music by Stephen Flaherty. Based on Rosa Guy's novel *My Love, My Love*. About race conflicts in the Caribbean, depicting a peasant girl's love for the son of a wealthy landowner. Prod. at Playwrights Horizons Mainstage Theatre, New York, opening May 6, 1990, for an undetermined run. Featuring

La Chanze, Kecia Lewis-Evans, Andrea Frierson, Afi McClendon, Gerry McIntyre, Milton Craig Nealy, Nikki Rene, Eric Riley, and Ellis E. Williams. **FURTHER REFERENCE:** *NY Post* 4–18–1990.

120 IN THE SHADE (1935). Touring vaudeville revue. Music and lyrics by Otis and Leon Rene. Prod. by Earl Dancer, Nat Perrin, and Eddie Joseph. Cast featured Etta Moten and Jeni LeGon.

ONE MORE SUNDAY (1985). Gospel folk opera. 2 acts. By Ja A. Jahannes. Described by the *Herald* (Savannah, GA, 1–23–1985) as "about a fictitious Black baptist church; and the machinations of a typical congregation, as they prepare for a special Sunday service, commemorating the life and death of Rev. Martin Luther King, Jr. . . . The play scenes covered a church committee meeting, a choir rehearsal, culminating with the memorial service to Rev. MLK." Premiered at the Johnny Mercer Theatre, Savannah Civic Center, Savannah, Jan. 13, 1985; presented at Kennedy Fine Arts Theatre, Savannah State Coll., the following day. The cast was composed primarily of nonprofessional actors and actresses, including local jazz singer Huxsie Scott (Sister Callie); Carol Gordon, a former local TV anchor, then on the faculty of Savannah State Coll. (SSC) (Mrs. Handy); Actie C. Maxwell II, an SSC student (Deacon Mack); Carol Bell, dir. of Central Services, City of Savannah (Sister Grace); Gussie Brown (Brother Bo); Charles Kitchen (Rev. Strong); Gary Swindell (Brother Jamil); and Norman Mizelle Wilkerson, a guest professional actor from New York (Rev. Day). The music consisted primarily of familiar gospel songs.

ONE MO' TIME (1979–87). Musical retrospective. Written and dir. by Vernel Bagneris. Music by various black composers and lyricists of the 1920s, including Henry Troy, Chris Smith, Clarence Williams, Alex Belledna, Andy Razaf, Spencer Williams, Henry Creamer, J. Turner Layton, Jo Trent, and others.

A re-creation of the golden era of black vaudeville in New Orleans during the mid-1920s, when Ma Rainey, Bessie Smith, Ethel Waters, and other black entertainers toured the TOBA circuit. The TOBA stood for Theatre Owners Booking Association, which was nicknamed by the performers Tough on Black Actors (also Acts and/or Asses). *One Mo' Time* tells the story of one fictitious touring company, the Bertha Williams Company, and the experiences the performers encounter while touring the TOBA circuit, focusing on the particular night that they perform at the Lyric Theatre in New Orleans, where the white manager is notorious for underpaying the black entertainers.

The show was developed in New Orleans in 1978 as a tribute to the black performers who once played at the Lyric Theatre. After a successful run in New Orleans, and apparently on tour of the college circuit, a tape of the show was sent to the owner of the Village Gate in New York, who came down to New Orleans to see the performance. He liked it and brought it back to New York. It opened at the Village Gate/Downstairs, Oct. 22, 1979, for a long run, continuing through the summer of 1982, when the show celebrated its 1,150th perf., and was honored by Mayor Edward I. Koch at New York's City Hall Plaza, with a certificate of appreciation.

Prod. in a touring version, after it closed at the Village Gate. Prod. in London at the Phoenix Theatre, where additional dialogue was created to clarify for British audiences the relationship of the black performers to the white theatre manager. In this version, a command performance was given for Queen Elizabeth. Also prod. at the Comedy Theatre in Melbourne, Australia; and at the Sands Hotel in Las Vegas, NV. In 1985, it was prod. by the Crossroads Theatre Company in New Brunswick, NJ, Sept. 18–Oct. 27. In 1987, it was still touring colleges and university campuses, under the management of Daedalus Productions.

The orig. cast included Sylvia "Kuumba" Williams (Bertha Williams), Thais Clark (Ma Reed), Topsy Chapman (Thelma), Vernel Bagneris (Papa Du), and °John Stell (Theatre Owner). The 1982 cast included Carol Woods (Bertha), Frozine Jo Thomas (Ma Reed), Peggy Alston (Thelma), Bruce Strickland (Papa Du), and °James "Red" Wilcher (Theatre Owner). Cast of the Crossroads Theatre Company prodn. included Elia English, Lynne Clifton-Allen, Sandra Reaves-Phillips, Roumel Reaux, and °Charles Woolfolk.

Songs and musical numbers: Act I—Overture (Orchestra), "Down in Honky Tonk Town" (Papa Du, Thelma & Ma Reed), "Kiss Me Sweet" (Thelma & Papa Du), "Don't Turn Your Back on Me" (Bertha), "Jenny's Ball" (Ma Reed), "Cake Walkin' Babies from Home" (Papa Du, Thelma & Ma Reed), "I Got What It Takes" (Thelma), "See See Rider" (Ma Reed), "He's In the Jailhouse Now" (Ma Reed), "He's Funny That Way" (Papa Du), "Tiger Rag" (Ma Reed), "Kitchen Man" (Orchestra), and "Just Wait Till You See My Baby" (Papa Du, Thelma & Ma Reed). Act II—"Muskrat Ramble" (Orchestra), "Black Bottom" (Ma Reed, Bertha & Papa Du), "The Pardy" (Company), "New Orleans Hop Scop Blues" (Papa Du), Exotic Dance (Thelma), "What It Takes to Bring You Back" (Papa Du & Bertha), "Everybody Loves My Baby" (Thelma), "You've Got the Right Key but the Wrong Keyhole" (Bertha), "After You've Gone" (Ma Reed), "My Man Blues" (Bertha & Thelma), "Papa De-Da-Da" (Papa Du & Company), "Muddy Waters" (Bertha), and "A Hot Time in the Old Town Tonight" (Company).

FURTHER REFERENCE: *DBlkTh* (Woll). *Ebony* 11–1982. *NYT* 12–7–1979; 8–31–1980.

ON THE TOWN (1944–46). Musical comedy. Book and lyrics by °Betty Comden and °Adolph Green. Music by °Leonard Bernstein. Bway show about the wonders of big-city life. Prod. at the Adelphi Theatre, opening Dec. 28, 1944, for 463 perfs., closing in March 1946. Blacks were integrated in minor roles throughout the large cast, including Royce Wallace in a singing/dancing role, and several blacks in the ensemble and chorus. The musical dir. of the orchestra was also a black musician, Everett Lee.

ON THE WAY TO BOSTON (1916). Vaudeville revue. Prod. by and costarring Frank Montgomery under the sponsorship of the Quality Amusement Co., and toured the theatres controlled by the company. Cast also included Fanny Wise, Mae Brown, Dewey Weinglass, Florence McClain, George Stamper, Alice Saunders, Blanche Harris, Josephine Lazzo, Marion Whitfield, Lillian Williams, Clarice Wright, Earl West, Howard & Mason, and Hattie James.

OPHELIA SNOW FROM BALTIMO' (1928–29). Vaudeville show in at least two eds. Prod. at the Lincoln Theatre in New York and on tour. Starring Andrew Tribble in the title role—a role he created and perfd. in several prodns. According to *BlksBf* (Sampson, p. 434), "This highly successful character was that of a single minded woman, careless, kindly, tough, and above all desirous [of] an affair of the heart just the same as her sisters blessed with more beauty." Cast also included Billy Mitchell, Dot Campbell, Carl Robinson, Harold Demund, Buddy Green, Elveta Brown, Kitty Arlanie, and a chorus of 8 ladies. Bessie Smith appeared in the Lincoln Theatre prodn.

OPPORTUNITY, PLEASE KNOCK (1969–70). Musical. By Oscar Brown, Jr. Prod. in Chicago and on national TV in 1969, with members of the Black P. Stone Rangers (a South Side Chicago youth gang), Oscar Brown, Jr., Jean Pace, B. B. King, Dick Gregory, and the Spencer Jackson family; dir. by the author. Revived briefly in Jan. 1970, with many of the orig. cast.

THE ORGANIZER (1938). Blues opera. 1 act. Libretto by Langston Hughes. Music by James P. Johnson. (see also *De Organizer*.)

Social propaganda piece dramatizing the underground struggle in the South to build a union of sharecroppers. The action takes place on a plantation in the South, where the sharecroppers have gathered to await the arrival of the Organizer, who will help them establish the union. Although the Overseer tries to break up the meeting, he is overpowered and runs away, promising to alert the Owner. But the sharecroppers now realize that in unity there is strength, and they know that they can now overcome their hardships together.

Perfd. at Carnegie Hall in 1940, as part of an International Ladies Garment Workers Union Convention. Although the cast is not known, the characters were assigned the following vocal parts: The Organizer (baritone), The Woman (contralto), The Old Man (bass), The Old Woman (soprano), Brother Dosher (tenor), Brother Bates (tenor), and The Overseer (bass).

Only one song from this show is known: "Hungry Blues," sung by Brother Dosher near the beginning of the action. This song establishes the theme of the opera—the dream of a better world where there is no hunger or racial prejudice.

ORIENTAL AMERICA (1896–99). Transitional musical show. 3 parts. Conceived and prod. by John W. Isham, dir. and co-proprietor.

A further departure from the minstrel tradition, which Isham had first attempted a year earlier with *The Octoroons (1895–1900), which continued to run simultaneously with this show. Still using the three-part minstrel format, and employing clever comedy routines and beautiful chorus girls, this was the first show that departed from the customary dance finale of the minstrel show, and presented instead a medley of operatic solos and choral selections as a finale. This practice was afterwards imitated by the *Black Patti Troubadours and other shows. *Oriental America* is also credited with being the first all-black musical to open "on Broadway proper" (*BlkManh* [Johnson], pp. 96–97).

Opened at Palmer's Theatre, on the northeast corner of Broadway and 30th Streets (later changed to Wallach's Theatre, and eventually demolished in 1915), August 3, 1896, where it was "not a huge success but was considered one of the best singing shows of the time" (*BlksBf* [Sampson], p. 62). Prominently featured in the orig. cast were Billy Eldridge (comedian) and his partner Jennie Eldridge (comedy and dancing), Belle Davis (singer), Inez Clough (dancer), Mattie Wilkes (leading soprano), Sidney Woodward (leading tenor), Ollie Burgoyne (dancer), Pearl and Maggie (Margaret) Scott (singers), Jesse A. Shipp, J. Rosamond Johnson, Edward Winny, William C. Elkins, the Meredith Sisters, Harry Fiddler, and Ruby Shelton.

Apparently toured the principal U.S. cities for the remainder of the 1896 season. The show was taken to Great Britain on the steamer *Alicia* in April 1897, where it landed in Liverpool, then began a tour of England and Scotland for the remainder of the year, during which it created a sensation. Although the European tour was an apparent success, Isham filed a petition of bankruptcy in Aug. 1899, and retired the following year.

The songs and musical numbers included solos and choruses from such operas as *Faust, Rigoletto, Martha, Carmen*, and *Il Trovatore*. This section comprised about 40 minutes of the show. According to one reviewer (*Morning Times*, Washington, DC 11–9–1896), the show that he witnessed included the bridal chorus sextette from *Lucia di Lammermoor*, in which all the stars appeared; "The Last Rose of Summer," sung by soprano Mattie Wilkes; an aria from *Rigoletto*, sung by tenor Sidney Woodward; the armorer's song from DeKoven's *Robin Hood*, sung by J. Rosamond Johnson; the hunting song and opening chorus from *The Belle(s) of Cornville*, sung by Belle Davis. Other popular songs were sung by Davis and Billy Eldridge.

A libretto is in the Rare Book Division, LC.

FURTHER REFERENCE: *BlksBf* (Sampson). *Ghost* (Sampson). *Just Before Jazz* (Riis). *NY Dramatic Mirror* 8–15–1896. Riis diss.

ORIENTAL SERENADERS (1924). Touring revue. Cast included Buster Lee and his wife "Boy," Elmira Washington (billed as "The Cut-Out Kid"), "Little Bits" Hall, Dorothy Dunbar, Margaret Warren, Little Jeff, and 3 musicians: Guy Jackson, James Hall, and John Ricketts.

ORIGINS (1969). Musical. 1 act. By Hazel Bryant, Beverly Todd, and Hank Johnson. Prod. at the Riverside Church Theatre, Oct. 1969.

O SING A NEW SONG (1934). Musical pageant. Prod. by the Century of Progress International Exposition at Chicago, 1933–34.

OUANGA (1932, 1941, 1948–49, 1950, 1956). Opera. 3 acts. Libretto by John Frederick Matheus. Music composed by Clarence Cameron White.

Based on the life of Dessalines, emperor of Haiti during the nineteenth century. The title means "talisman" or "charm" in Haitian Creole. As described by the critic of the *South Bend* (IN) *Trib.* (6–11–1949), who reviewed the premiere performance in 1949, "This is a rich score. The themes are on a rhythmic pattern that jolts and sways with a jungle beat and often sweeps to majestic, terrifying heights. The production was colorful and tumultuous. The settings were eye-filling and handsome."

Presented in concert form by the American Opera Society in Chicago, Nov. 1932. Auditioned at the New School for Social Research, New York, 1941. Broadcast over radio station WINS, New York, June 1948. Premiered in a full stage perf. by the Burleigh Music Association, at Central High School, South Bend, IN, June 10–11, 1949; conducted by the composer. Prod. by the Negro opera company of Philadelphia, Dra-Mu, at the Academy of Music in Philadelphia, 1950. Prod. in a concert version, with ballet, by the National Negro Opera Co., at the Metropolitan Opera House, New York, May 1956; the performance was repeated in Sept. 1956 at Carnegie Hall in New York City.

OUR FRIEND FROM DIXIE. See *THE DARKTOWN FOLLIES.*

OUT IN THE STREET (1914). Tabloid musical. Written and prod. by Billy King. Presented at the Star Theatre, Savannah, GA, for one week, with members of the Billy King Stock Co.

OUT OF BONDAGE / / Subtitled *Before and After the War* (c. 1875–c. 1891). Musical play. 3 acts. Adapt. by the Hyers Sisters (Anna Madah and Emma Louise Hyers) from a play by the Rev. °Joseph Bradford of Boston.

One of the earliest shows outside the minstrel tradition. The first musical show featuring black women; the first dramatic musical in which the Hyers Sisters appeared. A musical and comedic treatment of black life from slavery to emancipation, focusing on songs and melodies which exemplified the various stages of the slaves' experience. According to one extant program (1890), pub. in *BlksBf* (Sampson, p. 72), it was billed as "A Unique Comedy, picturing the Darky as he existed in Ante-Bellum Days, showing his humorous characteristics without burlesque. Introducing Musical Novelties and the Old-Time Southern Camp-Meeting and Jubilee Melodies." Another extant program in NYPL describes the three acts as follows: Act I: Uncle Eph's Cabin, down South Before the War; Act II: During the War; Act III: Up North, 5 years after.

Prod. as a touring show by the Hyers [Sisters] Musical [Comedy] Co., opening c. 1875, remaining in repertory for about 16 years. Originally starred the young Sam Lucas in the comedy role of Henry (which he reputedly made famous), Anna Madah and Emma Louise Hyers, and the then well-known tenor Wallace King. Cast of the 1890 show, prod. at the Los Angeles Theatre in Los Angeles, CA, opening on Feb. 20, included Louise Hyers (Kaloo, the Mischievous), Madah Hyers (Narcisse, Pet of the Plantation), Joe Davis [who was later replaced by Fred Lyons] (Henry, Always Full of Fun), Charles Moore (Uncle Eph, Patriarch of the Plantation), Miss Bedford (Aunt Naomi, Good Old Soul), James Ward (Prince, with Songs), George Freeman (Plumber Williams), and Joseph Brooks (Adolphus). Other characters included field hands, jubilee singers, and cotton pickers.

Songs and musical numbers included jubilee songs, dances, and choruses; specialties by the character portrayed as Henry; and the following specific titles: "The Yankees Are Comin'," "The Possum Supper," "Uncle Eph and Aunt Naomi in the Children's Happy Home," "Goodbye, Old Home," "Echoes from the Plantation," "You Can't Lose Me," and "Ah Those Golden Slippers" (finale).

Handwritten manuscript located in the Rare Book Collection/LC.
FURTHER REFERENCE: *Just Before Jazz* (Riis). Riis diss. Program in TC/NYPL.

OVER THE TOP (1919). Musical show. Written and prod. by Billy King. Music by J. Berni Barbour. About a black sea captain (Capt. Austin) who is denied admission to the Paris Peace Conference because of his color. He subsequently returns to the U.S., where he makes several speeches about the mistreatment of blacks in America. Presented by the Billy King Stock Co., first at the Grand Theatre, Chicago, then on U.S. tour, including the Lafayette Theatre in New York. The orig. cast included Billy Higgins, Gertrude Saunders, Theresa Burroughs Brooks, Margaret Scott, Ernest Whitman, Marcus Slayter, Ollie Burgoyne, Ida Forsyne, Birleanna Blanks, Ruth Cherry, Edna Hicks, and Rebecca "Dink" Thomas.
FURTHER REFERENCE: *BlksBf* (Sampson).

THE OYSTER MAN (1907–8). Musical comedy. Advertised as a "Song Play." Book by Flournoy E. Miller and Aubrey Lyles (Miller & Lyles). Music by Ernest Hogan and Will Vodery. Lyrics by Henry Creamer. Adapt. as *The Man from Baltimore* (1934).

A starring vehicle for Ernest Hogan, *The Oyster Man* was considered among the best of the early black musical comedies. It was a sequel to *Rufus Rastus* (1905–7), in which Hogan also starred. Rufus Rastus was also the central character in *The Oyster Man*. Whereas he was a down-and-out vaudevillian in the preceding show, in this show he plays the role of an oyster vendor in Baltimore, who travels with an entourage of Baltimoreans to the mythical island of Blazasus, a place of utopian splendor, where gin rickeys flow from the rocks like fountains and chickens grow on trees. There, amid scenes of primitive splendor, Rufus and his company have a number of memorable experiences, including narrow escapes, being captured by a band of savages, and other complications which permit them to display their comedic, singing, and dancing talents to the greatest advantage. This was the last show in which Hogan appeared before his death. He became ill with tuberculosis in early 1908, forcing him to leave the show after a year. He died in May 1909.

Under the management of °Hurtig & °Seamon, prod. and staged by J. Ed. Green, the show rehearsed for several weeks in New York, then was taken on an out-of-town tour for several weeks, prior to opening at the Yorkville Theatre in New York City, Nov. 25, 1907, where it was well reviewed. Cast: Ernest Hogan (Rufus Rastus, a Baltimore Oyster Vendor), John Rucker (Sunny Sam, Rufus' Friend), Carita Day (Angelea Gailiard, Society Leader, Graduate of Tuskegee), Muriel Ringgold (Oyster Man's Girl), Al F. Watts (Aunt Jemima), Harry Reed (Useless), Bob Kelly (Brother Peter Smith), Lawrence Deas (Samuel Austin), Craig Williams (George Oramos), Ella Anderson (Princess Ito), George Lynnier (Policeman), Charles Foster (Panama Jack), Ella Deas (Belle Cown), Billie Moore (Gazook Seventh Eleventh), George Lynnier (Ho Bo), Gus Hall (Gazabo), Newell Morse (Keno), J. H. Bolden (Bazo), James Worles (Debility), J. L. Grant (Delivery), Blanche Arlington (Ba La), Louise Salisbury (La La), and Ora Henry (Zamazi).

Songs and musical numbers: "Enough, That's Enough," "In the Shade of Morro Castle," "Yankee Doodle Coon," "When Buffalo Bill and His Wild West Show First Came to Baltimore," "Blazasus Chorus," "Contribution Box," "Hail to the King," "I Just Can't Keep My Eyes Off You," "Meet Me at the Barber Shop," "Mermaid's Chorus," "Mina," "No You Didn't, Yes I Did," "Swanee River," "Tomorrow," and "The Whitewash Brigade."

FURTHER REFERENCE: *Just Before Jazz* (Riis). *NY Age* 5–27–1907. *NY Dramatic Mirror* 12–9–1907. Riis diss. *Oyster Man* folder in Harvard Theatre Collection.

P

PANAMA (1908). Musical comedy. 3 acts. Book and lyrics by Marion A. Brooks and Charles A. Hunter. Music by James T. Brymn and H. Lawrence Freeman.

The inhabitants of Brandyville, a small Kentucky town, fall victim to a smooth-talking real estate swindler, who persuades them to invest money in a nonexistent parcel of land in Panama. The action moves from Kentucky to Panama, where the situation is eventually resolved.

Prod. by J. Ed. Green and the Pekin Stock Co., at the Pekin Theatre, Chicago, opening in Jan. 1904; featuring Harrison Stewart and Abbie Mitchell.

Songs and musical numbers include "Ebenezer Julius Caesar Johnson," "Awful," "What I Knows I Knows," "Put It Right in My Hand," "Happy Sam Crow," "Things Just Ain't Right," "The Summertime," and "I'd Like to Run Away with You."

PANSY (1929). Musical revue. Billed as "An All-Colored Musical Novelty." 2 acts. Book by Alex Belledna. Music by Maceo Pinkard.

Unsuccessful musical set on the campus of a southern university on commencement day. The plot concerned the love of a college girl, Pansy, for a young man named Bob, whom her father opposes in favor of Bill (the Proposition Kid). One of the good things about this otherwise forgettable show was that blues singer Bessie Smith made two stage appearances in Act II as herself, for which she received "wild applause" by the otherwise restless and disgruntled audience, and favorable reviews by the critics. Brooks Atkinson (*NYT* 5–15–1929) called *Pansy* "the worst show of all time," stating that it was a "nightmare of lost cues, forgotten words, embarrassed performers and frantic efforts backstage to avoid complete collapse behind the footlights."

Prod. by Pinkard at the Belmont Theatre, New York, May 14, 1929, for 3 perfs.; dir. by Frank Rye. Cast: Ralph Harris (Dean Liggett), Al Frisco (James), Cole Brothers (Tom and Austin: Campus "Cut Ups"), Ida Anderson (Miss

Wright), Alfred Chester (Bill, the Proposition Kid), Elizabeth Taylor (Miss Merritt), Pearl McCormack (Pansy [Green]), Speedy Smith (Ulysses Grant Green, father of Pansy), Amon Davis (Mrs. Green), Billy Andrews (Bob), Jackie Young (Sadie), W. Crumbly, L. Randall, H. Mattingly, and D. Davis (Penn Comedy Four), and Bessie Smith (as herself).

Songs and musical numbers: "It's Commencement Day," "Break'n the Rhythm," "Pansy," "Campus Walk," "I'd Be Happy," "Gettin' Together," "Shake a Leg," and "Fond Memories." Smith's songs included "If the Blues Don't Get You" and "A Stranger Interlude."
FURTHER REFERENCE: *NY Eve. Post* 6–21–1929. *NY Herald Trib.* 5–15–1929. *NYT* 5–15–1929.

PAPER BIRD / / Orig. title: *A New Breed Is Now the Seed* (1975). Musical. 2 acts. Story, lyrics, and music by Gerald W. Deas. Book and direction by Tad Truesdale. Title taken from a poem by Deas, which deals with man's universal desire to fly like an eagle, only to find out that he is just a paper bird. Explores some of the problems of survival in big-city ghettos through the story of conflict among black, Hispanic, and white street gangs. Prod. under its orig. title by William Hunter at Town Hall, New York, 1975. Prod. under its present title by Now the Seed Productions, Inc., at the Storefront Museum, Queens, NY, Nov. 17–Dec. 3, 1977, for 9 perfs.

THE PASSING SHOW OF 1913 (1913). White-oriented musical revue. The Winter Garden's annual extravaganza. Music and lyrics by °Harold Atteridge. Additional music by Andy Razaf and others. Prod. on Bway at the Winter Garden, July 25, 1913, for 116 perfs. With an all-white cast headed by °Charlotte Greenwood, °John Charles Thomas, °Carter De Haven, °Anne Dancrey, °Bessie Clayton, °Harry Gailfoil, °Charles & Molly King, and °Wellington Cross. Featured one song, "Baltimore," by Razaf.

THE PASSING SHOW OF 1915 (1915). White-oriented musical revue. The Winter Garden's annual extravaganza. Dialogue and lyrics by °Harold Atteridge. Music by °Leo Edwards, °William F. Peterson, and J. Leubrie Hill. Prod. on Bway at the Winter Garden, opening May 29, 1915, for 145 perfs. Included "My Trombone Man," by Hill and Atteridge, pub. by G. Schirmer, New York; copy in Moorland-Spingarn.

PECULIAR SAM / / Subtitled *The Underground Railroad* / / Orig. title: *Slaves' Escape; or, The Underground Railroad* (1880). Historical musical drama. 4 acts. By Elizabeth Pauline Hopkins.

Drama of slave life, with music, dancing, and heavy dialect, written especially for Sam Lucas and the Hyers Sisters. After his sweetheart Virginia is forced by her master to marry the black slave overseer Jim, whom the master has picked out for her, Sam (a mulatto slave) leads Virginia, his family, and their friends from the Mississippi plantation where they live to freedom in Canada. Their escape is briefly thwarted by Jim, who tries to capture the group, using a hundred dollars given him by the master to buy information concerning their whereabouts. Sam manages to outwit Jim, overpower him, and gain possession of the money; and with the aid of abolitionists and "stationmasters" of the Underground Railroad, they arrive safely in Canada with much rejoicing.

Prod. by the Hopkins Colored Troubadours, at Oakland Gardens, Boston, July 5, 1880, for one week; and perhaps on tour. Cast included the author, her parents, the Hyers Sisters (Anna Madah and Emma Louise), and a chorus of over 60 voices. Whether or not Sam Lucas played the leading role is not known. No record of specific roles played by the other performers and singers has been located. Characters include Sam [Lucas?], a Peculiar Fellow (1st tenor); Jim, Overseer (2nd tenor); Caesar, Station Master (baritone); Pete and Pomp, Friends to Sam (tenor/guitarist and bass); Virginia, Plantation Nightingale (soprano); Juno, Sister to Sam (alto); and Mammy, Mother to Sam (2nd soprano).

Songs and musical numbers indicated in the script include choruses, solos, quartets, lively banjo music, and dancing: Act I: Chorus (at curtain rise), Lively Dance (Sam & friends), Solo [Sam's dream] (Sam), Chorus (Jim, Caesar, Pete & Pomp), Solo [Sam's love of Virginia] (Sam), Chorus (Mixed Quartet), "Home, Sweet Home" (Virginia). Act II: "Steal Away" (Chorus), "Rise and Shine" (Chorus), "Way Over Jordan" (Chorus). Act III: "Old Kentucky Home" (Chorus), Song (Virginia & Chorus). Act IV: Song [after style of "Swanee River"] (Virginia), Dance [jig] (Juno), Songs (solos, quartets & Chorus), Finale: "Golden Slippers" (Sam [dancing] & Chorus).

Script pub. in *The Roots of African Am. Dr.* (Hamalian & Hatch).

PEPPER POT REVUE (1927). Vaudeville revue. Prod. in Harlem and on tour by Leonard Harper. The Harlem prodn. featured Bill Robinson, who danced up and down a flight of stairs; Madeline Belt; Small & May, billed as "two mahogany princes," who perfd. on ukulele and banjo, and sang "Under the Dixie Moon"; Byrd & Billy Higgins, who appeared in a comedy sketch; and Marie Preval, who sang "Emaline," while Robinson danced. The road show cast also included Flo Brown, Cecil Rivers, Monte Hawley, and Edgar Connors.

PEPPY STEPPERS (1927). Touring vaudeville revue. Prod. by and costarring Carter Lockhart, who perfd. as part of a blackface comedy team called Lockhart & Bozo. Also in the cast were Sol Speights & Myrtle, and Rose Brown.

PHILLIS (1986). Musical. Book by Leslie Lee. Music and lyrics by Micki Grant. Based on the life and world of the eighteenth-century black American poet Phillis Wheatley, a slave born in Senegal, who learned to read and write and gained international fame as America's first black woman poet to be published, which earned her the admiration of Presidents George Washington and Thomas Jefferson. Prod. by Ralph Madero Productions, in association with the

United Negro Coll. Fund. Previewed at the Apollo Theatre, New York, Oct. 30, 1986; dir. by Ronald G. Russo. Sched. to open at Ford's Theatre, Washington, DC, in late 1986; no record of the actual opening.

PICKINGS FROM DIXIE (1929–30). Touring vaudeville revue. Prod. and perfd. by Billy and Mary Mack. Billy was leading comedian with Leonard Rogers; Mary was leading lady. Also in the cast were straight man Charles Taylor, singer D. Bubiskit, tap dancer J. J. Mims, singer Irene Cooper, 6 chorus girls, and the "4 Periods": Charles Taylor, Bill Thomas, Leonard Rogers, and Ed Braxos.

PINKARD'S FANTASIES (1941). Musical revue. Written and prod. by Maceo Pinkard, New York, 1941. James P. Johnson was musical dir.

THE PINK SLIP. See *UNDER THE BAMBOO TREE*.

THE PLANTATION (1906–15). Opera. 3 acts. Written and composed by H. Lawrence Freeman. Set in America. Unperfd. The composer's best-known operas include *The Martyr* (1893), *Valdo* (1905–6), *Vendetta* (1911–23), and *Voodoo* (1921–28).

PLANTATION DAYS (1922–23, 1925). Musical revue. Music mainly by James P. Johnson (who was also musical dir.), with some "unauthorized interpolations" (later dropped) by Noble Sissle and Eubie Blake (Sissle & Blake).
    A touring show, with comedy and specialty acts, conceived to capitalize on the success of °Lew Leslie's *Plantation Revue* (1922–23), with which it is often confused. According to Ethel Waters (*His Eye Is on the Sparrow*, pp. 158–59):

Maury Greenwald, a white producer, . . . kept pestering me to sign up with a Negro musical he wanted to send to England. He'd heard that Lew Leslie was planning to ship his *Plantation Revue* to London, and Mr. Greenwald figured that if he got there first with his *Plantation Revue* [*sic*] he'd clean up, a Negro show being then an unheard of novelty around old Piccadilly Circus.

Although Miss Waters did not sign up with the show at that time, she did become associated with it at a later date (see below).
    The orig. *Plantation Days* toured from New York City in 1922, playing such eastern and midwestern cities as Pittsburgh, Detroit, Cleveland, Toledo, and Chicago; staged by Leonard Harper, with additional staging by Lawrence Deas. Starring the dancing team of Harper & Blanks (Leonard Harper and his wife, Osceola Blanks), comedian Eddie Green, James P. Johnson, and the Plantation Days Syncopated Orchestra.
    Following its U.S. tour, the show returned to New York City for a scheduled one-week perf. at the Lafayette Theatre on Feb. 24, 1923; but the perf. did not take place on that date because of a contract dispute concerning three of the

show's most popular numbers that had been pirated from the successful musical *Shuffle Along* (1921), which the company was forced to drop from the show under court order. After the contract was renegotiated, the show finally opened at the Lafayette for one week, beginning April 2.

After that engagement, the troupe, consisting of 35 members, including chorus and orchestra, hastily sailed to London, where, within a few days of their arrival, they were integrated as a 12-minute segment into a larger prodn., already being rehearsed, entitled *The Rainbow*, with music by °George Gershwin. (Composer Johnson is said to have collaborated with Gershwin on some of the musical numbers for *The Rainbow*, but no documentary evidence has been located.) The combined and integrated show presented a number of racial and professional problems for both the white English and the black American cast; it nevertheless opened at the Empire Theatre in mid-April, where it ran until early June 1923, after which the company returned to the U.S.

In addition to Harper, Blanks, Green, and Johnson, other members of the orig. cast included the Four [or Five] Cracker Jacks [also Crackerjacks], the Silverton[e] Four, Joyner & Foster, George Pasha, Austin & Delaney, the Pepper Choir, Dave & Tressie, Marjorie Sipp, Chappelle & Stinnette (Thomas Chappelle and Juanita Stinnette), the Three Eddies (Scott, Allen & Lee), Adams & Tunstall, Smith & DeForrest, Daisy Pizarro, Julia [or Julian] Mitchell, Seymour & Jeannette (Seymour James and Jeannette Taylor), a female chorus of Hula Girls, and a male chorus of Plantation Johnnies. Sam Wooding's Famous Syncopated Orchestra perfd. at the Lafayette Theatre.

After its London tour, the orig. stars and the composer left the company: Johnson began to work on his next and most important show, *Runnin' Wild* (1923–25); Harper & Blanks perfd. their act in an abbreviated version, first at Connie's Inn in July, then at the Lincoln Theatre in Aug. The rest of the *Plantation Days* company, also minus Eddie Green, toured the western states and Canada for the rest of the season. The reduced company consisted of Jones & Jones, Seymour & Jeannette, Austin & Delaney, the Three Eddies, Baby Theada Deas, and the Clarence Johnson Orchestra. Ethel Waters, who joined the company in Chicago for a two-week engagement in Aug. 1923, states that she was billed as an "extra added attraction" in order to "save" the "fast-flopping revue" (*His Eye Is on the Sparrow* [Waters], pp. 179–80).

After completing its tour of the West and Canada, the show was apparently revived in Chicago in 1925, with Blanche Calloway and some members of the orig. cast, including the Five Cracker Jacks and the Three Eddies. Blanche's brother, Cab Calloway, also toured with this ed. "as a replacement for the first tenor in a vocal quartet" (*HarlRenD* [Kellner], p. 65).

Songs and musical numbers: "Ukulele Blues" (a Hawaiian song), with melody by James P. Johnson and words by Merton Bories (Sphinx Music, 1922), is the only known original song from this show. The three hit tunes borrowed from *Shuffle Along* (and later dropped) were "Gypsy Blues," "I'm Craving for That Kind of Love," and "Bandanna Days," all by Sissle & Blake.

FURTHER REFERENCE: *NY Age* 2–17–1923; 3–3–1923; 8–1–1923; 9–1–1923. *NY Amsterdam N.* 2–14–1923; 2–28–1923; 3–28–1923; 4–4–1923; 4–13–1923; 7–25–1923; 8–1–1923. *Toledo Blade* 12–18–1922.

PLANTATION FOLLIES (1933). Touring musical revue. Prod. by James P. Johnson, who was also presumably the principal composer and musical dir. Cast included Joe Byrd, Bearnice & Scott, Carrie Marrero, Rogers & Rogers, Earl "Snakehips" Tucker, Maitland & Wheeler, Cecilia Williams, the Three Little Words, the Twelve Sepia Dancers, and James P. Johnson's Black Diamond Aces.

PLANTATION REVUE (1922) / / Prod. in London as part of *From Dover Street to Dixie*, the title later changed to *From Dover to Dixie* (1923) / / Revised for Bway prodn. as *Dixie to Broadway* (1924). Book by °Lew Leslie. Lyrics by °Roy Turk. Music by °J. Russell Robinson. Orchestra direction by Will J. Vodery.

A transitional musical expanded from a cabaret floorshow which had begun at the Plantation Club in New York City, and which was later metamorphosed into the more successful Bway show *Dixie to Broadway*, after receiving rave revues when the show was taken to England and France (see production information below). This song-and-dance revue, which featured Florence Mills and boosted her to stardom, was set on a southern plantation, where black life was depicted as happy and carefree; a large watermelon suspended from the flies dominated the stage motif, adding to the stereotypical minstrel atmosphere. Shelton Brooks was the master of ceremonies, introducing the various musical, dance, comedy, and specialty acts; the music was perfd. by Will Vodery's Plantation Orchestra.

Opened at the Forty-eighth Street Theatre in New York City, July 17, 1922, for 40 perfs. Cast included Edith Wilson, Juanita Stinnette, Chappy Chappelle, U. S. Thompson (Miss Mills' husband), Jonnie Dunn, Lew Keene, and the Six Dixie Vamps.

Opened in London on May 31, 1923, at the Pavilion Theatre, as part of a revue called *From Dover Street to Dixie*, with the "Dover Street" half depicted by white English actors as the first part, and the "Dixie" half featuring the *Plantation Revue* company, with Miss Mills and Will Vodery's Orchestra. Retitled *From Dover to Dixie*, the show was taken to Paris, and then on a successful tour throughout England, with a view to reaching Bway. However, the Dover half of the show was dropped prior to returning to the U.S., where an all-black American version was created, called *Dixie to Broadway*, which opened on Bway in 1924.

Musical numbers from the *Plantation Revue* included "The Bugle Call Blues," with Jonnie Dunn as the bugler; "Old Black Joe," with U. S. Thompson, Lew Keene, and the Plantation Quartet; "A Southern Hobby," with Thompson and the Quartet; "Robert E. Lee," with Edith Wilson and the Six Dixie Vamps;

"Southland," with Chappy Chappelle and Juanita Stinnette; "Mandy," with Mills and the Vamps; "Swanee River"; "Hawaiian Nights in Dixie"; "I Want to Be Vamped in Georgia"; and the finale, "Minstrels on Parade," with the entire company. The lively dance numbers included the buck and wing, the cakewalk, and various tap routines.

FURTHER REFERENCE: *NY Globe* 7–18–1922. *NYT* 7–18–1922. *Variety* 7–21–1922.

PLAYMATES (1928). Touring vaudeville revue. Prod. by and costarring Buster Lee. Cast also included Geneva Pichon, Laura Smith, Edna Brisco, Hattie Jones, Fred LaJoie, and James Langston.

POLICY KINGS (1939–40). Musical revue. Book by °Michael Ashwood, who also prod. the show. Music by James P. Johnson. Lyrics by °Louis Douglass.

Although the plot of this show is not known, the title and songs indicate that it concerned the numbers racket in Harlem.

Prod. at the Nora Bayes Theatre in New York on December 30, 1939, apparently for a short run; dir. by Louis Douglass. Musical arrangements by °Ken Macomber; dance direction by °Jimmy Payne; staged by Winston Douglass. Principal cast included Bill Cumby, Frankie Jaxon, Ray Sneed, Jr., Willor Guilford, Monte Norris, Robert Mason, Norman Astwood, George Jenkins, Enid Raphael, Edward Davis, Cora Green, Bessie DeSaussure, Irene Cort, Herbert Evans, Margie Ellison, and Henry Drake.

Musical numbers (by Douglass and Johnson): "Court House Scene," "Deed I Do Blues," "Dewey Blues," "Harlem Number Man," "Harlem Woogie," "Havin' a Ball," "I'm Gonna Hit the Number Today," "To Do What We Like," "Walking My Baby Back Home," and "You, You, You."

FURTHER REFERENCE: *NY Herald Trib.* 12–31–1938. *NY Post* 12–29–1938. *NY Sun* 12–31–1938. *NYT* 12–31–1938; 1–8–1939. *NY World Telegram* 12–31–1938. *Variety* 1–11–1939.

THE POLICY PLAYERS / / Orig. title: *4–11–44* (1899–1900). Ragtime musical. Billed as "A Musical Farce Comedy." 2 acts. Conceived by Williams & Walker. Book by George Walker and Jesse A. Shipp. Music and lyrics mainly by Bert Williams.

Moderately successful Williams & Walker musical, based on a reworking and rewriting of some of the material originally used in *A Lucky Coon,* which also revolved around a gambling plot. *The Policy Players* went on the road as *4–11– 44* (a winning policy number), but after it failed to draw an audience, "Jesse Shipp was called in as 'show doctor.' He rewrote several of the scenes, cut others, and suggested a change of title" (Belcher diss., p. 115).

A thinly disguised vaudeville show, with a slight plot that held together a number of specialty acts. According to the *NYT* (4–3–1900): "The farce-comedy has little to do with policy playing, but serves as an excellent means to present

Williams and Walker about whom are surrounded a large company who indulge in solos, duets, acrobatic feats, yarn spinning and negro eccentricities.''

After winning a fortune in a lottery, Bert Williams (as Dusty Cheapman) wishes to buy his way into high society. For a substantial fee, he is aided by Walker (a schemer named Happy Hotstuff), who arranges to have him invited to a swank affair, attended by the Negro uppercrust, called the Colored 400, where he is introduced as the ex-president of Haiti. The party is held at the palatial home of the Asterbilts, a wealthy white family, while they are out of town, by a financial arrangement with the butler, who wishes to become a member of the Colored 400. Complications arise, including the return of the Asterbilts, which make the affair both a fun-filled and a disastrous event.

Prod. by °Hurtig & Seamon, opening at the Star Theatre at the corner of Bway and 13th St. in New York City, Oct. 16, 1899. Next it moved to Hurtig & Seamon's Harlem Theatre, Oct. 21, 1899. Cast included Williams & Walker, Ada Overton (soon to become Mrs. George Walker), Hodges & Launchmere (singers), Mattie Wilkes (soprano), the Reese Bros. & Fred Douglass, the Mallory Bros., Williams & Walker Quartette, W. H. Chappelle, William C. Elkins, Richard Connors, George Catlin (impersonations), Lottie Thompson (later Mrs. Bert Williams), Ollie Burgoyne (dancer), and Odessa Warren. Frank Mallory was stage manager.

The show then toured through the spring of 1900. It played in small theatres throughout the East and Midwest, including Walker's hometown of Lawrence, KS, where it opened at the Bowersock Opera House in Jan. 1900. There Walker was presented with an engraved silver loving cup, in appreciation of the prominence which he had brought to the town by his success. Before closing, the show returned to New York City, opening April 3, 1900, for 8 perfs. at Koster & Bial's.

Songs and musical numbers pub. in *Williams and Walker's Album of Songs; From Their Original Musical Farce Comedy, The Policy Players* (Hurtig & Seamon, New York, 1899) include "Who's Gwine to Get the Money," "Dream Interpreter," "Gwine to Catch a Gig Today," "Ghost of a Coon," "The Colored Band," "The Broadway Coon," "Honolulu Belles," "The Medicine Man," and "Policy Players," by Williams & Walker; "I Certn'ly Was a Very Busy Man," by Benet & Northrup; "The Man in the Moon Might Tell," by Shipp; "Gladys," by Theodore E. Northrup; and "Take Me As I Am," by Hurtig & Lewis. Other songs: "I Don't Like No Cheap Man" (sung by Overton), "He's Up Against the Real Thing Now" (Williams), "Kings of the Policy Shop" (Williams), "Toughest in the Place," "Five Little Haytian Maids," "Moonlight," "Why Don't You Get a Lady of Your Own," and "Asterbilts Welcome Home."

FURTHER REFERENCE: *BlksBf* (Sampson). *Ghost* (Sampson). *Just Before Jazz* (Riis). *Nobody* (Charters). *NY Clipper* 4–20–1900. *NYT* 4–3–1900. Riis diss. *The Policy Players* folder in Harvard Theatre Collection.

PORGY AND BESS (1935–36, 1952–56, 1961, 1964, 1976, 1983, 1985). Subtitled "An American Folk Opera." 2 acts [7 scenes]. Book by °DuBose Heyward. Lyrics by Heyward and °Ira Gershwin. Music by °George Gershwin. Based on the play *Porgy* (1928), by °Dorothy and DuBose Heyward, dramatized from DuBose Heyward's novel by the same title (1925).

The best-known and most often revived opera by an American composer, which, in spite of its failure at the box office when it was first prod. in 1935, has since become an American classic. It is usually considered, in retrospect, the best all-black musical of the 1930s—a reference to the color of the cast only, since all of the principal creators were white. It has also been viewed as a symbol of the demise of black musical comedy, as it had traditionally flourished during the first third of the century; and in place of this genre, the serious black drama with music now began to become increasingly popular.

In the setting of the black ghetto of Catfish Row in Charleston, South Carolina, *Porgy and Bess* tells the love story of Porgy, a crippled beggar on his knees in a goat cart, for the beautiful Bess, who is the common-law wife of the dangerous and brutal, but sexually vital and appealing Crown. Early in the opera, Porgy is teased by his friends about his love for Crown's woman, which he unconvincingly denies; while Crown establishes his brutal nature by killing Robbins, the husband of Serena, in a crap game. When Crown flees to a coastal island to avoid prosecution, Porgy then becomes more open with regard to his love for Bess, and with the aid of an unscrupulous lawyer, he arranges a "divorce" from Crown for Bess, who now becomes "his woman." At a picnic, however, held on the same island where Crown is hiding, Crown detains Bess, warning her that she is still his, and forcing her to remain with him for the night. The picnic festivities are made more lively by the antics of Sportin' Life, a dope peddler, whose view of life is totally amoral and hedonistic. When Bess returns from the island, she is in a state of delirium, but after her recovery, which is aided by Porgy, she confesses her love for him, and he promises to protect her from Crown. Crown soon appears, attempting to kill Porgy, but Porgy uses Crown's own knife to kill him instead. When Porgy is taken to jail, Sportin' Life convinces Bess that Porgy will never be free to marry her, and under the influence of some of the "happy dust" (cocaine) that he persuades her to take, she agrees to go to New York with him. When Porgy is released from jail, he learns that Sportin' Life and Bess have gone, and he vows to go to New York in search of them.

First presented on Bway by the Theatre Guild at the Alvin Theatre, opening Oct. 10, 1935, for 124 perfs.; dir. by °Rouben Mamoulian. Cast: Ford L. Buck (Mingo), Abbie Mitchell (Clara), John W. Bubbles (Sportin' Life), Edward Matthews (Jake), Georgette Harvey (Maria), Olive Ball (Annie), Helen Dowdy (Lily), Ruby Elzy (Serena), Henry Davis (Robbins), Jack Carr (Jim), Gus Simons (Peter), Todd Duncan (Porgy), Warren Coleman (Crown), Anne Brown (Bess), Alexander Campbell (Detective), Harold Woolf and Burton McEvilly (Policemen), John Garth (Undertaker), George Lessey (Mr. Archdale), Ray Yeates

(Nelson), Helen Dowdy (Strawberry Woman), Ray Yeates (Crab Man), George Carleton (Coroner); Others: Residents of Catfish Row (the Eva Jessye Choir, conducted by Eva Jessye), Children, and the Charleston Orphan's Band. This prodn. went on tour for 5 months after closing in New York.

Revived on Bway by °Cheryl Crawford at the Majestic Theatre, opening Jan. 22, 1942, for 286 perfs.; dir. by °Robert Ross. With Todd Duncan, Anne Brown, Warren Coleman, Edward Matthews, Georgette Harvey, Helen Dowdy, Ruby Elzy, and J. Rosamond Johnson in their orig. roles. Major cast changes included Avon Long (Sportin' Life), Harriet Jackson (Clara), and Jimmy Waters (Mingo). Toured for a year and a half, with Todd Duncan succeeded by William Franklin and Anne Brown by Etta Moten.

Prod. on international tour beginning in June 1952 in Dallas, TX. It went to Europe in Sept. 1952, playing in Vienna, Berlin, London, and Paris. Opened at the Stoll Theatre in London, Oct. 9, 1952, for 142 perfs., and in New York at the Ziegfeld Theatre, March 10, 1953, for 305 perfs. Cast: William Warfield (London only); Le Vern Hutcherson, Leslie Scott, or Irving Barnes (Porgy); Leontyne Price or Urylee Leonardos (Bess); Cab Calloway (Sportin' Life); John McCurry (Crown); Helen Thigpen (Serena); Helen Colbert (Clara); Joseph James (Jake); Jerry Laws (Mingo); Georgia Burke (Maria); Helen Dowdy (Lily); and Moses La Marr (Frazier).

Toured the U.S. and Canada, Dec. 1953–Sept. 1954; Europe and the Middle East, Sept. 1954–June 1955; Latin America, July–Oct. 1955; Europe again, incl. the USSR, Nov. 1955–June 1956.

Twice revived by the New York City Center Light Opera Co., at the New York City Center, May 17, 1961, for 16 perfs., and May 6, 1964, for 15 perfs. Cast of the latter revival: William Warfield (Porgy, replaced by Irving Barnes), Veronica Tyler (Bess, replaced by Barbara Smith Conrad), William Dillard (Crown), Robert Guillaume (Sportin' Life), Marie Young (Clara), Irving Barnes (Jake), Tony Middleton (Mingo), Carol Brice (Maria), Gwendolyn Walters (Serena), and Al Fann (Frazier).

Revived by the Houston (TX) Grand Opera Company, with the first presentation of the complete score, Sept. 1976. This prodn. was presented in a pre-Bway tour which included performances in the Filene Theatre at Wolf Trap Farm Park in Vienna, VA. This prodn. was apparently presented in New York at the Uris Theatre in late 1976.

Revived by Radio City Music Hall, at Radio City Music Hall, New York, April 7–May 15, 1983, for 67 perfs., including 22 previews. With Robert Mosely, Jr., alternating with Michael V. Smartt (Porgy) and Priscilla Baskerville alternating with Elizabeth Davis (Bess).

Revived by the Metropolitan Opera Co., in repertory, as a 50th anniversary celebration of the opera's 1935 premiere, Feb. 4, 1985. With Simon Estes (Porgy) and Grace Bumbry (Bess). Again revived by the Metropolitan Opera, in an updated staging by Arvin Brown, Sept. 1989, with choreography by Arthur Mitchell. Cast: Michael Smartt (Porgy), Priscilla Baskerville (Bess), Marvis

Martin (Clara), Camellia Johnson (Serena), Gordon Hawkins (Jake), Marjorie Wharton (Maria), Ben Holt (Sportin' Life), and Gregg Baker (Crown).

Film version prod. by Samuel Goldwyn, 1959, dir. by °Otto Preminger; with Sidney Poitier (Porgy), Dorothy Dandridge (Bess), Sammy Davis, Jr. (Sportin' Life), and Pearl Bailey (Maria, the matriarch of Catfish Row). This 1959 film version was withdrawn from circulation by Ira Gershwin prior to his death in 1983.

A new, contemporary, innovative, urban version was most recently prod. in Great Britain by °Trevor Nunn, and first presented at Britain's Glyndebourne Festival in 1986. This prodn. was revived at London's Royal Opera House in Covent Garden Oct. 9–mid-Nov. 1992, and videotaped the following week for international TV and videocassette distribution. According to the *Washington Post* (11–22–1992), Ira Gershwin's widow desired Nunn's stage version to become the definitive film version, and vigorously worked toward the realization of this dream prior to her death in 1991. The two most innovative aspects of Nunn's conception were putting Porgy on crutches, instead of on his knees in a goat cart, and emphasizing the drug abuse motif, making it the principal motivation for the tragic events that occur—portraying Sportin' Life as a thoroughly immoral drug pusher. The videotaped version, which used special effects and a variety of locales outside of Catfish Row as suggested by the text, will be distributed by PBS and the BBC, prior to becoming available on videocassette.

Songs and musical numbers: "Summertime" (lullaby: Clara), "A Woman Is a Sometime Thing" (Jake & Ensemble), "They Pass By Singing" (Porgy), "Gone, Gone, Gone!" (Ensemble), "Overflow" (Ensemble), "My Man's Gone Now" (Serena & Ensemble), "Leavin' fo' de Promis' Lan' '' (train song: Bess & Ensemble), "It Takes a Long Pull to Get There" (rowing song: Jake & Fishermen), "I Got Plenty of Nuttin' '' (Porgy), "Woman to Lady" (divorce scene: Porgy, Bess, Frazier & Ensemble), "Bess, You Is My Woman Now" (duet: Porgy & Bess), "It Ain't Necessarily So" (Sportin' Life & Ensemble), "What You Want with Bess?" (duet: Crown & Bess), "Time and Time Again" (Serena & Ensemble), "I Loves You, Porgy" (duet: Porgy & Bess), "Oh, de Lawd Shake de Heaven" (Ensemble), "A Red Headed Woman" (Crown & Ensemble), "Clara, Don't Be Downhearted" (Ensemble), "There's a Boat That's Leavin' Soon for New York" (Sportin' Life & Bess), "Where's My Bess" (trio: Porgy, Serena & Lily), "I'm on My Way" (Porgy & Ensemble).

Orig. cast recording by Decca (DL 9024; with Todd Duncan and Anne Brown). Also recorded in a second Decca version (with Carmen McRae and Sammy Davis, Jr.); by Columbia's Odyssey label (with Lawrence Winters and Camilla Williams); by Bethlehem (with Mel Tormé and Frances Faye); by Camden (with Helen Jepson and Lawrence Tibbett); by RCA Victor (in two versions: one with Leontyne Price and William Warfield; the other with Lena Horne and Harry Belafonte); and Verve (with Ella Fitzgerald and Louis Armstrong).

FURTHER REFERENCE: *BlkMusTh* (Woll). *BlksBf* (Sampson). *Ebony* 10–1959. *NY Eve. Post* 10–11–1935. *NY Herald Trib.* 10–11–1935; 12–8–1935. *NYT* 10–6–1935; 10–11–1935; 10–20–1935; 9–19–1976. *Stage* 10–1935. *ThArts* 1–1936.

PORT TOWN (1960). Opera. 1 act. Libretto by Langston Hughes. Musical score by °Jan Meyerowitz.

The story of a typical seaport town, the sailors who come and go, the girls they become involved with and leave behind, and the bars they frequent. Based on Hughes' travels on the African coast and to other ports of the world.

Prod. as a summer workshop of the Boston Symphony Orchestra at the Berkshire Music Festival at Tanglewood in Lenox, MA, Aug. 4, 1950.

Unpub. librettos in JWJ/YUL and Moorland-Spingarn (the latter inscribed to Arthur Spingarn).

THE PRINCE OF BUNGABOO (1907–8). Musical comedy. 2 acts. Written by Salem Tutt Whitney, who starred in the title role.

Described by the St. Louis *Globe-Democrat* (2–7–1908) as ''a show that puts real significance in that much-abused term, musical comedy. The comedy and much of the music of this piece is furnished by 'Tutt' Whitney [Salem Tutt Whitney], as 'Lucky Bill,' who impersonates the prince. This artist is extremely funny as the ignorant moke, and has an abundance of really witty lines and ragtime songs.''

Prod. on tour by the *Black Patti Troubadours*, who, in Dec. 1907, began a week's engagement at the Elysium Theatre in Indianapolis, IN; starring Whitney. Cast also included Charles Bougia, Maria La Calas, and Emma Baynard.

Songs and musical numbers included ''Dagone, I'm Happy Now'' (Bougia), ''Sweet Coon from Dixie Land'' (Tutt), ''The Lady of Quality'' (Baynard), and ''Conversation Song'' (La Calas & Baynard).

A PRINCE OF DIXIE (1911). Musical farce. Prod. by George Taylor, who costarred as principal comedian. Possibly about a bogus prince who comes to a small town in search of an heiress for a bride, and is eventually exposed as a fraud. Prod. as a touring show. Cast included Frank Montgomery (Will Daley), Bessie Brady (Mamie Brown), James Brown (Mose Jenkins), Pearl Churchill (Rastus Brown), Elwood Woodring (Messenger), Eddie Stafford (Parson Brown), Mamie Jones (Aunt Mirandy), Lena Mitchell (Lilly Snow Jackson), Mamye Brown (Jube Jones), Maude Hudson (Sue Simpkins), George Tucker (Jeff Jackson), and Lizzie Hart (Teacher). Songs included ''All Wise Chickens Follow Me'' (Taylor), ''I Ain't Going to Walk Back Home,'' and ''I Am the Man with All the Dough.''

THE PRINCESS OF MADAGASCAR. See *URLINA, AFRICAN PRINCESS.*

PRINCESS ORELIA OF MADAGASCAR. See *URLINA, AFRICAN PRINCESS.*

THE PRODIGAL SISTER (1974). Biblical-inspired musical. 2 acts [8 scenes]. Book by J. E. Franklin. Lyrics by Franklin and Micki Grant. Music by Grant. Based on Franklin's play *Prodigal Daughter* (1962).

An upbeat, updated version of the biblical Prodigal Son, with a change of sex. A young girl becomes pregnant, leaves her home and family for the big city, and sinks into a life of degradation, before finally returning home to the love and protection of her family.

First prod. by the New Federal Theatre, New York, prior to opening Off-Bway at the Theatre De Lys, New York, Nov. 25–Dec. 29, 1974, for 40 perfs.; dir. by Shauneille Perry. With Paula Desmond in the title role. Cast: Desmond (Jackie), Frances Salisbury (Mother), Esther Brown (Mrs. Johnson), Ethel Beatty (Sissie), Leonard Jackson (Jack), Louise Stubbs (Essie & Baltimore Bessie), Saundra McClain (Lucille), Kirk Kirksey (Slick & Pallbearer), Frank Carey (Rev. Wynn & Employment Man), Joyce Griffen (Hot Pants Harriet), and Victor Willis (Dr. Patten, Caesar, & Jackie's Boyfriend).

Included 16 songs and musical numbers ranging from gospel to soul to rock: "Slip Away," "Talk, Talk, Talk," "Ain't Marryin' Nobody," "If You Know What's Good for You," "First Born," "Woman Child," "Big City Dance," "Sister Love," "Remember Caesar," "Superwoman," "Look at Me," "I Been Up in Hell," "Thank Your Lord," "Remember," "Celebration," and "The Prodigal Has Returned."

Libretto and musical score pub. by Samuel French, 1975.

THE PRODIGAL SON (1965). Subtitled "A Gospel Song Play." 1 act. By Langston Hughes.

A lively retelling of the biblical parable in the black idiom, through song, dance, and drama. The Prodigal Son is almost overcome by the temptations of Jezebel, the personification of evil, until virtue triumphs through the efforts of the good Sister Lord, the Exhorter, and the young man's gospel-singing mother.

First prod. Off-Bway at the Greenwich Mews Theatre, May 20, 1965, for more than 14 perfs.; dir. by Vinnette Carroll. Music arranged and dir. by Marion Franklin, pianist; Syvilla Fort, choreographer; Robert McCann, organist; and Willard Bond, percussionist. Cast: Dorothy Drake (Sister Lord), Robert Pinkston (Brother Callius), Philip A. Stamps (Prodigal Son), Ronald Platts (Father), Jeanette Hodge (Mother), Joseph Attles (Exhorter), Glory Van Scott (Jezebel), Marion Franklin (Brother John), Johnny Harris (Brother Alex), Jean Perry (Sister Anna), Sylvia Terry (Sister Waddy), Jeffrey Wilson (Brother Joseph), Teddy Williams (Brother Jacob), and Hattie Winston (Sister Fatima).

Went on European tour in the fall of 1965, playing in England, Belgium, the Netherlands, and France.

Songs and musical numbers: "Wade in the Water," "Take the Lord God," "Rock with Jezebel," "I Look Down the Road," "Devil Take Yourself Away," "How I'm Gonna Make It," "Feast at the Welcome Table," "When I Touch His Garment," "Fly Away (Wings)," "You Better Take Time to Pray," "I'm

Waiting for My Child," "Done Found My Lost Sheep," and "Come on in the House."

Script pub. in *Players* magazine, Dec. 1967–Jan. 1968. Unpub. script in Schomburg and in the Archives and Manuscript Div., State Historical Society of Wisc., at Madison. Earlier drafts in JWJ/YUL.
FURTHER REFERENCE: *Liberator* 10–1965. *NYT* 5–21–1965.

PROFESSOR EBENEZZER [*sic*] (1915). Vaudeville show. Prod. on tour by Harrison Stewart, who starred in the title role. Cast also included his wife Viola Stewart, Sam and Maude Gaines, Lawrence Chenault, Ethel and Loretta Jacobs, Gertrude and Pete Jones, Zenobia Allen, Beulah Brown, George Hall, Rena Blunt, Beulah Bishop, Sallie Walker, Hattie Wallace, Charles Cantry, Marie Gibson, Will Sulzer, Lottie Bryant, and J. C. Liverpool.

THE PROPHECY (1911). Opera. 1 act. By H. Lawrence Freeman. Set in America. Unperfd. The composer's best-known works include *The Martyr* (1893), *Valdo* (1905–6), *Vendetta* (1911–23), and *Voodoo* (1921–28).

THE PROVIDENCE GARDEN BLUES (1975). Play with music. By George Houston Bass. Music by Jonas Gwangwa. Concerns the problems of racism in Providence from the 1920s to the 1980s. Based on information gathered by Bass during an oral history research study. Prod. by Rites & Reason, at Brown Univ., Providence, RI, March 1975; dir. by Bass.

PURLIE (1970–74). Musical adaptation. Prologue, 2 acts [6 scenes], and epilogue. Book by Ossie Davis, °Peter Udell, and °Philip Rose. Based on the play *Purlie Victorious* (1961) by Ossie Davis. Lyrics by Udell. Music by °Gary Geld.

Possibly the most optimistic black musical of the 1970s, which made its social commentary on the racial problems of the American South with good humor and geniality, demonstrating that laughter and goodwill can be effective weapons against racial prejudice. Like the original play on which it was based, it broadly satirized traditional white and black stereotypes which had become deeply rooted in America's racial and cultural memory, including the benevolent but racist white master or plantation owner, the young white liberal or do-gooder, the black preacher as self-appointed messiah of his race, the Uncle Tom, the black mammy, the kitchen wench or maid, the matriarchal black family, the plantation structure of white society, segregation, integration, the black church, and numerous other stereotypical concepts and institutions.

The plot, which unfolds through flashbacks, tells the story of how Purlie (with the aid of Lutiebelle and others) tries to "reembezzle" $500 from Ol' Cap'n Cotchipee, the plantation owner, to establish an integrated church in the black community. The prologue is a celebration of the establishment of the church, Big Bethel, with a rousing funeral for Ol' Cap'n, who had died of shock, standing up; his coffin is borne in, in an upright position symbolic of the way he died, to the singing of a joyful gospel hymn, "Walk Him Up the Stairs." Acts I and II then relate the real and often imaginary events that led up to the death of Ol' Cap'n and the establishment of Big Bethel. The epilogue continues the lively funeral begun in the prologue.

Prod. on Bway by °Philip Rose, opening at the Broadway Theatre March 15, 1970; moved to the Winter Garden, Dec. 15, 1970, then to the ANTA (American National Theatre and Academy) Theatre, March 15, 1970, closing Nov. 7, 1971, for a total of 688 perfs.; dir. by Rose. Cast: Cleavon Little (Purlie), Linda Hopkins (Church Soloist), Melba Moore, replaced by Patti Jo (Lutiebelle), Novella Nelson, replaced by Carol Jean Lewis (Missy), Sherman Hemsley (Gitlow), °C. David Colson (Charlie), Helen Martin (Idella), and °John Heffernan (Ol' Cap'n). For their perfs., Little and Moore won Drama Desk Awards, Tony Awards, and *Variety*'s annual New York Drama Critics' Poll. Little also won the New York Drama Critics Circle Award.

Prod. on national tour by Philip Rose, opening Nov. 20, 1971, at the Shubert Theatre, Philadelphia, where it continued to play through May 1972. This prodn. returned to Bway, opening at the Billy Rose Theatre, Dec. 27, 1972, for 14 perfs. and 2 previews, closing Jan. 7, 1973; after which it continued its national tour. Cast: Robert Guillaume (Purlie), Shirley Monroe (Church Soloist), Patti Jo (Lutiebelle), Laura Cooper (Missy), Sherman Hemsley (Gitlow), °Douglas Norwick (Charlie), Helen Martin, replaced by Louise Stubbs (Idella), and °Art Wallace (Ol' Cap'n).

Prod. by the Repertory Company of the Virginia Museum Theatre, Richmond, VA, opening Nov. 8, 1974, dir. by Albert B. Reyes; choreography by Nat Horne. With Milledge Mosely, Monty Cones, Marie Goodman Hunter, James Kirland, Birdie M. Hale, Walter Rhodes, and Red Goodridge.

Songs and musical numbers: "Walk Him Up the Stairs" (Company), "New Fangled Preacher Man" (Purlie), "Skinnin' a Cat" (Gitlow and Field Hands), "Purlie" (Lutiebelle), "The Harder They Fall" (Purlie & Lutiebelle), "Charlie's Songs" (Charlie), "Big Fish, Little Fish" (Ol' Cap'n & Charlie), "I Got Love" (Lutiebelle), "Great White Father" (Cotton Pickers), "Skinnin' a Cat" (reprise: Gitlow & Charlie), "Down Home" (Purlie & Missy), "First Thing Monday Morning" (Cotton Pickers), "He Can Do It" (Missie & Lutiebelle), "The Harder They Fall" (reprise: Gitlow, Lutiebelle & Missy), "The World Is Comin' to a Start" (Charlie & Company), and "Walk Him Up the Stairs" (finale: Company).

Libretto pub. by Samuel French, 1971. Vocal selections pub. by Mourbar Music, 1970. Orig. cast recording by Ampex (A–40101).

FURTHER REFERENCE: *America* 12–9–1961. *Ebony* 3–1962. *Liberator* 4–1970. *Nation* 10–14–1961. *NewRepub* 11–6–1961. *NY Daily N.* 3–16–1970. *NYorker* 10–7– 1961; 11–14–1970; 12–23–1972. *NY Post* 3–16–1970. *NY Sunday Times* 3–22–1970. *NYT* 9–24–1961; 9–29–1961; 10–8–1961; 3–16–1970. *Reporter* 10–26–1961. *Sat. Rev.* 10–14–1961. *ThArts* 12–1961. *Time* 10–6–1961. *Wall St. J.* 3–19–1970. *Women's Wear Daily* 3–16–1970.

PUT AND TAKE (1921). Musical revue. 2 acts. Book by Irvin C. Miller. Lyrics and music by Spencer Williams, Perry Bradford, and Tim Brymn.

A reworking of Miller's successful touring show *Broadway Rastus, which had appeared in several eds. since 1915. According to the *NYT* review (8–24–1921, p. 12), *Put and Take*'s "first night audience found it lively and lilting entertainment, filled with excellent dancing, good singing and quite a dash of comedy." James Weldon Johnson (*BlkManh*, p. 189) stated that it was "by all standards . . . a good show, but it was overshadowed by the great vogue of [*] *Shuffle Along.*"

Although the prodn. attempted to avoid many of the minstrel stereotypes, and was considered by some critics as being too "white" a show for black performers, Miller himself perfd. his blackface comedy routines with Emmett "Gang" Anthony, who later became his partner in vaudeville as Miller & Anthony. According to *Jazz Dance* (Stearns & Stearns), the critics were most impressed with the dancing of the chorus and of the dancing star, Maxie McCree.

Toured for 30 weeks as *Broadway Rastus* (1921 ed.), before opening at Town Hall in New York City, Aug. 23–Sept. 23, 1921, for 23 perfs.; after which it continued to tour. Cast included Perry Bradford, Tim Brymn, Hamtree Harrington, Andrew Tribble in one of his famous female impersonations, Mildred Smallwood, Fred LaJoy, Florence Parham, Lillian Goodner, Mae Crowder, Maxie McCree, Earl Dancer, Bernie Barber, Hobart Shand, Violet Branch, Virgie Cousins, Essie Worth, Joe Peterson, George Braxton, Al Pizarro, Cora Green, Julius Foxworth, Roscoe Wickham, Chappelle & Stinnette, and Walter Richardson.

Songs and musical numbers: "Broadway Down in Dixieland," "Stop and Rest Awhile," "Georgia Rose," "Wedding Day in Georgia," "Dog," "Wedding Bells," "June Love," "Snagem Blues," "Beedle 'Em Boo," "Put and Take," "Creole Gal," "Chocolate Brown," "Yodle," "Old Time Blues," and "Stop! Rest a While." The last song was pub. by L. Wolf Gilbert, New York, 1921; copy in Moorland-Spingarn.

FURTHER REFERENCE: *Billboard* (J. A. Jackson's Page) 10–9–1921. *BlkMusTh* (Woll). *NY Dramatic Mirror & Th. World* 8–25–1921. *NYT* 8–24–1921. *NY Trib.* 6–20–1922. *Variety* 8–26–1921; 9–16–1921; 6–23–1922.

Q–R

QUEENIE PIE (1986). "Street Opera." Libretto by George C. Wolfe. Score by Duke Ellington. Score reworked by his son, Mercer Ellington, who also served as musical dir. Duke Ellington's last major work, completed prior to his death in 1974. It tells the story of an aging Harlem businesswoman who has made a fortune creating and selling cosmetics for black women, and who now travels to a mythical land hoping to find the ultimate secret of beauty, youth, and happiness. Played for a five-week engagement at the Kennedy Center's Eisenhower Theatre in Washington, DC; prod. by the American Music Theatre Festival and dir. and choreographed by Garth Fagan. Cast included Teresa Burrell in the title role, Larry Marshall, and Ken Prymus.

RACE HORSE CHARLIE'S LAST CHANCE (1926). Touring vaudeville revue. Prod. by Dad James. Cast included Melvin Butler, Gertrude Demond, Marion Ford, Annie Mason, and Hortense Lewis.

RADIO GIRLS (1922, 1925). Vaudeville revue in at least two eds. First prod. and perfd. by comedian Roscoe Montella, later in collaboration with his partner, under the name of Roscoe & Mitchell. The *1922 ed.* featured Kid Lips (the Charleston King). The *1925 ed.* featured Pauline Montella (his wife), Edmonia Henderson, Bessie Williams, Emma Johnson, Mamie Jefferson, Annie Mc-Reynolds, Bobby Powell, and Baby Badge.

RADIO SAM THE MELODY MAN (1929). Touring vaudeville revue. Prod. by George L. Barton, who also prod. *Steamboat Bill from Louisville* (1928).

RAGTIME (1933). Touring vaudeville revue. Prod. by musician and recording artist Earl B. Westfield. Cast included "Babe" Townsend, A. B. DeComathiere, Brown & Brown, and Frank Wilson.

RAG TIME BLUES (c. 1975). A musical history of Scott Joplin. Created by the AMAS Repertory Theatre of New York City, under the dir. of Rosetta LeNoire. Prod. New York, c. 1975, and apparently aimed for a Bway opening which was not forthcoming.

A RAGTIME FROLIC AT RAS-BURY PARK (1899). Musical skit. 1 act. Written by members of the *Black Patti Troubadours*.

One of the opening skits of the Troubadours' show, modeled after the group's very successful *At Jolly Coon-ey Island*, written by Bob Cole. In this show, the action is transferred from Coney Island to Asbury Park, presumably focusing on the typical characters who frequented the famous New Jersey resort including tourists, hustlers, vendors, performers, policemen, etc.

Prod. on tour as part of the Troubadours' show, 1899. Cast featured Dan Avery (Primrose Possom), Kid Frazier (Silas), Leslie Triplet (King Koon Kop, the park policeman), Mattie Philips, and Judson Hicks.

Musical numbers featured ragtime songs and dances.

RAGTIME SAILORS (1924, 1926). Vaudeville revue. Touring show prod. by Bob Russell. Cast of the *1924 ed.* featured his wife Josephine Russell, "Kid" Williams, Fred Lajoy, Freeman & McGinty, Petrona Lazzo, Creole Mays, Leonora Morgan, Ivy Black, Ethel Watts, Mabel Brown, Elenora (or Eleanor) Wilson, Carrie Huff, and E. E. Pugh. The *1926 ed.* also included Wilson, Mack, and Lajoy. Added to the show were Sam Robinson, Arthur Boykin, and the Rogers Duo.

RAGTIME STEPPERS (1925). Touring vaudeville revue. Prod. by Jules McGarr. Cast included Howell & Ogburn, Mabel Disworth, Fred Clarkson, Eugene Landrum, Melvin Hunter, and the Chicago Jazz Five.

RAIDING A CABARET (1917). Tabloid musical. Written and prod. by Billy King. Presented at the Grand Theatre, Chicago, with members of the Billy King Stock Co. Cast included King, Gertrude Saunders, India Allen, Ernest Whitman, Georgia Kelly, and Howard Kelly.

RAINBOW CHASERS (1926). Touring revue. Prod. by and costarring Salem Tutt Whitney and J. Homer Tutt (Whitney & Tutt). Cast also included Russian dancer Ida Forsyne; singers Mae Barnes, L. Baynard Whitney (tenor), Mabel Ridley (mezzo soprano), and Frankie Watts (contralto, blues singer); comedians Clarence Nance and Joseph Purnell; character actor Charles Hawkins; dancer Nona Marshall (billed as the "Queen of the Charleston"); the Melody Maids Trio; and a chorus of 6 ladies.

RAISIN (1973–81). Musical adaptation. 2 acts [14 scenes]. Book by °Robert Nemiroff and °Charlotte Zaltzberg. Based on *A Raisin in the Sun* (1959) by Lorraine Hansberry. Music by °Judd Woldin. Lyrics by °Robert Brittan.

Award-winning musical drama about the clash of dreams among the members of the Younger family in Chicago, who are eagerly awaiting the arrival of Mama Lena Younger's deceased husband's insurance settlement. The problems of what to do with the money and what actually happens to it provide most of the complications of the play. Mama wants to buy a home in an integrated neighborhood and to send her daughter Beneatha to medical school; Walter wants to buy a liquor store and become an independent businessman. Before any of their dreams can be actually realized, the money is stolen, and the family must come to grips with the more deeply rooted problems that cause their personal dissatisfactions and family division. Among the themes explored are black identity, power, and pride; assimilation versus separation of the races; black male-female relationships; the African roots of black American heritage; the generation gap; and numerous others.

Winner of a Tony Award as the best musical of 1973–74. Virginia Capers also won a Tony as best actress in a musical, for her portrayal of Mama Lena Younger. Ralph Carter was nominated for a Tony as best supporting actor in a musical and for a Drama Desk Award as the most promising young actor. Carter, Ernestine Jackson, and Joe Morton won *Theatre World* Awards as the most promising newcomers to Off-Bway prodns.

Opened at the Arena Theatre in Washington, DC, and went on a lengthy and successful tryout tour prior to being presented on Bway by Robert Nemiroff at the Forty-sixth St. Theatre, Oct. 18, 1973–Dec. 7, 1975, for 847 perfs.; dir. and choreographed by Donald McKayle. Cast: Al Perryman (Pusher), Loretta Abbott (Victim), Ernestine Jackson (Ruth Younger), Ralph Carter, succeeded by Paul Carrington (Travis Younger), Helen Martin (Mrs. Johnson), Joe Morton (Walter Lee Younger), Deborah Allen (Beneatha Younger), Virginia Capers (Mama Lena Younger), Elaine Beener (Bar Girl), Ted Ross, succeeded by Irving Barnes (Bobo Jones), Walter P. Brown (Willie Harris), Robert Jackson, succeeded by Herb Downer (Joseph Asagai), Chief Bey (African Drummer), Herb Downer, succeeded by Milt Grayson (Pastor), Marenda Perry, succeeded by Alyce Elizabeth Webb (Pastor's Wife), and °Richard Sanders (Karl Lindner); Others: People of the Southside.

Toured successfully, and presented in a number of revived versions until about 1981, and beyond. (Consult the *Best Plays* series for specific prodns.)

Songs and musical numbers: "Man Say," "Whose Little Angry Man," "Runnin' to Meet the Man," "A Whole Lotta Sunlight," "Booze," "Alaiyo," "African Dance," "Sweet Time," "You Done Right," "Same Old Color Scheme," "He Came Down This Morning," "It's a Deal," "Sidewalk Tree," "Not Anymore," and "Measure the Valleys."

Libretto pub. by Samuel French, New York, 1978. Vocal selections pub. by Blackwood Music, 1964. Cast recording by Columbia (KS–32754).

FURTHER REFERENCE: *America* 11–17–1973. *Dance Mag.* 4–1975. *Ebony* 5–1974. *Nation* 11–12–1973. *Newswk* 10–29–1973. *NYorker* 10–29–1973. *NYT* 5–31–1973; 10–27–1973; 10–28–1973; 11–4–1973; 11–19–1973.

RAISIN' CAIN (1923). Musical revue. 2 acts [8 scenes]. Book and music by Frank Montgomery, who also choreographed dances. Music possibly by James P. Johnson.

A musical journey from Africa (Act I) to New York's Harlem (Act II), apparently following the trail of a lost black soldier. In Africa, the three scenes move from (1) Senegambia, to (2) A Jungle trail, to (3) The Interior of Chief Nomo's Hut. In New York City, the five scenes shift from (1) a Music Store on Upper Seventh Ave. in Harlem, to (2) The Block of the Lafayette Theatre, to (3) The Restaurant of Bilo and Shaky, to (4) The Hotel Conservatory, to (5) The Hotel Ballroom. Act II ends with a passing review of the great Bway musicals, *Strut, Miss Lizzie*, *Plantation Revue*, *Shuffle Along*, *Liza*, *How Come?*, and a salute to the great comedy team of Williams & Walker.

Prod. by Nat Nazarro at the Lafayette Theatre, New York, July 9, 1923. Featured cast: Buck & Bubbles (Specialty), Emory Hutchins (Nomo, a Senegambian Chief & Slick, a Bad man), Jean Starr (Leila, the Chief's Daughter), Coressa Madison (Neila, the Chief's Daughter), Sam Russell (Bilo, a Lost Soldier), Josephine Gray (Mrs. Brown, Mother of Bilo & Weary, a Prophetess), George McClennon (Shaky, a Buddy of Bilo), Demos Jones (Flash Jones), Percy Wiggins (Leila's Chum), and Cliff (as Cliff).

Songs and musical numbers: Act I—Opening Chorus, "Tropical Chant" (Ensemble), "When My Man Comes Home," "Mammy's Black Baby" (Gray), "Jungle Jump" (Wiggins & Chorus), "Happenings" (Jones & Chorus), "Senegambian Moon" (Jones & Chorus), "Sentimental Oriental Blue" (Jones & Chorus), "Come Out" (Green & Chorus), "Let's Go" (Starr, Madison, Green, Jones & Company). Act II—"Harmony" (Ensemble), Specialty, "A Few Moments with Buck and Bubbles, World Famous Entertainers," "Laughing Clarinet" (McClennon), Dance (Bubbles), "Call a Cop" (Madison & Chorus), "Voice from the Congo" (Gray), "Barber Shop Harmony" (Buck, McClennon, Russell & Jones), "Hot Chops" (Ensemble), "Fattening Frogs for Snakes" (Madison & Green), "Raisin' Cain" (Jones, Green & Ensemble), "Oh, Foot" (Russell & McClennon), Specialty (Starr, with Fred Tunball at piano), "Passing Review" (of the musicals named above), Grand Finale (Company).

FURTHER REFERENCE: *NY Age* 7–7–1923. *NY Amsterdam N.* 7–4–1923.

RAMBLIN' AROUND (1923). Musical revue. Prod. in Chicago by Clarence Muse, who also costarred. Cast included Emmett Anthony, Blanche Calloway, Ollie Powers, Valaida Snow, and Esther Bigeou.

RANDY'S DANDY CIRCUS (1974). Children's musical. By Kelsie E. Collie. About a young boy who inherits a circus, but his envious aunt and uncle sabotage the opening by stealing all the animals. The story ends happily, however, with the help of the boy's friends. Prod. by the Howard Univ. Children's Theatre, Washington, DC, summer 1974.

RANG TANG (1927). Musical comedy. 2 acts [10 scenes]. Book by Kaj Gynt. Music by Ford Dabney. Lyrics by Jo Trent. Based on vaudeville routines of Miller & Lyles (Flournoy E. Miller and Aubrey Lyles).

Successful Miller & Lyles musical, involving African elements, conceived as a sequel to their *Shuffle Along*, in which they also played the roles of Sam Peck and Steve Jenkins. In this show, inspired by the Lindbergh flight over the Atlantic, Peck and Jenkins are two debt-ridden village barbers who escape from their creditors in Jimtown by stealing a plane and flying to Africa, where they hope to "make it rich" by finding a treasure. Forced to land their plane at sea near the island of Madagascar, they become involved in a series of hilarious misadventures among the natives and animals that they encounter in the forests, jungles, and deserts of this somewhat mythical, exotic, and often terrifying ancestral land. They eventually find the treasure they have been searching for and return to the U.S., finally arriving at a Harlem cabaret, where they celebrate in grand style their new status as two of the richest men in the world.

Prod. on Bway at the Majestic Theatre, opening July 12, 1927, for 119 perfs. Principal cast: Flournoy Miller (Steve Jenkins, a Barber), Aubrey Lyles (Sam Peck, Another Barber), Daniel Haynes (King of Madagascar), Zaidee Jackson (Magnolia), James Stranger (Barber Shop Customer, and member of the Chorus), Josephine Hall (Singer and Queen of Sheba), Marie Mahood (One of Chief Bobo's Six Wives), and Inez Draw (Singer).

Songs and musical numbers: "Everybody Shout," "Sammy and Topsy," "Brown," "Pay Me," "Sambo's Banjo," "Some Day," "Come to Africa," "Zulu Fifth Avenue," "Jungle Rose," "Monkey Land," "Sweet Evening Breeze," "Summer Nights," "Tramps of the Desert," "Voo Doo," "Harlem," and "Rang Tang."

FURTHER REFERENCE: *NY Eve. World* 7–13–1927. *NYT* 7–13–1927. *Variety* 1–18–1928.

RARIN' TO GO (1925–26). Touring musical revue. 2 parts. Music by Joe Jordan. Prod. by °Edward E. Daley on the Columbia Theatrical Circuit (white); with a cast of black and white performers. The whites perfd. separately in the first part; the blacks in the second. The black cast included Tim Moore, Lovey Taylor, Florence McClain, Jimmie Ferguson, Dancing Dane, Lena Wilson, Gertie Moore, and Gladys Smith.

RASTUS BROWN IN BAD COMPANY (1924). Touring vaudeville entertainment. Featuring comedian "Rastus" Brown, Billy English (billed as "Kansas City Brown"), Miss "Lindy," Sleepy Harris, Herbert Skinner, Albert Celeston, Billy Henderson, Virginia Barker, Beulah Gittins, and Stella Johnson.

A RAT'S MASS/PROCESSION IN SHOUT (1976). Jazz opera. Adapt. by Cecil Taylor from Adrienne Kennedy's avant-garde play *A Rat's Mass* (1963), which was described by John S. Scott (*Players* 2/3–1972, p. 13) as "a vitriolic struggle of a Black brother and his sister [characterized as Brother and Sister Rat] to rid themselves of white-Christian oppression." Prod. Off-Off-Bway by La Mama Experimental Theatre Club (E.T.C.), March 1976; also dir. by Taylor.

RECORD BREAKERS (1924). Touring show. Prod. by Joe Reed. Cast was headed by Billy Cumby (billed as "The Black Spear") and the Kewpie Doll Chorus.

REDEMPTION (1920s). Musical extravaganza. By J. Berni Barbour. Toured the western part of the U.S. during the 1920s.

RED HOT MAMA (1926–?). Seasonal musical show prod. by Irvin C. Miller. The theme of this show was "Glorifying the Brownskin Girl." First prod. during the 1926 season, starring Gertrude Saunders, and apparently went through a number of eds. after that time. (See also *Brownskin Models*.)

RED HOTS (1926). Touring revue. Featuring Baby Cox, Leo Edwards, Fred Clarkson, Hattie V. Snow (sister of Valaida Snow), and Lillian Barbrey.

THE RED MOON (1908–9). Operetta. Also called a musical comedy. Billed as "A Sensation in Red and Black." 3 acts. Book by Bob Cole. Lyrics and music by Cole, J. Rosamond Johnson, and Joe Jordan. Additional lyrics by Charles Hunter. Additional music by James Reese Europe, musical dir.

Described by James Weldon Johnson (*BlkManh*, p. 109) as "one of the first true Negro operettas," and considered by him to be unsurpassed in its "well-constructed book and . . . tuneful, well-written score." This opinion was sustained by both the *NY Dramatic Mirror* which called the score "often quite ambitious and always pleasing to hear" (5–4?–1909), and Edward B. Marks, the music publisher, who, in his 1934 autobiography, called *The Red Moon* "the most tuneful colored show of the century" (both quotations cited in *AmMusTh* [Bordman], p. 249).

The plot, which underwent some changes from the touring show to the Bway version, was built around the story of a part-black, part-Indian maiden who is abducted by her father, who had abandoned her 15 years earlier, and returned to his reservation in the West, where he hopes to marry her to an Indian brave. After many complications, she is rescued by two black men in disguise and returned to her mother. In the touring version, the abduction occurs at a government school for blacks and Indians in the Midwest, and the rescuers are two members of a traveling show who disguise themselves as a doctor and lawyer respectively. In the Bway version, the woman is abducted from her mother's home in Virginia, and the rescuers (a quack doctor and a bogus lawyer) disguise themselves as Indians. After the maiden is returned to her home, she falls in love with her principal rescuer (played by Bob Cole), and they have a tender romance which culminates in marriage. The Indian chief also becomes reunited with his black wife in the end. This musical also successfully broke with the long-standing taboo against romantic scenes between black lovers in shows presented to white audiences.

Toured successfully during 1908 and early 1909, before opening on Bway in its revised version at the Majestic Theatre, May 3, 1909, for 32 perfs.; dir. by Cole. Cast of the Bway prodn.: Bob Cole (Slim Brown), J. Rosamond Johnson (Plunk Green), Ada Overton Walker (Phoebe Brown), Abbie Mitchell (Minnehaha, the Indian maiden), Henry Gant (Bill Gibson), Wesley Jenkins (Bill Armour), Sam Lucas (Bill Webster), Benny Jones (Bill Simmons), Arthur Talbot (John Lowdog, Indian Chief), Frank Brown (Red Feather, Indian Brave), Harry Watson (Eagle Eye), Sam Lucas (Spread Eagle), Elizabeth Williams (Lucretia Martin), Mollie Dill (Amanda Gibson), Rebecca Delk (Lilly White), Fanny Wise (Truscalina White), and Marie Young (Waneta).

Songs and musical numbers: "Ada, My Sweet Potater," "Big Red Shawl," "Cupid Was an Indian Pickaninny," "I Ain't Had No Lovin' in a Long Time," "I Want My Chicken," "I've Lost My Teddy Bear," "Life Is a Game of Checkers," "My Indian Maid," "Phoebe Brown," "Run, Brudder Possum, Run," "Don't Tell Tales Out of School," "Pickaninny Days," "Bleedin' Moon," "As Long as the World Rolls On [or Goes Round]," "On the Road to Monterey," "Wildfire Dance," "Red Moon," "To-da-lo Two Step," "Sambo," and "Coola-Woo-La."

FURTHER REFERENCE: *BlksBf* (Sampson). *Just Before Jazz* (Riis). *NY Age* 7–14–1910. *NY Dramatic Mirror* 5–4–1909. *NY Eve. Sun* 5–5–1909. *NYT* 5–4–1909. Riis diss. *Red Moon* scrapbook in TC/NYPL.

RED PASTURES (1930). Touring show. Prod. by Irvin C. Miller. Cast included Jackie (later "Moms") Mabley, Billie Young, Mary Wheeler, Albert Jackson, Hayes Prior, and Edgar Martin.

REGGAE (1980). Caribbean-inspired musical. 2 acts [11 scenes]. Concept and prodn. by °Michael Butler. Story by Kendrew Lascelles. Book by Melvin Van Peebles, Lascelles, and Stafford Harrison. Music and lyrics by Ras Karbi, Michael Kamen, Kendrew Lascelles, Max Romeo, Randy Bishop, Jackie Mittoo, and Stafford Harrison.

A Bway show, set in Jamaica, built around reggae music and Rastafarian philosophy, both of which were beginning to achieve some popularity in the

U.S. About a Jamaican singer who returns to her country after achieving fame in the States. She becomes reunited with her lover, who is now a marijuana grower, and (because of that) they come into conflict with some gangsters who try to kill them. They are rescued by a group of Rastafarians, who eventually seek to convert them to their philosophy.

Prod. on Bway at the Biltmore Theatre, March 27–April 13, 1980, for 21 perfs.; dir. by Glenda Dickerson, with choreography by Mike Malone. Cast: Calvin Lockhart (Ras Joseph, Rastafarian leader), Alvin McDuffy (Anancy, the Spider), Sheryl Lee Ralph (Faith, the Singer) Michael Thomas (Esau, the Marijuana Farmer), Obba Babatunde (Rockets), Fran Salisbury (Mrs. Brown), Louise Robinson (Louise), Ras Karbi (Natti), Charles Wisnet (Corson), and Sam Harkness (Binghi Maytal).

Songs and musical numbers: "Jamaica Is Waiting," "Rise Tafari," "Farmer," "Hey Man," "Mash Em Up," "Mrs. Brown," "Everything That Touches You," "Mash Ethiopia," "Star of Zion," "Reggae Music Got Soul," "Talkin' 'Bout Reggae," "Rise Up Ja-Ja Children," "No Sinners in Jah Yard," "Banana, Banana, Banana," "Promised Land," "Rasta Roll Call," "Ethiopian Pageant," "Rastafari," "Roots of the Tree," "I and I," "Gotta Take a Chance," "Chase the Devil," and "Now I See It."
FURTHER REFERENCE: *AmMusTh* (Bordman).

A REIGN OF ERROR (1899). White-oriented musical farce-comedy. Main authorship unknown. Included a so-called coon song by Bob Cole and Billy Johnson entitled "I Wonder What Is That Coon's Name." A °Rogers Brothers show, starring Gus and Max Rogers, as Hans Wurse and Carl Leetlewurzer, who are constantly pursued by a stereotypical Italian stage villain, Dr. Dago Daggeri. Prod. at the Victoria Theatre on 42nd St., New York, opening March 2, 1899.

THE RETURN OF SAM LANGFORD (1916). Musical show. Prod. and perfd. on tour by Billy Watts, with members of the Watts Big Stock Co. Featured in the cast was Madam Patti Willis, with Watts as the principal comedian.

A REVIVAL (1969–72). Black ritual. Written by Charlie L. Russell. An evolving theatrework, completed in 1972 after almost three years of work, putting into dramatic form the unifying philosophy of the National Black Theatre, founded by Barbara Ann Teer, who directed and helped to shape this work. Utilizes a combination of music, drama, dance, "rap," and the rhythms and fervor of the black church tradition to teach black people to unite, love one another, and work together for meaningful change. Prod. by the National Black Theatre, July 1–Dec. 10, 1972, for 113 perfs.; dir. by Teer. Cast: Willie Faison (Jason), Beverly Williams (Cynthia), William Still (Robin), Jabulile (Sonia), Oba Babatunde (Pickwick), Ntombi (Candy), Ronnie Grant (Porky), LaVerne Moore (Beverly), Douglas Leslie Dunn (Clarence), Brenda Thomas Denmark (Miss Sylvia), Al

Samuel (Sugarfoot), Mary Giles (Bernice), Ifenu (Virginia), Michael J. Lythcott (Officer Green), Jingo (Officer Brown and Walt), LaVerne Johnson (Dara), Akinwole Babatunde (Mamadou), Yaa Shepherd (Thembi), Mathew Bernard Johnson, Jr. (Toussaint), Cecilia Talley (Georgia), Steven Tillman (Gregory), P. M. Bowdwin (Rita), Donald Faison (Preacher in Procession), Muhuanda Ali (Ayana), Charles Wood (Njonjo), Zuri Laini McKie (Oshun), and Akinwole Babatunde (Ancestor).

REVUE NÈGRE (1925). All-black revue. Conceived and prod. by °Caroline Dudley Reagon. This was the show that boosted Josephine Baker to international stardom. According to Bruce Kellner (*HarlRenD*, pp. 300–301), "Reagon, a rich, white socialite [from] Chicago . . . had fallen under the spell of black music and musicians. Married to a wealthy American in the foreign service, she seized on the idea of transporting something of the Harlem Renaissance to Paris, where she and her husband were stationed." The result was the *Revue Nègre*, which was eventually prod. at the Théâtre des Champs-Elysées in Paris, Sept. 1925, starring Baker. The cast featured a number of American performers and musicians that included Sidney Bechet, Maude de Forest, Hazel Valentine, Claude Hopkins and his band, and other dancers and comedians. According to Kellner, "From her first appearance onstage, wearing a girdle made out of bananas, Josephine Baker was one of the brightest black stars of the century" (p. 301).

RHAPSODY IN BLACK (1931–32). Musical revue. Billed as a "Jazz Concert." Conceived and prod. by °Lew Leslie. Lyrics and music by J. Rosamond Johnson, Cecil Mack, W. C. Handy, and several white writers including °George Gershwin, °Dorothy Fields, and °Jimmy McHugh. Vocal arrangements for spirituals and folk songs by Cecil Mack.

A transitional black revue, costarring Valaida Snow and Ethel Waters, in which Leslie broke away from his standard pattern used successfully in several of his *Blackbirds* revues, until this formula had become jaded. In this show he dispensed with the dancing chorus, the blackface comedians, and the stereotypical sketches that had characterized previous shows, and focused primarily on the black artists and their music. The *NYT* (5–5–1931) found the new trend toward simplicity "monotonous." But the *Washington Post* (4–13–1931) reported that the show "blew the theatre roof off with applause."

Prod. on Bway at the Harris Theatre, opening May 4, 1931, for 40 perfs. Cast: Ethel Waters, Valaida Snow, the Berry Brothers, Earl "Snakehips" Tucker, Eddie Rector, Blue McAllister, Al Moore, Cecil Mack Choir, Pike Davis' Continental Orchestra, Edith Wilson, Eloise Uggams, Ada Ward, and Geneva Washington. Although its Bway run was short-lived, Ethel Waters (*His Eye Is on the Sparrow*, pp. 265–66), reports that it had a profitable tour.

Songs and musical numbers: "Washtub Rub-sody" (Waters), " 'Till the Real Thing Comes Along" (Snow & Orchestra), "Dance Hall Hostess" (Waters), "What's Keeping My Prince Charming?" (Waters), "You Can't Stop Me from

Loving You'' (Waters), ''Harlem Rhumbola'' (Snow, Moore & Orchestra), ''Rhapsody in Blue'' (by Gershwin: sung by Snow, Choir & Orchestra), ''St. Louis Blues'' (by Handy), ''Dream of the Chocolate Soldier'' (Snow, Rector & Orchestra), ''Rhapsody in Black'' (Snow & Orchestra), ''Eli Eli'' (sung in Hebrew by Avis Andrews, Uggams & Choir), ''Chloe'' (Washington & Chorus), ''Great Gettin' Up Mornin' '' (Ernest Boyd & Chorus), ''I Found a Million Dollar Baby at the Five and Ten Cents Store,'' ''Exhortation'' (Ernest Allen & Choir), ''Rhythm in Rhapsody'' (dance: Tucker & Bessie Dudley), ''Rhapsody in Taps'' (dance: Rector), ''St. James Infirmary'' (Snow, Choir, & Orchestra), and ''Two Guitars'' (Snow & Choir).

FURTHER REFERENCE: *BlkMusTh* (Woll). *BlksBf* (Sampson). *DBlkTh* (Woll). *NYT* 5–6–1931. *Washington Post* 4–13–1931. *Rhapsody in Black* file in Theatre Collection, Philadelphia Free Library.

RHAPSODY IN RHYTHM (1945). Touring revue. Prod. by Paul Small. Cast was headed by Ethel Waters, Mantan Moreland, ''Dusty'' Fletcher, Timmie Rogers, the Savage Dancers, and the Four Step Brothers.

RHUMBA LAND REVUE (1931). Musical revue. Prod. in Harlem at the Lafayette Theatre; with Mamie Smith.

RHYTHM HOTEL (1935). Touring show. Written and prod. by Leonard Reed. Featured George Dewey Washington, Ida Brown, Show Boy & Ann, Rubie Blakely, and the Three Lightning Flashes.

THE RICH UNCLE / / Also known as **My Rich Uncle** (1918). Tabloid musical. Written and prod. by Billy King. Two con men, one a handsome city slicker (Howard Kelly), the other his accomplice (King), try to swindle a rich man out of his money by fulfilling his wish to marry into high society. Much of the comedy comes from the disguises employed by the accomplice (including one as a baby) to carry out this scheme. Perfd. by the Billy King Stock Co., at the Grand Theatre, Chicago.

A RIOT OF FUN (1928). Musical revue. Prod. in Harlem at the Lincoln Theatre; with Mamie Smith.

THE RIVALS (1916). Tabloid musical. Written and prod. by Billy King. Perfd. at the Grand Theatre, Chicago, with members of the Billy King Stock Co.

ROCK AND ROSEY LEE (1919). Vaudeville revue. Touring show prod. by Sandy Burns, with members of the Sandy Burns Stock Co.

ROCK DINAH (1927). Touring vaudeville revue. Prod. by and costarring Coot Grant and Kid Wilson (Grant & Wilson). "Big Boy" Anderson and Shorty Ford were the principal comedians; Baby Hines was the leading lady and principal singer; Johnny Bragg was the leading man; Raymond Shackelford played both light and comedy parts; Jeannette Jackson was the soubrette; and the chorus of 5 included Louise Shackelford, Mamie Ford, Elizabeth Chandler, Francis Tyler, and Billy Clay.

ROCK FANTASY (pre-1983). Rock musical. Music and lyrics by Alan Dones and David Daniels, with additional lyrics by Robert Alexander. A middle-aged black CPA (Albert Jackson) attempts to find refuge from his everyday problems by delving into rock-and-roll fantasies. He dreams that he has become a rock star. The contemporary new wave music incorporates Michael Jackson & Prince sounds with those of Grace Jones and Talking Heads. In 1983, it was under option to premiere at the Lorraine Hansberry Theatre in San Francisco; no record of the actual prodn.

ROCKING CHAIR REVUE (1931). Musical revue. Prod. at the Lafayette Theatre in Harlem; with Mary Stafford.

THE ROGERS BROTHERS IN CENTRAL PARK (1900). White-oriented vaudeville farce. 3 acts. Book by °John T. McNally. Lyrics by °J. Cheever Goodwin. Music by °Maurice Levi. With additional songs by Sidney Perrin, Bob Cole, James Weldon Johnson, and J. Rosamond Johnson.

One of a series of annual musicals starring °Gus and °Max Rogers, who portray two German yokels duped into buying Central Park—the one in Missouri, not New York.

Tried out on the road before opening on Bway, prod. by °Klaw & Erlanger, at the Victoria Theatre, Sept. 17, 1900, for 72 perfs. With an all-white cast that included °Della Fox, °Eugene O'Rourke, °Lee Harrison, °James Cherry, and the Rogers Bros. Taken back on the road after closing at the Victoria.

Black-authored songs included "Run, Brudder Possum, Run," by Cole & the Johnson Brothers; and "Lina, Ma Lady," a serenade, with music by Perrin and words by °Carol Fleming, the latter song pub. by Rogers Bros. Music Publishing Co., New York; copy in Moorland-Spingarn.
FURTHER REFERENCE: *AmMusTh* (Bordman). *BesPls 1899–1909.*

THE ROLLICKING GIRL (1905). White-oriented musical play. 3 acts. Libretto by °Sidney Rosenfield. Music by °W. T. Francis. Additional song by Grant Stewart and Tom Lemonier. Prod. by °Charles Frohman at the Herald Square Theatre, New York, May 1, 1903, for 192 perfs. With an all-white cast. Stewart & Lemonier's song was "My Cabin Door."

ROLLING ON (1928). Touring vaudeville revue. Prod. by and starring Russian-style dancer Dewey Weinglass. Also in the cast were Gertrude Saunders, Billy Mitchell, and Jackie Young.

ROLLIN' WITH STEVENS AND STEWART (1988). 2-man show. Conceived and directed by its stars, Ronald "Smokey" Stevens and Jaye Stewart. A 2-man salute to the genius of black entertainers who toured the TOBA circuit. Prod. at 1515 Broadway, Detroit, MI, Feb. 11–28, 1988.

ROLL-ON (1926). Touring vaudeville revue. Prod. and perfd. by Lillian Brown and her partner, under the name Brown & DuMont. Cast also included Wells & Wells, Freddie Tunsdall, "Slim" Jones, Allen & Allen, and Clifford & Battle.

ROMEO & JULIET: NEW WAVE / / Former prod. as *Romeo & Juliet (A Rock Musical)* and *Romeo-Rock & Juliet Jazzical* (1981–84). A punk/rock adaptation of Shakespeare's tragedy. By William Electric Black (Ian Ellis James).

This version of Shakespeare's play, which remains faithful to the language, is set in the Lower East Side, with Romeo wearing blue hair and a "No-shit" button, and Juliet as a free-wheeling liberated female who just wants to have fun. Although the *Village Voice* reviewer (3–13–1984, p. 79) felt that "the production [didn't] give enough room to explore the close relationship of death and eros in punk," he praised "the rock club ambiance [which made] the comic scenes delightfully vivid and [gave] the fight scenes more true street beat than any clash of Jets and Sharks" he had witnessed.

First prod. as *Romeo-Rock & Juliet Jazzical* at Club 57, New York, June 20–July 6, 1981, for 3 perfs. Prod. as *Romeo & Juliet (A Rock Musical)* at the Bridgehampton Theatre, Long Island, Aug. 1983. Prod. as *Romeo & Juliet: New Wave* at Entermedia Marquee, New York, Feb. 21–March 11, 1984. All prodns. were dir. by the author.

ROSELAND REVUE (1928). Touring vaudeville revue. Featured Dusty Fletcher, Andrew Tribble, the Gaines Brothers (acrobats), and the Pan American Four.

ROSIE'S WEDDING DAY (1923–24). Vaudeville show. Originated in Chicago, where it was prod. by Tim Moore and his Chicago Follies Co.; then on tour. The thin plot revolves around Rosie's plans to elope with her lover, and the parents' bitter opposition to their schemes. Moore, the principal comedian, played the part of Jake, a hired hand, who assists the lovers in gaining Rosie's parents' approval. Other cast members (specific roles not known) were Willie Singleton, Pete Gentry, Fred Moore (dancer), Fred Durrel (juvenile), Edna Brown, Early Smith, Rachel King, and Eva Simmons. Musical numbers include "Loving Song" (Gentry) and "Log Cabin Blues" (Singleton).

ROUND THE GLOBE (1926). Touring vaudeville revue. Prod. by Mary Mack (Mrs. Billy Mack) and her Merry Makers Co.

ROYAL AMERICAN SHOW (1939). Touring show. Prod. by Leon Claxton. Cast included snake dancer Hilda Smith, rhumba dancer Doris Williams, comedian "Too Sweet," rhythm and tap dancers Sparkey & Spencer, and Gwendolyn Bates.

A ROYAL COON (1909). Musical comedy. Written apparently by John Larkins, who starred in the title role. Presented by the *Black Patti Troubadours*, on transcontinental tour, including a perf. at the Park Theatre in Indianapolis, c. May 1907. Others in the cast included Al F. Watts (Garper, the miser), Charles Bougia (A Fisherman), John C. Boone (Henri, Marquis of Cornville [or, possibly, Coonville]), King & Bailey, Montrose Douglass (unicyclist), and Will A. Cook. Songs and musical numbers included "Flirting" (Marie Lacal, Emma Baynard & Chorus), "A Royal Coon" (Larkins), "Coon of Pedigree," "Dixie Boy," and "Happy Land."

ROYAL FLUSH REVUE (1927). Touring vaudeville revue. Featured comedians Skeeter Winston, Roscoe Montella, and Billy Mitchell; singer Pauline Montella; Campbell & Farrell; Garland Howard; Mae Brown; Bernice Robinson; Sterling Grant; and Julia Moody.

ROYAL SAM (1911). Touring vaudeville show. Prod. on tour by °Morrow & °Mindlin. Cast featured comedians "Jolly" John Larkins and Irvin "Boots" Allen, George McClain, J. Frances Mores, Ethel Johnson, Ethelyn Green, Ora Dunlap, Arthur C. Simmons, T. J. Sadler, Luke A. Scott, James A. Lilliard, Irene Tasker, Anna Tyler, and William Wilkins.

RUFUS RASTUS (1905–7). Musical comedy. Book by William D. Hall. Lyrics by Lester A. Walton, Frank Williams, Howard Herrick, Arthur Gillespie, and Hall. Music by Ernest Hogan, Tom Lemonier, Joe Jordan, and H. Lawrence Freeman.

A starring vehicle for Hogan, which was the culmination of a long-held dream of mounting his own show. About a down-and-out vaudevillian who owes a debt of $22, which he tries to pay by working at various jobs in the Ponce De Leon Hotel (including bootblack and laundry worker) and as doorkeeper at Madison Square Garden. These locations form the background for a number of the show's songs and specialty numbers, including acrobatic displays and operatic singing. Moreover, his various jobs give him an opportunity for numerous changes of attire and guises to suit his various professions. In any event, his jobs are insufficient to pay off his debt, which steadily increases as he tries to pay it off at $2 per week. Just as he is about to be jailed for nonpayment, he comes into possession of a large fortune (either $22,000 or $50,000, depending on which source is consulted—either by accidental discovery or by inheritance), which enables him to pay off his debt, live like a king in the hotel where he was formerly a lowly employee, and marry the girl of his dreams (Carita Day).

Organized in New York City as a road show, and taken on tour around 1905, under the management of °Hurtig & °Seamon. Opened at the American Theatre in New York, Jan. 29, 1906, where it received favorable reviews, the number of perfs. unknown. Cast: Ernest Hogan (Rufus Rastus), J. F. Mores (waiter), J. Leubrie Hill (Dr. Fo-Jo, dealer in lucky charms), Anna Cook Pankey (Sophronia, hotel housekeeper), Harry Fiddler (Hugo, the porter), A. D. Byrd (Mrs. Angelica Newcomb, looking for a job), R. A. Kelly (Rev. Nightingale Slipback Newcomb), Alice Mackey (Federica, the Newcombs' educated daughter), Muriel Ringgold (Snowflake, the Newcombs' youngest daughter), Theo Pankey (Enoch, the bell boy; Cousin Monk; and Casterphe), Henry Troy (Lazarus Tuttle, theatrical promoter), Carita Day (Selina Giltedge, prima donna of Coontown 400), Mamie Emerson (Mandy Jones, leading soprano of Ragtime Opera Co.), Harry Gilliam (Samsom Strong), Matt Housley (Officer), Pauline Hackney (Belmoral, Hugo the porter's sweetheart), Bill Moore (Floor Manager); Others: Hotel Help, Jubilee Singers, Minstrels, Terpsichorean Artists, Choristers, Scrub Women, Nurse Girls, Chambermaids, Laundresses, Bell Boys, Yardmen, Footmen, Chefs, and Newsboys.

Songs and musical numbers: "Oh, Say Wouldn't It Be a Dream" (the hit song: Hogan), "Dixie Anna Lou," "Cock-a-doodle-doo," "Eve Handed Adam a Lemon," "The Hornet and the Bee" (Day), "If Peter Was a Colored Man," "I'll Love You All the Time," "Is Everybody Happy?" (another hit song: Hogan), "The Isle of Repose" (Pankey), "Lilly's Wedding Day," "Mammy," "The Monkey and the Bear," "Moon Boy," "My Mobile Mandy" (Emerson), "On Grandma's Kitchen Floor," "Watermelon," "What We're Supposed to Do," "Consolation" (Troy), "Maude" (Mackey), "Old Kentucky Home" (Sally Green), "Goodbye, Old Dixie Land," and "Newsboys' Life."

FURTHER REFERENCE: *BlksBf* (Sampson). *DBlkTh* (Woll). *Just Before Jazz* (Riis). Riis diss. *Rufus Rastus* folder in Harvard Theatre Collection.

RUNAWAY SLAVES (1911). Touring vaudeville show. Featured Lee & Lee, Edna Campbell, and Edwards & Edwards. Songs included "Stop, Stop, Stop," "If Dreams Are True," "There Is No Place Like the Old Folks After All," and "That Was Me."

THE RUNAWAY'S RETURN (1914). Musical show. Prod. by Billy King at the Star Theatre, Savannah, GA, for one week, with members of the Billy King Stock Co.

RUN, LITTLE CHILLUN! / / Orig. title: ***Across the River, or Run Little Chillun*** (1933, 1938–39, 1943). Folk drama with incidental music. 2 acts [4 scenes]. Written, composed, and arranged by Hall Johnson.

The plot turns on a popular theme of the 1930s—the clash of Christianity and African paganism in the religious practices of southern rural blacks. In this play, the two opposing groups are the New Hope Baptists, a fundamentalist Christian sect which is intolerant of all pagan religions; and the New Day Pilgrims, a non-Christian cult from the Bahamas which practices a form of voodoo worship and hedonism. A crisis is precipitated when Jim Jones, the son of the New Hope Baptist minister, a young married man, falls under the spell of Sulamai, a beautiful young woman from the New Day Pilgrims, who seduces him and persuades him to leave his wife and church to join her group.

The war of the churches begins as the Baptists make a fervent effort to win the minister's errant son back to the fold. The leading prophet of the New Day Pilgrims, Elder Tongola, who also opposes the love affair, puts a curse on Sulamai, which apparently causes her to be struck by lightning. The victory of the Baptists is celebrated as the minister's son repents of his sins and is received back into the fold. The most exciting scenes of the musical, according to several critics, were the worship scenes of both churches—the revival practices of the New Hope Baptists, including spirituals, prayers, confessions, and sermons; and the orgiastic rituals of the New Day Pilgrims, which included singing, dancing, moon-worship, voodoo, and speaking in tongues. The *NYT* (3–2–1933), commenting on the orig. prodn., considered ''all of [the songs] more than good'' and ''some of them . . . superb.''

First prod. at the Lyric Theatre, New York, opening March 1, 1933, for 126 perfs.; dir. by °Frank Merlin. Music by the Hall Johnson Choir. Cast: Edna Thomas (Ella), Olive Ball (The Rev. Sister Luella Strong), Mattie Shaw (Sister Mattie Fullilove), Bertha Powell (Sister Flossie Lou Little), Ray Yeates (Brother Bartholomew Little), Walter Price (Bro. Esan Redd, Deacon of New Hope Baptist Church), Rosalie King (Sister Mahalie Ockletree), Pauline Rivers (Sister Judy Ann Hicks), Carolyn Hughes (Sister Susie Mae Hunt), Lula Hunt (Sister Lula Jane Hunt), Edward Broadnax (Brother George Jenkins), Milton Lacey (Brother Jeremiah Johnson), Service Bell (Brother Goliath Simmons), Harry Bolden (The Rev. Jones, Pastor of New Hope Baptist Church), Alston Burleigh (Jim, Rev. Jones's Son), Fredi Washington (Sulamai), James Boxwill (Brother Lu-te, Chief Singer of New Day Pilgrims), Gus Simons (Brother Jo-be, Herald of Joy), Ethel Purnello (Sister Mata, Priestess), Ollie Burgoyne (Mother Kenda, Daughter of Tongola), Waldine Williams (Reba, Daughter of Kenda), Jack Carr (Brother Moses, Young Priest), Harold Sneed (Elder Tongola, Prophet of the New Day Pilgrims), Bessie Guy (Belle, of Toomer's Bottom), Mabel Diggs (Mame, of Toomer's Bottom), Cecil Scott (Mag, Sulamai's Mother), Lula King (Sue Scott, of Toomer's Bottom), and Andrew Taylor (The Rev. Ebenezer Allen, Local Preacher).

Prod. by the Los Angeles Federal Theatre in Los Angeles and Hollywood, CA, for 11 months, 1938–39; with Alfred Grant and Florence O'Brien as Jim and Sulamai. Prod. by the Federal Theatre and Music Projects, at the Alcazar Theatre, San Francisco, opening Aug. 11, 1943, for 16 perfs.; dir. by Clarence Muse. With Caleb Peterson and Edna Mae Harris in the leading roles.

Unpub. scripts in LC, Schomburg, and Doheny Lib., Univ. of Southern California/Los Angeles.

FURTHER REFERENCE: *AnthANT* (Patterson). *Arena* (Flanagan). Hicklin diss. *Neg&Dr* (Bond). *NegPlaywrs* (Abramson). *NY Herald Trib.* 8–12–1933. *NYT* 3–2–1933; 3–12–1933; 4–30–1939; 6–14–1939; 7–14–1943. *Opportunity* 4–1933; 5–1941. *ThArts* 4–1933; 5–1933; 8–1942; 10–1943. *Th. Bk. of the Yr., 1943–44* (Nathan).

RUNNIN' DE TOWN (1930). Touring revue. Book by Leigh Whipper. Music and lyrics by J. C. Johnson. Prod. by Aubrey Lyles, apparently on tour. Cast: Ollie Perkins (Sister Rebecca), Marie Young (Sister Matilda), Susie Brown (Missie), Sam Cross (Brother Dixon), Muriel Rahn (Josephine Dixon), Leigh Whipper (Fred Briggs), Paul Ford (Bob Jenkins), Angeline Lawson (Sister Drucilla), Yank Brunson (Yaller), James McPheetus (Foots), Henry Davis (Happy), and Aubrey Lyles.

RUNNIN' SAM (1933). Touring musical revue. Featured Gertrude "Baby" Cox, Edith Wilson, Lorenzo Tucker, Speedy Smith, Lionel Monagas, and Madeline Belt.

RUNNIN' WILD (1923–25). Musical comedy. 2 acts [10 scenes]. Book by Flournoy E. Miller and Aubrey Lyles (Miller & Lyles). Music and lyrics by James P. Johnson and Cecil Mack.

Fast-paced musical, second in popularity only to *Shuffle Along* (1921), both created by and costarring Miller & Lyles, and built around their vaudeville routines. This show was also set in Jimtown, and was another episode in the misadventures of Steve Jenkins and Sam Peck; Peck was the con artist and Jenkins the boob. Here they are run out of town for failing to pay their board bill, and return, in disguise, as mediums. The show was especially praised for its lively singing and dancing, and its best-known contribution was the introduction of the Charleston dance to Bway.

Prod. by °George White, it toured in Washington, DC, and Boston, MA, prior to opening at the Colonial Theatre on upper Bway, Oct. 29, 1923, for 213 perfs., closing eight months later in 1924; with choreography by Lyda Webb. Cast: C. Westley Hill (Uncle Mose), Arthur D. Porter (Uncle Amos), Lionel Monagas (Tom Sharper), Revella Hughes (Ethel Hill), George Stephens (Jack Penn), Paul C. Floyd (Detective Wise), Mattie Wilkes (Mrs. Silas Green), Ina Duncan (Mandy Little), Adelaide Hall (Adelaide), Flournoy Miller (Steve Jenkins), Aubrey Lyles (Sam Peck), Eddie Gray (Willie Live), Tommy Woods (Chief Red

Cap), Billy Andrews (Head Waiter), Elizabeth Welch (Ruth Little), J. Wesley Jeffrey (Silas Green), James H. Woodson (Boat Captain), George Stamper (Sam Slocum), Katherine Yarborough (Lucy Lanky), and Georgette Harvey (Angelina Brown).

Presented at the Bronx Opera House, New York, opening Jan. 19, 1925, for an undetermined run.

Principal songs and musical numbers: +"Open Your Heart" (Stephens), "Log Cabin Days" (Harvey & Male Quartet), "Old Fashioned Love" (Duncan, Porter & Hall), "Ginger Brown" (Hall, Bob Lee [dancer] & Chorus), +"Charleston" (song & dance: Welch & Chorus), "Juba Dance" (Welch & Chorus), "Keep Movin' " (Clarence Robinson), and +"Love Bug." Others: "Set 'Em Sadie," "Red Caps Tappers," "Snowtime," "Roustabouts," "Ghost Recitative," "Lazy Dance," "Pay Day on Levee," "Swanee River," "Song Birds Quartette," "Ghost Ensemble," "Jazz Your Troubles Away," "Sun Kist Rose," "Showtime," "Heart Breaking Joe," "Slow and Easy Goin' Man," "The Sheik of Alabam' Weds a Brown-Skin Vamp," and "Watching the Clock."

Songs marked with a plus sign (+) pub. by Harms, Inc., 1923.

FURTHER REFERENCE: *Billboard* 9–15–1923; 11–10–1923. *NY American* 10–31–1923. *NY Eve. Post* 10–30–1923. *NY News* 11–2–1923. *NY Sun and Globe* 10–31–1923. *NYT* 10–30–1923. *NY Telegram* 10–30–1923. *NY Trib.* 10–30–1923. *NY World* 10–30–1923. *Variety* 8–30–1923; 11–1–1923.

S

SAHDJI, AN AFRICAN BALLET (1925). Dance drama. / / Also a ballet (1930). Scenario written by Richard Bruce (Nugent), in collaboration with Alain Locke (whose name appears on the copyright notice, although he was not originally listed as a collaborator). Ballet music score by William Grant Still. Based on Bruce Nugent's short story, "Sahdji," which originally appeared in Locke's anthology *The New Negro* (1925).

The narrator (a tribal chanter) interprets the action, which is in dance-pantomime. While an African chief is away on a hunting trip, his wife has an affair with his apparent successor. When the chief is killed in the hunt, the wife, by virtue of her marriage vows and the tribal custom, must commit suicide, as part of the funeral rites for her husband. While her lover watches helplessly and in grief, she kills herself with a dagger and falls upon her husband's bier.

First prod. as a dance drama at Howard Univ., Washington, DC, during the late 1920s. Prod. as a ballet by the Eastman School of Music, Rochester, NY, 1932.

Scenario pub. in *Plays of Negro Life* (Alain Locke and Montgomery Gregory, 1927); and by the Eastman School of Music, Univ. of Rochester, Rochester, NY, 1961. Manuscript score of Still's ballet, "in which is laid autobiographical comment in longhand by Alain Locke and Bruce Nugent, who collaborated on the scenario for this dance drama," is located in JWJ/YUL.

SAILORS' JAZZ (1924). Touring musical revue. Prod. by Bob Russell. Cast included Howard Mason, Freeman McGinty, and Elinor Wilson.

ST. LOUIS 'OOMAN (1929). Folk opera. Also called a music drama. Musical score by Will Marion Cook. Libretto by his son, Mercer Cook. About black life on the Mississippi River during the gay nineties. Apparently never prod.

ST. LOUIS WOMAN (1933, 1935, 1946). Subtitled "A Musical Play." 3 acts. Book by Arna Bontemps and Countee Cullen. Adapt. from Bontemps' novel *God Sends Sunday* (1931). Music of Bway version by °Harold Arlen; lyrics by °Johnny Mercer.

Set in a saloon in St. Louis during the 1890s, when black jockeys were in their heyday, this musical tells the story of the turbulent romantic involvement of one of these jockeys, Little Augie (Harold Nicholas), with the saloon keeper, Della Green (Ruby Hill), which causes him to kill his rival, Biglow Brown (Rex Ingram). Pearl Bailey also costarred as Butterfly, an earthy barmaid who sings two of the show's most memorable songs.

First prod. by the Gilpin Players at the Karamu Theatre in Cleveland, Nov. 22–26, 1933, for 5 perfs.; revived by the same group June 5–9, 1935, for 5 perfs.

Prod. on Bway, after an out-of-town tryout, at the Martin Beck Theatre, March 30–July 6, 1946, for 115 perfs.; dir. by °Rouben Mamoulian. Cast: Ruby Hill, Harold Nicholas, Rex Ingram, Pearl Bailey, Juanita Hall (Leah), Robert Pope (Barfoot), Fayard Nicholas (Barney), June Hawkins (Lila), Louis Sharp (Slim), Elwood Smith (Ragsdale), Merritt Smith (Pembroke), Charles Welch (Jasper), Maude Russell (The Hostess), J. Mardo Brown (Drum Major), Milton J. Williams (Mississippi), Frank Green (Dandy Dave), Joseph Eady (Jackie), Yvonne Coleman (Celestine), Herbert Coleman (Piggie), Lorenzo Fuller (Joshua), Milton Wood (Mr. Hopkins), Creighton Thompson (Preacher), and Carrington Lewis (Waiter).

Prod. in a second musical version entitled *Free and Easy*, 1959.

Songs and musical numbers: "Li'l Augie Is a Natural Man" (Badfoot), "Any Place I Hang My Hat Is Home" (Della), "I Feel My Luck Comin' Down" (Augie), "True Love" (Lila), "Legalize My Name" (Butterfly), "Cake Walk Your Lady," "Come Rain or Come Shine" (Della & Augie), "Chinquapin Bush" (Children), "We Shall Meet to Part, No Never" (Piggie), "Lullaby" (Della), "Leavin' Time" (funeral scene: Choral Group), "A Woman's Prerogative" (Butterfly), "Ridin' on the Moon" (Augie & Ensemble), "Least That's My Opinion" (Badfoot), and "Come On, Li'l Augie" (Ensemble).

Orig. cast recording by Capitol (DW 2742), 1946, reissued in 1947. Libretto pub. in *Blk. Th.: A Twentieth Century Collection of the Work of Its Best Playwrights* (comp. by Lindsay Patterson; New York: Dodd, Mead, 1971). Libretto also in Schomburg and FTP/GMU.

FURTHER REFERENCE: Alkire diss. *Cath. World* 5–1946. *Commonweal* 4–19–1946. *Complete Bk. of the Am. Mus. Th.* (Ewen). *Forum* 6–1946. *Life* 4–10–1946. *Modern Mus.* 4–1946. *Newswk* 5–15–1946. *NYorker* 4–6–1946. *NYT* 4–1–1946; 6–2–1946; 7–3–1946. *Phylon* 2nd qtr. 1946; 2nd qtr. 1947. *Pitts. Courier* 7–15–1946; 7–22–1946. *Sat. Rev.* 4–27–1946. *ThArts* 8–1946. *Time* 4–8–1946. *Variety* 4–3–1946. *World of Mus. Comedy* (Green).

SALLY IN OUR ALLEY (1902). White-oriented musical comedy. 2 acts. Book and lyrics by °George Hobart. Music by °Ludwig Englander. With two interpolated songs—one by Bob Cole, James Weldon Johnson, and J. Rosamond Johnson; the other by Bert Williams and George Walker.

Tells the story of a lively, good-hearted Jewish girl nicknamed "Sally" (whose real name is Sarah), focusing on her relationships with her father, her friends, and the people in her neighborhood whom she tries to help when they get into trouble.

Prod. at the Broadway Theatre, New York, opening Aug. 29, 1902, for 67 perfs.; starring °Marie Cahill as Sally and °Dan McAvoy as her father.

Cahill introduced the hit song of the evening and the turn of the century, "Under the Bamboo Tree," by Cole and the Johnson Brothers. The Williams and Walker song was "When It's All Goin' Out, and Nothin' Comin' In." Both songs pub. by Joseph W. Stern, New York; copy of the former in Moorland-Spingarn; the latter is pub. in *Nobody* (Charters, pp. 85–87).

FURTHER REFERENCE: *BesPls 1899–1909. BlkMagic* (Hughes & Meltzer).

SAMBO (1969). Subtitled "A Black Opera with White Spots." Previously subtitled "A Nigger Opera." 2 acts. Music by Ron Steward and Neal Tate. Lyrics by Tate.

Adapted characters from children's fairy tales to depict the black man's feeling of alienation from white society.

First prod. by La Mama Experimental Theatre Club, New York, opening June 14, 1969. Prod. as an indoor prodn. by the New York Shakespeare Festival (NYSF) Public Theatre, opening Dec. 12, 1969. Revived as an indoor prodn. by NYSF Mobile Theatre and presented at parks and playgrounds of the five boroughs of New York City, July 14–Aug. 8, 1970; dir. by Michael Schultz. The predominantly black cast (racial identities not certain) included Ron Steward (Sambo), Veronica Redd (Bo Peep), George Turner (Jack Horney [*sic*]), Judy White (Untogether Cinderella), Jane Stewart (Miss Sally Muffat [*sic*]), Sandi Morris (Tiger Lady), and Joe Darby (Tiger Man).

Musicians included Margaret Harris, Fred Waits, Ted Dunbar, Reggie Johnson, Hal Vick, and Wood Shaw.

FURTHER REFERENCE: *NYorker* 1–3–1970. *NYT* 12–22–1969; 1–11–1970; 7–23–1970; 7–24–1970.

SAMBO JONES IN NEW YORK (1917). Touring vaudeville show. Prod. by and starring dancer/comedian Seymour James and straight man Wallace Stovall (billed as James & Stovall).

SAMMY ON BROADWAY (1975). Celebrity one-person show, starring Sammy Davis, Jr., assisted by a few other artists. Presented at the Uris Theatre, New York, opening April 23, 1975, for a 2-week run.

SAM T. JACK'S CREOLE [BURLESQUE] COMPANY. See *THE CREOLE SHOW.*

SANDHOG (1954). Musical. Prod. in New York City during the 1954–55 season. Concerned the hardships endured by construction workers involved in the building of New York's Hudson River Tunnel during the 1930s. One of the laborers was portrayed by black actor Rodester Timmons.
FURTHER REFERENCE: *Phylon* 3rd qtr. 1955.

SANDS OF HONOLULU (1925). Touring show. Prod. by and starring comedian Sandy Burns. Cast included Sam "Bilo" Russell, Bonnie B. Drew, and Lee & Wise.

SANDY BURNS AND BILO (1930). Touring show. Prod. by and costarring comedians Sandy Burns and Sam "Bilo" Russell. Also in the cast was George Wiltshire.

SAVAGE RHYTHM (1931–32). Play with music. By °Harry Hamilton and °Norman Foster. Music and lyrics by James P. Johnson and Cecil Mack.
    Mystery-melodrama about a Harlem singer whose mother and grandmother are conjure women. She returns to her home in the South, where a murder occurs, and she discovers that she has inherited her family's power and is able to reveal the murderer.
    Prod. at the John Golden Theatre, New York, Dec. 31, 1931, for 12 perfs., ending in Jan. 1932; dir. by °Robert Burton. Cast: Inez Clough [at some point replaced by Vivian (Viviennne) Baber] (Orchid, a Harlem singer), Georgette Harvey (Her Sister), Mamie Cartier (Conjure Woman), Juano Hernandez (Orchid's hometown beau, Ernest Sweetback [disclosed as the murderer]), Vivian Baber (Sweetback's wife?), Joe Sobers and Raymond Bishop (Grandchildren), Olive Wanamaker (Flirt), John Robinson (A Young Neighbor), J. W. Mobley (Parson), Al F. Watts (Barbecue Man), James Daniels and Alvin Childress (Juveniles), and Fred Miller (Church Elder).

SEASON'S REASONS (1977). Musical. Written and dir. by Ron Milner. Music by Charles Mason. Prod. by the New Federal Theatre, New York, July 14, 1977, for 18 perfs.

SEEING CHINATOWN (1919). Musical revue. Prod. by the Quality Amusement Co.; staged by Jesse A. Shipp. Presented at the Lafayette Theatre, New York, and possibly on tour of theatres controlled by the company.

SELMA (1975). Dramatic musical. 2 acts [17 scenes]. Book, music, lyrics, and musical and choral arrangements by Thomas Isaiah Butler (also known as Tommy Butler).

Described by the Inner City Cultural Center's *ICCC Calendar* (5–26–1975), as a "celebration of the life and works of Dr. Martin Luther King, Jr., which tells the story of the Civil Rights Struggle of the '50s and '60s."

Co-prod. by the author and the ICCC, Los Angeles, opening March 16, 1975; dir. by Cliff Roquemore. Moved uptown to the Huntington-Hartford Theatre, Los Angeles, in 1976, backed by Redd Foxx Productions. Closed, after a nationwide tour, in 1977. Prod. Off-Bway by the New Federal Theatre, at the Louis Abrons Arts for Living Center, Feb. 16–March 4, 1984, for 15 perfs.; dir. by Roquemore. Musical dir., Neal Tate. The integrated cast (racial identities not certain) included Ernie Banks (Rev. Abernathy), James Curt Bergwall (Rev. Graetz), Jonathan Carroll (Young Boy & Black Panther), Daryl E. Copeland (Drunk & Black Panther), Cora Lee Day (Mama Sweets), J. Lee Flynn (Sheriff Barnside), Pat Franklin (Jackie, Nurse & Klansman), Michael French (Bus Driver, Deputy & Ensemble), Rita Graham-Knighton (Coretta), Joyce Griffen (Child & Klansman), Leverne (Ensemble), Paul M. Luksch (Deputy), George E. Morton III (Tillman), Cynthia I. Pearson (Teacher & Klansman), Sherrie Strange (Rosa), Pamela Tyson (Miss Anne & Ensemble), and Ronald Wyche (Woody).

Songs and musical numbers: "Nature's Child," "Working in the Name of King," "Celebration," "Martin Martin," "Niggerwoman," "Precious Memories," "The Time Is Now," "Wash Your Sins," "Pull Together," "You're My Love," "Isn't It Wonderful," "Freedom Liberation," "Jesus Christ," "Tell Us Martin," "Where's That Martin Boy?," "Do You Lie?," "Pick Up Your Weapon," "Boycott Trial Song," "I Can Feel Him," "When Will It End," "Klansmen Song," "Prison Song," "Higher," "I Hate Colored People," "Children of Love," "Poison Hiding," "Burn," "Listen to Me Jesus," "Selma," "Selma March," and "We Shall Overcome."

THE SENATOR (1917). Tabloid musical. Written and prod. by Billy King. Presented at the Grand Theatre, Chicago; with members of the Billy King Stock Co. Cast included King, Theresa Burroughs Brooks, and Gertrude Saunders.

SENEGAMBIAN CARNIVAL (1898) / / A reworking of materials from *Clorindy, the Origin of the Cakewalk* (1898). Touring ragtime musical show. With contributions by Bert Williams, George Walker, Will Marion Cook, and Paul Laurence Dunbar.

Williams & Walker's first black-authored show, built around *Clorindy*, a musical comedy sketch written especially for the comedy team by Cook (music) and Dunbar (lyrics). *Clorindy* had been successfully prod. on Bway earlier during the summer of 1898, with Ernest Hogan in the starring role after Williams & Walker were unable to appear. When the show closed in New York, the two comedians were invited to take it on the road. Realizing that *Clorindy* was only one hour long, they expanded it by the addition of a number of specialty acts, and the cakewalking numbers (the main feature of *Clorindy*) were exploited by the addition of 20 more dancers than there were on Bway.

The specialty acts, comprising the first part, included comedy routines and songs by the two stars; acrobatic performances by Goggins & Davis; feats of magic by Black Carl (Carl Dante); a sister act by Ada Overton (later Mrs. George Walker) and Grace Halliday, both also in the Chorus; songs by Hodges & Launchmere; and instrumental selections by the Mallory Bros.

Clorindy was presented as an afterpiece, as it had been on Bway. The orig. stars (Hogan and Belle Davis) were replaced by Williams & Walker, Abbie Mitchell (later Mrs. Will Marion Cook), and Lottie Thompson (later Mrs. Bert Williams). Other cast members included Maizie (or Mazie) Brooks, Henry Williams, Lord Bonnie, William Elkins, Charles L. Moore, and Mamie Emerson. Harry T. Burleigh led the orchestra in the Boston prodn.; however, Will Marion Cook apparently replaced him on the road as musical dir., conducting a small ragtime orchestra.

Prod. by °Lederer & McConnell (George W. Lederer and William McConnell) in the fall of 1898. Opened in Boston at the Boston Theatre, Sept. 5–7; then moved to Proctor's Theatre in New York City for a short run. Also played in Philadelphia, Washington, DC, Cincinnati, and Chicago. However, it did not draw the expected audiences and quickly closed—possibly for the reason given by Tom Fletcher (*100 Yrs*, p. 45), that "apparently the public was not too [well] acquainted with the word Senegambian"—a term of African reference, which Williams & Walker had used the previous year (1897), when they played an engagement at the Empire Musical Hall in London, billed as the "Tobasco Senegambians."

It is presumed that *Senegambian Carnival* used most of *Clorindy*'s songs and musical numbers (as given in the main entry for that show). "The Hottes' Coon in Dixie" was sung with great success by Walker. One song by Williams & Walker, "Why Don't You Get a Lady of Your Own," was also very successful.

THE SEPIA AND SWING REVOLUTION (early 1940s). Musical revue. By Noble Sissle and Eubie Blake (Sissle & Blake). Toured USO circuits at the beginning of World War II.

SEPIA STAR (1977). Musical. Book by Ed Bullins. Music and lyrics by °Mildred Kayden. Tells the story of an early black blues singer. Prod. at Stage 73, New York, Aug. 1977.

SEPIA VAGABONDS (1930). Touring revue. Featured Mamie Smith, Eloise Bennett, Kay Mason, Buddy Green, Alec Lovejoy, Bernice Bennett, and the Virginia Four (Quartet).

SEPTEMBER MORN (1920). Musical comedy. 3 acts. Touring show prod. by Arthur Gillespie and the Panama Amusement Co. Apparently conceived by Shelton Brooks, who also dir. the orchestra and chorus, and costarred. The plot turns on a scheme to steal a famous painting, *September Morn*, to have it altered by an artist to make it resemble the face of a Parisian dancer, and to use it to advertise the dancer's American debut by pretending that she was the subject of the painting. After a number of complications, the theft is discovered and the culprits exposed.

SERGEANT HAM / / Orig. title: *Sergeant Ham of the 13th District* (1917–19). Musical revue in at least 2 eds. Conceived and prod. by Perry "Mule" Bradford, who also costarred. *1917 ed*. Co-prod. under orig. title by Bradford & Jeanette. Cast included Bradford & Jeanette, Hatch & Hatch, Mason & Brown, Billy McLauren, blues singer Mamie Smith, and Elsie Perry. *1919 ed*. Prod. under present title by Bradford alone. Cast included Marion Bradford, Ruth Coleman, Jerome Johnson, Gladys Thompson, Charley Young, Larabell Wise, Anita Spencer, and the Dixie Four.

7–11 / / Also *Seven-Eleven* (c. 1922–c. 1926). Musical revue. Book by Barrington Carter, Garland Howard, and Sam Cook. Music by Speedy Smith.

Song-and-dance show which, according to *Pitts. Courier* (12–21–1929), featured "the hardworking 'Speedy' Smith, Mae Brown, and Garland Howard, a delux [*sic*] dancing combination; 'Chink' the best oriental impersonator of his day, and a chorus which, while not composed of high class beauties, stood as one of the best-trained group [*sic*] of girls this writer [William G. Nunn] has ever seen."

Apparently toured the black theatrical circuits, 1922–23, prod. by Barrington Carter. Prod. by °Jack Goldberg on the white Columbia Circuit, c. 1925–26. Cast of the *1923 ed*. Speedy Smith (Jack Storal), Garland Howard (Hotstuff Jackson), Rebecca "Dink" Thomas (Elder Berry), Bill [or Will] Grundy (Diamond Joe); Others: Evon Robinson, Mae Brown, Sam Cook, Barrington Carter, Elenora Wilson, Eddie Gray, and a chorus of over 20 singers.
FURTHER REFERENCE: *Billboard* (J. A. Jackson's Page) 1–28–1922; 11–11–1922.

SHADES OF HADES (1922–23). Musical revue. 2 acts [7 scenes]. Book by Tim Owsley. Music and lyrics by Dave Payton.

About a woman's attempt to cure her husband of jealousy by causing him to lose his memory. During the absence of his memory, his soul apparently goes to Hades (or Hell). The same action that causes his memory loss eventually restores it.

Prod. by the Lafayette Players, at the Lafayette Theatre, New York, 1922; dir. by Julia Rector. Then apparently went on tour. Cast of the 1923 ed.: Tim Owsley (Sam Green, Pullman Porter), B. B. Joyner (John Drinkmore), Laura Bowman (Green's Wife, a lawyer), Sidney Kirkpatrick (Satan); Others: Hester

Kenton, T. B. Thomas, Walter Richardson, Richard Gregg, Charles Moore, Ollie [or Allie] Smith, Mary Bradford, Earl Simms, Charles Grundy, Ora Johnson, and Isadora Mitchell.

Songs and musical numbers included "Carolina" (Thomas), "The Nashville Blues" (Kenton), and "Holiday in Hades Today."

SHADES OF HARLEM (1984). Musical retrospective. By Jeree Palmer (Mrs. Adam Wade). Frank Owns, musical dir. A re-creation of Harlem's famous Cotton Club, which flourished during the 1920s. Prod. at the Village Gate, New York City, Aug. 21, 1984–April 20, 1985, for 229 perfs.; dir. by Mical Whitaker. Cast included Palmer, Branice McKenzie, and Ty Stephens. Toured as a National Black Touring Circuit prodn., 1987–88. Included songs of Duke Ellington, Eubie Blake, Billie Holiday, and Kerry Mills, with some orig. songs by the musical dir., Frank Owns.

SHADOWS ON THE MOON (early 1930s). An allegorical musical dealing with the depression in Heaven. Book by Ralph Matthews. Music by Rivers D. Chambers. Prod. by Sheldon D. Hoskins and the Adam and Eve Prodn. Co. in Baltimore, MD, prior to 1934. (See also *Adam and Eva, Inc.*)

SHAKE, RATTLE AND ROLL (1927). Touring revue. Featured Jones & Jones, Viola McCoy, Westley Hill, Bobby Perry, George Hughes, George Stafford, Hatch & Hatch, and toe dancer "Honey" Brown.

SHAKE YOUR FEET (1923, 1925, 1929). Musical revue in at least 3 eds. Touring song-and-dance show which featured comedian Joe Carmouche in all three eds.

1923 ed. Prod. by Will Mastin (Sammy Davis, Jr.'s uncle), who also costarred. Cast included Charles Pugh (featured comedian), Vergie Richards, Joe Carmouche, Cleo Mitchell, and Harris & Holly (comedy sketch artists), who perfd. in a sketch entitled 'Push 'Em and Pull 'Em.'

1925 ed. Apparently prod. by Carmouche, who also costarred as second comedian. Cast also included Zachariah White (principal comedian), Billy McOwens (comedian), "Baby" Ernestine (child singer), Willie Oglesby (dancer), Susie Wroten (toe dancer), and Robert Wright (dancer).

1929 ed. Co-prod. by Carmouche and Cleo Mitchell, who also costarred. Cast included Van Epps and Beatie (singers/dancers), Grant Ross (tap dancer), Mattie Brown (singer), Bill Gunn and Henry Williams, Sue Parker (singer), Edna Young (toe dancer), and Mattie Hedgeman (dancer).

SHARLEE (1923). White-oriented musical comedy. 2 acts. Book by °Harry L. Cort and °George E. Stoddard. Music by C. Luckeyth Roberts. Lyrics by Alex C. Rogers. About a nightclub singer's efforts to find love and marriage. Prod. at Daly's (?) Theatre, New York, opening Nov. 22, 1923, with an all-white cast. Only one Rogers & Roberts song from this show has been identified: "Heart Beats"; copy in Schomburg.

SH-BOOM! (1984). Musical show. Music by Wilex Brown, Jr. and Eric Tait. Takes place during the rock and roll era of the 1950s and 1960s, and concerns the commercial takeover of black popular music (rhythm and blues) by white groups. Prod. at Symphony Space, New York City, Nov. 1984; featuring Jimmy Keyes and the Chords.

SHEBA (1972). Musical. 1 act. By Hazel Bryant. Music by Jimmy Justice. Apparently about the biblical queen who tested the wisdom of King Solomon. First prod. by the Afro-American Total Theatre, at the Riverside Church Theatre, Dec. 11–17, 1972. The premiere was sponsored by Guyana's ambassador to the United States, Frederick Talbot, and his wife. The perf. was attended by over 30 African, Asian, and Latin ambassadors and some 150 black American artists and celebrities in every area of the arts. Presented at the Third Annual Black Theatre Festival, at the Brooklyn Academy of Music, 1973. Remained in repertory until April 1974. Unpub. script in Schomburg.

THE SHEIK OF HARLEM (1923–24). Musical comedy. Harlem show, written and prod. by Irvin C. Miller and Donald Heywood. Described by Bruce Kellner (*HarlRenD*, p. 321) as "a popular Lafayette Theatre show, in which a girl falls in love with a macho type who disguises himself as an overdressed sissy." Prod. by the Lafayette Theatre in Harlem, 1923 and 1924.

   1923 ed. Cast included Irvin C. Miller, Quintard Miller, Paul Bass, Billy Mills, Edith Spencer, Hattie Reavis, Bessie Arthur, Ida Anderson, Alonzo Fenderson, and Will A. Cook. One song from this ed. was "It Don't Pay to Love a Northern Man in from the South," sung by Hattie Reavis to Will Cook.

   1924 ed. Perfd. by the cast of Irvin C. Miller's *Liza* company, with Miller and Ethel Ridley among the featured players.
FURTHER REFERENCE: *Messenger* 9–1923.

THE SHOO-FLY REGIMENT (1905–7). Musical comedy, also called an operetta. 3 acts. Book by Bob Cole. Lyrics and music by Cole and J. Rosamond Johnson. Additional lyrics by James Weldon Johnson.

   Because of its well-written book and musical score, this show was called by James Weldon Johnson "the first true Negro operetta" (*BlkManh* [Johnson], pp. 222–23). It concerned the participation and heroism of black soldiers in the Spanish-American War. Act I takes place at Tuskegee Institute, an industrial school in Alabama, where Hunter Wilson, a young graduate (played by Cole), is about to become a teacher when the Spanish-American War breaks out. Against the advice of the school board, his family, friends, and sweetheart, he volunteers for service with a Negro regiment that is being recruited for service in the Philippine Islands. Act II concerns the activities of the regiment in the Philippines, where Hunter becomes a hero. In Act III, he returns triumphantly, along with his fellow soldiers, marries his sweetheart, and resumes his intention to become a teacher.

First prod. by Cole & Johnson in Washington, DC, fall 1905; then went on tour throughout the South. Opened on Bway at the Bijou Theatre, Aug. 6, 1906, for 15 perfs. Also presented at the Park Theatre in New York. Cast: Bob Cole (Hunter Wilson) and J. Rosamond Johnson (Edward Jackson) as principal comedians and members of the Shoo-Fly Regiment, Arthur Talbot (Professor Maxwell), Frank De Lyons (Williamson), Nettie Glenn (Virginia), Henry Gant (Uncle July Jackson), Elizabeth Williams (Aunt Phoebe Jackson), Fannie Wise (Rose Maxwell), Andrew Tribble (Ophelia Snow, a spinster), Sam Lucas (Brother Doolittle, member of the Board of Education), Wesley Jenkins (Brother Dooless, Doolittle's partner), Molly Dill (Dilsey Lumpkins), Arthur Ray (Farmer Randolph, Napoleon Bonaparte Lumpkins & A Filipino Spy), Anna Cook Pankey (Lieutenant Dixon), William Phelps (Orderly), Edgar Connors (juvenile), Tom Brown and [Miss] Siren Navarro (comedy team), Matt Marshall (singer), Henry Amos, Daisy Brown, and Inez Clough.

Songs and musical numbers: According to NY Age (6–6–1907), "[J. Rosamond] Johnson furnishe[d] . . . a pleasing portion of the entertainment with his clever songs and piano playing." Principal songs include +"Floating Down the Nile" (Johnson & Johnson), +"I Can't Think of Nothin' in the Wide, Wide World But You" (Cole & J. R. Johnson; advertised as the hit of the show), +"On the Gay Luneta" (Cole & James Reese Europe), "Sugar Babe" (Cole & J. R. Johnson), "There's Always Something Wrong" (Cole & J. R. Johnson), +"Who Do You Love?" (sung by Tribble & Marshall), "If Adam Hadn't Seen the Apple Tree" (sung by Cole), "Bode of Education" (sung by Lucas), "Little Girl" (sung by J. R. Johnson & Chorus), "The Ghost of Deacon Brown" (sung by Cole & Chorus), and "Don't You Want to Be My Little Bear."

Songs marked with a plus sign (+) are pub. by Joseph W. Stern, New York; copies in Moorland-Spingarn. Libretto in Moorland-Spingarn. Musical score in MC/LC.

FURTHER REFERENCE: BlkMusTh (Woll). Just Before Jazz (Riis). NY Dramatic Mirror 6–15–1907. Riis diss. ThMag 9–1907. Shoo-Fly Regiment folder in Harvard Theatre Collection. Clipping scrapbook in TC/NYPL.

SHOW BOAT (1927–28, 1946, 1971, 1983). Musical drama. Also called an operetta. 2 acts [15 scenes]. Book by °Oscar Hammerstein II. Based on °Edna Ferber's novel by the same title (1926). Music by °Jerome Kern.

One of the longest-running, most influential, and most often revived musicals of the 1920s, which departed from the standard musical comedy format of the shows that preceded it to become the first successful musical play. It was also the first major musical show to deal with the problem of miscegenation—or interracial marriage between blacks and whites—in the story of Julie, a mulatto passing for white. This show provided the most famous song hit ever written for a black performer, "Old Man River," which was sung in successive productions by Jules Bledsoe, Paul Robeson, Kenneth Spencer, and William Warfield. It has also been included in the repertoire of almost every bass or baritone concert singer since it was first presented. Although its treatment of blacks seems outdated today, for its time the show dealt sympathetically with the plight of southern blacks, portraying them realistically as victims of oppression, rather than as inherently inferior.

Set in the 1890s, *Show Boat* tells the story of the members of a riverboat show troupe, focusing mainly on the romantic difficulties of two female singers—one (Magnolia), the daughter of the showboat captain who marries a professional gambler, and the other (Julie), the leading singer, a mulatto passing for white, whose racial identity is revealed after she has married a white man who truly loves her, and who stands by her even when she is exposed as part black. Julie is then forced to leave the show, and Magnolia takes over her singing role. For some reason, Julie's husband later deserts her, and she becomes a nightclub torch-singer who drowns her sorrows in alcohol. Two of the most memorable songs from *Show Boat* are sung by Julie, expressing her undying devotion to her husband: "Can't Help Lovin' Dat Man" and "Bill." Magnolia is also eventually deserted by her husband, who, soon after their marriage and the birth of their daughter, loses everything through gambling; and only at the end of the story do they become reunited.

The "genuine" black characters in the cast include Joe, a dockworker on the Mississippi levee, who is portrayed as a sort of earthy philosopher who comments on the events as they unfold—especially through the lyrics of the various songs he sings. His wife, Queenie, a cheerful cook, is a more stereotypical domestic who knows her place and accepts it, but is treated with dignity and respect by the whites. The members of the chorus function in singing, dancing, and atmospheric roles as stevedores, their women, maids, waiters, and entertainers.

First presented on Bway by °Florenz Ziegfeld at the Ziegfeld Theatre, opening Dec. 27, 1927, for 572 perfs.; dir. by Hammerstein. Principal cast included °Norma Terris (Magnolia), °Helen Morgan (Julie), Jules Bledsoe (Joe), and Tess Gardella (Queenie). After a successful tour, this prodn. returned to New York at the Casino Theatre for 180 perfs., with Paul Robeson replacing Bledsoe. Afterwards, it continued to tour for three months, with Bledsoe replacing Robeson.

Opened in London at the Drury Lane Theatre, May 3, 1928, for 350 perfs. With °Marie Burke (Julie), Paul Robeson (Joe), and Alberta Hunter (Queenie).

Revived on Bway, at the Ziegfeld Theatre, Jan. 5, 1946, for 418 perfs. With °Carol Bruce (Julie), Kenneth Spencer (Joe), Helen Dowdy (Queenie), Pearl Primus (Dahomey Queen), and Talley Beatty (dancer).

Revived in London, at the Adelphi Theatre, July 29, 1971, for 910 perfs. With °Cleo Laine (Julie), Thomas Carey (Joe), and Ena Cabayo (Queenie).

Revived on Bway, April 24, 1983, at the Uris Theatre, for 73 perfs. and 5 previews. With black actress Lonette McKee (Julie), Bruce Hubbard (Joe), and Karla Burns (Queenie).

Film versions: Prod. by Universal, with Stepin Fetchit, 1929. Prod. by Universal, with Paul Robeson and Hattie McDaniel, 1936. Prod. by MGM, with William Warfield, 1951.

Songs and musical numbers: "Cotton Blossom," "Make Believe," "Ol' Man River," "Can't Help Lovin' Dat Man," "Life Upon the Wicked Stage," " 'Till Good Luck Comes My Way," "You Are Love," "Why Do I Love You?," "I Might Fall Back on You," "Bill," "After the Ball," and "Dance Away the Night" (London only).

Libretto pub. by Chappelle & Co., Ltd., London, 1934.

FURTHER REFERENCE: Alkire diss. *Ency. of the Mus. Th.* (Green). *NY Herald Trib.* 1–7–1946. *Phylon* 2nd qtr. 1946. *Show Business Illus.* 10–3–1961. *ThArts* 4–1957; 11–1960. *World of Mus. Comedy* (Green).

SHOW FOLKS (1920). Touring show. Written, prod., and composed by songwriter Sidney Perrin. Performed by his High Flyers Co., featuring Iris Hall, George Wiltshire, Willie Richardson, and Jimmie Stewart.

SHUFFLE ALONG (1921–23, 1930, 1932–33, 1952). Musical comedy. 2 acts. Book originally by Flournoy E. Miller and Aubrey Lyles (Miller & Lyles). Lyrics and music originally by Noble Sissle and Eubie Blake (Sissle & Blake). Based on *The Mayor of Dixie,* a musical play by Miller & Lyles (1907).

The best-known, most sensational, and most influential musical up to its time, which was written, prod., directed, and perfd. by blacks, and which set the pattern for black musicals for many years thereafter. The thin plot had its setting in Jimtown in Dixieville on Election Day, and concerned the rivalry between Steve Jenkins and Sam Peck (Miller & Lyles), two ignorant storekeepers and business partners, both running for mayor of the town. The story served only as a framework for the elaborately staged and beautifully costumed musical numbers, the spectacular singing and dancing, the hilarious comedy routines, and the beautiful chorus girls for which the show was noted. The principal song, "I'm Just Wild About Harry," was later used by Harry Truman as his presidential campaign theme song.

Prod. by the Nikko Producing Co. (an all-black corporation), the 1921 ed. was tried out in Harlem, Washington, DC, New Jersey, and Philadelphia, before opening at the Sixty-third Street Musical Hall in New York City (then considered a part of Bway), May 23, 1921, where it remained for 504 perfs. before going on the road for another year, playing in white theatres all across the nation; staged by Walter Brooks. Dances by Charles Davis and Lawrence Deas; musical arrangements by William Vodery; orchestrations by William Grant Still; and orchestra direction by Eubie Blake, who was also "at the piano." Cast: Paul Ford (Jim Williams, Proprietor of Jimtown Hotel), Lottie Gee (Jessie Williams, His Daughter), Gertrude Saunders, replaced by Florence Mills (Ruth Little, Her Chum), Roger Matthews (Harry Walton, Candidate for Mayor), Mattie Wilkes (Mrs. Sam Peck, Suffragette), Noble Sissle (Tom Sharper, Political Boss), Flournoy Miller (Steve Jenkins, Candidate for Mayor), Aubrey Lyles (Sam Peck, Another Candidate for Mayor), Lawrence Deas (Jack Penrose, Detective), C. Westley Hill (Rufus Loose, War Relic), A. E. Baldwin (Soakum Flat, Mayor's Bodyguard), Billy Williams (Strutt, Jimtown Swell), Charles Davis (Uncle Tom), Bob Williams (Old Black Joe), Ina Duncan (Secretary to Mayor); Others: Board of Aldermen, Pedestrians, Traffic Cop, Secretaries, Vamps, Jazz Jasmines, Happy Honeysuckles, Syncopating Sunflowers, and Majestic Magnolias. Josephine Baker, Paul Robeson, and Adelaide Hall were members of the chorus during the run of this show.

Orig. songs and musical numbers: "I'm Just Full of Jazz" (Ruth & Steppers), "Love Will Find a Way" (Ruth & Harry), "Bandanna Days" (An Alderman & Company), "Sing Me to Sleep, Dear Mammy" (Harry & Aldermen), "Honeysuckle Time" (Sharper), "Gypsy Blues" (Jessie, Ruth & Harry), "Shuffle Along" (Pedestrians & Traffic Cop), "I'm Just Wild About Harry" (Jessie & Sunflowers), "Jimtown's Fisticuffs" (Jenkins & Peck), "Syncopated Stenos" (Mayor's Secretaries), "If You've Never Been Vamped by a Brown Skin, You've Never Been Vamped At All" (Jenkins, Peck & Vamps), "Uncle Tom and Old Black Joe" (Tom & Joe), "Everything Reminds Me of You" (Jessie & Harry), "Oriental Blues" (Sharper & Chorus), "I'm Craving for That Kind of Love" (Ruth), "Baltimore Buss" (Sharper & Steppers), and "African Dip" (Peck & Jenkins). Most songs pub. by M. Witmark, New York, 1921; copies in Moorland-Spingarn.

Shuffle Along of 1930. 2 acts [12 scenes]. Book by Flournoy E. Miller. Music by James P. Johnson and Thomas "Fats" Waller. Lyrics by Andy Razaf. A new version by Miller (without Lyles) and new songwriters, set in Ragtown, Virginia, the plot of which has not been located. Scenes: Act I, Scene 1— Construction of Ragtown School; Scene 2—Main Street of Ragtown; Scene 3— Exterior of Punk Willis' Home; Scene 4—Willow Tree; Scene 5—Main Street; Scene 6—Banjo Land. Act II, Scene 1—Equal Got League; Scene 2—Main Street, Ragtown; Scene 3—Interior of Punk Willis' Home; Scene 4—Valaida Snow; Scene 5—Ragtown Cemetery; Scene 6—Exterior of Punk Willis' Home. Cast: James Lillard (Green Ford, Foreman), Johnnie Virgel (Mose), Margaret Simms (Bess), Allen Virgel (Billy), Valaida Snow (Valaida), Hilda Perleno (Ruth), [An unknown performer posing as] Mr. Miller (Punk Willis), Billie Young (Mrs. Willis), [An unknown performer posing as] Mr. Lyles (Sam Peck), Derby Wilson (Jimmy Strutt), Howard Elmore (Tommee Taps), Herman Listerino (Tom), Herman Jenkins (Sambo), Herman Edwards (Andy); Others: Male Chorus, Ragtime Belles, Laborers, Virginia Four, and the Three Brown Spots. Songs and musical numbers: "Work, Work, Work" (Male Chorus & Ragtime

Belles), "Teasing Baby" (Perleno & Virgel), "Chocolate Bar" (Simms & Virgel), "Labor Day Parade" (Company), "Porter's Love Song" (Snow & Virgel), "Sippi" (Perleno), "Brothers" (Virgel & Male Chorus), "Willow Tree" (Snow & Chorus), Dance: "Taps and Wings" (Three Brown Spots), "Banjo Land" (Ensemble), "Shufflin' " (Virgel & Belles), "Rhythm Man" (Snow, Girls & Boys), "Loving Honey" (Perleno & Belles), "Taps" (Wilson), Dance (Miller's Dancing Girls), "Spirituals" (Virginia Four), "Poor Little Me" (Snow), and "Go Harlem" (Ensemble).

Shuffle Along of 1933. 2 acts [8 scenes]. Book by Flournoy E. Miller. Music by Eubie Blake. Lyrics by Noble Sissle. A new version by three of the four orig. authors (after the death of Aubrey Lyles). The plot was changed from a mayoral race to the problems of financing a molasses factory. The setting was Jimtown, Mississippi. Scenes: Act I, Scene 1—City Square; Scene 2—Caesar Jones' Cabin; Scene 3—U-Eat-Em Molasses Factory. Act II, Scene 1—City Square; Scene 2—Sugar Cane Field; Scene 3—Office of U-Eat-Em Molasses Factory; Scene 4—Ben's Taxi Stand; Scene 5—Roof of U-Eat-Em Molasses Factory. Prod. by Mawin Productions, Inc., at the Mansfield Theatre, New York, Dec. 26, 1932, for 17 perfs.; staged by Walter Brooks. Cast: Lavada Carter (Edith Wilkes), Marshall Rodgers (Taxi Ben), Edith Wilson (Mrs. Jones), Mantan Moreland (Caesar Jones), Louise Williams (A Customer), George McClennon (Dave Coffey), Noble Sissle (Tom Sharp), Flournoy Miller (Steve Jenkins), Clarence Robinson (Harry Walton), Vivienne Baber (Alice Walker), Howard Hill (Sam), Taps Miller (Farmer Taps), Joe Willis (Sheriff), James Arnold (Summons Server), Catherine Brooks (Stenographer), Herman Reed (Office Boy), Ida Brown (Telephone Girl), Romaine Johns (Shipping Clerk), and Adolph Henderson (Waiter). Songs and musical numbers: "Labor Day Parade," "Sing and Dance Your Troubles Away," "You Don't Look for Love," "Bandanna Ways," "Keep Your Chin Up," "Breakin' 'Em In," "In the Land of Sunny Sunflowers," "Sugar Babe," "Chickens Come Home to Roost," "Waiting for the Whistle to Blow," "Saturday Afternoon," "Here 'Tis," "Lonesome Man," "Arabian Moon," "If It's Any News to You," "You've Got to Have Koo Wah," and "Reminiscing (with Sissle and Blake)."

Shuffle Along of 1952. 2 acts [8 scenes]. Book by Flournoy E. Miller and Paul Gerard Smith. Lyrics by Noble Sissle. Music by Eubie Blake. An updated version of the orig. show, with the time changed to the end of World War II. Scenes: Act I, Scene 1—A castle in Northern Italy, Spring 1945; Scene 2—An Alpine pass; Scene 3—A street in Genoa; Scene 4—A cafe. Act II, Scene 1—A fashion salon in New York City; Scene 2—A Street; Scene 3—An office; Scene 4—A pier. Prod. unsuccessfully at the Broadway Theatre in New York City, opening May 8, 1952, for 4 perfs.; staged by George Hale and Paul Gerard Smith. Choreography by Henry LeTang. Cast: William Dillard (Bugler), James E. Wall (M/Sgt.), Thelma Carpenter (Cpl. Betty Lee), Avon Long (Lt. Jim Crocker), Earl Sydnor (Col. Alexander Popham), William McDaniel (Major Joseph Gantt), T. S. Krigarin (Capt. Frederick Graham), Delores Martin (Sgt.

Lucy Duke), Leslie Scott (Cpl. Louie Bauche), Napoleon Reed (Capt. Harry Gaillard), Flournoy Miller (Pvt. Cyphus Brown), Hamtree Harrington (Pvt. Longitude Lane), Laurence Watson (Chaplain), Mable Lee (Mable), Henry Sherwood (Fifeto), Louise Woods (Rosa Pasini), Harry Meller (SS Trooper), Urylee Leonardos (Laura Popham), Marie Young (Sgt. Mabel Powers), Sara Lou Harris (Margie), Noble Sissle and Eubie Blake (Themselves). Songs and musical numbers: "Falling," "City Called Heaven," "Bongo-Boola," "Swanee Moon," "Rhythm of America," "Farewell with Love," "I'm Just Wild About Harry," "Love Will Find a Way," "It's the Gown That Makes the Gal That Makes the Guy," "Bitten by Love," "You Can't Overdo a Good Thing," "My Day," and "Give It Love."

An archival re-creation of the 1921 prodn., entitled *Sissle & Blake's Shuffle Along*, featuring members of the orig. cast, was made by Recorded Anthology of American Music, Inc., and released by New World Records, 1976.

FURTHER REFERENCE: *AnthANT* (Patterson). *BlkDr* (Mitchell). *BlkMagic* (Hughes & Meltzer). *BlkMusTh* (Woll). *Broadway's Greatest Musicals* (Laufe). *Commonweal* 5–30–1952. *Complete Bk. of the Am. Mus. Th.* (Ewen). *Crisis* 9–1922; 5–1923. *DBlkTh* (Woll). *National Mag.* 10–1922. *NegAmTh* (Isaacs). *NewRepub* 7–6–1921. *NY Clipper* 5–25–1921. *NYorker* 5–17–1952. *NYT* 5–23–1921; 12–27–1932; 5–9–1952. *Phylon* 2nd qtr. 1950. *Reminiscing with Sissle and Blake* (Kimball & Bolcom). *ThMag* 8–1921. *Time* 5–19–1952.

SHU-SHIN-SHI (1925). Touring show. Prod. by Johnny Lee Long, who co-starred in the show with his Creole Chorus.

SIDEWALKS OF HARLEM (1930). Musical revue. Harlem show, prod. by Addison Carey and Charles Davis. Cast included John "Rareback" Mason, the Gaines Brothers, Doris Rheubottom, Johnnie Virgel, Struggles & Red, "Washer Board," and Jackie (later "Moms") Mabley.

SILAS GREEN FROM NEW ORLEANS (c. 1903–c. 1953). Orig. concept, book, and lyrics by Salem Tutt Whitney and J. Homer Tutt. Whitney & Tutt eventually shared ownership with Prof. Eph. Williams, a former dog and pony circus owner, who joined with them after losing "all of his [circus] paraphernalia except his dogs and ponies" (J. Homer Tutt, in *Afro-American* [Baltimore] 8–15–1936).

After "a big storm wiped the whole show out" in 1905, Whitney & Tutt gave the music, lyrics, and title of *Silas Green* to Williams, who "salvage[d] [it] out of the mud," and kept it on the road until his death in 1921, after which it was sold to °Thomas Collier. Under Collier's proprietorship, Tim Owsley was producer and S. H. Dudley, Jr., was stage manager during the 1930s. In 1943, the show was brought by °W. P. Jones, one of Collier's partners, and it apparently remained active until sometime in the early 1950s.

Although it toured the South for some fifty years, and was the longest running black show in history, no plot summary has as yet been located by this writer. It apparently centered around the marital difficulties of a philandering husband and his long-suffering, churchgoing wife, and the concern of his nosy neighbors and friends about his outrageous conduct. While she stays at home doing the house-keeping chores, he is out in the neighborhood having fun and flirting with the ladies.

Around this basic plot were assembled a number of variety acts and novel features which were constantly revised from season to season. "At the time of its organization," wrote Frederick W. Bond (*Neg&Dr*, p. 179), "the featured attractions were the antics of horses [*sic*] trained by Professor . . . Williams."

In 1910, Eph. Williams' [Famous] Troubadours toured the Southeast playing Silas Green with the following featured cast: William Mayfield (as Silas, the principal comedian), Jennie Hale (Mary Smith, leading lady and prima donna), Pearl Moon (Lula Jane Green, Silas' wife), George Baker (slack wire performer), Miss Polk (the Goo-Goo Singing Bird), R. H. Collins (band master), Eph. Williams (owner and manager), R. C. Puggsley (business manager), and Ross Jackson (advance agent). This was obviously an abbreviated list of players, which does not include the many townspeople and special added attractions that were more than likely among the features of the show.

Bond (*Neg&Dr*, p. 179) reports that in the show's history there have been only four main Silas Greens: Eddie Stafford, Larry Knox, Ford (or Fred?) Wiggins, and Happy Hampton. According to J. Homer Tutt (in *Afro-American* 8–15–1936), Silas Green became "an institution throughout the Southland," and "every big actor at one time or other" played in this show.

FURTHER REFERENCE: *Afro-American* (Baltimore) 8–15–1936. *BlksBf* (Sampson). *Chicago Defender* 4–6–1932; 8–22–1936; 3–12–1955. *Ebony* 9–1954. *Ghost* (Sampson). *Neg&Dr* (Bond).

SIMPLE MOLLIE (1908). Musical comedy. 1 act [3 scenes]. Music and lyrics by Henri Wise.

A love story, which moves from a picnic in Love Hollow to Main Street in Duckville, to the parlor of the Johnson home, where the wedding presumably takes place.

Prod. by Robert Motts and the Pekin Stock Co., at the Pekin Theatre, Chicago, 1908. Cast: Lottie Grady (Lucy Johnson), Tim Owsley (Jim Slick), Lew Lammer (Wild Bill), Augusta Stevens (The Preacher), Katie Milton (Mollie-O), Henri Wise (Jake Blossome), and Miss Boyd [first name unknown] (Singer).

Songs and musical numbers: "Sweet Molly-O" (Company), "Summer Time" (Boys & Company), "Poor Little Maid" (Milton), and "Taffy Finally" (Grady & Company).

SIMPLY HEAVENLY (1957–59). Billed as "A Comedy with Music." 2 acts [17 scenes]. Book and lyrics by Langston Hughes. Music by David Martin. Based on Hughes' nonmusical play, *Simple Takes a Wife* (1955), his four novels on Simple, which were in turn based on his Simple stories that appeared for many years in weekly columns in the *Chicago Defender* and later in the *NY Post*.

This is Hughes' most popular play, the plot of which revolves around the affairs and escapades of a colorful Harlem character (which he created) named Jesse B. Semple, nicknamed Simple by his friends, and particularly his efforts to get his girlfriend Joyce to marry him. Simple has been described by Hughes and °Milton Meltzer (*BlkMagic*, p. 231) as "a sort of Harlem Everyman, a sidewalk philosopher and genial commentator on the passing scene." The Harlem settings include Simple's tenement room, Joyce's room, Paddy's Bar, a hospital room, a sidewalk on Lenox Avenue, and a phone booth.

The parade of other Harlem characters who move in and out of the various scenes (as described by Hughes in his Program Notes in the pub. script) include Simple's "fat, comical and terrible" landlady Madame Butler, who "has a bark that is worse than her bite—but her bark is bad enough," who "runs her roominghouse as Hitler ran Germany"; Ananias Boyd, Simple's neighbor, a "serious-minded" intellectual whom "almost every Harlem bar" can find "among its regular customers"; Miss Mamie, a "plump," "hard-working domestic," who uses "biting words to protect a soft heart and a need for love"; Gitfiddle, a guitar player, who, with the help of "a barfly pianist," "furnishes all the music . . . for the songs and interludes"; and Zarita, "a lively barstool girl," "but not a prostitute," with whom Simple is also involved on the side.

First prod. Off-Bway by Stella Holt at the 85th Street Playhouse, May 21, 1957, for a short run; dir. by Joshua Shelley. Cast: Stanley Greene (Boyd), Javotte S. Greene (Mrs. Caddy [Joyce's landlady], Nurse & Party Guest), Marilyn Berry (Joyce), Lawson Bates (Hopkins, the bartender), Willie Pritchett (Pianist), Claudia McNeil (Mamie), Charles A. McRae (Bodiddly, a dockworker), Allegro Kane (a bar character), John Bouie (Melon [Watermelon] Joe, a fruit vendor), Ray Thompson (Gitfiddle), Ethel Ayler (Zarita), Josephine Woods (Arcie, Bodiddly's wife), Charles Harrison (John Jasper, Bodiddly's son), and Pierre Rayon (Ali Baba, a root doctor).

Prod. on Bway by °Vincent Cero and °Abel Enklewitz at the Playhouse Theatre, opening Aug. 20, 1957, for 62 perfs., with the same director and most of the orig. cast, except for the following: Wilhelmina Gray (Madame Butler), Dagmar Craig (Mrs. Caddy, Nurse & Party Guest), Duke Williams (Hopkins), Brownie McGhee (Gitfiddle), Anna English (Zarita), and Maxwell Glanville (Big Boy [Ali Baba] & Cop).

Transferred to Off-Bway beginning Nov. 8, 1957, at the Renata Theatre in Greenwich Village; with the same director and cast.

Prod. on the "Play-of-the-Week" television series in 1957, and was the first all-black play presented on this series.

An English prodn. opened in London at the Adelphi Theatre, May 20, 1958, following a successful tour of the British provinces.

Prod. May 5–June 27, 1958, and Sept. 15–Oct. 17, 1959, by the Gilpin Players at Karamu House in Cleveland. Also prod. by a number of black colleges and universities, including Howard, Talladega, and Florida A & M—the latter of which presented it on a seven-week tour of Europe, under the direction of

Randolph Edmonds. Prod. in a nonmusical version in Prague, Czechoslovakia, in 1959.

Songs and musical numbers include "Love Is Simply Heavenly" (Joyce & Simple), "Did You Ever Hear the Blues" (Mamie & Melon), "Deep in Love with You" (Simple), "I'm Gonna Be John Henry" (Simple), "When I'm in a Quiet Mood" (Melon & Mamie), "Look for the Morning Star" (Pianist & Joyce; reprise by Joyce & Simple and by Ensemble), "Let's Ball Awhile" (Zarita & Guests), and "A Good Old Girl" (Mamie).

Cast recording by Columbia (OL 5240). Music pub. by Bourne, Inc. Acting edition pub. by Dramatists, which controls the amateur acting rights and can furnish copies of the vocal and piano scores for prospective producers. Scripts pub. in *Langston Hughes Reader* (1959), *Five Plays by Langston Hughes* (Smalley, 1963), and *Blk.Th.* (Patterson). Condensed version for a recording script in Schomburg. Earlier drafts in JWJ/YUL.

FURTHER REFERENCE: *AnthANT* (Patterson). *Billboard* 9–30–1957. *BlkMagic* (Hughes & Meltzer). *Cath. World* 8–1957. *CLAJ* 6–1967; 9–1968. *Dr. Critique* Spr. 1964. *Nation* 10–5–1957. *NY Herald Trib.* 5–22–1957; 8–18–1957. *NYT* 5–22–1957; 5–23–1957; 8–21–1957; 6–2–1967; 2–2–1958. *Phylon* 3rd qtr. 1957. *Sat. Rev.* 9–7–1957. *Variety* 8–28–1957.

SING HALLELUJAH (1987). Gospel musical. Choreographed, staged, and dir. by Worth Gardner. A celebration of gospel music in song and dance. Prod. at the Village Gate, New York, Dec. 1987–Jan. 1988. Featuring Curtis Blake, Ann Nesby, Patricia Ann Everson, Clarence Snow, and Rose Clyburn. Instrumental music by Craig Harris, Richard Odom, Victor Ross, and Michael Terry.

SINGIN' THE BLUES (1931). Billed as "A Melodrama with Music." 2 acts [10 scenes]. Book by °John McGowan. Music and lyrics by °Jimmy McHugh and °Dorothy Fields.

A musical about Harlem night life, built around the melodramatic plot of the pursuit of a black fugitive from a Chicago poolroom to New York City's Harlem by two bumbling white detectives. After Jim Williams shoots a policeman during the raid of a dice game in Johnson's Poolroom in Chicago, he flees with his pal Knuckles Lincoln to Harlem, where he hides out in two nightspots, Crocker's Place and the Magnolia Club, which provide convenient settings for most of the show's musical numbers. He is aided by a nightclub singer, Susan Blake, with whom he falls in love. However, his whereabouts are revealed to the police by another jealous singer, Elise Joyce, but Williams manages to escape before he can be arrested, and he and Susan head for safety to Williams' hometown in Georgia.

Prod. at the Liberty Theatre, New York, opening Sept. 16, 1931, for 45 perfs.; dir. by °Bertram Harrison. Music by Eubie Blake's Orchestra. Cast: Mantan Moreland ("Knuckles" Lincoln), Isabell Washington (Susan Blake, a nightclub entertainer), Fredi Washington (Elise Joyce), Ashley Cooper ("Potato-Eyes"

Johnson), Frank Wilson (Jim Williams), John Sims ("Bad Alley" Joe), James
Young (Dooley), Joe Byrd (Colored Policeman), Johnny Reid (Rocky), Shirley
Jordan (Eddie), Jennie Sammons (Mazie), S. W. Warren (Jay), Jack Carter
(Dave Crocker, a nightclub owner), Esther Bernier (Edith), Ralph Theodore
(Sam Mason), Millard Mitchell ("Whitey" Henderson), C. C. Gill (Tod), Percy
Wade (Sid), Percy Verwayen (Jack Wilson), Maude Russell ("Sizzles" Brown),
James Stark (Officer Frank), Susaye Brown (A Singer), the Lindy Hoppers, the
Four Flash Devils, Wen Talbert's Choir, and the Magnolia Club Chorus.

Only two numbers from the McHugh/Fields' score are known: the title song
"Singin' the Blues" and "It's the Darndest Thing."

FURTHER REFERENCE: Alkire diss. *BlkMusTh* (Woll). *HarlRenD* (Kellner). *NYT*
9–17–1931. *Outlook & Independent* 9–30–1931. *Variety* 9–22–1931.

SING, MAHALIA, SING! (1985). Gospel musical. 2 acts [22 scenes]. Book
by George Faison. Music and lyrics by Richard Smallwood, George Faison, and
Wayne Davis. About the life and times of gospel singer Mahalia Jackson.

Prod. as an exclusive tour production by Kolmar/Luth Entertainment, Inc.,
opening March 18, 1985, at the Shubert Theatre in Philadelphia, then traveling
to 11 other cities during its run. With Jennifer Holliday (alternating with Esther
Marrow) in the role of Mahalia, supported by a cast of more than 20. All other
cast members were also members of the Ensemble. Cast: Carolene Adams-Evans
(Miss Ruth, Sister Russell), Sarita Allen (Rita the Manicurist, Mourning
Woman), Lisa Burroughs (Aunt Hannah, Sister Thomas), Felicia Y. Coleman
(Louise Lemon, Rosa Parks), Wayne Davis (Eddie Robinson), Germaine Ed-
wards (Redcap, Reporter), Marva Hicks (Young Mahalia), Jennifer Holliday or
Esther Marrow (Mahalia Jackson), Stephanie James-Rainey (Eastern Star Mem-
ber, Waitress), James Arthur Johnson (Chafalaya), Tyrone Jolivet (Angel of
God), Dottie Jones (Sue), Glenn Jones (Rev. Jenkins, Prince Johnson, Rev.
Jameson), Garry Q. Lewis (Master of Ceremonies, Floor Manager, Film Direc-
tor, Reporter, Policeman), Michelle Rene Lovett (Mildred Falls), Joe Lynn (Ike
Hunkenhull), Milton Craig Nealy (Male Swing Dancer), Stanley Wesley Per-
ryman (Radio Listener, Reporter, Policeman), Jackie Ruffin (Aunt Duke),
Brother John Sellers (Grandpa), Kiki Shepard (Sister Willis), Lynette Hawkins
Stevens (Mother Weeks), Paul W. Weeden, Jr. (Dr. Martin Luther King, Jr.),
and Allison M. Williams (Sister Smith).

Synopsis of scenes and musical numbers: Act I, Scene 1 (Chicago, 1963;
Greater Salem Baptist Church)—"Glorify the Lord" (Church Members &
Choir), "Sing, Mahalia, Sing" (Rev. Jenkins), "Come on Children, Let's Sing"
(Mahalia, Church Members & Choir), "Precious Lord" (Mahalia), "How I Got
Over" (Mahalia, Church Members & Choir); Scene 2 (New Orleans, 1911–
1927; Miss Ruth's Sporting House on Water Street)–"Louisiana" (Chafalaya,
Miss Ruth, Miss Ruth's Girls & Customers); Scene 3 (Aunt Duke's House on
Water Street)—"It Don't Cost Very Much" (Aunt Duke & Young Mahalia),
"Going to Chicago" (Chafalaya, Aunt Duke & Young Mahalia); Scene 4 (Miss

Ruth's Sporting House)—"Handwriting on the Wall" (Sanctified Church Member); Scene 5 (Baptist Church and the Water's Edge)—"Handwriting on the Wall" (Baptists), "I Surrender All" (Young Mahalia), "Baptismal" (Baptists & Baptismal Candidates), "Down by the Riverside" (Young Mahalia & Baptists); Scene 6 (Aunt Duke's House and the Cemetery)—"Father, I Stretch My Hands to Thee" (Aunt Duke, Young Mahalia & Mourners), "Just a Closer Walk with Thee" (Young Mahalia & Mourners); Scene 7 (Chicago, 1927–1939; Union Station and the Club De Lisa)—"Shake Your Ashes" (Redcaps, Travelers, Emcee, Chorines & Club Patrons); Scene 8 (Club De Lisa)—"Wait on the Lord" (Janitor), "His Eye Is on the Sparrow" (Mahalia); Scene 9 (Mahalia and Ike's Apartment)—"What You Gonna Do" (Ike), "I'm Gonna Live the Life I Sing About in My Songs" (Mahalia), "Be Faithful" (Angel of God & Angel Chorus); Scene 10 (Ebenezer Baptist Church)—"God Will Take Care of You" (reprise: Louise Lemon & Johnson Singers); Scene 11 (On Tour)—"God Will Take Care of You" (reprise), "Dig a Little Deeper" (Mahalia, Louise Lemon & Johnson Singers); Scene 12 (Basement of the Olivet Baptist Church)—"Not Up Here in This Pulpit" (Mother Weeks & Daughters of the Eastern Star); Scene 13 (The Olivet Baptist Church)—"Plead My Cause" (Mahalia and the Angel of God), "Lord, Search Her Heart" (Mother Weeks & Mr. Russell), "God's Gonna Separate the Wheat from the Tares" (Mahalia & Ensemble), "Didn't It Rain?" (Mahalia & Ensemble). Act II, Scene 1 (Kansas City, 1943; National Baptist Convention)—"So Glad I'm Here" (Women of Convention), "Call the Lord" (Delegate Ministers), "Sho Been Good to Me" (Conventioneers), "Benediction and Closing Remarks" (Secretary of Convention), "Elijah Rock" (Mahalia); Scene 2 (Mahalia and Ike's Apartment; Chicago, 1943–1949)—"When I Been Drinking" (Ike), "I've Got Something" (Mahalia); Scene 3 (Mahalia's Beauty Shop)—"Working on a Building" (Operators & Patrons), "He Won't Leave You" (Sue, Operators & Patrons); Scene 4 (New York City, 1950; Carnegie Hall)—"Move on Up a Little Higher" (Mahalia); Scene 5 (On the Air, 1954–1959)—CBS Radio Studio, Chicago: "Carolyn Rice" (Golden Gate Quartet), "His Eye Is on the Sparrow" (Golden Gate Quartet); NBC Television Studio, New York: "Dig a Little Deeper" (Mahalia); MGM Studio, Hollywood: "Soon I Will Be Done" (Mahalia); World Tour: "He's Got the Whole World in His Hands" (Mahalia); Scene 6 (Chicago, 1958; Mahalia's New Apartment)— "Come Over Here Where the Table Is Spread" (Party Guests), "I've Been Buked" (Party Guests); Scene 7 (The United States of America, Early 1960s; Civil Rights Movement)—"Ain't Gonna Let Nobody" (Demonstrators), "Motherless Child" (Rosa Parks), "Lord Come by Here" (Demonstrators); Scene 8 (Washington, DC, 1963; Lincoln Memorial)—"We Shall Overcome" (Dr. Martin Luther King, Jr.), "I Have a Dream" (Ensemble); Scene 9 (Chicago, 1963; Greater Salem Baptist Church)—"The Lord's Prayer" (Mahalia), "Sing, Mahalia, Sing" (Ensemble).

SIZZLING ORIENTAL SUNFLOWER REVUE (1929). Touring revue. Cast included Lovey Austin, Peat and Leroy White, Chippy Hill, Christine Russell, Jessie Taylor, Atta Blake, Dave Brown, and Lawrence Nash.

SKRONTCH!! (1975). Musical show. Based on show music composed by Duke Ellington for a number of theatrical productions including *Pousse Cafe*, **Beggar's Holiday*, **Jump for Joy*, and the Cotton Club revues. Prod. by the Theatre at Noon, at St. Peter's Church, New York, 1975.

THE SLAVE (1925). Opera. Written and composed by H. Lawrence Freeman. Part of an unperfd. tetralogy entitled *Zululand* (1925–47). His best-known operas include **The Martyr* (1893), **Valdo* (1905–6), **Vendetta* (1911–23), and **Voodoo* (1921–28).

SLAVES' ESCAPE; OR, THE UNDERGROUND RAILROAD. See *PECULIAR SAM*.

SLAVE SONG (1974). Musical. By Oscar Brown, Jr. Sched. for prodn. by the Lamont Zeno Community Theatre, Chicago, March 1974.

SLEEPING BEAUTY AND THE BEAST (1901–2). White-oriented musical extravaganza. 3 acts. By °J. Hickory Wood and °Arthur Collins; adapt. for the stage by °John J. McNally and °J. Cheever Goodwin. Lyrics by Goodwin. Music by °J. M. Glover and °Frederick Solomon. Additional music and lyrics by Bob Cole, James Weldon Johnson, and J. Rosamond Johnson.

An Americanized version of one of the Drury Lane Pantomimes brought over from London, which were the greatest spectacles that had ever been presented on the American stage. James Weldon Johnson reported that New York had never seen "such massing of performers, such lavishness of scenery, and such marvels of stage effects [including] the fairy parliament, the witch's cave, the palace of crystal, the prismatic fountains, and, above all, the flying ballet" (*Along This Way* [Johnson], p. 178).

Prod. on Bway with great success by °Klaw & Erlanger at the Broadway Theatre, opening Nov. 4, 1901, for 241 perfs.; dir. by °John Brooks. With an all-white cast headed by °Joseph Cawthorn, °Harry Bulger, °Viola Gillette, °Charles J. Ross, and °John Hyams.

The Cole & Johnson Brothers songs included "Tell Me, Dusky Maiden," pub. by Howley, Haviland & Dresser; "Nobody's Lookin' But the Owl and the Moon," pub. by Joseph W. Stern & Co. and included in *Ten Choice Negro Folksongs for Voice and Pianoforte* (New York: date and publisher unknown); and "Come Out, Dinah, on the Green." Copies of all 3 songs in Moorland-Spingarn.

SLIM SLIVERS (1927). Touring revue. Prod. by J. W. Jackson. Cast included Louis Deckail, Elvira Johnson, Alberta Pope, Edna Davis, Lionel Monagas, Frank Bradham, and Percy Wade.

SMALL TOWN DOINGS (1921). Touring show. Prod. by and costarring Salem Tutt Whitney and J. Homer Tutt (Whitney & Tutt). Perfd. by the *Smart Set Co.

(THE) SMART SET (CO.) (c. 1901–24). A popular name for several touring vaudeville and musical comedy companies, but especially °Gus Hill's *Smart Set Co.* (c. 1901–2), S. H. Dudley's *Smart Set Co.* (c. 1904–12), and Whitney & Tutt's *Smart Set Co.* (c. 1909–24).

Gus Hill's company was the first show using this title, and is often referred to as the original *Smart Set Co.* Prod. by white minstrel man Gus Hill, this show starred Ernest Hogan, who wrote his own songs and comedy material. Apparently it was a loosely constructed musical show, which featured vaudeville acts, comedy sketches, songs, and dances. The published music (see below) bears the inscription on the title page: "Introduced by the Smart Set in *Enchantment*," which was the title of the featured musical comedy sketch. However, the show seems to have closed after only one season, 1901–2, after which Hogan left the show. The big song hit from this show, which Hogan wrote and sang, was "Watermelon Time." As the orchestra played, he gave the audience a lesson in how to eat a watermelon and demonstrated as he sang. Other songs included "Roll On, Mr. Moon," a minstrel song, and "My Sweet Moana," a popular ballad, both by Hogan and Billy McClain; and "The Missionary Man," a minstrel song by Hogan and Steve Cassin—all pub. by Joseph W. Stern & Co., New York, 1902; copies in Moorland-Spingarn.

Two years after the demise of the original *Smart Set Co.*, S. H. Dudley organized a second company by this name in 1902, offering a seasonal repertoire of musical comedies, of which only 3 titles are known: *The Black Politician* (1904–8), *His Honor, the Barber* (1909–11), and *Dr. Beans from Boston* (1912). Dudley was the star of each of these shows; Bill Vodery trained the chorus and directed the orchestra; and James P. Johnson toured with the show as musical director. (See separate show titles for more complete information.)

The third *Smart Set Co.* (also called the *Southern Smart Set Co.* and the *Smarter Set Co.*) was organized by Salem Tutt Whitney and his brother J. Homer Tutt (Whitney & Tutt), and was modeled after the two preceding companies. Although exact information is difficult to locate, Whitney & Tutt's show apparently began touring in 1909, offering a changeable seasonal repertoire of musical comedies, farces, and sketches, all cowritten by the two brothers, and flourished until around 1924. Specific titles, which should be consulted for more information, include: *Blackville Strollers* (1908–9) [see note below], *The Mayor of Newtown* [also *Newton*] (1909, 1912), *How Newtown* [or *Newton*] *Prepared* (1916), *Darkest Americans* (1918–19), *(The) Children of the Sun* (1919–20), *Bamboula* (1921), *Up and Down* (c. 1919–22), *North Ain't South* (1923), *Who Struck John?* (1923–24), *Nut Brown Lady* (1924), and *When Malinda Sings* (1924–25).

[Note: Although the inclusive dates of the *Blackville Strollers* is given as

1908–9, Whitney & Tutt did not begin touring this show with the *Smart Set Co.* until 1909. It was first prod. by the *Black Patti Troubadours* in 1908, when Whitney & Tutt were associated with this show. Afterwards they left the show to form their own company.]

An undated poster (c. 1911) advertising a non-related tent show calling itself *Smart Set*, starring blues singer Ma Rainey, is pub. in *BlkMagic* (Hughes & Meltzer, p. 69). This show claimed to feature "50 celebrated theatrical circus and operatic stars," "a beautifully costumed singing and dancing chorus," and an "imperial troupe of tossing, turning, tumbling clowns in feats of daring."

According to Eileen Southern (*BioDAfMus*, p. 342), a *Smart Set* show was prod. by Al Wells during the 1920s, and there were occasional references in the black press to other companies by this name in "subsequent decades."

SNAPSHOTS OF 1921 (1921). Stage show. Music partially by Harry Brooks. Prod. New York, 1921.

SO DIFFERENT REVUE (1926). Touring revue. Featuring Beulah Benbow, Melvin Hunter, Jimmie Howell, J. Revis, Floyd Young, and Ethel Oydbraum.

SOLID SOUTH (1930?). Musical revue. Prod. New York; with Georgette Harvey.

SOME BABY (1921). Touring revue. Prod. by and starring Quintard Miller. Cast also included B. B. (or Beebee) Joyner, Lulu Whidby, Marguette (or Margaret) Lee, Jimmy Howell, Ruth Cherry, and Theresa Burroughs Brooks.

SOME PARTY (1922). White-oriented musical. Book and lyrics mainly by °R. H. Burnside. Music by °Sylvio Hein, °Percy Wennick, J. Turner Layton, and others. Prod. New York, April 15, 1922, for 17 perfs. With an all-white cast that included °De Wolf Hopper, °Jefferson DeAngelis, and °Lew Dockstader. No information concerning the music by J. Turner Layton.

SOMETHING FOR JAMIE (1972). Musical. Book by Holly Hamilton and Gertrude Greenidge. Music and lyrics by Hamilton. A black preacher of a storefront church is jailed when one of his female church members falsely accuses him of sexual molestation, thereby causing him to reevaluate his life. Prod. by the Franklin Thomas Little Theatre, New York City, Oct. 23–Nov. 2, 1975; dir. by Franklin Thomas. Prod. at Robeson House, Brooklyn, Sept. 25–Oct. 18, 1982.

THE SONG OF SHEBA (1989). Musical. Book and lyrics by Elmo Terry Morgan. Orig. score and music by Clarice LaVerne Thompson. A celebration of the contributions of five great black singers: Bessie Smith, Dinah Washington, Lena Horne, Billie Holiday, and Sarah Vaughan. Prod. by the National Black Theatre, New York; featuring Marsha Z. West, Clarice LaVerne, and Cheryl Hewitt.

SONGS MY FATHER TAUGHT ME (1973). Musical. By Thomasena (Sena) Davis Allen. A celebration of the spiritual truths and values which African Americans have inherited from their forefathers. Prod. by the Black American Theatre, Washington, DC, March 1974.

SONNY BOY SAM (1929). Touring show. Featuring Sam Robinson in the title role. About the determination of a black boy from the cotton fields of the South to gain fame and fortune by any means necessary. Cast also included Zablo Jenkins, Hunter & Warfield, C. D. Davis, James "Kid" Austin, O'Brien & McKenny, Paul Foster, Blake Morril, and Gertie Davis. Songs included "Sonny Boy," "Tomorrow," "Sweet Sue," and "There Must Be a Silver Lining."

THE SONS OF HAM (1900–1902). Vaudeville farce-comedy. Billed as a musical comedy. 3 acts. Based on concept and improvisations by Williams & Walker (Bert Williams and George Walker). Music by Will Marion Cook. Lyrics by Alex C. Rogers. Additional music and lyrics by Williams, Cecil Mack, Tim Brymn, Tom Lemonier, Will Accooe, Joe Jordan, Ernest Hogan, Bob Cole, J. Rosamond Johnson, and James Weldon Johnson.

A collection of vaudeville routines assembled around a thin plot, which underwent a number of revisions during the course of its run. The first successful Williams & Walker musical. With no apologies to either Plautus or Shakespeare, this show concerned two bums (played by the two comedians), who arrive in a Tennessee town and find themselves mistaken for a pair of twin brothers who are heirs to a large fortune, and who are expected to arrive from boarding school after a long absence. The father of the twins, Old Ham (played by Jesse Shipp), who has not seen his children in many years, quickly accepts Williams & Walker as his sons, and they, being down and out, readily enjoy their good fortune. Complications arise early, however, even before the real twins arrive, because it turns out that they have been studying to be acrobats and gun-jugglers; and in order to escape detection, Williams & Walker must try to avoid proving their lack of acrobatic and juggling skills. When the real twins turn up (played by the Reese Bros., professional acrobats), the impostors are exposed and run out of town. The prodn. included numerous other vaudeville specialty numbers, as well as a jungle scene finale for Act I and a cakewalk finale for Act III.

Organized and rehearsed for three weeks in New York in Sept. 1900; afterwards it toured the country for two seasons, during which it played in Washington, DC, at the Bijou Theatre, c. Sept. 20, 1901. Under the sponsorship of °Hurtig and Seamon, it opened at the Grand Opera House on March 3, 1902, for 8 perfs., and at the New York Theatre on March 22, 1902, also for about 8 perfs. Featured members of the orig. cast included Bert Williams and George Walker (as itinerant derelicts, mistaken for the real twins), Jesse Shipp (Old Ham, father of the twins; later replaced by Pete Hamilton), the Reese Brothers (Arthur and Ollie: the real twins—both acrobats), Ada Overton Walker (soubrette), George Catlin (Chinese imitation specialty), Anna Ross (old woman), and the rest of the company (Denver citizens and singers). Florence Mills reportedly made her debut in this show at age 8 at the Bijou Theatre in Washington, when, according to *BlksBf* (Sampson, p. 402), "she was billed as 'Baby Florence Mills, an Extra Added Attraction,' and . . . sang 'Miss Hannah from Savannah,' " the song hit first introduced by Ada Overton Walker, who taught it to the young Mills.

Songs and musical numbers: "Beyond the Gates of Paradise" (Lloyd Gibbs), + "The Leader of the Ball" (by Mack & Lemonier: sung by G. Walker), "Miss Hannah from Savannah" (by Mack & Lemonier: sung by A. Walker), + "My Castle on the Nile" (by Cole & the Johnson Bros.: sung by Williams), "The Phrenologist Coon" (by Hogan & Accooe: sung by Williams), "She's Growing More Like White Folks Every Day" (sung by Williams), "Society" (by Cook: sung by A. Walker), "My Little Zulu Babe" (sung by Williams & Walker), "Blackville Strutters," "Cairo," "Calisthenics," "Dinah," "Down Where the Cotton Blossoms Grow," + "Fortune-Telling Coon" (by Williams & G. Walker: sung by Williams), "Good Afternoon, Mr. Jenkins," "Josephine, My Jo" (by Mack & Brymn), "Old Man's Song and Dance," "The Promoters," "Sons of Ham," "When the Corn Is Wavin'," "When the Heart Is Young," and "Rag Time Schottische" (sung by G. & A. Walker). Songs marked with a plus sign (+) pub. by Joseph W. Stern, New York, 1901. "Josephine, My Jo" pub. by Shapiro, Bernstein & von Tilzer, 1901; copy in Hargrett Rare Book and Manuscript Lib., Univ. of Georgia Libraries. "Society" pub. by Keith, Prowse & Co., London, 1903.

A brief libretto is located in the Rare Book Room/LC.

FURTHER REFERENCE: *BlksBf* (Sampson). *Freeman* (Indianapolis) 12–14–1901. *Ghost* (Sampson). *Just Before Jazz* (Riis). *Nobody* (Charters). Riis diss.

SONS OF REST (1927). Touring show. Music and lyrics by Sidney Easton and Robert Warfield. Prod. by Sidney Easton and Joe Simms, who also perfd. in the cast. Other cast members include Angeline Lawson (A Spiritualist who has been cheated out of her land, and who employs both the law and the supernatural to get her property back), Coley Grant (Old Man), Harriet Williams (His Daughter), "Billy" Moore (Indian Chief), Paul C. Floyd (Government Agent), Addison Carey (Sheriff), Louise Williams and Arthur Noble (Juveniles), Taft Rice and Robert Warfield (Dance Specialties), Sam Davis (piano), and chorus.

SOPHISTICATED LADIES (1981–83). Musical retrospective, celebrating the music of Duke Ellington. 2 acts. Conceived, choreographed, and staged by Donald McKale, who apparently wrote the orig. libretto, with the assistance of several others, including Samm-Art Williams. Tap choreography by Henry LeTang. Additional staging and choreography by °Michael Smuin.

An elaborately staged and beautifully costumed song-and-dance show, built around the music of Duke Ellington, and starring Gregory Hines, Judith Jamison, and Hinton Battle as the leading dancers. Some 35 of Ellington's songs were played by an onstage band conducted by his son, Mercer Ellington. The *NYorker* (4–27–1981, p. 4) described it as an "exceptionally elegant" show, also writing that "Gregory Hines dances with a grace that ravishes the eye, and with a velocity that must alarm every cardiologist in the audience." Arnold Shaw (*Blk. Pop. Mus. in Am.*, p. 300) considered Hines as the "solo star"; and Gerald Bordman (*AmMusTh*, p. 700) said that "Gregory Hines' high-stepping stole the spotlight and brought down the house."

After an unsuccessful tryout in Washington, DC, Michael Smuin, co-director of the San Francisco Ballet, was called in as show-doctor, and he augmented the staging and choreography to turn the show into a hit. It opened on Bway at the Lunt-Fontanne Theatre, March 1, 1981, for 767 perfs. Cast: Gregory Hines, Judith Jamison, Hinton Battle (who won a Tony Award for his dancing), Phyllis Hyman (who received a *Theatre World* Award), Gregg Burge, Mercedes Ellington, °Terri Klausner, °Michael Lichtefeld, °P. J. Benjamin, °Claudia Asbury, and °Wynonna Smith. Costume designer Tony Walton also won a Tony Award for outstanding costume design.

Songs and musical numbers: "Take the 'A' Train," "I've Got to Be a Rug Cutter," "Music Is Woman," "The Mooche," "Hit Me with a Hot Note and Watch Me Bounce," "Love You Madly," "It Don't Mean a Thing," "Bli-Blip," "Solitude," "Don't Get Around Much Any More," "I Let a Song Go Out of My Heart," "Caravan," "Something to Live For," "Rockin' in Rhythm," "In a Sentimental Mood," "I'm Beginning to See the Light," "Satin Doll," "Just Squeeze Me," "Dancers in Love," "Cotton Tail," "Drop Me Off in Harlem," "Echoes of Harlem," "I'm a Lucky So-and-So," "Hey Baby," "Imagine My Frustration," "Kinda Dukish," "I'm Checking Out Goombye [*sic*]," "Do Nothing 'Til You Hear from Me," "I Got It Bad and That Ain't Good," "Mood Indigo," and "Sophisticated Ladies."
FURTHER REFERENCE: *BlkMusTh* (Woll). *NYT* 3-3-1981.

SO THIS IS AFRICA (1933). Touring show. Featured Wheeler & Woosey.

SOUL AT SUNRISE (1970). Musical pageant. 3 sequences. By J. W. Robinson Horne. A saga of the "Soul Man" (the American of African descent) from his golden age in Alkebu-lan (ancient Africa) to his arrival in America, where as a slave he gave birth to the sacred sound of "soul"—the spiritual—and as a free man he created the syncopated sound of soul—black gospel music. The three

sequences include 'Souls in the Sun,' 'Souls in Slave Ships,' and 'Souls' Sacred Sounds.' Prod. as a part of the annual Easter Sunrise Service at Second Baptist Church, Richmond, VA, 1970, 1973, and 1982; dir. by the author. Other musical pageants written and prod. by Horne for the annual sunrise service include: *The Garden [of Easter]* (1952, 1963, 1973), *The Acts of Four Men* (1959, 1969, 1975), *That Man John* (1961), *Great Day* (1964), *The People vs. the Nazarene* (1965, 1966, 1977), *Joy to Jesus Christ* (1972, 1979), *Miracle Morning* (1974), *Entrances and Exits* (1976), *Sisters* (1980), *Easter: A Jesus Jubilee* (1981), *Rejoice in the Redeemer* (1983), *Morningstar* (1985), and *Praises* (1986).
FURTHER REFERENCE: *Contemporary Blk. Am. Playwrs. and Their Pls.* (Peterson).

SOUL GONE HOME (1954). Opera. 1 act. Adaptn. with musical score by Ulysses Kay of Langston Hughes' play in 1 act by the same title. The "spirit" of a dead son accuses his prostitute mother of misconduct and neglect for his untimely death from tuberculosis. Unperfd. Libretto in JWJ/YUL.

SOUTH BEFORE THE WAR (1891–98). Integrated touring show. Prod. by °Whalen & °Martell.
This show, which had a predominantly white cast that included a number of blacks, consisted primarily of plantation scenes, songs, dances, and specialty numbers. Billy McClain, the leading black star and asst. stage manager, perfd. with the show for about four years. °Snyder & °Buckley were the leading white stars.
It toured the burlesque circuit in the East, Midwest, and West for about seven seasons. Among the black individuals and groups who appeared in this show during its long run were Billy Williams and William Ferry (human frogs), Cordelia McClain (one of the leading actresses), Florence Brisco, Pearl Woods (acrobat), Joseph Hodges, Tom McIntosh, John Wesley Jenkins, Henry Winfred, Albert Anderson and his brother York Anderson, J. Ed. Green (who played the role of ''Young Eph'') and directed his Black Diamond Quartet; and other quartets including the Standard Quartet, the Twilight Quartet, and the Eclipse Quartet.
Billy McClain was highly praised for his songs and dances. His songs included ''Old Schoolhouse Bells'' (1892), ''Hand Down de Robe'' (1894), and for a song he wrote for Billy Williams, ''Ise South Carolina Liza'' (1894). Among the dances which McClain introduced in the show was the cakewalk.
FURTHER REFERENCE: *BlksBf* (Sampson).

THE SOUTHERNERS (1904). Musical of plantation life. Billed both as ''A Musical Romance'' and as ''A Musical Study in Black and White.'' Book and lyrics coauthored by Will Mercer (pseudonym of Will Marion Cook) and °Richard Grant. Music by Cook (using his own name).
One of the earliest attempts at integration on the Bway stage, this musical was set in slavery days, with all the speaking characters portrayed by whites,

and blacks represented by a number of specialty acts, including a chorus of singers and dancers, a group of 6 children appropriately costumed for a number called "The Chipmunk and the Squirrel"; Ida Forsyne as a solo dancer; and Cook's wife Abbie Mitchell as a featured singer.

According to *NYT* (5–24–1904), although many feared that racial trouble would occur because of the integrated cast, these fears were soon dispelled after the opening night performance:

When the chorus of real live coons walked in for the cake [i.e., performed the cakewalk] at the New York Theatre, mingling with the white members of the cast, there were those in the audience who trembled in their seats. . . . [H]ere were scores of blacks and whites mingling. But it presently became evident that the spirit of harmony reigned. The magician was . . . the Negro composer Will Marion Cook, who all alone had succeeded in harmonizing the racial broth as skillfully as he had harmonized the accompanying score.

The play unfolds as an old ex-slave (played in blackface by °Eddie Leonard, a well-known minstrel dancer) dreams of the "good old days" on his master's plantation, some 80 years earlier. The dream depicts the young master as a benevolent slaveholder who wishes to free his slaves, but knows that this will not be socially acceptable. After a quarrel with his sweetheart, he joins the navy, giving instructions for the disposition of his slaves only to friendly slaveowners who will treat them kindly. Contrary to his wishes, a thoroughly disreputable and tyrannical slave dealer attempts to acquire his slaves, in order to possess one beautiful fair-skinned girl after whom he has long lusted. Through the efforts of the master's girlfriend, with whom he becomes reconciled, he returns just in the nick of time to prevent the sale and to continue to provide a good home for his slaves until they are emancipated.

Prod. and dir. by °George W. Lederer at the New York Theatre, New York, opening May 12, 1904, for 36 perfs. The speaking characters (all white) included °Eddie Leonard (Uncle Daniel, the old ex-slave), °William Gould (Leroy Preston, the young master), °Elfie Faye (Polly Drayton, the master's sweetheart), °Junie McCree (Branigan Bey, the lustful slave dealer), and °Vinie Daly (Parthenia, the beautiful slave girl). For black performers, see above.

Piano score pub. by York Music Co., 1904 (copy in Moorland-Spingarn), includes the following songs and musical numbers: "Julep Song (The good old mint julep for me)," "As the Sunflower Turns to the Sun," "Mandy Lou" (sung by Mitchell), "Where the Lotus Blossoms Grow," "Darktown Barbecue," "Allus the Same in Dixie," "Dandy Dan," "Slumber Song (Sweet dreams, dear one, of thee)," and "Good Evenin'." Other songs not in the above score are "Daisy Dean" and "The Amorous Star."

FURTHER REFERENCE: *Boston Eve. Transcript* 8–30–1904. *DBlkTh* (Woll). *Just Before Jazz* (Riis). *NY Herald Trib.* 5–24–1904. *NYT* 5–24–1904. Riis diss. *The Southerner* folder in Harvard Theatre Collection.

A SOUTHERN STAR. See *A CHRISTMAS MIRACLE*.

SOUTHLAND FOLLIES (1924, 1927). Musical revue in at least two eds. Touring show prod. by and costarring singer Joe Sheftell. *1924 ed*. Cast also included "Ukulele" Bob Williams (comedian), Russell Brown and Joe Peterson (dancers), Reuben Brown, and Nina Cato. *1927 ed*. Cast also included Johnny Woods, Little Henry, the White Brothers, Mamie Moon, Esther Bigeou, Charles Moore, and Dude Kelly.

SOUTHLAND REVUE (1927). Touring revue. Prod. by and costarring comedian Tim Moore. Cast also included Freddie Johnson, the Berry Brothers, Campbell & Farrow, Clinton "Dusty" Fletcher, Ethel Williams, and Viola Speedy.

A SPANISH REVIEW (1898). Musical sketch. Conceived and arranged by Bob Cole and William "Billy" Johnson, in celebration of the victory of the Spanish-American troops over Spain in the Spanish-American War. Apparently consisted of a drill or march of Spanish toreadors, during which the letters T-R-I-U-M-P-H were formed. Prod. on tour, as part of the *Black Patti Troubadours* show, after the Spanish-American War ended in 1898.

SPEEDING ALONG (1931). Musical revue. Written by "Jelly Roll" Morton. Prod. at the Jamaica Theatre, New York, May 1931.

SPICE OF 1922 (1922). White-oriented revue. Book by °J. Laid. Lyrics by °James F. Hanley. Music by miscellaneous composers. Included an additional song by Henry Creamer and J. Turner Layton. Prod. at the Winter Garden Theatre, New York, opening Aug. 6, 1922, for 73 perfs.; with an all-white cast. The Creamer & Layton song was "Way Down Yonder in New Orleans," a song which has become a classic; it was originally written for inclusion in *Strut Miss Lizzie* (1922), but was not used in that show.

SPOONY SAM (1911). Musical revue. 1 act. Touring show prod. by William M. Benbow and the Alabama Chocolate Drop Co. Cast included Benbow (Spoony Sam), Mose Graham, Rebecca Kinzy (the Black Swan), and Edna Benbow. Songs included "Tell Her No, That's All," "All That I Ask Is Love," and "In the Land of Harmony."

STAGGERLEE (1987). Rhythm and blues musical. Written and dir. by Vernel Bagneris. Music by Allen Toussaint. A 1950s musical, set in New Orleans during the Mardi Gras season. Prod. at the Second Avenue Theatre, New York City, during the summer of 1987; with choreography by Pepsi Bethel. Featuring Adam Wade, Ruth Brown, Marva Hicks, Juanita Brooks, Reginald Vel Johnson, and Carol Sutton.

STARS OVER BROADWAY (1936). Cabaret revue. Prod. at Connie's Inn in its downtown New York City location, 1936; starring Billie Holiday, who was replaced by Bessie Smith during Holiday's brief illness.

STEAMBOAT BILL FROM LOUISVILLE (1928). Touring show. Prod. by George L. Barton. Cast included comedians Billy Ewing and Sam Robinson, piano artists "Bozo" Nickerson and J. C. Davis, comedienne Hattie Joel, deluxe dancers Jackson & Jackson, eccentric dancer Tommy Woods, the Dixie Quartet, and the Brown Skin Radio Beauty Chorus.

STEAMBOAT DAYS (1928). Musical revue. Prod. by and starring blues singer Bessie Smith, on northern tour in 1928, finally opening at the Lincoln Theatre in Harlem on Jan. 14, 1929. Cast included Sam Davis (father of Sammy Davis, Jr.), Ethel Williams, Nat Cash, Lloyd Hollis, Bootsey Swan, and Hackback and Willie Holmes.

STEP ALONG (1922–24). Touring show. Prod. by Quintard Miller and blackface comedian Marcus Slayter. Apparently built around the comedy routines of Amon Davis (also in blackface), who played the part of a smart fellow, whose friends try to stump him with stupid questions, and in the end they always manage to do so. Also in the cast were Burch Williams, Eddie Lemons, Homer Hubbard, Belle Johnson, Irene Parker, Bessie Wrightson, Mildred Brown, Myrtle Bryson, Villa Williams, Edith Randolph, Gladys Mitchell, and Carrie Yates.
FURTHER REFERENCE: *Billboard* (J. A. Jackson's Page) 10–21–1922; 11–22–1922.

STEP ALONG (1926). Touring revue. Prod. by the Standard Amusement Co. Cast included Rose Henderson (billed as "Little Miss Jazz") and Marguerite Johnson.

STEP CHILDREN (1923). Touring show. Prod. by Boatner & Clark. About a stepmother who tries to defraud her two stepchildren out of their rightful inheritance so that it can go to her own two children. Cast included straight comedian Clem Mills, Eulalia Smith, Mary Hicks, Vergie Williams, Mary Green, and Katie Smith.

STEP LIVELY, BOY (1972). Musical adaptation. By Vinnette Carroll. From the antiwar play *Bury the Dead*, by Irwin Shaw. Music and lyrics by Micki Grant. Prod. by the Urban Arts Corps, New York, opening Feb. 7, 1972; dir. by Carroll.

STEP LUCKY GIRLS (1923). Touring revue. Prod. by Bailey & Harris (Laura Bailey and Stella Harris). Cast also included Johnny Bird and O. Robinson.

STEP ON IT (1922). Touring revue. Written, prod., and perfd. by Flournoy E. Miller and Aubrey Lyles (Miller & Lyles). Cast also featured Ada Brown. **FURTHER REFERENCE:** *Billboard* (J. A. Jackson's Page) 7–29–1922.

STEPPIN' BABIES (1926). Touring revue. Prod. by Eddie Lemons, who co-starred with his wife, Olive Lopez Lemons. Also in the cast were "String Beans" Price, Yanks Bronson, Charles A. Berry, Lulu Whidby, and Albert McClelland.

STEPPIN' HIGH (1924, 1925). Musical revue in at least two eds. Touring show starring Thomas & Russell (Rebecca "Dink" Thomas and "Strawberry" Russell) and the Three Black Aces (a dance team which included Eddie "Roch-ester" Anderson, his brother Cornie Anderson, and Lawrence "Flying" Ford). *1924 ed.* Prod. by and costarring William "Billy" Pierson. Cast also included Hazel Myers, Mary Richards, Glennie Cheesman [or possibly Chessnut], and Ernestine Porter. *1925 ed.* Prod. by Thomas & Russell. Cast also included Leonidas Simmons, Richard Courtney, Glennie Chessnut [or possibly Chees-man], and Webb King.

STEPPIN' TIME (1924). Touring revue. Prod. by and costarring Alex C. Rogers and C. Luckeyth Roberts. Cast also included Billy Higgins and Eddie Hunter.

STEPPIN' UP (1924). Touring revue. Book by Jessie Gines. Musical dir., "Doc" Perkins. Cast included Gines, Alice Perkins, Happy Holmes, Byrd & Byrd, May Allen, and "Kid" Bruce.

STILL DANCING! (1925). White-oriented musical revue. Main authorship un-known. Featured a popular song, "Lady of the Moon," by Noble Sissle and Eubie Blake. Prod. London, 1925. Musical score pub. by Keith Browne, London, 1925; copy in Moorland-Spingarn.

STOMPIN' ALONG (1985). Jazz musical. A retrospective view of the 1940s, with its glamourous entertainers—Cab Calloway, Billie Holiday, the Mills Broth-ers, and others. Prod. at the Downtown Cabaret Theatre of Bridgeport [CT], 1985.

STOP AND THINK (1990). Musical morality. "A new drug and racism rap musical" (*Blk. Masks* 1/2–1990). Prod. at the Phipps Plaza Theatre in Phipps Housing Complex, New York City, Feb. 1990; dir. by Rome Nea. Music and performance by Positively Black. Featuring Jermaine Farrar, Jason C. F. Spen-cer, Benja K., Sheila McGill, Robert "Mkhizi" Turner, and Mary "Rhodi" Striplin.

STOPPIN' THE TRAFFIC (1927). Touring revue. Prod. by and costarring Russian-style dancer Dewey Weinglass. Cast also included Slim Thomas and Billy McLaurin, Cecil Rivers, Bertha Roe, Flo Brown, Bloudina Stern, Lomax & Blue, Marion Moore, Lee Allen, Tommy Woods, "Birdie" Parker, and the Song Birds.

THE STORY OF SOUL (1978). Musical. By Owen Dodson and Gary Keyes. Combined poetry, music, and dance to tell the origin and meaning of "soul," an elusive term used to define the essence of black culture during the 1970s. Premiered at Howard Univ., Washington, DC, Dec. 1978.

STORYVILLE (1977). Musical comedy. By Ed Bullins. Music and lyrics by Mildred Kayden. "Set in New Orleans in 1917, a singer gets involved with a musician and they form their own band as they work their way up the river" (*Blk. American* 5–1977). Prod. at the Mandeville Theatre, Univ. of California/ La Jolla, May 1977.

STRAIGHT FROM THE GHETTO (1976–77). Musical revue. By Neal Harris and Miguel Piñero. Based on a book of poems written by members of the Black Osmosis Drama-Writers Workshop, New York, dir. by Harris. Prod. by the New York Shakespeare Festival, at Lincoln Center, and on tour throughout the New York State penal system, summer 1976 through Jan. 1977.

STRANDED IN AFRICA (1912). Musical play. Written by Frank Crowd. Prod. by the Freeman-Harper-Muse Stock Co., at the Globe Theatre in Jacksonville, FL, 1916. Starring Clarence Muse as King Gazu, whose makeup was praised for its creative artistry. Cast also included J. D. Taylor, William Burrell, Otis Hall, Oscar Hagamin, Leonard Harper, Essie Whidby, Lulu Whidby, Lucille Nelson, Annie Morgan, Gussie Freeman, and George Freeman.

STREET SCENE (1947). Folk opera. 2 acts. Libretto by °Elmer Rice. Lyrics by Langston Hughes. Musical score by °Kurt Weill. Based on Rice's play of the same title, which won the Pulitzer Prize in 1929.
    Tragedy of tenement life in New York City, revolving around the murder of an adulterous wife and her lover, and her daughter's romantic affair with a young Jewish intellectual. Often called "the first Broadway opera."
    Prod. on Bway at the Adelphi Theatre, Jan. 9–May 17, 1947, for 148 perfs.; dir. by °Charles Friedman. The integrated cast featured °Polyna Stoska, °Ann Jeffreys, and °Norman Gordon; with Creighton Thompson and Juanita Hall as the black janitor and his wife, and Wilson Woodbeck and Helen Ferguson (juvenile) in minor roles.
    Frequently revived by the New York City Opera, of which one perf. was telecast Oct. 27, 1979.
    Important songs include "I've Got a Marble and a Star" (sung by the black

janitor), "Moon-Faced, Starry-Eyed," "What Good Would the Moon Be?," "Remember That I Care," "Somehow I Never Could Believe," "Wouldn't You Like to Be on Broadway?," and "Lonely House."

Orig. cast recording by Columbia Records (COL 4139). Piano-vocal score pub. by Chappell & Co., New York. Script of lyrics in JWJ/YUL.

STRUT MISS LIZZIE (1922). Vaudeville revue, self-described as "Glorifying the Negro Beauty." Book by Henry S. Creamer. Lyrics and music by Creamer and J. Turner Layton.

A typical black revue of the 1920s, in frank imitation of the more successful *Shuffle Along*. Described by the *NYT* (6–20–1922) as "a generally entertaining if somewhat repetitious succession of songs, dances and comedy scenes." Also featured a medley of song hits by Creamer & Layton and a parody of *Il Trovatore*.

After a tryout in Harlem, and a brief downtown stint at the National Winter Garden (on Houston St.) in New York City, it moved to Bway's Times Square Theatre, opening June 19, 1922, for 32 perfs.; then to the Earl Carroll Theatre, for three weeks, before closing in the red; dir. by Creamer. Cast: Henry Creamer, J. Turner Layton, Hamtree Harrington, Brevard Burnett, George Harve, James Barrett, James Moore, Alice Brown, Cora Green, Grace Rector, Jean Rountree, Charles Frederick, Henderson & Halliday, and Williams & Taylor.

Songs and musical numbers: "Strut, Miss Lizzie," "Dear Old Southland," "Buzz Mirandy," "Darktown Poker Club," "Nobody's Gal," "My Hometown," "Creole Blues," "Lovesick Blues," "In Yama," "Crooning," "Wyoming Lullaby," " 'Way Down Yonder (in New Orleans)," "Hoola from Coney Isle," "Mandy," "I Wanna Dance," "Fan Tan Fannie," "When You Look in the Eyes of a Mule," "Four Fo' Me," "Jazz Blues," and "Sweet Angeline." "Strut, Miss Lizzie" pub. by J. Mills, New York, 1921; copy in Schomburg. "Buzz Mirandy" pub. by Shapiro, Bernstein, 1922; copy in Moorland-Spingarn. **FURTHER REFERENCE:** *BlkMusTh* (Woll). *NYT* 6–20–1922. *NY Trib.* 6–20–1922. *Strut Miss Lizzie* file in TC/NYPL.

STRUTTIN' (1988). Musical. Book, music, and lyrics by Lee Chamberlin. About two sisters from New Jersey who move to New York to seek fame and fortune during the depression. Prod. by the AMAS Repertory Theatre, New York, Feb. 11–March 6, 1988; dir. by Chamberlin. Choreography by Bernard J. Marsh; musical direction by Neal Tate. Starring Jillian C. Hamilton and Reaux Roumel, who both received AUDELCO Awards for outstanding performance in a musical (female and male, respectively). AUDELCO Awards were also received by Chamberlin (as director), Marsh (for choreography), and Shirley Prendergast (for lighting design).

STRUTTIN' ALONG (1923). Musical revue. Prod. by °Jack Joy. Touring show featuring Mamie Smith and her Jazz Hounds, which toured the West Coast in 1923. This was the show in which Eddie "Rochester" Anderson (who became Jack Benny's famed servant in the Jack Benny Show) began his professional career. Other members of the cast included John Rucker, Sid Perrin, Richard

Courtney, William Pierson, Frisco Nick, Zoe Rames, Carolyne Snowden, Susie Harris, William Mitchell, Lawrence Ford, Earl West, Norman Stewart, Billy Moore, C. Anderson, and Mlle. Augusta Petit.

STRUTTIN' ALONG LIZA (1924). Touring revue. Prod. by and apparently costarring Flournoy E. Miller and Aubrey Lyles (Miller & Lyles). Cast also included Lemons & Williams (Eddie Lemons and Birch Williams), Marcus Slayter, Lulu Whidby, and Wrightson & Williamson.

STRUTTIN' HANNAH FROM SAVANNAH. See ***4–11–44***.

STRUTTIN' SAM FROM ALABAM' (1927). Vaudeville revue. 2 parts [5 scenes]. Book, lyrics, and music by Charles Alpin. Prod. by °Arthur Rockwald.

Sam Brown (Struttin' Sam), a dancer from Alabama now living in San Francisco, somehow becomes involved with a princess from Samoa whom he meets in California. He takes her and a group of friends on an odyssey from San Francisco's Chinatown to Alabama, then to Samoa, and back to San Francisco, where a final celebration is held at the Dark Town Strutters' Club.

Prod. by Rockwald at the Majestic Theatre in Los Angeles, where the show was closed after a three-day run, because of the boycott of blacks who protested the theatre's Jim Crow policy. Cast: Tom Harris (Sam Brown), Frieta Shaw (Kukula, A Samoan Princess), Tom Cross (Officer Blue), Mildred Washington (Blossom), Malcolm Patten (Charles Towne), Buddy Brown (Chinatown Phil), Edward Tolliver (Tong Fuey), Boston Webb (Mandy), Amy Loften (Cleopatra), Margaret Jackson (Molano), Duke Johnson (Deacon Jones); Others: Creole Chorus, Street Sweepers, Chinese Girls, Alabama Strutters, Samoan Girls and Boys; Specialties: Ali Brothers, John Jackson, Charles Hart, Helena Justa & Boys, Tommy Gates, and Charles Weaver.

Songs and musical numbers: Part I—"Clever People, These Chinese" (Creole Chorus), "The Ragtime Struttin' China Girl" (Washington & Chorus), "Chin Chin Chinaman" (Tolliver & Chorus), "I'd Rather Be a Street Sweeper" (Harris & Street Sweepers), "Dancing on the Old Plantation" (Chorus), Specialties (Jackson, Ali Bros., Gates & Weaver), "Struttin' Sam Is Coming Back to Dixie" (Webb & Chorus), "The Girl I Left in Zanzibar" (Patten, Justa & Girls), "Don't Think Because My Name Is Cleopatra" (Loften), "The Samoan Dancing Girl" (Harris & Chorus), Finale. Part II—Specialty (Justa & Boys), "I'm a Samoan Maid" (Shaw & Chorus), "I'm the King" (Harris & Chorus), "Guide Me Mystic Moon to Dixieland" (Chorus & Quartette), "On Our Carolina Honeymoon" (Patten & Washington), "My Queen of Poppyland" (Justa & Dancing Boys), Specialty (M. Jackson, billed as "The Black Galli Curci"), 'Evolution of the Dance' (Shaw & Company): Quadrille (Johnson), Cake Walkers (J. Jackson, Billy Drew, Gladys Johnson, Aberdeen Ali [one of the Ali Bros.] & Ruth Edmondson), Pas-ma-la (Gates), Texas Tommy (Washington & Brown), Shimmy (Marbelle DeLandro), and Charleston (Weaver).

STRUTTIN' TIME (1924). Touring show. Book by Eddie Hunter. Prod. by and costarring Flournoy E. Miller and Aubrey Lyles (Miller & Lyles). Cast also included Eddie Hunter, Alex Rogers, Dink Stewart, Andrew Tribble, Ada Brown, Katherine Yarborough, Nina Hunter, Lena Roberts, and Alberta Hunter. Only one song has been identified: "Magnolia" (sung by Yarborough & Chorus).

STRUTT YOUR STUFF (1920). Musical revue. Book and lyrics by William "Babe" Townsend. Music and stage direction by Dave Payton. Touring show that featured Ida Forsyne, Margaret Ward Thomas, Billy Brown, Gertrude Saunders, Leonard Scott, Mary Bradford, Billy Gulfport, Charles Shelton, India Allen, and a chorus of 10 ladies. Musical numbers include "Hold Me" (Forsyne), "The Wedding Blues" (Thomas), "Darktime Dancing School," "Dancing Is the Work of the Evil One" (Scott), "I Want to Shimmy" (Bradford), "Louisiana Blues" (Gulfport), and "Summer Time" (Shelton).

STYLISH STEPPERS (1921). Musical revue. Touring show cited in *Billboard* (J. A. Jackson's Page) 3–26–1921.

SUBWAY SAL (c. 1909). Vaudeville comedy. Prod. by Eddie Green. Opened at the Crescent Theatre, New York, around 1909.

SUGAR CANE (1925–28, 1933). Musical revue in several eds. Apparently prod. in Harlem and on tour. A. D. Price has been cited as the orig. producer of the *1925, 1926 and 1927 eds.* Dewey "Pigmeat" Markham was one of the featured performers in all eds. The *1928 ed.* was prod. by and costarred Coleridge Davis. Cast included Markham, Jessie Cryor, D. Martin, John Davis, Geneva Washington, Harry James, Marie Williamson, Florine Jenkins, Alma Bell, and Willie Greek. This prodn. toured the Majestic Theatrical Circuit (white). The *1933 ed.* featured Markham, Harriet Calloway, Charles Ray, Lavanda Snow, Rudolph Craig, and Willie & "Smoak."

SUGAR HILL / / Also known as *Meet Miss Jones* (1931, 1947, 1949). Musical comedy. Subtitled "An Epoch of Negro Life in Harlem." Music by James P. Johnson. Lyrics by Jo Trent. Book originally by Aubrey Lyles, with revisions by °Charles Tazewell. Book revised in 1947 by Flournoy Miller and retitled *Meet Miss Jones*. Book and lyrics revised in 1949, and credited to Flournoy Miller alone.

Starring vehicle for Miller & Lyles, who provide new adventures for their vaudeville characters as Steve Jenkins and Sam Peck. As the title suggests, the setting was the swank Harlem district known as Sugar Hill, involving about ten blocks, which, according to Bruce Kellner (*HarlRenD*, p. 344), consisted of "a line of brick and granite townhouses and apartment buildings, with canopied entrances and uniformed doormen, [which] sheltered Harlem's aristocracy. Like

'Nob Hill' in San Francisco and 'The Main Line' outside Philadelphia, the name of the locale was used to suggest money and position.''

The single set was the exterior of one of the brownstone buildings, which, according to Gerald Bordman (*AmMusTh*, p. 473), ''led several critics to view [the play] as a musicalized, black [version of] [*]*Street Scene*. . . . In a further similarity to *Street Scene* a number of minor plots were woven into the main story line.''

Allen Woll has brought to light (*BlkMusTh*, p. 152) that *Sugar Hill* did have a strong relationship to *Street Scene* in that both were concerned with a murder involving a New York City apartment building. According to Woll, the Miller & Lyles show was built around the accidental killing of a baby in Harlem during a gangster shoot-out, in which four other children were also injured in the crossfire. The accounts of these deaths were reported in *NYT* (7–29–1931) and *Time* (7–10–1931).

In *Sugar Hill*, Miller and Lyles, as an iceman and an apartment house janitor, respectively, become involved in trying to solve the murder, and to help one of the tenants, a beautiful young woman, played by Etta Moten, whose fiancé is being threatened by the racketeers.

The *Houston Informer* (1–9–1932), reviewing the Bway prodn., described the show as a mixture of ''horseplay, comedy, a few plaintive songs, including 'Fate Misunderstood Me' and a great deal of shuffling . . . [which proved to be] at best a poor attempt to bring Negro laughter and gaiety to Broadway.'' Miles Jefferson (*Phylon* 2nd qtr. 1948, p. 106), who reviewed the 1947 prodn., which apparently departed greatly from the Bway version, stated that ''Flournoy Miller . . . should be jailed on [a] bread and water diet for the libretto,'' and that while Johnson's music recalled ''the simple melodies of 'Shuffle Along' and 'Runnin' Wild' days, . . . it lacked their nostalgic charm and originality.''

First prod. on Bway at the Forrest Theatre, New York, opening Dec. 25, 1931, for 11 perfs. Cast: Flournoy Miller (Steve Jenkins), Aubrey Lyles (Sam Peck), Juanita Stinnette (Loucinda), Chappy Chappelle (Jasper), Broadway Jones (Gyp Penrose), Carrie Huff (Sister Huff), Margaret Lee (Matilda Small), Albert Chester (Joe), Kay Mason (Mitzie), Etta Moten (Cleo), Tressa Mitchell (Tress), Harrison Blackburn (Uncle Henry), Andrew Copeland (Officer Brown), Ina Duncan (Cleo's Mother), and J. Louis Johnson (Parson Johnson).

Songs and musical numbers of the orig. prodn.: ''Boston,'' ''Fate Misunderstood Me,'' ''Fooling Around with Love,'' ''Hot Harlem,'' ''Hot Rhythm,'' ''Yes, I Love You Honey,'' ''Moving Day,'' ''Noisy Neighbors,'' ''Rumbola,'' ''Something's Gonna Happen to Me and You,'' ''What Have I Done,'' and ''I Don't Want Any Labor in My Job.'' Some songs pub. by Harms, Inc., 1931–32.

Prod. as *Meet Miss Jones* by the Negro Musical Comedy Experimental Theatre, at the American Negro Theatre in Harlem, Nov. 1947.

Revived as *Sugar Hill* (with subtitle *Meet Miss Jones*) in Los Angeles, CA, opening at the Las Palmas Theatre in Hollywood in June 1949, where it ran for three months but the producers were unable to find the financial backing to bring the show to New York.

Songs and musical numbers of the 1949 prodn.: "Apple Jack," "Bad Bill Jones," "Busy Body," "Caught," "Don't Lose Your Head, Then Lose Your Girl," "Faraway Love," "I Don't Want Any Labor in My Job," "I've Got to Be Lovely for Harry," "Keep 'Em Guessing," "Love Don't Need a Referee," "Lovin' Ain't My Aim," "Mr. Dumbell and Mr. Tough," "My Sweet Hunk of Trash," "Peace, Sister, Peace," "Sender," "Sepia Fashion Plate," "Smilin' Through My Tears," "That Was Then," "Until You Are Caught," "You're Going to Blitz the Ritzes," "What Kind of Tune Did Old Nero Play," "You Can't Lose a Broken Heart," and "You're My Rose." Most songs pub. by Mills Music, 1948–50.
FURTHER REFERENCE: *NYT* 12–26–1931.

SUGAR HILL (1990). A play with music. By °Robert Fernandez and Louis St. Louis. (Not related to the musical of the same title by Miller & Lyles [1931].) About three generations of black women in show business who resided in the Sugar Hill neighborhood of Harlem, from the 1920s through the 1950s. This neighborhood was a ten-block section from 145th to 155th Streets, between Amsterdam and Edgecombe Avenues, made famous by such artistic figures as Langston Hughes, Paul Robeson, and Duke Ellington. Prod. in the theatre at St. Peter's Church, New York City, opening April 18, 1990; dir. by Hattie Wilson.

SULTAN FOR A NIGHT (1917). Touring vaudeville comedy. Prod. by Irvin C. Miller, who played the title role and costarred with comedian Dink Stewart.

SULTAN SAM (1920). Vaudeville comedy. Prod. at the Lafayette Theatre in Harlem by Irvin C. Miller, who starred in the title role. Cast also included Emmett Anthony, Ada G. Brown, Blanche Thompson, Anita Wilkins, Ernest Whitman, Ralph Brown, and the Leggett Sisters.

SUMMER IN THE CITY (1965). Musical. By Oscar Brown, Jr., and Kent Foreman, who also dir. Although this was an integrated show, according to *Blk. World* (4–1973, pp. 28–29), "the gut and beauty of it came entirely from Black life." Prod. at the Harper Theatre in Hyde Park, Chicago, 1965.

THE SUN DO MOVE / / Orig. title: *Sold Away* (1941–42). Called by the author "A Music-Play." Prologue, 3 acts. By Langston Hughes.

A musical pageant of the black man's journey from slavery to freedom, depicted through a series of episodes interspersed with narrative and spirituals. Thematically akin to the author's more successful *°Don't You Want to Be Free* (1937). The title was taken from the famous sermon by John Jasper, an unlettered but popular black preacher of the nineteenth century.

The narrator is a porter who appears only in the Prologue, where he sweeps away the dust from the Negro's past, then sheds his porter's identity and assumes his rightful identity as an African. The three acts focus upon a young slave couple, Mary and Rock, carrying them from the auction block through the various events and crises in their lives. These include their separation when Rock is sold to another master, the birth of their son and his rearing by Mary alone, the individual hardships that each has to bear, Rock's unsuccessful attempt to escape and his recapture, the death of their son after trying to protect his mother from the brutality of her mistress, and Mary and Rock's eventual escape to freedom in the North through the Underground Railroad.

Sched. for prodn. under its orig. title by the Karamu Theatre, Cleveland, at the Brooks Theatre, during the 1941–42 season, but was cancelled because of Pearl Harbor.

First prod. by the Skyloft Players, Chicago, at the Good Shepherd Community House, spring 1942. Presented during the 1940s at Parkway House, New York.

Script mimeographed by the International Workers Order, New York, 1942; copies in Schomburg, TC/NYPL, and Moorland-Spingarn. Scripts and drafts in JWJ/YUL.

SUN FLOWER REVUE (1929). Touring show. Prod. by Lovey Austin. Cast included Clara & Della, Chippy Hill, Lida Lee, Dant & Roy, Rastus Jones, and Roy Blanks.

THE SUN GETS BLUE: A JAZZICAL (1982). Jazz musical. Book, lyrics, and choreography by William Electric Black (Ian Ellis James). Music by °Paul Shapiro. Described by Lionel Mitchell (*NY Amsterdam N*. 5–9–1982, p. 25) as "a staging of the Harlem riots in a way that doesn't allow us to forget the greater uprising of the people." According to him, the show was "very Aaron Copland [Billy the Kid ballet], ultra modern in sounds and movement." Prod. by the Frank Silver Writers Workshop (FSWW), at the Theatre of the Open Eye, New York, April 14–May 2, 1982, for 15 perfs.; dir. by Amy Brockway. Unpub. script in the FSWW Archives/Schomburg.

SUNKIST SOUTHERNERS (1921). Musical show. Cited in *Billboard* (J. A. Jackson's Page) 3–26–1921.

THE SUNNY SOUTH COMPANY / / Rockwell's Sunny South Company (c. 1906–8). Touring vaudeville company and show. 3 acts. °J. C. Rockwell, proprietor and manager.

This show promised two and a half hours of solid fun. Act I consisted of popular songs; Act II included specialty numbers, songs, and dances; and Act III concluded the show with a comedy skit or playlet.

Toured the Northeast for at least three seasons. Among the featured performers were James W. and Louise Turner, comedians; Clifford D. Brooks, leading tenor and stage manager; Bob Purcell and Nellie Thornton, comedians, singers, and dancers; singers Daisy Fox, Blanche and Robert Fuller, Lillian Weathers, Nellie Thornton, Albert Harris, Robert Edmonds, and Young Rastus; Green & Weather(s), unicyclists; the Colored Bells and Swells, singers and dancers; the Sunny South Ladies Quartette; and the Sunny South Male Quartette. Ed. A. Fox was band leader; and H. E. Wheeler (succeeded by W. Washington) was orchestra leader.

Program of the 1908 show: Act I—Plantation songs (Company), "On the Bank of the Ohio River" (opening medley: Company), Dance: Coons Prancing to Two-Step Rather than Waltz (Company?), "Let Me Be Your Lemon Coon" (Young Rastus), "Big Chief Battle Axe" (song: D. Fox), "My Old Kentucky Home" (Edmonds & Ladies Quartette), "Who Me, I'm Not the Man" (Brooks), "Be My Little Teddy Bear" (B. Fuller), "Good Old Georgia" (song: R. Fuller), "What the Rose Said to Me" (song: Weathers), "I Was Born in Virginia" (song: Thornton), Our Whirlwind Buck and Wing Dancers (Company, with J. W. Turner in his specialty portrayal of "Mammy"). Act II—Specialty performances by B. Fuller (the Sunny South Nightingale), J. and L. Turner (the Encyclopedia of Comedy), Purcell & Thornton (comedians, singers, and novelty Buck and Wing Dancers), D. Fox (the Little Magnet), Green & Weather(s) (novelty trick and fancy unicyclists), Male Quartette, Harris & Edmonds (singing old-time melodies and introducing the Colored Bells and Swells in songs and dances). Act III—Farce: 'Fun at Camp'; Cast of Characters: J. W. Turner (Jake, a new recruit), Brooks (Capt. Big Head, who thinks he knows it all), Purcell (Sgt. Nocount), L. Turner (Ambolinas Snow), Privates, and Visitors (Company). **FURTHER REFERENCE:** *Ghost* (Sampson).

SUNSHINE (1930). Musical revue. Prod. at the Alhambra Theatre in Harlem; featuring Trixie Smith.

SUNSHINE SAMMY. See *MOOCHIN' ALONG*.

THE SUNSHINE TRAIN (1972). Gospel musical. Conceived and dir. by William E. Hunt. Music dir. by Louis Hancock and Howard Nealy. Prod. at the Abbey Theatre, New York, June 15–Dec. 17, 1972, for 28 perfs. With the Carl Murray Singers (Carl Murray, Ron Horton, Ernest McCarroll, Joe Ireland, and Larry Coleman) and the Gospel Starlets (Mary Johnson, Dottie Coley, Peggie Henry, Barbara Davis, and Gladys Freeman). Songs and musical numbers: "The Sunshine Train," "Near the Cross," "On My Knees Praying," "Wrapped, Tied and Tangled," "Thank You, Lord," "Just Look Where I Come From," "His Eye Is on the Sparrow," "Troubled Waters," "Swing Low," "Beams of Heaven," "We Need More Love," "Jesus Loves Me," "All the World to Me," "Judgment Day," "Higher," "Come by Here," "Peace," "Stand Up for Jesus," and "God Be With You."

SUN-TAN FROLICS (1929). Musical revue. Prod. at the Lincoln Theatre in Harlem; featuring Mamie Smith.

THE SUPPER CLUB (1901). White-oriented musical comedy. By °Sidney Rosenfeld. With songs by Bob Cole, J. Rosamond Johnson, and James Weldon Johnson. The thin plot revolves around a tour of New York by a new millionaire and his friends. Prod. by the Sire Brothers at the New York Winter Garden, New York, Dec. 23, 1901, for 40 perfs. Partly staged by Cole, who also helped with choreography. The Cole & Johnson Brothers songs included "When the Band Plays Ragtime" and "Don't Butt In."

THE SURPRISE COMPANY (1928). Touring show. Prod. by Rosa Hostler. Cast included Rastus Murray, Louise Redder, Baby Doris Wallace, Sam Theard, and 6 chorus girls.

SWANEE CLUB REVUE (1928). Musical revue. Prod. by Leonard Harper at the Lafayette Theatre. Cast included Clara Smith, Willie Jackson, Doris Rheubottom, and Wells & Mordecai.

SWANEE RIVER HOME (1923). Touring musical show. 2 acts [13 scenes]. Book by Sandy Burns. Music by Benton Overstreet. Prod. by and starring Sandy Burns. Inez Dennis, stage dir. Cast also included Sam Russell, Helen Dolly, Inez Davis, Grace Smith, Millie Holmes, Alec Lovejoy, Fred Hart, George Wiltshire, Dinah Scott, Brownie Campbell, Al Curtis, Leroy & Rastus, and the Swanee Four.

SWEET CHARIOT (1930). Musical play. By °Robert Wilder. A speculative drama about what might have happened if Marcus Garvey had taken a group of blacks back to Africa as he proposed to do during the 1920s.

As described by *HarlRenD* (Kellner, p. 346), "After selling fake stock in his steamship company, Marius Harvey [played by Frank Wilson], becomes inspired by his own eloquence and transports a group of black Americans to Africa. . . . Once settled there they begin to long for the pleasures of their Saturday nights back home and subsequently desert Harvey to return to the United States."

Prod. at the Ambassador Theatre, New York, Oct. 23, 1930, for only 3 perfs. Cast: Frank Wilson (Marius Harvey), Fredi Washington (Lola), Vivian [or Vivienne] Baber (Delia), Alec Lovejoy (King), Harrison Blackburn (Futch), Percy Verwayen (Troll), Martin Mallory (Ship's Captain), Clay Cody (Port Officer), Dixie Reid (1st Negro), Hubert Browne (2nd Negro), Clara Smith (A Worker), Billy Andrews (Peter), Victor Esker (1st White Man), and George Dryden (2nd White Man).

SWINGIN' THE DREAM (1939–40). Musical adaptation. Swing version of Shakespeare's *A Midsummer Night's Dream*. Book by °Gilbert Seldes and °Erik Charrell. Music by °Jimmy Van Heusen. Lyrics by °Eddie De Lange.

This adaptation for an integrated cast, set in Louisiana in the 1890s, used whites for the upper-class characters and blacks for the artisans and wood fairies. The revels are staged for the benefit of the governor of Louisiana, and the lovers wander into a voodoo forest, where they are placed under a spell by a black Puck, played by Butterfly McQueen, who works her magic with a flit gun. Louis "Satchmo" Armstrong played the role of a trumpet-playing Bottom, in which he was apparently replaced during some performances by Benny Goodman, whose sextet perfd. the music for the show. As described by Rosamond Gilder (*ThArts* 2–1940, p. 93),

On the stage, Louis Armstrong blew his magic horn, Maxine Sullivan, a dusky, gentle Titania, crooned her strange rhythms, jitterbugs danced madly, fantastic creatures cavorted and sang, masses of brilliant costumes deployed against gay or fantastic settings, in the orchestra pit and on either side bands provided swing in every mood and mode. Yet never once did all these elements come together or reach out to the spectator and make him take part, even vicariously, in the festivities.

Prod. at the Center Theatre, New York City, opening Nov. 29, 1939, for only 13 perfs.; dir. by the producer and co-librettist, Erik Charrell. Danced by °Agnes de Mille. Cast: White characters/performers—°Herman Green (Majordomo), °Joseph Holland (Theodore, Governor of Louisiana), °Ruth Ford (Polly), °Catherine Laughlin (Crimson), °George LeSoir (Egbert), °Eleanor Lynn (Gloria), °Thomas Coley (Cornelius), °Boyd Crawford (Alexander), and °Dorothy McGuire (Helena). Black characters/performers—Nicodemus (Starveling), Jackie Mabley (Quince), Gerald de la Fontaine (Snug), Troy Brown (Snout), Oscar Polk (Flute), Louis Armstrong (Bottom), Alberta Perkins (Peaceful Pearl), Butterfly McQueen (Puck), Vivian Dandridge (First Pixie), Dorothy Dandridge (Second Pixie), Etta Dandridge (Third Pixie), Maxine Sullivan (Titania), Sunny Payne (Drummer Boy), and Juan Hernandez (Oberon). Black players in the opera "Pyramus and Thisbe": Jackie Mabley (Prologue), Louis Armstrong (Pyramus), Oscar Polk (Thisbe), Troy Brown (Wall), Nicodemus (Moon), Gerald de la Fontaine (Lion), and Bill Bailey (Cupid). Other black specialty performers: Bill Bailey (dancer), the Dandridge Sisters (Dorothy, Etta, and Vivian: singers), the Rhythmettes (Alberta Perkins, Cora Parks, and Auntie Mae Fritz), and the Deep River Boys (George Lawson, Harry Douglas, Vernon Gardner, and Edward Ware).

Songs and musical numbers: "Peace, Brother," "There's Gotta Be a Wedding," "Swingin' a Dream," "Moonland," "Love's a Riddle," "Darn That Dream," "Doing the Saboo," "Jumpin' at the Woodside," and "Pick-a-Rib."
FURTHER REFERENCE: *NYT* 11–30–1939.

SWING IT (1937). Musical comedy. Book and lyrics by Cecil Mack and Milton Reddie. Music by Eubie Blake.

An unsuccessful attempt to create the type of black musical popular during the 1920s. Described by the *NYT* (7–23–1937, p. 17) as "a potpourri of minstrelsy, singing, dancing, mugging, clowning, spirituals, jazz, swing, tapping, and the carrying of Harlem's throaty torch.'' The plot concerned some entertainers from a Mississippi showboat who try to find a better life in New York's Harlem, where they finally put on the show of shows. The principal comedians were Henry Jines and James Green (as Rusty and Dusty), Herbie Brown (as a dancing waiter), and Sherman Dickson and Frances Everett as the young lovers.

Prod. by the Variety Theatre Unit of the WPA Federal Theatre Project at the Adelphi Theatre, New York, opening July 22, 1937, for 60 perfs.; dir. by Cecil Mack and Jack Mason. Cast: Edward Frye (Jake Frye), George Booker (Gabby), Blanche Young (Skadmoose), Walter Crumbly (Nate Smith), Frances Everett (Bud), Genora English (Mame), James Mordecai (Ginger), Sonny Thompson (Steve), Sherman Dirkson (Bob), Henry Jines (Rusty), James Green (Dusty), Al Young (Chin Chin), Dorothy Turner (Su San), John Fortune (Jamaica Joe), Cora Parks (''Moms'' Brown), Richard Webb (Smoky), Leo Bailey (Sonny), Olena Williams (Gladys), Marion Brantley (Ethel), Norman Barksdale (Bill), Lawrence Lomax (Swipes), Frank Jackson (Flatfut), Al Young (Sheriff), James Boxwell (Jasper), and Anita Bush (Amy).

Songs and musical numbers: ''Huggin' and Muggin','' ''Ain't We Got Love,'' ''By the Sweat of Your Brow,'' ''Green and Blue,'' ''It's the Young in Me,'' ''Old Time Swing,'' ''Sons and Daughters of the Sea,'' ''Captain, Mate, and Crew,'' ''Rhythm Is a Racket,'' and ''Shine.''
FURTHER REFERENCE: *NYT* 7–23–1937. *Variety* 7–28–1937.

THE SWING MIKADO (1938–39). Swing version of the Gilbert & Sullivan operetta. 2 acts. Conceived by °Harry Minturn and Shirley Graham DuBois of the Chicago WPA Federal Theatre. Musical arrangements mainly by °Gentry Warden. Orchestrations mainly by °Charles Levy. (Not to be confused, as it often was, with *The Hot Mikado, starring Bill Robinson.)

DuBois, who was not credited with her part in the conception, was then director of the Negro Unit of the Chicago Federal Theatre. She stated in a May 1975 letter to Bernard L. Peterson that

[*The Swing Mikado*] indeed . . . was one of the Federal Theatre plays which led to the closing of the Federal Theatre because it was offering such competition to the regular Broadway theatre. *The Hot Mikado* was an attempt to capture attention which had been generated by the *Swing Mikado*. But there was absolutely no connection between the two.

This jazzed-up version of *The Mikado* was set on a mythical South Sea island, rather than in old Japan, against a background of palm trees, exotic and colorful flowers, the deep blue waves of the Pacific, and the golden, tropical moon. The characters wore mainly sarongs and loincloths. The songs and dialogue were rendered in an easy-flowing Caribbean accent, and the swing dances included the Big Apple, the Susie-Q, and the latest swing steps of the period.

First prod. by the Chicago Federal Theatre, opening in Sept. 1938, and running through the fall, for 22 weeks, as the hit of the season. It was then brought to

New York, where it opened at the New Yorker Theatre on March 1, 1939, playing to packed houses for 52 perfs. Moved to the 44th Street Theatre, May 1, 1939, where it played for another 28 perfs. Cast included Maurice Cooper (Nanki Poo), Lewis White (Pish-Tush), Herman Greene (Ko-Ko), William Franklin (Poo-Bah), Gladys Boucree (Yum-Yum), Frankie Fambro (Pitti-Sing), Mabel Carter (Peep-Bo), Mabel Walker (Katisha), and Edward Fraction (The Mikado).

FURTHER REFERENCE: *BesPls 1938–39* (two entries). *Crisis* 5–1977.

SYNCOPATED SUE (1929). Touring show. Featured Alice Stewart in the title role; with Inez Saunders as soubrette, Francis Wallace as female lead, Ralph Franklin as straight man, and William Jones and William Green as principal dancers.

SYNCOPATION (1927). Touring show. Cast included Inez Dennis, Billy McLaurin, and Monette Moore.

SYNCOPATIONLAND REVUE (1924). Musical revue. Prod. at the Lafayette Theatre in Harlem; featuring Mamie Smith.

THE SYSTEM (1972). Revolutionary black musical. By Clarence Young III. A musical psychodrama about life in America. Prod. by Theatre West, spring 1972, and presented on a number of college and university campuses, including Spelman Coil., Atlanta, Sept. 1972, and Cleveland State Univ., 1973.

T

TABASCO QUEENS (1928). Touring revue. Cast included Leona Williams, Joe Byrd, Billy Higgins, Vivian Brown, Hooten & Hooten, and Walter Thomas.

TABERNACLE (1969). Theatrical collage. 2 acts. By Paul Carter Harrison. Described by the pub. script as an articulation of "Black experience through a synthesis of all elements of the stage—plasticity of stage design, dance movement, music (African and jazz), masks, choral chants, verse, and improvisation" (*New Blk. Playwrs.*, paperback ed. [Couch, 1970]). Centered around the Harlem riots which occurred during the summer of 1964, it explores the theme of justice in the form of a staged ceremony, employing the elements of drama, the musical, and opera, to create a unique theatrical experience. First prod. by Howard Univ., Washington, DC, 1969. Prod. by the State Univ. of California/Sacramento, for a tour of California state universities, 1971. Prod. by the Afro-American Studio, New York, 1974, 1976, 1979, and 1981; dir. by Ernie McClintock. Pub. in *New Black Playwrights* (ed. by William T. Couch, Jr.; New York: Avon, 1970); and in *The Design of Drama: An Introduction* (ed. by Lloyd J. Hubenka and LeRoy Garcia; New York: David McKay, 1973).

TABOO (1922). Musical show. Cited in *Billboard* (J. A. Jackson's Page) 2–22–1922.

TAKE IT EASY (1924). Touring show. Prod. by and starring comedians Quintard Miller and Marcus Slayter (Miller & Slayter).

TAKE IT FROM THE TOP (1979). Musical. Books and lyrics by Ruby Dee. Music by her son, Guy Davis. Prod. Off-Bway by the New Federal Theatre, opening Jan. 18, 1979; dir. by Ossie Davis, who also perfd. in the cast. Unpub. script and tape recording in Hatch-Billops.

TALK OF THE TOWN (1924). Touring show. Cast featured James "Slim" Parker and Little Jeff.

TALLABOO (1913). Touring show. Book by N. R. Harper. Cast included Jeni Lacey, Nellie Lane, Fannie Hall, Clara Hutchinson, Aida Cunningham, George Hutchinson, A. C. Simms, George Gamway, and Slim Walls.

TAMBOURINES TO GLORY (1963). Called by the author "A Gospel Song Play." 2 acts [12 scenes]. By Langston Hughes. Music by Jobe Huntley. Evolved from some of Hughes' poems that had been previously turned into gospel songs by Huntley, an earlier play written around these songs, and Hughes' novel *Tambourines to Glory*.

In his Author's Notes to the pub. script, Hughes stated his intention that the play be perceived as "a fable, a folk ballad in stage form . . . —if you will, a comic strip, a cartoon—about problems which can only be convincingly . . . presented very cleanly, clearly, sharply, precisely, and with humor." In these Notes, he also described the play as a "dramatization of a very old problem— that of good versus evil, God slightly plagued by the Devil, but . . . always . . . winning in the end." According to Hughes' statement in the *NY Herald Trib. Mag.* (10–27–1963, pp. 12–13), this was his first play to make gospel music "an actual part of the play itself."

The plot revolves around the efforts of two women, assisted by the Devil in disguise (in the character of Buddy Lomax, a handsome hustler), to establish a storefront church in Harlem. The two women are contrasted very sharply: Essie is an elderly widow, strong in her religious devotion; while Laura is a very sensual and worldly woman, but essentially a good person. The Notes describe Essie as "the eternal mother image," "that of the good old earth, solid, always there come sun or rain, laughter or tears"; while Laura is "a compelling personality, one not merely pretty, but capable of projecting sunlight, laughter, easy-going summer, and careless love."

Prod. by °S. & H. Venture and °Sidney S. Baron at the Little Theatre, West 44th St., New York City, Nov. 2–23, 1963, for 24 perfs.; dir. by °Nikos Psacharopoulos; choir dir., Clara Ward. Cast included Louis Gossett (Buddy Lomax), Hilda Simms (Laura Wright Reed), Clara Ward (Birdie Lee), Rosetta LeNoire (Essie Belle Johnson), Robert Guillaume (C. J. Moore, a young saint), Clyde Williams (Youth, Brother Clyde, Deacon & Minister of Music), Rosalie King (Mattie Morningside, mistress of the robes), Rudy Challenger (Marshall & Policeman), Anna English (Gloria Dawn, a glamour girl), Helen Ferguson and Tina Sattin (The Gloriettas), Garwood Perkins (Bartender, Deacon & Warden), Brother John Sellers (Brother Bud & Deacon), Micki Grant (Marietta Johnson, Essie's daughter), and Joseph Attles (Chicken-Crow-for-Day, a saved sinner). Other characters include Deacons, Tambourine Temple Choir, Passersby, Cabaret Patrons, and Neighborhood Folk.

Recently prod. at the Red Carpet Theatre, Toura Coll., 240 E. 123rd St., New York City, Jan. 28–Feb. 28, 1988; dir. by Rey D. Allen.

Songs and musical numbers include "Tambourines to Glory" (sung in Prologue by Buddy & Ensemble; and in Finale by Ensemble), "Upon This Rock" (sung first by Essie & Laura, later by Brother Bud), "When the Saints Go Marching In" (Birdie Lee), "Scat Cat" (Gloriettas), "Hand Me Down My Walking Cane" (Gloria & Gloriettas), "New York Blues" (played first by piano, later sung by Buddy), "Love Is on the Way" (Laura), "As I Go" (Deaconess Hobbs), "A Flower in God's Garden" (Marietta), "Back in the Fold" (Crow-for-Day), "I'm Gonna Testify" (Birdie Lee), "The Ninety-and-Nine" (Laura), "Devil Take Yourself Away" (Buddy), "Little Boy, Little Boy" (Marietta & C. J.), "Moon Outside My Window" (C. J.), "What's He Done for Me" (Choir), "When I Touch His Garment" (Choir), "Home to God" (Essie), "Who'll Be a Witness?" (Laura), "Leaning on the Everlasting Arms" (Crow-for-Day), "Let the Church Say Amen" (Birdie Lee), "Thank God, I've Got the Bible" (Essie), "God's Got a Way" (Crow-for-Day), and "I Have Sinned" (Laura).

Songs pub. in *Tambourines to Glory Gospel Songs* by Hughes & Huntley, New York, 1958; also recorded by Folkways Records (GF–3538), sung by the Porter Singers, Hugh E. Porter conducting, with instrumental accompaniment, in New Canaan Baptist Church, New York City, Oct. 3, 1958. Script pub. in *Five Plays by Langston Hughes* (ed. Walter Smalley; Bloomington: Indiana Univ. Press, 1963). Earlier drafts in JWJ/YUL.

FURTHER REFERENCE: *AnthANT* (Patterson). *BlkMagic* (Hughes & Meltzer). Coleman diss. *Newswk* 11–18–1963. *NY Herald Trib.* 9–4–1963. *NYorker* 11–9–1963. *NYT* 10–27–1963; 11–4–1963; 11–22–1963. *NY World-Telegraph* 11–4–1963.

TAN TOWN TAMALES (1930). Musical revue. Prod. at the Lafayette Theatre in Harlem; with Ada Brown.

TAN-TOWN TOPIC REVUE (1933). Touring show. Cast included Jessie Belle Hicks, Pamela Moore, Dorothy Mayes, Helen Morrison, Dorothy Perry, Alice Duran, Ralph Wills, and Ruby Williams.

TAN TOWN TOPICS (1926). Musical revue. Written and prod. by Eddie Rector and Ralph Cooper, who were featured dancers in this show. Music by Thomas "Fats" Waller, written in collaboration with Spencer Williams. Prod. at the Lafayette Theatre in Harlem, 1926, for a run of three or four weeks; then went on tour of the Eastern Negro Theatre Circuit for about two weeks. Also in the cast were Maude Mills (sister of Florence Mills), comic Phillip Giles, singer Arthur Gaines, whistler Walter Brown, Gulfport & Brown (who perfd. in a sketch, 'Let My Wife Alone'), Adelaide Hall, Fats Waller and his band, Donald Heywood and his Orchestra, and 9 chorus girls. The hit tune of this show was "Senorita Mine."

THE TAP DANCE KID (1983–85). Musical drama. Prologue and 2 acts. By Charles Blackwell. Music composed by °Henry Krieger. Based on the novel *Nobody's Family Is Going to Change*, by Louise Fitzhugh, which had been prod. as a TV drama (also called "The Tap Dance Kid") by NBC, Oct. 24, 1978, with Blackwell in the role of the father.

About a black youth's aspiration to become a Bway dancer in spite of his father's objections. Blackwell's adaptn., according to *NY Amsterdam N.* (1–28–1984, p. 26), is built around the idea of "a nuclear Black middle-class family," and in this song-and-dance musical, he wished to show "that they could be upwardly mobile and strive for better things without being preachy."

Prod. on Bway at the Broadhurst Theatre, Dec. 21, 1983; then moved to the Minskoff Theatre in early 1974, where it remained until March 11, 1985, closing after 705 perfs. With choreography by Dannie Daniels, who won a Tony Award for best choreography. Starring Alfonso Ribeiro in the title role as Little Willie, who dreams of following in the footsteps of Bill Robinson and °Fred Astaire. With Samuel E. Wright as the father, a successful lawyer; Hinton Battle as Willie's Uncle Dipsey, a dancer-choreographer, who encourages Willie to pursue his dream; Hattie Winston, as Willie's mother, a former dancer; Alan Weeks, as Willie's grandfather, Daddy Bates, a former vaudevillian, who returns from the grave to inspire Willie by doing some of his old dance routines; and Martine Allard, Willie's big sister.

FURTHER REFERENCE: *AmMusTh* (Bordman). *NY Amsterdam N.* 1–28–1984; 3–3–1984; 4–21–1984; 12–29–1984.

A TEENAGE LOVE PLAY (1985). Musical. 2 acts. By Kenshaka Ali. About two aspiring young dancers, who must deal with child abuse, pregnancy, drug abuse, and other crises which threaten their ambitions. Sched. for prodn. by Mind Builders' Positive Youth Troupe, on tour of New York City public schools, March 1985; no record of the actual prodn.

TELL IT—SING IT—SHOUT IT—MAHALIA LIVES! (1986). Retrospective gospel musical. By Sandra Reaves-Phillips. Based on the life of gospel singer Mahalia Jackson. Prod. as a work-in-progress by the Laurelton Theatre of Performing Arts, at the Social Concern Building, Laurelton, NY, for an open run.

TELL IT TO TELSTAR (1960s). Musical play. 1 act. Subtitled "Ready to Live." By Langston Hughes. Utilizes soloists, dancers, and chorus to dramatize "the freedom struggle that connects slavery of Jews, Blacks, and prerevolutionary French poor to Buchenwald, Birmingham, Selma, and Little Rock" (*Blk. Playwrs.* [Hatch & Abdullah], p. 20). Unprod. Copy in JWJ/YUL.

TELL PHAROAH (1967, 1973, 1984). Concert drama. 2 acts. By Loften Mitchell.

A musical documentary in readers' theatre style, with traditional black music, retelling the history of the black man from Africa to America, emphasizing his struggle for freedom. The title is taken from the well-known spiritual "Go Down Moses," which includes the line, "Tell ole Pharoah / To let my people go!"

Prod. on a black-history-brotherhood program, at Golden Auditorium, Queens Coll., New York, Feb. 19, 1967. The all-star cast of professional actors included Micki Grant, Ruby Dee, Frederick O'Neal, Louis Gossett, Mary Alyce Glenn, and Gloria Daniel, assisted by the St. Albans Children's Choir and soloists Lucille Burney and Robert Alexander.

Prod. in New York as a benefit for the Schomburg Center for Research in Black Culture at the National Maritime Union Theatre, May 8, 1967, under the direction of Albert Grant; and at the Concord Baptist Church, with McKinley Johnson as the leading singer. Prod. by the Kutana Players, a theatre group from Southern Illinois Univ., at the Metropolitan Campus of Cuyahoga Community Coll., Cleveland, 1973. Prod. by the American Folk Theatre, at Symphony Space, New York, June 21, 1984; dir. by Henry Miller. Cast included Oscar Brown, Jr., Frances Foster, and Earl Hyman.

Script pub. in *The Blk. Teacher and the Dramatic Arts* (Reardon & Pawley).

THE TEMPLE OF JAZZ (late 1920s). Musical revue. Prod. either at the Lafayette or Lincoln Theatre in Harlem during the late 1920s; featuring Mattie Hite.

A TEMPORARY ISLAND (1948). Musical. With songs by Lorenzo Fuller. Prod. New York, 1948.

TEN DARK NIGHTS (1911). Touring show. Prod. by Rolf & Smith. Cast featured Jane Smith, Jimmie Brown, Henderson Smith, Alexander Wood, Wright Mobley, Martha Russell, the Haley Trio, and the Erie Quartet.

THAT GETS IT (1922). Musical revue. Prod. in Chicago, in New York (at the Lafayette Theatre), and on tour by Teenan Jones and Dave Payton, in partnership as the Chicago Producing Co. Cast included Tim Owsley, Laura Bowman, Sylvia Mitchell, Sidney Kirkpatrick, Birleanna Blanks, Charles Richardson, Susie and Jodie Edwards (Butterbeans & Susie), Robert Warfield, Mabel Gant, and Alberta Perkins.

THAT'S IT (1928). Musical revue. Prod. by °Jack Goldberg on the Majestic Theatrical Circuit (white). Cast included Edgar Martin, Elizabeth Smith, and Hazel Vanverlah.

THAT'S MY BABY (1926–27). Touring revue in at least two eds. Prod. by Irvin C. Miller. Cast of the *1926 ed.* featured Gallie DeGaston, John Henderson, Alice Gorgas, Aurora Greeley, Happy Simpson, George McArthur, and Albert Jackson (son of J. A. Jackson). The *1927 ed.* featured Bee Freeman, Elizabeth Smith, Harriet Calloway, John Alexander, Charles Hawkins, Lois Williams, and Hampton & Hunter.

THAT'S THE TIME (1919). Musical. Book, lyrics, and music by "Negroes in Baltimore Md.," according to *Crisis* (12–1919, p. 80). Presented with a cast of 50 actors at Albaugh's Theatre in Baltimore, 1919.

THEY'RE OFF (1919). Revived as ***Derby Day in Dixie*** (1921). Musical comedy. 2 acts. Written and prod. by Billy King. Music by J. Berni Barbour.

The plot is built around a horse race at Saratoga, which was apparently presumed to be in the South (as deduced from the song title "Derby Day in Dixie," after which the show was retitled in 1921. Act I takes place in the lobby of a hotel where the guests are waiting to be transported to the racetrack. Act II is at the track.

First presented at the Grand Theatre, Chicago, 1919, with members of the Billy King Stock Co.; dir. by Barbour. Then apparently went on tour, including the Lafayette Theatre in New York. Cast included Birleanna Blanks, Marcus Slayter, Laura B. Hall, Ernest Whitman, Edna Hicks, Gertrude Saunders, Ida Forsyne, Theresa Burroughs Brooks, Ollie Burgoyne, and Clarence Green.

Songs and musical numbers include "Dusting" (hotel maids), "Yama Blues" (Hicks), "You Can't Shake Your Shimmie Here" (Blanks), "Room 16" (Slayter), "Derby Day in Dixie" (Green), "Up in My Aeroplane" (Burroughs, who "flew over the audience" in a "real plane"), "Jungle Jazz" (King), "Hot Dog Ball" (Saunders), and "Brazil" (a classic dance by Burgoyne).

Revived at the Lafayette Theatre, New York, 1921, as *Derby Day in Dixie*. **FURTHER REFERENCE:** *BlksBf* (Sampson).

THIS AND THAT (1919–20). Musical revue. 2 acts [11 scenes]. Book and lyrics by Alex C. Rogers. Music by C. Luckeyth Roberts. Prod. by the coauthors at the Lafayette Theatre in Harlem, 1919–20; dir. by Rogers. Dances choreographed by Hazel Thompson. With a large cast that included Dink Stewart, Lottie Harris, Jesse Paschall, Al F. Watts, Percy Colston, Edna Brown, Charles Woody, Ellis Stevens, Eddie the Curry, Charles H. Williams, and Lelia Mitchell.

THIS OLE HAMMER. See ***NATURAL MAN.***

THIS ONE NIGHT (1922). Touring show. Prod. by Sandy Burns. Featuring members of the Sandy Burns Stock Co.

THIS WAY OUT (1922). Touring show. Prod. by Quintard Miller, who also was a principal member of the cast. A domestic musical comedy, about an unfaithful wife whose lover persuades her to leave her husband and infant child. The separation is averted, however, by the return of the husband in the nick of time. Cast: Quintard Miller (Husband), Henrietta Lovelass (Wife), Purcell Cuff (Lover), and Eugene Shields (Professor).

THOUGHTS (1972–74). Billed as "A Musical Celebration." Book, music, and lyrics by Lamar Alford. Additional lyrics by °Megan Terry and Jose Tapia.

Collection of musical sketches based on Alford's reminiscences of his growing up as a black youth in the South. As described by Jeff Sweet (*BesPls 1972–73*, p. 45), "Time and time again, the rhythms of gospel and soul roused the audience to hand-clapping, foot-stomping enthusiasm, a high point being Mary Alice's rendition of 'Sunshine.' "

First prod. Off-Bway at LaMama E.T.C. (Experimental Theatre Club), Dec. 6, 1972; dir. by Jan. Mickens. Presented Off-Bway, at Theatre De Lys, March 19–April 8, 1973, for 24 perfs.; dir. by Michael Schultz. Cast: Mary Alice, Jean Andalman, Martha Flowers, Robin Lamont, Baruk Levi, Bob Molock, Barbara Montgomery, Jeffrey Mylett, Howard Porter, Sarallen, and E. H. Wright. Presented in the Theatre De Lys version by the New Theatre Club of Washington, DC, at the Washington Theatre Club, Jan. 23, 1974, for 23 perfs.

Songs and musical numbers: "Opening," "Blues Was a Pastime," "At the Bottom of Your Heart," "Ain't That Something," "Accepting the Tolls," "One of the Boys," "Trying Hard," "Separate but Equal," "Gone," "Jesus Is My Main Man," "Bad Whitey," "Thoughts," "Strange Fruit," "I Can Do It to Myself," "Walking in Strange and New Places," "Music in the Air," "Sunshine," "Many Men Like You," "Roofs," and "Day Oh Day."

THREE FOR TONIGHT (1955). Musical revue. Bway revue which featured Harry Belafonte.
FURTHER REFERENCE: *BesPls 1954–55.*

THREE LITTLE MAIDS (1930). Musical show. Featured at least two songs by James P. Johnson: "My Idea of Love" and "Never Mind," both copyrighted by Shubert Theatre Corp., 1930; copies of songs reportedly in LC.

THREE SHOWERS (1920). Book by °William Cary Duncan. Lyrics and music by Henry S. Creamer and J. Turner Layton.

The plot centers around an old saying that if a person makes a wish on a day with three showers, that wish will come true. The girl, a "farmerette," with the unlikely name of Robert Lee "Bob" White (played by °Anna Wheaton), wishes for the man, Peter Fitzhugh (°Paul Frawley), and gets her wish. Prod. by °Mr. and °Mrs. Charles Coburn, who also costarred in this prodn.

First presented at the Empire Theatre, Syracuse, NY, before opening at the

Harris Theatre, New York City, April 5, 1920, for 48 perfs. One of the featured songs from the Creamer & Layton score (which was described as "lively, but not memorable" [*AmMusTh* (Bordman), p. 348]), was "It's Always the Fault of the Man," musical score pub. by Charles K. Harris, New York; copy in Moorland-Spingarn.
FURTHER REFERENCE: *NY Clipper* 4–14–1920. *NY Dramatic Mirror* 4–10–1920. *NYT* 4–6–1920. *ThMag* 5–1920.

THREE THIEVES (1927). Musical comedy. Touring show which featured Tim Owsley, Hazel Myers, Rags Cole, Silvertone Toya, and K. Pierson.

THE THREE TWINS (1916). Vaudeville farce. 2 acts. Lyrics by °C. A. Hauerback. Music by °Karl Hoschna. Although this show involved three sets of lovers, no information has been located as to the relationship of the "three twins" to the plot. Act I occurs in General Stanhope's home on the Hudson River. Act II is set in the sanitarium of Dr. Siegfrid Hartman, "a bug nut." Prod. by the Quality Amusement Co., 1916, and apparently presented at the Lafayette Theatre in Harlem, and in other theatres controlled by Quality. Cast: Tom Brown (General Stanhope, "suffering from Dyspepsia"), Walker Thompson (Tom Stanhope, the General's son), Abbie Mitchell (Kate Armitage, Tom's sweetheart), Gertie Townsend (Isabel Howard, the General's ward), J. Francis Mores (Ned Maryland, in love with Isabel), Susie Sutton (Molly Summer, "always happy"), E. R. Brown (Harry Winters, Molly's expected bridegroom), Laura Bowman (Mrs. Dick Winters, "a cheerful weeper"), Adell Townsend (Bessie Winters), George E. Brown (Dick Winters, "somewhat nervous"), Mildred Smallwood (Billy Winters, Dick's child), Babe Townsend (Dr. Hartman, director of the Hartman Sanitarium), G. G. Gibbs (Matthew, a Keeper); Others: Guests, Tennis boys and girls, Bathing girls, Yama Yama girls, Nurses, Keepers, Visitors, etc.

THROW DOWN (1986). Musical. Written and dir. by °Marvin Felix Camillo. A tribute in vignettes and songs to the careers of several boxing folk heroes, including Joe Louis, Muhammad Ali, Leon Spinks, Larry Holmes, Salvadore Sanchez, and Roberto Duran. Prod. and perfd. by the Family Repertory Company, New York, Jan. 8–Feb. 8, 1986.

TIGHT LIKE THAT (1930). Touring show. Cast featured George Crawford, Earl Edwards, Rivers & Brown, Simms & Bowie, and Barnes & Jackson.

TILL VICTORY IS WON (1965). Opera. Libretto by Owen Dodson. Musical score by Mark Fax. Traces the highlights of the black man's history from Africa to the present. Written for the centennial celebration of Howard Univ., and perfd. there in April 1965. An excerpt was presented in Bermuda, under the auspices of the Howard Univ. Alumni Assn.

TIMBUKTU! (1978–79). Musical adaptation. 2 acts [12 scenes]. Book by °Luther Davis. Based on the musical *Kismet* (1953), by °Charles Lederer and Luther Davis; from the play by °Edward Knoblock. Music and lyrics by °Robert Wright and °George Forrest; from the themes of Alexander Borodin and African folk music.

A remake of the operetta *Kismet* for an all-black cast, with the location changed to Timbuktu, a flourishing trade center in the ancient Empire of Mali, West Africa, during the year 1361 (the Islamic year 752). The plot follows that of the original musical, and concerns the beautiful daughter of a beggar-poet who falls in love with a prince. A starring vehicle for Eartha Kitt, which marked her comeback to Bway after many years of being blacklisted, allegedly through the actions of President and Mrs. Lyndon Baines Johnson, following a widely reported incident at a White House luncheon, where Kitt, as an invited guest, apparently insulted the First Lady by making a candid political remark. In this show, Kitt played the favorite wife of the Wazir, and Melba Moore and Gilbert Price played the young lovers.

Prod. on Bway at the Mark Hellinger Theatre, opening March 1, 1978, for 221 perfs.; dir. and choreographed by Geoffrey Holder. Cast: Eartha Kitt (Sahleem-La Lume, the Wazir's wife of wives), Ira Hawkins (Hadji), Melba Moore (Marsinah, daughter of Hadji), Gilbert Price (The Mansa of Mali), Obba Babatunde (The Chakaba: Stiltwalker, Witchdoctor, Orange Merchant & Antelope), Harold Pierson (Beggar & Witchdoctor), Shezawae Powell (Beggar & Woman in Garden), Louis Tucker (Beggar), Deborah Waller (Child), Daniel Barton (M'Ballah of the River), Eleanor McCoy (Najua & Bird of Paradise), George Bell (The Wazir), Bruce A. Hubbard (Chief Policeman), Miguel Goodreau (Munshi & Bird of Paradise), Luther Fontaine (Antelope), and Vanessa Shaw (Zubbediya).

After successfully completing its Bway run, it toured for a year, opening Sept. 20, 1978, at the Fisher Theatre in Detroit, and closing Feb. 4, 1979, at the Pantages Theatre in Los Angeles; all productions starring Eartha Kitt, with a different cast.

Songs and musical numbers: "Rhymes Have I," "In the Beginning, Woman," "Baubles, Bangles, and Beads," "Stranger in Paradise," "Gesticulate," "Night of My Nights," "My Magic Lamp," "Rahadlakum," "And This Is My Beloved," "Golden Land, Golden Life," "Zubbediya," and "Sands of Time."

TIME FOR A COMING OUT (1989). Gospel musical. Conceived and written by Hazel Smith. Music composed and dir. by Lucille Gaita. Prod. by Help Somebody Productions, at the Theatre of Riverside Church, New York, July 1– Aug. 27, 1989. Music by the TFCO Trio. Cast: Joyce Jordan, T. J. McGarrah, Linda Ransom, Ed Dewer III, Mark R. McKinley, Jannae Jordan, India Faison, Kenneth E. Glover, Annette Evans, Shawn La Re, Marcial Howard, Jamel Allen, Anthony Jarrett, and Darryl Sapp.

THE TIME, THE PLACE, THE HORSE (1920). Touring show. Prod. by the Stovall & Mack Stock Co.

TIM MOORE'S FOLLIES (1922). Touring revue. Prod. by Tim Moore, who also starred as the principal comedian. Cast included Gertie Moore, Eddie Stafford, Ethel Watts, Eva Smith, Kid Brown, Eugene Thomas, Jessie Conway, and Florence Seales.

TINTYPES (1980). Retrospective musical revue. Conceived by °Mary Kyte, with °Gary Pearle and °Mel Marvin. A nostalgic review of selected songs from 1876 to 1920. With an integrated cast of 6 that included Lynne Thigpen (understudied by S. Epatha Merkerson) as the only black performer.

TIP TOP REVUE (late 1920s). Musical revue. Prod. in Harlem either at the Lafayette Theatre or the Lincoln Theatre, late 1920s.

T K O (1989). Musical about boxing. Written and prod. by Cliff Roquemore and William "Mickey" Stevenson. Explores the rise and fall of a black welterweight world champion. Prod. by the Inner City Cultural Center, Los Angeles, April-May 1989. Winner of 1989 NAACP Theatre Awards for the coauthors.

T.O.B.A. REVUE (1925). Musical revue. Prod. by Albert Gibson, presumably on the TOBA Circuit. Cast included the Gibson trio (Albert Gibson, Little Albert, and Baby Corine); "Grasshopper," the comedian; and Wilton Crawley, the "human worm."

TOKIO (1928). Musical revue. Prod. by Irvin C. Miller, who also costarred as principal comedian with Emmett [or Emett] "Gang" Anthony. Cast included Queenie Price, Gladys Robinson, John Churchill, Edna Barr, and Jota (a dancer).

TOM BOYS—EASY BREEZY GIRLS (1914). Touring revue. Prod. by Billy Johnson, who costarred with Tom Brown as principal comedians.

TOM-TOM (1932). Opera. 3 acts [16 scenes]. Written and composed by Shirley Graham Du Bois (Mrs. William E. B. Du Bois). Music based on African and Negro folk melodies.

Developed from a three-act music drama by the same title which the author/composer wrote at Oberlin College during the late 1920s and early 1930s, when she was a student there, involved in research in African music. Although originally intended for student prodn., at the suggestion of the director of the Cleveland Opera Co., she built this drama into a full-scale, 16-scene opera.

Tom-Tom dramatizes the odyssey of the black man from the jungles of Africa to America, and his eventual arrival in New York City's Harlem. According to *Crisis* (8–1932, p. 258), Mrs. Du Bois (then Miss Graham) "used as a background for her melodic structures weird, unpublished, rarely heard Negro folk songs of the Southern swamps.'' In addition to African and native black American themes, the music utilized African instruments, including tom-toms, and the style of the recitative was based on African chants and the sermons of old-time Negro preachers.

The first act is set in a jungle before 1619. The second act shows the African as a slave in America. The third act moves to the Harlem of the 1930s. In a manner similar to that used in Eugene O'Neill's *The Emperor Jones*, the steady beat of the tom-tom underlies all the action. As described by Benjamin Brawley (*The Neg. Genius*, p. 305), ''The production . . . was spectacular, with a full orchestra [and] five hundred singers and dancers.'' The elaborate staging, according to *Crisis* (8–1932, p. 258), included ''elevated trains, subways, automobiles, cabarets, sailing vessels which explode . . . pantomimonists [*sic*], warriors, head-hunters, [and] gigolos [*sic*].''

First prod. in an abridged concert form over NBC Radio, June 26, 1932. Premiered in its first stage prodn. by the Cleveland Summer Opera Co., at Cleveland Stadium, where it was perfd. (according to the author) from June 29 to July 6, 1932. (Hamalian & Hatch, editors of the published script, give the prodn. dates as June 30–July 3, 1932.) Featured cast: Jules Bledsoe (Witch Doctor, Voodoo Man, & Garvey-like Leader), Charlotte Murray (Mother), Luther King (Boy), Lillian Coway (Girl), Hazel Walker (Mammy), and Augustus Grist (Tribal Chief, Plantation Preacher & Captain).

According to Hamalian & Hatch (*The Roots of African-American Drama*, p. 253):

Tom-Tom is the first black opera to be performed on a large scale and with a professional cast. (Harry Freeman had produced his opera [*]*Voo-Doo* [*sic*] at the Palm Garden four years earlier in New York, and his operetta [*]*Vendetta* would debut at the Lafayette Theatre.) *Tom-Tom* premiered . . . on a huge three-dimensional stage before an audience of ten thousand people and with an all-black cast of five hundred people drawn chiefly from local choirs, directed by Ernst Lert and Laurence Higgins.

To secure realism for the jungle scenes, the producers imported Indoxis Chiakazoa, a native African voodoo-man as production adviser.

Libretto pub. in *The Roots of Am. Dr.* (Hamalian & Hatch).

TOO MANY IN THE HOUSE (1909). Touring vaudeville show. Prod. by G. W. Allen, and featuring the Allen's Troubadours.

The show was apparently divided into two parts. Part I was a skit, and Part II consisted of songs and specialty numbers. The show toured the southern states with the following cast: Daisy Reynolds, Josephine Plummer, Richard Carr, G. W. Allen, Jolly Ed. Stewart, Sarah Terry, Annie Lee, Jim Brown, Mme. Lazelle Price, and Stella Carr.

Part I—'Trouble Over Black-Eyed Peas in Dryade Street Restaurant.' Cast of characters: Reynolds (Bluffey Ann, Proprietor of restaurant), Plummer (Old

Sloppy Sal, the cook), Carr (Copper Goodhill, the policeman), Allen (Hank, the black-eyed pea man), Stewart (Jim Hobbs, his partner); Customers of the restaurant: Terry (Winkle Lou), Lee (Butter Bean Lizzie), Brown (High Life Sam), Price (Cat Fish Mame), and Carr (Molly High Grass).

Part II—Songs and specialty numbers: "Picture Single Life" (Brown & Carr), "I Wish I Was in Heaven Sitting Down" (Allen & Price), "If I Had a Thousand Lives to Live" (Price, Carr, Reynolds, Terry & Company), "I Love My Wife, But Oh, You Kid" (Allen, Price & Stewart), "The Family Clock" (Price, Reynolds, Carr, Lee & Terry), "Merry Widow Chorus" (Allen), "Trans-May-nif-i-can-ham-dam-uality" (Price), "Oh, You Loving Gal" (Reynolds), "Good Evening, Caroline" (Company), "Too Many Men in the House" (Company).

TOPSY AND EVA (1924). Jazz version of *Uncle Tom's Cabin*. By °Catherine Chisolm Cushing. Music and lyrics by °Vivian and °Rosetta Duncan (the Duncan Sisters) who costarred as Eva and Topsy (in blackface) respectively. Prod. in Chicago for a lengthy run; then opened on Bway Dec. 23, 1924, where it ran through the Christmas holidays.
FURTHER REFERENCE: *BesPls 1924–25. HarlRenD* (Kellner). *NYT* 12–24–1924.

THE TOWER (1957). Comic opera. 1 act [15 scenes]. By Townsend Brewster. Musical score by Marvin David Levi. King Solomon attempts unsuccessfully to prevent the fulfillment of a prophecy that his daughter will marry the poorest man in the kingdom. Perfd. by the Santa Fe Opera, NM, during its initial season, Aug. 2, 1957. Pub. by Boosey & Hawkes, New York, 1958.

TOWN TOP-PIKS (1920). Musical revue. Touring show prod. by and costarring Aaron Gates. Music partly by Spencer Williams. Cast included Gulfport & Brown (Billy Gulfport and Will Brown), Gertrude Saunders, Ida Forsyne, Ollie Burgoyne, Leonard Scott, Edith Wilson, Ruth Allison, James Thomas, Anna Freeman, and Mary Bradford. Songs and musical numbers: "Land of Creole Girls" (Scott), "I'll Get Even" (Saunders & Brown), "Sweet Daddy" (Saunders), "Dixie Jazz" (Freeman), "Shimmy Shake" (Bradford), "Babylon" (Freeman), and "Mississippi Blues" (Gulfport).

A TRAGEDY ON THE TOWN (1913). Musical drama. Prod. apparently on tour by Porter & McDaniel. Featuring members of the Porter & McDaniel Stock Co.

THE TRAITOR (1913–14). Tabloid musical comedy. 2 acts. Book and lyrics by Alex C. Rogers and Henry S. Creamer. Music by Will Marion Cook.

Described by Cook in the *NY Age* (3–20–1913) as "a playlet . . . full of catchy songs, pretty tableaux, bright repartee, and good singing."

Prod. by the Negro Players Co., at the Lafayette Theatre, New York, March 17, 1913, for one week. Cast included Rogers & Creamer, Abbie Mitchell,

Grace Lee Cook, Chris Smith, Billy Harper, "Boots" Allen, and William Shelton.

Again prod. by the Famous Colored Players, also presumably at the Lafayette Theatre, 1914. Cast included Billy Harper, Charles H. Gilpin, Alice Gorgas, Grayce LeCook, Ruth Cherry, Andrew Bishop, Cassie Norwood, and the Invincible Quartet.

Songs included "After All I've Been to You" and "Lover's Lane."

TREEMONISHA (1907, 1915, 1972, 1975, 1985, 1991). Ragtime folk opera. Written and composed by Scott Joplin.

Joplin's second ragtime opera (the first was *A Guest of Honor*, 1903, now lost), which had to wait almost 70 years for its first full prodn. Set in the nineteenth century, just after the Civil War, it concerns a young woman, who as a child had been found under a tree on an Arkansas plantation by a childless slave couple (Ned and Monisha), who named her Treemonisha, and persuaded some white people to educate her. After Treemonisha comes of age and is about to begin teaching her people, she is abducted by a voodoo conjurer, Zodzetrick. She is eventually rescued and begins to pursue her mission as an educator.

Efforts to secure a prodn. at the Lafayette Theatre in 1913 did not materialize. A 1915 effort to attract backers by presenting an informal audition of the score for an invited audience at a small Harlem rehearsal hall came to naught. Its first public presentation was in a concert version in Atlanta in Jan. 1972, where it was perfd. by the Music Department of Morehouse College and the Atlanta Symphony Orchestra.

The first full-scale prodn. was given by the Houston Grand Opera in May 1975. This prodn. toured briefly before reaching New York, where it was presented on Bway at the Palace Theatre, Oct. 21, 1975, for a run of eight weeks, dir. by °Gunther Schuller. Featured cast: Willard White (Ned), Betty Allen, alternating with Lorna Myers (Monisha), Carmen Balthrop, alternating with Kathleen Battle (Treemonisha), Ben Harney (Zodzetrick), Curtis Rayam (Remus, who helps to rescue Treemonisha).

Perfd. by the Eden Theatrical Workshop, Denver, CO, Nov. 14, 16, and 17, 1985, as part of American Music Week, with the title role played by Marilyn Thompson, a soprano from New York City.

Presented most recently in a "semistaged performance" at Town Hall, New York City, Thursday, Dec. 5, 1991, in a collaborative production by the Harlem School of Arts and Opera Ebony, as a part of the Not Just Jazz Series. As described by the *NYT* (12–8–1991),

Tanya León conducted an orchestra at stage right. Opposite, a costumed chorus sang from risers and 11 principals took their turns out front. La-Rose Saxon [as Treemonisha] sang with a true, vibrato-rich soprano. Raymond Bazemore, Curtis Rayam and Clinton Ingram sang Ned, Remus and Andy respectively with unstinting conviction. Eddye Pierce Young [Monisha], Andre Solomon-Gover [Zodzetrick], John Amthony, Ray Gordon, Michael Loften, Lisa Polite and Melton Sawyer were all convincing. Not every bit of ensemble worked, but Ms. León, using Gunther Schuller's orchestrations, kept this happy music alive.

Libretto pub. by the author, 1911. Cast recording of the Houston Grand Opera prodn. by Deutsche Grammophon (2707–083), which includes libretto. Vocal selections pub. by Chappell, 1975.
FURTHER REFERENCE: *Ebony* 4–1972. *High Fidelity/Mus. Am.* 5–1972. *Neg. Hist. Bull.* 1–1974. *NY Post* 12–4–1991. *NYT* 12–8–1991. *Washington Post* 8–6–1972; 8–11–1972.

A TRIBUTE TO MALCOLM X (1988). Billed as "A Soul Musical." By Titus Walker. A Ujamaa Black Theatre prodn. which opened at the Lincoln Square Theatre, New York, May 20 and 27, 1988.

A TRIP AROUND THE WORLD (1921). Musical show. Written and prod. by Billy King. A pageant of the life and customs of some of the most picturesque and beautifully costumed nations of the world, including France, Spain, Italy, China, Japan, Turkey, Africa, and Cuba, in which King (as Kid Bumpsky) has numerous adventures, including bouts with an alligator and a bull. First prod. at the Grand Theatre, Chicago, and perfd. by members of the Billy King Stock Co.; then went on U.S. tour, including the Lafayette Theatre in New York. Cast included Marshall Rogers, Rebecca "Dink" Thomas, Birleanna Blanks, and Maude Russell.
FURTHER REFERENCE: *BlksBf* (Sampson).

A TRIP TO AFRICA (1908, 1910–11). Musical farce-comedy in two eds. Both eds. written by John Larkins and prod. by the Black Patti Musical Comedy Co., and featuring the *Black Patti Troubadours.*
    1908 ed. 2 acts. Music by Will Vodery. This ed. is important as the first all-black show to be presented before a white audience in the Bowery section of New York City in early 1908; also went on tour, including Chicago, where, after a short run in that city, the show was stranded and forced to close. Cast included "Jolly" John Larkins (King Jasper), Tom Logan (Jim Grafter), George Reese (A Bear), Herbert Sutton (Mail Carrier), Clarice Wright (Miss Sapollo), John Grant (Waiter), James Marshall (Detective); Others: Sissieretta Jones (Black Patti), Muriel Ringgold, and W. J. Jenkins. Songs and musical numbers: Act I—"Royal Coon" (Larkins), "Dolly Brown" (Larkins), "The Man in Grey" (Sutton); Act II—Opening Chorus, "Peekaboo" (Company), "Kentucky Home" (Sutton), "Hoodoo Man" (Jenkins), and "Dolly Brown" (Larkins).
    1910 ed. Billed as a "Revised Musical Comedy in 3 acts," "a new and delicious musical souffle, garnished with dressing of beautiful costumes and stage settings." Music by Dave Payton. According to the Indianapolis *Freeman* (2–26–1910), "The trip to Africa . . . was to rescue Lucinda Lee (Black Patti [Sissieretta Jones]), the favorite instructress at Long Creek College, from the Zamboo tribe by whom she had been made Princess Lulu. The rescue was

successfully accomplished after many ups and downs.'' Prod. on transcontinental tour, which included a three-day engagement at the Park Theatre in Indianapolis, c. Feb. 25, 1910. Cast: John Larkins (''Razz Jim''), Sissieretta Jones (Lucinda Lee), Sarah Green Byrd (Dinah Lee, a ''frisky'' teacher), H. Morgan Prince (Dr. Foolemall, a ''polished'' professor), Will A. Cook (Secret Service Agent), Charles Bougia (Sam Williams), George Taylor (Hank Williams), Louis Hunter (Kleptomaniac), Gus Hall (Chief Zamboo), J. A. Grant (Thomas Cott), J. C. Boone (Cat Maria), William Wilkins (Janitor), George Hayes (Chief Chef), and chorus. Songs and musical numbers (Note: According to the *Boston Transcript* [4–18–1911], ''before and through the African trip, the [show] was well furnished with ragtime ditties and dances to match.''): ''Suwanee River'' (Jones); ''Mother's Chile,'' ''All Hail the King,'' ''A King Like Me,'' ''A Trip to Africa,'' ''The Jungle Drill,'' and ''O You Loving Man'' (all sung by Larkins); Others: ''All I Want Is My Honey,'' ''I Ain't No Fool,'' ''In the Bright Moonlight,'' ''Rag-Time Baseball,'' ''I'm Going to Leave Today,'' ''Good Enough for Me,'' ''The Beaming Sun,'' ''Boola Boola,'' and ''In Zulu Land.'' According to the *Freeman* review, the dancing of Sarah Green Byrd was ''loudly applauded.''
FURTHER REFERENCE: *Boston Transcript* 4–18–1911. *Just Before Jazz* (Riis). Riis diss.

A TRIP TO ARABY (1927). Touring show. Prod. by Matt Housley. Cast featured ''Dink'' Thomas and Slim Austin (billed as the ''Sheiks of Araby''), Angeline Mitchell, Baby ''Kid'' Hall, Moxie Jackson, Josephine Dean, and Baby DeLeon.

TRIP TO CANNIBAL ISLE (1924). Touring show. Prod. by and costarring Drake & Walker (Henry Drake and Ethel Walker).

A TRIP TO COONTOWN (1897–1901). Musical farce, with vaudeville attractions. Billed by the authors as ''The First Black Musical Comedy.'' 3 acts. Book, music, and lyrics by Robert (Bob) Cole and William (Billy) Johnson, assisted by Sam Corker, Jr. Additional music and musical direction by Willis Accooe.

A landmark musical in the history of black theatre, which the *NYT* (4–16–1898) called ''a great success.'' One of the earliest shows to break with the minstrel tradition. Usually credited as being the first true black musical comedy, with a continuous plot, or story line, from beginning to end. Also considered the first musical show written, prod., dir., acted, and managed by blacks. The title was probably borrowed from *A Trip to Chinatown*, the most popular and longest-running white-oriented show of the 1890s, which also dealt with a visit to an exotic ethnic locality.

The thin plot was built around the efforts of Jim Flimflammer, a confidence man (played by Johnson), to swindle the well-to-do Old Man Silas Green out of his $5,000 pension—a swindle that is averted in the nick of time by Willie Wayside, a tramp (played by Cole in whiteface), around whom (with his bulldog

"Bo") much of the comedy is centered, through the numerous practical jokes that are played on him throughout the performance. The show is fleshed out with vaudeville specialty acts, including "original coon oddities" sung by Cole & Johnson, opera solos, juggling, and contortionist stunts.

According to the Indianapolis *Freeman* (10–20–1900), "A parlor in [Silas Green's] home is staged beautifully, where the solos are rendered [and where occurs] the reception of the Prince from Dahomey, who is none the less the very funny Bob Cole. The show is terminated with Cole & Johnson in their grand Oriental frolic in conjunction with the Coontown Carnival."

The show was cast and rehearsed at Proctor's Music Hall, New York, Aug. 1897. Apparently it was tried out in the Catskills in New York State and in South Amboy, NJ (on Sept. 27, 1897), before opening at Miler's Eighth Avenue Theatre in New York in late 1897. Unable to play the first-class theatres in New York City because of a lockout order by the New York Theatrical Syndicate, it toured the Canadian provinces, with engagements in Montreal (at the Queens Theatre, week of Feb. 16, 1898), Ottawa (at Victoria Park), and Toronto, where it received rave reviews.

°Klaw & Erlanger then, in defiance of the Syndicate's lockout order, booked the show at the Third Avenue Theatre, New York, April 4, 1898, for 8 perfs. Cast: Bob Cole (Willie Wayside, a tramp), Billy Johnson (Jim Flimflammer, a bunko artist), Jesse A. Shipp (Silas Green, the grand old man of Coontown; later replaced by Sam Lucas), Bob A. Kelley (Silas Green, Jr.), Tom Brown (Rube, Chinaman & Detective), Lloyd G. Gibbs (Opera Singer), George Brown (Sam; also the company's master of transportation), Walter Dixon (Capt. Fleetfoot), Jim Wilson (Boarder & equilibrist), Samuel King (Boarder), Molly Dill (Mrs. Fannie Brown), Clara Freeman (Flotinda), Margaret Rhodes (Marinda), Jennie Scheper (Clotinda; also wardrobe mistress), Maggie Davis (Florinda), Estella Ware (Aminda), Jennie Hillman (Dudinda), Juvia Roan (Opera Singer), Freeman Sisters (Pauline & Alice: acrobatic dancers), Bill Binkerton (Italian act), Camille Casselle (specialty), Henry Wise, Vincent Bradley, May Wynn, Theresa Ver Vallen, Gladys Hunter, and Sadie Robinson.

Toured for several weeks, then opened at the Grand Opera House in New York City, Sept. 12, 1898, for 8 perfs. Also played at the Casino Roof Garden (June 1899) before going on the road for two more seasons, closing in 1901. Although the show was a popular success, Cole & Johnson filed for bankruptcy in April 1901, and dissolved their partnership the same year. Other performers who moved in and out of the cast during the course of its run were Thomas Craig, Barrington Carter, George Ledbetter, Wiletta Duncan, Pearl LaVan, Myrtle Cousins, Albertina Martin, Willis Accooe, Alice Mackay (Mrs. Willis Accooe), Edna Alexander, Robert Slater and Bert Murphy (vaudeville team), Sam Cousins, George Brown, Lavinia Jones, Nettie Glenn, Vincent Bradley, and William Carl (Black Carl Danti [or Dante]).

Songs and musical numbers: "All Chinks Look Alike to Me," "Coontown Frolique," "The Coontown Regiment," "The Famous Black Moguls," "For

All Eternity," "Play 4–11–44," [+]"La Hoola Boola" (which apparently inspired the "Yale Boola" song), "I Can Stand for Your Color, But Your Hair Won't Do," "If That's Society, Excuse Me," "Here's a Hoping These Few Lines Will Find You Well," "I Must o'Been a Dreaming" (Cole), "In Dahomey," "The Italian Man," "I Wonder What Is Dat Coon's Game," "A Jolly Old Rube," "The Luckiest Coon in Town," "Ma Chicken," "Meet Me at the Gin Spring," "Miss Arabella Jones," [+]"No Coons Allowed!," "Old Kentucky Home," "Picken on a Chicken Bone" (Cole), "Sweet Savannah," [+]"There's a Warm Spot in My Heart for You, Babe," "Trio from Attila," "A Trip to Coontown," "Two Bold Bad Men," "The Way to Kiss a Girl," "The Wedding of the Chinee and the Coon," and "When the Chickens Go to Sleep." Songs marked with a plus sign ([+]) are pub. by Howley, Haviland and Co.; piano scores are located in Moorland-Spingarn.

FURTHER REFERENCE: BesPls 1894–99. BlkMusTh (Woll). BlksBf (Sampson). DBlkTh (Woll). Eve. Scimitar (Memphis, TN) 1–24–1901. Freeman (Indianapolis) 2–18–1899; 10–20–1900. Just Before Jazz (Riis). NY Dramatic Mirror 4–9–1898. NYT 4–16–1898. Riis diss. A Trip to Coontown folder in Harvard Theatre Collection.

TRIP TO SOUTH AFRICA (1919). Touring show. Prod. by Sandy Burns, with members of the Sandy Burns Stock Co.

TROPICAL REVIEW (1944–45). Dance review. Presentation of West Indian dances by Katherine Dunham and her dance troupe. Opened at the Century Theatre, New York, for a three-week engagement, with a racially mixed cast; dir. by Dunham. Bobby Capo, Cuban singer, and the Dowdy Quartet were also in the show.

TROPICANA (1941). Touring show. Prod. by Donald Heywood. Cast included Edna Mae Harris, Alec Lovejoy, Sister Rosetta Tharpe, George Wiltshire, Conway & Parks, Freddie Robinson, and the Mary Bruce Orchestra.

TROPICS AFTER DARK (1940). Musical revue. 2 acts. By Langston Hughes and Arna Bontemps. Music by Margaret Bonds. Prod. at the American Negro Exposition, Chicago, 1940. Cast included Katherine Day, Rubie Blakley, Mitzie Mitchell, "Sweetie Pie" DeHart, Jeanette Girder, Dick Landry, Pop & Lourie, Dick Montgomery, and Pork Chops Patterson.

TROUBLED ISLAND (1949). Opera. 4 acts. Libretto by Langston Hughes. Musical score by William Grant Still. Based on Hughes' play The Emperor of Haiti (1935).

Concerns the heroic rise and tragic fall of Dessalines, emperor of Haiti during the Napoleonic era. According to Raoul Abdul, literary assistant to Hughes for a number of years, "It [had] remained for many years unproduced. But when the New York City Opera celebrated its fifth anniversary . . . it presented this work in its gala world premiere at City Center" (*NY Amsterdam N.* 2-7-1987). Considered the best prodn. of a full-length black-authored opera up to its time.

Perfd. by the New York City Opera Company at City Center, New York, March 31, 1949. According to Hughes, Robert McFerrin was among the black singers, but "the leading roles were performed by white artists, Robert Weede, Helena Bliss and Maris Powers in blackface. They looked odd, but sang beautifully" (*BlkMagic* [Hughes & Meltzer], p. 147).

Pub. by Leeds Music Corp., New York, 1949. Libretto in TC/NYPL.
FURTHER REFERENCE: *Phylon* 2nd qtr. 1949.

TROUBLE ON THE RANCH (1931). A black-oriented musical western. Prod. at the Standard Theatre in Philadelphia, for a short engagement ending in July 1931. Starring Clara Smith and Jackie (later "Moms") Mabley.

TRULY BLESSED (1990). Gospel musical retrospective. Conceived and perfd. by Queen Esther Marrow. A tribute to the legendary gospel singer Mahalia Jackson, celebrating her life from her impoverished beginnings to the height of her fame—emphasizing the sacrifices which she made by refusing to sing commercially. Prod. at the Longacre Theatre in New York, opening April 22, for an undetermined run. Featuring Marrow (as Mahalia), Gwen Steward, Lynette G. DuPre, Carl Hall, and Doug Eskew.
FURTHER REFERENCE: *NY Post* 4-18-1990.

TRUMPETS OF THE LORD (1963, revised 1969). Gospel musical. By Vinnette Carroll. Adapt. from James Weldon Johnson's *God's Trombones* (1927).

One of several adaptns. by Carroll of the James W. Johnson classic. In the setting of a country church revival, seven of Johnson's sermons in verse are delivered by three black preachers (two men and a woman), intermingled with traditional Negro spirituals and gospel songs.

First prod. Off-Bway by Theodore Mann, in association with °Will P. Sandler, at the Astor Place Playhouse, New York, opening Dec. 21, 1963, for 160 perfs.; dir. by Donald McKayle. Cast included Al Freeman, Jr. (Rev. Ridgely Washington), Theresa Merritt (Sister Henrietta Pinkston), Lex Monson (Rev. Bradford Parham), and Cicely Tyson (Rev. Marion Alexander).

Opened on Bway, prod. and dir. by Mann, at the Brooks Atkinson Theatre, April 29-May 3, 1969, for 7 perfs. With the same cast, except for Freeman, who was replaced by Bernard Ward.

Songs and musical numbers: "So Glad I'm Here," "Call to Prayer," "Listen Lord—A Prayer," "Amen Response," "In His Care," "The Creation," "God Lead Us Along," "Noah Built the Ark," "Run Sinner Run," "Didn't It Rain," "The Judgment Day," "In That Great Gettin' Up Morning," "God Almighty Is Gonna Cut You Down," "Soon One Morning," "There's a Man," "Go Down Death," "He'll Understand," "Were You There?," "Calvary," "Crucifixion," "Reap What You Sow," "We Shall Not Be Moved," "We Are

Soldiers," "Woke Up This Morning," "Let My People Go," "We Shall Overcome," "Jacob's Ladder," and "God Be With You."
FURTHER REFERENCE: *NYT* 12–23–1963.

THE TRYST (1909). Dramatic opera. 1 act. By H. Lawrence Freeman. A drama of early American Indian life, set in Michigan, in which a young chieftain, trying to avoid being killed by his white pursuers, hurls a knife which kills his sweetheart instead. Perfd. by the Freeman Operatic Duo, at the Crescent Theatre in New York City, May 1909, for one week.

TUNES AND FUNNIES OF 1920 (1920). Touring revue. Prod. by Flournoy E. Miller and Aubrey Lyles (Miller & Lyles), who costarred as principal comedians. Cast also included Leon Diggs, Lem Ross, A. J. Twiggs, Edna Hicks, Bessie Tribble, Rosa Gordon, Julia Rector, Trixie Butler, Ethel Patton, Alma Jones, Mary Carpenter, and Cordelle Richardson.

TUNES AND TOPICS (1921, 1923). Touring revue in at least two eds. Prod. by Quintard Miller. *1921 ed.* Cast featured B. B. Joyner (billed as "Long Gone"), Johnny Hudgins (as "The Fashion Plate of Musical Comedy"), Lulu Whidby, Theresa Burroughs Brooks, James Howell, and Mildred Marlene. *1923 ed.* Co-prod. by Marcus Slayter. Opened at John T. Gibson's Dunbar Theatre in Philadelphia, Dec. 24, 1923 (Christmas Eve), with a cast of 60 performers headed by Bessie Smith. Other featured performers included Andrew Tribble, George Cooper, Miller & Slayter, Emmett [or Emett] Anthony, Carrie Yates, and Greenlee & Drayton.

20 DARK SPOTS OF JOY (1928). Touring vaudeville revue. Featured "Ornie" (Lollypop) Jones, Grace Rector, comedian Johnny Snow, character actress Anna Mae Fritz, Jazz Lips (juvenile), Lottie Harris, William Brown, dancers Wiley & Silvers, and a chorus of 10 women and one man.

20 MINUTES IN HELL (1918). Touring show. Prod. by Benbow's Merry Makers. Cast featured William Benbow, Baby Benbow, Bob Davis, and Williams & Taylor.

TWIT / / Orig. titles: *Twit for Twa'* and *Twit for 'Wat* (1974, 1986). Musical adaptation. Loosely based on Shakespeare's *Measure for Measure*. Book by Maxwell Glanville and Gertrude Greenidge. Musical score by Ben F. Carter. Additional lyrics by Bessye Scott.
   Like Shakespeare's dark comedy, *Twit* concerned the misuse of power and the way things are finally put to right. Costumed in Roman dress, and borrowing many of its comedy devices and trappings from the comedies of Plautus as well as Shakespeare, this musical farce was nevertheless set in the country of Blackolovia, "where Blacks rule and sex without marriage is a hanging offense" (*NY*

Amsterdam N. 6–28–1986, p. 32). As in the orig. play, the mayor (Pissy Mutton) hands over the government of his country to a hypocritical deputy (Mulan Black) who promptly revives an old edict banning fornication, thus bringing near tragedy into the lives of several characters, including Wishy Washy, who is arrested for impregnating his fiancée (Sally Sadass). Wishy Washy appeals to his sister (Jessa Maidenhead, a religious novice) to plead with the deputy mayor in his behalf, but the deputy mayor refuses to change his sentence—unless Jessa will give up her virginity to him. The real mayor remains on the scene in disguise, as Rev. Mike, and in the end villains are punished and everything ends happily for the others. A subplot, not in Shakespeare's comedy, involves an International Convention of the Blackolovian Order of Pimpdom (ICBOP), headed by Daddy Horebucks. At the Convention Picnic, the villains are unmasked.

Completed in 1974; music completed in 1979. Public reading at the New Florida Theatre, New York. Full prodn. by Cythia Belgrave Artists, Theatre Workshop, at Long Island Univ.'s Triangle Theatre, Brooklyn, June 19–29, 1986; dir. by Charles Turner. Musical direction by Neal Tate. Choreography by C. Abigail Farris. Prod. stage manager, John Crow. Cast: Beverly Bonner (New Ms. Head Ho', a prostitute), Stephen James Brown (Licky), Calvin Campbell (Doodoo), Janice Cornelius (Superior Maidenhead, Mother of a Convent), Edythe Davis (Sally Sadass, Wishy Washy's fiancée), Abigail Farris (Juga & Teenager), Randy Flood (Pissy Mutton, Mayor & Rev. Mike), Linda Brandon Ford (Holy Roller & Whore), °Orli Himmelweit (Teenager), Lawrence James (Mulan Black, Deputy Mayor), Gaye Leslie (Prologue & Townswoman), Michael Lyles (Main Man), David Morris (Wishy Washy, Jessa's brother & Sally's fiancé), David Parris (Cal & Agnew), John Saxton (Daddy Horebucks), Stephanie Sweeney (Townswoman), LeVerne Summers (Attila & Visiting Pimp), Donald Lee Taylor (Muzza Fuzza, the Sheriff), Michael Taitt (Teenager), Barbara Wise (Ms. Doneover, A Brothel Keeper), Lillias White (Jessa Maidenhead, Wishy Washy's sister), and Janet Young (Teenager).

Songs and musical numbers: "Let's Get on Down" (Company), "Someone Greater Than Me" (Pissy), "Oh for Like It Used to Was" (Juga, Licky & Main Man), "There Is Joy in This House" (Jessa), "Intercoursin' with Sin" (Jessa), "Why Did I Get It Up?" (Mulan), "Serious Joint" (Company), "Save His Soul Instead" (Jessa), "Why Is the Bottle Almost Empty?" (Doodoo), "Blues for Sally" (Sally), "Bite Your Tongue" (Rev. Mike), "Jessa's Mood" (Jessa), "It's Serious" (Company), and "Corruption High, Morality Low."

TWO BILLS FROM ALASKA (1912–14). Billed as "A Breezy Musical Comedy." Written and prod. by Billy King. Prod. by the first Billy King Stock Co. in Atlanta, GA, 1912. Again prod. by a second Billy King Stock Co. at the Lyric Theatre in Kansas City, MO, where it played for 21 weeks before moving to the Star Theatre in Savannah, GA, c. 1914, with the following cast: Billy King and Billy Higgins (comedians) as the "two Bills," Hattie McIntosh (Mrs. Billy King), Cordelia McClain, Howard and Georgia Kelly, Jack "Ginger"

Wiggins (specialty dancer), W. Henri Bowman, Ursell Burnett [or Ursel Burnette], and Walter Watkins.

THE TWO DETECTIVES (1917). Touring vaudeville comedy. Prod. by Frank Montgomery, who costarred with his wife, Florence McClain. Cast also included Sam Gaines, Garland Howard, and Hattie James.

TWO GENTLEMEN OF VERONA (1971–73). Musical version of Shakespeare's comedy. 2 acts. Adapt. by °John Guare and °Mel Shapiro. Music by °Galt MacDermott. Lyrics by Guare. Winner of both Tony and Drama Critics Circle Awards for best musical of 1971–72, and a Tony for best musical libretto. Prod. by °Joseph Papp and the New York Shakespeare Festival at the St. James Theatre, New York, Dec. 1, 1971–May 20, 1973, for 614 perfs. With an integrated cast that featured Clifton Davis and Jonelle Allen as Valentine and Sylvia (one of the two gentlemen and his love). Norman Matlock, succeeded by Elwoodson Williams, was also in the cast, as the Duke of Milan.

TWO NEIGHBORS (1921). Touring vaudeville comedy. Prod. by and starring Hardtack Jackson.

TWO NUTS FROM BRAZIL (1921). Touring vaudeville comedy. Prod. by and starring Hardtack Jackson.

TWO STORY (1911). Musical comedy. 1 act. Prod. by William M. Benbow and the Alabama Chocolate Drop Co. Cast included Mose Graham (as the Porter), Edna Benbow, Rebecca Kinzy, and William Benbow. Songs included ''China Town Rag'' and ''Miss Malinda.''

U

UBANGI CLUB FOLLIES (1935). Touring revue. Music and lyrics by Andy Razaf. Choreography by Lou Crawford. Prod. by Leonard Harper, with the following cast: Billy Daniels, "Dusty" Fletcher, Mae Johnson, Pearl Baines, Edna Mae Harris, Velma Middleton, Lee Simmons, Brown & Brown, the Three Speed Demons, Helen Smith, Bobby Evans, "Bunny" & Don, and Erskine Hawkins and his Bama State Collegians Orchestra.

UHURUH (1972). Musical revue. 2 acts. Book, music, lyrics, direction, and choreography by Danny Duncan. A showcase for Duncan and his company. Prod. at the City Center Downstairs, New York City, March 20–25, 1972, for 8 perfs. Starring Danny Duncan; with Walterine Ross, Samaki Zuri, David Gardner, Pamela Sweden, and Raymond Wade among an all-black cast of 12 singers and dancers.

ULYSSES (THE JAZZICAL) (1978). Jazz musical. Apparently based on Greek/Roman mythology. Written and dir. by William Electric Black (Ian Ellis James). Prod. at Southern Illinois Univ., April 1978. Prod. by Intermedia Marquee Theatre, New York, Aug. 25–Sept. 12, 1982; with music by °Hilary Schmidt.

UNCLE EPH'S CHRISTMAS (1899). Musical vaudeville sketch. 1 act. By Paul Laurence Dunbar. Music by Will Marion Cook. Written for vaudeville star Ernest Hogan. A dialect play with interpolated songs, depicting a Christmas celebration in Uncle Eph's cabin, where he resides with his wife, Aunt Chloe, and their children. Uncle Eph, in the spirit of the season, becomes intoxicated in the presence of his neighbors and guests, which include the church parson and the village gossip. The sketch ends with a cakewalk, a very popular dance finale of the 1890s. First prod. in the Boston Music Hall during Christmas week, Dec. 1899.

THE UNDERGROUND RAILROAD. See *PECULIAR SAM*.

THE UNDERTAKER'S DAUGHTER (1916). Tabloid musical. Written and prod. by Billy King. Prod. at the Grand Theatre, Chicago, with members of the Billy King Stock Co., including Billy Walker, Gertrude Saunders, William Benton Overstreet, and Howard Kelly.

UNDER THE BAMBOO TREE / / Orig. title: *The Pink Slip* (1922). Musical show. Book and lyrics by °Walter DeLeon. Music by °Sigmund Bomberg and Will Vodery.
   The last play in which Bert Williams starred, before his death. According to *Nobody* (Charters, p. 146),

It was a weak play about a resort hotel porter [played by Williams] who was an outstanding prevaricator. Possessing a deed worth a significant sum of money, he decided to tear up the deed and sell bits of it to various people in the hotel, with the promise of great rewards for their participation in the intrigue. Predictably there were numerous complications and a love interest before everything was settled to universal happiness.

   Prod. by °Al Woods, it went into rehearsal as *The Pink Slip* in Jan. 1922. After an out-of-town tryout, the show was revised and the title changed to *Under the Bamboo Tree*, taken from a popular song by Bob Cole and J. Rosamond Johnson, which had been introduced by °Marie Cahill in *Sally in Our Alley* (1902). The revised and retitled show opened in Chicago in Feb. 1922, where Williams caught a cold that quickly developed into pneumonia. He collapsed halfway through a performance on Feb. 25, after which the show closed. Williams died on March 4, 1922.

UNLOVED WIFE (1923). Touring revue. Featuring Bessie Allison and Evelyn Ellis.

UP AND DOWN (c. 1919–22). Musical farce-comedy. 2 acts. Book, music, and lyrics by Salem Tutt Whitney and J. Homer Tutt.
   Touring show, starring Whitney & Tutt as two get-rich-quick schemers, Ham Sanford (Whitney) and Sam Hanford (Tutt), who are pursued up and down the country by Silas Perkins (Amon Davis), who has been bilked out of some money by the two con men. The show featured a "Famous Bronze Beauty Chorus" (of 16 ladies, all named after the colors and the seasons) and an "army of First Line Entertainers."
   Prod. by Whitney & Tutt, with the *Smart Set Co.*, it reportedly played "at a theatre on 57th Street, New York City," prior to 1920 (*Neg&Dr* [Bond], pp. 53–54), where "it featured some who were later to be great stars; namely, Ethel Waters, Margaret Simms, Emmett Anthony, and Andrew Tribble." Toured for several years, c. 1920–c. 1922. In addition to Whitney, Tutt, and Davis, the cast of the 1922 ed. (which did not include Ethel Waters) was as follows: Blanche

Calloway (Miss Green), Jennie Dancey (Miss Pink), Alberta Jones (Miss White), Margaret Simms (Miss Sunshine), Virginia Wheeler (Miss Purple), Elizabeth Campbell (Miss Red), Helen Jackson (Miss Lavender), Nellis Brown (Miss Crimson), Marion Bradford (Miss Summer), Viola Mander (Miss Black), Elvira Davis (Miss Tempest), Edith Simms (Miss Yellow), Bobby Reno (Miss Winter), Helen Warren (Miss Maytime), Hazel Springer (Miss Fall), Joyce Robinson (Miss Autumn), J. Frances Mores (Dr. Sunnyside), Alfonzo Fenderson (Prof. Boosowisk), Henry Thompson (Jed Thompson), John Dancey (Bill Splivins), Nat Cash (Sergeant Oderly), Wilson Dyer (Jimmie Beets), George Phillips (Lee Lung Chang & Wilton Frayne), and Chester Jones (Elbert Singer).

Songs and musical numbers included "We Want to Booze" (Fenderson), "Backbiting Me" (Davis), "When You're Crazy Over Daddy" (Bradford & Chorus), "Male Vamps" (Tutt & Chorus), and "Rock Me, Daddy" (Dancey).

THE UPS AND DOWNS OF THEOPHILUS MAITLAND (1974, 1976). Musical. Conceived, adapt., and dir. by Vinnette Carroll from a West Indian folk tale. Music and lyrics by Micki Grant. An old man who has shocked his family and the people of the town by marrying a beautiful young woman discovers on his wedding night that he is impotent. After being advised by several doctors that there is nothing they can do, he finally consults a witch woman who cures him with one of her potions. Prod. by the Urban Arts Corps (UAC), New York, opening Nov. 13, 1974. Also presented by UAC at the Black Theatre Alliance annual festival, New York, 1974. Revived Nov. 1–Dec. 5, 1976.

UP STAIRS AND DOWN BELOW (1919). Touring revue. Prod. and perfd. by Miller & Lyles (Flournoy E. Miller and Aubrey Lyles).

UPTOWN . . . IT'S HOT (1985). Retrospective dance musical. Conceived, choreographed, and dir. by Maurice Hines. A nostalgic review of the most popular songs and dances from the 1930s to the 1980s. Prod. at the Tropicana Hotel & Casino, Atlantic City, NJ, late 1985. Opened on Bway at the Lunt-Fontanne Theatre, New York, Jan. 28, 1986, for an undetermined run. Cast included Hines, Jeffery V. Thompson, Marion Ramsey, Lawrence Hamilton, Tommi Johnson, and Alisa Gyse.

URBAN VOICES (1984). Musical collage. A program of music, dance, and poetry about life in the inner city. Prod. by the Theatre of Universal Images, Newark, NJ, Oct. 10–Nov. 4, 1984.

URLINA, AFRICAN PRINCESS / / Also known as *The Princess of Madagascar* and *Princess Orelia of Madagascar* (1877–79). African-inspired musical show. "Written especially for" the Hyers Sisters (Emma Louise and Anna Mada Hyers), according to the *San Francisco Pacific Appeal* (4–5–1879).

Described by the *San Francisco Chronicle* (3–31–1879) as "a new burlesque" about a royal African princess, in which the Hyers Sisters appear, and "themselves claim to be of African extraction. The music is taking, the singing is good, the costumes are bright and the scenery is effective, but the play lacks one element, a good amusing libretto."

According to Tom Fletcher (*100 Years*, p. 71), he and Sam Lucas appeared with the Hyers Sisters in *The Princess of Madagascar* in 1877. As *Urlina, African Princess*, the show was presented at the Bush Street Theatre, San Francisco, March 31, 1879, for a two-week engagement. The cast also included the tenor Wallace King and singer John Luca.

FURTHER REFERENCE: *BlksBf* (Sampson).

UZZIAH (1934). Opera. By H. Lawrence Freeman. One of his unperfd. works. His best-known operas include *The Martyr (1893), *Valdo (1905-6), *Vendetta (1911-23), and *Voodoo (1921-28).

V

VALDO (1905–6). Dramatic opera. 1 act. By H. Lawrence Freeman. Named for his son Valdo Freeman (1900–1922), this opera is set in Mexico and involves a case of mistaken identity which results in the hero's being challenged to a fatal duel by his sister's jealous fiancé, who believes that he is her lover. Perfd. by the Freeman Grand Opera Co., at Weisgerber's Hall, Cleveland, May 1906.

VAMPING LIZA JANE (1922). Touring revue. Prod. by and costarring Billy Ewing. Cast also included his wife, Goldie Ewing, and the team of Jenkins & Jenkins.

VANITIES (1926). (Not to be confused with the *Vanities of 1926.*) Touring show prod. by Earl Dancer, who costarred with Ethel Waters in this revue. Cast also included Billy King, Marshall Rogers, and Nuggle Johnson.

VANITIES OF 1926 (1926). Touring revue. Prod. by Edward Langford. Cast included George Aiken, Kitty Aublanche, Dandy Brown, ''Crackshot'' & Hunter, George Ray, Doris Rhinebottom, Rogers & Rogers, Gonzell White, and Bill Baisey's Band.

VANITIES OF 1932 (1932). Touring revue. Featuring the comedy team of Butterbeans & Susie (Jodie and Susie Edwards) and Jimmy Ferguson.

VELVET BROWN BABIES (1930). Touring revue. Prod. by and costarring Eddie Lemons. Cast also included Frank Lajoie, Sadie McKinney, Mike & Ike, Joe Sheftell, and Elizabeth Welch.

VENDETTA (1911–23). Dramatic opera. 3 acts. Written and composed by H. Lawrence Freeman. Dramatic story, set in Mexico, of the fatal rivalry between a nobleman and a toreador for the love of a beautiful, well-born lady. Completed 1911. Perfd. by the Negro Grand Opera Co., at the Lafayette Theatre, in Harlem, Nov. 12, 1923.

VIRGINIA (1937). White-oriented musical play. 2 acts. By °Lawrence Stallings and °Owen Davis. Music by °Arthur Schwartz. Lyrics by °Albert Stillman. A play set in the period of the American Revolution, perfd. mainly by English actors brought over from London's Drury Lane. John W. Bubbles (of the team of Buck & Bubbles) was cast in the role of Scipio, presumably a slave. Prod. at the Center Theatre, New York, opening Sept. 2, 1937, for 60 perfs.; dir. by Albert Stillman.

VOODOO (1912–28). Opera. 3 acts. By H. Lawrence Freeman. His best-known work. A dramatization of voodoo rites practiced by slaves on an old Louisiana plantation. Completed 1912–14. First presented in an abridged version over Station WGBS, New York, May 20, 1928. Presented in a full perf. with an amateur cast at the 52nd St. Theatre, New York City, Sept. 10–11, 1928, and was the first opera to be perfd. in the Bway district. Reportedly purchased by Paramount Studios to be filmed as a stage presentation in a condensed version (*Crisis* 10–1933). Earned for the composer a Harmon Award, 1930.

W

WALK DOWN MAH STREET! (1967). Subtitled "A Topical Musical Revue."
2 acts. Script, lyrics, choreography, and stage direction mainly by °Patricia
Taylor Curtis. Music composed and perfd. mainly by °Norman Curtis. With
contributions by members of the Next Stage Theatre Company.

A series of songs, skits, and musical numbers on racial subjects, based on
life in an urban ghetto.

First prod. in an adaptn. for television by "Camera Three," CBS-TV, New
York, 1967. Prod. Off-Bway by Audience Associates, Inc., at the Players Theatre, June 12–Nov. 6, 1968, for 135 perfs. With members of the Next Stage
Theatre Co., which included two blacks, Kenneth Frett and Gene Rounds, among
the cast of 7, which also included 2 or 3 Hispanic performers.

Program (including skits, songs, and other musical numbers): "We're Today,"
"Taxi!," "Walk Down Mah Street," "Is She or Ain't She," "Zap!," "If You
Want to Get Ahead," "Don't Be a Litterbug," "Just One More Time," "The
Buildings Slash the Sunlight," "Obie," "Where and With What?," "Mah
House," "I'm a Statistic," "Minus One," "Unknown Factor," "Someday, If
We Grow Up," "Candid Camera," "Basic Black," "What Shadows We Are,"
"Want to Get Retarded?," "What's for Dinner?," "Teeny Bopper," "Push
One," "Foster Child," "For Four Hundred Years," "Don't Have to Take It
Anymore," "Plus Two," "Lonely Girl," "The American Way," "Clean Up
Your Own Backyard," "Better We Should Start All Over," and "Walk Lordy,
Walk."

WALK TOGETHER CHILDREN (1968). One-woman show. 2 acts. Arranged,
adapt., and perfd. by Vinie Burrows. Taped music under the direction of Brother
Ahh (Robert Northern). A program of poetry, prose, and songs by black authors,
"depicting the Black journey from auction block to new nation time" (Program
Notes). First prod. Off-Bway by Robert Hooks at the Greenwich Mews Theatre,

Nov. 11–Dec. 1, 1968, for 24 perfs. Revived Off-Bway at the Mercer-Brecht Theatre, March 16–July 2, 1972, for 89 perfs.

WALK TOGETHER CHILLUN / / Also known as ***Walk Together Children*** (1936). Social drama with Negro spirituals. 3 acts. By Frank Wilson. Making a plea for black solidarity and unity, this play deals with a labor dispute between black workers in upstate New York and a group of southern black workers who have been brought up by whites from the South to supply cheap labor. First prod. by the New York Negro Unit of the Federal Theatre Project (FTP), at the Lafayette Theatre in Harlem, opening Feb. 2, 1936, for 19 perfs.; with an attendance of more than 10 thousand. With J. August Smith and Oliver Foster in the leading roles. Significant as the first FTP prodn. in New York City.

WALK WITH MUSIC (1940). White-oriented musical comedy. 2 acts. By °Guy Bolton, °Parke Levy, and °Alan Lipscott. Lyrics by °Johnny Mercer. Music by °Hoagy Carmichael. Stepin Fetchit perfd. in this play in the role of Chesterfield, a servant, among the otherwise all-white cast, which featured °Kitty Carlisle, °Mitzi Green, and °Betty Lawford. As the three Gibson girls, they move from a New England chicken farm to New York City, where they invest their funds in a scheme to win a rich husband for the eldest (Carlisle), while the other two pose as maid and chaperone. Although the scheme backfires, all three ladies find suitable husbands in the end. Prod. at the Ethel Barrymore Theatre, New York, opening June 4, 1940, for 15 perfs.; staged by °R. H. Burnside.

THE WALLS CAME TUMBLING DOWN (1976). Opera. 1 act. Libretto by Loften Mitchell. Music by Willard Roosevelt. Operatic version of Mitchell's play *Sojourn to the South of the Wall* (1973), about blacks in seventeenth-century New Amsterdam, NY, who attempted to persuade the Dutch to fight againt the British. Prod. by the Harlem School of the Arts at Alice Tully Hall, Lincoln Center, New York, March 1976.

THE WARRIOR ANT (1988). Multi-ethnic musical show. Written and dir. by °Lee Breuer. Music by Bob Telson. Combines African and Latin rhythms with the techniques of Japanese theatre to examine relationships between the sexes, the individual and society, and the social classes (working vs. elite) through the life of the warrior ant. Prod. at the Brooklyn Academy of Music, Brooklyn, NY, Oct. 19–30, 1988. Cast included Afro-Caribbean and Latin bands, African narrators, and Japanese puppeteers.

WATERMELON (1926–27). Musical revue in at least two eds. Prod. by °Jack Goldberg on tour of the Majestic Theatrical Circuit (white), 1927. About two con men who gain a fortune by getting some Mississippi townspeople to finance a scheme to make watermelons grow on trees overnight. The hustlers then go on a European pleasure tour, spending their ill-gotten fortune. *1926 ed*. Principal cast included Speedy Smith, Howard Garland, and Mae Brown. *1927 ed*. Principal cast included Andrew Tribble, Jacqueline and Guy Jines, Bob Bramlet, Elverta Brown, and Harriet Carter.

WATERMELON GIRLS (1923). Touring revue. Prod. by and costarring Charles Taylor. Cast also included Reggie Taylor, George and Emma Nash, Hattie Storey, Lillian Rankin, Cecil McKay, and Hattie Owen.

THE WEARY BLUES (1966). Musical adaptation. By Woodie King, Jr. From Langston Hughes' first book of poetry, *The Weary Blues* (1926), using additional prose and poetry from his other works, with the setting in Harlem, and W. C. Handy's blues added as an integral part of the concept. According to King (*Neg. Dig.* 4–1969, pp. 31–32), "The idea would be to follow a young Black American from a storefront church through the Harlem streets and finally to the foreign soil of some distant land," where he apparently meets his death while protecting his country. First prod. at the Lincoln Center Museum and Library, New York City, sponsored by the Equity Library Theatre, opening Oct. 31, 1966, for 3 perfs. Cast included Theresa Merritt, Eleo Pomare (as a junkie dancer), Norman Bush (as a preacher), and Cliff Frazier (as a hustler). Again prod. in New York by the Adventure Corps, Feb. 1968.

A WEDDING IN JAZZ (1919). Touring revue. Prod. by Stovall & Mack's Merry Makers, starring straight man Wallace Stovall and his partner, Billy Mack. Cast included Walker & Brown, Tim and Gertie Moore, Thomas & Martin, and Joe Sheftell and his Eight Black Dots.

WE GOT IT (1922, 1924). Touring revue in at least two eds. Prod. by and costarring comedian Joe Carmouche. *1922 ed*. Cast included E. Pugh and Cleo Mitchell. *1924 ed*. Cast included Troy "Bear" Brown, Mary Covington, S. H. Dudley, Jr., Cleo Mitchell, Willie Ognesby, and Susie Wrotan.

WE LOVE YOU ALWAYS (1980–81). Musical. By Rosetta LeNoire and Clyde Williams (who was also musical and stage dir.). Prod. by AMAS Repertory Theatre, New York, 1980–81. Asst. musical dir., David Davis. Stage managers, Thomas Yarnal and Eva Lopez. Cast (racial identities not certain): Bob Brooker, Joe Ginza, Debbie Liguori, Jacki Miles, Barbara Purdy, Charlie Rodriguez, Andrew Tabbat, and Diane Wilson.

WESLEY VARNELL'S REVUE (1922). Touring revue. Prod. by Wesley Varnell. Cast included Brown & Hudson, Coleman & Johnson, Houston & Houston, and Henry "Gang" Jines.

WE'S RISING (1927). Musical comedy. 2 acts [10 scenes]. By Porter Grainger and Leigh Whipper. Subtitled "A Story of the Simple Life in the Souls of Black Folks." Apparently prod. in Harlem, 1927. Typescript in Schomburg.

WE'VE GOT IT (1924). Touring revue. Prod. by and costarring Sam Robinson. Cast also included blues singer Ma Bailey, Wallace Curtis, C. S. Davis, Paul Foster, Bessie McKinney, and Jimmy Simmons.

WHAT'S UP (1925). Touring revue. Prod. by comedian Roscoe Montella, who costarred with his Radio Girls. (See also *Radio Girls*.)

WHAT'S YOUR HUSBAND DOING? (1917). White-oriented farce with music. By °George V. Hobart. Incidental music by James P. Johnson. Prod. New York, 1917. Johnson's music was not mentioned in the program; however, he led a five-piece band onstage during a short scene, presumably conducting his own music.

WHAT YOU GONNA NAME THAT PRETTY LITTLE BABY (1979). Gospel musical. Conceived and dir. by Vinnette Carroll. Prod. by the Urban Arts Corps, New York City, Dec. 1978, for 12 perfs.

WHEN HELL FREEZES OVER, I'LL SKATE (1979). Musical. Conceived and dir. by Vinnette Carroll. An optimistic view of the problems of black life in America, in poetry, dance, and song; using folk, gospel, and contemporary music. First prod. by the Urban Arts Corps, New York, Jan. 1979. Also presented in the Black Theatre Festival, held in New York City, May 1, 1979. Telecast on NET, 1980–81. Revived in a pre-Bway tryout at the Forrest Theatre, Philadelphia, April 1984.

WHEN LUCK BILL CAME TO TOWN (1914). Touring vaudeville show. Featured Nina Stovall, Billy Gross, McDaniel & White, and Robinson & Robinson.

WHEN MALINDA SINGS (1924–25). Tabloid musical. Title apparently based on the poem by Paul Laurence Dunbar. Prod. as a touring show by Salem Tutt Whitney and J. Homer Tutt (Whitney & Tutt). Perfd. by members of their *Smart Set Co.*, including Joe Purnell, Mabel Ridley, Charles Hawkins, Wilbur White, and the Duncan Sisters.

WHERE THE TRAIL ENDS IN MEXICO (1921). Touring revue. Prod. by and possibly starring Hambone Jones. About the kidnapping of a beautiful American girl by Mexicans, who take her across the border; and her eventual rescue by her fiancé, a U.S. army officer. Cast included S. H. Gray, Virginia Liston, Bob Davis, Rosa Knight, Dolly Brown, Henrietta Leggett, and Annie Bell Cook.

Musical numbers include "Loromba" and "Papa Loving Joe" (Liston), "From My Kentucky Home" (Knight, Brown & Quartette), "Old Man Shouts What a Time" (Gray, Davis & others), "In the Mexican Blues" (Liston & Chorus), and "Chili Beans" (Leggett).

WHIM WHAM WHARBLERS (1925). Touring show which played on the TOBA circuit. Prod. by and costarring Martin & Walker (Edgar Martin and Billy Walker). Cast also included Babe Brown, Sylvia Mitchell, Lawrence Nash, and Singing Slim Howard. See also *Wift Waft Warblers* (1921).

WHIRL OF JOY (1922). Musical show. Prod. by Bill King at the Grand Theatre, Chicago, with members of the Billy King Stock Co. See also *Whirl of Pleasure*.

WHIRL OF PLEASURE (1923). Prod. by Billy King at the Grand Theatre, Chicago, with members of the Billy King Stock Co. See also *Whirl of Joy*.

THE WHITEWASH MAN (1915). Touring vaudeville comedy. Prod. by and starring Harrison Stewart. With members of the Harrison Stewart Co.

WHITMAN SISTERS REVUE [or REVIEW] (c. 1899–c. 1936). Series of touring shows, prod. under this and other titles (see below), starring the Whitman Sisters: Mabel, Essie, Alberta ("Bert"), and later Alice Whitman.
   A vaudeville company and show which originated during the 1890s in Kansas City, MO, as a church trio consisting of the three older sisters, Mabel, Essie, and Alberta, who traveled with their father, the Rev. Albert Whitman, singing and playing the guitar in churches where he preached. Afterwards, around 1899, Mabel and Essie began singing professionally, billed as the Danzette Sisters, traveling through the south from Missouri to Florida under the management of their mother, also performing in a skit written especially for them by Will Accooe. Changing their name first to the Whitman Sisters Novelty Company, later to the Whitman Sisters New Orleans Troubadours, and intermittently to the Whitman Sisters Revue, they built up their act to a first class vaudeville show, with a company of 12 (at the beginning) traveling under the management of Mabel, the oldest sister. By 1910, they had played most of the major vaudeville circuits in the South, East and Northeast, including the Orpheum, Greenwald, Kohl & Castle, Keith & Proctor, Poli & Fox, Pantages, and the Independent Family United. During this period, Alice Whitman joined the show as a juvenile singer and tap dancer, billed as "Baby Alice." The sisters split up briefly between 1911 and 1913, with Alice leaving the show temporarily, Mabel doing a single act in southern houses, and Essie and Alberta forming a small vaudeville group which played throughout the East. By 1914, the Sisters were again united, along with Alice and a small company that included two "picks" (child performers in blackface) known as Aaron and Sambo. By the 1920s, their company was traveling with a group of 30, as a regular feature on the TOBA circuit, their act

now including Little Albert Whitman (Alice's son, a dancer, billed as "Little Pops"), who was to remain with the show for more than ten years. A typical Whitman Sisters Revue consisted of a beautiful leading lady (Alice), a featured singer (Essie), a lively, high-stepping chorus line, two blackface comedians (such as Mike Bow and Willie "Toosweet"), a male impersonator (Alberta), one or two juvenile performers (such as "Little Pops" and "Jazzlips"), a midget and her partner (Princess Wee Wee and Willie Bryant, who were a long-time feature of the show), and other musical, novelty, and specialty acts. Mabel was the company's manager and songwriter. Among the numerous performers who appeared with the Whitman Sisters through the years were Little Thomas Hawkins (the "Toy Comedian"), Billy Mills, Slim Henderson, Billy Earthquake, Gallie DeGaston (songs and recitations), Clyde Bernhardt (trombonist), Mattie Dorsey (singer), Hamilton & Hamilton (husband and wife team), Sambo Reed (comic), the Five OK Boys, the Four Cotton Pickers, and "Count" Basie (then known as William ["Bill"] Basie).

Among the known show titles used by the Whitman Sisters for various editions of their revues were *The Black Coachman* (1916), *Their Gang* (1924), *Goin' Some* (1925), *Rompin' Through* (1926), *Watermelon Morn'* (1926), *Miss New York* (1926), *Dancing Fools* (1927), *Hello Dixieland* (1929), *Faststeppers* (1930), *Spirit of 1930* (1930), *Wake Up Chillun'* (1930), *January Jubilee* (1931), *Step Lively Girls* (1931), and *Swing Revue* (1936).

FURTHER REFERENCE: *BlksBf* (Sampson). *Chicago Defender* 1–26–1918; 3–5–1927; 4–4–1936; 10–3–1936; 5–16–1942; 6–27–1964. *Freeman* (Indianapolis) 12–25–1915. *Ghost* (Sampson). *NY Age* 4–27–1935.

WHOOP-DEE-DOO (1903). White-oriented musical extravaganza. Book and lyrics by °Edgar Smith. Music mainly by °William T. Francis. With additional songs by Bob Cole, James Weldon Johnson, and J. Rosamond Johnson.

A silly farce set in a German beer garden perched, of all places, on the banks of the Seine in Paris, where it apparently is not attracting many customers. The plot revolves around the owner's attempts to unload his establishment on two unsuspecting yokels, played by °Weber & Fields.

Prod. at Weber and Fields' Broadway Music Hall, New York City, opening Sept. 24, 1903, for 151 perfs. With an all-white cast, including °Lillian Russell, °Peter F. Dailey, °Al Lewis, °Carter de Haven, and °Louis Mann. Reopened at the New Amsterdam Theatre, New York, May 16, 1904, for 14 additional perfs.

Two black-authored songs were introduced by Russell in this prodn.: "The Maid of Timbuctoo," by J. W. Johnson and Cole, and "The Flowers of Dixie Land," by J. Rosamond Johnson & Smith; both musical scores pub. by Joseph W. Stern, New York, copies in Moorland-Spingarn.

FURTHER REFERENCE: *AmMusTh* (Bordman). *BesPls 1899–1909*.

WHO'S DAT (1926). Touring revue. Prod. by Eddie Lemons, who costarred with his wife, Olive Lopez [Lemons]. Cast also included Rose Henderson, Eva Mason, Theresa Brooks, Elizabeth Scott, and Petway & Rector.

WHO'S MAMA'S BABY, WHO'S DADDY'S CHILD? (1985). Comedy with songs and dance. 2 acts. By Gertrude Jeannette. Music and lyrics by Louise Mike. About the trials and tribulations of a retired middle-class couple who, after successfully raising three children of their own, have now become foster parents to a talented group of abused and unwanted children. Prod. by the HADLEY Players and the Community Service Council of Greater Harlem, at 207 West 133rd St., New York, for four weekends, May 31–June 23, 1985.

WHO'S STEALIN' (1918). Musical comedy. By Flournoy E. Miller and Aubrey Lyles, who costarred in the show.

The story turns on the rivalry between two partners in an Iowa department store (Miller & Lyles), whose wives try to outdo each other to be known as the prettiest and best-dressed women in town. To accommodate their wives, each store owner (unknown to the other) institutes a system whereby his own wife can freely obtain the clothes that she desires "without cost." As a result, there is a loss of profits, which makes it appear that one of the partners is stealing. A private detective is called in, who is later revealed as a bogus detective and a crook, until the real detective arrives and uncovers the truth.

Prod. by Miller & Lyles in Harlem and on tour, 1918. Cast: Miller & Lyles (Department Store Co-owners), Bessie Miller and Mrs. Andrew Tribble (Their Wives), Cassie Slaughter (Mrs. Fairfax, a widow), Myrtle Porter Lyles (Adelaid, the widow's daughter), A. J. Twigg (Dr. Rockwell), Roger Jones (Crooked Detective), Andrew Tribble (Grocery Man), Leon Diggs, Daisy Collins, Julia Rector, and the Woods Sisters.

Songs and specialty numbers: "Hand in Hand" (Diggs & Chorus), "Just Like a Gypsy" (Diggs & Chorus), "Four Eyes Told Me So" (Collins), Oriental Dance (Rector), and Specialty (Woods Sisters).

WHO'S TO WIN (1913). Touring vaudeville show. Prod. by Bragg & Mahone, who costarred with Madame Endora Lockett.

WHO STRUCK JOHN? (1923–24). Prod. by and costarring Salem Tutt Whitney and J. Homer Tutt. Featuring the *Smart Set Co.

WHY GIRLS GO WRONG (1928). Touring revue. Prod. by comedian Joe Bright and the Record Breakers Co. Cast included "Cutout" & Leonard and Billy "Scarecrow" McOwens (blackface comedians), Katie Jones (comedienne), Alonzo Jackson (character actor), Willie Too Sweet (juvenile), Bobbie Toliver Bright, Baby Kid, Laura Miller, and chorus.

WHY SPOIL IT? (1922). Touring revue. Prod. by dancer/choreographer Frank Montgomery, who costarred with Florence McClain, his wife and partner, and Rebecca "Dinks" Thomas.

WHY WORRY? (1921). Touring revue. Prod. by Quintard Miller. Cast included Theresa Burroughs Brooks, Billy Higgins, James Howell, Margaret Lee, and Lulu Whidby.

WIDE WIDE RIVER (pre-1960s). Folk opera. Libretto by Langston Hughes. Music by Granville English. Adapt. from the play *The Shuffle Town Outlaws*, by William Norman Cox. Incomplete. Apparently unprod. Copy in JWJ/YUL.

THE WIDOW (1982). Unfinished opera. 1 [of 3 acts]. Words and musical score by Russell Atkins. Based on his play *The Corpse* (1954), about a mentally unstable widow who makes an annual visit to the tomb of her deceased husband to watch with pleasure his corpse's gradual deterioration and loss of identity. Apparently unperfd. Other musical stage works by Atkins include *The Abortionist* (libretto, 1 act, 1954), about a physician who gets revenge on his most despised colleague by performing a savage operation on the enemy's daughter, pub. in *Free Lance* magazine (Cleveland), 1954; and *The Nail* (libretto, 3 acts, 1957), adapt. from a short story of the same title by Pedro Antonio de Alarcon, about a female fugitive who is hunted down by her lover, pub. in *Phenomena* (a collection of plays by Atkins, Wilberforce, OH: Wilberforce Univ. Press, 1961). **FURTHER REFERENCE:** *Contemporary Blk. Am. Playwrs. and Their Pls.* (Peterson).

A WIFE WANTED (1924). Touring revue. Prod. by and costarring Drake & Walker (Henry Drake and Ethel Walker [Mrs. Drake]).

WIFT WAFT WARBLERS (1921). Musical revue. Conceived and prod. by blackface comedians Amon Davis and Eddie Stafford (Davis & Stafford), who also costarred.

The story concerns a wealthy father's desire to marry his daughter to the man of his choice, and her efforts to elope with the man she loves. The action centers around the pursuit of the eloping couple and the attempt by both the father and the rival suitor to prevent their marriage. In the end, the true lover wins the girl, and the father's choice proves to be a man of unsuitable character.

Prod. in Harlem and possibly on tour, 1921. Other cast members included Willie Carter, Elveta Davis, Harold Douglass, Alex Johnson, Harry Jackson, Josephine Leggett, Lester Miller, Julia Ray, Alfonso Robinson, Ethel Watts, and the Warblers' Quartet.

Songs and musical numbers: "Jail House Now" (Davis & Stafford), "My Home Town" (Johnson), "Once in a While" (Jackson), "Strutting Your Stuff"(Ray), "Old Fashioned Garden" (Watts & Girls), "Kaffir Babe" (Jackson), "Home Again Blues" (Miller), and "Down in China Town" (Watts).

THE WILD ROSE (1905). White-oriented musical comedy. Book by °Harry B. Smith, who also wrote many of the lyrics, assisted by °George V. Hobart. Music by various writers; with one song contributed by Will Marion Cook and Cecil Mack.

Concerns the rescue of a beautiful gypsy maid from a loveless marriage by a comic hypnotist.

Prod. at the Knickerbocker Theatre, New York, opening May 5, 1905, for 136 perfs. Starring the librettist's wife, °Irene Bentley, as the gypsy belle, °Eddie Foy as her rescuer, and an all-white cast which included °June McCree, °Marie Cahill, °Marguerite Clark, °Elsie Ferguson, and °Evelyn Florence.

According to *AmMusTh* (Bordman, p. 181), the score was filled with inter-polated, so-called coon songs, alternating with "the lilt of the Viennese waltz." "The Little Gypsy Maid," with music by Cook and lyrics by Mack and Smith, was one of the hit songs of the show.

WILLIAMS & WALKER (1986–87). Two-character musical retrospective. By Vincent D. Smith. Based on the lives of the legendary comedians Williams & Walker (Bert Williams and his partner, George Walker), who perfd. in vaudeville and in numerous musicals such as *In Dahomey, *Abyssinia, and *The Sons of Ham. After Walker's death, Williams rose to national stardom with the *Ziegfeld Follies, in which he appeared for nearly ten years. In this show, Williams & Walker are portrayed respectively by Ben Harney (later replaced by Alan Weekes) and Vondie Curtis-Hall, who entertain with biographical material, songs, and humorous stories. Prod. by the New Federal Theatre and the American Place Theatre at the American Place Theatre, New York, Feb. 27–March 16, 1986; dir. by Shauneille Perry. Neal Tate was musical dir.; Lenny Sloane was cho-reographer. Revived at the Davis Center in Harlem, Oct. 2, 1986, for a short run; then turned to the Crossroads Theatre, New Brunswick, NJ, Jan. 28–March 1, 1987. Recipient of 6 AUDELCO award nominations, including best actor in a musical (Vondie Curtis-Hall), best director of a musical (Shauneille Perry), and best costumes (Judy Dearing).
FURTHER REFERENCE: *NY Amsterdam N.* 10–11–1986.

WILL MORRISSEY'S FOLIES BERGERE REVUE. See *FOLIES BERGERE REVUE*.

THE WIZ (1975–76). Musical adaptation. Book by °William F. Brown. Based on °L. Frank Baum's *The Wonderful Wizard of Oz*, which had been made into a film starring °Judy Garland in 1939. Musical score by Charlie Smalls.

An all-black version of *The Wizard of Oz*, with a brand new book and score, both designed to distance it completely from the Judy Garland version. Actually, the show was a black satire on the all-white version, which had dominated the American psyche for nearly forty years. According to Bryan Rollins (*NY Am-sterdam N.* 1–11–1975), *The Wiz* said "something extra to blacks" through its numerous "symbols and associations, obvious and obscure, that relate to crucial aspects of the black experience and culture." This experience was reflected in the gospel, rock, soul, and rhythm & blues sounds which pervaded Charlie Smalls' score; in the flamboyant costume design and direction of Geoffrey Holder; and in the lively choreography of George Faison.

Although the show's early demise was predicted by the major critics, it was strongly supported by the black community after a vigorous selling campaign was initiated, which included television advertisements, with the backing of Twentieth Century-Fox, augmented by theatre parties and other concerted efforts to win over the black audience. Eventually it became a "hit," winning seven Tony Awards, including best musical, best musical score (Smalls), best choreography (Faison), best costume design (Holder), best direction (Holder), best supporting actor (Ted Ross), and best supporting actress (Dee Dee Bridgewater). It also won five Drama Desk Awards.

Prod. on Bway by Ken Harper at the Majestic Theatre, opening Jan. 5, 1975, for 1,672 perfs. Cast: Tasha Thomas (Aunt Em); Nancy (a dog: Toto); Stephanie Mills (Dorothy); Ralph Wilcox, succeeded by Albert Fann (Uncle Henry); Evelyn Thomas (Tornado); Phylicia Ayers-Allen, Pi Douglass, Andrew Torres, Carl Weaver & Joni Palmer (Munchkins); Clarice Taylor (Addaperle); Ronald Dunham, Eugene Little, John Parks & Kenneth Scott (Yellow Brick Road); Hinton Battle (Scarecrow); Wendy Edmead, Frances Morgan & Ralph Wilcox (Crows); Tiger Haynes (Tinman); Ted Ross (Lion); Phillip Bond, Pi Douglass, Andrew Torres, Rodney Green & Evelyn Thomas (Kalidahs); Lettie Battle, Leslie Butler, Eleanor McCoy, Frances Morgan & Joni Palmer (Poppies); Phylicia Ayers-Allen, Pi Douglass, Carl Weaver & Ralph Wilcox (Field Mice); Danny Beard (Gatekeeper); Andre De Shields (The Wiz); Mabel King (Evilene); Ralph Wilcox (Lord High Underling); Carl Weaver (Soldier Messenger); Andrew Torres (Winged Monkey); and Dee Dee Bridgewater (Glinda); Others: Emerald City Citizens.

Revived at the Lunt-Fontanne Theatre, New York, May 24, 1984, for 9 perfs.; starring Stephanie Mills.

Prod. in a 1978 film version starring Diana Ross, Richard Pryor, Lena Horne, and Michael Jackson.

Songs and musical numbers: "The Feeling We Once Had," "Tornado Ballet," "He's the Wizard," "Soon as I Get Home," "I Was Born on the Day Before Yesterday," "Ease on Down the Road," "Slide Some Oil to Me," "Mean Ole Lion," "Kalidah Battle," "Be a Lion," "Lion's Dream," "Meet the Wizard," "To Be Able to Feel," "No Bad News," "Funky Monkeys," "Everybody Rejoice," "Who Do You Think You Are?," "Believe in Yourself," "Y'All Got It!," "A Rested Body Is a Rested Mind," and "Home."

FURTHER REFERENCE: *BlkMusTh* (Woll). *Blk. Th. in the 1960s and 1970s* (Williams). *Encore* 4–21–1975. *Essence* 9–1975. *NY Amsterdam N.* 1–11–1975. *NYT* 12–28–1975; 3–3–1976.

THE WIZARD OF ALTOONA (1951). Musical. 3 acts. By Langston Hughes. Music by °Ellie Siegmeister. About carnival people, focusing mainly on their love affairs and business relationships. Apparently incomplete. Script in JWJ/YUL.

WOLVES AND LAMBS (1917). Musical revue. Prod. by and costarring James & Stovall (Seymour James and Wallace Stovall). James was dancer and principal comedian; Stovall was straight man. The show toured the TOBA circuit in 1917.

WORKING (1977). Musical. Adapt. and dir. by °Stephen Schwartz from the book by °Studs Terkel. With music and lyrics by Micki Grant and others. Prod. by the Goodman Theatre, Chicago, opening Dec. 30, 1977, for 40 perfs. Opened on Bway at the Forty-Sixth St. Theatre, May 14, 1978, for 30 perfs. Nominated for a Tony Award, 1977–78.

A WORLD OF PLEASURE (1915). White-oriented musical extravaganza. Book and lyrics apparently by °Harold Atteridge. Musical score by °Sigmund Romberg. Featured interpolated songs by J. Leubrie Hill. A series of vaudeville and prodn. numbers built around a slim plot involving the courtship of an heiress by a wealthy young suitor. Prod. at the Winter Garden, New York, Oct. 14, 1915. The all-white cast included °Richard Crawford (Tony Van Schuyler, the suitor) and °Venita Fitzhugh (the heiress). Hill's songs, apparently not memorable, included "Syncopation" and "Rosey Posey," the latter with lyrics by Atteridge; musical scores pub. by G. Schirmer, New York; copies in Moorland-Spingarn.

THE WORLD'S MY OYSTER (1948). Musical. By Lorenzo Fuller and Carley Mills. According to Miles Jefferson (*Phylon* 3rd qtr. 1956, p. 237), "The book was one of those long ago moth-eaten South Sea Island fantasies developed somewhat as if its writers had been stunned by [*]*Finian's Rainbow*." Prod. at the Actors Playhouse in Greenwich Village, New York, Aug. 1956, for 40 perfs. With Fuller as the romantic lead and Butterfly McQueen also in the cast.

WRAP IT IN BLACK (1931). Touring show. Prod. by and costarring Sam H. Gray. Cast also included Trixie Smith, Billy Mitchell, Sammy Paige, Doe Doe Green, George "Bugle Blues" Williams, Emmett "Gang" Anthony, Tim and Irene Robinson, Irene Castle, Jean Calloway, Paul Floyd, and Prof. Toby (the wonder horse).

THE WRONG MR. PRESIDENT (1913–14). / / Revised as *His Excellency, the President* (1914–15). Musical comedy. 2 acts. Book and lyrics by Salem Tutt Whitney and J. Homer Tutt (Whitney & Tutt). Music by Russell Smith and Taylor L. Corwell.

   In the setting of Ginger Springs, a health resort in Georgia, Whitney & Tutt play the roles of two tramps (Bud White and Dan Jenkins) who come into town just as the community is expecting the arrival of the president and secretary of the Republic of Haiti, who are traveling incognito. Believing that their seedy appearance is a part of some disguise, the townspeople greet White and Jenkins at the Ginger Springs Hotel as the two Haitian dignitaries, and the two are treated royally by their unsuspecting hosts. In order to avoid discovery of their mistaken identity, Whitney & Tutt get into numerous difficulties before the real president and secretary arrive, who are at first assumed to be imposters.

Prod. on tour by Whitney & Tutt, with the following cast: Salem Tutt Whitney (Bud White, a tramp, mistaken for His Excellency), J. Homer Tutt (Dan Jenkins, another tramp, mistaken for the Secretary to His Excellency), Greensbury Holmes (Monsieur LaFitz, Agent of the Haitian Rebel Faction), Alfred Strauder (Elias Simpson, Proprietor of the Ginger Springs Hotel), Frank Jackson (Senator Conback, U.S. Minister to Haiti), O. D. Carter (Willie Jump, Bell Boy), William "Babe" Townsend (Oh, Saymore, Real President of Haiti), James Woodson (Menee Lick, Ambassador of Abyssinia), Matt Johnson (Moore Menas, Secretary of the Haitian Legation), George Boutte (Sylam Bughouse, Resident of Ginger Springs), Blanche Thompson (Carmencia Gomez, Agent of the Rebel Faction), Douglas Barrymore (Mr. James Brown), Ethel Marshall (Dashing Widow), Pauline Parker (Lady Winterbottom, A Society Belle), Helen Clinton (Mandy Simpkins, Wife of Elias), Hattie Ackers (Lydia Harkfurst, Old Maid Suffragette), Emma Jackson (Dancer, Hotel Maid), and Others: Society Belles, Tango Dancers, Politicians, and Foreign Celebrities.

Songs and specialty numbers: Act I—"Tourists We Are" (opening chorus: Company), "What You Need Is Ginger Springs" (Strauder & Chorus), 'Good Advice' (comedy duo: Whitney & Tutt), "Come Out" (song and dance: Boutte, Carter & others), "Ye Old Quadrille" (square dance: Johnson & Company), "The Love You Can't Forget" (novelty: F. Jackson & Octette), "Romance Espagnola" (Thompson & Chorus), "Just a Pickaninny All Dressed Up" (Whitney & Tutt), "When Your Country Calls to Arms" (drill: Holmes & Chorus), "The Intruder" (finale Act I: Ensemble). Act II—"Hesitation Waltz" (Company), "All I Ask Is to Forget You" (Thompson), 'Have Patience, Don't Worry' (comedy duo: Whitney & Tutt), "Smart Set Tango" (Company), "We Welcome Thee" (Company), "Hawaiian Tango" and "Twilight Dreams" (demonstration of latest dances: Whitney & Tutt, Blanche Thompson & Hattie Ackers), "For Honor" (dramatic ensemble: Company), and "Tutt's Tudalo" (finale: Danced by Entire Company).

FURTHER REFERENCE: *BlksBf* (Sampson).

THE WRONG MR. RIGHT (1913). Musical revue. Prod. by the Pekin Stock Co., at the Pekin Theatre, Savannah, GA, 1913.

X–Y–Z

X (THE LIFE AND TIMES OF MALCOLM X) (1986). Opera. Written and composed by Anthony Davis. Perfd. by the New York City Opera, Lincoln Center, Sept. 7–Oct. 14, 1986, for 4 perfs.; conducted by Christopher Keene. Featuring Priscilla Baskerville, Marietta Simpson, Ben Holt, Thomas Young, and Mark S. Doss.

YALLER GAL (1924). Touring revue. Prod. by and costarring the dance team of Chappelle & Stinnette (Thomas Chappelle and Juanita Stinnette). Cast also included John Mason and Gertrude "Baby" Cox.

YEAH MAN! (1932). Musical revue. Book by Leigh Whipper and Billy Mills. Music and lyrics by Whipper, Mills, Porter Grainger, Al Wilson, °Charles Weinberg, and °Ken Macomber.

This show, starring comedian Mantan Moreland and dancer Eddie Rector, was described by the *NYT* (5–27–1932) as a "shrill and tuneless farrago, light on its feet and lugubrious in its humor," but the *NYT* had some faint praise for Moreland, "without whom none of these blackamoor capers is quite official." The reviewer went on to praise Moreland's smile, his tireless energy, and the way in which he smoked a cigar, took his falls, and "feign[ed] wide-eyed terror," with comic effect.

Prod. by °Walter Campbell and °Jesse Wank at the Park Lane Theatre (formerly Daly's Sixty-third St. Theatre), New York, opening May 26, 1932, for 4 perfs. Cast: Moreland, Rector, Mills, Whipper, Rose Henderson, Lilly Yuen, Hilda Perleno, Peggy Phillips, Marcus Slayter, Adele Hargraves, Jarahal, Walter Brogsdale, Russell Graves, Harry Fiddler, and the Melodee Four.

Songs and musical numbers: "Mississippi Days," "Gotta Get de Boat Loaded," "Dancing Fool," "At the Barbecue," "I'm Always Happy When I'm in Your Arms," "I've Got What It Takes," "Crazy Idea of Love," "Come

to Harlem," "The Spell of Those Harlem Nights," "Baby, I Could Do It for You," "Shady Dan," "Give Me Your Love," "Shake Your Music," "That's Religious," and "Qualifications."
FURTHER REFERENCE: *BesPls 1931–32. NYT* 5–27–1932.

THE YEAR 'ROUND (1953). Musical show. Sketches by °Charles Scheuer. Music and lyrics by J. C. Johnson. Additional material by °David MacMacin, Langston Hughes, Scheuer, Eva Franklin, and Gerri Major. Opened at the Harlem Musical Theatre, April 27, 1953.
FURTHER REFERENCE: *NYT* 5–6–1953.

YELLOW GAL (1926). Touring revue. Prod. by blackface comedian John "Rareback" Mason, who costarred with the Dixie Beach Girls Co.

YELLOW GIRL REVUE (1927). A Bessie Smith show, which originated in New York at the Lafayette or Lincoln Theatre before going on tour.

YES, GOD IS REAL (1988). Gospel musical. Book and lyrics by James M. Brown. Music by Thomas Jennings and the Rev. Charles Lyles. About a devout young man who loses his faith, but finally regains it. Prod. at the Apollo Theatre in Harlem, spring 1988; dir. by Al (Suavae) Mitchell; choreographed by Lydia Abarca Mitchell. With Wendy Mason, Betty Graves Scott, Bill Greene, and the Rev. Charles Lyles.

YES, SIR (1926). Touring revue. Prod. by and costarring comedians Martin & Walker (Edgar Martin and Billy Walker). Cast also included Babe Brown, Myrtle Quarrels, Ray Moore, and chorus.

YOUNG JOHN HENRY (late 1980s). Billed as "A Rollicking Family Musical." By Useni Eugene Perkins. Music by Wanda Bishop. About the early life of the legendary black railroad workers. Prod. by the ETA Creative Arts Foundation, Chicago, c. 1989; dir. by Runako Jaho.

THE YOUNG MR. BOJANGLES / / Orig. title: *Young Mr. Bo* (1986). By Billy Graham. Commissioned by the Harlem Cultural Council. About the early years of tap dancer Bill "Bojangles" Robinson. Prod. by One West Dinner Theatre, 1 W. 125th St., New York, fall 1986.

YOUR ARMS TOO SHORT TO BOX WITH GOD (1975–76, 1980–82). Gospel musical. Conceived and dir. by Vinnette Carroll. Music and lyrics by Alex Bradford. Additional music by Micki Grant.
    A joyous hand-clapping and foot-stomping, revivalist version of the biblical Book of Matthew (also known as the Gospel of Matthew), told in gospel songs,

drama, and dance, with the title taken from a poem in James Weldon Johnson's *God's Trombones* (1927), which has been the inspiration for several musicals by Carroll, Bradford, Grant, and other black writers.

Developed by the Urban Arts Corps (UAC), New York, for presentation at the Festival of Two Worlds, Spoleto, Italy, where it was first presented in 1975. American premiere held at Ford's Theatre, Washington, DC, opening Nov. 4, 1975, for 168 perfs.; then taken on U.S. tour for a year; starring Jennifer Holliday (then an unknown gospel singer who later became the star of *Dreamgirls*).

Opened on Bway at the Lyceum Theatre, Dec. 22, 1976, for 429 perfs.; choreographed by Talley Beatty; with Delores Hall (who won a Tony Award as best featured actress). Cast also included Adrian Bailey, Salome Bey, Deborah Lynn Bridges, Sharon Brooks, Clinton Derricks-Carroll, Sheila Ellis, Thomas Jefferson Fouse, Jr., Michael Gray, Cardell Hall, William Hardy, Jr., Bobby Hill, Edna M. Krider, Hector Jaime Mercado, Mabel Robinson, William Thomas, Jr., Leone [*sic*] Washington, Derek Williams, and Marilyn Winbush.

After a lengthy U.S. tour, the show returned to Bway at the Ambassador Theatre, June 2–Oct. 12, 1980, for 149 perfs.; starring Jennifer Holliday. With Adrian Bailey, Julius Richard Brown, Cleavant Derricks, Sheila Ellis, Ralph Farrington, Jamil K. Garland, Elijah Gill, William-Keebler Hardy, Jr., Linda James, Gary Q. Lewis, Linda Morton, Jai Oscar St. John, Kiki Shepard, Leslie Hardesty Sisson, Ray Stephens, Quincella Swyningan, Faruma S. Williams, Marilynn Winbush, Linda Young, and the Swing Dancers: Adrian Bailey and Linda James.

Taken on national tour, restaged by dancer-choreographer Ralph Haze, before playing on Bway at the Alvin Theatre, Sept. 9–Nov. 7, 1982, for 69 perfs.; starring Patti LaBelle, Al Green, and Ralph Haze.

Songs and musical numbers: "Beatitudes," "We're Gonna Have a Good Time," "There's a Stranger in Town," "Do You Know Jesus? (He's a Wonder)," "Just a Little Bit of Jesus Goes a Long Way," "We Are the Priests and Elders," "Something Is Wrong in Jerusalem," "It was Alone," "Be Careful Whom You Kiss," "Trial," "It's Too Late," "Judas' Dance," "Your Arms Too Short to Box with God," "Give Us Barabbas," "See How They Done My Lord," "Come on Down," "Can't No Grave Hold My Body Down," "Didn't I Tell You," "When the Power Comes," "Everybody Has His Own Way," "Down by the Riverside," "I Love You So Much Jesus," "The Band."
FURTHER REFERENCE: *NY Amsterdam N.* 3–19–1977; 9–11–1982. *NYT* 1–23–1977.

YOU'VE GOT TO STEP LIVELY (1927). Touring musical show. Prod. by and costarring Bailey & Wiggins (Laura Bailey and Jack "Ginger" Wiggins). Cast also included Jesse Gordon, "Dollar Bill" Jones, James Lancaster, Slim Russell, Anna Thomas, the Three Inkspots (dancers), and chorus.

ZIEGFELD FOLLIES [of 1910, 1911, 1914, 1915, 1916, 1917, 1919, 1921, 1922, 1931, 1936, and 1956] (1910–56). Series of annual musical revues or extravaganzas. Prod. continuously by °Florenz Ziegfeld from 1907 to 1932, then periodically until 1957. The above eds. were significant for their black content.

Bert Williams wrote songs for and starred in 8 eds. of the Follies as the only black member of an integrated cast. Several eds. featured contributions by other black songwriters, but other black performers did not appear in the show until the 1930s. This show was noted for its gorgeously gowned girls, beautiful scenery, extravagant stage effects, funny sketches and comic routines, excellent choreography, and the introduction of popular song hits written by the nation's top composers.

Ziegfeld Follies of 1910. 3 acts [14 scenes]. Book and lyrics by °Harry B. Smith. Music by °Gus Edwards. Prod. at the Jardin de Paris, New York, June 20, 1910, for 88 perfs. Included several songs by black writers: "That Minor Strain," by Ford Dabney and Cecil Mack; "Lovey Joe," by Will Marion Cook and Joe Jordan; ⁺"Constantly," with music by Bert Williams (words by Harry Smith and °James Burris), pub. by Jerome K. Remick, New York, 1910; ⁺"You're Gwine to Get Somethin' You Don't Expect," with music by Williams (words by °Vivian Bryan), pub. by Leo Feist, New York, 1910. Starring Bert Williams, who apparently sang his two songs as part of a scenic symphony entitled "That Apple Blossom Grove," in which several ladies jump into a pool of water and are transformed into seals while Williams sings. According to a review by Channing Pollock (*Green Bk. Album* 9–1910, pp. 502–5), Williams, in his opening night performance "somehow missed fire," which may have been caused by "first night nervousness," or by "a paucity of opportunity," or "because his songs, excepting one called 'Constantly' were distinctly unfunny— whatever the reason, Bert Williams did not provoke the gales of merriment that usually follow his caroling." Bert's two songs, marked with a plus sign (⁺), are located in Moorland-Spingarn.

Ziegfeld Follies of 1911. 2 acts [13 scenes]. Words and lyrics by °George V. Hobart. Music by °Maurice Levi and °Raymond Hubbell. Prod. at the Jardin de Paris, New York, June 26, 1911, for 88 perfs. Starring Bert Williams, who also wrote music for one of his three songs, "Dat's Harmony" (with words by °Grant Clark), pub. by Jerome N. Remick, New York, 1911; copy in Moorland-Spingarn. His other songs were "Woodman, Spare That Tree" and "In the Evening." Williams introduced his famous poker sketch in this show, which was described by Channing Pollock (*Green Bk. Album* 9–1911, pp. 568–69) as "a bit of pantomime, showing a hand at poker, that is very high," in which "Williams conveys the opening of a jack pot, and the losing of his stack," in a solo performance. "You watch his face and know just how many cards have been drawn by each player."

Ziegfeld Follies of 1912. 2 acts. Words by Harry B. Smith. Music by Raymond Hubbell. Prod. at the Moulin Rouge, New York, Oct. 21, 1912, for 88 perfs. Starring Bert Williams, who wrote the music for one of his songs, "Borrow from Me'' (with words by °Jean Ravez), pub. by Jerome N. Remick, New York, 1912; copy in Moorland-Spingarn. In this show, Williams perfd. in a sketch with °Leon Errol, with whom he costarred in several other *Follies* eds. As described by Channing Pollock (*Green Bk. Mag.* 1–1913, p. 72), this was ''a convulsingly [*sic*] funny scene between Bert Williams as the owner of a sea-going hack, Mr. Errol as a prospective fare with a load that wouldn't go into a procession of carriages, and indescribable property horse named Nicodemus.''

Ziegfeld Follies of 1914. 2 acts. Book and lyrics by George V. Hobart. Music by Raymond Hubbell. Additional music by black songwriter J. Leubrie Hill (songs unknown). Special numbers by °David Stamper. With additional lyrics by °Gene Buck. Prod. at the Winter Garden, New York, June 1, 1914, for 112 perfs. Starring Bert Williams, who wrote the music for two of his songs, ''I'm Cured'' (with lyrics by °Jean C. Havez) and ''The Vampire'' (with lyrics by Gene Buck and °Earl Jones; both pub. by Jerome H. Remick, New York, 1914; and perfd. his famous poker sketch, 'The Darktown Poker Club,' which was first introduced in the *Follies of 1911*. According to Gerald Bordman (*AmMusTh*, p. 295), in Williams' single-handed poker game, ''he was the only player, and his free hand became a hilarious dexterous computer.'' This skit generally has been considered his finest moment.

Ziegfeld Follies of 1915. 2 acts. Lines and lyrics by °Channing Pollock, °Rennold Wolfe, and Gene Buck. Music by °Louis Hirsch and David Stamper. Prod. at the New Amsterdam Theatre, New York, June 21, 1915, for 104 perfs. Starring Bert Williams, who played the role of an overworked houseboy. Nothing else is known of his perf.

Ziegfeld Follies of 1916. 2 acts. Book and lyrics by George V. Hobart and Gene Buck. Music by Louis Hirsch, °Jerome Kern, and David Stamper. Prod. at the New Amsterdam Theatre, New York, June 12, 1916, for 112 perfs. Starring Bert Williams, who appeared in a spoof of *Othello*. This prodn also featured a finale entitled ''Midnight Frolic Glide,'' with music and lyrics by Alex C. Rogers and C. Luckeyth Roberts, which apparently remained in the show for two consecutive seasons.

Ziegfeld Follies of 1917. 2 acts. Book and lyrics by Gene Buck and George V. Hobart. Music by Raymond Hubbell and David Stamper. Patriotic finale by °Victor Herbert. Prod. at the New Amsterdam Theatre, New York, June 12, 1917, for 111 perfs. Starring Bert Williams, who was teamed with °Eddie Cantor in blackface. Cantor played the college-educated son of a Pullman porter (Williams) who is ashamed of his father's illiteracy. Also featured was ''Unhappy,'' a song with lyrics by Henry Creamer and music by J. Turner Layton.

Ziegfeld Follies of 1919. Music by David Stamper, °Harry Tierney, °Irving Berlin, Victor Herbert, and °Albert Von Tilzer. Lyrics by Berlin, Gene Buck, °Joseph McCarthy, and °Lew Brown. Sketches by °Rennold Wolf, Buck, °George Lemaire, and Eddie Cantor. Prod. at the New Amsterdam Theatre, New York, June 16, 1919, for 171 perfs. Starring Bert Williams, who perfd. in 'The Follies Minstrels,' a sketch in which Eddie Cantor was Tambo and Williams was Bones.

Cantor and Williams also sang an Irving Berlin number, "I Want to See a Minstrel Show." In another prohibition sketch, Berlin wrote a special song for Williams, "You Cannot Make Your Shimmy Shake on Tea."

Ziegfeld Follies of 1921. Music by Victor Herbert and °Rudolph Friml. Sketches by °Willard Mack, °Raymond Hitchcock, and °James Reynolds. Lyrics by Gene Buck and others. Black songwriters Henry Creamer and J. Turner Layton (Turner & Layton) also contributed at least one song to this show, "Strut, Miss Lizzie," introduced by °Van & Schenk.

Other editions: *Ziegfeld Follies of 1922* introduced a song by Creamer & Layton, the title of which has not been located. *Ziegfeld Follies of 1931* featured the comedy team of Buck & Bubbles. *Ziegfeld Follies of 1936* featured Josephine Baker, in which she danced in a Calypso number entitled "Island in the West Indies," with music by °Vernon Duke and lyrics by °Ira Gershwin. *Ziegfeld Follies of 1956* featured singer Mae Barnes.

ZULIKI (1897–1900). Opera. 3 acts. By H. Lawrence Freeman. Set in Africa. Perfd. in parts of Cleveland, OH, 1900. For the composer's best-known works, see *The Martyr* (1893), *Valdo* (1905-6), *Vendetta* (1911-23), and *Voodoo* (1921-28).

ZULU KING (c. 1932). Opera. 1 act. Written and composed by H. Lawrence Freeman. Part of an unperfd. tetralogy entitled *Zululand* (1925–47). For the composer's best-known works, see *The Martyr* (1893), *Valdo* (1905-6), *Vendetta* (1911-23), and *Voodoo* (1921-28).

ZULULAND (1932–47). Operatic tetralogy. Written and composed by H. Lawrence Freeman. Includes four unperfd. 1-act operatic works: *Nada, *Allah, *The Zulu King, and *The Slave. For the composer's best-known works, see *The Martyr* (1893), *Valdo* (1905-6), *Vendetta* (1911-23), and *Voodoo* (1921-28).

ZUNGURU (1938, revived 1940). African dance opera, with English and African dialogue. Written and choreographed by Asadata Dafora Horton, a native of Sierra Leone.

The choreographer's second dance drama; the first was *Kykunkor* (1934). Although this work followed the same general "formula of his earlier work," and "was a more mature and better production," it "did not have the impact of *Kykunkor*," according to *Blk. Dance* (Emery, p. 251). *Time* (9–19–1938) described the 1938 version as "primitive in plot . . . a kind of savage vaudeville, with three blacks pounding African drums, brown girls strutting their stuff, a witch doctor gabbling and shrieking, a fire-eater munching lighted torches—all of it 'background' for Boy Meets Girl in Senegal." The *NY Herald Trib.* (4–28–1940) stated that this prodn. contained "the wildest dancing you ever saw," and was "untouched by the softening hands of civilization." The *NYT* (5–21–1940) praised it for its "tremendous gusto" and "vitality."

First prod. New York in Aug. 1938. A revised version was presented Off-Bway in May 1940.

FURTHER REFERENCE: *NY Herald Trib.* 4–28–1940. *NYT* 8–3–1938; 8–7–1938; 5–21–1940.

APPENDIX: CHRONOLOGY OF MUSICAL SHOWS

The following is a chronology of all musical stage works included in the main body of this encyclopedia, subdivided by decades and proceeding from *Free and Easy* (1873) to *Jelly's Last Jam* (1992). Outstanding musical shows are marked with a single dagger (†) for the benefit of those readers who are seeking some guidance in the study of the history of black American musical stage and who may wish to read about these musicals in the approximate order that they were first written or produced. Operas and operettas are usually indicated by (O), and adaptations by (adapt.). Shows with two or more editions are usually listed only once, during the decade of the first edition, with the dates of other editions given in parentheses.

1870–1879

Free and Easy (1873), Lyles & Lyles

†*Out of Bondage* (c. 1875–c. 1891), Hyers Sisters

†*Urlina, African Princess* (1877–89), Hyers Sisters

1880–1889

Blackville Twins (1889–91), Ganze & Piper/Hyers Sisters

1890–1899

†*The Creole Show* (1890–97), °S. T. Jack

Colored Aristocracy (1891), Hyers Sisters

†*South Before the War* (1891–98), °Whalen & °Martell

The Martyr (O, 1893), H. L. Freeman

†*Black America* (1895), B. McClain

†*The Octoroons* (1895–1900), J. W. Isham

The Belle of Cornville (O, 1896), Afro-Am. Opera Co.

Fred Douglass' Reception (1896), J. E. Green

†*The Gold Bug* (1896), with Williams & Walker

†*At Jolly Coon-ey Island* (1896–97), Cole & Johnson/Blk. Patti Troubadours

†*Courted into Court* (1896–97), Hogan & Harney (songs)

†*Darkest America* (1896–99), °Fields & °Scott

†*Oriental America* (1896–1899), J. W. Isham

†*(The) Black Patti Troubadours* (c. 1896–1915), various authors

The Good Mr. Best (1897), Perrin & Hillman (song)

Zuliki (O, 1897–1900), H. L. Freeman

†*A Trip to Coontown* (1897–1901), B. Cole & W. Johnson

†*At Jolly Coon-ey Island* (New Ed.) (1898), Hogan & Raynes/Blk. Patti Troubadours

†*Clorindy, The Origin of the Cakewalk* (1898), Cook & Dunbar

†*Kings of Koon-dom* (1898), W. Isham

†*Senegambian Carnival* (1898), Williams & Walker

A Spanish Review (1898), Cole & Johnson

†*A Lucky Coon* (1898–99), Williams & Walker

By the Sad Sea Waves (1899), E. Hogan (song)

Dream Lovers (O, 1899), Dunbar & Taylor

†*A Ragtime Frolic at Ras-bury Park* (1899), Blk. Patti Troubadours

†*A Reign of Error* (1899), Cole & Johnson (song)

Uncle Eph's Christmas (1899), Dunbar & Cook

†*The Policy Players* (1899–1900), Williams & Walker

†*Whitman Sisters Revue* (c. 1899–c. 1936), Whitman Sisters

1900–1909

†*The Belle of Bridgeport* (1900), Cole & Johnson Bros. (songs)

Coontown Carnival (1900), B. Cole

A Country Coon (c. 1900), Hogan & Dunn

A Darktown Frolic at the Rialto (1900), Blk. Patti Troubadours

†*Jes Lak White Fo'ks* (1900), Cook & Dunbar

The King of Spades (1900), B. Cole

Madge Smith, Attorney (1900), E. Hogan (songs)

†*The Rogers Brothers in Central Park* (1900), Cole & Johnson Bros. (songs)

†*The Casino Girl* (1900–1901), Cook & Accooe (songs)

†*The Sons of Ham* (1900–1902), with Williams & Walker

King Rastus (1900–1905), Cole & Johnson

In Old Kentucky (c. 1900–c. 1915), °C. L. Dazy

African Princes (1901), J. E. Green

†*The Cannibal King* (1901), Cook, Dunbar & others

Champagne Charlie (1901), Cole & Johnson Bros. (songs)

The Liberty Belles (1901), W. Accooe (song)

Medicine Man (1901), J. E. Green

†*The New Yorkers* (1901), Cook & Perrin (songs)

The Supper Club (1901), Cole & Johnson Bros. (songs)

†*The Little Duchess* (1901–2), Cole & Johnson Bros. (songs)

Sleeping Beauty and the Beast (1901–2), °Wood & °Collins

Lady Africa (1901–4), Anderson & Anderson

†*The Ex-President of Liberia* (1901–9), S. T. Whitney

†*(The) Smart Set (Co.)* (c. 1901–24), various companies

A Filipino Misfit (1902), Blk. Patti Troubadours

Foxy Grandpa (1902), Lemonier & Gerard (song)

†*The Girl from Dixie* (1902), Cole & Johnson Bros.

The Hall of Fame (1902), Johnson Bros. (songs)

Huckleberry Finn (adapt., 1902), C. Mack & others (songs)

The Octoroon (O, 1902), H. L. Freeman

†*Sally in Our Alley* (1902), Cole & Johnson Bros.

†*In Dahomey* (1902–5), with Williams & Walker

An African Kraal (O, 1903), H. L. Freeman

A Bogus Prince (1903), S. Perrin

†*Darktown's Circus Day* (1903), B. Cole/Blk. Patti Troubadours

The Girl with the Green Eyes (c. 1903), S. Perrin (song)

†*A Guest of Honor* (1903), S. Joplin

†*Mother Goose* (1903), Cole & Johnson Bros. (songs)

Mr. Bluebeard (1903), Dunbar, Cole & Johnson

†*Nancy Brown* (1903), Cole & Johnson Bros. (songs)

Whoop-Dee-Doo (1903), Cole & Johnson Bros. (songs)

†*Silas Green from New Orleans* (c. 1903–c. 1953), Whitney, Tutt & Williams

Alabama Blossom (1904), Cole & Johnson (songs)

†*Cooney Dreamland* (1904), B. Cole/Blk. Patti Troubadours

An English Daisy (1904), Cole & Johnson Bros. (songs)

A Little Bit of Everything (1904), Cole & Johnson Bros. (songs)

†*The Southerners* (1904), Cook & °Grant

†*In Newport* (1904–5), Cole & Johnson Bros. (songs)

†*The Black Politician* (1904–8), S. H. Dudley & others

†*Humpty Dumpty* (1904–8), Cole & Johnson Bros. (songs)

The Rollicking Girl (1905), Stewart & Lemonier (song)

†*The Wild Rose* (1905), Cook & Mack (song)

Valdo (O, 1905–6), H. L. Freeman

†*Rufus Rastus* (1905–7), E. Hogan

†*The Shoo-Fly Regiment* (1905–7), Cole & Johnson Bros.

†*Hottest Coon in Dixie* (1906), °Ferdos & °Carter

Marrying Mary (1906), C. Smith & others

†*Abyssinia* (1906–7), with Williams & Walker

†*The Sunny South Company* (c. 1906–8), °J. C. Rockwell

The Plantation (O, 1906–15), H. L. Freeman

†*The Man from 'Bam* (1906–7, 1920, 1923), Miller & Lyles

†*The Grafters* (1907), J. Ed. Green

The Mayor of Dixie (1907), Miller & Lyles

In Zululand (1907), J. E. Green & others

†*The Oyster Man* (1907–8), Miller & Lyles, Hogan & Vodery

†*The Prince of Bungaboo* (1907–8), S. T. Whitney

†*Bandana Land* (also *Bandanna Land*, 1907–9), with Williams & Walker

†*The Husband* (1907–9), Miller & Lyles

†*Captain Jasper* (1907–13), Blk. Patti Troubadours

†*Captain Rufus* (1907, revived 1914), J. E. Green & others

†*Treemonisha* (O, 1907, 1915, 1972, 1975, 1985, 1991), S. Joplin

The Boys and Betty (1908), W. M. Cook (song)

†*The Colored Aristocrats* (1908), Miller & Lyles

†*The Czar of Dixie* (1908), Lincoln Stock Co.

Dr. Knight (1908), Miller & Lyles

†*The Emperor of Dixie* (1908), Perrin & Crumbly (?)

†*Ephraham Johnson from Norfolk* (1908), Miller & Brooks

The Merry Widower (1908), V. H. Smalley

†*Panama* (1908), M. A. Brooks & others

†*Simple Mollie* (1908), H. Wise

†*Blackville Strollers* (1908–9), Whitney & Tutt

†*The Red Moon* (1908–9), Cole & Johnson

†*A Trip to Africa* (at least 2 eds., 1908, 1910–11), J. Larkins/Blk. Patti Troubadours

De Cider Man (1909), E. Denton

†*My Friend from Kentucky* (1909), Whitney & Tutt

A Royal Coon (1909), J. Larkins/Blk. Patti Troubadours

Subway Sal (c. 1909), E. Green

†*Too Many in the House* (1909), G. W. Allen

†*The Tryst* (O, 1909), H. L. Freeman

†*Mr. Lode of Koal* (1909–10), Shipp & Rogers

†*The Mayor of Newtown* (also *Newton*, 1909, 1914), Whitney & Tutt

1910–1919

†*The Census Taker* (1910), J. Mills

George Washington Bullion (1910), Whitney & Tutt

Judy Forgot (1910), W. M. Cook (song)

The Music Man (1910), with T. Lockhart

†*A Night in New York's Chinatown* (1910), J. A. Shipp

No Place Like Home (1910), J. A. Shipp

†*A Blackville Corporation* (adapt., 1910, 1915), J. L. Hill

†*The Darktown Follies* (1910–16), J. L. Hill & others

†*Ziegfeld Follies* [of 1910, 1911, 1912, 1914, 1915, 1916, 1917, 1919, 1921, 1922, 1931, 1936, and 1956] (1910–56), B. Williams, Roberts & Rogers, Creamer & Layton

Dr. Herb's Prescription, or It Happened in a Dream (1911), J. A. Shipp

The Ham Tree (1911), W. Benbow

Hello, Paris (revised ed., 1911), Johnson & Hill (songs)

†*In the Jungles* (1911), Cook & Watts/Blk. Patti Troubadours

Little Miss Fix-It (1911), Johnson & Johnson (songs)

A Prince of Dixie (1911), G. Taylor

The Prophecy (O, 1911), H. L. Freeman

Royal Sam (1911), °Morrow & °Mindlin

Runaway Slaves (1911), with Lee & Lee

Spoony Sam (1911), W. M. Benbow

Ten Dark Nights (1911), Rolf & Smith

Two Story (1911), W. H. Benbow

The Hottest Coon in Dixie (1911–12), with H. Morgan & others

†*In Ethiopiaville* (1911–13), F. Montgomery

Vendetta (O, 1911–23), H. L. Freeman

†*Dr. Beans from Boston* (1912), S. H. Dudley & others

Happy Sam from Bam (1912), Miller & Paschal

Stranded in Africa (1912), F. Crowd

Happy Girls (1912–13), W. Vodery

Two Bills from Alaska (1912–14), B. King

Voodoo (O, 1912–28), H. L. Freeman

The Cabaret (1913), Miller & Lyles

Captain Bogus of the Jim Crow Regiment (1913), Star Stock Co.

The Frog Follies (1913), W. M. Cook & others

The Lady Barber (c. 1913), Russell & Owens

The Passing Show of 1913 (1913), A. Razaf (song)

Tallaboo (1913), N. R. Harper

A Tragedy on the Town (1913), Porter & McDaniel

Who's to Win (1913), Bragg & Mahone

The Wrong Mr. Right (1913), Pekin Stock Co.

†*The Old Man's Boy* (1913–14), Rogers & Creamer

†*The Traitor* (1913–14), Rogers, Creamer & Cook

†*The Wrong Mr. President* (1913–14), Whitney & Tutt

Carnation (1914), B. King

The Girl from Utah (1914), C. Smith

†*Lucky Sam from Alabam'* (1914), H. Stewart/Blk. Patti Troubadours

†*Mr. Ragtime* (1914), Miller & Vodery

Now I'm a Mason (1914), B. King

Out in the Street (1914), B. King

The Runaway's Return (1914), B. King

Tom Boys—Easy Breezy Girls (1914), B. Johnson

When Luck Bill Came to Town (1914), N. Stovall & others

†*Darkydom* (1914–15), H. Troy & others

†*His Excellency, the President* (1914–15), S. T. Whitney

The Darktown Politician (1915), S. T. Whitney

†*George Washington Bullion Abroad* (1915), Whitney & Tutt

The Passing Show of 1915 (1915), J. L. Hill (song)

Professor Ebenezzer (1915), H. Stewart

The Whitewash Man (1915), H. Stewart

†*A World of Pleasure* (1915), J. L. Hill (songs)

Athalia (O, 1915–16), H. L. Freeman

Bombay Girls (1915–23), Drake & Walker

†*Broadway Rastus* (1915–28), I. C. Miller

45 Minutes to Broadway (1916), with A. Mitchell & others

From Speedville to Broadway (1916), F. Montgomery

Good Times Tonight (1916), Drake & Walker

An Hawaiian Idyll (1916), A. M. Dunbar-Nelson

†*How Newtown Prepared* (also *Newton*, 1916), Whitney & Tutt

Lizzie and Pete of the Cabaret Show (1916), M. Decard

On the Way to Boston (1916), F. Montgomery

The Return of Sam Langford (1916), B. Watts

The Rivals (1916), B. King

The Three Twins (1916), °Hauerback & °Hoschna

The Undertaker's Daughter (1916), B. King

Holiday in Dixie (at least 2 eds., 1916–22), W. Mastin & others

The Bon Ton Minstrels (1917), F. Montgomery

The Face at the Window (1917), B. King

Hotel Nobody (1917), B. King

The Kidnapper (1917), B. King

Lady for a Day (1917), B. King

The Lonesome Mile (1917), B. King

A Mother-in-Law's Disposition (1917), B. King

Neighbors (1917), B. King

Raiding a Cabaret (1917), B. King

Sambo Jones in New York (1917), James & Stovall

The Senator (1917), B. King

The Two Detectives (1917), F. Montgomery

What's Your Husband Doing? (1917), J. P. Johnson (music)

Wolves and Lambs (1917), James & Stovall

The Final Rehearsal (1917–18), B. King

The Heart Breakers (1917–18), B. King

My People (1917–18), Whitney & Tutt

Sergeant Ham [of the 13th District] (at least 2 eds., 1917–19), P. Bradford

At the Beach (1918), B. King

†*Board of Education* (1918), B. King

†*Catching the Burglar* (1918), B. King

The Charming Widow (1918), B. Russell

Chief Outlanchette (1918), B. King

†*The Con Man* (1918), B. King

Goodbye Everybody (1918), B. King

His Honor, the Mayor (1918), Lafayette Players

In the Draft (1918), B. King

Mr. Jazz from Dixie (1918), B. King

My Wife's Sweetheart (1918), Miller & Lyles

The Night Raid (1918), B. King

The Rich Uncle (1918), B. King

20 Minutes in Hell (1918), Benbow's Merry Makers

†*Who's Stealin'* (1918), Miller & Lyles

†*Darkest Americans* (1918–19), Whitney & Tutt

Bowman's Cotton Blossoms (1919), W. H. Bowman

Darktown After Dark (1919), P. Bradford

Exploits in Africa (1919), King & Barbour

The Hunter Horse (1919), S. Burns

Over the Top (1919), King & Barbour

Rock and Rosey Lee (1919), S. Burns

Seeing Chinatown (1919), Quality Amusement Co.

That's the Time (1919), "Negroes in Baltimore, Md."

†*They're Off* (1919), King & Barbour

Trip to South Africa (1919), S. Burns

Up Stairs and Down Below (1919), Miller & Lyles

A Wedding in Jazz (1919), Stovall & Mack

†*Baby Blues* (1919–20), Rogers & Roberts

†*(The) Children of the Sun* (1919–20), Whitney & Tutt

This and That (1919–20), Rogers & Roberts

†*Hello 19–* (at least 4 eds., 1919–22), F. Montgomery

†*Up and Down* (c. 1919–22), Whitney & Tutt

1920–1929

†*An African Prince* (1920), Quality Amusement Co.

Arrival of the Negro (1920), J. B. Barbour

Beale Street to Broadway (1920), A. Gates

Black Bottom (1920), P. Bradford

Bringing Up Husband (1920), H. Jones

†*Broadway Brevities [of] 1920* (1920), °Le Maire & Williams

Broadway Gossips (1920), Q. Miller

†*Canary Cottage* (1920), Carrol, Brooks & others

China Town (1920), B. King

The Cotton Brokers (1920), H. Jones Co.

Follies and Fancies of 1920 (1920), Montgomery & McClain

Folly Town (1920), with 10 blk. performers

Fun in a Music Shop (1920), Gaines Bros.

Hello Dixieland (1920), B. King

Lime Kiln Club (1920), B. King

Maid in Harlem (1920), with M. Smith

The Midnight Rounders (1920), Sissle & Blake (song)

Miss Nobody from Starland (1920), S. Brooks

September Morn (1920), S. Brooks

Show Folks (1920), S. Perrin

Strutt Your Stuff (1920), Townsend & Payton

Sultan Sam (1920), I. C. Miller

†*Three Showers* (1920), Creamer & Layton

The Time, The Place, The Horse (1920), Stovall & Mack

Town Top-Picks (1920), A. Gates

Tunes and Funnies of 1920 (1920), Miller & Lyles

†*Alabama Bound* (1920–21), I. C. Miller

New Americans (1920–21), B. King

†*Bamboula* (1921), Whitney & Tutt

The Broadway Rounders (1921), F. Horton

Chocolate Brown (1921), I. C. Miller

Cotton Tops (1921), Authorship unknown

Darktown Frolics (1921), with Mme. Branin & others

Dixie Girls (1921), P. Williams

Fun at the Picnic Grounds (1921), H. Jackson

†*George White's Scandals* (1921, 1922, 1926, 1931 eds.), °G. White

Hello Sue (1921), S. Burns

High Flyers (1921), S. Perrin

In Mexico (1921), D. D. Green

The Insane Asylum (1921), E. Hunter

Joyland Girls (1921), E. Martin

Mexico (1921), D. D. Green

Midnight in Chinatown (1921), Scott & Scott

Miss Nobody's Hotel (1921), H. Jackson

Noyes and Watts Musical Comedy Co. (1921), Noyes & Watts

†*Put and Take* (1921), I. C. Miller & others

Small Town Doings (1921), Whitney & Tutt

Snapshots of 1921 (1921), H. Brooks

Some Baby (1921), Q. Miller

Stylish Steppers (1921), Authorship unknown

Sunkist Southerners (1921), Authorship unknown

A Trip Around the World (1921), B. King

Two Neighbors (1921), H. Jackson

Two Nuts from Brazil (1921), H. Jackson

Where the Trail Ends in Mexico (1921), H. Jones

Why Worry? (1921), Q. Miller

†*Wift Waft Warblers* (1921), Davis & Stafford

Daffy Girls (1921–22), with Larue & Larue

Darktown Scandals of 1921 (1921–22), Q. Miller

Tunes and Topics (at least two eds., 1921, 1923), Q. Miller

Creole Belles (at least 3 eds., 1921–26), E. Lee & others

†*Shuffle Along* (1921, 1930, 1932–33, 1952), Miller & Lyles, Sissle & Blake

Abraham the Barber (1922), E. Hunter

Africana (1922), G. Taylor

All Aboard (1922), Authorship unknown

Anita Bush Company (1922), A. Bush

Beulah Benbow's Dancing Fools (1922), B. Benbow

†*Blue Monday Blues* (1922), °G. Gershwin & others

†*Bon Bon Buddy, Jr.* (1922), Miller & Pinkard

Breezy Times (1922), Byron & Muse

Broadway Strutters (1922), Authorship unknown

Business Before Pleasure (1922), Authorship unknown

Chappelle and Stinnette Revue (1922), Chappelle & Stinnette

The Charleston Steppers (1922), V. Brown & others

Chuckles (1922), B. Pierson

Clorifena's Wedding Day (1922), with Simms & Warfield

The Coal Heavers (1922), Crescent Players

Creole Jazz Babies (1922), with S. Henderson

Creole Revue (at least 2 eds., 1922–24), J. Berry and others

Darktown Jubilee (1922), B. King

The Devil (1922), Q. Miller

Dixie Flyers Girls (1922), J. Cox

†*Dumb Luck* (1922), °L. Rosen

Geechie (1922), Creamer & Johnson

Go Get It (1922), S. H. Dudley

Hardtack Jackson's Company (1922), H. Jackson

Hearts of Men (1922), Q. Miller

Hello Rufus (1922), Authorship unknown

Hello Sue (1922), King & Overstreet

Henri Bowman's Cotton Blossoms (1922), W. H. Bowman

High Life Scandals (1922), Benbow & Cohen

Hoola-Boola (1922), C. Muse

Hot Dogs (1922), I. C. Miller

In Honolulu (1922), Kemp & Ragtime Steppers

In Old Virginia (1922), Authorship unknown

In Slam (1922), Byrd & Byrd

Jump Steady (1922), Whitney & Tutt

Keep It Up (1922), °I. M. Weingarden

Me and You (1922), J. P. Johnson

†*Moonshine* (1922), B. King

†*Mutt and Jeff* (1922), °Fisher & °Carroll

†*Oh Joy!* (1922), Whitney & Tutt

Some Party (1922), °R. H. Burnside

Spice of 1922 (1922), Creamer & Layton (song)

Step on It (1922), Miller & Lyles

†*Strut Miss Lizzie* (1922), Creamer & Layton

Taboo (1922), Authorship unknown

That Gets It (1922), Chicago Producing Co.

This One Night (1922), S. Burns

This Way Out (1922), Q. Miller

Tim Moore's Follies (1922), T. Moore

†*Under the Bamboo Tree* (1922), with B. Williams

Vamping Liza Jane (1922), B. Ewing

Wesley Varnell's Revue (1922), °W. Varnell

Whirl of Joy (1922), B. King

Why Spoil It? (1922), F. Montgomery

Creole Follies [Revue] (1922–23), Coleman Bros.

†*Shades of Hades* (1922–23), Owsley & Payton

Hits and Bits (1922–24), B. King

†*Liza* (1922–24), Miller & Pinkard

†*Plantation Revue* (1922, 1924), °L. Leslie & others

Step Along (1922–24), Miller & Slayter

We Got It (at least 2 eds., 1922, 1924), J. Carmouche

†*Plantation Days* (1922–23, 1925), °Greenwald & Johnson

Radio Girls (at least 2 eds., 1922, 1925), R. Montella

†*7–11* (also *Seven-Eleven*, c. 1922–c. 1926), B. Carter & others

Burgleton Green vs. Spark Plug (1923), B. King

Chocolate Town (1923), R. Day

Elsie (1923), Sissle & Blake (music)

The Frolics (1923), L. Harper

The Girl with the Beauty Spot (1923), I. Edwards & others

†*Go-Go* (1923), Roberts & Rogers (songs)

Hot Chops (1923), J. Trent

The Jazz Express (1923), Whitney & Tutt

Jones Syncopated Syncopators (1923), J. Jones

Just for Fun (1923), I. C. Miller

K of P (1923), Hayes & Hayes

Let 'Em Have It (1923), Byrd & Ewing

The Mayor of Jimtown (1923), Miller & Slayter

Mr. Sambo from Gaston, South Carolina (1923), Delaney & Delaney

†*North Ain't South* (1923), Whitney & Tutt

Oh, Yes (1923), H. Jenkins & others

†*Raisin' Cain* (1923), Montgomery & Johnson

Ramblin' Around (1923), C. Muse

Sharlee (1923), Roberts & Rogers (songs)

Step Children (1923), Boatner & Clark

Step Lucky Girls (1923), Bailey & Harris

Struttin' Along (1923), °J. Joy

Swanee River Home (1923), Burns & Overstreet

Unloved Wife (1923), with Allison & Ellis

Watermelon Girls (1923), C. Taylor

Whirl of Pleasure (1923), B. King

†*Come Along Mandy* (1923–24), Whitney & Tutt

†*Dinah* (1923–24), I. C. Miller & others

Follow Me (1923–24), with V. Snow & others

†*In Bamville* (1923–24), Sissle & Blake

Rosie's Wedding Day (1923–24), T. Moore

†*The Sheik of Harlem* (1923–24), Miller & Haywood

Who Struck John? (1923–24), Whitney & Tutt

†*Dixie to Broadway* (1923–25), °L. Leslie & others

†*How Come?* (1923, revived 1925), E. Hunter & others

†*Runnin' Wild* (1923–25), Miller & Lyles

Get Set (1923, revived 1926), J. Bright & others

The Chocolate Scandals (1923, 1927), S. Russell

Shake Your Feet (at least 3 eds., 1923, 1925, 1929), with J. Carmouche

André Charlot's Revue of 1924 (1924), Sissle & Blake (song)

Annie Oakley (1924), Miller & Slayter

The Broadway Vamps (1924), Mason & Townsend family

Brown Skin Vamps (1924), B. McLaurin

Cotton Land (1924), J. P. Johnson

The Darktown Bazaar (1924), Allen & Stokes

The Devine (1924), with S. Martin & others

Ethiopia Shall Win (1924), J. Bright

From Baltimore to Turkey (1924), J. Bright

The Girl from Philly (1924), Drake & Walker

Happy Days (1924), Dancing Demons & others

Happy Go Lucky (1924), M. Ashton & others

Hide and Seek (1924), Whitney & Tutt

Hit and Run (1924), Smith & Carter

Honey (1924), Miller & Lyles

Hot Feet (1924), J. Cooper

Jolly Time Follies (1924), L. Deppe & others

Let's Go (1924), F. Clark & others

Milinda's Wedding Day (1924), J. Bright

Negro Nuances (1924), Mitchell, Miller & Lyles

Nut Brown Lady (1924), with Whitney & Tutt

Oh Honey (1924), A. Smith

An Oil Well Scandal (1924), F. Johnson

Oriental Serenaders (1924), with Lee & Lee

Rastus Brown in Bad Company (1924), "R." Brown

Record Breakers (1924), J. Reed

Sailors' Jazz (1924), B. Russell

Steppin' Time (1924), Rogers & Roberts

Steppin' Up (1924), J. Gines

Struttin' Along Liza (1924), Miller & Lyles

Struttin' Time (1924), Hunter, Miller & Lyles

Syncopationland Revue (1924), with M. Smith

Take It Easy (1924), Miller & Slayter

Talk of the Town (1924), with J. Parker

Topsy and Eva (1924), °C. C. Cushing

Trip to Cannibal Isle (1924), Drake & Walker

We've Got It (1924), S. Robinson

A Wife Wanted (1924), Drake & Walker

Yaller Gal (1924), Chappelle & Stinnette

†*Aces and Queens* (1924–25), Grainger & Johnson

Backbiters (1924–25), F. E. Miller

†*The Chocolate Dandies* (1924–25), Sissle & Blake

New Orleans Vampires (1924–25), J. Green

Steppin' High (1924, 1925), with Thomas & Russell

When Malinda Sings (1924–25), Whitney & Tutt

Black and White Revues (1924–26), with S. Bechet

Brown Beauties (1924–26), M. Wilson

Georgia Red Hots (1924–26), J. Cox

Mamie Smith Revue (at least 2 eds., 1924, 1926), with M. Smith

Ragtime Sailors (at least 2 eds., 1924, 1926), B. Russell

Southland Follies (at least 2 eds., 1924, 1927), J. Sheftell

Alabama Fantasies (1925), S. Wooding

Brown Babies (1925), I. C. Miller

Brown Skin Quinan Revue (1925), °L. Leslie

Chocolate Kiddies (1925), Trent & Ellington

Darktown Puzzles (1925), S. Russell

De Board Meetin' (1925), Grainger & Whipper

Dusty Miller Revue (1925), D. Miller

Fan Fan Follies (1925), E. B. Westfield

Get-It-Fixed (1925), J. Bright

Go Getter Revue (1925), J. Mason

Happy Days in Dixie (1925), Carmouche & Mitchell

†*Harlem Rounders* (1925), Montgomery & Johnson

Harlem Strutters (1925), O. Burgoyne

Hello Dixie (1925), A. Downey

Hottentot Revue (1925), Petway & Rector

How've You Been (1925), D. Heywood

Melody Lane Girls (1925), E. Seals & others

Miss Georgia Brown (1925), I. C. Miller

†*Moochin' Along* (1925), Shipp & Johnson

A Night in Turkey (1925), Carmouche & Mitchell

Non-Sense (1925), Whitney & Tutt

Ollie Burgoyne and Her Darktown Strutters (1925), O. Burgoyne

Ragtime Steppers (1925), J. McGarr

Revue Nègre (1925), with J. Baker

†*Sahdji, An African Ballet* (1925), Still & Nugent

Sands of Honolulu (1925), Burns & Russell

Shu-Shin-Shi (1925), J. L. Long

The Slave (O, 1925), H. L. Freeman

Still Dancing! (1925), Sissle & Blake (song)

T.O.B.A. Revue (1925), A. Gibson

What's Up (1925), R. Montella

Whim Wham Wharblers (1925), Martin & Walker

Chocolate Box Revue (1925–26), J. Gibson

Ebony Vampires (at least 2 eds., 1925–26), B. Watts

†*Lucky Sambo* (1925–26), Grainger & Johnson

Rarin' to Go (1925–26), J. Jordan (music)

Get Happy (1925–27), W. Benbow

Harlem Frolics (1925–27), with B. Smith

†*Sugar Cane* (several eds., 1925–28, 1933), with D. Markham

Nada (O, 1925–47), H. L. Freeman

†*Brownskin Models* (1925–c. 1954), I. C. Miller

Atlantic City Follies (1926), B. Mitchell

Bamville Dandies (1926), S. H. Dudley

Bessie Smith Revue (1926), with B. Smith

Blue Moon (1926), Miller & Heywood

Bon Ton Revue (1926), S. Sutton

Broadway Brevities (1926), Miller & Slayter

Brownskin Vamps (1926), L. Payton

Charleston Fricassee (1926), Miller & Slayter

Charleston Syncopators (1926), Bruce & Skinner

Chicago Loop (1926), Johnson & Creamer

Chicago Pacemakers (1926), with D. Wiles

Club Alabama Revue (1926), Straine & Brown

†*Deep River* (O, 1926), °Stallings & °Harling

Desires of 1927 (1926), Razaf & Johnson

Dixiana (1926), J. L. Long

Dixie Strutters (1926), I. Saunders & others

Dots and Dashes (1926), O. Williams

A Dream of Enchantment (1926), E. C. Foster

Everybody's Talking (1926), S. T. Whitney

4–11–44 (1926), E. Hunter

Fun Festival (1926), L. Fisher

Golden Brown Reasons of 1926 (1926), with S. Martin & others

Harlem Butterflies (1926), Miller & Slayter

The Harlem Scandals (1926), B. Crumby

Hello Sambo (1926), J. McGarr

†*Jr. Blackbirds* (1926), T. Waller

Kentucky Sue (1926), Chappelle & Stinnette

Lincoln Follies (1926), with A. Hall & L. Hegamin

Louisiana Mess-Around (1926), with M. Young & others

Ma Rainey and Her Georgia Jazz Hounds (1926), M. Rainey

†*Miss Calico* (1926), Dancer & Haywood

Miss Dinah of 1926 (1926), Miller & Slayter

†*My Magnolia* (1926), Rogers & Hunter

A Night at the Cabaret (1926), J. Clark

Nobody's Girl (1926), Harrington & Green

Race Horse Charlie's Last Chance (1926), D. James

Rainbow Chasers (1926), Whitney & Tutt

Red Hots (1926), with B. Cox

Roll-On (1926), L. Brown

Round the Globe (1926), M. Mack

So Different Revue (1926), Benbow & others

Step Along (1926), Standard Amusement Co.

Steppin' Babies (1926), E. Lemons

Tan Town Topics (1926), Rector & Cooper

Vanities (1926), with E. Waters

Vanities of 1926 (1926), E. Langford

Who's Dat (1926), E. Lemons

Yellow Gal (1926), J. Mason

Yes, Sir (1926), Martin & Walker

†*Blackbirds of 1926* (1926–27), °L. Leslie & others

Charleston Dandies (1926–27), C. Muse

Connie's Inn Frolics (1926–27), Connie's Inn

Hey, Hey! (1926–27), A. A. Garvey

Red Hot Mama (1926–27), I. C. Miller

That's My Baby (1926–27), I. C. Miller

Watermelon (1926–27), °J. Goldberg

Dixie Brevities (1926–28), Miller & Slayter

Earl Carroll's Vanities (1926, 1930), J. P. Johnson (songs)

Ace High Revue (1927), with M. Wilson

†*Africana* (1927), Dancer & Heywood

A La Carte (1927), Creamer & Johnson (songs)

All Nation's Revue (1927), I. C. Miller

An American Romance (O, 1927), H. L. Freeman

Aunt Jemima's Revue (1927), with E. Ringgold

Bare Facts (1927), Q. Miller

Black Bottom Revue (1927), °J. Goldberg

†*Bottomland* (1927), C. Williams

Broadway Flappers (1927), R. Johnson

Brown Sugar (1927), Garvey & Manning

Chicago Plantation Revue (1927), C. Muse

Club Kentucky Revue (1927), L. Harper

Darktown Scandals (1927), E. Hunter

Dashing Dinah (1927), E. Lemons

Gay Harlem (1927), I. C. Miller

Great Temptations (1927), Heywood & Marshall

The Harlem Follies (1927), with B. Smith

The Harlem Strutters (1927), C. D. Fletcher

Heebee Jeebies (1927), J. Cooper

His Honery, the Judge (1927), Our Gang Revue Co.

Fanticies of 1927 (1927), with E. Howard & others

Jigfield Follies (1927), with Mitchell & Calloway Sisters

Keep Movin' (1927), E. E. Daley

Look Who's Here (1927), with J. Mabley

Louisiana Blackbirds (1927), with M. Rainey

Lulu Belle (1927), J. W. Jackson

Mannequins of 1927 (1927), J. L. Long

Midnight Steppers (1927), L. Harper

Miss Bandanna (1927), C. Muse

Modern Cocktail (1927), N. Thomas

'Neath the Southern Moon (1927), B. Pierson

Pepper Pot Revue (1927), L. Harper

Peppy Steppers (1927), C. Lockhart

†*Rang Tang* (1927), with Miller & Lyles

Rock Dinah (1927), Grant & Wilson

Royal Flush Revue (1927), S. Winston & others

Shake, Rattle and Roll (1927), with Jones & Jones

Slim Slivers (1927), J. W. Jackson

Sons of Rest (1927), Easton & Warfield

Southland Revue (1927), T. Moore

Stoppin' the Traffic (1927), D. Weinglass

Syncopation (1927), with I. Dennis & others

Three Thieves (1927), T. Owsley & others

A Trip to Araby (1927), M. Housley

We's Rising (1927), Grainger & Whipper

Yellow Girl Revue (1927), B. Smith

You've Got to Step Lively (1927), Bailey & Wiggins

Blue Baby (1927–28), I. C. Miller

†*Show Boat* (1927–28, 1946, 1971, 1983) °Kern & °Hammerstein

Ace of Clubs (1928), Thomas & Parvus

A La Carte (1928), W. Douglass

All Girl Revue (c. 1928), I. C. Miller

Bandanna Days (1928), °J. Goldberg

Benbow's New York Colored Follies (1928), W. Benbow

Black Diamond Express (1928), with M. Smith

Black Scandals (1928), G. Smithfield

Bubbling Over Revue (1928), Mitchell & Rector

Bubblin' Over (1928), Mitchell & "Weevil"

Butterbeans and Susie Revue (1928), Butterbeans & Susie

Carolina Nights (1928), D. D. Green

Circus Day Revue (1928), with S. Thompson & others

Clara Smith Revue (1928), C. Smith

Dancing Days (1928), J. Simms

The Dixie Vagabond (1928), Montella & Montella

Dusky Follies (1928), °J. Goldberg

Ebony Follies (1928), S. H. Dudley

Fancy Trimmings (1928), A. Carey

Gettin' Hot (1928), S. Smith

Happy Go Lucky (1928), Johnson & Lee

Here We Are (1928), E. E. Daley

Highlights of Harlem (1928), with T. Smith

Jazz Town Capers (1928), M. Rogers

†*Keep Shufflin'* (1928), Miller & Lyles

Levee Days (1928), A. Rogers & others

Mandy Green from New Orleans (1928), °J. Goldberg

Miss Broadway (1928), "B." Hope

Mississippi Steppers (1928), H. Jenkins

New York Revue (1928), with T. Smith

Next Door Neighbors (1928), with T. Smith

(The) Nifties of 1928 (1928), S. Brooks

Playmates (1928), B. Lee

A Riot of Fun (1928), M. Smith

Rolling On (1928), D. Weinglass

Roseland Revue (1928), with D. Fletcher & others

Steamboat Bill from Louisville (1928), G. L. Barton

Steamboat Days (1928), B. Smith

The Surprise Company (1928), R. Hostler

Swanee Club Revue (1928), L. Harper

Tabasco Queens (1928), with L. Williams & others

That's It (1928), °J. Goldberg

Tokio (1928), I. C. Miller

Why Girls Go Wrong (1928), J. Bright

†*Blackbirds of 1928* (1928–29), °L. Leslie & others

†*Deep Harlem* (1928–29), Whitney & Tutt

Midnight Steppers (1928–29), with B. Smith

Ophelia Snow from Baltimo' (1928–29), with A. Tribble

Abraham from Alabam' (1929), W. H. Bowman

Adam and Eve in Harlem (1929), L. Harper

†*Bamboola* (1929), °Marcus & °Martin

Birth of the Blues (1929), Watts & Ringgold

Blackouts of 1929 (1929), Brooks & Higgins

Brown Gal (1929), J. Henderson

Chocolate Blondes (1929), with Hite & Rector

The Circus Showman (1929), I. C. Miller

Crazy Quilt Revue (1929), with J. Johnson

†*Darktown Affairs* (1929), G. Howard & others

Devil's Frolics (1929), with J. Mabley

Dreamgirls and Candied Sweets (1929), with C. Smith

Fioretta (1929), J. Trent (song)

Gee Whiz (1929), with A. Ramsey

George Stamper's Revue (1929), G. Stamper

Georgia Peaches (1929), Jenkins & Idaho

†*Great Day* (1929), °Wells & °Duncan

Harlem Darlings (1929), C. Davis

†*Hot Chocolates* (1929), A. Razaf & others

Hot Ella (1929), E. B. Moore

It's a Plenty (1929), R. Simmons & others

Jazz Regiment (1929), with Saunders & Gorman

Jumble Jazzbo Jamboree (1929), Watts & Wills

Late Hour [Tap] Dancers (1929), with B. Smith

Leonard Harper's Revue (1929), L. Harper

Load of Coal (c. 1929), Waller & Razaf

Loose Feet (1929), J. Carmouche

Make Me Know It (1929), with A. B. DeComathiere & others

Malinda (1929), D. Donoghue & others

†*Messin' Around* (1929), Bradford & Johnson (songs)

Midnight Frolic (1929), with M. Bonds & others

Miss Creola (1929), W. Mastin

Miss Inez (1929), B. Benbow

My Gal (1929), G. Howard

†*Pansy* (1929), Belledna & Pinkard

Radio Sam the Melody Man (1929), G. L. Barton

St. Louis 'Ooman (1929), Cook & Cook

Sizzling Oriental Sunflower Revue (1929), with L. Austin & others

Sonny Boy Sam (1929), with S. Robinson

Sun Flower Revue (1929), L. Austin

Sun-Tan Frolics (1929), with M. Smith

Syncopated Sue (1929), with A. Stewart

†*Gingersnaps* (1929–30), Tutt & Heywood

A Great Day in N'Orleans (1929–30), Miller & Johnson

Hottentots of 1930 (1929–30), B. Benbow & others

The Jail Birds (1929–30), Drake & Walker

Pickings from Dixie (1929–30), Mack & Mack

Betwixt and Between (1920s), Whitney & Tutt

Black Propaganda (1920s), J. B. Barbour

Ethiopia (1920s), J. B. Barbour

Fly Round, Young Ladies (1920s), C. Mack (songs)

Follies of the Stroll (1920s), Rogers & Roberts

Lovin' Sam from Alabam' (1920s), Greenlee & Drayton

Midnight Follies (1920s), with B. Smith

Redemption (1920s), J. B. Barbour

The Temple of Jazz (late 1920s), with M. Hite

1930–1939

The Arkansas Swift Foot (1930), with M. Rainey

Bandana Babies (1930), with M. Rainey

†*Blackbirds of 1930* (1930), °L. Leslie & others

Broadway Revue (1930), with B. Smith

†*Brown Buddies* (1930), °Rickman & Jordan

Bubble Along (1930), Authorship unknown

†*Cabaret Prince* (1930), Miller & Slayter

†*Change Your Luck* (1930), G. Howard & others

Dixie on Parade (1930), N. Sissle

Fireworks of 1930 (1930), Waller & Johnson

Folies Bergere Revue (1930), °Morrissey & Blake

†*Funny Money* (1930), T. Owsley

Harlem Girl (1930), I. C. Miller

Hello Everybody (1930), Drake & Walker

Hollywood Revue (1930), S. Fetchit

Hot Heels (1930), °L. Azorsky

†*Hot Rhythm* (1930), D. Markham & others

The Joy Boat (1930), with Fletcher & Mabley

Kitchen Mechanics Revue (1930), Johnson & Razaf

Lily White (1930), with T. Smith

Happy Times (1930), with B. Smith

Maytime Revue (1930), J. L. Long & others

Midnight Steppers (1930), Saunders & Dancy

Miss Broadway (1930), B. Pierson

My Wife (1930), Drake & Walker

Red Pastures (1930), I. C. Miller

Runnin' de Town (1930), Whipper & Johnson

Sandy Burns and Bilo (1930), Burns & Russell

Sepia Vagabonds (1930), M. Smith & others

Sidewalks of Harlem (1930), Carey & Davis

Solid South (1930?), with G. Harvey

Sunshine (1930), with T. Smith

†*Sweet Chariot* (1930), °R. Wilder

Tan Town Tamales (1930), with A. Brown

Three Little Maids (1930), J. P. Johnson (songs)

Tight Like That (1930), G. Crawford & others

Velvet Brown Babies (1930), E. Lemons

†*The Green Pastures* (1930–35), °M. Connelly

Adam and Eva, Inc. (early 1930s), R. Matthews

Shadows on the Moon (early 1930s), R. Matthews

Chocolate Scandals (1931), with Moreland & Brooks

Club Hollywood Revue (1931), I. C. Miller

Cock o' de World (adapt., 1931), L. Hughes

Echoes of a Plantation (1931), E. Dancer

†*Fast and Furious* (1931), °F. Randolph

Gossiping Liza (1931), with B. Smith

Hot from Harlem (1931), with B. Robinson

Lazy Rhythm (1931), Miller & Lyles

Leah Kleschna (O, 1931), H. L. Freeman

Lucky to Me (1931), with E. Waters & others

Rhumba Land Revue (1931), with M. Smith

Rocking Chair Revue (1931), with M. Stafford

†*Singin' the Blues* (1931), °J. McGowan & others

Speeding Along (1931), "J. R." Morton

Trouble on the Ranch (1931), with C. Smith

Wrap It in Black (1931), S. H. Gray

†*Rhapsody in Black* (1931–32), °L. Leslie

Savage Rhythm (1931–32), Johnson & Mack

†*Sugar Hill* (1931, 1947, 1949), Miller & Lyles

†*Blackberries of 1932* (1932), Green & Heywood

Cocktails of 1932 (1932), with P. Markham

Dear Old Southland (1932), with M. Stafford

Deep Central (1932), Larkins & Lovejoy

Do Your Stuff (1932), R. Thomas

Ebony Scandals (1932), with M. Barnes

†*Ham's Daughter* (1932), D. Donoghue

Hot Rhythm (1932), D. Weinglass

Old Kentucky (1932), C. Smith & others

†*Ol' Man Satan* (1932), D. Heywood

†*Tom-Tom* (1932), S. G. DuBois

Vanities of 1932 (1932), Butterbeans & Susie

†*Yeah Man!* (1932), Whipper & Mills

Zulu King (O, c. 1932), H. L. Freeman

Harlem Hotcha (1932–33), Connie's Inn

Allah (O, 1932–47), H. L. Freeman

Zululand (O, 1932–47), H. L. Freeman

†*Ouanga* (1932, 1941, 1948–49, 1950, 1956), Matheus & White

†*As Thousands Cheer* (1933), with E. Waters

Christmas Revels (1933), with B. Smith

Cotton Club Parade of 1933 (1933), Cotton Club

Hot Stuff of 1933 (1933), Butterbeans & Susie

†*Hummin' Sam* (1933), °Nutter & °Hill

Plantation Follies (1933), J. P. Johnson

Ragtime (1933), E. B. Westfield

Runnin' Sam (1933), G. "B." Cox & others

So This Is Africa (1933), with Wheeler & Woosey

Tan-Town Topic Revue (1933), with J. B. Hicks & others

†*Blackbirds of 1933* (1933–34), °L. Leslie & others

†*Run, Little Chillun!* (1933, 1938–39, 1943), H. Johnson

†*St. Louis Woman* (1933, 1935, 1946), Bontemps & Cullen

Jim Crow (pre-1934), D. Heywood & others

†*Africana* (O, 1934), D. Heywood

Dixie Follies (1934), with W. Crawley & others

Fan Waves (1934), with B. Smith

Flying Down to Harlem (1934), "R. L." Williams

†*Four Saints in Three Acts* (1934), °Stein & °Thomson

Harlem Scandals (1934), I. C. Miller

Goin' to Town (1934), J. Richardson & others

†*Kykunkor* (1934), A. D. Horton

†*The Man from Baltimore* (1934), °J. Raines & others

O Sing a New Song (1934), Century of Progress International Exposition

Uzziah (O, 1934), H. L. Freeman

Get Lucky (1934–35), Q. Miller

†*At Home Abroad* (1935), with E. Waters

Blue Steel (O, 1935), W. G. Still

Cotton Club Parade (1935), Cotton Club

Honeymoon Cruise (1935), E. Partello

120 in the Shade (1935), Rene & Rene

Rhythm Hotel (1935), L. Reed

Ubangi Club Follies (1935), A. Razaf

†*Porgy and Bess* (1935–36, 1952–56, 1961, 1964, 1976, 1983, 1985), °Gershwin & °Heyward

†*Black Rhythm* (1936), D. Heywood

Darktown Scandals (1936), with I. Cox & others

Harlem Broadcast (1936), I. C. Miller

The League of Rhythm (1936), with B. Smith

Menelek (O, 1936), P. Lovingood

Stars Over Broadway (1936), Connie's Inn

Walk Together Chillun (1936), F. Wilson

†*Natural Man* (1936–37, 1941), T. Browne

Broadway Rastus (1937), with B. Smith

Harlem Is Heaven (1937), with C. Williams

Little Black Sambo (adapt., 1937), S. G. DuBois (music)

Swing, Gates, Swing (1937), T. Browne

†*Swing It* (1937), Mack & Reddie

Virginia (1937), with J. W. Bubbles

†*Don't You Want to Be Free?* (1937, revised 1963), L. Hughes

De Organizer (1938), Hughes & Johnson

Dixie Goes High Hat (1938), F. E. Miller

†*The Organizer* (1938), Hughes & Johnson

†*The Swing Mikado* (1938–39), °Minturn & DuBois

Zunguru (1938, revived 1940), A. D. Horton

†*Blackbirds of 1939* (1939), °L. Leslie & others

Class Struggle in Swing (1939), Hughes & Johnson

Ecstatic Ebony (1939), R. Cooper

Hollywood Revue (1939), F. E. Miller

†*The Hot Mikado* (adapt., 1939), °M. Todd

Royal American Show (1939), L. Claxton

†*Policy Kings* (1939–40), °Ashwood & Johnson

†*Swingin' the Dream* (1939–40), with L. Armstrong

1940–1949

Black Ritual (1940), °A. deMille

De Gospel Train (1940), J. H. Tutt & others

John Henry (1940), °R. Bradford

Tropics After Dark (1940), Hughes & Bontemps

Walk with Music (1940), with S. Fetchit

†*Cabin in the Sky* (1940–41), °L. Root & others

Cavalcade of the Negro Theatre (1940–41), Hughes & Bontemps

Harlem on Parade (early 1940s), Sissle & Blake

The Sepia and Swing Revolution (early 1940s), Sissle & Blake

A Bayou Legend (1941), Still & Avery

Bronze Manikins (1941), D. Kay

Here 'Tis (1941), J. James & others

†*Jump for Joy* (1941), D. Ellington (music)

Pinkard's Fantasies (1941), M. Pinkard

Tropicana (1941), D. Heywood

†*The Sun Do Move* (1941–42), L. Hughes

Harlem Cavalcade (1942), °E. Sullivan

†*Born Happy* (1943), with B. Robinson

†*Early to Bed* (1943–44), °Marion & Waller

†*Carmen Jones* (adapt., 1943–46), °O. Hammerstein

Africa (O, 1944), A. D. Horton

On the Town (1944–45), °L. Bernstein

Tropical Review (1944–45), K. Dunham & troupe

Bloomer Girl (1944–46), with D. Wilson & others

†*Blue Holiday* (1945), with E. Waters & J. White

†*Carib Song* (1945), with K. Dunham & troupe

Harlem Express (1945), I. C. Miller

†*Memphis Bound* (1945), °Barker & °Benson

Rhapsody in Rhythm (1945), P. Small

Annie Get Your Gun (1946), with 3 blk. performers

Atlantic City Follies of 1946 (1946), J. Johnson

Bal Nègre (1946), K. Dunham & troupe

Call Me Mister (1946), with 3 blks.

The Choreography of Love (O, 1946), Brewster & °Goldreyer

†*Beggar's Holiday* (adapt., 1946–47), °Latouche & Ellington

Caribbean Carnival (1947), P. Primus

Finian's Rainbow (1947), °Harburg & °Saidy

Kitchen Opera (1947), Johnson & Miller

†*Street Scene* (1947), Hughes, °Rice & °Weill

A Temporary Island (1948), L. Fuller (songs)

The World's My Oyster (1948), Fuller & Mills

The African Chief (1949), J. H. Brown

†*Troubled Island* (1949), Hughes & Still

†*Lost in the Stars* (1949–50, 1958, 1968, 1972, 1987), °Weill & °Anderson

Adam and Eve and the Apple (O, pre-1950), L. Hughes

Five Foolish Virgins (pre-1950), Hughes & °Meyerowitz

1950–1959

Arms and the Girl (1950), with P. Bailey

†*The Barrier* (1950), Hughes & °Meyerowitz

Bless You All (1950), with P. Bailey

Carmen (1950), translated by T. Brewster

Hansel and Gretel (1950), translated by T. Brewster

Just a Little Simple (1950), L. Hughes

Just Around the Corner (1951), L. Hughes & others

King Solomon (O, 1951), Elmsie & Brown

The Wizard of Altoona (1951), Hughes & °Siegmeister

New Faces (1952, 1956), with E. Kitt & T. Haynes

Almanac (1953), °J. N. Anderson

Ankles Away (1953), with T. Carpenter

At Home with Ethel Waters (1953), with E. Waters

Little Girl, Big Town (1953), T. Brewster

The Year 'Round (1953), J. C. Johnson (songs)

By the Beautiful Sea (1954), W. M. Barnes

Sandhog (1954), R. Timmons

Soul Gone Home (1954), Hughes & Kay

†*House of Flowers* (1954–55), °Capote & °Arlen

†*Mrs. Patterson* (1954–55, 1957), Seebree & °Johnson

Experiment in Black (1955), W. B. Branch

Three for Tonight (1955), with H. Belafonte

†*Mr. Wonderful* (1956–57), with S. Davis, Jr.

Adjoah Amissah (1957), M. Angelou

The Tower (1957), Brewster & Levi

†*Esther* (1957–58), Hughes & °Meyerowitz

†*Jamaica* (1957–58), °E. Y. Harburg & °Saidy

†*Simply Heavenly* (1957–59), Hughes & Martin

The Body Beautiful (1958), with Satin & McNair

A Christmas Miracle (O, 1958), Dodson & Fax

Flower Drum Song (1958), with J. Hall

Free and Easy (1959–60), °H. Arlen

Wide Wide River (pre-1960s), Hughes & English

1960–1969

Ballad of the Brown King (1960), Hughes & Bonds

Cabaret for Freedom (1960), Angelou & Cambridge

†*Port Town* (1960), Hughes & °Meyerowitz

†*Fly Blackbird* (1960–62), Jackson & °Hatch

†*Man Better Man* (1960, 1962, 1969), E. Hill

Kicks & Company (1961), O. Brown, Jr.

†*Kwamina* (1961–62), °Aurthur & °Adler

A Lady of Consequence (1961–62), Cruse & Fields

†*Black Nativity* (1961–64), L. Hughes

†*Gospel Glow* (1962), L Hughes

†*Ballad for Bimshire* (1963), Burgie & Mitchell

Gentlemen, Be Seated! (1963), °Moross & °Eager

†*Tambourines to Glory* (1963), Hughes & Huntley

†*Jerico–Jim Crow* (1963–64, revived 1968), L. Hughes

†*Trumpets of the Lord* (1963, revived 1969), V. Carroll

Fade Out—Fade In (1964), with T. Haynes

Josephine Baker (1964), with J. Baker

†*Golden Boy* (adapt., 1964–65), with S. Davis, Jr.

†*The Prodigal Son* (1965), L. Hughes

Summer in the City (1965), Brown & Foreman

Till Victory Is Won (1965), Dodson & Fax

Jonah (1966), °P. Goodman

Joy (1966), O. Brown, Jr.

The Weary Blues (adapt., 1966), W. King, Jr.

A Hand Is on the Gate (1966, revived 1976), R. L. Browne

And People All Around (1967), °Sklar & Bradshaw

Curley McDimple (1967), with B. Mc-Queen

†*Walk Down Mah Street!* (1967), °Curtis & °Curtis

†*Hallelujah, Baby!* (1967–68), °A. Laurents & others

How to Be a Jewish Mother (1967–68), °S. Vall & others

†*Hello, Dolly!* (1967–71), All-blk. version

†*Tell Pharoah* (1967, 1973, 1984), L. Mitchell

Ballad of a Blackbird (1968), Mitchell & Lucas

†*The Believers* (1968), Walker & Jackson

The Confession Stone (1968), Dodson & Da Costa

The Funhouse (1968), G. H. Bass

Her First Roman (1968), with L. Uggams

How to Steal an Election (1968), °Brown & °Brand

Walk Together Children (1968), V. Burrows

†*God Is a (Guess What?)* (1968–69), R. McIver

Jacques Brel Is Alive and Well and Living in Paris (adapt., 1968–71), °Blau & °Shuman

Ask Your Mama (1969), L. Hughes

(The) Black Cowboys (1969), Rivers & Taylor

Black Expo (1969), Authorship unknown

Down in the Valley (1969), °K. Weill

Fiesta (1969), K. Collie

High John De Conquer (1969), Primus & Banks

A Hip Rumplestiltskin (1969), C. Goss

The Lonely Crowd (1969), V. Whitfield

Mae's Amees (1969), H. Bryant & others

Oh Lord, This World (1969), G. H. Bass

Origins (1969), H. Bryant & others

†*Sambo* (1969), Steward & Tate

Tabernacle (1969), P. C. Harrison

†*Buck White* (1969–70), O. Brown, Jr.

Opportunity, Please Knock (1969–70), O. Brown, Jr.

†*But Never Jam Today* (1969–70, 1979), V. Carroll

Tell It to Telstar (1960s), L. Hughes

1970–1979

Akokawe (1970), A. Ajayi

†*Billy Noname* (1970), Mackey & Brandon

Makin' It (1970), H. Bryant & others

Soul at Sunrise (1970), J.W.R. Horne

†*Don't Play Us Cheap!* (1970–72), M. Van Peebles

†*The Me Nobody Knows* (adapt., 1970–72), °Livingston & °Schapiro

†*Don't Bother Me, I Can't Cope* (1970–73), Carroll & Grant

†*Black Circles 'Round Angela* (1970–74), H. Bryant

†*Purlie* (1970–74), O. Davis & others

Black Magic Anyone? (1971), B. Emeruwa

Croesus and the Witch (1971), Carroll & Grant

A Day in the Life of Just About Everyone (1971), °E. Wilson, Jr.

Jesus Christ—Lawd Today (1971), Dickerson & Barrett

†*Ain't Supposed to Die a Natural Death* (1971–72), M. Van Peebles

Inner City (1971–72), °Miller & °Merriam

Lady Day (1971–72), Rahman & Shepp

†*Jesus Christ Superstar* (1971–73), with B. Vereen

Two Gentlemen of Verona (1971–73), with Davis & Allen

Miss Truth (1971–72, 1978), G. Van Scott

Lady Plum Blossom (1972), Brewster & Ollinger

Sheba (1972), H. Byrant

Something for Jamie (1972), Hamilton & Greenidge

Step Lively, Boy (adapt., 1972), V. Carroll

The Sunshine Train (1972), W. E. Hunt

The System (1972), C. Young III

Uhuruh (1972), D. Duncan

†*The Great MacDaddy* (1972–74), P. C. Harrison

†*Thoughts* (1972–74), L. Alford

†*Changes* (1973), Whitfield & Smith

The Cocktail Sip (1973), Brewster & Da Costa

Down on Beale St. (1973), L. Frazier

Harlem Heyday (1973), Voices, Inc.

House Party (1973), R. LeNoire

The Hymie Finklestein Used Lumber Company (1973), Snipes & Fann

I Am (1973), A. Early

It's Fun to Be Black (1973), A. Browning

Kojo and the Leopard (1973), G. Cooper

Mama Etta's Chitlin Circuit (1973), G. H. Bass

Songs My Father Taught Me (1973), T. D. Allen

†*Raisin* (adapt., 1973–81), from L. Hansberry's play

All the King's Men (adapt., 1974), Carroll & Dodds

Big Man (1974), Adderley & Adderley

An Evening with Josephine Baker (1974), J. Baker

The 5th Dimension, with Jo Jo's Dance Factory (1974), with 5th Dimension & Dance Factory

Hound Dog Party (1974), AMAS Rep. Th.

Jerry Bland and the Blandelles Featuring Miss Marva James (1974), C. Fuller

†*The Prodigal Sister* (1974), Franklin & Grant

Randy's Dandy Circus (1974), K. E. Collie

Slave Song (1974), O. Brown, Jr.

†*Me and Bessie* (1974–76), Hopkins & °Holt

The Ups and Downs of Theophilus Maitland (1974, 1976), Carroll & Grant

Twit (1974, 1986), Glanville & Greenidge

†*Bayou Legend* (1975), Dodson & °Landron

Bessie (1975), with L. Hopkins

Black Love (1975), C. Young

†*Black Picture Show* (1975), Gunn & Waymon

The Cable (1975), T. Brewster

Doctor Jazz (1975), B. Davis

Fat Tuesday (1975), R. Furman

Mama Do Blew (1975), G. H. Bass

Mikado AMAS (adapt., 1975), AMAS Rep. Th./R. LeNoire

Oh, My Pretty Quintroon (1975), Brewster & Rivers

Paper Bird (1975), Truesdale & Deas

The Province Garden Blues (1975), G. H. Bass

Rag Time Blues (c. 1975), AMAS Rep. Th.

Sammy on Broadway (1975), S. Davis, Jr.

†*Selma* (1975), T. Butler

Skrontch!! (1975), D. Ellington

†*The Wiz* (1975–76), °Brown & Smalls

Your Arms Too Short to Box with God (1975–76, 1980–82), Carroll & Bradford

America More or Less (1976), A. Baraka & others

The Godsong (adapt., 1976), T. Truesdale

†*Guys and Dolls* (1976), All-blk. version

I'm Laughin' But I Ain't Tickled (1976), Carroll & Grant

The Morning Duke Ellington Praised the Lord and Seven Little Black Davids Tap-Danced Unto (1976), Dodson & Gill

The Mystery of Phillis Wheatley (1976), E. Bullins

A Rat's Mass/Procession in Shout (O, 1976), from A. Kennedy's play

The Walls Came Tumbling Down (O, 1976), L. Mitchell

Straight from the Ghetto (1976–77), Harris & Piñero

How's Your Sex Life (1977), A. Browning

How to Be Happy Though Married (1977), A. Browning

In De Beginning (1977), O. Brown, Jr.

Season's Reasons (1977), Miller & Mason

Sepia Star (1977), Bullins & °Kayden

Storyville (1977), Bullins & °Kayden

Working (1977), M. Grant (songs)

Alice (1978), Carroll & Grant

A Broadway Musical (1978), °Brown & °Strouse

Cartoons for a Lunch Hour (1978), L. Mitchell

Goin' Downtown to See Jesus (1978), S. W. Branchcomb

The Last Minstrel Show (1978), J. T. Ford

The Story of Soul (1978), Dodson & Keyes

Ulysses (The Jazzical) (1978), W. E. Black

†*Timbuktu!* (1978–79), with E. Kitt

†*Eubie!* (1978–80), Sissle & Blake (songs)

†*It's So Nice to Be Civilized* (1978–80), M. Grant

Dancin' (1978–81), °B. Fosse

Mahalia (1978–82), Evans & Lewis

†*Ain't Misbehavin'* (1978–82, 1988), T. Waller (songs)

Ain't Doin' Nothin' But Singin' My Song (1979), J. Brandon

The All Night Strut! (1979), °F. Charnas

†*Comin' Uptown* (adapt., 1979), with G. Hines

†*Daddy Goodness* (adapt., 1979), R. Miller & S. Perry

Isabel Rising (1979), H. Brummit

Money (1979), Baraka & °Gruntz

Take It from the Top (1979), Dee & Davis

What You Gonna Name That Pretty Little Baby (1979), V. Carroll

When Hell Freezes Over, I'll Skate (1979), V. Carroll

†*One Mo' Time* (1979–87), V. Bagneris

Blues Life of Billie Holiday (1970s), P. R. Allen

Mascara and Confetti (1970s–1987), T. Brewster

1980–1989

Billy Stars & Kid Jupiter (1980), Black & °Shapiro

†*Black Broadway* (1980), H. Coles & others

†*Blues in the Night* (1980), S. Epps

Changes (1980), °D. Love & others

Daddy! Daddy! (1980), Truesdale & Cook

†*Jane White, Who?* . . . (1980), White & °Masteroff

†*Jazzbo Brown* (1980), °S. H. Lemberg

Jazz Set (1980), Milner & Roach

Jill Reed, Read!? (1980), M. Dinwiddie

†*1999: The Beginning of the End . . . The End of the Beginning* (1980), C. Alonzo

No Crystal Stair (1980), AMAS Rep. Th.

†*Reggae* (1980), M. Van Peebles

Tintypes (1980), with L. Thigpen

The Crystal Tree (1980–81), AMAS Rep. Th.

Mo' Tea, Miss Ann? (1980–81), AMAS Rep. Th.

We Love You Always (1980–81), LeNoire & Williams

†*Mama, I Want to Sing* (1980–91), V. Higginsen

The First (1981), °Siegel & °Charnin

Jerry's Girls (1981), Herman & Alford

L.A. Sunset (1981), W. E. Black

Louis (1981), D. Evans

Makin' It (1981), H. Brummit

†*Sophisticated Ladies* (1981–83), D. Ellington's music

†*Romeo & Juliet: New Wave* (1981–84), W. E. Black

†*Dreamgirls* (1981–89), °Ewen & °Krieger

Barca! Men of Lightning (1982), Grimes & Bacon

Can't Help Singing (1982), with 2 blk. singers

The Sun Gets Blue: A Jazzical (1982), Black & °Shapiro

The Widow (O, 1982), R. Atkins

†*Adam* (1983), °Tansey & °Ahlert

†*Amen Corner* (adapt., 1983), from J. Baldwin's play

5-6-7-8. . . . Dance! (1983), with A. McQueen

†*The Gospel at Colonus* (adapt., 1983), with M. Freeman

Haarlem Nocturne (1983), DeShields & °Horowitz

Miss Waters, to You (1983), Mitchell & LeNoire

†*The Tap Dance Kid* (1983–84), C. Blackwell

A . . . My Name Is Alice (1984), °Silver & °Boyd

Anonymous (1984), °V. Stornaiuolo

Brer Rabbit Whole (1984), G. H. Bass

†*Funnyhouse of a Negro* (1984), Kennedy & Moore

Gullah (1984), A. Childress

A Hot Summer Night (1984), Grenoldo

Jericho (1984), °Brussell & °Brown

Shades of Harlem (1984), J. Palmer

Sh-Boom! (1984), Brown & Tait

Urban Voices (1984), Th. of Universal Images

†*Oh! Oh! Obesity* (1984–87), Deas & Howard

Almos' a Man (adapt., 1985), T. Thompson

Bingo (1985), Davis & Gilbert

The Dream Team (1985), R. Wesley & others

Flat Street Sa'dy Night (1985), Solomon & Tooks

Frankenstein: New Wave (1985), W. E. Black

Hot Rags (1985), S. Joplin's music

Jack (1985), °Melli & °Wess

One More Sunday (1985), J. A. Jahannes

Sing, Mahalia, Sing! (1985), G. Faison

Stompin' Along (1985), Downtown Cabaret Th.

A Teenage Love Play (1985), K. Ali

Uptown . . . It's Hot (1985), M. Hines

Who's Mama's Baby, Who's Daddy's Child? (1985), G. Jeannette

†*A Celebration* (1985–86, revived 1988), S. Perry

Big River (adapt., 1985–87), °R. Miller

No Name in the Street (1985, 1987), V. D. Fisher

The Choice (pre-1986), Ashby & Ashby

The Duffers (pre-1986), Ashby & Ashby

Back in the Big Time (1986), Brandon & °Kroll

La Belle Helene (1986), AMAS Rep. Th.

Big Deal (1986), °B. Fosse

Blues for a Gospel Queen (1986), D. Evans

Broadway Runs Through Harlem—II (1986), HADLEY Players

Club Fifty (1986), Wade & Palmer

†*The Colored Museum* (1986), G. C. Wolfe

Crispus (1986), Patterson & °Torraca

De Obeah Man (1986), C. Douglass

Dorothy Fields (1986), °B. Fosse

Elizabeth Welch: Time to Start Living (1986), E. Welch

In the House of the Blues (1986), D. Charles

Just So (1986), with A. DeShields

Phillis (1986), Lee & Grant

Tell It—Sing It—Shout It—Mahalia Lives! (1986), S. Reaves-Phillips

Throw Down (1986), °M. F. Camillo

X (The Life and Times of Malcolm X) (O, 1986), A. Davis

The Young Mr. Bojangles (1986), B. Graham

Williams & Walker (1986–87), V. D. Smith

Abyssinia (1987), °Kociolek & °Rascheff

Blazmatazz (1987), Th. of Universal Images

Conrack (adapt., 1987), AMAS Rep. Th.

Diary of Lights (1987), A. Kennedy

E-Man (1987), Dagley & Tooks

Sing Hallelujah (1987), W. Gardner

Staggerlee (1987), Bagneris & Toussaint

Don't Get God Started (1987–88), R. Milner

The Legacy (1987–90), G. Nelson

Anchorman (O, 1988), Harrison & Hemphill

Into the Woods (1988), with P. Rashad

The Little Tommy Parker Celebrated Colored Minstrel Show (1988), C. Brown

Martin (1988), L. Alford

Mio (1988), Perry & Williams

Rollin' with Stevens and Stewart (1988), Stevens & Stewart

Struttin' (1988), L. Chamberlin

A Tribute to Malcolm X (1988), T. Walker

The Warrior Ant (1988), °Breuer & Telson

Yes, God Is Real (1988), J. M. Brown

God's Trombones (adapt., 1988–89), V. Carroll

God's Creation (1989), H. Hardy

Goree (1989), M. Manaka

The Gospel of the Harlem Renaissance (1989), T. Walker

Hang Tough (c. 1989), U. E. Perkins

I Have a Dream (1989), °J. Greenfield

It's About Time (1989), Brown & Brown

Let the Music Play Gospel (1989), V. Higginsen

Mood Indigo (1989), J. Swain

The Song of Sheba (1989), Morgan & Thompson

Time for a Coming Out (1989), Smith & Gaita

T K O (1989), Roquemore & Stevenson

†*Black and Blue* (1989–90), °Segovia & °Grezzoli

Count Your Blessings (1989, revised 1990), J. M. Brown & others

Cute Root (1980s), T. Brewster

Esprit de Corps II (1980s), Nickelson & Betts

Queenie Pie (late 1980s), Ellington & Ellington

Young John Henry (late 1980s), U. E. Perkins

1990–1992

The African American (1990), Overton & Overton

Once on This Island (1990), Ahrens & Flaherty

Stop and Think (1990), Positively Blk.

Sugar Hill (1990), Fernandez & St. Louis

†*Can't Take Her Nowhere* (1991), R. Harris

Junebug Jack (1991), Junebug Prodns. & Roadside Th.

Kingdom of Gold (1991), Chocolate Chips Th. Co.

The First Lady (1992), C. Fields

†*Jelly's Last Jam* (1992), G. Wolfe

INFORMATION SOURCES

LIBRARIES AND REPOSITORIES

The following libraries and repositories have strong collections in black musical theatre, and may be useful in locating further information on the musicals included in this directory. [Abbreviations used for citing the most frequently used collections are given in brackets.]

AMERICAN ACADEMY OF ARTS AND LETTERS LIBRARY

633 W. 155th St.

New York, NY 10032

  (Langston Hughes Papers)

AMISTAD RESEARCH CENTER

Dillard University

400 Esplanade Ave.

New Orleans, LA 70116

  (Countee Cullen Papers; Manuscript Collection)

BOSTON PUBLIC LIBRARY

666 Boylston St.

Boston, MA 02117

  (Drama and Theatre Collections)

CHICAGO PUBLIC LIBRARY CULTURAL CENTER

75 E. Washington St.

Chicago, IL 60602
   (Chicago Theatre Collection)

CLARK ATLANTA UNIVERSITY RESEARCH CENTER
Robert W. Woodruff Library
111 James P. Brawley Drive, S.W.
Atlanta, GA 30314
   (Countee Cullen/Harold Jackman Collection; Hoyt Fuller Collection)

DETROIT PUBLIC LIBRARY
Music and Performing Arts Dept.
5201 Woodward Ave.
Detroit, MI 48202
   (E. Azalia Hackley Memorial Collection)

DuSABLE MUSEUM OF AFRICAN-AMERICAN HISTORY
3806 S. Michigan Ave.
Chicago, IL 60653
   (Library Collection)

EDWARD L. DOHENY MEMORIAL LIBRARY
University of Southern California
University Park
Los Angeles, CA 90089
   (Theatre Collection)

FISK UNIVERSITY LIBRARY AND MEDIA CENTER
17th Ave., N.
Nashville, TN 37203
   (Theatre Collection; Papers of Pauline Hopkins, Langston Hughes, and others)

HARVARD UNIVERSITY LIBRARY
Cambridge, MA 02138
   (Harvard Theatre Collection)

HATCH-BILLOPS COLLECTION
491 Broadway
New York, NY 10012
   (Published and Unpublished Play Collection; Oral History Collection; Owen and Edith
   Dodson Memorial Collection) [Hatch-Billops]

HOWARD UNIVERSITY LIBRARIES
Moorland-Spingarn Research Center Library
2400 Sixth St., N.W.
Washington, DC 20059
  (Moorland Collection; Spingarn Collection) [Moorland-Spingarn]

LIBRARY OF CONGRESS
10 First St., S.E.
Washington, DC 20540
  (Manuscript Division; Rare Book Collection; Music Collection) [LC]

MUSEUM OF THE CITY OF NEW YORK
1220 5th Avenue
New York, NY 10029
  (Theatre Archives)

NATIONAL ARCHIVES
Pennsylvania Ave. and Eighth St., N.W.
Washington, DC 20408
  (Federal Theatre Project Collection)

NEW YORK PUBLIC LIBRARY
Performing Arts Research Center
111 Amsterdam Ave.
New York, NY 10023
  (Theatre Collection, also known as the Billy Rose Theatre Collection; Music Collection)
  [TC/NYPL]

NEW YORK PUBLIC LIBRARY
Schomburg Center for Research in Black Culture
513 Malcolm X Boulevard
New York, NY 10037
  (Schomburg Collection; Music Collection; Rare Book Collection; Manuscript Collection) [Schomburg]

OHIO HISTORICAL SOCIETY
Interstate 71 and 17th Ave.
Columbus, OH 43211
  ([Paul Laurence] Dunbar Collection)

PHILADELPHIA FREE LIBRARY

Logan Square

Philadelphia, PA 19103

  (Theatre Collection)

RESEARCH CENTER FOR THE FEDERAL THEATRE PROJECT

(Also called the Institute on the Federal Theatre Project and New Deal Culture)

George Mason University

4400 University Drive

Fairfax, VA 22030

  (Federal Theatre Project Collection) [FTP/GMU]

STATE HISTORICAL SOCIETY OF WISCONSIN

Archives and Manuscript Division

816 State St.

Madison, WI 52706

  (Langston Hughes Papers)

UNIVERSITY MICROFILMS INTERNATIONAL

300 N. Zeeb Road

Ann Arbor, MI 48106

  (Dissertations, Theses, Out-of-Print Books, Black Newspapers in Microform)

YALE UNIVERSITY

Beinecke Library

New Haven, CT 06520

  (James Weldon Johnson Memorial Collection) [JWJ/YUL]

REFERENCE BOOKS AND CRITICAL STUDIES

   Includes specific studies of black contributions to the American musical stage, as well as more general resource materials pertinent to the subject. [Abbreviations used for citing the most frequently used reference books are given in brackets. Other standard abbreviations from the list of Other Bibliographical Abbreviations in the front of the book are also used in citing many of the references in this bibliography. Because of the subject matter of this study, abbreviations are used throughout for Black (Blk.), Negro (Neg.), Musical or Music (Mus.), Theatre (Th.), and Drama (Dr.).]

Abramson, Doris E. *Negro Playwrights in the American Theatre, 1925–1959.* New York: Columbia Univ. Press, 1969. [*NegPlaywrs*]
The Afro-American Encyclopedia. 10 vols. North Miami, FL: Educational Book Publishers, 1974.

Andrews, Bert, et al. *In the Shadow of the Great White Way: Images from the Black Theatre*. New York: Thunder's Mouth Press, 1989.

Arata, Esther Spring. *More Black American Playwrights: A Bibliography*. Metuchen, NJ: Scarecrow Press, 1978.

Arata, Esther Spring, and Nicholas John Rotoli. *Black American Playwrights, 1800 to the Present: A Bibliography*. Metuchen, NJ: Scarecrow Press, 1976.

Archer, Leonard C. *Black Images in the American Theatre*. Brooklyn: Pageant-Poseidon, 1973.

ASCAP Biographical Dictionary [of Composers, Authors and Publishers]. 4th ed. New York: R. R. Bowker, 1980. Also earlier eds.

Atkinson, Brooks. *Broadway*. rev. 3rd ed. New York: Macmillan, 1974.

Atkinson, Brooks, and Albert Hirschfeld. *The Lively Years*. New York: Association Press, 1975.

Baker, Houston A., Jr. *Modernism and the Harlem Renaissance*. Chicago: Univ. of Chicago Press, 1987.

Baldwin, James. *Notes of a Native Son*. New York: Bantam, 1964.

Barbour, Floyd B. *The Black Seventies*. Boston: Sargent, 1970.

Baskin, Wade, and Richard N. Runes. *Dictionary of Black Culture*. New York: Philosophical Library, 1973.

Beckerman, Bernard, and Howard Siegman. *On Stage: Selected Theatre Reviews from the New York Times, 1920–1970*. New York: Arno Press, 1973.

Bergman, Peter N., and Mort N. Bergman. *The Chronological History of the Negro in America*. New York: Bergman Publishers, 1969; distributed by Harper and Row; and by Mentor/New American Library, 1969.

The Best Plays of 1894–1899/1990–1991. (The Burns Mantle Theatre Yearbook, also known as The Burns Mantle Best Plays Series.) Ed. by Burns Mantle, succeeded by John Chapman, Louis Kronenberger, Henry Hewes, and Otis Guernsey. Boston: Small, 1920–1925; New York: Dodd, Mead, 1926–1991. [*BesPls*]

The Biographical Encyclopedia & Who's Who of the American Theatre, ed. by Walter Rigdon. [Revised as *Notable Names in the American Theatre*, ed. by Raymond D. McGill, 1976.] New York: James H. Heineman, 1966.

Blum, Daniel, and John Willis, eds. *A Pictorial History of the American Theatre: 1860–1976*. 4th ed. New York: Crown, 1977.

Bond, Frederick W. *The Negro and the Drama: The Direct and Indirect Contribution Which the American Negro Has Made to Drama and the Legitimate Stage, with the Underlying Conditions Responsible*. Washington, DC: Associated Publishers, 1940; reprinted by McGrath, 1969; graphic reprints also available from Univ. Microfilms International. [*Neg&Dr*]

Bontemps, Arna. *The Harlem Renaissance Remembered*. New York: Dodd, Mead, 1972.

Bontemps, Arna, and Jack Conroy. *Anyplace But Here*. [A revised and enlarged version of Bontemps' *They Seek a City*, 1945.] New York: Hill and Wang, 1966.

Bordman, Gerald. *American Musical Revue*. New York: Oxford Univ. Press, 1978.

———. *American Musical Theatre: A Chronicle*. expanded ed. New York: Oxford Univ. Press, 1986. [*AmMusTh*]

———. *The Oxford Companion to the American Theatre*. New York: Oxford Univ. Press, 1984.

Bradford, Perry. *Born with the Blues: Perry Bradford's Own Story. The True Story of the Pioneering Blues Singers and Musicians in the Early Days of Jazz.* New York: Oak Publications, 1965.

Brawley, Benjamin. *The Negro Genius.* New York: Dodd, Mead, 1937.

Brown, Scott E. *James P. Johnson: A Case of Mistaken Identity.* In volume with *A James P. Johnson Discography,* comp. by Robert Hilliard. Metuchen, NJ: Scarecrow Press and the Institute of Jazz Studies, Rutgers Univ., 1986.

Brown, Sterling. *Negro Poetry and Drama.* Included in *Negro Poetry and Drama and the Negro in American Fiction,* a combined printing of two of Brown's books. Originally pub. by Associates in Negro Folk Education; reprinted by Atheneum, 1968, and by Arno Press.

Brown, Warren, comp. *Check List of Negro Newspapers in the United States, 1827–1946.* Jefferson City, MO: Lincoln Univ. Press, 1946.

Butcher, Margaret Just. *The Negro in American Culture.* Based on materials left by Alain Locke. Revised and updated ed. New York: Mentor/New American Library, 1971.

Campbell, Georgetta Merritt. *Extant Collections of Early Black Newspapers.* Troy, NY: Whitson, 1981.

Charters, Ann. *Nobody: The Story of Bert Williams.* New York: Macmillan, 1970. [*Nobody*]

Clarke, John Henrik. *Harlem: A Community in Transition.* Syracuse, NY: Citadel Press, 1964, 1979.

————. *Harlem, U.S.A.* Berlin: Seven Seas, 1964; revised ed., New York: Collier/Macmillan, 1966.

Clurman, Harold. *The Naked Image: Observations on the Modern Theatre.* New York: Macmillan, 1966.

Craig, E. Quita. *Black Drama of the Federal Theatre Era: Beyond the Formal Horizons.* Boston: Univ. of Massachusetts Press, 1980.

Cruse, Harold. *The Crisis of the Negro Intellectual.* New York: William Morrow, 1967.

Cunard, Nancy, ed. *Negro Anthology [1931–1933].* London: Wishart, 1934; reprinted in an unabridged facsimile ed. by Negro Universities Press; abridged by Frederick Ungar Publishing Co., 1970.

Cuney-Hare, Maud. *Negro Musicians and Their Music.* Washington, DC: Associated Publishers, 1936. [*NegMus&M*]

Cunningham, Virginia. *Paul Laurence Dunbar and His Song.* New York: Dodd, Mead, 1948.

Davis, John P. *The American Negro Reference Book.* Yonkers, NY: Educational Heritage, 1966.

Davis, Sammy, Jr., and Jane and Bert Boyer. *Yes I Can: The Story of Sammy Davis, Jr.* New York: Pocket Books, 1966.

Detweiler, Frederick G. *The Negro Press in the United States.* College Park, MD: McGrath, 1968.

Dickinson, Donald C. *A Bio-Bibliography of Langston Hughes, 1906–1967.* 2nd ed. Hamden, CT: Archon, 1972.

Dorman, James H., Jr. *Theater in the Ante-Bellum South, 1815–1861.* Chapel Hill: Univ. of North Carolina Press, 1967.

Dramatists Play Service. *Complete Catalog of Plays, 1984–1985.* New York: Dramatists Play Service, 1984. Also earlier eds. and later supplements.

The Ebony Handbook, eds. of *Ebony* Magazine. (Formerly *The Negro Handbook* [1966].) Chicago: Johnson Publishing Co., 1974.

Ellington, Duke. *Music Is My Mistress*. Garden City, NY: Doubleday, 1973.

Emanuel, James A. *Langston Hughes*. New York: Twayne, 1967.

Emery, Lynne F. *Black Dance in the United States from 1619 to 1970*. Palo Alto, CA: National Press Books, 1972. [*Blk. Dance*]

Engel, Lehman. *The American Musical Theatre: A Consideration*. CBS Legacy Collection Book; distributed by Macmillan, New York, 1957.

Ewen, David. *All the Years of American Popular Music*. Englewood Cliffs, NJ: Prentice-Hall, 1977.

———, ed. *Complete Book of the American Musical Theatre*. rev. ed. New York: Holt, 1959.

Fabre, Geneviève. *Drumbeats, Masks and Metaphor: Contemporary Afro-American Theatre*. Trans. by Melvin Dixon of Fabre's *Le Théâtre noir aux États-Unis* (Black Theatre in the United States). Originally pub. Paris: Editions du Centre National de la research scientifique, 1982. Cambridge: Harvard Univ. Press, 1983.

Feather, Leonard. *The Encyclopedia of Jazz*. New York: Horizon Press, 1955; rev. 1960, 1970, and 1976 (coauthored with Ira Gitler).

The Federal Theatre Project: A Catalog-Calendar of Productions, comp. by the Staff of the Fenwick Library, George Mason Univ. Westport, CT: Greenwood Press, 1986.

Flanagan, Hallie (Hallie Ferguson Flanagan Davis). *Arena: The History of the Federal Theatre*. New York: Duell, Sloane, and Pearce, 1940; republished by Benjamin Blom, 1965. [*Arena*]

Fletcher, Tom. *The Tom Fletcher Story: 100 Years of the Negro in Show Business*. New York: Burge, 1954. [*100 Yrs*]

French, Samuel, Inc. *Basic Catalog of Plays, 1985*. New York: Samuel French, 1985.

Gottfried, Martin. *Opening Nights: Theatre Criticisms of the Sixties*. New York: Putnam, 1969.

Green, Stanley. *Encyclopedia of the Musical Theatre*. New York: Dodd, Mead, 1976; reprinted by Da Capo Press, New York, 1980.

———. *The World of Musical Comedy*. New York: A. S. Barnes, 1974.

Hamalian, Leo, and James V. Hatch, eds. *The Roots of African American Drama*. Detroit: Wayne State Univ. Press, 1991.

Harrison, Paul Carter. *The Drama of Nommo*. New York: Grove Press, 1972.

Hartnoll, Phyllis, ed. *The Oxford Companion to the Theatre*. 3rd ed. New York: Oxford Univ. Press, 1970.

Hatch, James V. *Black Image on the American Stage: A Bibliography of Plays and Musicals, 1770–1970*. New York: DBS Publications, 1970.

Hatch, James V., and Omanii Abdullah. *Black Playwrights, 1823–1977: An Annotated Bibliography of Plays*. New York: R. R. Bowker, 1977. [*Blk. Playwrs.*]

Hatch, James V., ed., and Ted Shine, consultant. *Black Theater, U.S.A.: Forty-Five Plays by Black Americans, 1847–1974*. New York: The Free Press, 1974. [*BlkThUSA*]

Hewes, Henry. *Famous Plays of the 1940s*. New York: Dell, 1960.

Hill, Errol. *The Theater of Black Americans: A Collection of Critical Essays*. 2 vols. Vol. 1: *Roots and Rituals/The Image Makers*. Vol. 2: *The Presenters/The Participators*. Englewood Cliffs, NJ: Prentice-Hall, 1980.

Hitchcock, H. Wiley, and Stanley Sadie, eds. *The New Grove Dictionary of American Music*. 4 vols. New York: Macmillan, 1986.

Houseman, John. *Run-Through*. New York: Simon and Schuster, 1972.

Howard University Library, Washington, DC. *Dictionary Catalog of the Arthur B. Spingarn Collection of Negro Authors.* 2 vols. Boston: G. K. Hall, 1970.

————. *Dictionary Catalog of the Jesse E. Moorland Collection of Negro Life and History.* 9 vols. Boston: G. K. Hall, 1970.

Huggins, Nathan. *Harlem Renaissance.* New York: Oxford Univ. Press, 1971. [*Harl. Ren.*]

Hughes, Catherine R., ed. *New York Theatre Annual, 1976–77/1977–78,* vols. 1 and 2. Also: *American Theatre Annual, 1978–79/1979–80.* (Title changed to cover regional theatre companies and national touring companies, in addition to New York prodns.) Detroit: Gale Research, 1978–1981. Also later vols.

Hughes, Langston, and Milton Meltzer. *Black Magic: A Pictorial History of the Negro in American Entertainment.* Englewood Cliffs, NJ: Prentice-Hall, 1967; rev. 1971. [*BlkMagic*]

————. *A Pictorial History of the Negro in America.* New York: Crown, 1956. Rev. and retitled *A Pictorial History of Black Americans,* ed. by Hughes, Meltzer, and C. Eric Lincoln. New York: Crown, 1973.

Hurston, Zora Neale. *Dust Tracks on the Road.* Philadelphia: Lippincott, 1942; reprinted by Arno Press, 1970.

Isaacs, Edith J. R. *The Negro in the American Theatre.* New York: Theatre Arts, 1947; reprinted by McGrath. [*NegAmTh*]

Jahn, Janheinz. *Neo-African Literature: A History of Black Writing.* Orig. pub. as *Geschichte der neoafrikanischen Literatur.* Trans. from the German by Oliver Coburn and Ursula Lehrburger. London: Faber and Faber, 1958; New York: Grove, 1968.

Johnson, James Weldon. *Along This Way.* New York: Viking Press, 1935.

————. *Black Manhattan.* New York: Alfred A. Knopf, 1930; reprinted by Arno Press and Atheneum. [*BlkManh*]

Kaplan, Mike, ed. *Variety Presents the Complete Book of Major U.S. Show Business Awards.* (Rev. ed. of *Variety Major U.S. Showbusiness Awards,* 1982.) New York: Garland, 1985.

————. *Variety Who's Who in Show Business.* New York: Garland, 1983.

Kellner, Bruce. *The Harlem Renaissance: A Historical Dictionary for the Era.* Westport, CT: Greenwood Press, 1984. [*HarlRenD*]

Kimball, Robert, and William Bolcom. *Reminiscing with Sissle and Blake.* New York: Viking, 1973.

King, Woodie, Jr. *Black Theatre: Present Condition.* New York: Publishing Center for Cultural Resources, 1981.

King, Woodie, Jr., and Ron Milner. *Black Drama Anthology.* New York: Columbia Univ. Press, 1972. [*Blk. Dr. Anth.*]

Kirkeby, Ed. *Ain't Misbehavin': The Story of Fats Waller.* New York: Dodd, Mead, 1966.

Kramer, Victor. *The Harlem Renaissance Re-examined.* New York: AMS Press, 1986.

Laufe, Abe. *Broadway's Greatest Musicals.* New York: Funk & Wagnall, 1969.

Leiter, Samuel, ed. *The Encyclopedia of the New York Stage, 1920–30/1940–50.* Westport, CT: Greenwood Press, 1986–1992.

Lewis, David Levering. *When Harlem Was in Vogue.* New York: Oxford Univ. Press, 1989.

Little, Stuart W. *Off-Broadway: The Prophetic Theatre.* New York: Coward, McCann and Geoghegan, 1972.

Logan, Rayford W., and Michael R. Winston, eds. *Dictionary of American Negro Biography*. New York: Norton, 1982. [*DANB*]

Mapp, Edward. *Directory of Blacks in the Performing Arts*. Metuchen, NJ: Scarecrow Press, 1978.

Mathews, Jane DeHart. *The Federal Theatre, 1935–1939*. Princeton, NJ: Princeton Univ. Press, 1967.

Mikolyzk, Thomas A. *Langston Hughes: A Bio-Bibliography*. Cambridge, MA: Harvard Univ. Press, 1966.

Mitchell, Loften. *Black Drama: The Story of the American Negro in the Theatre*. New York: Hawthorn, 1967. [*BlkDr*]

———. *Voices of the Black Theatre*. Clinton, NJ: James White, 1975.

Nathan, George Jean. *Passing Judgment*. New York: Alfred A. Knopf, 1933.

———. *Testament of a Critic*. New York: Alfred A. Knopf, 1931.

———. *The Theatre Book of the Year, 1943–1944*; also *1946–1947*; *1947–1948*. New York: Alfred A. Knopf, 1944, 1948.

The Negro Handbook, eds. of *Ebony* Magazine. (Superseded by *The Ebony Handbook.*) Chicago: Johnson Publishing, 1966.

The Negro Handbook, 1942; *1944*; *1946–47*; *1949*, ed. by Florence Murray. Various New York pubs.: Wendell Malliet, 1942; Current Reference Publications, 1944; Current Books, 1947; Macmillan, 1949.

Negro Yearbook: An Annual Encyclopedia of the Negro, 1912/1937–38, ed. by Monroe N. Work. Tuskegee, AL: Negro Year Book Co., 1912–38. Continued as *Negro Year Book: A Review of Events Affecting Negro Life, 1941–46*, and *1952*, ed. by Jessie P. Guzman. Tuskegee, AL: Dept. of Records and Research, Tuskegee Institute, 1947, 1952.

New York Public Library. *Dictionary Catalog of the Schomburg Collection of Negro Literature and History*, 9 vols., 1962. *1st Supplement*, 2 vols., 1967. *2nd Supplement*, 4 vols., 1972. *Supplement* 1974, 1976. Boston: G. K. Hall, dates as indicated. Also later Supplements, as issued.

New York Times (Reference Services). *The New York Times Directory of the Theatre*. [A separate issue of the index of *The New York Times Theatre Reviews*, cited below, covering the period 1920–70.] New York: Arno Press, 1973. Also later eds. and supplements.

———. *The New York Times Theatre Reviews*. Originally 16 vols. plus index, 1870–1970. Also later eds. and supplements, as issued. New York: New York Times Books, 1971–

Notable Names in the American Theatre, ed. by Raymond D. McGill. [A revision of *The Biographical Encyclopedia & Who's Who of the American Theatre*, ed. by Walter Rigdon, 1966.] Clinton, NJ: James T. White; distributed by Gale Research, 1976.

Patterson, Lindsay, ed. *Anthology of the American Negro in the Theatre: A Critical Approach*. New York: Publishers Co., under the auspices of the Association for the Study of Negro Life and History, 1967. [*AnthANT*]

———. *The Negro in Music and Art*. New York: Publishers Co., under the auspices of the Association for the Study of Negro Life and History, 1969.

Peterson, Bernard L., Jr. *Contemporary Black American Playwrights and Their Plays: A Biographical and Dramatic Index*. Westport, CT: Greenwood Press, 1988.

———. *Early Black American Playwrights and Dramatic Writers: A Biographical Di-*

rectory and Catalog of Plays, Films, and Broadcasting Scripts. Westport, CT: Greenwood Press, 1990.

Ploski, Harry A., and Roscoe C. Brown. *The Negro Almanac.* New York: Bellwether Publishing, 1966. (Superseded by *Afro USA.*)

Ploski, Harry A., and Ernest Kaiser. *Afro USA: A Reference Work on the Black Experience.* (An expanded and enlarged version of *The Negro Almanac,* cited above.) New York: Bellwether Publishing, 1971; distributed by Afro-American Press.

Rampersad, Arnold. *Life of Langston Hughes.* 2 vols. Cambridge, MA: Harvard Univ. Press, 1986–88.

Reardon, William R., and Thomas D. Pawley, eds. *The Black Teacher and the Dramatic Arts: A Dialogue, Bibliography, and Anthology.* Westport, CT: Greenwood Press, for Negro Universities Press, 1970.

Richards, Stanley. *Great Musicals of the American Theatre.* New York: Chilton, 1976.

Riis, Theodore Laurence. *Just Before Jazz.* Washington, DC: Smithsonian Institution Press, 1989.

Salem, James A. *A Guide to Critical Reviews. Part II: The Musical, 1909–1974,* 2nd ed. Metuchen, NJ: Scarecrow Press, 1976.

Sampson, Henry T. *Blacks in Blackface: A Source Book on Early Black Musical Shows.* Metuchen, NJ: Scarecrow Press, 1980. [*BlksBf*]

———. *The Ghost Walks: A Chronological History of Blacks in Show Business, 1865–1910.* Metuchen, NJ: Scarecrow Press, 1988. [*Ghost*]

Seller, Maxine Schwartz, ed. *Ethnic Theatre in the United States.* Westport, CT: Greenwood Press, 1983.

Shaw, Arnold. *Black Popular Music in America: From the Spirituals, Minstrels, and Ragtime to Soul, Disco, and Hip-Hop.* New York: Schirmer Bros., 1986.

Smith, Jessie Carney, ed. *Images of Blacks in American Culture: A Reference Guide to Information Sources.* Westport, CT: Greenwood Press, 1988.

Southern, Eileen. *Biographical Dictionary of Afro-American and African Musicians.* Westport, CT: Greenwood Press, 1982. [*BioDAfMus*]

———. *The Music of Black Americans: A History.* New York: W. W. Norton, 1971; rev. 1983. [*MusBlkAms*]

———, ed. *Readings in Black American Music.* New York: W. W. Norton, 1983.

Stearns, Marshall, and Jean Stearns. *Jazz Dance: The Story of American Vernacular Dance.* New York: Schirmer Books, 1968.

Theatre World, 1950–1951/1990–1991. (Annual ''Complete Pictorial and Statistical Record of the . . . Broadway and Off-Broadway Theatrical Season.'') Title varies: Originally called *Theatre World*; later called *Blum's Theatre World*; now mainly listed as *John Willis' Theatre World.* Ed. by Daniel Blum, 1950–55; currently ed. by John Willis, 1956–91. New York: Crown, 1951–1991.

Toll, Robert C. *Blacking Up: The Minstrel Show in Nineteenth Century America.* New York: Oxford Univ. Press, 1974.

University Microfilms International. Various catalogs and updates, including: *The Arts: A Catalog of Current Doctoral Dissertation Research,* 1983. *The Arts: A Catalog of Selected Doctoral Dissertation Research,* 1985. *Black Studies: A Dissertation Bibliography,* 1977. *Black Studies II: A Dissertation Bibliography,* 1980. *A Catalogue of Out-of-Print Titles from the Negro in the United States.* Ann Arbor, MI, dates as indicated.

Van Vechten, Carl. *"Keep A-Inchin' Along"*: *Selected Writings by Carl Van Vechten about Black Arts and Letters*. Ed. by Bruce Kellner. Westport, CT: Greenwood Press, 1979.

Waters, Ethel, with Charles Samuels. *His Eye Is on the Sparrow*. New York: Doubleday & Co., 1950.

Williams, Mance Raymond. *Black Theatre in the 1960s and 1970s: A Historical-Critical Analysis of the Movement*. Westport, CT: Greenwood Press, 1985.

Wittke, Carl. *Tambo and Bones: A History of the American Minstrel Stage*. Durham, NC: Duke Univ. Press, 1938, 1968.

Woll, Allen. *Black Musical Theatre: From "Coontown" to "Dreamgirls."* Baton Rouge: Louisiana State Univ. Press, 1989. [*BlkMusTh*]

————. *Dictionary of the Black Theatre: Broadway, Off-Broadway, and Selected Harlem Theatre*. Westport, CT: Greenwood Press, 1983. [*DBlkTh*]

Work, Monroe. *A Bibliography of the Negro in Africa and America*. New York: H. W. Wilson, 1928; reprinted by Octagon Books, 1965, and Argosy-Antiquarian Ltd., 1965.

WPA [Works Progress Administration] Federal Theatre Project. *A List of Negro Plays*. New York: National Service Bureau, Publication No. 24–L, 1938. Xerographic prints available from Univ. Microfilms International.

DISSERTATIONS AND THESES

Where order numbers are given in parentheses, dissertations and theses are available in paper or microform copies from University Microfilms International, P.O. Box 1764, Ann Arbor, MI 48106. For current pricing information, call the Dissertation Hot Line, 1–800–521–3042, toll free.

In the main body of the encyclopedia, dissertations are abbreviated by the author's last name, followed by the type of dissertation or thesis and the date: e.g., Abramson (Ph.D. diss., 1969). A further abbreviation is used in the References at the end of an entry, e.g., Abramson diss.

Abramson, Doris Elizabeth. "A Study of Plays by Negro Playwrights, from 'Appearances' to 'A Raisin in the Sun' (1925–1959)." Ph.D. diss., Columbia Univ., 1969. (BEJ67–14016) [Published as *Negro Playwrights in the American Theatre, 1925–1959*. See Reference Books and Critical Studies, above.]

Adubato, Robert A. "A History of the WPA's Negro Theatre Project in New York City, 1935–1939." Ph.D. diss., New York Univ., 1978. (BWK78–18122)

Alkire, Stephen Robert. "The Development and Treatment of the Negro Character as Presented in American Musical Theatre, 1927–1968." Ph.D. diss., Michigan State Univ., 1972. (BEJ73–05314)

Archer, Leonard Courtney. "The National Association for the Advancement of Colored People and the American Theatre: A Study of Relationships and Influences (Vols. I and II)." Ph.D. diss., Ohio State Univ., 1959. (BEJ59–02728) [Published as *Black Images in the American Theatre*. See Reference Books and Critical Studies above.]

Belcher, Fannin Saffore, Jr. "The Place of the Negro in the Evolution of the American Theatre, 1762–1940." Ph.D. diss., Yale Univ., 1945. (BEJ69–17658)

Bond, Frederick W. "The Direct and Indirect Contribution Which the American Negro Has Made to the Drama and the Legitimate Stage, with the Underlying Conditions

Responsible." Ph.D. diss., New York Univ., 1938. (BWK78–13518) [Published as *The Negro and the Drama*. See Reference Books and Critical Studies, above.]

Buchanan, Singer Alfred. "A Study of the Attitudes of the Writers of the Negro Press Towards the Depiction of the Negro in Plays and Films: 1930–1965." Ph.D. diss., Univ. of Michigan, 1968. (BEJ68–13288)

Caldwell, Hansonia Laverne. "Black Idioms in Opera as Reflected in the Works of Six Afro-American Composers." Ph.D. diss., Univ. of Southern California, 1974. (GAX75–06403)

Cochran, James P. "The Producer-Director on the New York Stage, 1890–1915." Ph.D. diss., State Univ. of Iowa, 1968.

Coleman, Edwin Leon, Jr. "Langston Hughes: An American Dramatist." Ph.D. diss., Univ. of Oregon, 1971. (BWK72–08518)

Davidson, Frank C. "The Rise, Development, Decline and Influence of the American Minstrel Show." Ph.D. diss., New York Univ., 1952.

Davis, (Brother) Joseph Morgan. "A Compilation and Analysis Concerning the Contributions of the Negro to the American Theatre in 1950–1960." Master's thesis, Catholic Univ., 1962.

Dickenson, Donald Charles. "A Bio-Bibliography of Langston Hughes, 1920–1950." Ph.D. diss., Univ. of Michigan, 1964. (BWK65–05891)

Goodman, Gerald Thomas. "The Black Theatre Movement." Ph.D. diss., Univ. of Pennsylvania, 1974. (BEJ75–14566)

Hicklin, Fannie Ella Frazier. "The American Negro Playwright, 1920–1964." Ph.D. diss., Univ. of Wisconsin, 1965. (BWK65–6217)

Johnson, Evamarii Alexandria. "A Production History of the Seattle Federal Theatre Project Negro Repertory Company, 1935–1939." Ph.D. diss., Univ. of Washington, 1981. (SAB82–12556)

Lawson, Hilda Josephine. "The Negro in American Drama." Ph.D. diss., Univ. of Illinois, 1939. [Abstract pub. in *Bulletin of Bibliography*, in two installments: Part I, Jan./April 1940; Part II, May/Aug. 1940.]

Lewis, Ellistine Perkins. "The E. Azalia Hackley Memorial Collection of Negro Music, Dance and Drama: A Catalog of Selected Afro-American Materials." Ph.D. diss., Univ. of Michigan, 1978. (BWK79–07122)

McLaren, Joseph. "Edward Kennedy (Duke) Ellington and Langston Hughes: Perspectives on Their Contributions to American Culture, 1920—1966." Ph.D. diss., Brown Univ., 1980. (GAX81–11144)

Miller, Jeanne-Marie Anderson. "Dramas by Black American Playwrights Produced on the New York Professional Stage (from 'The Chip Woman's Fortune' to 'Five on the Black Hand Side')." Ph.D. diss., Howard Univ., 1976. (BWK78–05440)

Monroe, John Gilbert. "A Record of the Black Theatre in New York City, 1920–29." Ph.D. diss., Univ. of Texas/Austin, 1980. (SAB881–09212)

Nash, Rosa Lee. "Characterization of Blacks in the Theatre of the Sixties." Ph.D. diss., Yeshiva Univ., 1971. (BEJ62–11162)

Ogunbiyi, Yemi. "New Black Playwrights in America (1960–1975): Essays in Theatrical Criticism." Ph.D. diss., New York Univ., 1975. (BEJ76–19529)

Pitts, Ethel Louise. "The American Negro Theatre: 1940–1949." Ph.D. diss., Univ. of Missouri/Columbia, 1975. (BEJ76–07538) [Abstract pub. as "The American Negro Theatre," in *The Theatre of Black Americans*, vol. 2, ed. by Errol Hill. Englewood Cliffs, NJ: Prentice-Hall, 1980.]

Richards, Sandra. "Bert Williams: His Stage Career and Influence on American Theatre." Ph.D. diss., Stanford Univ., 1973.

Riis, Thomas Laurence. "Black Musical Theatre in New York, 1890–1915." Ph.D. diss., Univ. of Michigan, 1981. (GAX82–04745) [Pub. as *Just Before Jazz*. See Reference Books and Critical Studies, above.]

Ross, Ronald Patrick. "Black Drama in the Federal Theatre, 1935–1939." Ph.D. diss., Univ. of Southern California, 1972. (BJ72–27693) [Abstract pub. as "The Role of Blacks in the Federal Theatre, 1935–1939," in *The Theatre of Black Americans*, vol. 2, ed. by Errol Hill. Englewood Cliffs, NJ: Prentice-Hall, 1980.]

Sandle, Floyd Leslie. "A History of the Development of the Educational Theatre in Negro Colleges and Universities from 1911 to 1959." Ph.D. diss., Louisiana State Univ. and A. & M. Coll., 1959. (BEJ59–05527)

Sheffey-Stinson, Sandi. "The History of Theatre Productions at the Los Angeles Inner City Cultural Center, 1965–1976." Ph.D. diss., Kent State Univ., 1979. (BWK80–03484)

Silver, Reuben. "A History of the Karamu Theatre of Karamu House, 1915–1960." Ph.D. diss., Ohio State Univ., 1961. (BEJ62–0081)

Thompson, Sister Francesca. "The Lafayette Players, 1915–1932: America's First Dramatic Stock Co." Ph.D. diss., Univ. of Michigan, 1972. [Abstract pub. as "The Lafayette Players, 1917–1932," in *The Theatre of Black Americans*, vol. 2, ed. by Errol Hill. Englewood Cliffs, NJ: Prentice-Hall, 1980.]

Williams, Mance Raymond. "The Color of Black Theatre: A Critical Analysis of the Black Theatre Movement of the 1960s and 1970s." Ph.D. diss., Univ. of Missouri/Columbia, 1980. (KWN81–08856. [Pub. as *Black Theatre in the 1960s and 1970s: A Historical-Critical Analysis of the Movement*. See Reference Books and Critical Studies, above.]

Wilson, Robert Jerome. "The Black Theatre Alliance: A History of Its Founding Members." Ph.D. diss., New York Univ., 1974. (BEJ74–30055)

Woods, Porter S. "The Negro on Broadway: The Transition Years, 1920–1930." D.F.A. diss., Yale Univ., 1965. (BEJ70–24050).

Young, Artee Felicita. "Lester Walton: Black Theatre Critic." Ph.D. diss., Univ. of Michigan, 1980. (GAX81–06254)

PERIODICALS

The following list includes journals, magazines, newspapers, newspaper magazines, newsletters, and bulletins, both active and no longer published, that are cited in the entries or listed among the references and sources for one or more of the musical shows in this encyclopedia. Abbreviations used in citing these periodicals are given in brackets. For the most frequently cited periodicals, such as the *New York Times*, special abbreviations may be used [e.g., *NYT*], which are also listed in the Bibliographical Abbreviations in the front of the book. For most other periodicals, only standard or familiar abbreviations are used.

No attempt has been made to list individual articles in these or other periodicals. For bibliographies of articles in periodicals, consult the pertinent reference books, dissertations, and theses listed in the two preceding sections. Especially useful in this regard are the following studies: *Black American Playwrights, 1800 to the Present: A Bibliography* (Arata & Rotoli, 1976); *More Black American Playwrights: A Bibliography* (Arata, 1978);

Black Playwrights, 1823–1977: An Annotated Bibliography of Plays (Hatch & Abdullah, 1977); *Black Theatre in the 1960s and 1970s: A Historical-Critical Analysis of the Movement* (Williams, 1985); *Dictionary of the Black Theatre: Broadway, Off-Broadway, and Selected Harlem Theatre* (Will, 1983); and *Black Musical Theatre: From "Coontown" to "Dreamgirls"* (Woll, 1989).

Afro-American (Baltimore)

America

Billboard (esp. J. A. Jackson's Page, 1921–25)

(The) Black American [*Blk. American*]

Black Art [*Blk. Art*]

Black Masks (Black theatre in NY, NJ, and CT) [*Blk. Masks*]

Black Perspectives in Music [*Blk. Perspectives in Mus.*]

Black Theatre (Nos. 1–6, ed. by Ed Bullins; New Lafayette Theatre, New York, 1968–72) [*Blk. Th.*]

Black World (formerly *Negro Digest*) (esp. annual black theatre issues, April 1971–April 1976) [*Blk. World*]

Bookman

Boston Evening Transcript [*Boston Eve. Transcript*]

Boston Transcript

Catholic World [*Cath. World*]

Chicago Defender

Chicago Whip

Christian Science Monitor Magazine [*Christian Science Monitor Mag.*]

CLA Journal [*CLAJ*]

The Colored American (Washington, DC)

Commonweal

Competitor

Connoisseur

Crisis (NAACP)

Cue

Dance Magazine [*Dance Mag.*]

Dissent

Drama Critique [*Dr. Critique*]

Dramatics

Ebony

Encore

Essence

Evening Scimitar (Memphis, TN) [*Eve. Scimitar*]

Forum

Freeman (Indianapolis)

Globe-Democrat (St. Louis)

Golden Book Magazine [*Golden Bk. Mag.*]

Green Book Album [*Green Bk. Album*]

Green Book Magazine [*Green Bk. Mag.*]

High Fidelity/Musical America [*High Fidelity/Mus. Am.*]

Houston Informer

ICCC Calendar (Inner City Cultural Center, Los Angeles)

Inter-State Tattler (New York)

Jet

Journal and Guide (Norfolk, VA) [*J. & Guide*]

Herald Tribune Magazine (New York) [*Herald Trib. Mag.*]

Houston Informer

Liberator

Life

Literary Digest [*Literary Dig.*]

Look

Los Angeles Daily Times [*L.A. Daily T.*]

Massachusetts Review [*Mass. Rev.*]

Messenger

Milwaukee Journal [*Milwaukee J.*]

Modern Music [*Modern Mus.*]

Morning Times (Washington, DC)

Musical America [*Mus. Am.*]

Nation

National Magazine [*National Mag.*]

Negro Digest [*Neg. Dig.*]

Negro History Bulletin [*Neg. Hist. Bull.*]

New Republic [*NewRepub*]

Newsday

Newsweek [*Newswk*]

New Theatre [*New Th.*]

New York [*NY*]

New York Age [*NY Age*]

New York American [*NY American*]

New York Amsterdam News [*NY Amsterdam N.*]

New York Clipper [*NY Clipper*]

New York Commercial [*NY Commercial*]

New York Daily Mirror [*NY Daily Mirror*]

New York Daily News [*NY Daily N.*]

New York Dramatic Mirror [*NY Dramatic Mirror*]

New York Dramatic Mirror and Theatrical World [*NY Dramatic Mirror & Th. World*]

New Yorker [*NYorker*]

New York Evening Journal [*NY Eve. J.*]

New York Evening Post [*NY Eve. Post*]

New York Evening Sun [*NY Eve. Sun*]

New York Evening World [*NY Eve. World*]

New York Globe [*NY Globe*]

New York Graphic [*NY Graphic*]

New York Herald [*NY Herald*]

New York Herald Tribune [*NY Herald Trib.*]

New York Journal American [*NY J. American*]

New York Journal of Commerce [*NY J. of Commerce*]

New York Magazine [*NY Mag.*]

New York Mail [*NY Mail*]

New York Mirror [*NY Mirror*]

New York Morning Telegraph [*NY Morn. Telegraph*]

New York Native [*NY Native*]

New York News [*NY News*]

New York Post [*NY Post*]

New York Review [*NY Review*]

New York Sun [*NY Sun*]

New York Sun and Globe [*NY Sun & Globe*]

New York Sunday News [*NY Sunday N.*]

New York Sunday Times [*NY Sunday T.*]

New York Telegram [*NY Telegram*]

New York Telegraph [*NY Telegraph*]

New York Times [*NYT*]

New York Tribune [*NY Trib.*]

New York World [*NY World*]

New York World Telegram [*NY World Telegram*]

New York World-Telegraph and Sun [*NY World-Telegraph & Sun*]

One-Act Play Magazine [*One-Act Play Mag.*]

Opportunity (National Urban League)

Outlook

Outlook and Independent [*Outlook & Independent*]

Philadelphia Record

Phylon

Pittsburgh Courier [*Pitts. Courier*]

Playboy

Players

PM

Reporter

San Francisco Call

San Francisco Chronicle

San Francisco Pacific Appeal

Saturday Review of Literature [*Sat. Rev.*]

School and Society [*School & Society*]

Sepia

Show

Show Business Illustrated [*Show Business Illus.*]

Soho Weekly News [*Soho Weekly N.*]

South Bend (IN) *Tribune* [*South Bend* (IN) *Trib.*]

Stage

The State (Columbia, SC)

St. Louis Post Dispatch

Theatre Arts (Monthly) [*ThArts*]

Theatre Magazine [*ThMag*]

Time

Toledo (OH) *Blade* [*Toledo Blade*]

Toronto Daily Star

Variety

Village Voice

Vogue

Wall Street Journal [*Wall St. J.*]

Washington Post

Women's Wear Daily

NAME INDEX

This index includes the names and page references for most individuals and performing groups cited in this encyclopedia, as well as the names of a number of black theatres that supported their own resident companies, and the main producing and touring companies that regularly booked black shows. Individuals include not only performers, librettists, lyricists, composers, and others involved in the creation of shows, but also directors, producers, choreographers, stage managers, musicians, and others also involved in the production of shows. Names of performing animals listed among the casts of characters have also been included. Since the billing of theatrical names often varies through the years, and since this volume includes thousands of names culled from a variety of sources, some less reliable than others, the author has tried scrupulously to correct the obvious glaring errors, but not all the variations in spelling and usage that frequently appear in the cast lists of shows. Therefore, an attempt has been made in this index to resolve these variations by using the longest or most popular version of the name, and giving the variant forms in brackets or parentheses. Brackets are most often used for questionable and possibly erroneous variations. Parentheses are most often used for established or recognized name variations, as well as for providing additional information about the individual or group. Closely similar names are often listed as separate entries, unless there is strong evidence that they identify the same person or group. Cross references have been used liberally throughout this index.

446 NAME INDEX

Clarke, Hope, 64, 111, 160, 198, 223
Clarke, Jerry, 108
Clarke, Robert, 73
Clarkson, Fred, 284
Clarkston (strong man), 143
Clary, Wilston, 28
Claude Hopkins' Orchestra, 89. See also Hopkins, Claude
Claxton, Leon, 295
Clay, Billy, 293
Clayton, Bessie, 268
Clement, Patricia A., 121, 132
Clemons, Mary, 192
Cliff [sic], 286
Clifford & Battle, 294
Clifton-Allen, Lynne, 64, 260
Clifton & Batis, 85
Clinton, Helen, 181
Clough, Inez, 82, 117, 186, 262, 304, 310
Club Baron (Harlem), 205
Clyburn, Rose, 318
Coats, Sherman, 93
Cobert, Helen, 276
Cobb, Jessie, 59
Coburn, Mr. and Mrs., 351
Cody, Clay, 340
Coffin, Maurice, 177
Cohen, Allen, 161
Cohen, Margie, 144. See also Benbow and Cohen
Cohn, Art, 175
Coker, Bebe, 243
Cole, Billy, 78. See also Flash Devils, Four
Cole, Bob (Robert), 12, 19, 20, 31, 44, 45, 69, 76, 93, 102, 122, 146 183, 184, 190, 209, 210, 216, 228, 243, 247, 254, 288, 289, 290, 293, 303, 307, 308, 310, 321, 324, 329, 340, 359, 360, 378. See also Cole & Johnson; Cole & the Johnson Brothers
Cole, Carol, 45
Cole, Cozy, 73
Cole, Doris, 50
Cole, Happy, 151
Cole, Louis, 55
Cole, Nora, 76
Cole, Rags, 352
Cole & Johnson (Bob Cole and William "Billy" Johnson, or possibly Bob Cole & J. Rosamond Johnson), 171, 183, 238, 360. See also individual names
Cole & the Johnson Brothers (Bob Cole, James Weldon Johnson, and J. Rosamond Johnson), 31, 76, 122, 146, 183, 216, 247, 303, 340, 393. See also individual names
Cole Brothers (Tom and Austin), 267
Coleman, Cecilia, 83, 166
Coleman, Charles, 51

Coleman, Desiree, 32, 225
Coleman, Ed Lea, 189
Coleman, Edna, 189
Coleman, Edwin Leon, Jr., 113
Coleman, Felicia Y., 319
Coleman, Herbert, 219, 302
Coleman, Larry. See Carl Murray Singers
Coleman, Marilyn B., 11, 255
Coleman, W. D., 110
Coleman, Warren, 219, 275, 276
Coleman & Johnson, 375
Coleman Brothers Creole Follies Co., 91
Coles, Honi, 40, 41
Coles, Zaida, 29
Coley, Thomas, 341
Collie, Kelsie E., 130, 287
Collier, Thomas, 315
Collins, Arthur, 183, 238, 321
Collins, Daisy, 379
Collins, Gene, 234
Collins, George, 254
Collins, H. D., 252
Collins, James, 163
Collins, Nora, 237
Collins, R. H., 316
Collins, Rise, 51
Colson, C. David, 281
Colston, Percy, 80, 81, 82, 186, 204, 246, 350
Colston, Vinna, 154
Columbia Univ. Opera Workshop (New York), 28
Colvan, Zeke, 168
Comacho, Leu [sic], 180
Comathiere (DeComathiere), A. B., 117, 258. See also DeComathiere, A. B.
Comden, Betty, 127, 159, 260
Committee for the Negro in the Arts (New York), 205
Comstock, F. Ray, 27
Cones, Monty, 281
Connell, Gordon, 32
Connelly, Marc, 18, 154
Conners [Connors], Edgar ("Sambo"), 28, 173, 242, 269, 310
Conners [Connors], Richard, 188, 274
Connie's Inn (New York), 88, 164, 173, 218, 271, 330
Conoly, Joseph, 243
Conoway, Grace, 61
Conrad, Barbara Smith, 276
Conrad, Con, 207
Conroy, Pat, 89
Conway, Dianne, 167
Conway, Dick, 204, 242
Conway, Jessie, 354
Conway, Lillian, 355
Conway & Parks, 361

"Jazz Lips," Jr., 86
J. D. Steele Singers (possibly Javetta Steele),
    152
Jeannette, Gertrude, 59, 119, 219, 379
Jeedman, Will, 146
Jefferson, Carlene, 121
Jefferson, J., 14
Jefferson, Mamie, 283
Jefferson, Miles, 72, 119, 383
Jefferson, "Peg Leg," 102
Jefferson, Raymond, 98, 202
Jefferson, Rosetta, 6
Jeffrey, J. Wesley, 299
Jeffrey, "Onions" [Jeffries, "Onion"], 178,
    235
Jeffreys, Ann, 332
Jeffries, Herb (Herbert) (Herb Jeffrey), 203
Jeffries, "Onion" [Jeffrey, "Onions"], 178,
    235
Jenkins, Daniel H., 32
Jenkins, Dorothy, 256
Jenkins, Florine, 335
Jenkins, George, 273
Jenkins, Hezekiah, 143, 237, 256. See also
    Jenkins & Idaho
Jenkins, Jill Holly, 70
Jenkins, W. J. [possibly Wesley (John) Jen-
    kins], 358
Jenkins, (John) Wesley, 289, 310, 327. See
    also Jenkins, W. J.
Jenkins, Zablo, 324
Jenkins & Idaho (Hezekiah Jenkins and [Ber-
    tha] Idaho Jordan), 143. See also individual
    names
Jenkins & Jenkins, 371
Jennings, Fred, 82, 165, 186
Jennings, Thomas, 386
Jepson, Helen, 277
Jesse A. Shipp's Stock Co., 252. See also
    Shipp, Jesse A.
Jessye, Eva (Alberta), 136, 232, 276. See also
    Eva Jessye Choir
Jimmy Johnson's Syncopators, 131. See also
    Johnson, James P.
Jimmy Keyes and the Chords, 308
Jines, Henry ("Gang"), 37, 57, 106, 246,
    342, 375
Jines, Jacqueline & Guy, 375
Jingo [sic], 291
Jo, Patti, 281
Joe Jordan's Orchestra, 169. See also Jordan,
    Joe
Joel, Hattie, 330
Johanson, Don, 198
John Paul II, Pope, 43
Johns, Al, 187
Johnson, Adel, 100
Johnson, Alan, 132

Johnson, Alex, 380
Johnson, Allie, 139
Johnson, Alonzo, 120
Johnson, Arlove, 162
Johnson, "Babe," 88
Johnson, "Baby" Juanita, 127
Johnson, Bayne, 94
Johnson, Belle, 330
Johnson, Bennie, 120
Johnson, Bernard, 23
Johnson, Billy. See Johnson, William "Billy"
Johnson, Bob, 249
Johnson, Camellia, 277
Johnson, Charles E., 93. See also Johnson &
    Dean
Johnson, Dora Dean. See Dean, Dora; Johnson
    & Dean
Johnson, Dot, 236
Johnson, Duke, 334
Johnson, Eleanor, 240
Johnson, Eloise, 57, 84
Johnson, Elvira, 184, 222, 321
Johnson, Emma, 283
Johnson, Ethel, 295
Johnson, Evamarii Alexandria, 248
Johnson, Fats, 81
Johnson, Francine Palmer, 256
Johnson, Freddie, 5, 221, 256, 329
Johnson, Frederick, 225
Johnson, Grace, 100, 102, 113
Johnson, Greer, 240
Johnson, Hall, 297. See also Hall Johnson
    Choir
Johnson, Hank, 223, 263
Johnson, Hardtack, 138
Johnson, J. C., 59, 61, 77, 106, 169, 298,
    386
Johnson, J. Louis, 68, 78, 95, 147, 336
Johnson, J. Rosamond, 31, 39, 59, 68, 69,
    76, 122, 128, 129, 137, 146, 160, 164,
    168, 173, 183, 184, 190, 216, 228, 238,
    243, 247, 262, 276, 288, 289, 291, 293,
    303, 308, 310, 321, 324, 340, 378. See
    also Cole & the Johnson Brothers; J. Rosa-
    mond Johnson's Troubadour Band; Rosa-
    mond Johnson's Choir
Johnson, J. S., 49
Johnson, Jack, 91, 121
Johnson, James Arthur, 319
Johnson, James P., 13, 79, 84, 90, 105, 119,
    131, 141, 153, 164, 207, 231, 233, 241,
    249, 261, 270, 271, 272, 273, 286, 298,
    304, 313, 335, 351, 376. See also James P.
    Johnson's Black Diamond Aces; Jimmy
    Johnson's Syncopators
Johnson, James Weldon, 12, 31, 69, 76, 99,
    122, 146, 147, 148, 160, 183, 190, 216,
    243, 247, 262, 282, 288, 293, 303, 308,

Jones, Sergeant W., 71
Jones, Sheryle R., 132
Jones, Sidney, 146
Jones, (Madame) Sissieretta (Black Patti), 44, 45, 71, 101, 191, 222, 358, 359. *See also* Black Patti Troubadours
Jones, "Slim," 294
Jones, Teenan, 349
Jones, W. P., 315
Jones, Walter, 125
Jones, William, 73, 343
Jones, Willie, 189
Jones & Allen, 183
Jones & Johnson, 175
Jones & Jones, 271, 308
Joplin, Scott, 156, 176, 284, 357
Jordan, Gladys, 173, 215
Jordan, (Bertha) Idaho, 143. *See also* Jenkins & Idaho; Idaho, Bertha
Jordan, Jannae, 353
Jordan, Joe, 26, 59, 104, 105, 128, 152, 169, 184, 192, 227, 228, 287, 288, 295, 324, 388. *See also* Joe Jordan's Orchestra
Jordan, Joyce, 353
Jordan, Shirley, 319
Jordan, Tenita, 115
Jordan & Jones, 67
Joseph, Eddie, 259
Joseph, Stephen M., 232
Jota [*sic*], 354
Joy, Jack, 333
Joyce, Adrian, 53, 181
Joy Makers Co., 250
Joyner, B. B. (Beebee), 37, 57, 102, 174, 227, 228, 307, 323, 363
Joyner & Foster, 36, 107, 271
J. Rosamond Johnson's Troubadour Band, 164. *See also* Cole & the Johnson Brothers; Johnson, J. Rosamond; Rosamond Johnson's Choir
Julian, Doris, 94
Junebug Productions (New Orleans), 205
Justa, Helen[a], 115; and her Dancing Boys, 334
Justice, Jimmy, 105, 224, 308

Kamen, Michael, 289
Kane, Allegro, 317
Kane, Gene, 174
Kani, John, 151
Karamu Theatre (Cleveland), 9, 184, 302, 317
Karbi, Ras, 289, 290
Katherine Dunham Dancers [Dance Troupe], 25, 50, 68, 72. *See also* Dunham, Katherine
Katzman, Lew, 54
Kay, Don, 59
Kay, Ulysses, 327
Kayden, Mildred, 306, 332

Kaye, Judy, 70
Kean, Jeanne, 119
Keane, Lew. *See* Keene, Lew
Keck, Michael, 205
Keels, Jim, 6
Keene, Christopher, 385
Keene [Keane], Lew, 108, 272, 336
Keith, Frank, 139, 201
Kellner, Bruce, 291
Kelly, Bob A., 254, 265, 360
Kelly, Dude, 329
Kelly, Georgia, 166, 284
Kelly, Howard, 21, 52, 75, 80, 88, 127, 131, 151, 166, 191, 250, 252, 284, 292, 364, 368
Kelly, Joy, 243
Kelly, Paul, 13
Kelly, Paula, 14, 111
Kelly, R. A., 296
Kelly, W. *See* W. Kelly's Orchestra
Kelly & Catlin, 137
Kelsey, Louis, 155
Kelso Brothers, 162
Kemp, Bobby, 53, 89, 102
Kemp, Emma, 61
Kemp, Mabel, 215
Kemp, Mae (Mabel), 189, 215, 252
Kennedy, Adrienne, 106, 138, 288
Kennedy-Overton, Jane, 9
Kennetts, The, 195
Kenney, Isador, 100
Kennon-Wilson, James, 167
Kenton, Hester, 307–308
Kepplinger, Louis, 91
Kermoyan, Michael, 133
Kern, Jerome, 70, 146, 310, 389
Kerry, C. Herbert, 238
Kersands, Billy, 49, 209
Kert, Larry, 77
Kewpie Doll Chorus, 288
Key, Alice, 203
Keyes, Bert, 64
Keyes, Evelyn, 208
Keyes, Gary, 332
Keyes, Jimmy, 308
Keyes, Joe, 112
Keyes, Lloyd, 82, 186
Khumalo, Sibangile, 151
Kid Brown, 67, 79, 239, 240, 354; Kid Brown's Company, 239
"Kid" Bruce, 331
"Kid" Country, 56
"Kid" Frazier, 70, 284
Kid Hawks, 236
"Kid Lips," 79, 168, 283
Kid Thomas, 249
"Kid" Williams, 284
Kid Wilson, 293

Williams, Marion, 43
Williams, Mary Lou, 50
Williams, Miles, 172
Williams, Milton J., 68, 155, 302
Williams, Mose, 79
Williams, Musa, 39
Williams, Olena, 342
Williams, Pal, 107
Williams, Robert, 110
Williams, "Rubber Leg," 134
Williams, Ruby, 347
Williams, Samm-Art, 326
Williams, Spencer (composer/lyricist), 38, 81, 259, 282, 349, 356
Williams, Spencer (performer), 108
Williams, Steve, 225
Williams, Sundra, 29
Williams, Sylvia "Kuumba," 260
Williams, Teddy, 279
Williams, Terri, 96
Williams, "Ukulele" Bob, 329
Williams, Vergie, 330
Williams, Villa, 330
Williams, Viola, 61
Williams, Waldine, 297
Williams, Willie, 28
Williams & Ferguson, 40
Williams & Grant, 120
Williams & Melburn, 254
Williams & Scott, 207
Williams & Taylor, 333, 363
Williams & Walker (Bert Williams and George Walker), 3–4, 5, 26, 27, 47, 53, 84, 85, 149, 150, 171, 187, 213, 220, 238, 273, 274, 303, 305, 306, 324, 381. *See also individual names*
Williams & Walker Quartette, 274
Williamson, Marie, 335
Williams Sisters, 70
Willie & "Smoak," 335
Willie Gunn's Beauty Chorus, 231
Willie Too Sweet, 379
Willinger, David, 106
Willis, Joe, 128, 314
Willis, Joseph, 60
Willis, Lovel, 227
Willis, Marie, 53
Willis, Ralph, 347
Willis, Victor, 279
Will Mastin Trio (Sammy Davis, Jr., Sam Davis, Sr., and Will Mastin), 240. *See also individual names*
Wills, Anna, 250
Wills, Mme. Patti, 120. *See also* Watts & Wills
Will Vodery's Orchestra, 61, 212. *See also* Vodery, Will
Wilson, Al, 385

Wilson, Anita, 255
Wilson, Billy, 62, 123, 145
Wilson, Bobby, 190
Wilson, Bootsie, 201
Wilson, Clarence G., 181
Wilson, Derby, 37
Wilson, Diane, 193, 375
Wilson, Dooley, 49, 68
Wilson, Earl, Jr., 104
Wilson, Edith, 36, 39, 41, 61, 120, 172, 173, 175, 183, 232, 272, 291, 298, 314, 356
Wilson, Eleanor [Elenor, Elinor, Elenora], 165, 168, 195, 284, 301
Wilson, Flora, 195
Wilson, Frank, 232, 283, 319, 340, 374
Wilson, George, 93
Wilson, Ida, 162
Wilson, Inez Richardson, 155
Wilson, Jeffrey, 279
Wilson, Jesse, 174
Wilson, Jessie, 143, 169
Wilson, Jim, 360
Wilson, John, 230
Wilson, Joe. *See* Midnight Steppers
Wilson, Lelia, 6
Wilson, Lena, 104, 173, 221, 250, 287
Wilson, Lester, 150, 231
Wilson, Louise, 190
Wilson, Mae, 5, 59
Wilson, Ocey, 114, 225
Wilson, Pasean, 214
Wilson, "Peaches," 235
Wilson, Rastus, 181
Wilson, Robin, 6
Wilson, Speedy, 47
Wilson, Theodore, 147
Wilson, Woodrow, 47
Wiltshire, George, 32, 79, 107, 170, 177, 178, 237, 304, 312, 340, 361
Winans, Vickie, 132
Winbush, Marilyn, 64, 387
Winde, Beatrice, 11, 12
Winfield, Evelin, 252
Winfield, Helmsley, 128
Winfield, "Rastus," 144, 252
Winfred, Fannie, 213
Winfred, Henry, 61
Winfred & Brown, 109
Winfred & Mills, 36
Winfrey, C. B., 184
Wing, Ted, 79
Winifred, Henry, 7
Winifrey, Claude, 141
Winkins, Al, 7
Winkler, Leona, 156
Winn, Lorine, 175
Winny, Edward, 262
Winstead, Daniel. *See* Ace, King and Jack

SONG INDEX

This is an index of songs and musical numbers cited for various shows throughout the encyclopedia. If variant titles are used for the same song, the earliest or best-known title is given first and the variant title is given in parentheses, or the variant words are enclosed within brackets. Where identical (or very similar) titles are used for more than one song, each title is listed separately and numbered consecutively—(1), (2), (3)—followed by specific page numbers. A page number in *italics* indicates that brief commentary or additional information about that song is given on that page.

GENERAL INDEX

This is an index of subjects, themes, genres, and other pertinent categories of information that may be of interest to users of this encyclopedia.

Abductions and rescues, 97, 191, 288–89, 376, 381

Adaptations, 9, 13, 14, 15, 18, 30, 32, 33, 47, 64, 69, 89, 93, 95, 105, 121, 138, 147, 148, 150, 151, 169, 183, 190, 195, 196, 205, 216, 226–27, 235, 240, 251, 280, 285, 288, 294, 341, 346, 353, 362, 375, 383. *See also* Black versions of successful white shows; Swing, and jazz versions of classical plays

Africa and Africans: back to Africa movement, 187; ballet/dance drama about Africa, 301; musicals about Africa, 7, 9, 10, 69, 125, 151, 211, 212, 286, 287, 332, 337–38, 358 (Abyssinia/Ethiopia, 3, 80, 232; Belgian Congo, 8; Dahomey, 187; Ghana, 7; Hannibal crossing the Alps with elephants, 28; Liberia, 125; Madagascar, 369–70; Nigeria, 12; South Africa, 219; Timbuktu, 353; Wagandu, Kingdom of, 209; West Africa, 47; Zululand, 14, 192); operatic works about Africa, 7, 8, 14, 232, 390 (Congo, 8; Ethiopia, 123; Zululand, 390); songs and musical numbers about Africa, 8, 18, 28, 38

African culture: celebration of, 12; conflicts of, with American culture, 3–4; conflicts of, with European culture, 8–9. *See also* Black American heritage, African roots of

Alabama (as setting; also called Alabam, Bam, Bamville), 3, 12, 13, 26, 162, 222, 227, 305, 336

Awards: Audelco Awards, 132, 333 (nominations for, 15); Burns Mantle selection, "Best Play," 11 ("Off-Off-Broadway Best Play," 43); Clarence Derwent Award, 62; Drama Desk Awards, 10, 11, 32, 62, 111, 281, 285, 382; Grammy Awards, 11, 63; NAACP Image Award, 111; NY Drama Critics Award, 10; Obie Awards, 111, 138, 153; Outer Critics Circle Awards, 10, 111; Pulitzer Prize, 154; Stanley Award (Wagner Coll.), 138; *Theatre World* Awards, 11, 62, 285, 326; Tony Awards, 10, 11, 32, 115, 190, 198, 281, 285, 326, 382 (nominations for, 11, 45, 62, 111, 112, 198, 285); *Variety's* annual New York Drama Critics' Poll, winner of, 281

Barbers, 3, 171, 213, 287

Biblical-inspired musicals and operatic works, 6, 7, 24, 42, 88, 123, 147, 152, 189, 200, 201, 210, 251, 258, 279, 309

Biographies and tributes (non-theatrical): Attucks, Crispus, 93; Bloomer, Dolly, 49; Davis, Angela, 41; Dessalines, Emperor of Haiti, 263, 361; Hannibal, Carthaginian general, 28; King, Martin Luther, Jr., 24, 185, 229, 259, 305; Malcolm X, 358, 385; Menelek, Emperor of Abyssinia (Ethiopia), 232; Powell, Adam Clayton, Jr., 6; Robinson, Jackie, 131; Truth, Sojourner, 238; Wheatley, Phillis, 246, 269. *See also* Retrospective musicals and theatrical tributes

Black American heritage: African roots of, 30, 104, 285; celebration of, 290, 324

Blackface: black performers in, 7–8, 12–13, 21, 26, 29, 32, 36, 53, 56, 57, 63, 69, 78, 96, 117, 143, 153, 162, 202, 215, 226,

About the Author

BERNARD L. PETERSON, Jr., is Professor Emeritus of English and Drama at Elizabeth City State University, Elizabeth City, NC. The author of *Contemporary Black American Playwrights and Their Plays* and *Early Black American Playwrights and Dramatic Writers* (Greenwood Press, 1988, 1990), both of which were named Outstanding Academic Books by *Choice* magazine, he is planning additional reference books on black achievement in American theatre.